For my parents, Gordon and Margaret

I don't lie. I merely make the truth a little more interesting . . .
I don't break my word – I merely bend it slightly. . . .

ROALD DAHL, from his *Ideas Books*, No. 1 (c. 1945–48)

Contents

List of Illustrations

Roald Dahl's paternal grandfather Olaus Dahl, c.1890. (© Roald Dahl (France))

Roald's father Harald Dahl, c.1895. (© Bryony Dahl)

Roald with his mother, Sofie Magdalene, c.1919. (© RDNL. Permission courtesy of The Roald Dahl Museum and Story Centre)

Roald and his sisters gathering corn at Ty Mynydd. (© RDNL. Permission courtesy of The Roald Dahl Museum and Story Centre)

Asta, Else, Alfhild and Roald, c.1924. (© RDNL. Permission courtesy of The Roald Dahl Museum and Story Centre)

Dahl with camera at Repton, c.1932. (© RDNL. Permission courtesy of The Roald Dahl Museum and Story Centre)

Geoffrey Fisher, photographed by Dahl. (Reproduced by permission of Repton School)

Priory House, Repton, summer 1931. (© RDNL. Permission courtesy of The Roald Dahl Museum and Story Centre)

Annabella Power. (© Getty Images)

Dahl with Ernest Hemingway, London, 1944. (© Bettmann/CORBIS)

Vice President Henry Wallace, 1940. (Time & Life Pictures/Getty Images)

Gabriel Pascal with one of his cows, 1945. (Time & Life Pictures/Getty Images)

The Roosevelts photographed at Hyde Park by Dahl, 1943. (© RDNL. Permission courtesy of the Roald Dahl Museum and Story Centre)

Charles Marsh around the time Dahl first met him in 1942. (© Robert Haskell. Reproduced with his permission)

Portrait of Dahl taken for the publication of *Over to You* in 1945. (© RDNL. Permission courtesy of The Roald Dahl Museum and Story Centre)

Dahl c.1948. (© RDNL. Permission courtesy of The Roald Dahl Museum and Story Centre)

Dahl c.1951. (© RDNL. Permission courtesy of The Roald Dahl Museum and Story Centre)

Dahl and Patricia Neal on honeymoon in Rome, 1953. (© RDNL. Permission courtesy of The Roald Dahl Museum and Story Centre)

Pat and Olivia in the aviary at Gipsy House. (© RDNL. Permission courtesy of The Roald Dahl Museum and Story Centre)

Dahl and Olivia, 1958. (© RDNL. Permission courtesy of The Roald Dahl Museum and Story Centre)

Lunch with Igor Stravinsky

ROALD DAHL THOUGHT BIOGRAPHIES were boring. He told me so while munching on a lobster claw. I was twenty-four years old and had been invited for the weekend to the author's home in rural Buckinghamshire. Dinner was in full swing. A mixture of family and friends were devouring a platter brimming with seafood, while a strange object, made up of intertwined metal links, made its slow way around the table. The links appeared inseparable, but Dahl had told us all they could be separated quite easily by someone with sufficient manual dexterity and spatial awareness. So far none of the guests had been able to solve it. As I waited for the puzzle to come round to me, I tried to respond to Roald's disdain for biography. I mentioned Lytton Strachey, Victoria Glendinning, Michael Holroyd. But he wasn't having any of it. Sitting in a high armchair, at the head of his long pine dining table, he leaned back, took a swig from his large glass of Burgundy, and returned to his theme with renewed relish. Biographers were tedious fact-collectors, he argued, unimaginative people, whose books were usually as enervating as the lives of their subjects. With a glint in his eye, he told me that many of the most exceptional writers he had encountered in his life had been unexceptional as human beings. Norman Mailer, Evelyn Waugh, Thomas Mann and Dr Seuss were, I recall, each dismissed with a wave of his large hand, as tiresome, vain, dreary or insufferable. He knew I loved music and perhaps that was why he also mentioned Stravinsky. "An authentic genius as a composer," he declared, throwing back his head with a chuckle, "but otherwise quite ordinary." He had once had lunch with him, he added, so therefore he spoke from experience. I tried to think of subjects whose lives were as vivid as their art: Mozart, Caravaggio, Van Gogh perhaps? His intense blue eyes looked straight at me. That wasn't the point, he said. Why on earth would anyone choose to read an assemblage of detail, a catalogue of facts, when there was so much good fiction around as an alternative? Invention, he declared, was always more interesting than reality.

As I sat there, observing the humorous but combative glint in his eye, I sensed that, like a boxer, he was sparring with me. He had thrown a punch and been pleased that I jabbed back. Now he had thrown me another. This one was more difficult to parry. It would be hard to take it further without the exchange becoming detailed and perhaps wearisome. I hesitated. I wondered at his own life. He had just written two volumes of memoirs, one of which he had given to me to read in draft. So I knew the rough outline of his first twenty-five years: Norwegian parents, a childhood in Wales, miserable schooldays, youthful adventures in New-foundland and Tanganyika, flying as a fighter pilot, a serious plane crash, then a career as a wartime diplomat in Washington. I had already told him privately that I found the books compelling. Did he want me to re-peat the compliment over dinner as well? It was hard to tell. At that mo-ment the metal links were presented to me and the conversation moved on. Soon, too, his huge pointy fingers had plucked the puzzle from my inept hands and he had begun confidently to demonstrate its solution. Later on, at the end of a meal which had concluded with the offer of KitKats and Mars Bars dispensed from a small red plastic box, he took his two dogs out into the garden. A few minutes later he returned, wished everyone good night, and retired theatrically from the public space of the drawing room into the privacy of his bedroom.

Half an hour later, I was walking up the frosty path from the main building to the guest house in the garden. The atmosphere was absolutely still. A fox shrieked in the distance. I stopped for a moment and looked up at the clear winter sky. I was struck by how many stars I could see. Great Missenden was less than an hour's drive from London, but the lights of the city seemed far, far away. Some cows stirred in a nearby field. I looked about me. Gentle hills curved around the garden on all sides. At the top of the lane a vast beechwood glowered. The dark outline of the 500-year-old yew tree that had inspired *Fantastic Mr Fox* loomed over me. In the orchard, moonlight glinted on the gaily painted gypsy caravan that he had recreated in *Danny the Champion of the World*. An owl fluttered low into the yew. I turned and opened the door to my room.

Soon, I found myself examining the books in the bookcase by my bedside. There was certainly no biography here. Most of it was crime fiction: Ed McBain, Agatha Christie, Ellery Queen, Dick Francis. As I pulled out a volume, I noticed some ghost stories too, an insect encyclopedia, the diary of a Victorian priest, and a book of poetry by D. H. Lawrence. All of the books looked as if they had been read. I reflected again on our exchange over dinner, and wondered whether Roald had actually met Stravinsky. Perhaps he had simply made that remark to disconcert me? Before I switched off the light, I remember thinking that next day I would flush him out. I would ask him how he had come to have lunch with the great composer. Needless to say, I got distracted and forgot to do so.

It was then February 1986. I had known Dahl six months. The previous autumn, as a fledgling documentary director in the BBC's Music and Arts Department, I had proposed making a film about him for *Bookmark*, the corporation's flagship literary programme. Nigel Williams, the producer, himself an established playwright and novelist, had decided that the Christmas edition of the show would be devoted to children's literature. Twenty-five years ago this was still a field that many people in the UK arts affected to despise, and for once none of the programme's older, more experienced directors seemed keen to put forward any ideas. I was the most junior on the team. I wanted desperately to make a film. Any film. So I took my chance. It was an obvious suggestion – a portrait of the most famous and successful living children's writer. The motivation however behind my plan was largely opportunistic. At that point, I had read none of Dahl's children's fiction other than *Charlie and the Chocolate Factory*. On the other hand, as a thirteen-year-old, I had read most of his adult short stories, feasting on them with concentrated relish from behind a school desk during maths lessons. My adolescent mind had revelled in their grotesqueries, their complex twists and turns, and their spare, elegant, strangely sexy prose.

I remember Nigel Williams's smile. How he looked at me when I mentioned Roald Dahl. It was knowing, almost wicked. "Okay," he said. "If you can persuade him to do it." I paused. Was he thinking about money? The programme had a tiny budget and always paid its contributors the most modest of disturbance fees. It wasn't cash, however, that was on Nigel's mind. "You know his reputation?" he asked rhetorically. "Unbelievably grumpy and difficult. He'll never agree to take part." I nodded, although this was actually news to me, for my impression of Dahl the man at that point was in fact one of singular lightness. Four years earlier, while I was an undergraduate, he had taken part in a debate at the Oxford Union. "Romance is bunk" was the motion. Dahl had contributed to it memorably, arguing that romance was no more than a euphemism for the human sex drive. He was a great entertainer – witty, subversive, and often risqué. At one point he challenged a young woman in his audience to try and "get romantic" with a eunuch. At another he joked that a castrated male was similar to an aeroplane with no engine, because neither could get up. As I walked out of Nigel's office, all this was still fresh in my memory. Maybe Dahl will be cantankerous, I thought, but I am sure he will be funny, too. I discovered from press cuttings that he lived in a village called Great Missenden. I searched a telephone directory for Dahl, R. and there was his phone number. Ten minutes later I was calling him to discuss the project. Our conversation was brief and to the point. "Come to lunch," he said. "There are good train services from Marylebone."

A week later, I was standing outside the bright yellow front door of Gipsy House, his modest eighteenth-century whitewashed home. I rang the bell. An explosion of dogs barking heralded the arrival of a gigantic figure in a long red cardigan. He looked down at me. He was six foot five inches tall, craggy and broad of beam. His body seemed larger than the doorway and far, far too big for the proportions of the cottage. He ushered me through into a cosy sitting room where a log fire burned generously in the fireplace. He seemed a trifle surprised. I asked if I had got the date wrong. "No," he said. "I was expecting you." He asked me to wait a moment, then left the room. His strides were huge and ponderous, but strangely graceful – a bit like a giraffe. On one wall a triptych of distorted Francis Bacon heads glared out at me alarmingly, reminding me that for years, Dahl's adult publishers had dubbed him "the Master of the Macabre". On an adjacent wall, another Bacon head – this one a distorted swirl of green and white – returned my gaze. Around them a dazzlingly eclectic group of paintings and artefacts decorated the room: colourful oils, a collection of outsize antique Norwegian pipes, a primitive mask, a sober Dutch landscape and some stylized geometric paintings. I learned over lunch that these were the works of the Russian Suprematists: Popova, Malevich and Goncharova.

His wife Liccy (pronounced "Lici" as in the middle two syllables of her name, Felicity) returned five minutes later and suggested I go through into the dining room, where he was waiting for me. Over a lunch of smoked oysters, served from a tin – I don't recall any wine – we discussed the documentary. In the week leading up to our meeting I felt I had become an expert on his work and had read everything of his that I could get my hands on. I asked him some questions about his early life and about childhood. He told me how easy he found it to see the world from a child's perspective and how he thought that this was perhaps the secret to writing successfully for children. His memoir of childhood, *Boy*, had recently been published. I wanted to use this as the backbone of the film and so we talked about Repton, the school where he had spent his teenage years, fifty years earlier. He told me what a miserable time he had had there and we talked about the ethics of beating, for which the school was famous. We pencilled some provisional shooting dates in his diary. Then I asked whether I could see his writing hut. I had read about it and wanted to film there. I anticipated he might say no and tell me that it was too private a place to show to a film crew. But he did not bat an eyelid, and, after lunch, he took me to see it. We walked down a stone path bordered with leafless lime saplings, tied onto a bamboo framework that arched gently over our heads. He explained to me that in time the saplings would grow around the structure and make a magical, shady tunnel.

He opened the door to the hut and I went inside. An anteroom, stuffed with old picture frames and filing cabinets, led directly into his writing space. The walls were lined with aged polystyrene foam blocks for insulation. Everything was yellow with nicotine and reeked of tobacco. A carpet of dust, pencil sharpenings and cigarette ash covered the worn linoleum floor. A plastic curtain hung limply over a tiny window. There was almost no natural light. A great armchair filled the tiny room – Dahl frequently compared the experience of sitting there to being inside the womb or the cockpit of a Hurricane. He had chopped a huge chunk out of the back of the chair, he told me, so nothing would press onto the lower part of his spine and aggravate the injury he suffered when his plane crashed during the war. A battered anglepoise lamp, like a praying mantis, crouched over the chair, an ancient golf ball dangling from its chipped arm. A single-bar electric heater, its flex trailing down to a socket near the floor, hung from the ceiling. He told me that by poking it with an old golf club he could direct heat onto his hands when it was cold.

Everything seemed ramshackle and makeshift. Much of it seemed rather dangerous. Its charm, however, was irresistible. An enormous child was showing me his treasures: the green baize writing board he'd designed himself, the filthy sleeping bag that kept his legs warm, and – most prized of all – his cabinet of curiosities. These were gathered on a wooden table beside his armchair and included the head of one of his femurs (which had been sawn off during a hip replacement operation twenty years earlier), a glass vial filled with pink alcohol, in which some stringy glutinous bits of his spine were floating, a piece of rock that had been split in half to reveal a cluster of purple crystals nestling within, a tiny model aeroplane, some fragments of Babylonian pottery and a metal ball made, so he assured me, from the wrappers of hundreds of chocolate bars. Finally, he pointed out a gleaming steel prosthesis. It had been temporarily fitted into his pelvis during an unsuccessful hip replacement operation. He was now using it as an improvised handle for a drawer on one of his broken-down filing cabinets.

The shooting went without incident. Though it was the first time he had ever been filmed in his writing hut, and indeed the first time that the BBC had made a documentary about him, there were no rows, no difficulties, and no grumpiness. Roald charmed everyone and I occasionally wondered how he had come to acquire his reputation for being irascible. His short fuse had not been apparent to me at all. Years later, however, I discovered that I just missed seeing it on my very first visit. Not long after he died, Liccy explained why I had been abandoned in his drawing room. For, standing in his doorstep, I had not made a good impression. Roald had gone straight to her study. "Oh Christ, Lic, they've sent a fucking child," he had groaned. Liccy encouraged him to give me a chance and I think my youth and earnestness eventually became an asset. I even felt at the end of the two-day shoot as if Roald had become a friend. In the editing room, putting the documentary together, I was reminded of the suspicion that still surrounded Dahl in literary circles. Nigel Williams, concerned that Dahl appeared too sympathetic, insisted that I shoot an interview with a literary critic who was known to be hostile to his children's fiction. This reaction may have been largely a result of a trenchantly anti-Israeli piece Dahl had written for *The Literary Review* two years earlier. The article had caused a great deal of controversy and fixed him as an anti-Semite in many people's minds. But there was, I felt, something more than this in the atmosphere of wariness and distrust that seemed to surround people's reactions to him. Something I could not quite put my finger on. A sense perhaps that he was an outsider: misunderstood, rejected, almost a pariah.

I must have visited Gipsy House six or seven times in the next four years. Gradually, I came to know his children: Tessa, Theo, Ophelia and Lucy. Many memories of those visits linger still in the brain. Roald's excited voice on the telephone early one morning: "I don't know what you're doing next Saturday, but whatever it is, you'd better drop it. The meal we're planning will be *amazing*. If you don't come, you'll regret it." The surprise that evening was caviar, something he knew I had never tasted. True to the spirit of the poacher at his heart, he later explained that it had been obtained, at a bargain price, in a furtive transaction that seemed like a cross between a John Le Carré spy novel and a *Carry On* film. The code phrase was: "Are you Sarah with the big tits?" Another evening, I remember him opening several of the hundreds of cases of 1982 Bordeaux he had recently purchased and that were piled up everywhere in his cellar. The wines were not supposed to be ready to drink until the 1990s, but he paid no attention. "Bugger that," he declared. "If they're going to be good in the 1990s, they'll be good now." They were. I recall his entrances into the drawing room before dinner, always theatrical, always conversation-stopping, and his loud, infectious laugh. Being in his company was always invigorating. You never quite knew what was going to happen next. And whatever he did seemed to provoke a story. Once, on a summer's morning outside on the terrace, he taught me how to shuck my first oyster, using his father's wooden pocketknife. He told me he had carried it around the world with him since his schooldays. Years later, when I told Ophelia that story, she roared with laughter. "Dad was having you on," she explained. "It was just an old knife he had pulled out of the kitchen."

Roald's physical presence was initially intimidating, but when you were on your own with him, he became the most compelling of talkers. His quiet voice purred, his blue eyes flashed, his long fingers twitched with delight as he embarked on a story, explored a puzzle, or simply recounted an observation that had intrigued him. It was no surprise that children found him mesmerizing. He loved to talk. But he could listen, too – if he thought he had something to learn. We often discussed music. He preferred gramophone records and CDs to live performances – his long legs and many spinal operations had made sitting in any sort of concert hall impossibly uncomfortable – and he enjoyed comparing different interpretations of favourite pieces, seeming curiously ill at ease with relative strengths and merits. A particular recording always had to come out top. There had to be a winner. This attitude informed almost every aspect of life. Whether it was food, wine, painting, literature or music, "the best" interested him profoundly. He liked certainty and clear, strong opinions. I don't think I ever heard him say anything halfhearted. And despite a life that had been packed with incident, he lived very much in the present and seldom reminisced. I recall only one brief conversation about being a fighter pilot and none at all about dabbling in espionage, or mixing with wartime Hollywood celebrities, Washington politicos and New York literati.

Occasionally he name-dropped. I recall him telling me, for no particular reason, that one well-known actor had been a bad loser when Roald beat him at golf. And then, of course, there was that improbable lunch with Stravinsky. But, though he was clearly drawn both to luxury and to celebrity, he took as much pleasure in a bird's nest discovered in a hedge as he did in a bottle of Château Lafleur 1982 or the bon mots of Ian Fleming and Dorothy Parker. He delighted in ignoring many of the usual English social boundaries and asking people personal questions. He did it, I suspect, not because he was interested in their answer, but because he revelled in the consternation he might provoke. In that sense he could be cruel. Yet, though his fuse was a famously short one, I actually saw him explode only once. He was on the telephone to the curator of a Francis Bacon exhibition in New York, who wanted to borrow one of his paintings and had called while he had guests for dinner. She said something that annoyed him, so he swore at her furiously and slammed the phone down. I recall feeling that the gesture was self-conscious. He was playing to an audience. His temper subsided almost as soon as the receiver was back in its cradle.

Even then, I was dimly aware that this showy bravado was a veneer, a carapace, a suit of armour created to protect the man within: a man who was infirm and clearly vulnerable. Several dinner invitations were cancelled at short notice because he was unwell. Once, Liccy told me on the phone that the "old boy" had nearly met his maker. Yet he always rallied, and the next time I saw him, he would look as robust and healthy as he had been before. Always smoking, always drinking, always controversial, he appeared a life force that would never be extinguished. So his death, in November 1990, came as a shock. At his funeral, a tearful Liccy, who knew my passion for classical music, asked if I would help her commission some new orchestral settings of some of Roald's writings and thereby achieve something he had wanted: an alternative to Prokofiev's *Peter and the Wolf* that might help attract children into the concert hall. I had just left the BBC to go freelance and jumped at the opportunity. Over the next few years, I encountered Roald's sisters, Alfhild, Else and Asta, as well as his first wife, Patricia Neal. They all took part in another longer film I made about Dahl in 1998, also for the BBC, which Ophelia presented, and in which she and I explored together some of the themes of this book for the first time. Many of the interviews with members of his family quoted in this book date back to this period.

Shortly before he died, Roald nominated Ophelia as his chosen biographer. In the event that she did not want to perform this task, he also made her responsible for selecting a biographer. This came as something of a shock to her elder sister Tessa, who had hoped that she would be asked to write the book. Nevertheless, it was Ophelia who took up the challenge of sifting through the vast archive of letters, manuscript drafts, notebooks, newspaper cuttings and photographs her father had left behind him in his writing hut. Living in Boston, however, where she was immensely busy with her job as president and executive director of Partners in Health, the Third World medical charity she had co-founded in 1987, made the research time-consuming, and she found it increasingly hard to find time to complete the book. Eventually, when she got pregnant in 2006, she decided to put her manuscript on the shelf and asked me whether I would like to try and take up the challenge of writing her father's biography. It was a tremendous leap of trust on her part to approach me – a first-time biographer – to write it. She did so, she told me, because I was outside the family, yet also because I had known her father and liked him. She felt that someone who had not met him would find it almost impossible to put together all the disparate pieces of the jigsaw puzzle that made up his complex and extravagant personality. Everything in the archive – now housed in the Roald Dahl Museum and Story Centre at Great Missenden, which had opened the previous year – was placed at my disposal. With characteristic generosity, Ophelia even allowed me to draw on the manuscript of her own memoir. Tessa too, despite an initial wariness, has subsequently freely given me her time and energies. I could not possibly have written the book without their cooperation as well as that of their siblings Theo and Lucy. I am profoundly grateful to all of them.

There were many surprises and puzzles in store for me on the journey – not least the discovery of how many contradictions animated his personality. The wild fantasist vied with the cool observer, the vainglorious boaster with the reclusive orchid breeder, the brash public schoolboy with the vulnerable foreigner, who never quite fit into the English establishment although he liked to describe himself as "very English . . . very English indeed".[1] A delight in simple pleasures – gardening, bird-watching, playing snooker and golf – counterbalanced a fascination for the sophisticated environment of grand hotels, wealthy resorts and elegant casinos. His taste in paintings, furniture, books and music was refined and subtle, yet he was also profoundly anti-intellectual. He could be a bully, yet prided himself on defending the underdog. For one who always relished a viewpoint that was clear-cut, these incongruities were not entirely unexpected. With Roald there were seldom shades of grey. I was also to learn that, as he rewrote his manuscripts, so too he rewrote his own history, preferring only to reveal his private life when it was quasi-fictionalized and therefore something over which he could exert a degree of control. Many things about his past made him feel uncomfortable and storytelling gave him power over that vulnerability.

So now, in 2010, a wheel has come full circle. Little did I imagine when Roald and I had that conversation over dinner in 1986 that, twenty-four years later, I would finally answer his challenge by writing this book. It is an irony that I hope he would have appreciated. For seldom can a biographer have been presented with such an entertaining and absorbing subject, the narrative of whose picaresque life jumps from crisis to triumph, and from tragedy to humour with such restless swagger and irrepressible brio. Presented with so much new material – including hundreds of manuscripts and thousands of letters – I have tried, everywhere possible, to keep Dahl's own voice to the fore, and to allow the reader to encounter him as I did, "warts and all". Sometimes I have wished that I could convey the chuckle in his voice or seen the twinkle in his eye that doubtless accompanied many of his more outrageous statements.

Moreover, his tendencies to exaggeration, irony, self-righteousness, and self-dramatization made him a particularly slippery quarry, and my attempts to pick through the thick protective skein of fiction that he habitually wove across his past may not always have been entirely successful. I have tried to be diligent and a good fact-checker, but if a few misjudgements and errors have crept in, I hope the reader will pardon them. I make no claim to be either encyclopedic or impartial. I am not sure either is even possible. Nevertheless, I have tried to write an account that is accurate and balanced, but not bogged down in minutiae. That is something I know Roald would have found unforgivable. So, while I remain uncertain if he ever had lunch with Igor Stravinsky, I have to confess that now I no longer care. It was perhaps a storyteller's detail, a trifle. Compared with so much else, whether it was true or false seems ultimately of little importance.

CHAPTER ONE

The Outsider

IN JULY 1822, *The Gentleman's Magazine* of Parliament Street, Westminster, reported a terrible accident. Its correspondent described how a few weeks earlier, in the tiny Norwegian hamlet of Grue, close to the border with Sweden, the local church had burned down. It was Whit Sunday and the building was packed with worshippers. As the young pastor warmed to the themes of his Pentecostal sermon, the aged sexton, tucked away in an unseen corner under the gallery, had felt his eyelids becoming heavy. By his side, in a shallow grate, glowed the fire he used for lighting the church candles. Gently its warmth spread over him and very soon he was fast asleep. Before long, a smell of burning was drifting through the airless building. The congregation stirred, but obediently remained seated as the priest continued to explain why the Holy Spirit had appeared to Christ's apostles as countless tongues of fire. The smell got stronger. Smoke started to drift into one of the aisles. The sexton meanwhile snoozed on oblivious. By the time he awoke, an entire wall of the ancient church was ablaze. He ran out into the congregation, shouting at the worshippers to save themselves. Suffocating in the thick smoke, they pressed against the church's sturdy wooden doors in a desperate attempt to escape the flames. But the doors opened inwards and the pressure of the terrified crowd simply forced them ever more tightly shut. Within ten minutes, the entire church, which was constructed almost entirely out of wood and pine tar, became an inferno. That day over one hundred people met, as the magazine described it, "a most melancholy end", burning to death in what is still the most catastrophic fire in Norwegian history.

Only a few people survived. They did so by following the example of their preacher. For Pastor Iver Hesselberg did not join the rush toward the closed church doors. Instead, he jumped swiftly down from his pulpit and, with great practical purpose, began piling up Bibles under one of the high windows by the altar. Then, after scrambling up them to the relative security of the window ledge, he hurled himself through the leaded glass and out of the burning edifice to safety. Some might have called his actions selfish, but all over Europe newspapers praised the cool logic of the enterprising priest, who thought his way out of a crisis and did not succumb to the group stampede. Here was a man of his time, they wrote, a thinker: an individual who stood outside his flock. Grateful for his second chance in life, Pastor Hesselberg evolved into a philanthropist and public figure. A contemporary remembered him as "a strict man who preached fine sermons", a staunch Lutheran who was also a liberal idealist, visiting the poor and teaching them arithmetic, as well as how to read and write. He even founded a parish library.[1]

Hesselberg ended his days as a distinguished theologian and eventually a member of the Norwegian parliament, where he helped to ensure that all public buildings in Norway would in future be built with doors that opened outwards. His son, Hans Theodor, attempted to follow in his footsteps. He trained for the priesthood and married into one of Norway's most distinguished families. His wife was a descendant of Peter Wessel, a Norwegian naval hero, who had been killed in a duel in 1720.[2] They settled at Vaernes,* a large farm not far from Trondheim, the ancient capital of Norway, whose magnificent Romanesque cathedral, built on the shrine of Norway's patron saint, St Olave, almost a millennium ago, evokes a virtually forgotten age when Scandinavia was a key spiritual centre of Christian Europe.

In Vaernes, Hans Theodor raised eleven children, but he lacked his

---

*Most of the Vaernes farmlands have now been subsumed into Trondheim Airport, but the actual building Hans Theodor owned is still standing. He is buried nearby in the cemetery of Vaernes Church.

father's shrewd judgement and talent for hard work. He drank excessively, managed his estates incompetently, and never practised as a priest. He was also an incorrigible – and unsuccessful – gambler. Bit by bit, he was forced to sell off his lands to pay his gaming debts. One evening he went too far. He staked the village storehouse in a game of cards and lost. Outraged at this disregard for his responsibilities to his flock, the local community forced him to sell what remained of the farm. Hans Theodor moved to Trondheim, where he died a pauper in 1898.[3] But his children went out into the world and prospered – many entering the burgeoning Norwegian middle classes. Two became merchants, one became an apothecary, another a meteorologist. Yet another, Karl Laurits, trained as a scientist, then studied law and eventually went to work in Christiania, now Oslo, as an administrator in the Norwegian Public Service Pension Fund. In 1884 he married Ellen Wallace, and the following year, his first daughter, Sofie Magdalene, was born in Kristiania.† Thirty-one years later, on a crisp autumn day in South Wales, she would give birth to her only son, Roald.

Roald Dahl himself was not that interested in his ancestry or in historical detail. Though proud of his Norwegian roots, archives and public records were not his domain, and when, in his late sixties, he wrote his own two volumes of memoirs, *Boy* and *Going Solo*, he seems to have known nothing of his great-great-grandfather Hesselberg's extraordinary escape from the church fire or of the streak of reckless gambling and alcohol addiction that had emerged in his descendants.[4] Yet Pastor Hesselberg's story would almost certainly have fascinated Roald. He would have admired his ancestor's resourceful ingenuity, as well as his ability to think both laterally and practically in the face of a crisis. These were qualities he admired in others and they were attributes he gave to the heroes and heroines of many of his children's books. In his own life, too, Dahl would face many moments of crisis and struggle, and seldom were his resources of tenacity or inventiveness found wanting. His psychology and

---

†Confusingly, the capital of Norway has undergone several changes of name. Ancient Norse Oslo was renamed Christiania in 1624 after King Christian IV of Norway rebuilt it following a disastrous fire. In 1878, Christiania was refashioned as Kristiania, and in 1925, the city became Oslo once again.

philosophy was always positive. "Get on with it," was one of his favourite phrases, recommended to family, friends and colleagues alike, and one that he put into practice many times in his life when dealing with adversity – whether that was accident, war, injury, illness, depression or death. Like Pastor Hesselberg, he seldom looked behind him. He infinitely preferred to look forward.

Yet this was only one side of the man. His daughter Ophelia once described her father to me as "a pessimist by nature",[5] and a depressive streak ran through both sides of his family. Many of his adult stories revealed a jaundiced and sometimes bleak view of human behaviour, which drew repeatedly on man's capacity for cruelty and insensitivity. His children's writing is sunnier, more positive – though even there, early critics complained of tastelessness and brutality.[6] It was a charge against which he always energetically defended himself, for underneath the exterior of the humourist and entertainer lurked a fierce moralist. But he found it hard because, like many writers, he hated analysing his own writing. I remember asking him on camera why so many of the central characters in his children's stories had lost one or both parents. He was taken aback by the question and at first even denied that this was the case. However, when, on reflection, he realized that he had made a mistake, his brain searched swiftly for a way out. He compared himself to Dickens. He had used "a trick", he said, "to get the reader's sympathy". In a rare confession of error, he admitted with a smile that he "had been caught out a bit".[7] What struck me most profoundly was that he seemed to make no conscious connection between his own life – he had lost his own father when he was three years old – and the worlds he created in his stories. It suggested, I thought, a kind of unexpected innocence and naivety.

Dahl's writing career would take many twists and turns over the course of his seventy-four years, and these convolutions were intimately bound up with a complex private life that held many hidden corners, secrets and anxieties. Together they made a powerful cocktail – for Dahl was full of contradictions and paradoxes. He loved the privacy of his writing hut, yet he liked to be in the public eye. He described himself as a family man, living in a modest English village, yet he was married to an

Oscar-winning movie star, and kept the company of presidents and politicians, diplomats and spies. He was fascinated by wealth and glamour. He often bragged. He gambled. He had a quick and discerning eye for great art and craftsmanship. He was drawn to the good things in life. Yet he was also a simple man, who preferred the Buckinghamshire countryside to life in the city – a man who grew fruit, vegetables and orchids with obsessive passion, who surrounded himself with animals, who bred and raced greyhounds, and who kept the company of tradesmen and artisans. He was generous, although his kindness was usually quiet and low key. Often only the recipient was aware of it. Roald himself however was no shrinking violet. He enjoyed public appearances, and delighted in being controversial. He was a conundrum. An egotistical self-publicist – notoriously brash, even oafish, in the limelight – he could also behave as slyly as the foxes he so admired. If he wanted, he could cover his tracks and go to ground.

As a writer, he was the most unreliable of witnesses – particularly when he spoke or wrote about himself. In *Boy*, his own evocative and zestful memoir of childhood, he begins by disparaging most autobiography as "full of all sorts of boring details."[8] His book, he asserts, will be no history, but a series of memorable impressions, simply skimmed off the top of his consciousness and set down on paper. These vignettes of childhood are painted in bold colours and leap vividly off the page. They are infused with detail that is often touching, and always devoid of sentiment. Each adventure or escapade is retold with the intimate spirit of one child telling another a story in the playground. The language is simple and elegant. Humour is to the fore. Self-pity is entirely absent. "Some [incidents] are funny. Some are painful. Some are unpleasant," he declares of his memories, concluding theatrically: "All are true." In fact, almost all are, to some extent, fiction. The semblance of veracity is achieved by Dahl's acute observational eye, which adds authenticity to the most fantastical of tales, and by a remarkable trove of 906 letters he kept at his side as he wrote. These were letters he had written to his mother throughout his life, and which she hoarded carefully, preserving them through the storms of war and countless changes of address.

In these miniature canvases, Dahl began to hone his idiosyncratic talent for interweaving truth and fiction. It would be pedantic to list the inaccuracies in *Boy* or its successor *Going Solo*. Most of them are unimportant. A grandfather confused with a great-grandfather, a date exaggerated, a slip in chronology, countless invented details. *Boy* is a classic, not because it is based on fact but because Dahl had a genius for storytelling. Yet its untruths, omissions and evasions are revealing. Not only do they disclose the author's need to embellish, they hint as well at the complex hidden roots of his imagination, which lay tangled in a soil composed of lost fathers, uncertain friendships, a need to explore frontiers, an essentially misanthropic view of humanity, and a sense of fantasy that stemmed in large part from the Norwegian blood that ran powerfully through his veins.

Norway was always important to Dahl. Though he would sometimes surprise guests at dinner by maintaining garrulously that all Norwegians were boring, he never lost his profound affection for and bond with his homeland. His mother lived in Great Britain for over fifty years, yet never renounced her Norwegian nationality, even though it sometimes caused her inconvenience – most notably when she had to live as an alien in the United Kingdom during two world wars. Although she usually spoke to her children in English and always wrote to them in her adopted language, she made sure they also learned to speak Norwegian at the same time they were learning English; and every summer she took them to Norway on holiday. Forty years later, Roald would recreate these summer holidays for his own children, reliving memories that he would later immortalize in *Boy*. "Totally idyllic," was how he described these vacations. "The mere mention of them used to send shivers of joy rippling all over my skin."[9] Part of the pleasure was, of course, an escape from the rigors of an English boarding school, but for Roald the delight was also more profound. "We all spoke Norwegian and all our relations lived over there," he wrote in *Boy*. "So, in a way, going to Norway every summer was like going home."[10]

"Home" would always be a complex idea for him. His heart may have sometimes felt it was in Norway, but the home he dreamed about most of the time was an English one. During the Second World War, when he was in Africa and the Middle East as a pilot and in Washington as a diplomat, it was not Norway he craved for, nor the valleys of Wales he had loved as a child, but the fields of rural England. There, deep in the heart of the Buckinghamshire countryside, he, his mother and his three sisters would later construct for themselves a kind of rural enclave: the "Valley of the Dahls", as Roald's daughter Tessa once described it. Purchasing homes no more than a few miles away from each other, the family lived, according to one of Roald's nieces, "unintegrated . . . and largely without proper English friends".[11] For though Dahl was proud to be British and though he craved recognition and acceptance from English society, for most of his life he preferred to live outside its boundaries, making his own rules and his own judgements, not unlike his ancestor, Pastor Hesselberg.

As a result, English people found him odd. His best friend at prep school admitted that he was drawn to Roald because he was "a foreigner".[12] And he was. Though born in Britain, and a British citizen, in many ways Dahl retained the psychology of an émigré. Later in his life, people forgot that. They interpreted his behaviour through the false perspective of an assumed "Englishness", to which he perhaps aspired, but which was never naturally his. They saw only a veneer and they misunderstood it. In truth, Roald was always an outsider, the child of Norwegian immigrants, whose native land would become for their son an imaginative refuge, a secret world he could always call his own.

As with many children of emigrants, Roald would take on the manners and identity of his adopted home with the zeal of a convert. His sister Alfhild complained that her brother did not "recognize more how strong the Scandinavian is in us as a family".[13] Ironically, however, the one British ancestor he did publicly acknowledge was the Scots patriot William Wallace. Dahl was immensely proud of the family tree that showed his direct lineage to the rebel leader who, legend has it, also stood over six foot five inches tall. Wallace had defeated the invading English armies at the Battle of Stirling Bridge in 1297, but he was to meet a grisly end at their hands eight years later, when he was captured, taken to London, and executed. The brutal details of his death would not have eluded Dahl's antennae, which were acutely sensitive to human cruelty. Wallace was stripped naked, tied to a horse and dragged to Smithfield, where he was hanged, cut down while still alive, then publicly castrated and disembowelled. His body was hacked into four parts and his head placed as a warning on a spike atop London Bridge, along with those of two of his brothers. The English then tried to exterminate the rest of the Wallace family and they largely succeeded in doing so. A few of them escaped, making a perilous journey by boat across the North Sea to Bergen in Norway, where they settled and began a Norwegian Wallace line that survives to this day. Dahl's grandmother, Ellen Wallace, was a descendant of those plucky fourteenth-century refugees. She married Karl Laurits Hesselberg, the grandson of the resourceful pastor who had escaped the church fire in Grue.

His father's side of the family were somewhat different.[14] If the Hesselbergs were grand, middle-class, philanthropic intellectuals, the Dahls were grounded in earth and agriculture. They were ambitious, canny, uneducated and rough – albeit with an eye for craftsmanship and beauty. Roald's father, Harald Dahl, was born in Sarpsborg, a provincial town some 30 miles from Christiania, whose principal industries in the nineteenth century were timber and brewing. Roald described his paternal grandfather Olaus as a "prosperous merchant who owned a store in Sarpsborg and traded in just about everything from cheese to chicken-wire".[15] But the records in the parish church in Sarpsborg describe him simply as a "butcher",[16] while other legal documents refer to him as "pork butcher and sausage maker". They came, as it were, from the other side of the tracks. Indeed, Roald once admitted to Liccy that his mother's family, the Hesselbergs, thought themselves "a cut above" the provincial Dahls and rather looked down their noses at them.[17]

Dahl is a common enough name in Norway. There are currently about 12,000 of them in a population of 4.75 million. But until the nineteenth century there were hardly any at all. Olaus Dahl indeed was not born a Dahl. He was christened Olaves Trulsen on May 19, 1834, the son of Truls Pedersen and Kristine Olsdottir. After his own given name, he took his father's first name and added *sen* (in English "son of") onto the end of it in the traditional Scandinavian manner. In this way surnames changed from generation to generation, as they still do in many Icelandic families. Spelling too was erratic – in records Olaus appears also as Olavus, Olaves and Olav. But at some point in his twenties he took the decision to "Europeanize" himself and acquire a fixed family name. Many others around him were doing the same, including his future wife Ellen Andersen, who changed her name to Langenen. Why Olaus chose Dahl, which means "Valley", is uncertain, although it seems to have been a popular choice with others who came from the lowlands rather than the mountains.

Olaus's story is typical of that of many Norwegians in the mid-nineteenth century. He was born into a small farming community, where his parents eked out a miserable existence. There, the short summers were filled with endless chores, while the winter brought only darkness and misery. The fogs swept in from the sea, swathing their primitive homestead and few acres of land in a damp, suffocating cloak of gloom. For much of the year, life was unbearably monotonous. If contemporary accounts are an accurate guide, in one corner of their two candlelit rooms, perched above the snorting animals, his mother would probably be spinning. In another his father was getting drunk. For generations, rural families had lived like this; subsisting, struggling simply to survive, grateful for the land they owned, yet tied to it like slaves. They were illiterate and uneducated. There was little or no scope for self-improvement. They aged prematurely and died young. Olaus would not have been alone in feeling the need to escape from a landscape that drained his energies and sapped his need for change. So, at some point in his late teens, he abandoned the countryside, and went to the expanding industrial town of Sarpsborg, some 20 miles away, where the railway would soon arrive. There he got a job as a trainee butcher and set up home with Ellen, from nearby Varteig. After a few years, he opened his own butcher's shop.

Early twenty-first-century Sarpsborg is a grim place. Gray and ugly, it is dominated by a sullen 1960s concrete and steel shopping centre, which crouches next to the mournful remains of the nineteenth-century town. The outskirts are relentlessly, oppressively industrial. It is a far cry from the ancient splendours of Trondheim, the civilized serenity of Oslo, or the picturesque fjords and fishing villages of the western coast. On a dull Saturday afternoon in November, drunken and overweight supporters of Sparta, the ailing local football team, stagger from bar to bar. The occasional raucous cheer suggests an attempt at rowdiness. But one senses their hearts are not quite in it. Depression stalks the streets. In quiet corners, solitary older inhabitants drink furtively, seeking out the darkest corners of gloomy cafés in which to hide. Others huddle in groups, saying nothing. No trace remains of the butcher's shop where Olaus plied his trade, or of the house in Droningensgade where he raised his family and where he lived with his servant Annette and his assistant Lars Nilssen. Like so many other older Sarpsborg buildings, they have long since been destroyed.

When Olaus died in 1923 at the age of eighty-nine, Roald was only six. It is not clear that he ever met him, although in *Boy* he confidently describes his paternal grandfather as "an amiable giant almost seven foot tall".[18] Some of the other detail he gives about the man is entirely fictitious. For example, he claimed that Olaus was born in 1820, some fourteen years earlier than he actually was. Perhaps he confused him with his great-grandfather Hesselberg, the son of the pastor from Grue, who was indeed born that year. Perhaps not. Yet this lack of concern for detail blinded him to one unexpected anomaly of his own family history. Olaus and his wife Ellen had six children: three sons and three daughters over a period of thirteen years. Harald was born in 1863, Clara in 1865, Ragna in 1868, Oscar in 1870, Olga in 1873, and finally Truls in 1876.[19] Examining the local baptism and marriage records, however, reveals a surprising and perhaps significant detail: Roald's father was illegitimate. Harald was born in December 1863, but his parents did not actually marry until the following summer. He was christened on June 26, 1864, when he was six months old, and just five days after his parents' wedding. Whether Harald was aware that he was born a bastard is unclear, but in a small community like Sarpsborg, it was unlikely that fact would have been kept a secret from him for long, and the associated stigma may well have fuelled his desire to start a new life elsewhere.

Harald undoubtedly had a hard childhood. In *Boy*, Roald tells the gruesome story of how, aged fourteen, his father fell off the roof of the family home, where he was repairing loose tiles, and broke his arm. A drunken doctor then misdiagnosed a dislocated shoulder, summoning two men off the street to help him put the shoulder into place. As they forcibly manipulated young Harald's arm, splinters of bone started to poke through the boy's skin. Eventually the arm had to be amputated at the elbow. Dahl tells the tale with his usual lack of sentiment, explaining how his father made light of his disability – sharpening a prong of his fork so he could eat one-handed, and learning to do almost everything he wanted, except cutting the top off a hard-boiled egg, with a single hand. It's a good tale. Suspiciously good. So it is not surprising to discover that Roald confessed to one of his American editors, Stephen Roxburgh at Farrar, Straus & Giroux, that he had invented much of it and that he had particularly enjoyed devising the detail of the sharpened fork.[20] Photographs confirm that his father's arm was certainly amputated. But it's also possible that Dahl's version of the accident hid a more squalid domestic truth and that it was a drunken parent rather than a drunken doctor who was responsible for the amputation. We don't know if Harald was a fabricator of the truth – his wife certainly was, and she was the one who passed the family legends down to Roald – but he was studious, thoughtful, and had a passion for beautiful things. He had little in common with his father: the obstinate and rough-hewn butcher, who squandered his money betting on local trotting races.[21]

Harald and his brother Oscar must have elected to leave Norway some time in the 1880s. Writing a hundred years later, Roald describes the decision in characteristically simple terms:

> My father was a year or so older than his brother Oscar, but they were exceptionally close and soon after they left school they went for a long walk together to plan their future. They decided that a small town like Sarpsborg in a small country like Norway was no place to make a fortune. So what they must do, they agreed, was to go away to one of the big countries, either to England or France, where opportunities to make good would be boundless.[22]

Both went to Paris, but their motivations for leaving were almost certainly more complex than Roald made out. To begin with, the two brothers were nothing like the same age. There was a seven-year gap between them. So, even if Oscar had just left school when he departed for France, Harald would have been a young man in his twenties. The fact that Roald also maintained his grandfather "forbade" his two sons to leave and that the two men were forced to "run away"[23] suggests it took a while for the slow-burning Harald to pluck up the courage and defy him. Two more of Olaus and Ellen's children also left Norway at this time: Clara went to South Africa and Olga to Denmark. Only Ragna and her youngest brother, Truls, stayed behind. Truls became his father's apprentice and eventually took over the butcher's shop, staying with him, one suspects, largely for business reasons.

The two older Dahl brothers left Norway on a boat. It's quite possible they worked on ships for a considerable period of time before they ended up in Paris, for both of them later went into careers that involved quite detailed knowledge of shipping. What exactly they did when they got to the French capital remains unclear. Family legend has it that they went there to be both artists and entrepreneurs – an improbable combination of skills perhaps, but one that would define Roald, in whose mind there was always a natural link between making art and making money. It was the same with his elder sister Alfhild. Sitting in the garden of her house in the Chiltern Hills, a stone's throw away from where her brother lived, her weathered features broke into a wrinkly grin as she recalled her father and uncle, seventy years earlier. "They left Norway to become artists, you see," she told me. "They went to make their fortune. They just assumed they could do it."[24] It was as if her brother were speaking. The crackly voice, the clipped, matter-of-fact delivery, the wry chuckle.

The big picture, too, is similarly vivid and compelling, always uncluttered with qualifications or a surfeit of detail. For Alfhild, Harald and Oscar were typical Nordic bohemians, who came to Paris for its glamour, its freedom, and its artistic energy. Fictionalized versions of these Scandinavian visitors appear in literature of that period – Oswald in Ibsen's *Ghosts*, for example, or Louise Strandberg in Victoria Benedictsson's play

The Enchantment. They left the stern world of the North for a "great, free glorious life"[25] among the boulevards and cafés, where geniuses mixed cheek-by-jowl with the indigent, where anarchists plotted social revolution, and where painting was in a ferment of change that had not been seen in one place since Renaissance Florence.

Fading sepia photographs give us a glimpse of the lost world they lived in: days at the races, fancy-dress parties, lunches on summer lawns in Compiègne and Neuilly. And then they painted. It was the golden age of Norwegian painting, and in Paris Harald would almost certainly have mixed with the leading Scandinavian painters of the day, including Edvard Munch and Frits Thaulow. Not that Harald was a modernist. He was a craftsman, who carved mirrors, picture frames and mantelpieces, and painted rural scenes. A few examples of his work survive – subtle, well-crafted landscapes in the Scandinavian naturalistic style. At Gipsy House, one of them, an impressionistic pastel in green, blue and brown, still hangs by Liccy Dahl's bedside. It is reminiscent of the dismal rural setting from which Harald's father had fled. A clump of straggly spruces tremble by the side of a placid lake, like a skeletal family tentatively approaching the chilly waters. No sunlight illuminates the scene, nor is there any sense of human habitation. In the foreground, reeds are tugged by a gust of wind. In the background, the bare mountains rise up into the haze toward the distant sky.

The visual arts were an important and little understood aspect of Roald Dahl's life and formed a continuous counterpoise to his literary activities. All his life he bought and sold paintings, furniture and jewellery – sometimes to supplement his literary earnings. He even opened an antique shop. That connection between business and art, which came as naturally to him as breathing, would puzzle and irritate many of Dahl's English literary contemporaries, who resented his skill at making money and disliked the pride he took in his own financial successes. It frequently caused misunderstandings. The British novelist Kingsley Amis was typical. In his memoirs, he described his only meeting with Dahl. It was at a party given by Tom Stoppard in the early 1970s. There, Roald apparently suggested to Amis that, if he was suffering from "financial problems", he should consider writing a children's book, and went on to describe how he might go about doing so. Amis, who had no interest in children's fiction, felt he was being patronized by Dahl's suggestion that his own writing was not bringing him enough money. Dahl, for his part, was in precisely the kind of English literary environment he loathed. He knew that Amis, like most of the guests, did not respect children's writing as proper literature and this attitude made him feel vulnerable. Drunk and ill at ease, he probably felt that the only way to keep his head up with Amis was to talk money. The clash of attitudes was bitter and fundamental. Noting that Dahl departed by helicopter, Amis concluded: "I watched the television news that night, but there was no report of a famous children's author being killed in a helicopter crash."[26]

The need for financial success was in Roald's blood. His father and his uncle Oscar had both evolved into shrewd businessmen. When the two brothers eventually separated in Paris, Oscar travelled to La Rochelle, on the west coast of France, with his new wife, Thérèse Billotte, whom he had rescued from a fire in 1897 at the Bazar de la Charité. As with the fire in Grue, this had killed over one hundred people.[27] Billotte was from a family of painters. Her grandfather was the French writer and artist Eugène Fromentin, most famous for his naturalistic depictions of life in North Africa, while her uncle, René Billotte, was a commercial landscape painter, whose murals of exotic scenes still decorate *Le Train Bleu*, the elaborate gilded dining room of Paris's main railway station to the South, the Gare de Lyon. In La Rochelle, Oscar started a company of fishing trawlers called Pêcheurs d'Atlantique. His fleet began the practice of canning its catch on board ship, and became so successful that Roald could justifiably boast after the war that his uncle was "the wealthiest man in town".[28] With the money he made, Oscar indulged himself. He purchased the Hôtel Pascaud, an elegant eighteenth-century town house, and filled it with exquisite objects. Roald would later fondly describe it as "a museum dedicated to beauty".[29]

Oscar was a complex character. He was an aesthete but, like his father Olaus, also something of a bully. Roald would always have a turbulent relationship with him. During the war Oscar remained in Occupied

France, collaborating with the Nazis, while his son fought in the Resistance. One family legend has it that, after the war was over, he was publicly tarred and feathered by a group of bitter locals and that father and son never spoke again. However, what is certain is that this exotic French uncle, with his Viking appearance and fastidious taste, left an indelible impression on his young nephew – if only for his facial hair.

> My late uncle Oscar . . . had a massive hairy moustache, and at meals he used to fish out of his pocket an elongated silver scoop with a small handle on it. This was called a moustache-strainer and he used to hold it over his moustache with his left hand as he spooned his soup into his mouth with his right. This did prevent the hair-ends from becoming saturated with lobster bisque . . . but I used to say to myself, "Why doesn't he just clip the hairs shorter? Or better still, just shave the damn thing off altogether and be done with it?" But then Uncle Oscar was the sort of man who used to remove his false teeth at the end of dinner and rinse them in his finger-bowl.[30]

Harald's temperament, like his moustache, was less extrovert than his brother's. And he remained in Paris a little longer. However, some time in the 1890s, when he decided that he was tired of the vie bohémienne, he headed not to La Rochelle but to South Wales, to the coal metropolis of Cardiff, where he had heard that enterprising Norwegians could make their fortune.

CHAPTER TWO

Shutting Out the Sun

THE HISTORY OF TRADING between Norway and South Wales goes back well over a thousand years. Medieval chroniclers writing of the land of Morgannwg, now Glamorgan, in the period between the Roman settlement and the Norman Conquest celebrated the visits of Norwegian traders, comparing them favourably to the "black heathens",[1] the Danes, whose intentions often seemed more inclined toward rape and pillage than commerce. Curiously, recent evidence suggests that Welsh men and women, captured in the valleys and sold into slavery, may have been the first major commodity exported from Wales to Norway;[2] however, by the mid-nineteenth century, trade in human souls had given way to a sophisticated, booming and lucrative business relationship based on timber, steel and above all, coal. Boats from Norway, already the third largest merchant fleet in the world, arrived in Cardiff with timber, mostly to use as pit props (which the Welsh miners called "Norways"), and left carrying coal and steel to all parts of the globe. In twenty years the city's population doubled as it became the world's major supplier of coal. By 1900, Cardiff was exporting 5 million tons of coal annually from more than 14 miles of seething dockside wharfage. Two thirds of these exports left in Norwegian-owned vessels. The city was consequently awash with commercial opportunities for an enterprising, intelligent young expatriate, tired of his sojourn in Paris and eager to make his fortune.

Cardiff, of course, already boasted a considerable number of resident Norwegian nationals. But the majority were transient sailors. In 1868, the

Norwegian Mission to Seamen had constructed a little wooden church between the East and West Docks on land donated by the Marquis of Bute. It was a place of worship, but also a place where the ships' crews, many of whom were as young as fourteen, could relax and read Norwegian books and newspapers, while the cargo on their boats was loaded and unloaded. A model ship hung from the ceiling, and the walls were decorated with Scandinavian landscapes and pictures of the royal families of Sweden, Denmark and Norway. The tables were even decorated with miniature Norwegian flags.

Up to 75,000 seamen passed through the Mission's doors each year, eager for reminders of home in this hostile industrial environment. The docks were noisy, filthy, and could be terrifying – particularly to anyone from a rural background. An experienced Norwegian sea captain described the city: "It's not difficult to find Cardiff from the sea," he told his young nephew, who was about to sail there for the first time; "you just look for a very black sky – that's the coal dust. In the middle of the dust, there is a white building, the Norwegian Seamen's Church. When we see that we know we are home."[3] The tiny church, with its plucky spire, quickly became a symbol for the Norwegian community in Cardiff, although most who settled there integrated with the local Welsh community, and used it simply for births, marriages and deaths.[4] Today it stands restored, looking out at redeveloped Cardiff Bay, as if saluting the most famous of its congregation, who was christened there in the autumn of 1916, and whose name now graces the public area between the church and the grey slate, golden steel modernity of the new Wales Millennium Centre: Roald Dahl.*

Exactly when Harald Dahl arrived in South Wales is not clear. He does not figure in the UK census of 1891; however, by 1897 a mustachioed and dapper Harald is posing for a portrait photographer in Newport, some 15 miles along the coast from Cardiff. His long, flat face,

---

*The church was dismantled, removed from its original site at Bute West Dock in 1987, and rebuilt in the regenerated Cardiff Bay in 1992. Roald Dahl was the first president of the Norwegian Church Preservation Society that supervised the restoration. In the process the building lost its corrugated iron roof and acquired a grander tiled one. It now overlooks Roald Dahl Plass (*Plass* is Norwegian for "Plaza"), formerly the Oval Basin, which was renamed after the author in 2002.

round forehead and confident, sardonic eyes bear little resemblance to the oafish features of his father, which scowl out of an earlier page in the same family photograph album.[5] It's likely that this photograph of Harald, despatched to sisters and friends in Paris, was taken not long after he arrived in the Cardiff area and began learning his trade in shipping. In 1901 the census records that he was still single, working as a shipbroker's manager and lodging near the docks in a small redbrick terrace at No. 3, Charles Place, Barry, in the house of a retired land steward called William Adam, his wife Mary and their two adult daughters. Yet, despite his relocation to South Wales, a significant part of Harald's heart had remained in France. He had fallen in love with a glamorous doe-eyed Parisian beauty named Marie Beaurin-Gressier. Later in the summer of 1901, he returned to Paris and married her.

Her granddaughter Bryony describes Marie as coming from "a posh *ancien régime* family that had become rather impoverished and down on its luck".[6] Certainly, the Beaurin-Gressiers were not bourgeois. Though they had houses in Paris and in the country, near Compiègne, they seemed more inclined to sport and leisure than to commerce. Rugby was a dominating interest. Two of Marie's brothers, Guillaume and Charles, played for Paris Stade Français, the latter representing his country twice against England, while one of her sisters married the captain of the French team that won a gold medal at the 1900 Olympics. Another sister went to Algeria and married an Arab. Another brother ran a well-known Parisian fish restaurant. Yet another was an auctioneer. Marie was the most beautiful. Waiflike, elfin and delicate, she had a pale complexion, a mop of thick dark hair and sad, serious eyes. Fifteen years her senior, Harald must have had enormous charm, as well as good financial prospects, to succeed in stealing her away from her warm and adoring family. A snapshot of her on her wedding day, on a sunny veranda in the French countryside, beaming with delight and surrounded by admirers, suggests that she was very much in love. But it also suggests her innocence. She can surely have had little sense of what life in industrial Cardiff would offer her. Perhaps to counteract any potential feelings of homesickness, Marie brought some reminders of France with her to South Wales. Her trousseau boasted a diverse collection of jewellery, paintings and furniture, including a rosewood bedstead, various antique tables, chairs, secretaires, cabinets, an astronomical clock and an elaborate Louis XVI timepiece. Touchingly there was also a gilt mirror "carved by Mr Dahl and presented to Mrs Dahl".[7]

Shortly after the newlyweds returned to Cardiff, Harald went into business with another expatriate Norwegian, three years younger than he was: Ludvig Aadnesen. The two men had become acquainted with each other in Paris, but the Aadnesens, who came from Tvedestrand, near Kragerø, the birthplace of Edvard Munch, were already part of Harald's extended family. One of them had married Harald's sister Clara, and emigrated to South Africa with her.† Ludvig, a lifelong bachelor, shared Harald's fascination for painting and became his confidant and closest friend.

Financially, it was a good move. Over the next two decades the shipbroking firm of Aadnesen & Dahl, which supplied the ships that arrived in the docks with fuel and a host of other items, would expand from its small room in Bute Street to acquire offices in Newport, Swansea and Port Talbot, as well as large premises in Cardiff, which at one point also housed the Norwegian Consulate. Gradually the partnership began to trade in coal as well as simply supplying ships, and both men became rich. Dahl and Aadnesen were business partners, but they were also immensely close, and Ludvig occupied "an incredibly special place"[8] in Harald's affections. In the family he was always referred to as *"Parrain"* (the French for "Godfather"), and when Harald died, he bequeathed to

---

†The exact links between the Dahls and the Aadnesens are complex and hard to discern. Census records reveal that Harald's sister Clara Dahl married an Aadnesen and went to live with him in South Africa, where she gave birth to a son, Harald Dahl Aadnesen, in Durban in 1895. Either Aadnesen died or the couple were divorced, for by 1900, Clara was back in Oslo, living with her father and her five-year-old son. By the time Olaus died in 1923, Clara had remarried a local machinist called Siegfried Cammermeyer. Oscar Dahl took a benevolent interest in his nephew, Harald, who spent much time with his own son, Erik. Oscar's family photograph albums show the two boys playing with each other, skiing in thick snow, and there are several shots of Harald's wedding in France. What happened after that is unclear. Either Harald died young or his connection with Ludvig Aadnesen became increasingly tenuous. When Ludvig died in Whitchurch, Glamorganshire, in 1956, at the ripe old age of ninety, he left the bulk of his estate to his nieces Helga and Elizabeth and a nephew called Torolf. There was no mention at all of the South African-born Harald.

his "good old friend and partner" the only named object in his will: a painting by Frits Thaulow called *Harbour Scene*. The painting, now lost, must have symbolized many shared memories for the two men. It spoke, of course, of ships and the sea that had caused them both to move to Wales, but it also evoked their youth together in Norway.

Harald's marriage to Marie began promisingly. He rented an Arts and Crafts seafront house near the docks in Barry, round the corner from where he had been lodging, with a first-floor balcony that offered a fine view of the bay. There, their first child, Ellen Marguerite, named after Harald's mother, was born in 1903, and a son Louis, named perhaps after her elder brother, three years later in 1906. Those are the bare statistics. Yet while archival research can reconstruct the landmark events of a vanished life – its births, marriages and deaths – it cannot bring to life the personality that lived between these records without more personal, idiosyncratic evidence. Harald left diaries, letters, paintings, odd pieces of carving, and other artefacts that hint at his character. The contents of the expensive French leather wallet that was in his pocket when he died, for example, now carefully preserved at the Roald Dahl Museum and Story Centre in Great Missenden, complete with postal orders and railway season ticket, testify both to his good taste and meticulous habits. Of Marie, however, nothing remains. Even the gilt mirror is no longer in the family.‡ It is consequently hard to hypothesize how she coped with her new life in Barry. But it's more than likely she suffered. Far away from her family and from the world she loved, the grime and dust of Cardiff Docks must have seemed a poor replacement for the elegance of Paris or the delights of summer days in Compiègne. Living with a Norwegian husband, fifteen years older than she was and accustomed to solitude, also cannot have been easy.

On October 16, 1907, while heavily pregnant with their third child,

‡According to Bryony Dahl, most of Marie's furniture eventually went to her daughter Ellen, who used it to furnish the house in Hampstead, where she lived with her husband Ashley Miles. When Ashley and Ellen died, within a few weeks of each other early in 1988, everything was left to Ashley's secretary, Barbara Prideaux, who had by then become their carer. She too died shortly afterwards, leaving two Beaurin-Gressier portraits to Bryony. She subsequently sold these along with the two pieces of Marie's furniture that had been left to her father, Louis: an "elaborate marquetry cabinet" and a "ridiculous marble and ormolu clock" – presumably the Louis XVI timepiece mentioned in the marriage settlement – Bryony Dahl, Conversation with the author, 01/17/08.

Marie died. She was twenty-nine years old. Her death certificate indicates that she collapsed and died of a massive haemorrhage caused by *placenta praevia* – an obstetric complication, where the placenta lies low in the uterus and can shear off from it, causing sometimes fatal bleeding. Someone called Mary Henrich, probably a nurse or nanny as she was also living at the house, was present when Marie died and reported her death to the authorities. Marie's granddaugther Bryony however remembers a rumour whispered in the family (perhaps stemming from Roald's mother, Sofie Magdalene) that Marie had been depressed and died from a failed abortion.[9] While it is possible that an attempt to terminate the pregnancy artificially might produce similar symptoms to *placenta praevia* haemorrhage, the risks for the abortionist if the pregnancy was advanced would have been enormous. So, unless Marie had attempted somehow to do it herself, the official version seems a good deal more plausible.

Marie's death left Harald devastated. He had almost completed building a splendid new whitewashed house for his family, far from the commotion and noise of the docks, in leafy Llandaff – a medieval town that the railway had made a suburb of Cardiff. Harald had designed many of the building's details himself and proudly named his new home "Villa Marie" in honour of his young wife. Sadly, she never saw it finished. It survives today, though its name has changed,[10] but its steeply sloping gables and idiosyncratic Arts and Crafts appearance, with leaded windows and faux medieval buttresses, suggest how much Harald himself had contributed to the design and how much he must have looked forward to a settled and happy family life there. Instead, at forty-four, he found himself suddenly on his own – left to raise two tiny children, aged three and one, neither of whom would ever remember the dusky, wide-eyed waif whose beauty had so bewitched him.

Following Marie's death, her mother Ganou came over from Paris to help look after Ellen and Louis. Harald drowned his sorrows in hard work, spending long hours in his office and obsessively tending Villa Marie's substantial garden.[11] Four years passed. Then, one summer, Harald went away to visit his sister Olga, who was now living in Denmark.[12] Whether he was lonely and went consciously in search of a new bride, as Roald maintained in his memoir *Boy*, is uncertain, but it was in Denmark, not Norway, as Roald later claimed, that the Dahls and the Hesselbergs finally connected. Sofie Magdalene Hesselberg, who was visiting friends, had strong, almost masculine features that were in sharp contrast to Marie's delicate, almost doll-like appearance. Within a matter of weeks she and Harald were engaged.

It was a convenient match for both of them. She was twenty-six years old, sturdy, strong-willed and eager to break the tie with her parents. He was prosperous, established, and old enough to have been her father. Harald however had to overcome strong opposition from Sofie Magdalene's parents. Karl Laurits and his wife Ellen were by now wealthy in their own right. He was treasurer of the Norwegian Public Service Pension Fund and both were very controlling personalities. Their only son had recently died, and their three daughters were now the focus of their attention. Sofie Magdalene was considered the least attractive of them, and felt herself in some ways the "Cinderella" of the trio.[13] Nevertheless Karl Laurits was disconcerted that his eldest wanted to marry a man only ten years younger than he was. Worse still was the fact that she planned to leave Kristiania and live in Wales. But Sofie Magdalene was determined, and her parents were eventually forced to consent grudgingly to the wedding.

Her stubbornness in doing so may also have been farsighted. Ahead of her, she may have seen the fate that would befall Ellen and Astri, her two younger sisters. They failed to escape their father's thrall and were destined to live out their entire lives in the parental home. Increasingly eccentric, they became a growing source of curiosity and amusement for their younger relations, who remembered them, either drunk or drugged, sitting on the veranda of their home in Josefinegate, like characters in an Ibsen play, methodically picking maggots out of raspberries with a pin.[14]

Harald took his new wife to Paris on her honeymoon, kitting her out in the French fashions he adored, and buying her a cape made of black satin that she kept for the rest of her life. They visited his brother Oscar and his wife in La Rochelle, before returning to the Villa Marie. Sofie Magdalene immediately took charge in a manner that was both decisive and somewhat brutal. She turfed the beloved Ganou out of the house, and hired a Norwegian nanny, Birgit, to look after the children. This alienated Ellen and completely traumatized the five-year-old Louis, for whom Ganou had become a surrogate mother. For weeks after she left he would stand at the garden gate looking desperately down Fairwater Road and screaming for her to come back. No longer was French to be spoken at home. From now on, only Norwegian and English were permitted. The sensitive Louis found it hard to cope with these changes and suffered psychologically. Once he appeared on the Dahls' front doorstep with a classmate who announced to an uncomprehending Sofie Magdalene that the unhappy boy had had "an accident in bags" during a lesson and needed to come home to wash his bottom. Though Louis would in time grow to be fond of his stepmother, these initial experiences caused a fault line between Sofie Magdalene and her stepchildren that would lead to tension later on.

The new bride, however, was deliriously happy in the Villa Marie. Fifty years later she would still describe it as her "dream home" – the place where she had been happiest of all.[15] She was soon pregnant and a rejuvenated Harald excitedly insisted that she take a series of "glorious walks" through the surrounding countryside, because he believed these would imbue the unborn child in her womb with a sense of beauty and a love of nature. Within five years Sofie Magdalene had given birth to four children: Astri (1912), Alfhild (1914),§ Roald (1916)[16] and Else (1917). All four were indeed to manifest a strong artistic leaning and profound love of the countryside, qualities they shared with both their parents. Nevertheless, the idea that these "glorious walks" had somehow influenced their emotional development became deeply ingrained in their psychologies. Astri was Harald's favourite. A snapshot of him roaring with delight as his one-year-old daughter takes a puff from his pipe is the only photograph to survive that shows him with anything but a sober, almost sombre, countenance. Roald was named after the Norwegian explorer Amundsen,

---

§Alfhild was named after Sofie Magdalene's late brother, Alf, who had died in his twenties. Astri Newman [daughter of Alfhild], Conversation with the author, 10/15/07.

who had successfully reached the South Pole in 1911, and whose nephew, Jens, worked briefly for Aadnesen & Dahl during the war.[17] He was his mother's "pride and joy", her only boy, and therefore treated with special care. His siblings affectionately dubbed him "the apple of the eye".[18]

The First World War brought the need for registration cards for Harald and Sofie Magdalene, and resentment among some locals that Norway remained neutral throughout the conflict. Harald and Sofie seem to have been immune from this – perhaps because Harald was working so hard to keep the merchant fleet going. His wartime secretary, J. Harry Williams, recalled Harald as a model employer, conscientious, diligent and responsible. He was "my first ideal", he told Roald. "Nobody has ever come higher in my experience."[19] Alfhild too remembered her father working long hours, coming home tired late in the evenings, and her mother trying to cheer him up with her Norwegian cooking. The war did no harm to his business and, as it prospered, Harald sold Villa Marie in 1917 and bought Ty Mynydd, a large Victorian farmhouse at Radyr, further out of Cardiff, a few stops down the Taff Vale railway. It had 150 acres of land, its own electricity generator, a laundry and a collection of farm outbuildings that included a working piggery. Roald later recalled with nostalgia its grand lawns and terraces, its numerous servants, and the surrounding fields filled with shire horses, hay wagons, pigs, chickens and milking cows. The purchase of the farm even merited an article in the local press, which described Mr Dahl as a man "with many years association with the shipping trade of South Wales" and "prominent in Docks circles". "His firm is a very large business," the article concluded, "especially with Norwegian shipowners, whose vessels have continued to trade with the district all through the war."[20]

Harald bought paintings and antique furniture for the new house, and carved wooden picture frames. He collected alpine plants, going out in all weathers to stock the new garden with what he had collected. At one point he also bought his young wife a secondhand De Dion Bouton car, and tried to persuade her to take up driving. It was a mistake. On her way to visit a friend who had just had a baby, she put her foot on the accelerator instead of the brake and crashed the car into a cartload of eggs. When she finally got to her friend's house, she found that the baby had died. She never drove again.[21] At home, Harald was not the easiest of husbands. He could be withdrawn and undemonstrative, sometimes almost cold, as he absorbed himself in his many private interests. Years later, Sofie Magdalene would tell her granddaughter, Lou Pearl, that at times she even felt frightened of him.[22]

As 1920 dawned, Harald would have been forgiven for looking back on his life with some satisfaction. He had come a long way since he left his family in Sarpsborg for the delights of bohemian Paris. Business was booming. He had survived the sudden death of his first wife, to find unexpected happiness with Sofie Magdalene. Though he had started his family late – when he was forty – he was now in his mid-fifties and had six happy, healthy multilingual children around him.¶ Two were already at boarding school. His eldest daughter Ellen was at Roedean, a grand English fee-paying school for girls, set high atop a cliff in Sussex overlooking the English Channel, while Louis had just started at nearby Brighton College. If he did not see his younger children as much as he would have liked, he still occasionally found the time to relax and unwind with them – chasing a giggling Alfhild round the dining-room table, for example, while singing Grieg's Troll Dance at the top of his voice.[23]

Now Sofie was pregnant again. Everything seemed idyllic. But these halcyon days were not to last. At the beginning of February, Astri, Sofie's eldest daughter, awoke in the middle of the night with a fierce stomach-ache. Her younger sister, Alfhild, who shared a room with her, went to fetch her mother, complaining that Astri's cries of pain were keeping her awake. A doctor was summoned and Astri was diagnosed with acute appendicitis. The doctor operated at home, on the scrubbed nursery table, but by then it was too late. The appendix had burst and Astri had peritonitis. She never came round from the anaesthetic. About a week later, she died from the infection. She was seven years old.

Harald never recovered from the blow. "Astri was far and away my

---

¶Learning two languages at the same time may have been one of the reasons Roald was so slow to start speaking. According to family legend, his first words were a complete sentence, spoken in Norwegian: *"Pappa, hvor for har du ikke tøfflene dine på deg – Daddy, why aren't you wearing your slippers?"*

father's favourite," Roald wrote in *Boy*. "He adored her beyond measure, and her sudden death left him literally speechless for days afterwards. He was so overwhelmed with grief that when he himself went down with pneumonia a month or so afterward, he did not much care whether he lived or died."[24] Writing those words, Roald knew only too well what his own father was feeling, for with vicious symmetry, some forty years later, he too was to lose his own eldest daughter – also aged seven. The son's understanding of his father's psychology was acute, but he also recalled his father's anguish from a child's perspective. He remembered the laurel bushes, which his father had been pruning when he first became ill and which, for the rest of his life, would always be associated with death. And he remembered his father's refusal to do battle with the disease. The eyes of the adult and child blended together as he described Harald's death, more than sixty years after it happened. "My father refused to fight," he wrote. "He was thinking, I am quite sure, of his beloved daughter, and he was wanting to join her in heaven. So he died. He was fifty-seven years old."[25]

Wracked with pneumonia, Harald articulated his regrets in his journal, torturing himself for having worked too hard and not having sufficiently enjoyed his dead daughter's brief life. "How little we understand about putting a price on the world's many good things? How seldom does the door to our hearts stand wide open? We put the blame on the fact that we have too much to do, that we must have peace and quiet to think and work, and so we shut out the sun. Only when it is too late do we see what we have missed."[26] Ironically, even as he noted these observations, he was unable to change his habits. As the coughing worsened and the fever soared, and as his eldest son Louis cycled around the garden with his five-year-old half sister Alfhild squealing with delight atop the handlebars,[27] Harald made minute and fussy adjustments to his will. Attended by two nurses, he cut out a small bequest to a distant cousin and instructed that all death duties arising from any of his other legacies were to be paid by the beneficiaries. Two days later, he was dead. He was buried in the medieval churchyard of St John the Baptist, Radyr, next to his daughter, Astri, on whose grave the earth was still fresh.

Above their joint resting place, not far from a 1,000-year-old yew tree,

Sofie Magdalene erected an elaborate pink granite cross. It stands still in the little churchyard that was once surrounded by fields and farmland and is now besieged by an ugly 1970s housing estate. The monument thrusts prominently above the surrounding gravestones, its Celtic ornamentation and circled cross suggesting perhaps a public commitment the Dahl family had made to the Welsh soil in which they had put down their roots. If that was the case, Sofie Magdalene was hedging her bets as well. For she also ensured that both coffins were lined in lead so that they could be dug up and transported back to Norway if she chose to return there in the future.[28]

The funeral was grand and formal. All the children dressed up. Alfhild wore a specially made check dress, with black bows. She remembered the huge house filled with flowers, the servants all dressed in black, and the heady perfume of the early spring narcissi, which lay strewn in piles upon the coffin. She also remembered the stoicism of her mother. For Sofie Magdalene never showed her pain. Others wept, but she did not. Much rested on her shoulders. She was thirty-five years old and had five children in her care – Ellen (sixteen), Louis (thirteen), Alfhild (five), Roald (three), and Else, barely one. A sixth was on the way. She was already looking forward. She intended to concentrate her energies on the living rather than the dead.

CHAPTER THREE

Boy

THE EDWARDIAN CHILDREN'S WRITER Edith Nesbit thought that the most important quality in a good children's writer was an ability vividly to recall their own childhood. Being able to relate to children as an adult, she believed, was largely unimportant. Roald Dahl could do both. His seductive voice, the subversive twinkle in his eye, and his sense of the comic and curious gave him an ability to mesmerize almost every child who crossed his path – yet he could also remember and reimagine his own childhood with astonishing sharpness. The detail might sometimes be unreliable, but what never failed him was an ability instinctively to recreate and understand the child's point of view. It was something of which he was very proud. He knew he could do it and that a great many others could not. Sitting in his high-backed faded green armchair by the fire at Gipsy House, a glass of whisky in one hand, he once talked to me about it with considerable pride. "It's really quite easy," he would say. "I go down to my little hut, where it's tight and dark and warm, and within minutes I can go back to being six or seven or eight again." Or, as his alter ego, Willy Wonka, put it in an early draft of *Charlie and the Chocolate Factory:* "In my factory I make things to please children. I don't care about adults." [1]

Dahl seldom dwelt on the traumatic early years of his childhood, and he generally made light of any connection between his fiction and his own life, yet the parallels between the two are intriguing. His fictional childhood bereavements, for example, are never maudlin. His child heroes or heroines always follow the positive pattern that Roald and his own sisters established after their father's death. Sophie in *The BFG* has lived in an orphanage almost as long as she can remember, but does not dwell on what might have been. "Oh you poor little scrumplet!" cries the Big Friendly Giant, when he discovers that Sophie has no father or mother. "Is you not missing them very badly?" "Not really," replies Sophie, "because I never knew them."[2] This pragmatism was characteristic of Dahl himself. Perhaps because he never really knew his father, he does not seem unduly to have felt his absence.

This attitude contributed to an unsentimental, frequently subversive view of families, which was reflected strongly in his children's fiction. The child always stands at the centre of things. Survival is often his or her main motivation, and enemies are as likely to come from within the family as from outside it.

Sometimes, the enemy is parents themselves – particularly if they are dreary or unimaginative. Occasionally, a good one appears – the "sparky" father figure in *Danny the Champion of the World* is probably the best example – but more often they feature as a negative force that the child must learn to endure, evade or subvert. To achieve this, the young hero must usually find an unexpected friend, who appreciates that child's special qualities and allows them to bloom. Charlie Bucket's soulmate in *Charlie and the Chocolate Factory* is neither mother, father, sibling nor schoolmate, but his quirky Grandpa Joe, and ultimately the great chocolate maker Willy Wonka himself. The orphaned narrator of *The Witches* has a similar relationship with his eccentric Norwegian grandmother. James in *James and the Giant Peach* finds salvation in nonhuman friends, a group of outsize and wacky bugs, while Sophie in *The BFG* finds her affinity in the person of a lumbering, good-natured giant. Sophie and James are both orphans and so have no parents to reject. Matilda Wormwood, on the other hand, the child heroine of Dahl's last major book, *Matilda*, has parents from hell – conniving, vulgar imbeciles who ignore their daughter and try to crush her love of reading. They are comic caricatures, but also capable of brutal insensitivity, being "so gormless and so wrapped up in their silly little lives" that Dahl doubts they would have noticed had their daughter "crawled into the house with a broken leg".[3] Matilda's exceptional connection with her teacher Miss Honey is the emotional core of the story, and in the end, she chooses to desert her dysfunctional family to live with her new adult friend – an option many children may have dreamed of in sulkier moments. In each case, the love Dahl celebrates is not the traditional one between parent and child, but a close friendship established by the child, on its own terms, and in an unfamiliar context.

In many instances his books are a kind of imaginative survival manual for children about how to deal with the adult world around them. They offer the vision of an existence freed from parental controls, a world full of imagination and pleasure, where everything is possible. Escapist perhaps, but not sentimental. For Dahl always remembered that children were programmed to be survivors. Several times in conversation he described them as "uncivilized creatures", engaged in a battle with a world of adults who were constantly telling them what to do. Once, in a radio interview, he even argued that most children unconsciously view their parents as "the enemy" and that there was "a very fine line between loving your parents deeply and resenting them".[4] It was a perception he developed early and one that remained with him until he died. It gave him the confidence to claim, at the end of his life, that he spoke for young people, that he was their advocate in a world that largely ignored them. Indeed, by then he often claimed that he preferred the company of children to that of adults.

Roald himself was blessed with an extraordinarily strong and influential Norwegian mother, who single-handedly raised him and did much to shape his attitudes. He described her as "undoubtedly the primary influence on my own life", singling out her "crystal clear intellect" and her "deep interest in almost everything under the sun" as two of the qualities he admired most in her. He acknowledged her as the source for his own interest in horticulture, cooking, wine, paintings, furniture and animals. She was the "materfamilias", his constant reference point and guide.[5] "She devoted herself entirely to the children and the home. She had no social life of her own," recalled her daughter Alfhild, adding that her mother "was very like Roald . . . a bit secret, a bit private".[6] Sofie Magdalene was undoubtedly a remarkable woman: brave, stubborn, eccentric and determined, a survivor who was able to face almost any difficulty or disaster with equanimity. "Practical and fearless,"[7] was how her youngest daughter described her. "Dauntless"[8] was the adjective Roald used in *Boy*, while pointing out that she was always the only member of the family not to get seasick on the two-day ferry crossing from Newcastle to Norway. He admired her toughness, her lack of sentiment, her buccaneering spirit and her laissez-faire attitude toward her offspring. His description of her, a non-swimmer, in a small motorboat, guiding seven children, all without lifebelts, through mountainous waves in the open Norwegian seas was typical. "That was when my mother enjoyed herself most," he wrote, revelling in behaviour most parents would consider reckless in the extreme. "There were times, I promise you, when the waves were so high that as we slid down into a trough the whole world disappeared from sight. Then up and up the boat would climb, standing almost vertically on its tail, until we reached the crest of the next wave, and then it was like being on the top of a foaming mountain." Dahl's description may be exaggerated, childish, but the implied metaphor is telling of his admiration for her as a parent. "It requires great skill to handle a small boat in seas like these," he concluded, "but my mother knew exactly how to do it and we were never afraid. We loved every minute of it."[9]

If his mother was the principal source of Roald's sense of adventure, she may unwittingly have been the source of some of his talents as a writer as well. For according to Roald's niece Bryony, Sofie Magdalene was also a born storyteller, and sometimes a gossip too, who enjoyed "weaving fantasies about members of the family, interspersed with downright lies". Bryony here hints at the division in Sofie Magdalene's attitude toward her blood children and her stepchildren, to whom one suspects she was always dutiful but less loving. They were usually the victims of her more malicious stories. "She used to have dreams about members of the family and say terrible things about what was going to happen to them," remembered Bryony, "and she loved to spread foul rumours about." It seems likely she was the source for the story of Marie Beaurin-Gressier's abortion and she once put it about the village that her stepson Louis's wife Meriel (Bryony's mother) was starving her husband. In hefty old age, confined to a wheelchair and dressed in black, Sofie talked less, but could still petrify her grandchildren and stepgrandchildren. "Witchy", "terrifying" and "like a spider" were some of the many descriptions of her. But she was not the only fabulist in the family. Alfhild and Roald both quickly honed their skills in that department, under the tutelage of their half sister Ellen, who also enjoyed an exaggerated yarn. Nevertheless, Sofie Magdalene was in a different league. "She was the *real* storyteller," Bryony recalled with a wistful chuckle. "I reckon Roald got it all from her." [10] And one of the first and most enduring legends she created for her children was about their father.

Roald was only three years old when his father died. The tales of Harald's personality and background, both real and invented, became therefore unquestioned, unexamined truths for his children. And Sofie Magdalene was largely responsible for all of them. As the years passed, she gradually cut off contact with almost all the other Dahls, creating a situation where few could contradict her version of events. The entrepreneur who left his family in Norway to find success abroad; the one-armed survivor, undaunted by adversity, who learned to cope with everything life could throw at him; the craftsman/painter living the high life in fin-de-siècle Paris; the lover of nature, the proponent of "glorious walks"; the grieving father, who lost the will to live. All these aspects of Harald's personality came to acquire talismanic qualities for his young son, who used them to help define himself. In later life, when things got difficult, sometimes he found himself looking for father figures who could measure up to this ideal. But he never inquired too deeply as to the veracity of the stories about his own father. They were too ingrained in his own personality. The legend of Harald, passed on to his children by his devoted wife, was perhaps the most powerful of the many myths of which his mother was the prime architect. Much of what she said, of course, was true. Yet Sofie Magdalene would later admit, in moments of weakness, that her husband had not been an entirely easy man to live with. For her young children, however, and for Roald in particular, Harald would always be the ideal "papa".

Roald criticized his father for only one thing: leaving an intricate, complex and controlling will, which suggested a distrust of his wife and which made the family's day-to-day survival much more difficult than was necessary. His plans were predicated on the assumption that Sofie Magdalene would marry again, so the bulk of the estate was left in a trust that was constructed more in favour of his children than his wife. But she remained a widow, and the result was that she was left with very little direct control of the family finances. Although she was one of the trustees, Sofie Magdalene still had to get approval from the other two trustees, her brother-in-law Oscar, and Ludvig Aadnesen, for almost everything she bought for the household. This was time-consuming and Sofie Magdalene sometimes also found it humiliating. The estate was large. In 1920, it was valued at over £150,000.[11] In today's terms its equivalent could be reckoned about £5 million (or $7.5 million). Harald's family in Norway were not entirely forgotten, but the bequests to them were small ones. He left £100 to each of his sisters, but to his eighty-six-year-old father, Olaus, who was still alive, and living in poverty in Kristiania in a tiny flat, and to his brother Truls, who had taken over the family business as pork butcher and sausage maker, he left nothing. Almost all of his wealth was left to his children.

One might have thought that the income from the modern-day equivalent of £5 million would have been enough for the Dahl family to go on living in Radyr, but it was not, and their life as rural landowners was abruptly terminated soon after Asta – "Baby", as she became known – was born in the autumn of 1920. By Christmas, the beloved farm was put on the market, the animals auctioned off, and the servants dismissed. From that moment onward, Radyr, with its turrets and fields, occupied an idealized place in the minds of the Dahl children, and the house came to embody a kind of paradise, irretrievably taken from them at a very young age. This sense of loss is echoed in many of Roald Dahl's books, most strikingly perhaps in *James and the Giant Peach*, where, on the very first page "the perfect life for a small boy" – which in this instance involved beaches, sun and sand rather than horses, fields and servants – comes to an abrupt end. James's parents had been up to London to go shopping (always a mistake in Dahl's eyes) and there they met a terrible, if hilarious fate – "eaten up in full daylight, mind you, and on a crowded street, by an enormous angry rhinoceros that had escaped from London Zoo". Though this was "a rather nasty experience" for them, Dahl reflects, "in the long run it was far nastier for James". His parents' end had been swift and relatively painless. Their son, on the other hand, was left behind, cut off from everything familiar and everyone he loved: "alone and frightened in a vast unfriendly world".[12]

So Radyr was sold. The family, with Birgit the nanny and a couple of maids, moved back to Llandaff, into a "pleasant medium-sized suburban villa"[13] called Cumberland Lodge, now part of Howell's School, which was also near the home of Ludvig Aadnesen. It was a comfortable existence, if less grand than life in Radyr. But there were consolations for a young boy. Its principal attraction was a large garden, with a swing and some rudimentary cricket nets, where Roald, already a keen sportsman, could practise his batting. Even more important than the garden was the man who worked there – a fellow whose real name was Jones, but whom the children called Joss or Spivvis. "Everyone loved him," Dahl would later recall, "but I loved him most of all. I adored him. I worshipped him, and whenever I was not at school, I used to follow him around and watch him at his work and listen to him talk." Every Saturday in the winter, when there was a home match, Joss would take young Roald to Ninian Park, to see Cardiff City, the local football team. Roald was already tall enough to see over many people's heads and clearly relished the experience of being away from a house full of women. "It was thrilling to stand there among those thousands of other men," he later wrote, "cheering our heroes when they did well and groaning when they lost the ball." The experience gave him "an almost unbearable sense of thrill and rapture", and contrasted with his feelings toward his first school: a local kindergarten called Elm Tree House, run by two sisters, Mrs Corfield and Miss Tucker. Their "sweet and smiling" faces made little impression on him and few memories of his short time there would linger in his brain.[14] One alone remained fresh. The swashbuckling thrill of riding his new tricycle down the road to school and leaning into the corners so steeply that only two of the cycle's three wheels touched the ground.

Roald's next school would be much more memorable. Llandaff Cathedral School, an elegant three-storey Georgian building, constructed in the shadow of a medieval cathedral, is an educational institution with a pedigree that dates back to the ninth century. Roald's elder brother Louis had been sent there, and though Sofie Magdalene was already planning a move to England, she was not yet quite ready to leave Wales. The school was also a stone's throw from Cumberland Lodge and so it was the natural place to send Roald after his year with the smiling sisters. He went there in 1923, at the age of seven, and stayed for two years. Of all the incidents he would later recall there, one adventure stood out above the others. It was both exciting and traumatic, and contained three ingredients that would come to characterize his later children's fiction: a sweetshop; a foul old hag; and violent retribution. In *Boy*, he introduces the story with a fanfare that is both swaggering and yet deliciously ironic. "When writing about oneself, one must strive to be truthful," he begins. "Truth is more important than modesty. I must tell you therefore, that it was I and I alone who had the idea for the great and daring Mouse Plot. We all have our moments of brilliance and glory," he concludes, "and this was mine." [15]

The story is a simple one. A boy finds a dead mouse under the floorboards at school. Along with a group of friends, Roald decides to use it to play a trick on the ugly and bad-tempered proprietor of the local sweetshop, Mrs Pratchett. He takes the dead mouse into the shop and when she is not looking, drops the mouse into a glass jar of sweets. Mrs Pratchett is so shocked when she opens it and finds the dead rodent that she drops the jar to the ground, where it shatters in pieces. Furious, she tracks down the offenders and takes revenge on them by ensuring they are ferociously beaten. A simple enough tale of a schoolboy prank that goes wrong, you might think. But not for Roald Dahl. For his sensitive child's antennae, this is an adventure story of grandiose proportions – enacted with buccaneering style and panache. Its setting, a sweetshop, is the centre of the universe. It is "what a bar is to a drunk, or a church is to a Bishop" – the most important place in town. Despite the suspicion that the tasty liquorice bootlaces may be made from rat's blood, or that the Tonsil Ticklers are infused with chloroform, the contents of its jars and boxes are objects of reverence and profound fascination. Dahl and his young accomplices are a "gang of desperadoes", locked in mortal combat with the hideous villain of the piece, Mrs Pratchett, a comic distillation of the two witchlike sisters who, it seems, ran the shop in real life.[16] She is "a small, skinny old hag with a moustache on her upper lip and a mouth as sour as a green gooseberry". She has "goat's legs" and "small malignant pig-eyes". Her "grimy hands" with their "black fingernails"[17] dig horrifyingly deep into the fudge as she scoops it out of the container. She is a typical Dahl enemy – cruel, bony, repulsive and female – and she wreaks a savage revenge on her five child tormentors, insisting that they are each caned by their headmaster while she sits in a chair, enthusiastically egging him on to greater violence.

Dahl's description of corporal punishment and adult unkindness in *Boy* is memorable and utterly convincing. It is the first time that any of the five boys have been beaten, so the tension is tremendous, as they venture ever deeper into the adult world, arriving at the inner sanctum of the enemy, the headmaster's study, with its forbidding smell of tobacco and leather. Mr Coombes, the headmaster, has so far seemed comic – a sweating, pink-faced buffoon. No longer preposterous, however, he is now transformed into a chilling agent of retribution: a giant, dangerously flexing his curved yellow cane. Roald's friend Thwaites is the first to feel its sting. As he bends over and touches the carpet with his fingers, Roald cannot help noticing "how small Thwaites' bottom looked and how very tight it was".[18] Each stroke of the cane is exaggerated, as the rod cracks "like a pistol shot" and boys shoot into the air, straightening up "like elastic".

But when Roald's own turn comes, the tone loses all comedy. The pain of the first stroke causes him to gasp so deeply that it "emptied my lungs of every breath of air that was in them". Aiming the strokes of the rod so that they come down in the same place has been a source of abstract comment, even admiration for the young boys. Now it is revealed as an act of cruel brutality. "It is bad enough when the cane lands on fresh skin," he declares, "but when it comes down on bruised and wounded flesh, the agony is unbelievable."[19] No surprise then to find that when his mother sees "the scarlet stripes" that evening at bathtime, she marches over to the school to give the headmaster a piece of her mind. No surprise either that, a term later, she takes Roald away from the school. But the outraged Sofie Magdalene does not then send her son to a gentler institution. Instead, she packs him off to St Peter's, a boarding school, across the Bristol Channel, which would prove to be even more draconian than the one in Llandaff.

The journey was taken on a paddle-steamer that "sloshed and churned" its way through the water from Wales to England for twenty-five minutes, before a taxi ferried boys to the school, which lay just outside the "slightly seedy" Somerset seaside resort of Weston-super-Mare. It was a typical English prep school of the period, as Dahl described it, "a purely money-making business owned and operated by the headmaster", educating about seventy boys,* aged between eight and thirteen, in a three-storey, ivy-clad Victorian Gothic mansion, surrounded by playing fields, tennis courts and allotments. In hindsight the school was to remind Dahl of "a private lunatic asylum",[20] an opinion corroborated by another celebrated St Peter's alumnus, some twenty years Dahl's junior, the writer and comedian John Cleese.[21] Looking at a faded postcard of the school dining room as it was, one might think it a civilized place. Light floods in through high sash windows onto tables laid with starched white tablecloths. Portraits of notables hang on the walls. Vases of fresh flowers even decorate the tables.

But, if Dahl and his contemporaries are to be believed, this was all a terrible illusion – a temporary image thrown up to persuade potential clients to part with both their offspring and their cash. For, once the parental back was turned, the picture became much uglier. Douglas Highton, Dahl's best friend for the last two of his four years at the school, agreed with Roald that it was a grim place, describing the headmaster, Mr Francis, as a "beastly cane-happy monster" with a "nasty collection" of rods on top of his bookshelves, who "seemed to enjoy beating little boys

---

*Not 150, as Dahl recalls in *Boy*, p. 72.

on the slightest pretext". It was an almost entirely male environment. The headmaster kept his "finicky and fussy" [22] wife and two unattractive daughters under lock and key, away from the eyes of the boys, and so the only feminine presence was a "female ogre" – the Matron, who "prowled the corridors like a panther" and obviously "disliked small boys very much indeed". [23]

Each boy was assigned one of four curiously named houses into which the school was divided: Duckworth Butterflies, Duckworth Grasshoppers, Crawford Butterflies and Crawford Grasshoppers. Dahl was a Duckworth Butterfly. Competition was encouraged at all levels, as each house vied with the others in both work and games to see who would come out top. Every boy in the school received either stars or stripes for successes or failures in the schoolroom or playing field and these were tallied up at the end of each term, when winners and losers were declared. Three times a year, a twenty-page magazine was professionally published, which formally chronicled and categorized these achievements, listing each boy's scores in a series of tables. It was taken very seriously. "Congratulations to you all, Butterflies, for you have this term risen from bottom place to second, and you were very nearly top," declares Duckworth Butterfly housemaster Mr Valentine Corrado in the December 1927 issue, adding grandly, as if reflecting on the outcome of a military battle, "to the very end it was uncertain whether you or the Duckworth Grasshoppers would triumph".

Corrado, who taught Latin when he was not trying to seduce the school matron, [24] was just one of the motley band of five or six schoolmasters who taught there. Most had fought in the First World War, many still hung on to their army rank, and some of them still bore the mental and physical scars of that conflict. All were eccentrics. They stare out of the school photographs that have immortalized them with a melancholy confidence – garbed in heavy tweed, moustaches trimmed, hair slicked back, jaws thrust forward. There is something untrustworthy yet forlorn about them. The shell-shocked grunting bully Captain Lancaster, for example, renamed Captain Hardcastle in *Boy*, whose thick orange moustache constantly twitched and bristled, or timid Mr S. K. Jopp, nicknamed "Snag" because that was one of his favourite words, who had only one hand and whose face had been deformed by an RAF flying accident.[25] It was to this peculiar collection of men, whose pleasures included stamp collecting,[26] and chasing the boys around the school on tea trolleys,[27] that Sofie Magdalene entrusted her nine-year-old son. Odd though they seemed, they instilled a sense of self-discipline and self-protection into their young charges. "They were tough, those masters," Roald wrote in *Boy*, "and if you wanted to survive, you had to become pretty tough too."[28]

The boys slept in dormitories. Between fifteen and twenty uncomfortable iron beds were lined up against the walls of each room, and Roald's first letter home mournfully reported that none of the mattresses had springs.[29] Under each was a bedpan (you were not allowed to go to the lavatory at night unless you were ill), and in the middle of the dormitory, a huddle of basins and jugs filled with cold water, for washing. It was a terrible shock for a young boy, used to a warm, comfortable and largely female environment, and Roald was initially homesick. He slept in his bed the wrong way round, facing the window that looked out toward the Bristol Channel, across which lay his home and his family, tantalizingly close, yet completely out of reach. He feigned appendicitis (having seen his half sister operated on at home a few months earlier, he knew the symptoms) and was sent home, where the local doctor in Llandaff quickly discovered his ruse. Another advocate of hardship as essential to the empire-building spirit, he too reinforced Dahl's survival mentality. "'I expect you're homesick,' he said. I nodded miserably. 'Everyone is at first,' he said. 'You have to stick it out. And don't blame your mother for sending you away to boarding school. She insisted you were too young, but it was I who persuaded her it was the right thing to do. Life is tough, and the sooner you learn how to cope with it, the better for you.'"[30] They struck a deal. In return for the doctor pretending he had a severe stomach infection and giving him an extra three days at home, Roald promised him he would go back to St Peter's and that he would never try the same trick again.

When he returned to Weston-super-Mare, Roald gradually began dealing with his homesickness. His main salvation was sport, something which the boys did almost every day and at which he showed a natural talent. His height and ranginess made him a good rugby player and a competent footballer, cricketer and boxer, though his school report for the summer of 1926 describes him as "overgrown" and "slow".[31] His weekly letters home to his mother, however, are brimful of his sporting exploits: swimming lengths of the pool underwater, learning to ride horses, scoring goals in soccer and striking boundaries in cricket. "I hit two sixes," he writes at one point, explaining dramatically to his mother that "you get a six when the ball goes full pitch into the boundary. One hit the pavilion with a tremendous crash and just missed a window."[32] His height was blamed for a "ponderous"[33] boxing technique, as were a number of other problems. Sent to a local optician because of recurrent headaches, he was told that there was nothing wrong with his eyes, but that he was "run down, due to growing too quickly".[34]

The academic standards at St Peter's were high and, initially, Roald was thrown in with a group of boys, including Douglas Highton, who were mostly a year and a half older than he was. He struggled to keep up, finding arts subjects – particularly languages – difficult. A report from Easter 1927 described him as "a little on the defensive" and exhorted him "to have more confidence". "He imagines he is doing badly," the report continued, "and consequently does badly."[35] So in September 1927 he stayed down in the 4th Form for a term, regaining his self-esteem and earning a record number of stars for Duckworth Butterflies.† But when he was promoted back to the higher year, things once more became academically difficult and again he became withdrawn. Douglas Highton, whose family lived in Asia Minor, and who was one of the most academic boys in the school, remembered Dahl as an outsider, with few friends. "Roald had a different individuality . . . he was very much an immigrant from Norway, and I was an immigrant from Turkey, where my mother's family had been established for about two hundred years. We were both foreigners." The two misfits became firm

---

†This was equivalent to year four in current UK educational practice and sixth grade in the United States and Canada.

friends, walking side-by-side on school trips to Weston-super-Mare, and indulging their mutual contempt for "what we regarded as stupid or unnecessary rules". They saw themselves as "subversives", developing a love of word games, enjoying a similar sense of humour, and sharing a sense of "the ridiculous nature of the English". A sprightly ninety-three when I spoke to him, Highton remembered that – even as a nine-year-old – his friend could be stubborn and dogmatic, "but I didn't mind," he continued. "I knew as soon as I met him, this was a chap I wanted to be with." [36]

Roald's letters home from St Peter's were always written in English, and he later recalled that after the family's Norwegian nurse left their employment in the mid-1920s, "the whole household started going over to English". [37] For his first year he always signed himself "Boy". It was the way he had defined himself in a house full of women and it was not until he was almost ten that he started to call himself Roald. The letters reveal many of the enthusiasms that would continue into later life: natural history, collecting (initially stamps and birds' eggs), food (mostly sweets and chocolates) and sport, where perhaps his most impressive achievement was at conkers.‡ Highton remembers that Roald was an "ace" – selecting his chestnuts "with great care and technical skill" and inventing a process to harden them "to such a degree of indestructibility that he almost always won". [38] One year he was the school champion, writing home to his mother with pride that he had "the highest conker in the school – 273". [39]

His tone to her was usually confident, often bossy, and his letters are full of detailed and highly specific instructions and requests. "I'm sending some things out of Toblerone chocolate, if you collect forty of them you get shares in the company," [40] he writes at one point, complaining bitterly at another that the toy submarine she has bought him from Harrods does not dive properly. In this context his mind strays to the store's famous pet department and he wonders how much a monkey might cost. "It would

---

‡In the traditional form of the game, as played by generations of schoolchildren, the seed of a horse chestnut, a conker, is suspended on a string and then used to strike another conker similarly suspended. When one of the two is destroyed, the survivor is declared victorious. A winning conker assumes the score of all its victim's preceding foes.

be rather nice to have one," he suggests hopefully.[41] Indeed, Roald often seemed more concerned about the well-being of his pets – which included turtles, dogs, rats, tortoises and a salamander – than he was about his family. His occasional letters to his sisters are generally brief and often patronizing. When Alf got a place at Roedean, for example, Roald merely commented: "What a miracle Alfhild has passed . . . she was jolly lucky; personally I didn't think she would."[42]

Roald was part of a generation of British children for whom the natural world was a source of immense stimulation and pleasure. As he grew up, he was constantly observing the countryside around him – noting unusual phenomena and picking up anything that attracted his attention. His collection of 172 birds' eggs, lovingly preserved in a glass cabinet with ten drawers, ranged from a tiny wren's to those of hawks, gulls and carrion crows. The eggs were things of great beauty for him, each with its own unique colours and speckles. Some were collected from sheer cliff faces, others from the tops of tall trees, and he recalled them with great affection. "I could always remember vividly how and where I had found each and every egg," he wrote a few months before he died, adding that he thought collecting eggs was "an enthralling hobby for a young boy and not, in my opinion, in the least destructive. To open a drawer and see thirty different very beautiful eggs nestling in their compartments on pink cotton-wool was a lovely sight."[43]

In childhood, Roald's curiosity about the world was insatiable, and his letters from St Peter's reveal clearly how much the natural world meant to him. The "snow-white passages" and "beautiful fossils" in the nearby Mendip caves[44] counterpoise a lecture on bird legends, in which the boys are told how the thieving blackbird got its black plumage and yellow beak, and – this appealed to him most – how the tiny wren defeated the eagle to become king of the birds. As a correspondent, he treats his mother as someone constantly in need of education, earnestly recounting what he has learned in school: how owls spew up the remains of the food they've eaten in pellets,[45] how kangaroos box, and how, in Nigeria, "black people live in mud huts".[46] An eclipse of the sun, which he views through special glasses he has got from a children's newspaper, fascinates him,[47] as does the precise means of making fire with wood and a piece of cord.[48] And just in case Sofie Magdalene can't quite grasp it, he makes a careful series of drawings and diagrams for her. His sense of adventure and curiosity is constantly stimulated. A film of the pilot Alan Cobham's flight to the Cape of Good Hope,[49] a lecture by Captain Morris who has been on an expedition to Mount Everest,[50] and a newsreel about travelling from Tibet to India in a motorcar,[51] compete with a school trip to the caves of the Cheddar Gorge, a nearby local attraction, in a charabanc, where the boys were squashed into the open-topped coach "like sardines in a tin".[52] Fire too is another source of wonder and always exciting – even when Roald's hand is badly burned by a "jackie jumper" firework.[53] And, when three shops burn down in the local town, the masters lead a school expedition there the following day so that the boys can inspect the smouldering ruins.[54]

Despite its Spartan discipline, the school exposed its pupils to the classics, to literature and to music. At home Roald had begun by reading Beatrix Potter stories, moving on to A. A. Milne, Frances Hodgson Burnett's *The Secret Garden*, which he would later describe as "the most enduring of all children's books", and the fairy tales of Hans Christian Andersen. Hilaire Belloc's *Cautionary Verses*, however, were the first to leave "a permanent impression".[55] They made him laugh, and by the age of nine he had learned them all by heart. St Peter's pushed him further. By the time he was twelve, Roald was familiar with compositions by Beethoven, Mozart, Tchaikovsky and Grieg,[56] and had encountered many of Shakespeare's plays, three Dickens novels, Stevenson's *Treasure Island*,[57] and a great deal of Rudyard Kipling. He was already very comfortable with literature. There were books at home and his mother was an avid reader – Horace Walpole, Thomas Hardy and G. K. Chesterton were among her favourites.

Her son's tastes were catholic, but his preference was generally for exotic tales of action, adventure and the imagination: the adventure stories of G. A. Henty, C. S. Forester, and Henry Rider Haggard, for example, as well as espionage thrillers such as *Secret of the Baltic* by T. C. Bridges and J. Storer Clouston's *The Spy in Black*, a First World War adventure set in the Orkneys that would later become Michael Powell and Emeric Pressburger's first film. Together with Douglas Highton, Roald also developed a fascination with Victorian ghost stories and Gothic fantasy, which he was to maintain for the rest of his life. The two boys read M. R. James and Edgar Allan Poe together, and Roald gave his friend a copy of Ambrose Bierce's 1893 collection of grand guignol short stories *Can Such Things Be?* as a birthday present. Dahl later admitted that Bierce's tales of ghosts, ghouls, psychics, robots and werewolves "scared me a lot",[58] adding elsewhere that the book was so frightening he "couldn't turn the light off at night".[59] He believed it "profoundly fascinated and probably influenced" him.[60] The book was so important to him that, almost sixty years later, Roald asked his friend whether he could have it back. Highton obliged and, in return, Roald sent him a signed copy of *Boy* with a warm dedication apologizing for a few of his more lurid descriptions of St Peter's. These were, he confessed, "coloured by my natural sense of fantasy".[61]

This love of fantasy did not transfer itself to things medical, for which Dahl was already developing a sharply observant eye. Accident and disease-prone throughout his life, Dahl's childhood was packed with grisly medical encounters and *Boy* is full of hair-raising (and mostly true) accounts of these. His nose is "cut clean off" in a car crash and stitched back on by a doctor at home on the kitchen table. Then, on holiday in Norway, a doctor with a "round mirror strapped to his forehead" and a nurse "carrying a red rubber apron and a curved enamel bowl" remove his adenoids without using anaesthetic. Dahl often uses the adjective "curved" when he wants to describe something sinister, while gleaming metal also usually presages pain. Here a "long shiny steel instrument", with a blade that is "very small, very sharp and very shiny", disappears high up into the roof of his mouth. The doctor's hand gives "four or five very quick little twists" and the next moment, "out of my mouth into the basin came tumbling a whole mass of flesh and blood".[62] Looking at the "huge red lumps" that had fallen out of his mouth, Dahl's first thought was that the doctor had cut out the middle of his head.

Back at school it is not long before he has another encounter with doctor and scalpel. This one has another "long steel handle" and a "small pointed blade". The young victim in this instance was not Dahl himself, but a fellow patient in the sickroom, Ellis, who has "an immense and angry-looking boil on the inside of his thigh. I saw it," Roald boasts enthusiastically. "It was as big as a plum and about the same colour." Ellis's outraged screams of pain and his floods of tears, as the doctor throws a towel over his patient's face and lances the purple swelling, driving the knife deep into the boil, provoke no sympathy from either doctor or the "mountainous-bosomed" Matron. "Don't make such a fuss about nothing," is all she says. Dahl himself is only marginally more sympathetic, admitting that he thinks the doctor "handled things rather cleverly". "Pain," he concludes, "was something we were expected to endure." [63]

Some things, however, were too much for his young readers. In the first draft of *Boy*, for example, Ellis was referred to by his real name, Ford, and Dahl added a coda to the story of the boil-lancing, which he removed before the book was published, almost certainly because he felt it was too sombre and gloomy. Ford survived the boil, he wrote, adding that "tragically it was all for nothing", [64] and explaining that, two years later, during an outbreak of measles at the school, the boy died. In this omission also Dahl may well have been being true to his unsentimental child's eye, for in his letters home from school the death is barely mentioned. His own exploits on horseback and a description of a toy motor canoe, with an automated rower, "whose joints move like real", [65] get far more attention.

It is possible too that, in this regard, Roald was looking after his mother by protecting her from bad news. Perhaps he was keeping his word to the doctor in Llandaff, and taking trouble not to worry her. Certainly, his own accidents and ailments are only reported when the patient is on the mend. And there are never any complaints. Instead, he learns early how to use misfortune as entertainment. "On Bristol station," he tells her, "Hoggart was sick, and when I looked at it, I was sick, but now I am quite all right." [66] Moreover, behind the desire to entertain and shock, there are traces of great sensitivity. Writing to comfort his mother on the seventh anniversary of his sister Astri's death, he comments: "I don't suppose the grave has ever looked nicer than it does now, with all the heather on it." [67] But drama is what excites him most. A trip into Weston to see the Duke and Duchess of York (the future King George VI and Queen Elizabeth), who were in town to open a new hospital, is memorable because their train ran someone over and because a local ironmonger got so excited that he fired six blank shots into the air and terrified the nervous duke.[68] By his final year at St Peter's in 1929, a thuggish quality was starting to reveal itself. After playing rugby against a local team, Roald writes boastfully of his own school's "rough plays", which were strongly censured by the match referee. "We got four of their chaps crying," he brags to his mother, as if pleased that he can now inflict injury as well as receive it.[69]

By the age of twelve he has also started to notice class and accents, remarking to his mother that the man who cleans his boots calls Highton "Oiton" and himself "Dorl",[70] and that while playing football, he has overheard some navvies arguing with the referee on a neighbouring pitch. Their language fascinates him. "Garn, stop yer gob, ref, or I'll come along and clump you over the ear!"[71] he records with evident delight. With Highton, he starts doing the *Daily Telegraph* crossword puzzle, and experimenting with his own clumsy but original word games. A competitor in the school boxing finals is described as "a lump of very conceited mass",[72] while a singer practising in the music room below him is evoked in terms that prefigure some of the language of *The BFG*. "The noise," he writes, "closely resembles that of a fly's kneecap, rattled about in a bilious buttercup, both having kidney trouble and lumbago!"[73] His eye for the quirky and absurd is also developing fast. He is intrigued by a letter from his sister Ellen, who had reported seeing "electrified frogs",[74] while, in a film about a silver mine, he laughs out loud when he sees "a lot of fat old women" mashing up the slurry "in order to get the silver out".[75] Obesity is always a source of comment, usually of amusement and sometimes of condemnation. A passenger at Yatton Station is "at least nine feet around the tummy in circumference",[76] and when "two elderly females" come to the school to act out Shakespeare's *Twelfth Night*, Roald observes critically that "the fattest, in a purple dress, didn't know it well, so had to hold a book all the time".[77] Even Sofie Magdalene is not exempt from his fat-detecting eye. In the summer of 1929, while on holiday in Cornwall, he writes to his mother warning her that although they are saving her a large room with a double bed, "I am sure your hips will protrude from each side."[78]

In April 1927, Sofie Magdalene sold Cumberland Lodge, and the Dahl family moved to Bexley in Kent. The spacious new house, Oakwood, was only 15 miles from Central London, yet had two acres of tree-filled grounds tended by a gardener called Martin, and, much to Roald's delight, a hard tennis court.[79] It had good railway connections to Roedean, where Alfhild was about to start school, and where Sofie Magdalene hoped Else and Asta would shortly follow. The sophisticated maverick Douglas Highton remembered it as "luxurious and civilized" – with a selection of cooked food laid out on the table each morning at breakfast, and a billiard room with full-sized table, which was used each night after a dinner, over which Sofie Magdalene presided in her "gentle and dignified way".[80] But a few years later, other more conventional guests found the Dahls running wild. One was amazed at the "filthy language" used by the children, to which their mother "paid no regard", sitting "stone deaf", while Roald and his sisters indulged themselves in a torrent of swearing.[81] His youngest sibling, Asta, agreed that the children "didn't have many restrictions" and that, by English standards, they were kept on a pretty loose leash. Once Roald sent her up a cedar tree in the garden, "absolutely padded out with cushions", so that he could shoot at his ten-year-old sister with his air rifle and see how far the bullets would penetrate.[82] She gleefully consented. On another occasion he rigged up an elaborate aerial "chariot" made out of Meccano, containing soup cans of cold water, and suspended it on a long wire so he could "bomb" local ladies, as they walked their dogs along the lane at the bottom of the garden. The result pleased him hugely. "The ladies who had halted and looked up on hearing the rushing noise of my chariot overhead, caught the cascade of water full in their face. . . . It was tremendous," Dahl remembered. And, despite his mother's "steely eye" when she discovered what he had done, "for days afterwards I experienced the pleasant warm glow that comes to all of us when we have brought off a major triumph".[83]

If holidays at home were like paradise for the children, going away was even better. Easter was usually spent on the coast of Wales, at the

picturesque seaside resort of Tenby, where the family rented a house in
the Old Harbour, right on the seafront. There, accompanied by both of
their maids from Bexley, Roald took donkey rides on the beach, collected
winkles from the rock pools, walked with the dogs on the clifftops, and
occasionally took the boat to nearby Caldy Island, where he gathered
seabirds' eggs. He also indulged his rich schoolboy sense of humour. Else,
his younger sister, remembers Roald asking her to lean out of the window
of the house and shout at the passersby: "One skin, two skin, three skin,
four skin!"[84] without understanding why her brother was rolling on the
floor with laughter.

But Tenby was as nothing compared to the summer holidays in Norway. After a candlelit dinner in Oslo, at the home of their Hesselberg
grandparents and their two eccentric spinster aunts, the children and
their indomitable mother would head off to the coast and the countless islands that lay scattered through the fjords. These afforded endless
opportunities for swimming, fishing, sunbathing, eating seafood, and
yet more pranks, such as replacing the tobacco in their future brother-
in-law's pipe with goat droppings and waiting to see how he would react
when he smoked it. Asta remembered sailing in Louis's boat *The Hard
Black Stinker* and handing up buckets to be filled with fresh prawns from
the returning shrimp boats, while Roald revelled in the lyrical pleasures
of fishing. "On our summer holidays in Norway we would often row out
into the fjord in the early evenings to fish," he wrote later. "We dropped
anchor and baited our hooks with mussels and let out the lines until the
weights hit the bottom. Then, unless we were after flat fish, we pulled
our lines up two good arms-lengths above the seabed and waited. Each of
us held the line in the proper manner around the back of the first finger
with the thumb on top, hardly daring to speak because, although the
fjord was deep, we weren't certain that the fish mightn't hear us."[85]

And in the evenings, Sofie Magdalene told stories. Sometimes they
were English ones, read from books, but often the fare was darker and
more Scandinavian. These were the ones Roald and Alfhild remembered:
fairy tales, either freshly invented or adapted from the nineteenth-century
collections of Peter Christian Asbjørnsen and Jørgen Moe.[86] These ac-

counts of wicked trolls and other mythical Norwegian creatures that lived in the dark pine forests were unsentimental yarns, usually with a highly developed sense of the fantastical and the grotesque. They featured satires on the consequences of greed, stories about battling giants and cloud monsters, tales of children who soared high into the sky on the backs of eagles, and a series about outsize insects and frogs entitled *Have Animals Got Souls?* They were to have a profound influence on the young Roald and shape his sense of what a story should be. Fables such as *The Boy Who Challenged a Troll to an Eating Competition, The Hare Who Laughed Until His Jaws Cracked* and *The Tabby Cat Who Ate Too Much* overflow with zany black humour. They clearly struck a chord with Roald, for he would reuse their themes and reinvent them in his own manner many years later.

These tales were illustrated by an artist called Theodor Kittelsen. Kittelsen was a Norwegian mystic – a visionary and fantastical painter, much loved by the Dahls. He was born in 1857 on the west coast of Norway, in Kragerø, the birthplace of Ludvig Aadnesen. Like his contemporary Edvard Munch, many of his paintings and illustrations are not for the fainthearted. He too was fascinated by the grotesque. His drawings of the bubonic plague, for example, which raged through medieval Norway, are remarkable for their evocations of death and loneliness in a dark, hostile landscape; yet he was also able to depict the evanescent swiftness of a running stream, the misty stillness of an autumn sunrise, and the strange shapeless wonderland of a familiar human landscape transformed by a heavy fall of snow. His eye is sharply observant, and his sense of humour usually coarse and hard-edged in a way that prefigures Dahl's own. In *Morbid Love*, for example, a bedraggled green mosquito and a frog in a crumpled white ball gown embrace by the side of a tranquil blue lake. A distant sun is setting. At the water's edge stands an empty bottle of wine. Beside it a drained glass lies on its side. The two animal lovers are parting. Both are weeping. But the pathos of this melancholy moment will soon be shattered. For, unbeknown to them, a mischievous crab has emerged from the water and is about to nip the grasshopper's leg, while on a branch above their heads a warbling bird has just evacuated its bowels. In a moment the resulting mess will splatter all over the lovers' tear-stained faces.[87]

This dimension of the ironic and absurd masked Kittelsen's profound fascination for the natural world. A fellow painter, Erik Werenskjold, praised his concern with "man's pettiness and absurdity, his vindictiveness and jealousy", which was set against "the lofty and unfathomable grandeur of Nature, as revealed in snowclad mountains, desolate hills or a tiny fragrant blossom".[88] This combination of the satirist and the naturalist, the fantasist and the observer, also defined an important aspect of Dahl's own aesthetic. His sisters, particularly the sharp and observant Alfhild, saw the link at once between their brother's tales and those Norwegian legends they had been told as children, recognizing in both a distinctive blend of humour and fear, combined with a sense of the solitary majesty of the natural world.[89] Recalling his childhood diaries, scribbled high up in the branch of an ancient chestnut tree, far away from other humans and deep within the realm of nature, Dahl himself would later write: "In springtime, I was in a cave of green leaves surrounded by hundreds of those wonderful white candles that are the conker trees flowers. In winter it was less mysterious, but even more exciting because I could see the ground miles below me as well as the landscape all around. Sitting there, above the world, I used to write down things that would have made my mother and my sisters stretch their eyes with disbelief had they ever read them. But I knew they wouldn't."[90]

This acute sense of the ecstasy and agony of childhood – of the strange opposition of happiness and sadness, reality and fantasy, success and failure – was something that Dahl never forgot. It remained familiar to him all his life. He remembered with ease how a child sees the world, how isolated he or she can feel even within the bosom of the family, how quickly they must adapt to new experiences, and how odd the world of adults can seem when viewed through younger eyes. As he was to write of the young matron at St Peter's, "it made no difference whether she was twenty-eight or sixty-eight because to us a grown-up was a grown-up and all grown-ups were dangerous creatures".[91] In later life, some adults would find this "childish" aspect to his personality irritating. They objected to it either in his writing, which they accused of coarseness and vulgarity, or when it was manifested personally in boastfulness, bragging or contentiousness. Yet, what came with it was an ever present sense of wonder. This imaginative verve was essential to his nature and in many ways, the keystone of all his writing – both for adults and children. It could result in the grotesque and repulsive, for which he would become notorious, but it could also be tender and elegiac, dark and mysterious. Expressed in spare, simple prose that sometimes verged on the poetic, Dahl's sense of the child's perspective was always sure-footed, and often immensely powerful. "I cannot possibly describe to you what it felt like to be standing alone in the pitchy blackness of that silent wood in the small hours of the night," he wrote in *Danny the Champion of the World*, describing a child who has got lost in the forest. "The sense of loneliness was overwhelming, the silence as deep as death, and the only sounds were the ones I made myself. . . . I had a queer feeling that the whole wood was listening with me, the trees and the bushes, the little animals hiding in the undergrowth and the birds roosting in the branches. All were listening. Even the silence was listening. Silence was listening to silence."[92]

CHAPTER FOUR

Foul Things and Horrid People

ON A CHILLY JANUARY morning in 1930, Roald Dahl set off for his first day at Repton School. He had bidden farewell to his pet mice, Montague and Marmaduke, at home, and to his mother and sisters at Bexley Station, where he caught the train for London. At Charing Cross, he loaded his luggage aboard a taxi and crossed the city, arriving at the neoclassical grandeur of old Euston Station, through its magnificent Doric arch – the largest ever built – and into the spectacular Great Hall, with its galleries, murals, gilded ceilings and the awe-inspiring double staircase, which swept down from the gallery level to the bustling station floor below. Gaggles of Reptonians, all immediately recognizable by their distinctive uniform of pinstripe trousers and long black tailcoats, chattered and joked as they waited to board the Derby train. A porter loaded Roald's trunks, each stamped with his name, onto the train, and an hour later it steamed out of the station on the 130-mile journey north.

On board, Roald struck up a conversation with one of his fellow pupils, Ben Reuss. He was a year older than Roald and had already been at the school for a term. He was a good ally for a new boy. Despite natural first-day nerves, Reuss was struck immediately by Dahl's "unconventional" manner[1] and his madcap sense of humour. By midafternoon, as the train pulled into Derby Station, the light was already fading. Roald then boarded one of a series of taxis that drove the boys and their luggage out of the grimy city and into a damp and dismal surrounding countryside. After about ten miles his cab drifted past St Wystan's Church, whose honey-coloured stone seemed dark grey in the dim light and whose tall spire, "as slender as a sharpened pencil",[2] to use a simile of one of his contemporaries, looked down upon the twelfth-century arch, where the main school buildings of Repton lay. A minute or so later, it came to a halt outside the doors of Priory House, the building that was to be Roald's home during term time for the next four years. He was thirteen years old.

Repton is a dour place. Squatting in the foothills of the Peak District, and sandwiched into a strip of countryside between the industrial towns of Derby and Burton-on-Trent, its stone and Victorian redbrick buildings cluster together in a tight huddle alongside Repton Brook, as if sheltering from the fierce winds that whistle down off Darley Moor to the north. Now, as in the 1930s, the town is dominated by the presence of the school, whose buildings lie scattered around its centre, but Repton itself has an ancient history, which goes back well over 1,500 years. It was once an early centre for English Christianity. An abbey was founded there and two Anglo-Saxon kings, Ethelbald and Wiglaf, were buried in the crypt, before the Vikings sailed down the Trent and destroyed the abbey in 873. In the twelfth century a magnificent priory was founded on the Saxon ruins, but this too was destroyed during the Reformation, in a spasm of Puritan zeal. Secretly, however, the old religion lingered on, and in 1553 Popish prayers were answered when the Catholic Mary Tudor acceded to the throne.

Three years later, a rich and devout local Catholic, Sir John Port, died. In his will, he set aside money to found a school in Repton, stipulating that its headmaster should be a priest. To this end, his executors purchased what remained of the old Priory and set about creating the college. Port's charity had an element of self-interest. He wanted a chantry founded at the school so that schoolboys could sing masses daily to speed his soul to heaven – a practice that had been outlawed the previous decade, but which under Mary was now legal again. His wishes were thwarted. In 1558, Mary died and her half sister, Elizabeth, a Protestant, ascended the throne. Thus Repton was established as an Anglican school. In the subsequent four and a half centuries, it experienced many ups and downs. By the late eighteenth century, one corrupt headmaster and his staff were employed to teach just a single pupil. Fifty years later, Repton was remodelled to conform to the values of Thomas Arnold, the head-master of Rugby School and one of the founding fathers of the Victorian ethos of hard work, discipline and duty. Arnold placed the cultivation of religious and moral principles above academic instruction, defining his object at Rugby as being "to form Christian men – for Christian boys I can scarcely hope to make".[3] His implication, that boys were naturally wild and undisciplined and that schooling was about creating a train-ing ground where rigorous moral values might be instilled within them, resonated at one level with Roald Dahl. He too believed that children were born savage, but he would celebrate the innocent anarchic attitudes of each "uncivilised little grub".[4] For Arnold, however, as for many of the staff at Repton in 1930, the opposite was true. They viewed that youthful freedom of spirit as something subversive that needed to be crushed.*

Sofie Magdalene had promised her dying husband that their children would all be educated in England, but precisely why she chose Repton for Roald is not immediately clear. The son of a family friend in Radyr was already there, and Captain Lancaster, the twitching orange-haired terror from St Peter's, was also an alumnus, or "Old Reptonian". One might think that this connection would have deterred young Roald. But it does not seem to have done, although the elaborate uniform put him off a bit. The stiff butterfly collar, attached to a starched shirt with studs, pinstripe trousers, twelve-button waistcoat, tailcoat and straw boater struck him as entirely ludicrous. He later described the tailcoat as "the most ridiculous garment I had ever seen"; he thought the costume made him look "like an undertaker's apprentice in a funeral parlour".[5] However, it was thus attired, with accompanying umbrella to keep the Peak District rain off the vulnerable boater, that Roald arrived for his first night at The Priory – one of nine boarding houses that were scattered around the town. Each house was a community of around fifty boys, about twelve from each year. Apart from some team sports and lessons, which were taught in

---

*In many respects, Repton was the archetypical contemporary British public school. As such it was chosen as the setting for the classic movie version of *Goodbye, Mr Chips* (1939), with Robert Donat and Greer Garson.

forms drawn from the entire school, the house was the focus of a boy's discipline, loyalties and social life. It was where he ate, slept, studied, and where he made friends. Dahl himself described that existence as "a curious system . . . you never walked to class with a boy from another House. You rarely spoke to boys from other houses and you seldom knew their names."[6]

The Priory is a steeply gabled redbrick building, with turrets and Gothic chimneys, a few hundred yards down the High Street from the Arch. Constructed by Geoffrey Fisher, the headmaster between 1914 and 1932, it contained a series of small dormitories known as "bedders", a collection of studies where boys worked in groups of five to seven, a panelled dining room, a tarmac yard at the front with fives courts, and a garden at the back called the Deer Park, in which there was a small plunge pool that was filled in the summer and in which the boys bathed naked. It also contained living quarters for the housemaster, J. S. Jenkyns, and his family.

Jenkyns was a classic interwar schoolmaster. Bald, with toothbrush moustache, tweed jacket, and polished leather brogues, he had already been at the school for twenty-four years when Roald arrived, and he would remain on the staff there for another sixteen. Educated at Winchester and Balliol, he had fought in the trenches during the First World War and his experiences there had made him gloomy, nervous and a trifle forbidding. In photographs he looks world-weary. "Twitchy", was how Dahl was often to describe him in his letters home. Jenkyns's youngest daughter Nancy admitted that sometimes even his children were "a bit frightened" of their father. "He could snap your head off," she recalled and could on occasions be "scratchy".[7] Yet Tim Fisher, Geoffrey Fisher's youngest son, believed that Jenkyns – or "Binks", as the boys called him – was adored by many of his pupils.[8] He certainly took a liking to his young six-foot Norwegian charge, and sometimes played fives with him. Dahl liked the sport, describing it as a "subtle and crafty" game played with a small hard leather ball that is struck at great speed by gloved hands and sent shooting around a court with "all manner of ledges and buttresses". On the fives court, his nervous housemaster could relax, "rushing about", as Roald described it, "shrieking what a little fool he is, and call-ing himself all sorts of names when he misses the ball".[9]

Perhaps the most curious aspect to the way pastoral care worked in The Priory was that Binks and his family were usually distant from the boys. His study was part of the "house", but his living quarters were elsewhere – in a separate wing at the top of the main staircase, where he resided with his "rather cold" wife[10] and their three boisterous daughters, Peggie, Rachel and Nancy. Rachel remembered Roald Dahl as a good-looking lad, twice her age and height. However, since she only saw the boys from afar, she could recall little else about him, except that he was "Scandinavian by birth and had had an unhappy early life".[11] Nancy, the youngest, a mischievous six-year-old with a shock of unruly dark hair, remembered a little more. She was fascinated by the older boys, peering over the banisters of the staircase to watch them go into the dining hall, or spying out who was being sent to her father's study to deliver their "blue" – a form of punishment in which a boy had to write out the same line of text up to 240 times in blue ink.

Nancy divided the house into "goodies" and "baddies" – Dahl was one of the goodies – but made clear that the opportunities for her to encounter any of them were rare. She did recall with relish one occasion, when Dahl and another goodie, Peter Ashton, were brought over to her side of the house for a few days and "put together in the spare room, which was up near the nursery". Then she got to spend some time with them.[12] Roald, used to the company of his sisters, must have longed to entertain the Jenkyns girls, or "the Binklets",[13] as he called them, more often. But opportunities to do so were rare. Ten years earlier, at a different boys' boarding school, the novelist Graham Greene had found himself in a similar situation. Greene's predicament was even more extreme because he was both a pupil and the headmaster's son, perhaps the most invidi-ous situation a child could imagine. He was haunted by the green baize door which for him seemed to symbolize the division between these two worlds. Beyond the warmth and civilization of one lay "a savage country of strange customs and inexplicable cruelties; a country in which [he] was a foreigner and a suspect, quite literally a hunted creature".[14] Emerging from Binks's family back into the harsh environment of The Priory, Roald must have had similar feelings. And in this brutal world – which offered no privacy and where even the outside lavatories had no doors – it was not the adults who wielded day-to-day power but the boys themselves.

Discipline was maintained by the senior boys, and in particular by four or five prefects, or "boazers", as they were known at Repton. They wielded great power. Each house was, as Dahl put it, "actually ruled by a boy of seventeen or eighteen who was the Head of House. He himself had three or four House Prefects. The House Prefects were the Gods of the House, but the Head of House was the Almighty." [15] Power was codified into a complex system of hierarchies, of "rules and rituals", which every new boy had to learn. Each study, for example, had at least five members. Its head was a study-holder, usually in his last year at the school. Sometimes the study-holder was also a boazer, which made him particularly "dangerous" for junior boys, because boazers had "the power of life and death" over them. [16] Below him there were two or three senior boys called "seconds" and two junior boys called "fags". The fags were treated as the study-holder's servants, "personal slaves", as Dahl would later call them, [17] and the system was justified by the rationale that it gave a new boy a sense of place and order. "He was straightaway in a study with five people," explained Tim Fisher. "He was the *bim fag*, the junior fag. Then there was the *tip fag*, the senior fag, in his second year, who would have shown his junior the ropes and helped him to discover how the school worked." [18]

The fag's tasks included cleaning the study, supplying it with coal for the fire, keeping the fire lit, and polishing the study-holder's shoes, buttons, badges and buckles. The boys received regular parcels of food from home to supplement what the school provided, and once or twice a week the fags cooked meals for the other members of their study in the communal bathroom, on portable paraffin primus stoves that they brought with them from home. With ten or more fags cooking at the same time, the bathroom would quickly fill with thick black smoke. To the young Dahl, the sight was exciting, reminiscent of "a witch's cauldron". [19] The power structure, however, lent itself easily to abuse. Boazers had only to yell "Fa-a-ag" at the top of their voice and every fag within earshot would have to drop what he was doing and run toward the needy prefect. The last to get there had to perform whatever task the senior boy required of him. There was almost no limit to what a boazer could request. One service, commonly demanded of the younger boys in winter, was to heat the wooden seats of the outside lavatories, by sitting on them, bare-bottomed, for long enough to ensure that the boazer himself did not have to place his own flesh onto an ice-cold seat. In *Boy*, Dahl memorably describes his first experience of doing this. "I got off the lavatory seat and pulled up my trousers. Wilberforce [the boazer] lowered his own trousers and sat down. 'Very good,' he said. 'Very good indeed.' He was like a wine-taster sampling an old claret. 'I shall put you on my list,' he added. I stood there doing up my fly-buttons and not knowing what on earth he meant. 'Some fags have cold bottoms,' he said, 'and some have hot ones. I only use hot-bottomed fags to heat my bog seat. I won't forget you.'"[20]

For the first two weeks of his time at Repton, a new boy was exempt from the rigors of fagging, but after that he bore its full force. Reading the early drafts of *Boy*, one senses a long-pent-up bitterness about Dahl's years there bubbling to the surface. It was a resentment that he clearly struggled to control, and in the final version, many of his most traumatic memories were expunged or watered down. Even so, the book caused considerable controversy amongst Old Reptonians when it was published in 1984. But the first draft was far rawer and more contentious. It painted a portrait of a profoundly melancholy boy, for whom the pleasures of youth had been stifled by an unfair system that was devoid of affection and feeling, and whose chief memories of his time there seem to have been those of loneliness and fear. "Four years is a long time to be in prison," Dahl writes. "It becomes twice as long when it is taken out of your life just when you are at your most bubbly best and the fields are all covered with daffodils and primroses. . . . It seemed as if we were groping through an almost limitless black tunnel at the end of which there glimmered a small bright light, and if we ever reached it we would be eighteen years old."[21] He continues with a description of "plodding endless terms", "grey classrooms" and "incredibly dull teachers . . . who never stopped to talk to you".[22] The images of isolation and misery are relentless. "At Repton the teachers gained no respect from us nor did they try to. As for the senior boys, they were so busy acting the part of being senior and so conscious of the power they wielded that they never bothered to be friendly. They didn't have to be. They ruled us by fear."[23] Independence of spirit and wit in the younger boys was stamped on and regarded as "side". And being "sidey" to a boazer was unthinkable. "You hardly dared speak to him, let alone be sidey."[24] Roald then recounts an incident that could have come straight out of *Tom Brown's Schooldays*.

> *Once, during my second year when I was fifteen, I was "sidey" to a boy called W. W. Wilson, who was sixteen. W. W. Wilson wasn't even a study-holder. He was just a second, but he didn't like what I had said, and at once he rounded up half-a-dozen seconds his own age and they hunted me down. I ran into the yard where they cornered me and grabbed hold of my arms and legs and carried me bodily back into the "house". In the changing room they held me down while one of them filled a bath brimful of icy-cold water, and into this they dropped me, clothes and all, and held me in there for several agonising minutes. "Push his head under water!" cried W. W. Wilson. "That'll teach him to keep his mouth shut!" They pushed my head under many times, and I choked and spluttered and half-drowned, and when at last they released me and I crawled out of the bath, I didn't have any dry clothes to change into.*[25]

Thankfully, Dahl's friend Peter Ashton gives this episode a redemptive twist, providing a spare suit for the soaking Roald, who is deeply grateful for this rare "act of mercy" in a world that was filled almost entirely with loneliness and terrors.

Repton also boasted an entrenched system of corporal punishment for offences as minor as forgetting to hang up your football kit in the changing room. In the 1930s, the cane or the strap were, as Tim Fisher described it, "an automatic and assumed part of the growing up process . . ."[26] They were part of a culture of toughening children up that would survive in England well into the 1950s and 1960s. As an adult,

Dahl too did not see any particular harm in boys having their bottoms "tickled" from time to time, if only the human dimension of the beater could be removed. He once even playfully speculated to me that a beating machine, "with knobs on it, like boiled eggs, for hard, medium or soft", might be a solution.[27] But he objected profoundly to the culture of violence he felt existed at Repton and most of all to the fact that the great majority of beatings there were performed by other boys. "Our lives at school were quite literally ruled by fear of the cane," he wrote. "We walked, with every step we took, in the knowledge that if we put a foot wrong, the result would be a beating."[28]

The white-gloved boazer Carleton, searching his study for the speck of dust that would justify a thrashing was typical. In Dahl's eyes, he was simply a sadistic thug, with a licence to inflict pain, in search of an easy victim. Carleton (actually a boy called Hugh Middleton) was perhaps the worst of Nancy Jenkyns's "baddies" and the most dreaded of Dahl's boazers. He was a "supercilious and obnoxious seventeen-year-old", with a cane that became an object of fetishistic interest to the other boys. His "creamy-white monster about four feet long with bamboo-like ridges all along its length and a round bobble the size of a golf-ball where the handle would have been" struck terror into a fag's heart. "Other Boazers used their OTC (Army) swagger-sticks when they beat the Fags, but not Middleton."[29]

The beatings were usually performed in the boazer's study shortly before going to bed. The victim had a choice between whether to have fewer strokes with his dressing gown off or more with it on. The latter was generally believed to be the less painful alternative. Afterwards the boy had to thank the boazer for his thrashing and return to his dormitory, where he would undergo a ritual inspection of his wounds. In *Boy*, Dahl describes such an occasion. The ace cricketer, Jack Mendl, had just beaten him, delivering four strokes, "so fast it was all over in four seconds".[30] Now back in the "bedder", his fellows insist Roald take down his trousers to show them his damaged buttocks. Dahl does not dwell on the "excruciating burning pain"[31] he is suffering. Instead, he recalls the boys' detailed analysis of Mendl's handiwork. "Half a dozen experts would crowd around you and express their opinions in highly professional language. '*What* a super job.' 'He's got every single one in the same place!' 'Boy that Williamson's [Mendl] got *a terrific eye!*' '*Of course* he's got a terrific eye! Why d'you think he's a Cricket Teamer?'"[32]

The scene is comic. At the end, the self-satisfied Mendl himself even appears slyly in the dormitory, "to catch a glimpse of my bare bottom and his own handiwork". However, the first draft of *Boy* also contains a piece of psychological analysis, unusual in Dahl's writing, that reveals much about his own state of mind: "It is clear to me now, although it wasn't at the time, that these boys had developed this curiously detached attitude towards these vile tortures in order to preserve their sanity. It was an essential defensive mechanism. Had they crowded round and commiserated with me and tried to comfort me, I think we would all have broken down."[33] Among its other influences Repton was conditioning Dahl to suppress many of his own fundamental emotional responses and to find consolation in disconnection and standing apart.

Mendl's beatings, though fierce, were clinical and dispassionate. With Middleton, it was different. Middleton was not simply the real Carleton, he was also the model for the bully, Bruce Foxley, in Dahl's adult short story "Galloping Foxley", which he wrote in 1953. This was the first time Dahl had revisited his schooldays in fiction, and his descriptions of the fagging and corporal punishment there are strikingly similar to those he later penned in *Boy*. Middleton is evoked more deftly perhaps in the earlier story, with his pointed Lobb shoes, his silk shirts, his "arrogant-laughing glare", his "cold, rather close eyes", and his hair, "coarse and slightly wavy, with just a trace of oil over it, like a well-tossed salad". But the events and settings are the same. Foxley's specialty is to bound down the corridor at full tilt before inflicting each blow. The actual gallop down the changing rooms, "cane held high in the air", may be an exaggeration, but what are we to make of the narrator's admission that his schooldays at Repton made him "so miserable" that he had contemplated suicide?[34] Hardened by his experiences at St Peter's, Dahl was already a survivor. He does not seem a likely candidate for suicide. However, it is also possible that the loneliness and the bullying might have led him to consider this option, if only briefly.

On top of it all, he was frequently unwell. As his sister Alfhild put it, Roald "caught everything" at Repton.[35] Apart from growing pains, for which he took calcium supplements to strengthen his bones, and a heart condition that required him to visit specialists,† he was also prone to respiratory problems. His letters home are filled with requests for a huge variety of medications for everything from corns on his toes to headaches and constipation. With Heath and Heather lozenges, Mistol, Nostroline, Lynol, Kalzana, Ostelin and Radiostoleum, the letters can sometimes read like a 1930s pharmacology handbook. These illnesses, which are clearly catalogued in his letters, and which do not feature at all in *Boy*, make a poignant appearance in *Galloping Foxley*. There the narrator bemoans the many colds he caught on his long walks around Orange Ponds, in the rain, gathering wild irises for his tormentor Middleton.

Dahl's school reports also suggest that he was miserable. "Rather dazed", "curiously dense and slow", exhibiting "fits of childishness" and "fits of the sulks" are just some of the many negative descriptions that characterize the way he was perceived there. His academic record was poor. "A persistent muddler, writing and saying the opposite of what he means" was his English teacher's verdict halfway through his first term. Eighteen months later, little had changed. His mathematics master is dismissive: "He has very little ability and is inclined to be childish." The following year is no better. Dahl is accused of "idleness", "apathy", and "stupidity"; he is "lethargic", "languid", and "too pleased with himself". His housemaster also notices "a vein of obstinacy in him",[36] which he compliments, but his pupil's happiness or unhappiness never appears to be an issue. Partly this was because these issues were just not considered important and also partly because Roald hid his feelings well from those around him. Constructing a protective facade of indifference, he both

---

†Dahl told his mother in 1931 that he had been made to go to see the school doctor about his heart despite the fact that he had already been to a number of specialists. Hodie, the school medic, apparently "said the same as Dr Goodall." What that was he did not specify – Letter to his mother, 09/31 – RDMSC RD 13/1/7/2.

preserved his sanity and avoided appearing like a potential victim. The same is true of his letters home, which give absolutely no indication of the melancholy he evoked in his first draft of *Boy*, and which are packed instead with amusing anecdotes and descriptions. It is as if the letter writing itself had become a means of escape from the greyness of school life. As if, out of the gloom, he had constructed a sunnier alternative reality, which not only reassured his family back in Bexley but entertained the writer at the same time.‡

By the age of fifteen, Roald was a sophisticated humorist and entertainer as well as a skilled and dextrous narrator. The exuberance of St Peter's has given way to a more jaundiced and critical view of the world, where he enjoys finding fault and making negative judgements. For example, though he proudly describes The Priory as "easily the nicest house",[37] the others are dismissed as "nasty little dirty looking hovels". His sharp eye takes pleasure in the discomfiture of the masters, who are "awfully nervous and dithering"[38] when school inspectors arrive to vet the lessons, and when Matron Malpas leaves, her replacement is described as having "hair like a fuzzie-wuzzie, and two warts on her face . . . I think I shall offer her my corn paint".[39] Yet he can be sensitive and empathetic, too. When an opponent's cap falls off in a hockey match to reveal "an absolutely bald head, his wig remaining in his cap", Dahl, like his teammates, feels only sympathy toward the "wretched fellow".[40] At other times he recounts escapades, in language reminiscent of the adventure books he enjoyed reading, and often with unexpected comic detail. Tobogganing, rioting on a train,[41] powder fights in his "bedder",[42] firing pencils out of his rifle,[43] and climbing illicitly up the tower of Repton Church to make the bells ring[44] all get this treatment.

But, as he comes to the end of his second year at Repton, he is already longing to live his life on a bigger canvas, and he seizes eagerly on any-

---

‡Sofie Magdalene seems to have had little inkling of what torments lay behind the wild irises she saw in her son's bedder. Visiting Roald during his first summer at the school, she wrote to her daughter Else that she was "very pleased with Repton. . . . It is much nicer than I expected it to be . . . Roald's study was absolutely crammed with flowers" – Sofie Magdalene Dahl, Postcards to Else Dahl, 06/27/30 – RDMSC RD 20/9/2 and RD 20/9/3.

thing dramatic. The inevitable fire that destroyed his study was the kind
of thing that really gave him a chance to flex his writing muscles:

> *The flames were enormous and the heat was colossal. The whole place*
> *stank of burning . . . and it got in your throat. I coughed all night.*
> *However we got to our bedrooms, which the firemen assured us were*
> *safe, but to us they looked as though they were being held up by two*
> *thin planks. We picked our way gingerly up the stairs (which were*
> *black and charcoaly) of course all the electric light had fused long ago.*
> *We got into our beds which were brown and nasty and I don't know*
> *how but I managed to get some sleep. The place looked grimmer than*
> *ever by daylight. All the passage was black and in our study absolutely*
> *nothing was left.*[45]

In his second year at Repton, Dahl also formed an important friendship, with Michael Arnold, a boy a year and a half older than he was, and
two years above him academically. Arnold was something of a celebrity
at Repton. He was quick-witted, subversive, and highly intelligent. In his
first term, Dahl described him to his mother as a "very clever boy", who
was "going to make the house a three-valve wireless".[46] By the following
year, he was hailing him proudly as "the cleverest boy in England".[47] In
house photographs, Arnold stares out confidently, casually, hands in his
pockets or arms folded, his hair slicked back in the manner of a young
W. H. Auden. Like Dahl he despised the school and saw himself as an
outsider. According to their contemporary, Ben Reuss, Arnold had no
friends at all until Dahl "took him up". Reuss found their friendship "a
little bit strange".[48] But Dahl and Arnold were very much kindred spirits.
Arnold's son Nicholas observed that both of them were "independent
and individualistic".[49] They were also both profoundly curious about
the natural world, and enjoyed searching the countryside for fruit, hunting crayfish in Orange Ponds, and conducting crazy experiments. Once
they put an unopened tin of pea soup in front of the fire, then, when it
was superheated, they punctured the can. From behind the shelter of an
unfurled Repton umbrella, they watched with delight as the hot soup

sprayed all over the study. The can, Dahl observed with relish, "continued to shoot for about two minutes".[50] Together they also obtained the key of the school darkroom and began to print photographs.[51] Soon Arnold became Michael – the only boy Roald ever referred to by his first name. He even wrote specifically to his mother to make sure she did the same. Roald invited Michael to Norway with his family in 1932, the summer before Arnold was scheduled to take the scholarship examination to Magdalen College, Oxford. "I expect he'll get it,"[52] Roald wrote confidently to his mother in December. He did. That Christmas he came down to Bexley to stay with the Dahls. Michael had become family.

Roald's friendship with Michael and the fact that he was no longer a fag began to make Repton more tolerable, as did the fact that he had successfully smuggled one of his pet rats into the school to keep him company. He told his shocked friend Ben Reuss that there was "no animal more intelligent or cleaner".[53] His fascination with photography deepened. Increasingly he spent hours on his own in the school darkroom. "I was the only boy who practised it seriously,"[54] he would later write, and after the summer of 1931, the subject dominates his letters home. His mother is bombarded with a stream of requests for lenses, photographic films and paper, while his latest set of prints – mostly of buildings, landscapes and the occasional botanical specimen – are usually enclosed for comments. "I've got a marvellous one of the baths, with reflection in it, so that you can hardly tell which way up it is," he writes in June 1931. "Dr Barton the science master is going to give me eight shillings for it."[55] Two years later, Dahl was winning competitions. Music too – mostly in the form of the gramophone – was another escape. Roald's taste was largely classical – the Austrian tenor Richard Tauber was a favourite – while he was also a fan of the black American bass, Paul Robeson and opera arias sung by Enrico Caruso and Luisa Tetrazzini. His art master, Arthur Norris, encouraged his interest in painting, too, and particularly the works of the French Impressionists.

Bizarrely for a school that was so brutal, by the 1920s Repton had also developed quite a reputation for the arts and literature. The novelists Christopher Isherwood and Edward Upward were pupils during the

First World War, while Isherwood's friend, the poet W. H. Auden, had been named by his father – an Old Reptonian – after the local church, St Wystan's. Dahl absorbed these literary values – even if Auden and Isherwood would never be his favourite writers. He never acknowledged it, but his English teacher, the war poet and cricketer John Crommelin-Brown, was another early influence, encouraging him to use imaginative language, but expressed correctly and elegantly. A contemporary, David Atkins, recalled "Crummers" repeatedly urging his pupils never to use a long word where a short one would do, and always "to keep your sentences free of froth".[56] Roald too would later recall that his education was "relentlessly directed" toward writing short, clear sentences that "said precisely what one meant them to say".[57] Sometimes this was achieved with puzzles, such as this example of why one needs to punctuate properly:

> *If you go to the zoo you will see elephants playing the saxophone you first take a breath and swallow the mouthpiece is then taken between the lips and firmly to boot polish people are proud to be or not to be is what Hamlet said when bathing the baby care must be taken to clean up his sparking plugs should be the regular practice of every driver who wants easy running does are female wives may forgive husbands never tell took a bow and shot the apple through the inside left raced down the field and shot a gaol civilisation being what it is is still necessary for locking up the undesirable flies fly and pigs don't brown is a dentist and can be seen any day drawing stumps is a sign that the match is over.*[58]

Roald sent it on to his mother, with a sealed, correctly punctuated version, in case she could not work it out.

His surviving school essays are notable for their celebration of the imagination. Many already display an acute use of dialogue and a delight in the possibilities of the unexpected. Some anticipate his children's writing forty or fifty years later. In an essay on Nursery Rhymes, Dahl writes of a child wandering into a vegetable garden, "enchanted to think that Jack is probably hiding up one of those large beanstalks". Similarly, he describes another child, Little Jill, climbing out of bed at night and tiptoeing to the window "to peep through a chink in the curtains, at the cows in the field below. Oh when, oh when, would she see one jump over the Moon . . ." He contrasts Little Jill's sense of fantasy scornfully with a "detestable" boy called Pip, who is "self-centred and unimaginative, with no vestige of excitement about him".[59] And his most striking Repton essay is about dreaming itself. A series of interrupted poetic reveries that remind his teacher of Tennyson also reveal a more modern, sometimes Wildean sensibility. An iceberg, "hard and cold, like some great fragment of an icy coast, far away, Northward" gives way to a scene where a tap drips onto a delicate crane fly. Its drops "welled limpid, on the lip, and fell with a little splash upon the insect below". Then waves like a "wounded tiger" boil over in "a turmoil of green and white", while overhead hang "wet black clouds, heavy with rain, like airships of paper filled with oil".[60] One by one the images tumble onto each other in a kaleidoscope of colour and sensation before they finally shatter, as Dahl is roughly awakened. Four boys have lifted up his bed and are trying to tip him out of it onto the cold floor of the dormitory.

Roald's unexpected similes reinforce David Atkins's memories of competing with Dahl for a school poetry prize. The subject apparently was "The Evening Sky". Atkins's attempt was romantic and constructed in formal metric rhyme. Dahl's apparently was bitter and anarchic, beginning: "Evening clouds, like frog spawn, spoil the sky." Atkins recalled playing fives with Dahl afterwards and taking him to task for his sourness, whereupon Dahl confessed to him that "Life isn't beautiful and sentimental and clear. It's full of foul things and horrid people, and incidentally, rhyming is old hat."[61] It was a rare moment of openness from a writer who had already learned to keep his emotional cards close to his chest. However, his main weapon for keeping "foul things and horrid people" at bay was not his sullenness, but a wicked, quirky and decidedly vulgar sense of humour – one which he retained well into old age, describing himself with great pride on a number of occasions as a "geriatric child".[62] "Laughter temporarily prevents gloomy thinking and melancholy brooding," he wrote in a schoolboy essay that concluded anarchically, "What an infinitely superior animal a dog would be if he laughed aloud when his master fell off a ladder." [63] Roald himself was proud of his skills as a humorist and enjoyed sharpening his talents in his letters to his mother, who shared his taste for absurdist comedy. In an exchange about whether dried figs were flattened by being trodden down, for example, her son wrote home one day with an exciting new development: "One fellow in my study, who claims to have licked an Arab's foot, said he recognised the taste on the surface of his fig. I said, 'Not really?' and he answered, 'No, on second thoughts, perhaps they are Italians' feet!'" [64]

Sport was another refuge. Dahl was a competent footballer and cricketer, but he excelled at squash and fives, rapidly becoming the best player in the school. And, despite his delight in the luxuries of life, such as good food and beautiful flowers, he was not without a fascination for Spartan values. In training for a football match, he tells his mother proudly he has to observe the following rules: "No eating between meals, except fruit which you may eat as much as you like. No fizzy drinks. A certain amount of 'charged' exercise every day. Skipping after prayers in the evening. No soaking in hot baths. A cold shower after baths. No playing on the yard. A good walk on Sunday afternoon." [65]

His height and size – he was six foot five by his mid-teens – also meant that for his final two years at Repton he was largely left alone. David Atkins, though from a different house, felt that even when Dahl was a junior boy there was something intimidating about him. [66] Roald certainly learned to enjoy this sense of otherness and isolation, and his long walks through the countryside gave him ample opportunity to indulge his imagination. In his very first letter home he wrote that "the best bit [of life at Repton] is we are allowed to go anywhere we like when nothing is happening", [67] while in the first draft of *Boy* he described himself simply as "rather dreamy". [68] It was while he was out walking on his own, smoking his pipe, [69] fishing, collecting bird's eggs, berries or crab apples, that he honed his observations of the natural world. These country walks were a constant feature of his life at Repton. They kept him sane and gave him a context both to watch and to dream. It was the same for another unhappy contemporary of his at school, the artist and writer Denton Welch.

Welch had arrived in September 1929, a term before Roald. Though they were not in the same house and did not become friends, they were certainly aware of each other. Both loathed the school, but while Dahl toughed it out, Welch caused a scandal by running away. In the first draft of *Boy*, Dahl wrote admiringly of his contemporary: "There was another boy in the school while I was there who was later to become a writer like me. His name was Denton Welch, and a fine writer he became. He wasn't in the same house as me, so I never got to know him, but every day I used to see Denton Welch walking to class all on his own, a tall frail bespectacled boy who looked totally miserable. He must have had more courage than me, or possibly less tolerance, because he refused to put up with it all. One day he escaped and ran away and never came back."[70]

In fact, Welch did come back but only for a few weeks, before his father secured a passage for his son to join him in Shanghai. By the time he was in his sixties, Roald had forgotten this detail. Fifty years earlier he had told his mother precisely what happened. He could not possibly admit to her that he too longed to escape – after all, he had made his promise to the doctor in Llandaff – so his tone remained, as always, positive and upbeat. "There are two Brothers in Brook House called Welch," he wrote, "and one did not want to come back to school, so at the station he told his bro. that he was going to buy a paper. But he didn't return. And no one knew where he was. The truth of the matter was he had bottled & taken a train to Salisbury, where he went to a cousin aged 63 & told him a pack of lies. The next day, he went to Exeter. He had to pawn his watch to get money & was found by a Policeman wandering about in the streets of Exeter at midnight with tenpence in his pocket. He slept the night in a cell. He is now back at school, & seems quite happy!!!!"[71]

Ironically, in *Maiden Voyage,* Welch's own account of life at Repton, this "escape" turned him into something of a celebrity, and on his return, he was treated with new respect by many of the boys and the masters. "'Good God, Welch, have you come back?'" one boy exclaims. "'I heard that you had got hold of forty pounds and gone off to France, and someone else told me that Iliffe had taken you to Italy.'" Iliffe, Welch adds, was an older boy who "had shown a frank interest in people younger than himself". Welch's Repton memoir was, in many respects, a twin of Dahl's. Both shared a horror of the open lavatories and of the school's many tortures, which included boys being stripped naked and having chewing gum rubbed into their pubic hair, or an initiation procedure where a child was forced to hang from a wooden ceiling beam and kiss a set of lips that had been painted onto the timber, while his naked body was flicked at with wet towels. "I had been told that you could lift the skin off someone's back in this way," Welch wrote. "I always waited, half in horror, to see a ribbon of flesh come off."[72]

Welch's ability to catch the child's fear of uncertainty, the dread of what may happen next, is something that he shared with Dahl.§ But, unlike his contemporary, what he also explores is a sexual dimension to life at Repton. Welch's own burgeoning homosexuality may have made the all-male environment of a public school more immediately charged in this respect than it was for Roald, but it's interesting that the latter, who was later to take some pleasure in tales of sexual perversity, never mentioned this aspect of his schooldays. Welch's description of a Repton beating evokes *Galloping Foxley* in its bounding assailant, its descriptive detail and its economy of style. But it also addresses the adolescent sexual confusion that these beatings provoked. "'Bend over the desk please.' The moment had come. I held my tongue between my teeth, biting on it, trying to make it hurt; then I put my hands over my eyes and burrowed inwards to myself. My eyes bored down long passages of glittering darkness as I waited. I heard Newman's feet shuffle lightly on the boards, then the faint whine of the cane in the air. There were two bars of fire eating into the ice, then nothing. . . . Through the pain that was biting into me I felt a surge of admiration for Newman, yet I hated myself for liking him. The other part of me wanted to smash his face into a pulp. My mind was rocking about like a cart on a rough road."[73]

Dahl seldom publicly discussed his own sexual experiences, although when he did, it was usually to a humorous end. The tale of his housemaster's explanation of the perils of masturbation, which alluded to a

§Curiously, when John Betjeman wrote to Dahl in 1961 to congratulate him on his collection of stories *Kiss Kiss*, he also made that comparison. He described the book as "a triumph of humour, poetry, the macabre, the unexpected – as though Denton Welch had become H. C. Anderson" – Betjeman, Letter to Roald Dahl, 01/01/61 – RDMSC RD 16/1/2.

torch with a limited power supply and concluded with the stern advice "not to touch it – or the batteries will go flat" was honed to comic perfection over many years of public speaking. But that, it seems, was as far as Dahl's sex education went at school. Charles Pringle, who overlapped with Roald in his first year at The Priory and who was his fag for a term, similarly remembered how uncomfortable J. S. Jenkyns was discussing sex, although he could not recall the story of the torch.[74] And, despite the permissive atmosphere at Oakwood, Sofie Magdalene did not think this was part of her maternal responsibilities either. Roald's sister Else told her daughter Anna that her mother had done nothing to prepare her for her first period. In pain and frightened by the bleeding, Else went to Sofie Magdalene for reassurance and was given short shrift. "Go and talk to your sister," was her response. Alfhild was apparently no more helpful. "It was Birgit [the nanny] who told everyone the facts of life," Else recalled. "Extremely inaccurately".[75] By the summer of 1933, Roald was longing for contact with girls outside his family. Having taken a course of dancing lessons, the sixteen-year-old was eager to monopolize Kari, a Norwegian friend of his sisters, at the school's end-of-year dance. Louis, his twenty-seven-year-old half brother, had also been invited to the event, and Roald was desperately concerned that Kari would find him more attractive. He told his mother that Louis should stick to dancing with Ma Binks.[76]

There were girls in the village, and others in Derby, who formed friendships with Repton boys. Some were even jokingly referred to as "so-and-so's wife".[77] However, it's likely that Dahl's own adolescent sexual desires were largely unfulfilled until he left the school. His stature and aloofness probably made him immune to the sexual advances of older boys such as the dandy Middleton with his silk cravats, or the bully W. W. Wilson, with his exotic hybrid chrysanthemums, nor is there much evidence that he had close friendships with younger boys. David Atkins recalled that Roald had had more than the distant contact he admitted with Denton Welch. Atkins wrote that he remembered them in English lessons together, the six-five Dahl, "voice already broken", playing Romeo to Welch's Juliet in a reading of the Shakespeare play, and that a "romantic friendship" formed between the two boys.[78] Atkins even re-

membered Dahl making a "determined grab" for Welch's private parts on
the first day of term.[79] "Welch was a natural target for cruelty," he wrote
elsewhere, "and Dahl was sometimes protective, but also enjoyed hurting
him. Welch, surely a masochist, would pretend to run away; Dahl would
catch him and twist his arm behind his back until tears came. He also applied Chinese burns to the skin of Welch's wrist. The rest of us stood and
watched; we were all a little frightened of Dahl."[80]

That Dahl and Welch might have been drawn to one another is not
surprising. Welch, like Michael Arnold, was an outsider. But he was gone
by the summer of 1932. Nor would Michael Arnold survive his full term
at Repton. The circumstances of Arnold's departure reveal again how
much Dahl kept from his mother, and how much his letters are to some
degree early essays in fiction. It all began when "Binks" brought Arnold,
the subversive, into the fold and made him a boazer, with all the powers
that entailed. In January 1933, during a "devilishly cold" spell of weather,
Roald told his mother that he and Michael had been out illicitly skating.
"But he must be careful what he does now," he added, "as he's just been
made a house prefect."[81] Things soon began to go wrong for Arnold. Not
that there is any trace of this in Roald's letters home, which continue as
ever in their chatty, upbeat descriptions of pike fishing, fox-hunting, and
killing rooks with a catapult.[82] On May 7, he told his mother that he
was in Michael's study again this term,[83] regaling her with details about
a photograph of a grasshopper he was enlarging and requesting her to
send patent leather shoes for a dancing lesson. But the following week he
delivered a bombshell:

> Do you know what has happened; Michael has had a severe mental
> breakdown and has had to go away for the rest of the term before he
> goes to Oxford. He is staying in a lonely inn, up in Westmoreland all
> alone + perfect quiet, which is essential for him to have. I don't think
> he'll mind it, because he rather enjoys tramping about on moors &
> things alone all day. I have had quite a lot to do arranging all his
> things, returning all his books to the masters from whom he had bor-
> rowed them, packing a crate full of his books, & putting everything else

in his trunk. I'm very sorry he's gone, but now I go about with Smith,
that fellow from Bromley. To show how darned popular he was – half
the house has written to him already.

As if deliberately to play down what he has just told her, he adds a comic
footnote:

Last night after lights I was shaving in the dark, when Palairet, whose
bed was within reach of my basin, said, I'll strike a match for you, so
you can see. I had my back to him, & when he struck the match, as it
was still fizzing he pushed the end against my bottom, burnt a hole in
both me & my pyjamas. He had to be sat on.[84]

But horseplay was something of a cover story. And the "character"
Dahl had created for his mother since his first letters home at St Peter's
was about to be exposed as something of a fake. After receiving Roald's
letter, a sympathetic Sofie Magdalene suggested to her son that she invite Michael to come and stay at Bexley. Roald replied that he thought
this was not a good idea, but did not explain why.[85] Sofie Magdalene,
ignoring her son's advice, must then have written to Michael's parents
and from them, or from Michael himself, learned the truth: that he had
been expelled for homosexual activity with younger boys. Shocked less
by Michael's behaviour than by the fact that Roald had not been honest with her, she then wrote to her son, accusing him of being a liar and
implicating him in what had been going on. In a panic, Roald went to
his housemaster for advice. Binks wrote Sofie Magdalene the following
letter:

Dear Mrs Dahl,

Roald came to me last night in considerable distress, because you
thought that he must have been concerned in the unfortunate events
which led to Michael Arnold leaving Repton.
*   He had not told you about that, because he did not want to*

distress you; but owing to the turn that events have taken, I think I
had better tell you about it. Early this term it came out that Arnold
had been guilty of immorality with some small boys last term. As he
was a prefect and in a position of trust in the house, and as his acts
had been quite deliberate, we decided that he must go. It was a very
unpleasant business for everybody and especially for Roald; not only
because he lost his chief friend, but also because people were likely to
think that he was implicated. But as a matter of fact there was no
sort of suspicion attaching to him, in fact I am convinced that he had
done his best to make Arnold give up his bad ways; but the latter is
very obstinate and would not listen to him.

When boys are sent away for this sort of thing, there is naturally
some difficulty in accounting to their acquaintances for their leaving
school. As a matter of fact Roald consulted me at the time about what
he should say. I did not think it necessary to tell you about it – as he
was not himself implicated – at least not at present, when he could
only communicate by letter. So when Arnold's father ascribed it to a
mental breakdown, I thought he had better use that explanation.

I may have been wrong in this – if so, I am sorry. But in any case
you may set your mind at ease about Roald. I am convinced that he is
perfectly straight about it all and has not been concerned in Arnold's
misdeeds.

As to the letter: Some of these very clever boys have an abnormality
in their minds, which makes them resentful of authority, and diffi-
cult to deal with, and may lead to disaster as in his case. Arnold was
apparently convinced (quite wrongly) that he was not appreciated at
his true worth here, and took up a defiant and revolutionary attitude
to assert his independence. It was of course a very wicked and self-
ish method of doing so, as he deliberately tried to start small boys off
wrong. It is a sad business, as he has many good qualities: I only hope
he will be able to control his "complex" in future.

But my chief object in writing is to set your mind at rest about
Roald – I'm sure he is straight and I hope you will tell him that you

trust him to go right. It is of great importance that he should feel you
believe in him.

> *Yours sincerely*
> *SS Jenkyns*[86]

The letter clearly reassured Sofie Magdalene, and Roald added his
own gloss later the same day when he wrote to her:

Yes, I knew Michael had been expelled, and had asked Binks what I
should say to you about it, and he said that it would be by far the best
for all concerned to conceal the fact under a pretext of mental break-
down. But please don't think that I had anything to do with him in
that way at all. I was his friend and I knew that he had a kink about
immorality. I had tried to stop him, as Binks knew, but it was no
good. I have asked Binks, who knows my character here a good deal
better than most, to assure you that I had nothing to do with it at
all. By your letter I concluded that you thought I had been behaving
badly and might be expelled if I was not careful. Well, please believe
me when I tell you that I had absolutely nothing to do with it. But it
was for the sake of everyone's feelings that Binks and I thought it best
to conceal the fact of his expulsion. The Boss [the Headmaster] told
me that it was not homosexuality, but merely the natural outlet for a
rather over-sensuous mind, often met hand in hand with great brain.
He has asked him to come down to the school again in a year's time.[87]

Ben Reuss thought Roald was lucky to avoid being expelled himself.
"He was terribly clever at sliding out of problems and trouble," he remembered. "He always got away with it."[88] But whatever Roald's own
involvement, the episode probably ensured that he would remain anti-
establishment, outside the fold. Michael Arnold, on the other hand,
went to Oxford and became a respected industrial scientist, marrying
before the war and fathering three sons, one of whom he sent to Repton.
He never told his children that he had been expelled and seems quickly

to have put the incident behind him. For Dahl, it was more complicated. The incident lingered in his subconscious and it subtly altered his
relationship with his mother. His letters to her became more factual, less
self-consciously effervescent because the happy-go-lucky mask he had
created for both of them had been damaged. The make-believe alternative Repton he had constructed was now tainted.

Surprisingly, the episode did not adversely affect Roald's affection
for Michael Arnold. It almost seems to have reinforced it. The two men
remained in regular contact for the next fifty years – one year Dahl and
Arnold took their young families away to Norway on holiday together
– until a violent argument in old age finally put an end to the friendship.[89] Roald however continued to believe that his friend had been
badly treated by Repton – not so much because he had been expelled,
but because he had been brutally beaten beforehand. This punishment
affected him more deeply than any injury he himself received – perhaps
because the beater in this instance was not a boazer, but his headmaster,
"the Boss". By the time he came to write *Boy*, his memories of that beating surged back with some ferocity. And this was one incident from the
initial draft that he did not censor. His final account is almost entirely
as he first described it. "Michael was ordered to take down his trousers
and kneel on the Headmaster's sofa with the top half of his body hanging over one end of the sofa," he wrote. In between each "tremendous
crack administered upon the trembling buttocks", the Boss would light
his pipe and "lecture the kneeling boy about sin and wrongdoing".[90]
Arnold, Dahl remembered, was subjected to ten strokes, although Ben
Reuss recalled that there were twelve, six with a "heavy cane" and six with
a "whippy one".[91]

"At the end of it all," Roald continued, "a basin, a sponge and a small
clean towel were produced by the Headmaster, and the victim was told
to wash away the blood before pulling up his trousers."[92] Ben Reuss corroborated Dahl's memory of the bloody "mopping up operations" and
added that the beating made a considerable impression on everyone in
the school.[93] And, although both his sisters Else and Asta maintained that
the Dahls had all been "brought up with no religion whatsoever",[94] Roald

would later claim that the incident made him begin "to have doubts about religion and even about God".[95] In his mind, it was all the more shocking and hypocritical because the perpetrator was Geoffrey Fisher, the man who later went on to become Archbishop of Canterbury.

Unfortunately, Roald had made a mistake. Not for the first time, he sounded off before he had fully checked his facts. For the culprit was not Fisher at all, but his successor John Christie. The beating happened in the summer of 1933, a year after Fisher, as Dahl records in his own letters home, had left Repton to become Bishop of Chester.[96] More than fifty years later, however, Dahl blamed the "shoddy bandy-legged" Fisher for the caning, and painted him as a sanctimonious hypocrite. "I would sit in the dim light of the school chapel and listen to him preaching about the Lamb of God and about Mercy and Forgiveness and all the rest of it and my young mind would become totally confused. I knew very well that only the night before this preacher had shown neither Forgiveness nor Mercy in flogging some small boy who had broken the rules."[97] That description was exaggerated. Beatings such as Michael Arnold's were unusual. Arnold himself was not a small boy, but an eighteen-year-old who had abused younger boys.¶ Moreover it was a surprising case of mistaken identity. For there is no evidence that Roald particularly disliked Fisher – either while he was at school or after he left it.

Indeed, in many of his letters, his headmaster comes across as an object of affection. In the summer of 1931, for instance, Roald took a photo of the Boss laughing uproariously during a cricket match. Thirty years later, he sent Fisher a copy of his collection of short stories *Kiss Kiss*. He enclosed a copy of that photograph and alluded with warmth to the same incident. On the first page he wrote:

> *The headmaster was roaring with laughter. There was a "click" behind him. He looked round and saw the thin boy holding a camera in his hands. "Dahl," the headmaster said sternly, "if it is ribald you will*

¶Probably both out of respect for Arnold's privacy and because *Boy* was directed at young readers, Dahl failed to mention the nature of Arnold's offence in his book. The reader is consequently left rather in the dark as to why his friend has been treated so savagely.

suppress it!" Today, thirty-two years later, the boy is a little frightened
that the headmaster will feel the same way about these stories. But he
offers them, nevertheless, with gratitude and affection.[98]

The inscription is dated December 1962. It was sent shortly after Roald
had turned to his headmaster for consolation after the death of his seven-
year-old daughter Olivia. Returning to Repton in the 1970s, to give a
generally lighthearted and entertaining speech to the pupils, he described
his former headmaster as a "thoroughly good" man, although "not guilt-
less" when it came to inflicting violence on younger boys.[99] By contrast,
Christie made little impression, except as something of a Christian zealot.
In the summer of 1932, Roald wrote to his mother explaining why he
had not invited her to his confirmation and telling her that there was no
question he would ever become seriously devout. "Talking about religious
fanatics," he continued, "this new Boss is one. He's most frightfully nice,
but he's a religious fanatic. Far too religious for this place."[100]

It has been suggested that when Dahl published *Boy*, he deliberately
falsified the truth about Michael Arnold's beating in order to create a sensation. Fisher went on to be Archbishop of Canterbury, crowning Queen
Elizabeth II at her coronation in 1953, while Christie was simply a public
school headmaster who later became principal of Jesus College, Oxford.
However, there is no evidence at all that this mistake was anything other
than a lapse of memory. Dahl had already mistaken the identity of Michael
Arnold's assailant eight years earlier, when he recounted the story of his
friend's beating on his visit to Repton in 1975. There, on home turf as it
were, he told the tale as vividly as he was to do in *Boy*, describing the flogging in terms of a "medieval religious inquisitorial exercise".[101] Strangely,
perhaps, on this occasion it caused no stir. Moreover, Dahl also related "an
interesting sequel" to this story, explaining that when he had been to visit
the now ennobled Lord Fisher in Sherborne eleven years earlier, the Boss,
who he declared had "an astonishing memory", could remember nothing of
the beating. Perhaps this should have flashed a warning light that something
was wrong. It didn't. And so the error became set in stone.

But when *Boy* was published in 1984, there was a furore. Family and former students rushed to Fisher's defence. Dahl's final head of house, John Bradburn, summed up their feelings when he wrote: "The Boss was a wise and stern headmaster . . . but always fair; and in general held in great respect, admiration and indeed affection."[102] It was curious that no one at the time stumbled on the fact that Dahl had simply accused the wrong man. Michael Arnold, presumably, could have set the record straight, but chose not to. Why he did not do so, we will probably never know.

From that incident onward, Dahl's final months at Repton were a kind of holding pattern. He had lost his soul mate. He was not made a prefect. So his energies turned even further inward. As he wrote slightly resentfully in *Boy*, "the authorities did not like me. I was not to be trusted. I did not like rules. I was unpredictable. . . . Some people are born to wield power and to exercise authority. I was not one of them."[103] He also had another secret consolation: his motorbike. For Christmas 1932 his mother had bought him a 500cc Ariel. He hid it in the barn of a local farm and it gave him a huge sense of independence and freedom. At weekends he would take it out and ride through the Derbyshire country-side, sometimes venturing into Repton itself and annoying masters and boazers, as he whizzed noisily past them, incognito beneath his old over-coat, rubber waders, helmet and goggles. He got a summons for speeding, but managed to keep that secret as well.[104]

Eventually, he took his School Certificate exam in the summer of 1933, passing with credit in Scripture Knowledge, English, History, French, Elementary Mathematics and General Science. He had already decided that he neither wanted to go to university nor to do "missionary work or some other fatuous thing".[105] His father's trust would provide him with a modest income from the age of twenty-five, so there was no immediate pressure to find a job. What he desired was adventure. So he chose to join an oil company and go to work abroad.** His mother, "desperate" at what she saw as his lack of ambition, sent off to have his

---

** In eschewing university, Dahl was doing the same as most of his fellows. According to the Repton archivist, of the eighteen pupils who arrived with Dahl in January 1930, only two were listed in the school register as going on to university when they left. Of the thirty-four pupils who left with him in July 1934, ten went on to get a university education.

horoscope professionally read. Years later she told her daughter Else that the psychic predicted Roald was going to be a writer.[106]

His final weeks at the school were spent building gigantic fire-balloons, which he and his friends constructed out of tissue paper, wire and paraffin. The biggest, he claimed, was 18 feet high.[107] Making these fire-balloons was something he would do on and off for the rest of his life. He enjoyed the thrill of seeing them rise up into the night sky and would chase them for miles across the countryside to see where they landed. At that point in his life they must also have seemed a symbol of freedom and escape. Because he had not become a boazer, he was leaving Repton uncorrupted and with his rebellious nature uncurbed. He may have been occasionally cruel – giving Denton Welch Chinese burns, or teasing an elder boy whom he dubbed "The Vapour" because he farted a lot[108] – but he had never wielded the force of school authority. And he had never beaten anyone. Had he been given an official position, perhaps it would all have been different, although, as his daughter Ophelia observed, "the typically English 'it happened to me, so it will happen to you' attitude was never part of his mentality".[109] His schoolfriend Ben Reuss was not so sure. "The powers-that-were mistrusted him and he got no promotion at all in a very hierarchical society. Probably a great mistake. No doubt it was feared that he would be subversive," Reuss concluded, "but in these cases the poachers generally make the best gamekeepers."[110] So, just as the photograph is fixed in the darkroom, Dahl was "fixed" at Repton. Already immensely self-reliant, he now further turned his back on English protocol and pecking orders. From now on, where possible, he resolved to control his own destiny. John Christie, his headmaster, concluded Dahl's final school report with these words: "He has ambition and a real artistic sense . . . If he can master himself, he will be a leader."[111]

CHAPTER FIVE

Distant Faraway Lands

IN AUGUST 1934, WHILE the rest of his family were frolicking in the Oslo Fjord, Roald boarded the RMS *Nova Scotia* as a member of the Public School Exploring Society. Fifty volunteers from across Britain had each paid £35 for the dubious pleasure of a four-week trek across a remote and unexplored area of the island of Newfoundland off the coast of northern Canada. The purpose was ostensibly to map an uncharted part of what was then still a British dominion, but no one really cared very much about that. What mattered far more to the organizers of the expedition was the business of character-building: instructing young empire builders how to survive in the wild, far away from the luxuries of civilization. For twelve of the fittest (that included Dahl) the journey culminated in a twenty-day Long March through soaking mosquito-infested bogs with between 60 and 100 pounds on their backs, living under canvas on a diet that consisted essentially of pemmican (a mixture of pressed meat, fat and berries), boiled lichen, mud and reindeer moss. It was a tough undertaking. The would-be explorers waded knee-deep down the Great Rattling Brook. They trudged through desolate swamps collecting plant and insect samples. They attempted to fish for trout and trap rabbits, but had little success at either. Their tents leaked and eventually they ran out of food. For most of the time they were hungry, wet and cold. As Roald recorded plaintively in his daily journal, "honestly I don't think any one of us has ever been so miserable".[1]

The week-long sea journey from Liverpool to St John's, the capital of Newfoundland, began in high spirits. Roald and another friend of his from Repton, the boisterous Jimmy Horrocks, got drunk and Horrocks had to be carried back to his cabin in a stupor. In between avoiding contact with a "silly little missionary" who wanted to talk about Labrador, and flirting with Ruth Lodge, a twenty-year-old actress who was also aboard the boat, Roald found time to make friends with a crew member from British Guiana called Sam. It was typical of him to look outside his immediate peer group for a kindred spirit, and Sam's freewheeling Caribbean attitudes were much more appealing than those of most of his fellow explorers who, apart from Jimmy Horrocks, scarcely get a mention in his journal. "He's a marvellous fellow, black curly hair & a blue beret," Dahl wrote of Sam to his mother, adding that he had asked Sam to shave his head for him – leaving only "a tiny bit of bristle on the top". Roald thought that he "looked fine"[2] with his new haircut, and Sam gave the seventeen-year-old boy his blue beret to keep his head warm. Dahl gratefully added it to a pack that, as he was the expedition's official photographer, included a camera and eighteen rolls of film in lead cases, as well as 14 ounces of tobacco, two pipes and a mouth organ.

The expedition was led by fifty-seven-year-old Surgeon Commander "Admiral" George Murray Levick, the founder of the Public Schools Exploring Society, and a survivor of Scott's doomed expedition to the Antarctic. Murray Levick was an eccentric British penguin expert, who advocated Spartan values in the education of young men. For many on the expedition, including one of his three assistants, a journalist called Dennis Clarke, he was tantamount to a national hero. In his official history of the trip, Clarke eulogized his leader's asceticism as well as his obsessive desire to put his feet where no other had trod before, boasting that, "if exploring were a crime . . . Commander Levick would have been hanged several times over".[3] He shared his commander's delight in the pleasures of bathing naked in ice-cold rivers, marching through unknown landscapes, and rejoiced in what we might now call the culture of male bonding. He celebrated Levick's disgust, for example, at having to travel first class on the 250-mile train journey inland from St John's to Grand Falls, where the expedition began, rather than "roughing it" on the third-class tickets he had specifically requested. Roald too clearly enjoyed the sense of pitting himself against a hostile natural environment – though perhaps not quite to the same degree as his commander. His journal records his battle with hunger and the elements in pithy detail, with occasional forays into imaginative fantasy, when things got really tough. "That night the water . . . soaked into our little bog and the water level in the tent rose several inches," he wrote one evening. "If some great giant, wandering by that night, having caught a cold in the wet the previous day had, in need of a handkerchief, seized up our tent, we would all have drifted away in our sleeping bags."[4]

It was not long too before another characteristic Dahl trait began to reemerge: a dislike of authority. This manifested itself in a growing sense of annoyance at "Admiral" Murray Levick. Roald was already suspicious of people who inflated themselves with unnecessary rank or title, and Murray Levick, who had been a surgeon commander but was certainly no admiral, and had been retired from the Royal Navy since 1918, instantly aroused his irritation. Roald found him both absurd and bogus. And that was not all. The "Admiral" defecated publicly each morning in full view of anyone who happened to be around: "Breakfast at 6.45," Roald noted in his journal. "The Admiral craps in the middle of the camp – quite unashamed and very successful – we all wish he wouldn't." And, as the Long March progressed and things started to go wrong, this distaste soon escalated into contempt. Roald began to believe that the "filthy old boy" was also a fool – albeit a tough one. He became particularly infuriated by one specific issue: Murray Levick's insistence that his team build a makeshift raft to row across a lake, when walking round it would have both been safer and increased their chances of finding food. At this point the young explorers were not in good shape. One of them was seriously ill with mumps, while Roald's footwear had disintegrated to such an extent that on one foot he had been forced to improvise a boot out of a canvas bucket. With their supplies of food almost exhausted, talk in his tent quickly began to get "revolutionary".[5] Eventually, Roald and two veterans of other Murray Levick expeditions, Michael Barling and Dennis Pearl, decided they must face the Admiral down and persuade him to return to base.

"We led a mutiny, he and I," remembered Dennis Pearl. "It didn't really get us very far, but it was what drew Roald and I together."[6] In fact, the trio made quite an impression. Even Clarke was struck by the intelligence and eloquence of their pleas, recording that although Murray Levick did not actually turn back, he did abandon his plan to cross the lake by raft. Whether he was irritated by the fact that one of his mutineers had been named after Roald Amundsen, who had triumphed over Scott in the race to the South Pole, was not mentioned. The final days of the bad-tempered journey were spent in silence as the marchers fought off their hunger pangs. Eating dominates the closing pages of Roald's journal. "You see our only thoughts were on food, more food and even more food still." At night, in their tents, the boys fantasized about imaginary meals in London restaurants – Simpsons, perhaps, or Ye Olde Cheshire Cheese. "It really was marvellous to talk about such things and to realise that they still existed," Dahl observed, adding that then the conversation would turn to literature or music. Those were the subjects that "gave us the greatest pleasure to talk about".[7] He returned to England in September, with "large side whiskers and beard",[8] and a new friend, Dennis Pearl. His suspicions of the pomposities and absurdities of certain elements of the British establishment had been reconfirmed, but so had his confidence that he could deal with them. He believed himself "fit and ready for anything".[9]

A few days later, Roald took up his job as a probationary member of staff with the Asiatic Petroleum Company, later to become a part of Royal Dutch Shell. He worked at St Helen's Court, in the heart of the City of London, and his salary was £130 per annum.* The job offered him few challenges. Commuting up each day from the family home in Bexley, he fell into a pleasurable rut of undemanding office work, punctuated by weekends playing golf, going racing, listening to Beethoven on his gramophone, and reading American crime stories. He was not a natural office worker. Bored by his time in the Accounts Department, with its chattering clerks seated on stools at their high desks,[10] and uninterested in the

---

*The equivalent of about £25,000 in 2010.

technicalities of refining petroleum, he dreamed only of travelling abroad. Inspired by the stories of Rider Haggard and Isak Dinesen,† he had asked to be posted to East Africa, but for many months the furthest he got from his desk was to the Shell Central Laboratories in West London, where he was made to study the composition of petroleum products.[11] In the summer of 1936 he was despatched to a refinery and oil wharf in Essex, on the lower reaches of the Thames. There too he found little to stimulate him. "Spent most of today on top of an enormous petrol tank – very hot and nearly suffocated by the fumes," he complained to his mother. "In the evening watched a tanker discharging a cargo of lubricating oil from Mexico."[12] A sales trip around the West Country the following year was a little more interesting, mainly for the opportunities it gave him to take photographs.

It took almost four years for the African posting to come through. Part of the reason for this delay may have been that Dahl was not a full British national when he joined Shell and needed to secure a British passport in order to travel abroad with them.‡ He may also have been considered just too unreliable. One contemporary of his at Shell remembered thinking that Roald would not last the training course because he was such an "independent person" and "didn't like an awful lot of direction".[13] Yet he was enjoying his release from the prison of school and his emergence into the longed-for sunlight of freedom. So wait he did.

If the four years in the rambling house at Bexley with his mother and sisters were without particular incident, they were perhaps as happy and carefree times as Dahl was to experience until the last decade of his life. There, he and his siblings moved gently together into adulthood. In April 1930, his chatty and intense half sister Ellen had married Ashley Miles,

---

†His sister Alfhild maintained that it was principally the tales of the Danish Karen Blixen that made her brother long to go to East Africa – Conversation with author, 08/07/92.

‡Letter from Asiatic Petroleum Company Ltd. to Roald Dahl, 07/16/34 – RDMSC RD 13/1/9/53. This letter, reminding Dahl that he could not take up a foreign posting with Shell without having British citizenship, suggests that at that point he may have had a Norwegian passport. The possibility that Roald was not a UK citizen until at least 1934 is reinforced by the fact that his sister Alfhild remembered none of the girls could join the British Forces until after Norway entered the war, and that, although they were British-born, they were treated as "foreigners and spies" – Conversation with the author, 08/07/92.

the talented young pathologist – later an eminent immunologist – whose pipe Roald had once filled with goat droppings on holiday in Norway. Soon the couple had settled into the comfortable professional gentility of Hampstead, in North London. The gentle Louis was more bohemian and took longer to leave the family nest. After a series of professional failures that included some months at Aadnesen & Dahl§ – where he discovered that, like his half brother, he disliked office life – and working as a jacka-roo on a remote Australian sheep station, he went to London to study at St Martin's College of Art, after which he took on a job as a commercial illustrator.[14]

While at St Martin's, Louis had converted the top floor of the house in Bexley into a studio. There he spent hours painting, often to a soundtrack of Sibelius symphonies on the gramophone. Sometimes he would venture out with Alfhild in the evening to a concert in London at the Queen's Hall. In 1936, he got engaged to a vicar's daughter, Meriel Longland, and he married her in Cambridge later that year. The newlyweds then moved up to London, first into rented accommodation in Marylebone and then to a house in Shepherd's Bush. Alfhild, who also aspired to be an artist, and was frustrated that Sofie Magdalene told her the family did not have enough money to send a daughter to art school,[15] found solace living a rather "fast" London existence, where she had affairs with the composer William Walton and the conservative historian Arthur Bryant, as well as with Roald's friend, Dennis Pearl. Her sister Asta recalled that she was often to be found "coming home on the milk train".[16] Else, a year younger than Roald, was shier and quieter. Initially she had refused to follow her sisters to Roedean, going briefly to Lindores College in Bex-hill[17] and a "very expensive" school in Switzerland instead, both of which she left after a single term.[18] "I expect she's quite a connoisseur of schools now,"[19] Roald commented wryly to his mother after the Swiss episode, where Else ate her train ticket on the station platform so she would not

---

§Aadnesen & Dahl continued in existence until the late 1950s, but by 1930, Ludvig Aadnesen "Parrain" was spending much of his time travelling in Norway and France. A bon viveur, without children of his own, he was a generous and supportive godfather to the Dahl children, who always spoke of him with enormous warmth and affection.

be able to board the train. She finally joined her younger sister, Asta, at Roedean in September 1933.

As Sofie Magdalene approached fifty, and her family responsibilities began to diminish, she was becoming increasingly arthritic, immobile and concerned with the welfare of her many animals. She had quarrelled with Oscar, her brother-in-law, over his administration of Harald's estate, accusing him of abusing his position as a trustee and humiliating her by making her submit receipts for every purchase she made. He in turn had threatened to sue her. But her children and stepchildren, led by the vociferous sixteen-year-old Roald, had rallied round. "I should jolly well sue him, get ten thousand and not care what anyone said!"[20] he told her. "Get Ellen and Louis to entice him to Bexley; take him up to Dartford . . . and push him into that most useful and old-established institution – the Dartford Mental Home, where he could spend his time writing lavatory roll after lavatory roll of concentrated libel – for writing libel seems to be his pet hobby nowadays."[21] As her family grew up, Sofie Magdalene's zest for travelling to Norway also began to wane. She preferred to take her Cairn terriers down to Tenby or to Cornwall instead, provoking her mother to accuse her of caring more for her puppies than her own parents.[22] Gradually she retreated into her own space and let her children get on with their own lives. She would be there if they needed her. Otherwise, she kept herself to herself.

In Bexley, Roald had set up his own "very smart"[23] darkroom with shuttered windows and zinc-lined sink. He spent much of his spare time there developing photographs and entering them for competitions. He also began to dabble in writing spoofs and sketches, including a short comic piece called *Double Exposure* which has survived as perhaps his first adult literary work. It is set in America some time in the future when the government has decreed that all couples must produce a child within five years of marriage. The plot tells of the aptly named Mrs Barren, who has failed to get pregnant and therefore faces a visit from a government official whose job it is to impregnate her – or, as Dahl puts it, to "go through the usual routine prescribed under the code" to ensure "continued propagation of the race". The humour is built on a premise of mistaken identity. On her fifth wedding anniversary, Mrs Barren is visited not by the government stud, but by Mr Litmus F. Lenser, a photographer of children who is trying to sell his services to her. A series of lewd double entendres ensues, as Mr Lenser talks about his "baby work" and Mrs Barren becomes increasingly alarmed by the number and variety of sexual acts she imagines she will have to perform with him. "I have reduced it to a science," says Lenser typically. "I recommend at least two in the bath tub, one or two on the couch, and a couple on the floor. You want your children natural, don't you?" [24]

Dahl found other outlets too for this madcap inventiveness. In Norway, in 1935, he had taken a photo of his bare-chested half brother Louis, playing a harmonica, and looking "not unlike a native of Honolulu. Brown granite looks white next to his skin".[25] In September 1937, however, this same photograph appeared in a very different context: *The Shell Magazine*. In a section entitled "Whips and Scorpions", the man in the photograph was identified as a Mr Dippy Dud, and Shell employees from the unlikely town of Whelkington-on-Sea were invited to rugby-tackle him to the ground when they saw him on the promenade. If they floored him while carrying a copy of *The Shell Magazine*, the article declared, a prize would be theirs. "Mr Dud," the anonymous writer continued, "is a keen musician, but do not be misled if he is not playing a mouth organ when you see him. He is an equally adept performer on the harmonica, also on the harmonium, euphonium, pandemonium, saxophone, vibraphone, dictaphone, glockenspiel and catarrh . . . Don't be afraid to tackle anyone you think may be Mr Dud. People who are mistaken for him enter heartily into the fun of the thing, especially town councillors, archdeacons and retired colonels." Dahl was surely the author of this piece, whose subversive tone and extravagant comic vocabulary anticipate the language of one of his most famous fictional characters: Willy Wonka.

It is hard to imagine these four years of relaxed normality – travelling up to London six mornings a week on the 8.15 train from Bexley, with trilby hat and furled umbrella, alongside a "swarm of other equally sombre-suited businessmen" [26] They simply do not fit in with the rest of Dahl's extraordinarily eventful existence. Perhaps in hindsight not even

Roald himself could believe it. In *Boy*, he telescopes these four years into two and suggests that he was in East Africa for much longer than the single year he spent there. Yet Dahl's time in the leafy suburbs was important in forming him as a writer for it was at this time that he became a voracious reader. "The best reading times I ever had were in the 1930s," he declared less than a year before he died, in a speech at the Sunday Express Book Awards, where he listed the novels by Waugh, Greene, Hemingway, Faulkner, and Fitzgerald that had thrilled him in his twenties. "We never had it so good,"[27] he continued, celebrating these novels for being entertaining, well-plotted, elegant and yet serious. One story of Damon Runyon's particularly excited him – for its terseness, its present-tense narrative and the fact that its style "broke all the rules".[28] Those years in Bexley also confirmed his ideal of family life. The carefree, easygoing atmosphere of Oakwood – a huge Edwardian house on three floors with rambling gardens, studios, well-stocked wine cellar, conservatory, grotto and servants – set a kind of standard for Dahl as to what a family house should be. It was relaxed. And there were few, if any, rules. It would become a model for the kind of lifestyle Dahl tried to create for himself and his own young family in rural Buckinghamshire twenty years later.

When not in his darkroom, Dahl could often be found playing golf. He had started playing as an eleven-year-old on the beach at Weston-super-Mare,[29] and joined Dartford Golf Club as a Junior Member in 1927, where he went almost every day of the holidays with Alfhild.[30] By 1936, when he was runner-up in the Shell Championship,[31] he had become almost a scratch player.[32] If not on the golf course, he was likely to be at the races, gambling either on horses or greyhounds. Dennis Pearl remembered Roald being introduced to the world of racing greyhounds by Dick Wolsey, a wealthy bookmaker who played at Dartford Golf Club. Wolsey was from the wrong side of the tracks. He had left school aged twelve, sometimes carried £1,000 in cash in his back pocket, and kept a Rolls-Royce that he only drove at night, "in case the tax man saw him".[33] He was perhaps the first of many self-made entrepreneurs to whom Dahl found himself instinctively drawn.

Wolsey took his young friend to the newly opened Catford Stadium, nine miles away, to see his own dogs racing, and Roald was instantly hooked. From then onwards he would spend most Saturday evenings there, often wagering his week's earnings on the races. Pearl remembered his friend's fascination with the other gamblers too and how intrigued Dahl was by "the way in which they gambled, and the effect that gambling had on them".[34] It was the beginning of a love affair with betting that would last to the end of his life. Indeed, he once told his daughter Ophelia that winning on the horses or at blackjack gave him more pleasure than receiving a royalty check from his writing.[35]

Shell did not offer much in the way of paid holidays, but whenever he could, Roald got away. Twice he went to Norway with Michael Arnold and Dennis Pearl. There, he swam, fished, went boating, chased girls, and reconnected with his cousin Finn, the son of his uncle Truls. Once he sketched out notes for a tale about an absurd encounter with a local mechanic, which some years later, relocated to wartime Greece, would become the basis of his poignant story "Yesterday Was Beautiful". He also indulged a sense of fun that could at times be distinctly oafish. Once on a climbing trip to Snowdonia, with Dennis Pearl and Jimmy Horrocks, Roald set fire to Dennis Pearl's sleeping bag while he was asleep inside it. This provoked outbursts of helpless laughter from the anarchic Horrocks, whom Pearl described as "an early version of the druggy dropout".[36] Next day, while taking a bath in the local hotel, Horrocks also flooded the bathroom. When the owner asked him for some money to repair the damage, Roald told his mother with delight that his friend had simply replied: "My dear sir, I don't think you know what you're talking about. I just washed your floor for you!"[37]

On the way up to Snowdonia, Pearl also remembered his friend inventing stories about characters glimpsed through the car window, creating detailed situations and plots simply from the look on someone's face or the way they were walking.[38] Most of the key threads that would characterize Dahl's fiction were subtly coming together in his psyche: an acute observational eye for detail, a madcap relish for fantasy, a sense of the irreverent, a delight in invention and a crude, childish sense of humour. Storytelling too was becoming part of his makeup. But he was a long way from doing it in an organized manner, let alone contemplating it as a means of earning his living. It was a diversion. For the moment, he seemed quite content to remain what he was – a young professional, with a salary and private income, whose spare hours were mostly spent playing golf, gambling, listening to music and practising his seduction techniques.

"I went into oil because all girls go for oilmen," Dahl told his Reptonian friend David Atkins, who sometimes had lunch with him in the City.[39] But if Dahl thought Shell would provide him with a glamorous social life, he was disappointed. For this, he was forced to look elsewhere, largely following in the wake of his vivacious elder sister Alfhild, and her friend the clever, larger-than-life Alfred Tregear Chenhalls, who worked as business manager for the actor Leslie Howard. "Chenny" was another misfit who became part of the Dahl clan – "a curious character," as Alfhild would later describe him, "a bit of a womanizer, but a bit of something else as well. You never quite knew what he was."[40] Chenny provided the Dahls with witty conversation and party opportunities in London. He taught Else and Alfhild to play piano duets and invited Sofie Magdalene, who "adored him", on holiday to his family home in Cornwall.[41] He helped Roald to get his job with Shell.[42] He was also "randy as hell" and liked to chase the girls. Alf had "a whale of a time" with him, but Else and Asta used to set traps for him on their bedroom doors in case he prowled the corridors when he stayed overnight.[43]

However, while Roald enjoyed talking about sex, he was somewhat buttoned up when it came to his own love life. As far as romance was concerned, Alfhild later recalled that Roald "didn't really discuss himself".[44] Dennis Pearl, who had had a row with his own parents and was now living at Oakwood too, remembered that his friend's first romances were often secretive. Several originated from his local golf club and at least two involved adultery.[45] One was with a peer's wife (he would always be attracted to aristocrats) and another with a woman from Bexley, whom he saw only when her husband was away on business.[46] "He tended to choose something which created difficulties," Pearl recalled. "He seemed to like mystery."[47] By the time his posting to Africa finally came through in September 1938, Roald had been dating a girl of his own age called Dorothy O'Hara Livesay, whom he had met through Alfhild's future husband, Leslie Hansen. "Dolly", as she called herself, was of Belgian-Irish descent,[48] and joined Roald's family on the pierside at London Docks to wave him goodbye on his trip to East Africa. "Look after her, Dennis," said Roald to his friend as he boarded the SS *Mantola*. Pearl took the advice to heart. Not long afterwards he got her pregnant and Dolly became the first Mrs Dennis Pearl.[49]

For Dahl, aged just twenty-two, a new chapter of his life was beginning. After a two-week journey on the *Mantola* to Mombasa in Kenya, in the company of some empire-building Englishmen and their "bright, bony little wives",[50] he took a small coastal steamer, a "bloody little ship",[51] down the African coast to Dar es Salaam. His letters home from the voyage describe none of the eccentric passengers he would later evoke in his memoir, *Going Solo* (1986): the nudist athletes Major Griffiths and his wife, for example, or the rupophobic Miss Trefusis. Not even the bewigged Mr U. N. Savory gets a mention. Most of these delightful characters were almost certainly invented as an entertaining alternative to his real companions on the journey, who were dismissed in a letter to his mother as "pretty dull". The welfare of some of the animals on board concerned him more: dogs that needed exercise and, in particular, a horse "doomed to stand in his box in which he can't even turn round".[52] By the end he longed to reach Tanganyika.

Occupying more than 350,000 square miles of land between the Indian Ocean and three of the African great lakes, this territory of around 5 million inhabitants had been a German colony from the 1880s until 1919, when, following Germany's defeat at the end of the First World War, it became a League of Nations-mandated territory, and subject to British colonial administration.¶ In 1936, Shell set up an oil terminal on the coast, in the capital, Dar es Salaam, and Dahl was appointed as the most junior of the three-man team charged with running it. Most of the company's business there involved supplying fuel and lubricants for farm

---

¶Originally known as German East Africa, Tanganyika finally became independent in 1961. In 1964 it merged with the neighbouring island of Zanzibar to become the United Republic of Tanzania.

equipment, but Dahl was particularly excited that he was put in charge of "all aviation business".[53] This involved meeting the flying boats that arrived in the harbour every two or three days, as well as dealing with the regular air services from Dar es Salaam to Mombasa and Nairobi. Much of the rest of the job was drudgery – a far cry from the exotic glamour of the bush evoked in Isak Dinesen's stories – but at least there was plenty of time for leisure. "Everything is OK," he wrote to his mother shortly after he arrived. "Life's rather fun. Bloody hard work. Bloody hot – golf or squash or something every evening and about four baths a day."[54] Best of all was the fact that there were new surroundings to observe and that he was no longer a commuter. "I loved it all," he reflected later. "There were no furled umbrellas, no bowler hats, no sombre grey suits and I never once had to get on a train or a bus."[55]

Dahl spent most of his year there living with two colleagues, Panny Williamson and George Rybot. They shared a large, spacious villa called Shell House, set in lush gardens some fifty yards from the beach at Oyster Bay, just south of the centre of Dar es Salaam. Much of his spare time was spent playing squash, darts and golf at the whites-only Dar es Salaam Club, or socializing at the colonial cocktail parties. "As far as I can see," he told his mother, "the average person . . . gets drunk at least twice a week out here. They have these things called 'sundowners' starting at about seven or eight o'clock – cocktail parties really – but no cocktails, only whisky, beer and gin . . . Actually it does you no harm and you never have a hangover because you sweat it all out in the night – it's so hot! I only get drunk once a week and then not properly drunk – just merry – I think it's good for you."[56] As his alcohol intake increased, Roald boasted that he was developing "hollow legs",[57] and complained about the vast amounts of money he had to spend on beer and spirits. The drunker he got, the more raucous his behaviour became, while his instinctive dislike of anything that smacked of bourgeois good taste led to clashes with the more conformist values of his peers. He dismissed most of his Shell colleagues as "either hearty or dumb",[58] and the expatriates in general as "awful twits really, full of manners, and getting up when women come in etc. etc. I don't do it and I'm always in the shit." [59] He once disgraced himself at a drinks party in Government House, stealing into the bedroom and returning to the drawing room with the Governor's chamberpot upon his head. But he found a kindred spirit in his house-mate, George Rybot.

> *George and I were asked to go and have a drink at Mrs Wilkin's house. Mrs Wilkin is a frightful old hag who weighs nineteen and a half stone (and is proud of it) and looks like a suet dumpling covered in lipstick & powder. Well, George went into the drawing room and I went down to the basement to have a widdle. Down there I came across the most marvellous crimson tin pi-jerry[chamberpot], so with a whoop of joy I seized it and dashed upstairs to show it to George, entering the draw-ing room waving the thing above my head. Well, I wasn't to know that there were twenty other people in the room, sitting primly around sip-ping their pink gins. There was a horrified silence. Then George started giggling – then we both got a fit of giggling while I pushed the frightful apparition under the nearest sofa and muttered something about "what a pretty colour it was and didn't they all think so".* [60]

Chamberpots and their contents interested him in other ways, too. Like many of his contemporaries, Roald was profoundly concerned about the frequency and quality of his bowel movements, and his letters home are full of scatological details and jokes about urination,[61] enemas,[62] and the regularity or irregularity of his motions. For a while he was taken with a contemporary bestseller his mother had sent him called *Culture of the Abdomen*, by Professor F. A. Hornibrook. Subtitled "The Cure of Obesity and Constipation", Hornibrook argued that maintaining a par-ticular exercise regime, and adopting a squatting posture when on the lavatory, were the most effective means both of thoroughly evacuating the bowel and of remaining fit and healthy. Dahl was fascinated. He quickly renamed the author "Horniblow" and persuaded his housemates to have a go at all the exercises. "Horniblow" soon became a byword for anything involved with the lower bowel at Shell House: native dancers, rhinoceros droppings, the antics of his dog Samka, all got the treatment. "We do Horniblow every morning – it's the funniest thing you've ever seen," he wrote to his mother, "George, Panny and I sprawling over the floor of my bedroom groaning, panting and sweating and cursing the old Professor. But I think it's done me lots of good."[63] He would remain concerned about his daily "deposit in the bank of good health"[64] until the end of his days.

For Roald as for all the Dahls, domestic life was unimaginable without pets, and so Shell House rapidly acquired a menagerie of peculiar animals. Many of these soon made regular comic appearances in his letters home. Chief among them were the tick-infested Samka, "a guard dog with the biggest tool and the longest tail (always wagging) that I've ever seen",[65] and two cats, Oscar and Mrs Taubsypuss.** Dog Samka is "such an important person in this house", Roald told his mother, "that when he is ill or off colour the whole household is disorganized".[66] Samka's escapades were recounted with generous dollops of picaresque detail, as the adventures of an insatiable canine Casanova, who suffered a postcoital hangover most mornings because of his propensity to "go out and roger himself silly at the slightest opportunity".[67] At one point he disappeared and no one could find him. Eventually, after much searching, he was discovered locked in the local chemist's shop. "We consoled ourselves," Roald reported, "with the thought that by now he would probably have had a very good meal of vanishing cream with a dessert of orange skin food and perhaps a bottle of *Nuits de Paris* or *Blue Grass* to wash it down . . . They say that when he trotted out his lips were rouged and he'd powdered his balls . . . Interviewed later, Dog Samka was heard to remark: I found french letters fried in liquid paraffin very nourishing, I shall always carry a packet with me in future in case of emergencies."[68]

One of the reasons that Dahl took such delight in chronicling the sexual exploits of his pets was because he was finding it difficult to have any himself. He wrote enviously of his sisters "gadding about" in Paris,

---

**Thirty-four years later, Mrs Taubsypuss would also make a cameo appearance as the US president's cat in *Charlie and the Great Glass Elevator*.

adding rather dolefully that "there's no-one here worth gadding about with".[69] A week later, his mood was more humorous. Describing how the damp made everything rot, he told his mother: "Golf balls go yellow, but that's nothing – mine do too, like everything else that's not used."[70] This was typical of the ribald detail Roald adored and which was enthusiastically lapped up by Sofie Magdalene and his three sisters. Dirty jokes abound in almost every letter. Some of these were quite straightforward, but others already verged on the surreal. When his mother was recovering from dental surgery, for example, Roald asked his sisters to "tell her the joke about the person who had all teeth out & couldn't be fed through the mouth. So the doctor said – I'll have to feed you with a tube through your anus – what would you like for your first meal? A cup of tea please doctor – Right, here goes. Hi, stop doctor, stop what's the matter, what's the matter, is it too hot? No, there's too much sugar in it."[71] His sisters, particularly Alfhild, usually responded in kind. And Roald often complimented them on how well their own jokes had been received at the club. Nevertheless, there was much more to Dahl's time in Africa than playing the fool. If he was not getting the *Out of Africa* experience of which he had dreamed, he was seeking out its equivalent secondhand among the characters he encountered in Dar es Salaam, be they Brahmin Shell employees, a septuagenarian orchid collector whom he nicknamed "Iron Discipline", or the servants in Shell House.

Shell House had its own cook and gardener and each of its three white residents had their own personal servant, or "boy". Roald's was called Mdisho. He was about nineteen, just three years younger than his master. "I get woken up by my boy at 6.30," Roald wrote to his mother shortly after his arrival. "He brings tea and an orange – a marvellous orange tasting quite different to anything you've ever had . . . I eat my orange and drink my tea that is after the boy has removed the enormous mosquito net that is suspended about six feet above you." Mdisho would then run his morning cold bath and lay out all Roald's clothes for the day ahead. Initially, Dahl enjoyed this power over "the natives",[72] but soon he became fascinated by the "tall and graceful and soft-spoken"[73] Mdisho, who was from a tribe of "magnificent fighters".[74] Mdisho travelled everywhere with him, showing "absolute loyalty" to his "young white master".[75] In turn, Roald looked after Mdisho, advising him on his finances, teaching him to read and write, and even acting as his banker when he wanted to save money to buy a wife.[76] Mdisho's lack of guile and his simple, honest view of the world resonated with Dahl, who was also impressed when Mdisho boasted that his tribe had been the only ones ever to defeat the much-feared Masai.†† Dahl evoked him with respect and affection in *Going Solo*, and celebrated their friendship.[77] Mdisho's innocent loyalty and toughness may even have helped inspire the hero of Dahl's most famous children's book, *Charlie and the Chocolate Factory*. For when Dahl first sketched out the story, he made his young hero a black boy, drawing a little picture of him and describing him as "the tiniest seven-year-old that you could ever find anywhere . . . as bright and clever as any other boy of his age in the town, and as brave as a lion and as kind and nice and cheerful as anyone you could meet".[78]

As a young man in Tanganyika, Dahl was guilty of making largely unflattering generalizations either about the native Africans, or the Indians, who made up a large part of the professional classes in Dar es Salaam. His endlessly feuding Goanese clerks, Carrasco and Patel, provoked him to complain that "they're all the same, these bloody Hindus", and to assert that their minds "grind exceedingly low". When his shipping clerk invited him to his house, he was appalled by the family's cramped and filthy living conditions, "their thousands of bloody relations" and "no less than eight horrible little naked children".[79] While he may have been repelled by their living conditions, Dahl was nevertheless curious about the lives of nonwhites and seized with enthusiasm the rare opportunities that occurred to explore their world. On one occasion, he and George Rybot stopped their car to help another car that had broken down at the side of the road. The occupants turned out to be "an educated native all done up in smart suit & trilby hat, his two wives & two children aged about 4 & 7". By way of thanks, they took Dahl and Rybot to "a bloody

††In *Going Solo*, Dahl describes Mdisho as coming from the nonexistent Mwanumwezi tribe. It is likely he intended to write Nyamwezi – the main tribe from the area in northwest Tanzania where Mdisho was born.

great native fair" that was celebrating "the big Mahomedan holiday of Id Ul Haj". Roald told his mother he found the experience "damn'd interesting."

> *There were lots of frightful old hand-operated roundabouts . . . made out of coconut trees etc, slip ways down which you slid on coconut matting finishing up amidst a throng of yelling blacks; the most frightful sort of swing boats which were made, by some means or other to revolve round an enormous coconut tree, and at full speed they stood out (that's the wrong word) parallel to the ground. Then there were native bands, with the players getting drunker & drunker on that frightful brew of theirs called Pombe, and beating the drums in the most weird fashion. But the best thing of all were the native dances. We saw the real thing – these blokes with nothing on except a bit of coconut matting & masses of white & red paint, yelling & swaying their hips in a manner which would make Mae West look like a fourth-rate novice. As each dance progresses, the dancers got more & more worked up, & yelled & shouted & leapt about until they just couldn't go on any longer and another tribe came on and took their place. The way they wobbled their tummies would have earned for them the fullest approval of our friend Proffessor [sic] Horniblow.*[80]

This response may have been unsophisticated and naive, but it was much more tolerant and embracing than that of many other whites around him. And as he grew older, Dahl became increasingly critical of his own youthful attitudes. In a speech at Repton in 1975, he described himself in Dar es Salaam as "a ridiculous young pukka-sahib", and in his last year of life, he admitted that he was "mildly ashamed" by his tacit acceptance of certain British imperial attitudes while he was in Tanganyika, regretting his failure at the time to see that the whole colonial situation was just "not right". He blamed it on the values he saw around him and on the fact that he had not yet learned to think independently. "When you're very young, you just swim along with what everyone else is doing," he told an Australian radio interviewer. "You can't buck the tide. It was the last days of the British Empire."[81]

Over forty years earlier, in his short story "Poison", he had been even more forthright, revealing a surprising empathy for the Indians he had once dismissed as "bloody fools". The tale is set in India. There, a white man, Harry Pope, lies in bed, sweating with fear because he believes a krait, a venomous nocturnal snake, has slithered under the sheets and curled up on his stomach. The narrator, discovering his terrified friend, sends for the local Indian medic, Dr Ganderbai, who eventually pumps chloroform under the covers in an attempt to anaesthetize the deadly creature. In an atmosphere of tense drama the sheet is eventually removed to reveal: nothing. The snake has been a figment of Pope's imagination. Humiliated, Pope turns on Ganderbai, shouting at him and calling him a "dirty little Hindu sewer rat" and other "terrible things", as the embarrassed narrator thanks the doctor for his trouble and ushers him apologetically toward his car. As published, it was clear that Dahl (in the person of the narrator) is totally on the side of Ganderbai. However, an earlier incarnation of the tale included a paragraph (later removed) that was even more overt in its condemnation of British colonial snobbery:

> *Dr Ganderbai was worried about his reputation and I must say I couldn't blame him. It was probable that he had never been called in to attend a European. None of them bothered with him much, except perhaps the British upon whom, in those days, his job depended, and who noticed him only in order to be politely offensive – as only the British can be. I imagined that even now little Ganderbai could hear the thick, fruity voice of Dr James Russell in the lounge at the club, saying, "Young Pope? Ah yes, poor fellah. Not a nice way to go. But then if people will call in a native witch doctor, what can they expect?"*[82]

Dahl's own encounters with venomous snakes were few and far between. Once he encountered one outside his home. "These black mambas are real bastards," he told his mother. "Not only are they one of the few snakes that will attack without provocation, but if they bite you, you stand a jolly good chance of kicking the bucket in a few hours unless you receive treatment at once." This one was reportedly "eight feet long and as thick as my arm and as black as soot".[83] Roald killed it with his hockey stick. Another time he saw one through the window of his car driving back from a cricket match in Morogoro.[84] In *Going Solo*, however, he recounts a host of exotic African animal adventures, including a close encounter with another mamba at the home of a customs official in Dar es Salaam and one with a man-eating lion, who steals into the garden of the District Officer's homestead and abducts his cook's wife. None of these incidents is recorded in his letters home. Aside from the snakes, and a glimpse of a "bloody great leopard"[85] in his back garden, his letters chronicle much more mundane experiences, such as climbing up trees to pick coconuts,[86] Dog Samka's attempts to impersonate the Empress of Australia in a swimming costume,[87] and countless visits to the club for a "snifter".[88] His life frustrated as much as it exhilarated and Dahl was clearly often bored with an existence that was often little more than one "long string of sundowners".[89] Trips into the interior were extremely rare and a lot of the time he was forced to admit that there was "bugger all to do except sweat",[90] complaining that, even with his car (a Ford 10 that he bought for £40), "you can't go up country more than a few miles, the roads are too bad".[91] The more exotic tales recounted in *Going Solo* are likely either to be compelling recreations of stories heard from others or just flights of pure fancy, written in the manner of his heroes Rider Haggard and Isak Dinesen.

These African experiences did fire his imagination, however, and give him the feeling that he had something special to write about. One of his earliest short stories, "An Eye for a Tooth", eventually published in 1946 as "An African Story", used a plot device that hinged upon another snake, a black mamba, which had learned to suckle milk from a cow. It was a bizarre and unlikely idea. Concerned that the tale was implausible, his literary agent at the time, Ann Watkins, contacted a certain Dr Bogert, an expert at the Museum of Natural History in New York, to ascertain whether such a thing might indeed be possible. Assured by Dr Bogert that it was not, a potential publisher rejected the story. This irritated Dahl, not only because he had lost a sale but also because he believed the event to have been entirely credible. In his own mind, he now saw himself as an expert on Africa and, in any event, it was quite against his nature to admit that he could ever be in the wrong. Writing to Ann Watkins, he acknowledged that perhaps as far as strict accuracy was concerned, he had indeed "slipped up". "Nevertheless," he continued, "I still maintain that if Dr Bogert or any of his learned friends go to Africa and talk to some of the native tribes there, they will tell them they have seen that sort of thing happen. But let us forget it. Send me back the story and I will keep it to read to my children." [92] To his mother, a week later, he wrote that, though the story had been declined, "morally and metaphorically I count it a sale". [93]

His time in Tanganyika was also formative in other ways. He learned to run a house, adopting the role of housekeeper and "holding court" each morning with Mpishi the cook and Mwino the head boy; paying wages, deciding menus, planning recipes and devising social events. He also indulged himself in the role of present giver and treatmaker, regularly sending back ornate jewellery, unusual furs and curios to his family. Hardly a letter goes by without mention of a gift he is seeking out or having made for one of them.‡‡ His love of classical music deepened, as did his pleasure in listening to his records at a very high volume. He sent long and detailed lists of exactly what he wanted to his family back in Bexley, declaring that listening to his music gave him "a hell of a kick". [94] His taste for his own company intensified as well. A few months before Dahl left Dar es Salaam, he chose to rent a remote house on his own rather than live in the club or share with others. "It'll be rather fun living there alone," he wrote, "plus wireless and gramophone and about three boys for whom incidentally there are special quarters built beyond the house. The rent is bloody high . . . but the rest of the blokes would give me piles to

---

‡‡"I've got a present in the offing for you," he told his mother in May 1939. "It's a large unlined fur made of a special rare & very beautiful kind of rabbit which is found only on the lower slopes of Mt Kilimanjaro. It would make a lovely coat – or otherwise a car rug. The deal is not yet completed" – Dahl, Letter to his mother, 05/07/39 – RDMSC RD 14/3/36.

live with."[95] One evening, listening to Beethoven symphonies, he studied the antics of two transparent lizards hunting on the ceiling of his sitting room. It was "very exciting", he told his mother, watching the gecko "fixing his unfortunate victim – often a small moth – with a very hypnotic eye".[96] He nicknamed the two reptiles "Hitler" and "Mussolini".

Those two names were frequently on his lips during his year in East Africa, for the political background to his time there was one of increasing certainty of war between Britain and Germany. As Roald set sail on the *Mantola*, German troops were occupying the disputed Sudetenland territory on the border with Czechoslovakia. By the time he arrived in Dar es Salaam, the British prime minister Neville Chamberlain had returned from his meeting with Adolf Hitler in Munich and announced to the world that he had won peace for his time. Dahl was one of many who did not believe it. He sided with the outsider Winston Churchill, who argued that Britain had suffered an "unmitigated defeat", that it had succumbed to a bullying German regime, and that soon all of Czechoslovakia would be "engulfed in the Nazi regime".[97] Two years earlier, Benito Mussolini's Fascists had occupied Abyssinia, now Ethiopia, with little international opposition. Now, it seemed to Dahl, Hitler was being allowed to do the same. Listening to the BBC's Empire Broadcasts on his short-wave radio in Shell House, he kept abreast of the growing international crisis. Sometimes he tried to make light of it, wishing that Mussolini would take up a useful hobby like "collecting bird's eggs instead of countries", but adding ruefully that the Italian dictator would "probably say it was cruel".[98]

In March 1939, Churchill's predictions were realized when the German Army occupied the remainder of Czechoslovakia. It left Chamberlain's "peace with honour" exposed as empty rhetoric. From then onwards, Dahl was convinced that war was inevitable. Repeatedly he urged his mother to get out of their house in Bexley, which he rightly believed would be directly under the flight path of any German bombers attacking London. He hoped that his mother and sisters would move to their holiday haunt on the Welsh coast in Tenby. There he believed they would be safe. "If war breaks out you've jolly well got to go to Tenby otherwise you'll be bombed," he wrote. "None of you must stay in London . . . Don't forget, you've got to go if war breaks out."[99] But Sofie Magdalene was stubborn. She did not want to move. And neither did her daughters, who were enjoying their social life in London too much and had no desire to relocate to the remote Welsh seaside. They elected to stay on, believing that Oakwood's large cellar would make an effective air-raid shelter against any attack.

Roald was infuriated by his mother's refusal to bend to his logic and repeatedly tried to make her change her mind. But mother and son were as obstinate as each other. By the end of September, the Germans had invaded Poland, Britain was formally at war, and Roald was desperate. "I say once more," he wrote, certain that the Luftwaffe raids were about to begin, "that you've no right to be sitting in one of the most dangerous places in the world at the moment, quite happy in the mere thought that you've got a cellar – That cellar's no good once the real raids start, which presumably they must before very much longer."[100] Roald's fears, though amply justified, would prove somewhat premature, as his family got a stay of execution from the bombs for another year. The "Phoney War" continued for another eight months, until May 1940, when Germany invaded France, while air raids on London did not begin in earnest until four months after that, in September 1940.

The impending war in Europe may have been thousands of miles away, but it had an immediate manifestation in Tanganyika, where the majority of white settlers were still German nationals. By the summer of 1939, significant tensions had already begun to develop with the British. Never the diplomat, Dahl's unbridled sense of mischief soon got him into trouble. One day at the Gymkhana Club, he and two of his friends drew a picture of a naked Hitler on a blackboard and spent an hour throwing darts at it. He described the game in some detail: "Hitting his balls with a dart counted 10, hitting his tool counted 15, his navel counted 5, his moustache 20 etc." A German member of the club made a formal complaint. "There was a frightful show . . . the little bugger whipped straight off to the German Consulate . . . and the Club Committee were called to an extraordinary General Meeting and all that sort of bullshit . . . There's one hell of a showdown – you see there are so many Germans in this place and everything is rather on the boil," he told his mother. Dahl was formally reprimanded, but he didn't care. The only lesson he had learned was: "Don't throw darts at Hitler's balls in public. They're private parts."[101]

By the late summer of 1939, the British authorities were preparing internment camps across Tanganyika for all German nationals should war be declared. On September 1, Hitler's invasion of Poland, to whom Britain was pledged as an ally, appeared to make that declaration inevitable. Roald had enlisted as a Special Constable. He was given a platoon of native soldiers to command and charged with guarding a stretch of road running south from Dar es Salaam to the border with Portuguese East Africa, now Mozambique. His job was to arrest any escaping German nationals and escort them to one of these internment camps. "If war breaks out it'll be our job to round up all the Germans," he had written to his mother on August 27, adding that he hoped they "would allow themselves to be rounded up quietly".[102] According to the report which Sir Mark Young, the Governor of Tanganyika, sent back to Whitehall almost two weeks after war was eventually declared, that is exactly what happened. Sir Mark told Malcolm MacDonald, the secretary of state for the colonies, that, despite his anxieties, the local Nazis under their leader Herr Troost had been unexpectedly cooperative, urging German nationals to submit to arrest and bear their fates with dignity and honour. "No resistance was offered by any enemy national and for the most part they submitted cheerfully and good-humouredly," Sir Mark noted. "In no single case was opposition reported."[103]

On September 2, Dahl and his six armed native Askaris from the King's African Rifles spent the night sleeping rough in the bush by the road from Dar es Salaam to Portuguese East Africa. Shortly after one o'clock the following afternoon, the field telephone rang and Dahl heard a "grim voice" announcing: "War has been declared – arrest all Germans attempting to leave or enter the town." His own account of the ensuing events, in a letter written a few days later, concurred with the Governor's report that the Germans offered no resistance, though he gave few specific details in case the "ruddy censor" held up the letter.[104] His early short story "The Sword" painted a similar picture: "The Germans started coming . . . as fast as they could. Some were in trucks and some were in private cars, Fords and Chevrolets mostly, and we rounded them up bit by bit without much difficulty. They saw our machine-gun and very quickly gave themselves up." [105] A later story, "Lucky Break" (1977), was more expansive, but also followed a similar pattern. There, Dahl described how he marched about two hundred German civilians back to Dar es Salaam, "where they were put into a huge camp surrounded by barbed wire . . . There was no battle. The Germans, who after all, were only civilian townspeople, saw our machine-guns and our rifles and quickly gave themselves up." [106] Less than ten years later, in *Going Solo*, Dahl was to embellish the story grandly. Now an angry bald German, whose movements are "full of menace", threatens him by the roadside. In a style reminiscent of Ian Fleming, he describes how the man points a Luger pistol to his chest and how one of his own Askari guards shoots the German through the face: "It was a horrible sight. His head seemed to splash open and little soft bits of grey stuff flew out in all directions. There was no blood, just the grey stuff and fragments of bone. One lump of the grey stuff landed on my cheek. More of it went all over my khaki shirt. The Luger dropped onto the road and the bald man fell dead beside it." [107]

This is the first of two unlikely deaths that conclude the African adventures in *Going Solo*. The second comes later that night when Dahl discovers that his good-natured servant Mdisho, excited by the declaration of war, has run off into the bush and murdered a rich local German landowner with an eighteenth-century ceremonial Arab sword that Dahl kept hanging on his wall. Running several miles through the night, Mdisho arrived at the homestead of this "unpleasant bachelor", who was rumoured to beat his employees with a whip made from rhinoceros hide, and sliced his head off as he stood in his back garden throwing pieces of paper onto a fire. Dahl recounts with relish Mdisho's proud but grisly description of his deed. "Bwana, it is a beautiful sword. With one blow it cut through his neck so deeply that his whole head fell forward and dangled down onto his chest, and as he started to topple over I gave the neck one more quick chop and the head came right away from the body and fell to the ground like a coconut and the most enormous fountains of blood came spurting out of his neck." Dahl then explains to the uncomprehending young man that he has committed a crime and must keep quiet about it or risk arrest. Mdisho is dumbfounded, but thrilled when Dahl presents him with the sword as a gift for his bravery. He concludes that the two men are now "exactly equal",[108] as both have been involved in killing a German.

This story was in essence a reworking of "The Sword", where Mdisho is replaced by an older boy called Salimu. That was presented as fiction. In *Going Solo*, it is presented as fact. In each case, however, the symbolism is clear. A rite of passage has been enacted. By killing a man, as young Masai warriors traditionally kill a lion, the two men have left their youth behind and become adults. They have grown up. It was a powerful fable and one that clearly resonated with Dahl himself. Whether it was presented as fact or fiction was of little interest to him. In much the same way as he had done at Repton, he simply constructed for himself a world that evolved naturally from his impulse to tell a story. As time went by, that imaginary world, revisited, relished and refined in storytelling, gradually became more real and more alive than the reality it had replaced. Sitting in his writing hut in the English countryside in the early 1980s, his interest was not with facts, but rather with visceral memories and narrative possibilities.

Unlike the early drafts of *Boy*, those of *Going Solo* are not tortured with changes and emendations. They flow with ease and speed. Occasionally one even senses Dahl dropping his entertainer's mask and pausing for a moment almost to moralize. The tale of Mdisho and the sword, for example, serves as a poignant curtain-raiser to the violence and absurdity of the coming war. There normal values will be turned on their heads and a single comprehensible killing, like Mdisho's of the brutal German, will be replaced by something much more faceless and inhuman. The little parable seems to be telling us something important – about life and death, about masters and servants, about whites and blacks, about innocence and experience, about youth and adulthood. Perhaps it also tells us something about the author himself. For Mdisho's viewpoint, even if fictional, was one to which Dahl himself was powerfully drawn. He too saw himself trapped by English values and manners to which he did not entirely relate and which he did not completely understand. The loner listening to Beethoven and watching geckos, the scatological humorist, the fantastical chronicler of Dog Samka's amorous adventures – all of these set him apart and, despite his efforts to fit in, compounded his reputation as the club's subversive misfit. Mdisho's fictional predicament was thus rather like his own. "I looked at him and smiled. I refused to blame him for what he had done. He was a wild Mwanumwezi tribesman who had been moulded by us Europeans into the shape of a domestic servant, and now he had broken the mould." [109]

Within days of the outbreak of war, Dar es Salaam began to fill up with soldiers. Dahl instinctively disliked the army, and described the new arrivals with thinly disguised contempt: "Fellows in uniform and cockade hats all over the place and a frightful lot of snobbishness. All bullshit." Joining this invasion of khaki did not appeal to him at all. Its regulations and pomposities reminded him only of school. Pointedly, he told his mother he had invented an "oxometer" designed to measure "the amount of bullshit talked and written by the military".[110] He had another plan. Inspired by his friend the pilot Alec Noon, who flew small commercial aeroplanes out of Dar es Salaam, Dahl had decided how he would finally see the Africa of which he had long dreamed, but which his job in Shell had largely denied him. He would join the Royal Air Force and become a pilot.

It was a fateful decision, perhaps the most important he ever made. That October, Noon had taken him on a patrol flight along the Tanganyikan coast to Mafia Island. Dahl was thrilled, writing home lyrically of the views and the "long, long line of sandy beach with palm trees on it and an endless white surf breaking".[111] A few days later he went up to Nairobi for his RAF medical, which he passed "with flying colours" despite the disadvantage of being just over six foot five inches tall. Reassuring his mother not to be alarmed by "this flying business", he told her it was all just "very good fun",[112] that he would get £1,000 worth of flying lessons for free, and that it would be "a bloody sight better than joining the army out here and marching about in the heat from one place to another doing nothing special".[113]

Dahl returned to Dar es Salaam, packed most of his clothes into mothproof trunks, paid his bills, resigned from his club, and wrote to his mother asking her not to send him a luxury Christmas hamper "because it will be difficult to eat those things . . . in an airmen's mess. I can imagine a pot of pâté de foie gras going in one meal, and someone who's never had it before saying they prefer bloater paste."[114] Two weeks later, in a large three-seater Chevrolet, he drove 900 miles north to Nairobi. The journey gave him time to contemplate the glories of the African landscape and ponder what the future had in store for him and his family. He talked to giraffes, crossed fast-running rivers on wooden rafts, watched Masai warriors demonstrating their skill with bows and arrows, and reflected philosophically on the gentle beauty of a family of elephants. "They are better off than me," he mused, "and a good deal wiser. I myself am at this moment on my way to kill Germans or be killed by them, but those elephants have no thought of murder in their mind."[115]

In Nairobi, Dahl was one of sixteen pilots enrolled in the Initial Training School. Only three would survive the next two years. Yet thoughts of death were far from his mind as he squeezed into his tiny two-seater Tiger Moth and someone chased the grazing zebra off the airfield. Nonetheless, he faced one significant problem. At six foot five, perched on top of his parachute, Dahl's head stuck so far over the top of the windshield that once the plane was airborne, its powerful slipstream made it almost impossible for him to breathe. Every few seconds he had to duck down behind the shield just in order to take a breath. Characteristically, he soon devised a solution: a thin cotton cloth tied over his nose and mouth allowed him to avoid being choked while flying. His love affair with this new element was immediate and intense. "I've never enjoyed myself so much,"[116] he wrote his mother. After seven hours and forty minutes, he went solo and was soon flying alone over the wide African savanna, soaring high through the Great Rift Valley and around Mount Kenya, then swooping down to only 60 or 70 feet above the ground, causing giraffes to look up in amazement and herds of wildebeest to stampede. He felt at one with his aeroplane and took an intense delight in the experience of being alone in the vast open spaces of the sky, from where he could view the landscapes about which he had fantasized for so long, from the vantage point of a god. He learned to navigate, to loop the loop, and make forced landings with his engine cut.

Then, after eight weeks, and with about fifty hours' flying time in their logbooks, the young pilots were all put on a train to Kampala in Uganda, where "bursting with energy and exuberance and perhaps a touch of self-importance as well, because now we were intrepid flying men and devils of the sky",[117] they went, via Cairo, to complete their flying training in Iraq – at a vast base called Habbaniya. After six months there in the fierce desert heat, "the worst climate in the world," where they were to live "only for the day we will be leaving",[118] in September 1940 Dahl found himself heading for action in the Western Desert of North Africa, ferrying an out-of-date and unfamiliar biplane toward a camouflaged airstrip just behind the Allied front line.

CHAPTER SIX

A Monumental Bash on the Head

ON SEPTEMBER 19, 1940, a tiny aircraft landed at a remote military airfield in northern Egypt. It was just after 5 p.m. and the sun was already falling low in the Western sky, causing the small machine to cast distorted shadows on the bright blue sea as it came in on its final approach. There was a light wind from the northwest. Visibility was good. The Gloster Gladiator, barely 27 feet long, touched down on the primitive airstrip and taxied rapidly to a standstill. The pilot switched off the single 830hp Bristol Mercury radial engine and all was silent. A couple of engineers approached the aircraft. As they did so, the canopy tilted backwards and a tall, gangly figure emerged from the tiny cockpit. He was wearing a light cotton flying suit. A route map was strapped to his knee. Pilot Officer Roald Dahl was just twenty-four years old and he was understandably nervous, for it was his first venture into a field of war. He had been in the air for much of the afternoon, ferrying the new Gladiator from an airstrip on the Suez Canal to join 80 Squadron at a secret location somewhere in the North African desert. At Amiriya, near Alexandria, where he had stopped to refuel an hour earlier, he had landed in a sandstorm. Now he was tired. He had yet to discover his final destination, which was still confidential. In a few moments' time, the airstrip's commanding officer would tell him its coordinates and he could depart. He asked directions to the CO's tent, hoping the end of his journey would not be far away.

The tiny coastal airstrip at Fouka was no more than a huddle of tents and parked aircraft – around it sand and water stretched as far as the eye could see. Less than 100 miles west was the front line. The invading Italian Army, which had crossed over from Libya the week before, was now encamped further down the coast at Sidi Barrani. Fouka was the last place of safety. Beyond it lay the real war – a war for which Dahl knew he was largely unprepared. He was flying a plane with which he was relatively unfamiliar and had received no air-to-air combat practice during his six months of advanced training. The sand blew against the tents, making the canvas rustle and sometimes flap violently. Inside one of them, the commanding officer made a phone call. He asked the pilot for his map. "Eighty Squadron are now there," the officer declared, pointing to a spot called Sidi Heneish in the middle of the Libyan Plateau 30 miles south of Mersah Matruh, another small coastal town on the edge of the Mediterranean. "Will it be easy to see?" Dahl asked. He knew the airstrip was camouflaged and it was already beginning to get dark. "You can't miss it," was the reply.

At 6.15 p.m. the aeroplane took off from the landing strip at Fouka and headed southwest. The windsock by the runway stood out straight like a signpost. Dahl estimated the journey would take fifty minutes at most. It would not be properly dark until seven-thirty, so he should just have time to get to there before night fell. He had calculated his bearings carefully, but navigating across desert was always dangerous. He flew low, at about 800 feet, but now he was travelling away from the coast. Now, the reassuring white foamy guideline, running between blue sea and yellow sand, was no longer there to keep him on track. The terrain below him was quite different. It offered no visual landmarks to help him on his way, and dusk was the most difficult time to fly. With no cloud cover, the winds could suddenly change direction, sometimes even by 180 degrees, as the temperatures over the sand plummeted. He might easily be thrown off course. An error of 1 degree would leave him a mile away from his destination; an error of more than 5 or 10 would be disastrous. He began to wonder if he should not have stayed overnight at Fouka and joined his squadron early the following morning instead.

As the minutes passed, the ground beneath him became a mottled canvas of browns, yellows and reds, shifting and darkening as the sun moved toward the horizon. The desert seemed to stretch away forever, featureless and hostile. He felt lonely, but protected, within the tight womb of the cockpit. Sometimes he wondered if he was the only living thing left in the world. The Gladiator's engine whirred away in front of him, but its deep song no longer delighted his ear. Fifty minutes was up. And now, as the sun began to set, the young man began to sweat. There was no sign of an airstrip anywhere – just an endless vista of boulders, ruts and dried-out gullies. Had he been given the wrong coordinates? Had he miscalculated his bearings? Or become a victim of a sudden change in wind direction? He circled the area – scouring the ground below for aircraft, tents, any signs of human habitation. He flew around to the north, south, east and west, but all he could see was sand, rock and camel-thorn.

The last rays of the setting sun illuminated the desert with a fierce red glow. Soon it would be really dark. His fuel was low. Going back to Fouka was not an option. He had only one possibility left – a forced landing. That was what he had been trained to do in these circumstances. He would land in the desert and spend the night there. Tomorrow morning a search party would be sent to find him. It was not the way he had planned to arrive at his squadron for his first day in action, but now there was no alternative. Desperately, he looked for somewhere to land the tiny craft. He skimmed low over the bumpy ground but could find nothing suitable. The sun disappeared behind the horizon and he knew his time had run out. He must land the plane immediately. He took a chance, throttling back and touching down at about 80 miles an hour, praying the wheels would not strike a rock. But luck was not on his side. The undercarriage hit a boulder and collapsed instantly into a pile of twisted metal and rubber, burying the nose of the plane into the ground. He was thrown violently forward against the front of the canopy. His nose was driven back into his face, his skull was fractured, and he was knocked unconscious.*

---

*I have pieced these events together as accurately as I can from Roald Dahl's own pilot's logbook, RAF records, interviews with other pilots, and Dahl's many written descriptions of the events of that day, principally in "Shot Down Over Libya" (1942), "Missing: Believed Killed" (1944), "A Piece of Cake" (1942–46),

It was a humiliating start to a flying career that had promised great things. Dahl had been one of the top trainees on his training course in Iraq, finding "great joy"[1] in all the flying exercises undertaken there, despite the fact that he thought the station at Habbaniya – "Have a Banana", as it was known in RAF slang – tedious and enervating.[2] Later he recalled it as "an abominable, unhealthy, desolate place . . . a vast assemblage of hangars and Nissen huts and brick bungalows set slap in the middle of a boiling desert on the banks of the muddy Euphrates river miles from anywhere".[3] Nevertheless, at least initially, he was awestruck by the sheer size of this city in the sand, constructed 60 miles away from Baghdad and boasting as many as 10,000 inhabitants. Cataloguing its many buildings, which included churches, a cinema, a dental hospital and a mineral water factory, Dahl added ruefully to his mother that "women do not come this way, so amongst numerous other things . . . they will have to be forgotten. But that will not be difficult because we are working and flying so hard."[4] The trainees flew almost every day, mostly in the mornings. There were navigational, technical and meteorological classes in the afternoons. His instructors had praised Dahl's flying skills as "well above average", judging his aerobatic skills "exceptional".[5] His written tests too had been excellent and he was an assiduous student – although he did occasionally find time to venture out into the surrounding territory. Once he went to see the ruins of Babylon and several times he went to bandit-infested Baghdad, shopping in the street markets and playing poker with the infamously knife-wielding, gun-toting natives. They were, he reported, "a treacherous crowd".[6]

Dahl's response to the locals had initially been one of interest and wonder. The Bedouin tribesmen he encountered in Palestine on the way to Habbaniya had fascinated him with their "huge sheepskin coats and furry hats".[7] But in Iraq it was a different matter. There the first responses to the RAF airmen were almost invariably hostile. Iraqis

---

"Lucky Break" (1977), and "Going Solo" (1986). Eighty Squadron's own accident report is brief, noting drily that "Pilot Officer Dahl was ferrying an aircraft from No. 102 Maintenance Unit to this unit, but unfortunately not being used to flying aircraft over the desert he made a forced landing two miles west of Mersah Matruh. He made an unsuccessful forced landing and the aircraft burst into flames. The pilot was badly burned and he was conveyed to an Army Field Ambulance station" – PRO Air 27, 669.

hurled stones at the planes and took potshots at the pilots with their rifles. Dahl's trips into the capital, to haggle with the coppersmiths and the silversmiths, excited him, and he was filled with admiration for the skills of the jewellers and craftsmen, but he was also horrified by the squalor he found there and revolted by the "horde of horrible little boys" who always followed him around. He described Baghdad as "a bloody awful town. Easily the dirtiest I've been to yet. The whole place is literally falling down. On either side of most of the streets you have mud brick ruins, in which people live, with the most loathsome smells issuing from their doorways. The pavements are simply packed with every conceivable kind of person – Arabs, Syrians, Jews, Negroes, Indians and the majority who are just nothing at all, with faces the colour of milk chocolate, and long flowing, but very dirty robes." After driving back through bandit country, and being chased by pariah dogs, cackling Bedouin hags, and "blokes with guns and knives who don't think twice about cutting your balls out for the sake of getting your brass fly buttons",[8] he was probably more relieved than he admitted to get back to the air-conditioned tedium of RAF Habbaniya.

Named after the Arabic word for the oleanders that had been planted along its avenues, in a futile attempt to soften the ferocity of the desert sun, Habbaniya may have been dull, but its conveniences made the harsh desert conditions tolerable. While Dahl was there, however, it was also to prove unexpectedly vulnerable to the elements. The camp had been constructed on a location that was prone to flooding, and that spring, when a swollen Euphrates threatened to burst its banks, thousands of inhabitants were forced to abandon their duties for six weeks, and build themselves a tented city on higher ground nearby. It was a miserable task, made worse by heat, scorpions, flies, sand vipers, and incessant 40mph sandstorms. Eventually the danger passed, everyone returned to the relative luxury of their messes and Nissen huts, and flying training resumed once more. The sandstorms ground down everyone's spirits. But they also brought out the Stoic in Dahl. "It's an excellent thing," he wrote his mother, "to experience discomforts which are so intense that you can be tolerably certain that you will never have to experience ones which are worse." He concluded that when, if ever, his flying training resumed, he would probably be "a sort of fossilised sand mound".[9]

In high summer, as temperatures soared to over 50 degrees Celsius in the shade, the pilots were only able to train between 4 a.m. and 9 a.m. The rest of the day was spent skulking indoors, avoiding the heat. Then the boredom was acute and Dahl could not wait to get away. "All we do is to fly in the early mornings, sleep and sweat in the afternoons, and listen to the news on the wireless for the rest of the time," he told his mother. "And anything more dismal than listening to the wireless these days it would be hard to find."[10] He likened the heat to that of a Turkish bath, joking that if he got through the war, he would be "well-qualified to become an attendant in one".[11] He was now flying Hawker Harts and Audaxes, light bombers armed with machine guns, in which he had his first lessons in how to shoot down other planes. He found these experiences "exhilarating".[12] By mid-August 1940, with more than 150 hours in his logbook, he had been made a pilot officer, passing out, he told his mother, with "Special Distinction" and being assessed as having "exceptional" flying ability.[13]

In his final exams, Dahl passed out third out of forty. The only two men to pass with higher marks had already flown as civilian pilots before the war.[14] Now, proudly wearing his RAF flying badge, he returned to Egypt, to the RAF station in Ismailia, where he was posted to 80 Squadron in the Western Desert. But he never arrived there. Instead, on the eve of his first day as a combat pilot, he destroyed his own plane, crashing it in the desert, before he had fired a shot in anger.

The smell of petrol stirred his consciousness. He tried to open his eyes, but he could see nothing. Moments later both the Gladiator's fuel tanks exploded and the craft itself caught fire. Blinded and numb, Dahl contemplated what seemed to be a certain death. "All I wanted was to go gently off to sleep and to hell with the flames,"[15] he wrote later. But something forced him to act, to extricate his damaged body from its parachute straps, push open the cockpit canopy, and drop out of it onto the sand beneath. His overalls were burning too, but he put out the fire by rolling on the ground. It was not bravery, Dahl later noted, simply a "tendency to remain conscious"[16] that saved him from being burned to death. "All I wanted was to get away from the tremendous heat and rest in peace. The world about me was divided sharply down the middle into two halves. Both these halves were pitch black, but one was scorching hot and the other was not."[17] In terrible pain, Dahl crawled slowly away from the burning wreckage. But he was not yet out of danger.

My face hurt most. I slowly put a hand up to feel it. It was very sticky. My nose didn't seem to be there. I tried to feel my teeth to see if they were still there, but it seemed as though one or two were missing. And then the machine guns started off. I knew right away what it was. There were about fifty rounds of ammunition left in each of my eight guns and, without thinking, I had crawled away from the fire out in front of the machine, and they were going off in the heat. I could hear them hitting the sand and stones all round, but I didn't feel like getting up and moving right then, so I dozed off.[18]

All the bullets missed him. Later that night, three infantrymen from the Suffolk Regiment, who had seen the plane come down some two miles west of their base in Mersah Matruh, went out to inspect the wreckage and found the injured pilot, barely conscious, but still alive. His flying overalls were so burnt and his face so disfigured that he was almost unrecognizable as an RAF officer. The soldiers carried him back to the underground Army Field Ambulance Station in Mersah, where one of the army doctors initially mistook him for an enemy Italian.[19] Eventually, he was patched up, sedated, and sent by train to the Anglo-Swiss Hospital in Alexandria, where he was treated for burns, severe concussion and spinal trauma. Initially, his face was so swollen that he could not open his eyes and it was impossible to assess whether the accident had blinded him. The doctors did not know whether he would ever see again.

For Dahl, it was a time of existential crisis. For almost a month he inhabited a hazy world of total darkness, uncertain of time or surroundings.† Concussed, blind and isolated from family and friends, he was disoriented and helpless. His imagination ran wild. It was a situation he recreated in an early short story, "Beware of the Dog":

> *The whole world was white and there was nothing in it. It was so white that sometimes it looked black, and after a time it was either white or black, but mostly it was white. He watched it as it turned from white to black, then back to white again, and the white stayed a long time, but the black lasted only a few seconds. He got into the habit of going to sleep during the white periods, of waking up just in time to see the world when it was black. The black was very quick. Sometimes it was only a flash, a flash of black lightning. The white was slow, and in the slowness of it, he always dozed off.* [20]

Dahl later wrote that the possibility of losing his sight did not frighten or depress him and that "blindness, not to mention life itself, was no longer too important . . . the only way to conduct oneself in a situation where bombs rained down and bullets whizzed past was to accept all the dangers and all the consequences as calmly as possible. Fretting and sweating about it all was not going to help." [21] As he lay in his bed, he also learned that the family house in Bexley had been hit by German bombers (his mother and sisters had survived, but had been forced to evacuate the property) and that the tent in Ismailia, where his air force kit, including camera and photographs, was being kept, had also been destroyed in an air raid. It was a low point, but it confirmed in him the sense that – despite the pleasure that the good things in life could bring – all material possessions were ultimately transitory. He and his family had survived. That was what mattered.

Gradually, his condition began to improve. The cranial swelling subsided and he was able to see again. Nevertheless, he was still sleeping more than sixteen hours a day and would remain immobilized for more

---

†Although he told his mother he was only blind for a week, he later told his editor at Farrar, Straus, Stephen Roxburgh, that he had "said that so as not to alarm her. It was much, much longer . . ." – Letter to Stephen Roxburgh, undated, FSG.

than another month. His features were reconstructed by a Harley Street plastic surgeon, now working for the army, who Dahl later claimed had modelled his new nose on the movie star Rudolph Valentino's.[22] But his first letter back home to his mother, written almost two months after the accident, was probably closer to the truth, as he described how the ear, nose and throat surgeon "pulled my nose out of the back of my head and shaped it". He added that his new nose looked "just as before except that it's a little bent about".[23] His injuries were sufficiently severe that his doctors suggested Dahl be invalided back to England on the next convoy, but he resisted their advice, because he had been told that he might yet fly again, and if that were possible, he wanted to remain close to his squadron. It cannot have been an easy decision. He was in great pain. He had not seen his family for more than two years. And, as he had yet to meet any of his fellow pilots from 80 Squadron, which had by that time moved from North Africa to Greece, where it was engaged in a successful counterattack against the invading Italians, he had no real comrades to rejoin. But Dahl was brave, stubborn and eager for action. Moreover, although the RAF had concluded that he was "not to blame" for destroying the Gladiator and that pilot inexperience had caused his accident,[24] he wanted to prove his fighting skills, and put behind him what had been an ignominious beginning to his career as a fighter pilot.

Dahl later claimed that an RAF inquiry had revealed that the commanding officer at Fouka had given him the wrong coordinates and that 80 Squadron's desert airstrip was actually 50 miles further south of the place where he had crashed his plane.[25] Now we will only ever have his word for it, as the official records of that inquiry were destroyed in the 1960s.[26] Dahl also implied that the crash was partly due to systemic planning failures within the RAF itself, maintaining that he was quite unused to flying Gloster Gladiators and that he only saw one for the first time less than twenty-four hours before he was due to ferry it from Ismailia into the desert. He added that when he had asked for some training, a "supercilious" officer pointed out to him that, as there was only one cockpit, he would have to teach himself. "This was surely not the right way of doing things," he concluded.[27] The aviation writer and historian Derek O'Connor has subsequently observed that what Dahl failed to mention in that context was that he had spent the preceding two weeks at Ismailia learning how to fly an almost identical aircraft: the Gloster Gauntlet. According to O'Connor, the Gladiator was essentially "an improved version of the Gauntlet with an uprated Bristol Mercury engine and an enclosed cockpit".[28] Dahl's need to rewrite history here speaks of more than a great storyteller embellishing the truth to entertain his reader. It suggests instead the intensity of his need to tell the story of the crash in a way that exonerated him of any slur of incompetence. The RAF records were not enough. He also needed a version of events that absolved him from responsibility and pointed the finger of blame elsewhere. Inevitably, it contributed to his later repeated fiction that instead of wrecking his plane, he was "shot down" in combat over the desert.

These was one final piece of mythmaking. On almost every occasion that he retold the events of that evening in the last forty years of his life, Dahl recounted them as if he was entirely on his own. But there was another pilot involved. This man flew with him from Fouka in a different Gladiator, safely put his machine down on the sand close by the wreckage of Dahl's plane, and comforted the burned and bleeding Roald through the long cold desert night. And in Dahl's earliest versions of these events, "Shot Down Over Libya" and "A Piece of Cake", both of which were written in wartime, he too is present in the narrative. In fiction, this man was called "Shorty" or "Peter". In reality, he was Douglas McDonald. McDonald, who had grown up in Kenya and learned to fly before the war at the Aero Club of East Africa, saw his friend "Lofty" that night in extremis – demoralized, tortured by pain and profoundly physically vulnerable. So vulnerable indeed that until, fifty years later, when he had to face the final days of his own terminal illness, he would always recall it as the worst moment of his life.[29] Dahl had always liked to appear strong. His position, since childhood, as the dominant male in his family household inclined him to support others, to be the paterfamilias. In this narrative, there was little place for weakness and incapacity. Consequently, "Shorty" or "Peter" soon disappeared from his retelling of the events of the crash. Yet in a remarkable letter written to Douglas McDonald's widow, Barbara, in 1953 – not long after her husband's death in a plane crash in the foothills of Mt Kilimanjaro – Roald offered a tiny glimpse of just how exposed he felt that evening and how much he had needed the simple consolation of human warmth and company:

> *I expect he's told you a little of what happened that evening in the desert when we both came down, and I crashed. But I doubt he explained how really marvellous he was to me, and looked after me and tried to comfort me, and stayed with me out there during a very cold night, and kept me warm. Well, he did. And I shall always remember it most vividly, even some of the things he said (because I was quite conscious) and most of all how, when he ran over and found me not dead, he did a sort of dance of joy in the sand and it was all very wonderful, because after all we were not very far away from the Italians and he had a great many other things to think about.*[30]

The letter is significant not just because it makes plain exactly what happened that night, but also because it also gives us a rare insight into Roald's sense of vulnerability. This was not a side of his personality that he normally disclosed to the world, preferring to present in its place the image of the stalwart problem solver or the ebullient humorist. These of course were real enough qualities as well, but sometimes they served also to mask feelings of inadequacy or weakness. The pattern had started in his youth. For his mother's sake, he had cultivated a stiff upper lip and taken pains to conceal his own suffering. This attitude would continue throughout his life. His earliest short stories about flying do reveal occasional cracks in the facade, and nowhere is this more pronounced than in his earlier versions of the immediate aftermath of the crash, where in the "bitter cold" of the desert, "Peter lay down close alongside so we could both keep a little warmer . . . I do not know how long we stayed there . . . Later I remember hot thick soup and one spoonful making me sick. And all the time the pleasant feeling that Peter was around, being wonderful, doing wonderful things and never going away."[31]

Before he left the Anglo-Swiss Hospital, Roald spent all of the money that had accumulated in his bank account buying a gold watch for each of the three nursing sisters who had looked after him. It was an act of characteristic generosity. Giving presents had been and would always be an essential part of his psychological makeup. Within the family, this could sometimes be interpreted as reinforcing his position as the dominant successful male, but with others the impulse was usually entirely altruistic. It was an attitude that would soon be echoed in the behaviour of others toward him – most strikingly, a wealthy English couple, Major Teddy Peel and his wife Dorothy. Following a new set of medical examinations, Dahl was sent back to Alexandria to convalesce at their home. Like many of the wealthier British inhabitants of Alexandria, the Peels made a point of visiting injured officers in hospital, and Dorothy had taken a particular liking to the charming, fragile giant, persuading him to abandon his plans to recuperate in the Kenyan Highlands and insisting that he stay as a guest in their spacious villa on the rue des Ptolemées. There, Roald told his mother that he spent most of his time "doing practically nothing at all with the greatest possible comfort". Dahl, of course, had been raised without financial worries. He was used to servants and now had a small private income from his father's trust. Nevertheless, he was amazed by the lavish expatriate Alexandrian lifestyle, noting – perhaps a little critically – that even in wartime, everyone there seemed to have "pots of money".[32]

His hosts were admiringly described as "probably the nicest and richest people" in town, with five cars, a large motor yacht, and a twin-engined aeroplane of their own.[33] In their house he slept on silk and linen sheets, often for twelve hours at a stretch, listened to Beethoven, Brahms and Elgar on the gramophone, made occasional conversation, and tried to regain some of the 30 pounds he had lost since the accident. Once or twice he even ventured out to play a few holes of golf. But his recovery was slow. He tired easily, his mind often felt sluggish, and he suffered from severe and prolonged headaches. He complained that he could not even concentrate sufficiently to play a hand of bridge and was prone to blackouts – particularly when he went out of the house.

After a month with the Peels, Dahl's headaches had become less frequent, and in February 1941, he was sent to RAF Heliopolis, near Cairo, where he was put on "light duties", looking after air force pay packets and ferrying messages across town in a chauffeur-driven car. One day, on a trip into Cairo, he accidentally ran into Lesley Pares, a friend of Alfhild's, who was working for the Air Ministry. Lesley was immediately struck by Roald's good looks and rakish charm. In our conversations, she recalled him nonchalantly performing Beethoven's three-minute baga-telle, *Für Elise*, in the bar of the Metropolitan Hotel in Cairo as if he was an accomplished pianist, then later confessing to her privately that it was the only thing he could play. She found him unpredictable, attractive and compelling. But she also found him indiscreet, which unsettled her, as did the fact that he could be argumentative and dogmatic. She tried to avoid encounters between him and another friend of hers who was a conscientious objector, because Roald was "rather fierce" on the subject of pacifism.[34]

For his part, Roald took an immediate liking to Lesley, describing her to his mother as "much nicer than the average Judy one meets here – most of them are bloody awful".[35] Her forthrightness, lack of pretension and disregard for unnecessary politesse reminded him of his family. "I like Lesley because she's the first woman I've met since I left home to whom I can swear or say what I bloody well like without her turning a hair," he wrote, adding humorously that she had probably been "well-trained" by his sister Alfhild.[36] She became a regular companion. They went on pic-nics into the desert together, where they talked about his family, argued about politics (she remembered him being quite socialist), and discussed poetry.

Wartime Egypt had a thriving British expatriate social scene, and a fertile literary subculture that included the writers Elizabeth David and Lawrence Durrell, who both moved there in 1941, after the Nazis in-vaded Greece. Lesley Pares would get to know them both and come to be extremely close to Elizabeth David. But Dahl was concentrating on his recovery and literary soirées held little interest for him. He preferred listening to his gramophone, animated only by occasional forays into the routine colonial existence of golf clubs, cocktails, dinner parties, and games of bridge. His contribution to Egyptian artistic life was limited to exhibiting two of the Iraqi photographs that had survived the destruction of his kit at an exhibition in Cairo, organized by a friend of his mother's from London, Dr Omar Khairat. One of them, an aerial photograph of the mighty 2,000-year-old Arch of Ctesiphon, won him a silver medal. He had taken it from the cockpit of his plane while flying from Habbaniya. However, his head injuries remained slow to heal and a return to the air was beginning to seem increasingly unlikely. Blinding headaches could still force him to abandon the simplest of tasks and retire to his room, and he was dogged by a sense of lethargy and lightheadedness. So he waited, hoping that his health would improve and that he would be able, at last, to fly in action. For, despite the doctors' pessimistic prognosis about his head injuries, his "one obsession was to get back to operational flying".[37]

"A monumental bash on the head" was how Dahl once described his accident in the Western Desert, claiming that it directly led to his becoming a writer.[38] This was not just because his first published piece of writing was a semifictionalized account of the crash, but also because he suspected that the brain injuries which he received there had materially altered his personality and inclined him to creative writing. His daughter Ophelia recalled her father's fascination with tales of people who had experienced dramatic psychological and physiological changes – such as losing or recovering sight – after suffering a blow to the head. He also told her that he was convinced something of this sort had happened to him, as it explained why a budding corporate businessman, without any particular artistic ambition, was transformed into someone with a burning need to write and tell stories.[39] This hypothesis was doubtless attractive too because it pushed potentially more complex psychological issues about the sources of his desire to write into the background.

Nowadays doctors might well have diagnosed Dahl as suffering from what is called postconcussive syndrome.[40] The initial symptoms of this condition are normally forgetfulness, irritability, an inability to concentrate and severe headaches. Dahl suffered from all of these. In some patients the symptoms disappear, but leave behind longer-lasting behavioural changes, which are usually associated with mood swings and an increased lack of inhibition. In some cases, too, it can also result in a fundamental alteration of the perception of the self. With Dahl, these alterations were marginal, but they were nonetheless significant. His sense of embarrassment – already minimal – was further diminished, his sense of fantasy heightened, while his desire to shock became even more pronounced. He emerged from his crisis more confident, more determined to make a mark. His first brush with death doubtless also played a significant part in this change in his own perception of himself, making him more aware of his vulnerability, more reflective, yet also intensifying the sense of himself as a survivor, as a figure of destiny.

This heightened sense of self was closely linked to the very act of flying. From its ecstatic beginnings, swooping over the Kenyan bush, the sense of being alone and free in an unfamiliar element stimulated Roald's sense of the mystical. It reinforced his sense of isolation. The sky became an alternative world: a place of tranquillity and gentle beauty, a refuge either from the horrors of war or the cruelties of human behaviour that could be magical, transformative, even redemptive. Most of his early adult stories are profoundly connected to this spiritual dimension of flying, and it is also a feature of many of Dahl's most well loved children's books. In the first of these, *James and the Giant Peach*, the child protagonist, James, who has escaped from his cruel aunts to find shelter inside an enormous peach, stands at night on the surface of the giant fruit, accompanied by a group of equally outsize bugs. They are all flying high above the Atlantic Ocean because the peach has been borne aloft by a flock of seagulls. Contemplating the heavens above him, James is filled with an overpowering sense of mystery and wonder. "Clouds like mountains towered over their heads on all sides, mysterious, menacing, overwhelming . . . ," Dahl writes. "The peach was a soft, stealthy traveller, making no noise at all as it floated along. And several times during that long silent night ride high up over the middle of the ocean in moonlight, James and his friends saw things that no-one had seen before."[41] It is a sense of epiphany similar to that which affects Charlie Bucket, the hero of Dahl's next children's book, *Charlie and the Chocolate Factory*, when, flying high over the factory inside a great glass elevator, Willy Wonka hands over his world to the young boy.

The glory of flight also suffuses Dahl's last book, *The Minpins*, in which a small boy, Little Billy, flies on the back of a swan into a dark and magical nocturnal landscape, filled with extraordinary natural wonders. Here, fifty years after he himself last flew on his own, Dahl powerfully evokes that sense of separation between the solitary flyer and the rest of humanity that he had felt when launching his schoolboy fire-balloons, and which, through flying a fighter plane, had been fixed at the centre of his psychology. Boy and bird, moving as one, witness things that neither will ever be able to understand or explain. And what they see is theirs alone. "They flew in a magical world of silence, swooping and gliding over the dark world below, where all the earthly people were fast asleep in their beds."[42] This mystical connection between boy and bird was familiar territory for Dahl, who had explored it fifteen years earlier in one of his cruellest and most powerful tales, "The Swan". Here, another small boy is hunted and bullied by a ruthless pair of child tormentors. They torture him and deliberately kill the nesting swan he has been watching with their rifle. Cutting the wings off the dead bird, they strap them to the terrified boy and force him to climb high up a nearby tree. Then they dare him to fly. When he refuses, they shoot him in the thigh in an attempt to make him jump. Wounded and bleeding, the boy spreads his wings and dives off the branch. However, he does not fall to the ground. Instead, he soars into safety toward "a light . . . of such brilliance and beauty he was unable to look away from it".[43] Dahl viscerally understood that situation: the dazzling bright aviator's light, the fine thread that separates life from death. He had experienced that, too.

In March 1941, after five weeks in Heliopolis, he was surprisingly declared fit enough to be sent up to RAF Ismailia on the banks of the Suez Canal for some further training, prior to joining his squadron. There, he was relieved to discover that the outdated Gloster Gladiators had now been replaced by "a much more modern type of fighter"[44] – a Mark I Hurricane. But he was also shocked again at how little time he was given to learn to fly it and prepare for aerial combat.‡ His accident was now seven months in the past. But in early April 1941, he once again found himself in almost exactly the same position as he had been in September 1940 – ferrying an unfamiliar aircraft into alien territory. Only this time he was going to Greece rather than Libya. Another thing had changed as well. The pilot. He was no longer the nervous youth flying recklessly into the desert night. He had passed though a marking point, a division between innocence and experience, between a kind of happy-go-lucky view of life and a darker, more critical view of human nature. He had not yet flown a sortie in anger, but the crash and his months in hospital had brought him face-to-face with death and had caused him to reflect on the reasons for living. The next two weeks would only intensify this sensation, as each new day brought with it the imminent prospect of his own demise.

‡In *Going Solo*, Dahl claims he was given just a "couple of days" to master the Hurricane and fly it to Greece. Yet in Ismailia, after a refresher course flying Miles Magisters and Gloster Gauntlets, Dahl had been sent on a two-week Hurricane conversion course. As Derek O'Connor commented, this was not "an immense amount of time to come to terms with a monoplane equipped with retractable landing-gear and a variable-pitch propeller, but there was a war on" – O'Connor, "Roald Dahl's Wartime Adventures", p. 47.

CHAPTER SEVEN

David and Goliath

IN ONE OF THE drawers of a cabinet in his writing hut, Roald Dahl kept a battered black Herculex address book. Purchased in 1941, and used for more than thirty years, it contains many a famous name: Walt Disney, Hoagy Carmichael, Max Beaverbrook, Ginger Rogers, Lillian Hellman, Ben Travers and Ian Fleming are just a few of the well-known figures from show business, politics and the arts who played bit parts in Dahl's life and whose contact details ornament the book's yellowing pages. The scruffy, tattered little volume is more than a testament to his fascination with celebrity: it offers a number of clues to his personality and tiny insights into his life in the 1940s and 1950s. On one page are scribbled memories of a lunch with Noël Coward. On another, a betting forecast. Most intriguingly, on the inside front cover is a list of names. These run in an irregular column down the right-hand side and there are no related addresses or telephone numbers. A corner of the address book is water-damaged and the ink has run off the page, so some of the names are indecipherable. Several are misspelled. Most however are still clearly legible: Tap Jones, Oofy Still, Timber Woods, Trolly Trollip, Pat Pattle, Bill Vale, Keg Dowding, Jimmy Kettlewell, Doc Astley, Hugh Tulloch, George Westlake, David Coke. A digit is scrawled beside each of them and against several Dahl also marked an X. At the end of the list, the writing curling away toward the bottom of the page, he added: "Self 5". Above all these names, underlined and in capitals, is the heading: "80 SQUADRON, GREECE".[1]

When the Italian Army opportunistically entered the northern Greek province of Epirus in late October 1940, it did not expect to encounter any significant resistance. But despite inferior firepower and an air force that consisted of outdated planes, the Greeks had fought back with unexpected tenacity, and by mid-November the Italians had been forced back into Albania. Great Britain, a guarantor of Greek independence, had responded to an immediate call for air support by despatching two squadrons of fighters, one of Gladiators (80 Squadron) and another mixed squadron of Blenheims (112 Squadron) from their already overstretched operations in North Africa. Based initially in the northern Greek airfields of Larissa, Trikkala and Ioannina, 80 Squadron's twelve Gloster Gladiators provided support for the Greek ground forces and made several "kills" of enemy aircraft in the border area, before winter rains waterlogged the grass airfields and forced the squadron to return south, to Elevsis, on the coast, a few miles west of Athens.

Six weeks later, in February 1941, an Allied Expeditionary Force, made up largely of Australians and New Zealanders, was sent from Egypt to bolster the Greek resistance. Then, as the weather improved, 80 Squadron – assisted by reinforcements from 33 Squadron – moved north again toward the Albanian border to support them. Under the command of South African-born Marmaduke "Pat" Pattle, the RAF's top fighter ace in the war, and flying largely in outdated biplanes, they scored a remarkable series of victories, destroying over a hundred Italian aircraft, against the loss of eight British fighters and two pilots. On one memorable day at the end of February, the RAF destroyed twenty-seven enemy planes without a single loss of their own. It was 80 Squadron's finest hour, and their victories were celebrated across Greece, with the pilots fêted as heroes by the grateful locals. Their successes were rewarded with the arrival of six brand-new Mark I Hawker Hurricanes, a single-engined, highly manoeuvrable fighter, whose fuselage, though still covered with doped linen, was constructed from modern high-tensile steel rather than the wood of the Gladiators. Each was equipped with eight wing-mounted Browning machine guns which fired simultaneously when the pilot's thumb depressed his gun button. Pattle himself claimed the new plane's first victim over

Greece, a Fiat G.50, which exploded before his eyes in a spectacular fireball with his first touch of the button. Beyond the mountains to the east that separated Greece from Yugoslavia, however, lurked vast numbers of the German Luftwaffe, who were advancing south through the Balkans. As their Italian allies struggled to hold the Greek counterinsurgents, it became inevitable that they would soon be drawn into the conflict.

On April 6, 1941, the Nazi invasion of Greece began. It was a ruthlessly effective assault. Within two days the Germans had occupied the northeastern city of Salonica (now Thessaloniki), and soon the Allied forces were in full retreat. While 80 Squadron withdrew south to Elevsis to be refitted entirely with Hurricanes, the inspirational Pat Pattle was despatched from 80 Squadron to the front line to command 33 Squadron, which – alongside 112 Squadron – was now bearing the brunt of the German offensive. Eighty Squadron remained behind at Elevsis to defend Athens. The odds against the British and Greek pilots were enormous: approximately 800 German and 300 Italian planes against a motley force of 192 British and Greek machines – or, as one the pilot described it, "a pleasant little show. All the wops in the world and half the Jerries versus two men, a boy and a flying hearse."[2] The mountainous terrain and the thick clouds and driving rain ensured that there were occasional lulls in the fighting. One lasted almost a week. But the calm was only temporary. And everyone was aware of it. It was into this gloomy mind-set that Dahl was despatched from Egypt on April 14. He evoked its awful fatalism in an early short story, "Katina": "The mountains were invisible behind the rain, but I knew they were around us on every side. I had a feeling they were laughing at us, laughing at the smallness of our numbers and at the hopeless courage of our pilots."[3]

As he climbed into his Hurricane at Abu Suweir, once again Dahl felt that the military establishment were being reckless both with human life and with their own machinery. "I had no experience at all flying against the enemy," he was later to write. "I had never been in an operational squadron. And now they wanted me to jump into a plane I had never flown in before and fly it to Greece to fight against a highly efficient air force that outnumbered us by a hundred to one."[4] He may have exaggerated the odds, but his scepticism was more than justified. Dahl was entering a conflict where the only possible outcome was defeat. The cockpit of his Hurricane was cramped and uncomfortable, particularly for someone of his height. He was also carrying gallons of extra fuel in tanks strapped to the wings just so he could complete the journey without refuelling. For nearly five hours he flew over the Mediterranean, contorted into "the posture of an unborn baby in the womb".[5] When he landed on "the red soil of the aerodrome at Elevsis", dotted with tents, temporary latrines, washbasins, and grey corrugated iron hangars along one side,[6] he was suffering from "excruciating cramp" and could not climb out of the plane. He had to be lifted out by ground crew.[7]

In *Going Solo*, Dahl dwells on the pointlessness of the Greek campaign. His spanking new plane "won't last a week in this place", declares one of the men who help him out of the cockpit, while explaining the full extent of the awesome opposition the squadron is facing. Half an hour later, a fellow pilot confirms the situation, telling Roald that their position is "absolutely hopeless". None of this unduly worried him, he claimed. "I was young enough and starry-eyed enough to look upon the Grecian escapade as nothing more than a grand adventure. The thought that I might never get out of the country alive didn't occur to me. It should have done, and looking back on it now I am surprised that it didn't." He was surely being disingenuous. Naturally he felt a sense of triumph that he had overcome his injuries and made it to the front line. He was a member of his squadron at last – even if, as his commanding officer Edward "Tap" Jones sarcastically noted, he was reporting for duty "six months late".[8]*

Yet, since his crash, Dahl had also lost the young pilot's protective sense of invulnerability. Walking across the airfield, with its myriad wildflowers "blossoming blue and yellow and red",[9] he must have pondered with foreboding what the future held in store. In the desert he had brushed against death and lived to fight another day. Now, in the ancient

---

*With his broad shoulders and bushy moustache, Tap Jones was clearly the model for Monkey, the squadron leader in Dahl's unpublished short story, "The Ginger Cat". There Dahl describes him as "a big fine man with a black moustache" – RDMSC 5/14/1–3.

blue skies of the Mediterranean, once again he had to face its cold, silent whisper. That sense of dread, of death as a character, haunts many of his early short stories.

> *Each time now it gets worse. At first it begins to grow upon you slowly, coming upon you slowly, creeping up on you from behind, making no noise, so that you do not turn round and see it coming. If you saw it coming, perhaps you could stop it, but there is no warning . . . It touches you gently on the shoulder and whispers to you that you are young, that you have a million things to do and a million things to say, that if you are not careful you will buy it, that you are almost certain to buy it sooner or later, and that when you do you will not be anything any longer; you will just be a charred corpse. It whispers to you about how your corpse will look when it is charred, how black it will be and how it will be twisted and brittle, with the face and the fingers black and the shoes off the feet because the shoes always come off the feet when you die like that.*[10]

It was not an easy situation for the young pilot. He was joining a squadron at the end of a campaign which many of his fellow pilots had been fighting for almost six months and which was now falling apart. By the time he got to Elevsis, the remains of 112 Squadron had abandoned its northern bases and retreated south to join 80 Squadron there. The following day, 33 Squadron did the same, merging to fight the unhappy endgame of a campaign that could only have one outcome. It was hardly surprising then that on his first evening Dahl found most of his eighteen fellow pilots uncommunicative. An exception was David Coke, a son of the Earl of Leicester, who took Dahl "under his wing" and gave his tentmate some useful tips on how to shoot at the kind of German planes he was likely to be facing the following day. The rest kept themselves to themselves. "They were all very quiet. There was no larking about. There were just a few muttered remarks about the pilots who had not come back that day. Nothing else."[11]

The next morning, at 10 a.m. on April 15, Dahl's logbook indicates that he went out on his first patrol and intercepted a German plane attacking shipping coming into the harbour at Piraeus, just outside Athens. Next day near Khalkis, some 40 miles north of the airfield, he chased six Junkers 88 bombers back into the mountains and downed one of them. He did not actually see the aircraft hit the ground, but he saw all three crew bale out and abandon their machine to its fate. He had shot down his first enemy plane.† However, when he returned to Elevsis, his sense of triumph was swiftly stifled by the discovery that one of his small band of pilots, Frankie Holman, had been killed. And the manner of Holman's death must have been particularly chilling for Roald because it was so familiar: a crash-landing. Hitting a rock at around 100 mph, his plane turned over on itself. There was no fire. But Holman was found lifeless, hanging upside down in his straps with no visible wounds. He had broken his neck.[12]

On April 17, the sense of impending defeat was reinforced by the departure of the remaining RAF bombers from Elevsis to Crete. It seemed to the fighter pilots and their maintenance crews that everyone was getting out except them. The local Greeks were dejected. In an attempt to boost Athenian morale, the British sent their sixteen serviceable Hurricanes up together to make a low pass over the city. It was an impressive sight and Dahl himself revelled in his dramatic proximity to one of the ancient cradles of civilization. But this stirring exercise in formation flying could not disguise the fact that, further north, the Allies were now completely on the run. The following day, on patrol near Khalkis, Dahl passed yet another combatant's milestone. He intercepted a Junkers 88 that was attacking a Greek ammunition ship. Diving down from above over the brilliant blue waters of Khalkis Bay, Dahl shot at the German plane and sent it plunging headfirst into the sea, in full view of the ships below. He had claimed his second victim. This time, however, the pilot

---

†These "kills", reported in *Going Solo* and confirmed in Dahl's logbook whose entries were signed off by "Tap" Jones, are not mentioned in 80 Squadron's operations record book, which credits all nine confirmed successes on those days to other pilots. Yet in this instance Dahl's own account is probably the more reliable. The squadron's own records were destroyed before they left Greece, so reconstructing what actually happened there relied largely on intelligence summaries and on the vagaries of human memory. Individual logbooks were rarely used, although these often provided the most accurate firsthand evidence of events.

did not bale out. This time it was not just a machine he had destroyed. This time he had killed someone.

Did he realize the significance of what he had done? It is hard to say. The high sides of the Hurricane cockpit gave it a womblike feeling that made a pilot feel strangely secure – both separated and protected from the outside world. Another pilot later remarked that it was hard to believe that only a few pieces of plywood stood between you and a 20mm bullet, so there was already a detachment to the killing.[13] Moreover, the "kill" had been detached and cold-blooded – an exercise in aerial skill and accurate marksmanship rather than a bloody close-up combat. Nonetheless, the issue of taking a life, the question "Whom shall I kill tonight?" would doubtless go on to haunt him, as it haunted the pilot protagonist of his 1945 short story "Someone Like You". For the moment, however, he and other pilots adopted a manner that was terse and matter-of-fact. Little was discussed or overtly reflected upon. Particularly death. "Formalities did not exist," Dahl later wrote. "Pilots came and pilots went. The others hardly noticed my presence. No real friendships existed." Each man was just another flyer, "wrapped in a cocoon of his own problems".[14] This situation caused a certain coolness to develop in his own personality that created a tension with his own natural exuberance. Writing in 1945 to an American friend, he tried to analyse where this indifference "to going home, to losing large sums of money . . . to everything else which men usually care about" had come from. In a strikingly honest, almost tormented letter, Dahl explained how easily young fighter pilots could become detached from almost everything. "Think," he wrote, "if you learn to be indifferent to death, sudden death, or if you learn to pretend to be indifferent to it, then you must surely first learn to be indifferent to everything else which is less important. To young people nothing is less important than death because there is very little philosophy in them."[15] As Dahl grew older, and reflected more, that attitude would soften, but the strange disconnection would never completely leave him.

On April 18 he went up on patrol three times without great incident, noting in his logbook that southern Greece was now within range of the versatile and dangerous Messerschmitt 109 fighters. This was a sure sign that the German Army was not far away and that Athens itself would shortly come under attack. That same day, 80 Squadron also lost the happy-go-lucky, ginger-haired pilot Oofy Still. This smiling, freckled flyer would become a curious kind of literary everyman for Roald, who wrote him memorably into an early draft of his very first story, "A Piece of Cake". His description was so vivid it provoked his hard-nosed New York agent Harold Matson to declare that it made him feel he knew Oofy personally.‡ When Roald proposed another story, this time set in Greece, he told Matson that "Oofy unfortunately got killed over there tackling about thirty Messerschmitt 109s single-handed. I loved him dearly".[16] His demise left just fifteen Allied pilots in Elevsis to greet the dawn of April 20, a day that would witness the climactic finale of 80 Squadron's "Greek Adventure".

Dahl described the Battle of Athens as "a long and beautiful dogfight in which fifteen Hurricanes fought for half an hour with between one hundred and fifty and two hundred German bombers and fighters".[17] That description for once corresponds with the operations record book, which details a series of "confused" encounters fought against "overwhelming odds", as three fragmented squadrons faced an opposition that outnumbered them by ten to one. For over half an hour these opposing forces engaged one another in a series of memorable aerial combats. It was David against Goliath. The underdog against the bully. However, far from being afraid, Dahl – like many of his pilot comrades – was thrilled by the intensity of the drama in which he found himself.

It was truly the most breathless and exhilarating time I have ever had in my life. I caught glimpses of planes with black smoke pouring from their engines. I saw planes with pieces of metal flying off their fuselages. I saw the bright red flashes coming from the wings of the Messerschmitts as they fired their guns, and once I saw a man whose Hurricane was in flames, climb calmly out onto a wing and jump off.

‡ Harold Matson, Letter to RD, 18/05/42 – RDMSC RD 1/1/1/4. Dahl later rewrote "A Piece of Cake", removing Oofy completely, and replacing him with another pilot alter ego called Peter, who was based on Douglas McDonald. One senses that many of the characters in his early stories – Fin, Stuffy, the Monkey, and the Stag, for example – were based on pilots he had met during his short time in 80 Squadron.

*I stayed with them until I had no ammunition left in my guns. I had
done a lot of shooting, but whether I had shot anyone down or had
even hit any of them I could not say. I did not dare to pause for even a
fraction of a second to observe results.*[18]

In clear blue skies over the harbour at Piraeus, the battered British
planes, riddled with bullet holes and in a state that would normally have
rendered them unserviceable, achieved twenty-two confirmed "kills", at
least one of which was later credited to Dahl. But they incurred heavy casualties. Five of their own machines were destroyed, and three of their pilots
died. South African Harry Starrett tried to get his damaged Hurricane back
to Elevsis, but it blew up on landing and he was consumed in the flames,
dying of burns two days later. "Timber" Woods was attacked by what a fellow combatant, the Canadian Vernon Woodward, described as "a swarm of
Ju88s protected by masses of Messerschmitt 110s".[19] Woods was an experienced pilot who had been flying since the summer of 1940. But he did not
have a chance. Not even his trusty silver medallion of St Christopher could
protect him against such overwhelming numbers. Woods and his blazing
Hurricane vanished into the deep waters of Elevsis Bay.[20]

Moments later, the twenty-six-year-old wizard Pat Pattle, stricken
with influenza and flying his third sortie of the day, also perished. He had
been trying to protect Woods when his plane was hit simultaneously by
two German Messerschmitts. The Hurricane exploded in midair, tumbling into the waves to join that of Timber Woods in the depths. Pattle
had just registered what was perhaps his fiftieth kill – an extraordinary
record, made even more remarkable by the fact that for much of the time
he had been flying antiquated biplanes. Dahl shared his fellow officers'
profound admiration for his commanding officer, recalling him in *Going
Solo* as "very small . . . and very soft-spoken", with "the deeply wrinkled
doleful face of a cat who knew that all nine of its lives had already been
used up".§ Only twelve pilots returned to the aerodrome at Elevsis,

§Though he regularly misspells Pattle's name in his logbook, Dahl agreed with those who hailed the South
African ace as the "top-scoring" RAF pilot of the war – See Christopher Shores, Brian Cull and Nicola
Malizia, *Air War for Yugoslavia, Greece and Crete 1940–1941* (London: Grub Street, 1987).

soaked in sweat and with their Hurricanes riddled with bullet holes. Dahl was one of them. Years later, he would reflect bitterly on the unnecessary loss of life he had witnessed that day, but his foremost emotion remained one of pride in the part he played in that gallant, if Pyrrhic, Athenian victory. Indeed, many years later he quietly drew Ophelia's attention to the verdict of the campaign's historian, Christopher Buckley. "In terms of heroism in the face of odds," Buckley wrote, "the pilots of these fifteen fighters deserve to rank with the heroes of the Battle of Britain."[21]

Early that evening, when the battered Hurricanes had returned to Elevsis and been patched up, some were deposited in hangars on the edge of the airstrip. The Germans had not attacked the corrugated iron buildings in their previous raids and it was felt it might be safer to put some of the planes there rather than leaving them out in the open where they were obvious targets. It was an error of judgement. Just before dusk there was a huge German raid and the hangars were targeted. Four Hurricanes were destroyed.¶ Elevsis was now clearly an untenable base, and on April 22, all remaining British and Greek aircraft were evacuated – initially to Megara a few miles down the coast, and a day later to Argos on the Peloponnese peninsula, the most southerly region of mainland Greece. At Megara, Dahl and the seven remaining pilots of 80 Squadron encountered Air Commodore Grigson, the man in charge of the retreat. There, Dahl remembered, the pilots protested the absurdity of their situation. Greece was being abandoned, they told him, and they felt like sitting targets. Their aircraft were needed elsewhere. They urged him to let them fly their planes to North Africa, where they could play a more effective part in the desert war. But Grigson did not listen. He told them they were there to defend shipping and gave Dahl a package – presumably the records of the campaign – which he wanted delivered to a mysterious stranger, who would be waiting for him back at Elevsis. On no account, he told Dahl, was the package to fall into enemy hands.**

¶Shores, Hill and Malizia describe the raid as taking place on the following morning, but Dahl's logbook makes clear it happened that evening.

**Interestingly, Dahl recounts this story the other way round in his short story "Katina". There he is given the package in Elevsis by a man "in civilian clothes" and carrying "a revolver in one hand and a small bag in the other" – *Collected Stories*, p. 42.

The air commodore's unresponsive manner touched Dahl's anti-authoritarian nerve. Perhaps it even reminded him of "Admiral" Murray Levick in Newfoundland. This time, however, there was no mutiny. Only bitter incomprehension. "I stared at him," he wrote. "If this was the kind of genius that had been directing our operations, no wonder we were in a mess." [22] He got back into his Hurricane, took off, delivered the parcel, and rejoined his comrades. Twenty minutes later, they landed at Argos. Dahl described the landing ground there as "just a kind of small field . . . surrounded by thick olive groves into which we taxied our aircraft for hiding". [23] It had no defences and "the narrowest, bumpiest, shortest" landing strip any of the pilots had ever seen. [24] Their living quarters, white tents dotted about the olive groves, were easily visible from the air. To compound the absurdity of their situation, next morning five new Hurricanes arrived from Crete as reinforcements. Within hours, a German reconnaissance plane had spotted them, and after that, it was only a matter of waiting for the inevitable.

The Luftwaffe attack came shortly after 6 p.m., while Dahl and four other pilots were on patrol, searching for nonexistent Allied ships to defend. They returned two hours after the attack to find the olive grove shrouded in a thick cloud of black smoke. Using the large rock that marked the end of the landing strip as a guide, the five planes plunged into the gloomy haze, each pilot wondering what vision of destruction he would find if he managed to land successfully. The runway, it transpired, was clear of debris, but Dahl alighted from his machine to discover that the Germans had destroyed thirteen Hurricanes and a huge number of the "peculiar, ancient" [25] Greek planes that had been parked with them in the olive groves. From the deep slit trenches where they had run for cover, those on the ground had been reduced to using rifles to defend themselves against the ground-strafing Messerschmitts. [26]††

A few hours later, the Greek "fiasco" was officially over. The most se-

---

††Perhaps Dahl remembered this detail and used it as the inspiration for the child Katina, who at the climax of the short story he named after her stands amidst the flames at Argos and shakes her fist in anger at the attacking German planes. Ironically, Dahl was probably unaware that John Grigson, the pompous air commodore who had asked him to fly back to Elevsis with that secret package, was also identified by Bill Vale as the symbol of this futile resistance. In the centre of the field, with rifle to shoulder and aircraftman to load for him, the two men stood "as calmly as if they were on the grouse moors, while the 109s fairly plastered the place" – Wisdom, *Wings Over Olympus*, p. 199.

nior pilots ferried the five serviceable Hurricanes that remained back to Crete. Dahl was among those evacuated back to Egypt in a light bomber with nothing but their logbooks and the clothes they were wearing. He had been in Greece barely ten days.

The Lockheed plane landed in a remote part of the Western Desert in the early hours of the morning. The passengers disembarked: filthy, tired and without any Egyptian money. Dahl hitched a ride into Alexandria and went straight to the home of Teddy and Dorothy Peel. In *Going Solo*, he claims that he also took the other eight pilots there, but his letter to his mother makes no mention of this. He simply says that he arrived on the doorstep "looking like a tramp with nothing but my flying-suit and a pair of khaki shorts".[27] This is the more plausible image. For, despite occasional attempts to suggest otherwise, Dahl, like many successful fighter pilots, was essentially a loner who kept himself to himself. He had come late to his squadron, when its winter glory days were over, arriving just in time to witness its rout and the death of two of its most senior pilots.[28] On top of this, he was still struggling to keep his persistent headaches at bay and needed to conserve his energies, to concentrate on survival. He wrote to his mother a few days later from the Peels' garden, summarizing his time in Greece, and reassuring her he was in good health. He tried to make light of it all, to reconnect with the swashbuckling schoolboy optimism of ten years before. But he could not do it. He simply concluded: "I don't think anything as bad as that will happen again."[29]

While 80 Squadron was being re-formed in Palestine, Dahl spent almost a month relaxing as a house guest of the Peels. His mother had arranged for him to be sent some money. With it he bought a small car, which in early June he drove across the Sinai peninsula and up toward Haifa (now in Israel), where the squadron was now based. "I loved that journey," he wrote later. "I loved it, I think, because I had never before been totally without sight of another human being for a full day and night." The harsh magnificence of the desert inspired him. He revelled in the sense of solitude it gave him. It was an interlude in sharp contrast to the three weeks that followed. In Haifa, his squadron's task was to provide support for an expeditionary force of British and Australian troops whose aim was to occupy Syria and Lebanon, where planes from Vichy French air bases had been regularly attacking Allied shipping. Dahl reserved a particular venom for these "disgusting pro-Nazi Frenchmen". In his eyes, not only had they willingly acquiesced to the occupation of their homeland, but he blamed their "fanatical loyalty" to the pro-German Vichy regime in France for the unnecessary loss of thousands of lives.[30]

When he got to Haifa, he found some familiar faces – including David Coke's – and twelve new pilots.‡‡ The biblical landscape around the air base excited him and he delighted in the proximity of a warm sea and in the many orange, grapefruit and lemon groves that lay scattered across the rolling hillsides. It was, as he told his family, a land "definitely flowing with milk and honey".[31] But he had little time to enjoy it. Though the campaign, which began in early June, was ultimately successful, the flying was intense and also dangerous. In the course of the first three weeks, Dahl shot down two French planes, while his squadron lost four more of its pilots. "What a lot of flying," he told his mother. "We never stopped – you see there weren't many of us. Ground-strafing, escorting, intercepting etc. etc. Some days we did seven hours a day which is a lot out here, where you sweat like a pig from the moment you get into the cockpit to the moment you get out."[32] In fact, the pressure was too intense. As he wrote that letter, the headaches from which he had been suffering in Greece began to become unbearable. He described them later as like having a knife driven into your forehead. Then the blackouts started. Five days later, he was suspended from flying. A few days after that an RAF medical board examined him, declared him no longer fit to fly, and sent him home. His days as a combatant were over.

Before Dahl departed from Palestine, he was involved in one other curious incident. He was sent to report on the viability of an alternative landing ground, in the event that the runways at Haifa were bombed. This potential airstrip was at a small village called Ramat David. It had

---

‡‡Coke was "almost inevitably" killed in action later that year – *Going Solo*, p. 201.

been cut in a field of maize that was part of one of the earliest kibbutzes – one named after the British prime minister David Lloyd George, whose government had issued the 1917 Balfour Declaration that Great Britain "viewed with favour" the idea of establishing a Jewish homeland in Palestine. Quite ignorant of this background, Dahl was startled to encounter a Zionist settler and a group of Jewish orphans when he landed there. The settler, a bearded man with a strong German accent, who, Dahl remembered, "looked like the prophet Isaiah and spoke like a parody of Hitler", tried to explain to the naive RAF pilot the need for a Jewish homeland. Dahl was unconvinced, but also fascinated by the settler's quiet sense of conviction and particularly by his startling eyes, whose pupils "seemed larger and blacker and brighter than any I had ever seen". "'You have a lot to learn,'" the man told Dahl as he got back into his Hurricane. "'But you are a good boy. You are fighting for freedom. So am I.'"[33]

Dahl, who later in life became publicly anti-Zionist, returned to Haifa and reported to his commanding officer only that the landing strip was "quite serviceable" and that there were "lots of children for the pilots to play with" should the squadron need to relocate there.[34] They did. Within days, Haifa had been attacked and 80 Squadron, following Dahl's advice, decamped to the kibbutz, to live once more among tents and olive groves. But by this time Dahl himself had moved on.

Dahl profoundly regretted the fact that he was no longer able to fly. "It's a pity," he commented when he told his mother the news, "because I've just got going."[35] Alfhild also later recalled that being invalided out of the war "hit him hard".[36] From now on he would no longer be in the thick of the battle. That solitary joy of being a flyer – of swooping, diving and floating in the air – would be his no more. He would miss it for the rest of his life. Combat, however, had altered him and made him more reflective, more inclined to relax and to celebrate life. "All the dreadful masculine aggressions of youth" had been "squeezed out" of him. From now on, Roald would live his life in a "lower gear".[37]

And he was going home. He drove back to Egypt, sold his car, and two weeks later boarded a troop ship, travelling back to England around the coast of Africa, stopping at Durban, Cape Town and Freetown in

Sierra Leone, where he indulged himself buying presents for his family: sackfuls of citrus fruit, chocolate, marmalade and expensive silks for his sisters. On the final leg of the journey, the convoy in which he was sailing was attacked by German bombers and U-boats and three ships were sunk. After disembarking at Liverpool, Dahl took a train to London, where he spent a night with his half sister Ellen and her husband Ashley Miles. In the morning he travelled by train and bus to Grendon Underwood in Buckinghamshire, where his mother was now living. She was waiting for him by the roadside. "I signalled the bus-driver and he stopped the bus for me right outside the cottage, and I flew down the steps of the bus straight into the arms of the waiting mother." [38] He had been away from home for almost three years.

That is where Dahl himself left off his memoirs. But *Going Solo* ends as it begins – with a liberal measure of embroidery and fabrication. Not satisfied with the relief of an ordinary homecoming, Dahl could not stop himself injecting an extra measure of tension for his readers: he tells us that he has heard nothing from his family for months, that he has no idea they have moved from Bexley, and that he is haunted by the fear that they have all been killed by a stray bomb. A disconnected phone line at his former home seems to confirm his anxieties, while a helpful telephone operator searches through phonebooks for other Dahls. An S. Dahl in Grendon Underwood is ignored because he has never heard of the village. All of this was untrue. Dahl was quite aware his house in Bexley had been bombed, and that his family was safe. He also knew exactly where his mother was living. He had been writing to her there ever since he recovered from his crash in the desert. Yet just as tales of lions and snakes animated the reality of endless sundowners in Dar es Salaam, so here, in war-torn London, he used these invented details to heighten a mood he wanted to create.

It was about coming home. Coming home to his sisters, to his beloved mother and to the Buckinghamshire countryside that he had yet to taste, but which would become his own favourite landscape. His sisters Else and Asta described this false ending as "slushy" and "sentimental".[39] Yet those closing pages of *Going Solo* are charged with genuine emotion. An emotion so powerful that when, shortly after they were written, Dahl read them in public, to an audience at the National Theatre in London, his daughter Ophelia remembered him crying.[40] It was perhaps the only time he ever showed emotion like that in public. His tears were testimony to the power of his relationship with his mother, and of the emotion of homecoming itself after three years away in which he had tasted the strange, exhilarating and disturbing experiences of war. "They never recede with time," he once wrote of these tumultuous events. "They were so vivid and violent that they remain etched on the memory like something that happened last month."[41]

Dahl's time as an active fighter pilot lasted barely a month, but those thirty-two days reconfirmed him both as a loner and as a survivor. They gave him the need to write as well as something to write about. Indeed, it is impossible to imagine any of Dahl's first stories being written without his experience as a flyer. All of them are intimately bound up with it. Many touch on the ecstasy of flying itself. Others deal with the confused tangle of human emotions he experienced in that short but intense four weeks in Greece. Most reveal a deeply fatalistic streak, so much so that one is tempted to wonder whether writing them may initially have been a kind of therapy, a way of making some sort of sense out of the muddle of conflicting emotions to which he had been exposed. Later, that act of writing would become habitual, a necessary escape from another reality. Then his claustrophobic, dark writing hut itself became a surrogate cockpit – a place where, in "tight, warm, dark"[42] surroundings, he could reconnect with that potent mixture of excitement, fear, beauty, horror, humour, wonder and exaltation that he had felt as a fighter pilot and that first animated his desire to tell stories. There, he could let his guard down. There, he surely penned that list of pilots in his address book, with the number of kills beside each name and an X against those who had died in combat.

Each name must have reminded him of the hard reality that lay behind so much of his literary fantasy. Some were the briefest imaginable record of a human life that had been extinguished in a random and unnecessary manner, perhaps by the tiniest jink on an aerial turn or the slightest misjudgement of pressure from a foot on the rudder bar. The list may even have become a kind of talisman. A covenant, almost, between the writer and his past; between Roald and those who had not been so fortunate as he. In that sense it may even represent the very germ of his literary imagination.

CHAPTER EIGHT

Alive But Earthbound

SOFIE MAGDALENE WAS AN incurable optimist. All through the summer of 1939, despite constant pressure to move from Bexley to the remote seaside resort of Tenby, where the family had spent so many holidays together, she remained determined to sit out the war in her big, rambling home with her two younger daughters and their menagerie of animals, believing that somehow she would manage to evade the German bombers there. For a while, it looked as if her stubbornness would pay off, as the "Phoney War", which had begun in September that year, continued on into winter and then into spring. Spring even moved into early summer with none of the predicted German attacks. Food rationing and blackout restrictions aside, for the average British civilian there was little tangible sense of being involved in military conflict. Moreover, as long as Neville Chamberlain remained prime minister, there was still an outside chance that some sort of peace might eventually be concluded with the Nazis.

Ironically for the Dahls, the series of events that precipitated the end of this twilight war began when the Nazis invaded Norway on April 10, 1940. In response, the British despatched an Expeditionary Force there to support their new Norwegian allies, but the short-lived campaign was so badly planned and mismanaged that, a month later, it forced Chamberlain's resignation. After a short struggle for the premiership with Viscount Halifax, Chamberlain's aloof and patrician foreign secretary, Winston Churchill, the maverick leader of the anti-Nazi Conservative faction in Parliament, emerged as the new prime minister. The same day that he entered Downing Street as the leader of a new all-party wartime government, Hitler invaded Luxemburg, Holland and Belgium. Within forty-eight hours, German Panzer divisions were pushing into France. As French defences collapsed, almost a quarter of a million British troops had to be evacuated back to the United Kingdom from Dunkirk. By mid-June, Paris was occupied, and France on the brink of surrender that became reality a few days later. Suddenly Britain was alone. On June 18, Churchill announced to the nation grimly that the Battle of France was over and that the Battle of Britain was surely about to begin. Nevertheless, as British forces retreated from mainland Europe, he brushed aside any suggestion of making peace with the Nazis. "We shall fight on," he declared. Hitler felt he had no option but to launch his attack on Britain.

Listening to the news from his training base in Iraq, Dahl was desperate. On June 8, he wrote to his sister Else's fiancé, a fellow RAF pilot named John Logsdail, asking him to try again where he had failed and persuade his mother to move either to Wales or Cornwall. His logic was clear. He knew that Bexley lay close to two potential targets: Woolwich Arsenal and the Vickers Armament works in nearby Crayford. He also suspected that the German bombing was likely to be ill-directed, and that his mother's house would almost certainly be hit in the raids. "You probably feel as worried about it as I do," he wrote his future brother-in-law. "No one will realise that there is any danger of a bomb actually dropping on or near their own house until it happens, and there is therefore a very natural tendency to sit back and say 'It's not worth moving.'"[1] But neither Roald nor John Logsdail could influence Sofie Magdalene and her two younger daughters, Else and Asta, who remained determined to stay in Kent.

In early July, as Dahl was completing his flying training, the first air skirmishes of the Battle of Britain began. The following month, the Luftwaffe were bombing air bases all over southern England. Their intention was to knock out British coastal defences prior to a land invasion, *Operation Sealion*, that Hitler had planned for later that autumn. But they failed to achieve their aim. The success of the British fighter pilots in fighting off their German aggressors took Hitler, and perhaps the British themselves, somewhat by surprise. With their highly manoeuvrable Hurricanes and Spitfires, assisted by the invention of radar, the RAF prevailed to such an extent that by the second week of September, Hitler was forced to change his tactics. Abandoning his assault on strategic airfields, and in direct response to an RAF raid on Berlin, which had killed ten civilians, he decided to weaken British morale by deliberately bombing civilian targets. Thus began the long-feared Blitz.

Shortly after teatime on Saturday, September 7, an eerie, endless droning filled the London air, and the clear late summer skies over the capital were darkened by countless black dots, swarming in from the south and east. For roughly an hour, more than three hundred bombers, in two waves, turned large areas of the London docks into wastelands of fire and rubble. Eyewitnesses described it as a kind of medieval vision of hell. Flames leapt hundreds of feet into the sky as warehouses filled with sugar, wheat, timber and paint were set ablaze. Oil depots exploded, sending viscous dark torrents of burning tar flowing into the debris-ridden streets. Water pipes and gas mains were destroyed, telephone communications severed. Barges, freed from their moorings, became floating infernos of destruction, drifting up and down the Thames at the mercy of the tide. Every fire engine in London was summoned to the disaster, but often the firefighters could do nothing but let the buildings burn.

Then, at around eight o'clock in the evening, the German bombers returned. This time the raid lasted more than eight hours and now, as Dahl had predicted, Woolwich Arsenal was hit. Storehouses of high explosives erupted, causing thunderclaps that could be heard all over southeast England and shattered windows for miles around. The all-clear was not sounded until almost 5 a.m. In the morning, Churchill came to the East End of London to inspect the damage and was reduced to tears by what he saw. Fourteen hundred people had been killed. And later that day the bombers came again. More than two hundred of them this time, in a nine-hour raid. It was the beginning of fifty-seven consecutive days of aerial bombing on London. The East End got the worst of it, but the bombs fell everywhere. Many ancient and much-loved buildings disappeared. The Chamber of the House of Commons was destroyed. Buckingham Palace was hit. No one was unaffected. For most of London's residents, it was an autumn where, as the writer Elizabeth Bowen remembered, leaves were always "swept up with glass in them".[2]

Sofie Magdalene, with Else and Asta, both now in their early twenties, bravely endured these early raids. For about a week they sheltered in the cellar of their big Victorian house in Bexley. One night five small bombs fell in the garden and shattered all the windows. The next day, to keep out rain and maintain the blackout, they prised linoleum up from the kitchen floor, cut it to size and nailed it into the empty window frames. Another night, while they were trying to sleep on their camp beds, a rogue bomb sent one of the ceilings crashing down above them. There was little they could do about that. The cellar, however, was well supplied with high-quality champagne and cognac, so, as the bombs fell down around them, and the night sky to the north was illuminated by the red glow of a burning London, they kept up their spirits with large amounts of fine alcohol – "drinking ourselves silly," as Asta put it, and doing their best to calm the nerves of their seven agitated and excitable dogs.

For ten days they lived like this. At that point, the British Army took the decision out of Sofie Magdalene's hands, requisitioning the house – apparently for use as an officers' mess.[3] She had twelve hours to leave and find alternative accommodation. Tenby and Cornwall (Roald's preferred choices) were rejected. Instead, Sofie Magdalene turned to her eldest daughter, Alfhild, who the previous year had married Leslie Hansen, a Danish neighbour of theirs in Bexley, and was now living some 40 miles northwest of London in Ludgershall. Alfhild quickly persuaded a farmer in nearby Quainton to let her family stay as paying guests on his farm. So, after putting what remained of their paintings and furniture into storage in a local barn,* the three women piled a few necessities into their little Wolseley Hornet, and set off with their dogs for Buckinghamshire.[4]

To get there, they travelled straight through London – the most direct

---

*An inventory dated May 22, 1934, now in the possession of Astri Newman, showed that their possessions were valued at over £6,400. They included a Bechstein 3/4 grand piano, and paintings by Daubigny, Samuel John "Lamorna" Birch, Frank Brangwyn, Laura Knight and their relative René Billotte.

route, but also by far the most dangerous. They had to drive through bomb-damaged streets, negotiate burst water mains, avoid smoulder-ing buildings and keep a lookout for unexploded ordnance. Street signs had been removed to make navigation difficult for an invading German army, so finding their way was fraught with complications. Furthermore, the Dahls (with the exception of Roald) were still alien nationals and, as such, liable to be viewed with suspicion by the authorities. None of them yet had British passports. They also had to face the possibility of getting caught in an air raid – a potential threat that soon turned into reality when the sirens sounded midway through their journey. With character-istic pluck, the three women stuck out the raid in their car, because the shelters would not accept animals and none of them wanted to abandon their dogs. They were lucky. No bombs fell close by. When they finally arrived at Woodlands Farm in Quainton, they were exhausted. Their 75-mile journey had taken the best part of a day. But their troubles were not over. The farmer's wife balked at the number of animals, and, after a few days, Sofie Magdalene had to move on again.[5]

To make matters worse, the terms of her late husband's will made it difficult for Sofie Magdalene to rent, let alone buy, a home. The strictures of the family trust were already onerous and had certainly made no provi-sion for a war that had already caused the loss of her one major asset, the family home. Even before the outbreak of hostilities, Sofie Magdalene had been finding it difficult to deal with her two other trustees, whose consent was required before any money could be released from the fund. Ludvig Aadnesen was now an old man and often travelling in Norway or France. He was difficult to contact, while her brother-in-law, Oscar, was frequently unhelpful and sometimes mean. Moreover, as the value of shares in Aadnesen & Dahl declined in the late 1930s, so did the family wealth. Sofie Magdalene was forced to reduce the household drastically. By the time war broke out, her only remaining servant was a gardener. Now, deprived of her only significant asset (there was no compensation for a requisitioned home), she faced serious financial difficulties. For-tunately, Alfhild, now married and of age, was able to help. Realizing some of her own capital in the trust, she bought her mother a redbrick thatched cottage opposite Wayside Farm, in Ludgershall, from the niece of General Alan Brooke – the man who was shortly to become Churchill's senior military adviser. It cost £700.

By the end of 1940, Sofie Magdalene was beginning to feel more settled. On New Year's Eve, she presided over Else's wedding to John Logsdail at the church in Ludgershall. It was a quiet family occasion. The young couple had bought themselves a house in nearby Grendon Underwood, so mother and her three daughters were still all within five miles of each other. Soon, Sofie Magdalene too would move into the village. As Norway and Britain were now Allies, restrictions on what Norwegian citizens could do for the war effort were lifted and Roald's siblings had more options than to "test gas-masks in the gas chambers".[6] Alfhild became a Land Girl, helping with agricultural production; Else honed her skills as a metalworker, making field kitchens for the army; while Asta, emulating her brother, eventually joined the Women's Auxiliary Air Force (WAAFs), where she worked as a radio operator, before helping to set up the gigantic barrage balloons whose thick metal cables were designed to protect London from low-level aerial bombardment. Eventually the Dahl sisters would all obtain UK passports. Sofie Magdalene alone remained the foreigner, continuing to report to the local police each week. Alfhild's daughter, Astri Newman, remembered her grandmother in the late forties as "very foreign in her appearance and in the way she spoke", but also "very outgoing and very much at home" in the Buckinghamshire countryside.[7]

Roald, on the other hand, understandably felt somewhat dislocated when he returned to England in the autumn of 1941. Gone was the security of the grand house in Bexley, with his pack of siblings roaring around its spacious corridors, rooms and gardens. In its place a small sixteenth-century thatched cottage in a rural village of no more than a hundred people, many of whom lived without mains drainage. His role in his own family had diminished, too. His mother had learned to live without him, as had Alfhild and Else, now married with homes of their own. Even his younger sister, the headstrong Asta, was frequently away. Roald missed the sense of freedom, glamour and adventure he had experienced as a pilot, and, while he busied himself in his mother's garden, planting vegetables and a raspberry bed of which he was particularly proud, he found it hard to adjust to being an invalid. Moreover, wartime Britain, with its stern regime of food rationing and its culture of austerity, shocked and frustrated him after the plenty of Africa and the Middle East. And he found his mother's cottage a difficult place in which to live – largely because of the cramped rooms and lack of privacy.[8]

Grendon Cottage is still much as it was seventy years ago – quaint and rambling, with thick, dark thatch and impossibly low ceilings. The garden is smaller and less tranquil today, because much of the land was sold off after the war to help build a new village school. Nevertheless, the place still feels quintessentially rural, and though the village has grown in recent years, it still feels not much more than the "piddling little place" one of its wartime inhabitants remembered – with a pub, a church, a tiny school, a few shops and some thirty thatched cottages, in one of which Shakespeare was reputed to have stayed.[9] It was the embodiment of a sleepy English village and Roald loved that.

One evening, Else introduced her brother to another RAF pilot, who lived in a particularly ancient wattle-and-daub house a short walk away, with his young wife and two small boys. He ran a flying training school nearby at Weston-on-the-Green and the two men struck up a friendship. Then, a few weeks after they met, the young pilot was killed in a midair collision over the airfield. Strikingly, Roald responded to the disaster by concentrating his energies on the children rather than on his friend's bereaved wife. Every afternoon he would wander down the road and comfort the two boys by creating an alternative, imaginary fictional reality for them. Under the canopy of an enormous elm, he enthralled them with a series of tales about gremlins, the mischievous horned creatures that RAF pilots blamed for mechanical failure in their planes. Jeremy, the elder of the two, still remembers these afternoons with the gigantic storyteller as "quite magical".[10] His aunt, Pauline Hearne, also recollected that children seemed mysteriously drawn to Roald, who told her he was much happier talking to them than he was dealing with adults. She was probably the first of many who would describe him as "a kind of Pied Piper".[11]

For their part, his family found Roald changed by his three-year absence. Some of his good humour seemed to have disappeared and, as Alfhild remembered, he had begun hiding things about himself. In particular, she resented the fact that he began to deny his Scandinavian origins. She blamed the RAF for that. "'I'm just an ordinary British fellow,'" she recalled him once saying to a friend of hers. "No, you're not," she thought. "You're Norwegian. Like I am." It was a tension that was to haunt Dahl all his life, and one perhaps that he, unlike his siblings, never quite resolved. He remained proud of his Norwegian blood, but he also felt himself culturally British. In Greece he had been prepared repeatedly to risk his life for his adopted country, and had thrived on a sense of belonging to the RAF community. Despite his criticisms of some of the decisions made by its top brass, it was perhaps the first British institution that had accepted him and of which, at least on the front line, he had felt completely a part. Now that sense of community had been taken away from him, along with the spiritual succour of flying that had meant so much to him. He missed both terribly. As he was to write with characteristic hyperbole the following year, "to a pilot, being alive but earthbound is worse than not being alive at all".[12] He also had to make a big decision about his future. Neither of his two most likely career options – taking a desk job in the RAF or becoming a flying instructor – appealed to him in the slightest, while other possibilities were very thin on the ground.

Exactly how Dahl fell into the world of public relations and intelligence work is almost impossible to establish with any degree of certainty, as there is so little firsthand evidence. Dahl himself was strikingly reticent on the subject. When he did speak, his tone was characteristically casual. He told two interviewers in the early 1970s that he had been stationed at an RAF training camp in Uxbridge, just outside London, trying to get fit enough to become a flying instructor, and that one of his fellow officers, "a middle-aged, baldheaded fellow", had invited him to supper one evening in late March 1942, at the intimate basement dining table of Pratt's, one of London's smallest and most exclusive all-male clubs.[13] There, while the servants were "sizzling lamb chops over a wooden fire".[14] he met the witty and convivial former First World War flying ace, Harold Balfour, who was now a Conservative member of Parliament and under secretary for air – a junior ministerial post created to support the man who was responsible for the RAF in Churchill's War Cabinet.† Dahl impressed Balfour with his sophisticated and amusing conversation, his exuberant battle stories – and his skill at bridge. The minister, it seems, was looking for someone charismatic to fly the RAF flag in the United States, and so the following day he summoned Dahl to his Whitehall office and told him that he would be joining the staff of the British Embassy in Washington, as assistant air attaché.[15]

Initially, Dahl was not at all keen to go. "'Oh no, sir, please, sir – anything but that, sir!'" was his response.[16] But Balfour was insistent, and three days later Dahl, now with diplomatic stamps in his passport, was on a train to Glasgow, where he boarded a requisitioned Polish ship, the SS *Batori*,[17] bound for Canada. He dismissed most of his fellow passengers as the usual British "types", who could think of nothing but "eating themselves silly" and then complaining of chronic constipation.[18] However, two unusual RAF men did intrigue him. One was his eccentric intelligence officer from 80 Squadron in Haifa, who always travelled with an imaginary dog called Rex;‡ the other was an ex-pilot, the dashing and witty Douglas Bisgood, who had raced motorcars at Brooklands, and become notorious for coining his own squadron's unofficial motto, "*Semper in Excreta*" – or "*Always in the shit*". Bisgood, too, was an invalid and on his way to work as a flying instructor in Canada. But he was also a man after Dahl's own heart – a Battle of Britain veteran, who had won the Distinguished Flying Cross and survived a head-on Hurricane crash. It was a significant meeting. The two men spent much of the sea voyage trading stories about gremlins. Dahl was already fascinated by the folklore that had grown up around the little imps and had begun to invent stories about them. Bisgood too had devised his own gremlin subculture. Together they let their sense of fantasy run free. By the end of the journey both had become true "gremlinologists", to use a phrase that Dahl would later make his own.

---

†Dahl told a slight variant of this story to another interviewer, the Australian journalist Terry Lane, in which he claimed the man he impressed was the secretary of state himself, Sir Archibald Sinclair.

‡Dahl later recreated this character in his short story "Someone Like You".

He arrived in Canada on April 14, 1942, and was immediately intrigued by the difference between the culture of plenty he found in North America and the starved, meagre life he had left behind in England. A local newspaper with forty pages in it, people eating ice cream in the snow, and grown men drinking bottles of milk with a straw were just three of the many things that struck him as curious. On the sleeper train from Halifax to Montreal he was impressed by the comfortable beds, the vast menu, the iced drinks, and the enormous number of "gadgets" on board – including air conditioning, spittoons, thermos flasks and underfloor heating. At the Ritz Carlton, a "swank joint" in Montreal, where he was lodged for a night, he was by turns fascinated and appalled by the conspicuous consumption he found there. As he sent his mother a birthday telegram and posted off her first monthly food parcel of cheese, chocolate, marmalade and lemons, he also wrote describing his evening meal in the hotel, which included "lettuce hearts like giant cabbages" and "steaks like doormats, only thicker", served by men wearing "fantastic gold and diamond rings" whose teeth were "like piano keys". Around him buzzed hordes of alluring "females [with] baby faces" who, he admitted slyly, look like they are "strolling from the bathroom into the bedroom – and they usually are".[19] The pace and energy of life excited him, as did the hotel elevator, which travelled ten floors in five seconds. "You usually arrive at a place well before you get there," he joked to his mother, "and you start to get ready to go after you've left."[20] The next morning he took a train down to Washington, crossing into the United States on a bitterly cold spring day and continuing on via New York, Philadelphia and Baltimore. By the time he arrived at the Willard Hotel in DC, where he would be lodging until he found himself an apartment, winter chill had given way to balmy spring. As he noted with delight, "the whole place is covered with the most magnificent double cherry blossom".[21]

Roald liked Washington. It was civilized. And most of its inhabitants were eager to talk to the tall, handsome pilot in his unfamiliar uniform. Indeed, they would often stop him in the street to ask him all about it, which was exactly what the British authorities wanted, because one of Dahl's principal functions as an assistant air attaché was to use his experiences as a wounded fighter pilot to help tie the Americans ever more closely into the British war effort. Only four months earlier the Japanese raid on the US Pacific Fleet in Pearl Harbor had destroyed five warships, almost two hundred aircraft, and killed more than two thousand men. This act of aggression had finally brought the United States into a war that many of its citizens had desperately tried to avoid, believing that American interests were best served by remaining neutral. Within weeks of the attack, Winston Churchill flew over to Washington to show solidarity with the American people and ensure that President Roosevelt's war aims were synchronized as much as possible with his own. Speaking to Congress, Churchill stressed his own American roots and the need for his former kinsmen to abandon isolationism and lead the free world to a common victory against Nazism. The United States, he confidently declared to Congress on December 26, 1941, had "drawn the sword for freedom and cast away the scabbard". Despite this trenchant rhetoric, that scabbard was never entirely out of sight. Isolationism and anti-imperial sentiment remained still a potent force in American politics. Dahl would be part of a team based at the British Embassy whose job was to ensure that – as far as possible – the exponents of these ideas were neutralized.

His office was in the Air Mission, a nondescript annex of the British Embassy, a grand neoclassical villa designed in the mid-1920s by the British architect Sir Edwin Lutyens. The building, which also served as the ambassador's residence, consciously evoked the appearance of an English country house from the early eighteenth century, with red bricks, tall chimneys, and elaborate formal gardens. It was the perfect setting for the effete, tight-lipped, fox-hunting ambassador, Lord Halifax. A former Viceroy of India, who as foreign secretary had been one of the architects of the British government's policy of appeasing Hitler, his power within the Conservative Party was such that Churchill felt compelled to keep him in that role for nine months, before deftly sidelining him to Washington. The philosopher Isaiah Berlin, then working as the embassy's information officer, likened his boss to the provost of an Oxford college, "very grand, very viceregal"[22] and "not of this century".[23] Dahl, who sometimes played tennis with Halifax and was his polar opposite in terms of personality, described him initially as "a courtly English gentleman". That reaction was magnified among Americans, where a contemporary profile in *Time* magazine described the ambassador drily as "obviously not the kind of man who ever could or ever would quite clear his throat of British phlegm".[24] In his letters home, each one opened and read by the censor, Roald damned his boss with faint praise, describing him simply as "nice" and "decent" with seldom an exuberant word and never one of affection.

He had to hit the ground running. Within a week of his arrival at the Air Mission, he was speaking about his experiences in Greece to the Masonic Lodge of West Orange, New Jersey, with a further three lectures scheduled for the following ten days in Washington and New York.[25] He did not enjoy it. After the extreme experiences he had encountered as a flyer, he concluded that he had landed "a most ungodly unimportant job". His brief, ironically, was not to tell the truth but to create the right image. And, on this subject, even for someone with great gifts of fantasy, this was a difficult task. "I'd just come from the war. People were getting killed. I had been flying around, seeing horrible things," he later admitted to William Stevenson. "Now, almost instantly, I found myself in the middle of a pre-war cocktail mob in America. I had to dress up in ghastly gold braid and tassels. The result was, I became rather outspoken and brash."[26] It was hardly surprising. The embassy was snobbish, humourless, hierarchical and studiedly intellectual – in short it was just the kind of place Dahl loathed. His colleagues who worked in the Lutyens grandeur of the main building also regarded the poky quarters of the Air Mission with something close to condescension. They looked down on it, Isaiah Berlin recalled, "rather as a grammar school was looked on by public schoolboys, at least in those days".[27] This attitude must have rankled with Dahl. The embassy's strutting and posturing, its luxury and safety, its chicanery, contrasted horribly with the bloody immediacy of war he had witnessed in Greece and Palestine, while the glib haughtiness of those who had not risked their own lives for the war effort threw the memories of those who had died in 80 Squadron ever more sharply into focus.

Then, ten days after he had arrived in the capital, a short, bespectacled man in his mid-forties shuffled into the young air attaché's office. It was the British novelist C. S. Forester, whose swashbuckling tales of mari-time adventure had enthralled Roald as an adolescent. Forester was now living in Washington and trying to help the British war effort. He had been commissioned to write a story based on Dahl's flying experiences for the *Saturday Evening Post*, a high-profile American weekly magazine with a circulation of over 3 million. The magazine's editorial line had, at least until Pearl Harbor, been largely isolationist, but it was now fully committed to the US war effort. Dahl later admitted he was a trifle disap-pointed by the novelist's nondescript appearance and particularly by his thick steel-rimmed spectacles. "I expected sparks to have been shooting out of his head, or at the very least he should have been wearing a long green cloak and a floppy hat with a wide brim,"[28] he wrote, observing in the same breath that there are always two sides to any writer of fiction, the ordinary exterior and the extraordinary interior – a tension that the flamboyant and showy Dahl would sometimes find harder to resolve than the retiring inventor of Captain Hornblower. Forester took the young at-taché out to lunch in a local French restaurant. There, while both enjoyed a hearty roast duck, Dahl offered to save the writer the trouble of making notes and eating at the same time by writing up his experiences himself and sending them on to Forester the next day.

That evening, true to his word, Dahl started to write. In his story "Lucky Break", he describes the experience as a kind of epiphany. With a glass of Portuguese brandy in his hand "to keep him going", he found himself transforming his own experiences and observations into the imaginative landscape of prose. Almost inevitably, the tale of an inexperienced pilot who lost his way and crash-landed his plane unsuccessfully became the story of a battle-hardened flyer trying to land an aeroplane that had been badly damaged by enemy fire. He simply could not help himself. "For the first time in my life," he admitted, "I became totally absorbed in what I was doing." In five hours he had finished. He had written neither notes, nor a piece of journalism, but a story. He called it "A Piece of Cake".§

---

§This contemporary expression, widely used at the time for something that could be done with ease, was often ironically used by RAF pilots to signify particularly difficult or dangerous missions.

The next day he sent it on to Forester, and a few days later Forester's secretary wrote to him with the news that his agent Harold Matson had sold it to the *Saturday Evening Post*. Dahl later claimed he was paid $1,000 for it.[29] This was an exaggeration. He was actually paid $300, which was reduced to only $187.50 after the agent took his commission and the Internal Revenue Service had taken off tax.[30] Matson was nonetheless impressed, describing the tale to Forester's secretary as "a remarkable piece" and Dahl as "a natural writer of superior quality".[31] Roald would also later claim that the magazine had published the story without changing a word.[32] This too was inaccurate. In reality he quickly became involved in a tussle over numerous details which the editors wanted to alter. They had deleted expletives and cut out RAF slang, proposing a number of American substitutions he considered completely inappropriate. Already immensely confident about his writing, soon he was penning an angry letter complaining about their insensitivity and lack of respect for his style.

Matson did his best to help his client out, but the aim of the story was propaganda. As a result, the piece that was eventually published in the *Saturday Evening Post* on August 1, 1942, was markedly different from that Dahl had initially submitted. That final version, entitled "Shot Down Over Libya", carried the byline: "a factual report written by a pilot officer presently invalided in the USA". None of his initial drafts of the story have survived,[33] so whether this angle was added by the wartime editors in an attempt to make the story "more dramatic", as Dahl later claimed,[34] or whether he encouraged it himself remains unclear. In any event, Dahl probably felt that being shot down was an improvement on a crash-landing and that a tale of a successful RAF raid on a squadron of Italian planes was preferable in every respect to one about youth, insecurity, incompetence and bad judgement. He was irritated by the change of title, which accentuated the journalistic aspect of the piece, and he described the editor's decision to alter it as "bloody". He also remained insistent that it should be published anonymously – almost certainly because he knew how far supposed fact had sailed into the territory of fiction. As Dahl reminded his mother, the piece had been written solely "to impress the American public and to do some good over here".[35] Its accuracy was not important. He had written it "purely in my line of duty".[36]

The issue of the *Saturday Evening Post* that carried "Shot Down Over Libya" was typical of the potpourri of eclectic wartime journalism that now characterized its copy. The tale appeared among articles about the training methods of US Marines, the wartime rubber shortage, the building of the Trans-Alaskan Highway, and human interest stories about a fencing schoolmistress called Beulah Bunny, and a girl called Effie who found satisfaction working as a female riveter. Yet, as Matson and Forester observed, there was something more to "A Piece of Cake" than just journalism. Roald Dahl had made his literary debut.

Dahl was generous in his praise of Forester, not only crediting him with his "lucky break" as a writer but also attributing to him his own awareness of the importance of precise observation in establishing a story's plausibility and atmosphere.[37] He uses this technique frequently in "Shot Down Over Libya" and it is a feature of almost all his early writing. Whether it was the shining steel glimpsed beneath the flaking paint of the aeroplanes, or the exact sound of the Browning guns being fired – "a quick, muffled sort of rattle" – his judicious use of circumstantial detail is usually telling. Dahl heightens this effect by his self-conscious use of RAF slang and technical jargon, which he presents with a simplicity, almost a naivety, that stemmed perhaps from his own admiration of the prose of Ernest Hemingway, but was also distinctively his own.

Outside, the Hurricanes were waiting, looking very dirty in their desert camouflage, which was just a coat of light-brown paint the colour of sand. At a distance they merged into their surroundings. They looked a little thin and underfed, but very elegant. Under the wings of each, in the shade, sat a fitter and rigger playing noughts and crosses in the hot sand, waiting to help start up.

"All clear."

"All clear, sir." I pressed the button; she coughed once or twice, as though clearing the sand from her throat, and started. Check the oxygen, check the petrol, brakes off, taxi into position behind Shorty,

airscrew into fine pitch, mixture control to "rich", adjust tail trimmer; and now Shorty's holding his thumb up in the air. Yes, O.K. O.K. Thumb up, and everyone else does the same.[38]

Despite Dahl's sharp eye for this sort of detail, he was always very open about his essential lack of interest in factual accuracy – particularly in any sort of autobiographical memoir. "I enjoy least of all writing about my own experiences," he noted in "Lucky Break". "For me the pleasure of writing comes with inventing stories."[39] Sometimes, that delight in invention would show a flagrant disregard for the truth. The crash in the desert was a good example. Until he was almost seventy, he would often claim that he had been shot down by enemy action. He did so most strikingly in "Lucky Break", where he maintained that "Shot Down Over Libya" was a piece of pure factual journalism, and quoted in full a letter from Forester to himself which in reality was completely fake.¶ The fiction occurs again in various letters,[40] interviews,[41] magazine articles, and once more in his memoir, *Boy*.[42] It was only in *Going Solo* that he attempted to put the record straight. Yet he did so with almost childish reluctance, admitting only "an implication" that he had been shot down in earlier stories, and blaming this false impression entirely on his wartime editors.[43]

In May 1942, Dahl moved out of the Willard Hotel and into a small rented house in Georgetown, with pale blue front door and window shutters. There he settled into a comfortable routine, rising just after eight o'clock, breakfasting on grapefruit and a glass of freshly squeezed orange juice which his "half-time negro servant" Annie had prepared for him the previous evening.[44] He listened to some music – usually Sibelius or Bach – before going upstairs to shave and dress. Then he drove to work in his chief luxury: a large olive green Buick, which he had purchased for $550 from a rich cigarette manufacturer and family friend, who lived in Bexley and frequently travelled to the United States on business.[45] He generally arrived at his office shortly after ten o'clock. Most of his day

---

¶Dahl had created it by paraphrasing Matson's letter to Forester's secretary and then exaggerating all the details wildly.

was spent writing speeches, dictating letters to his Canadian secretary or making phone calls. In the evening, if he was not required for "official stuff",[46] or the thing he dreaded most, "boring dinner invitations from social hostesses",[47] he would come home around seven and start writing. Sometimes he would prepare a meal for friends, boasting on several occasions that he had become a "very fine cook indeed".[48] He was not so good at clearing up afterwards, admitting that after one particular evening, his maid left him a note saying: "Mr Dahl – I am exaspated [sic] woman – have never, never, never seen such mess!" Once, just before Christmas, he and his guests acted out his sketch *Double Exposure* and Roald dressed up in leopard skins to play the part of Mr Keep M. Clean.[49] Few of his dinner guests seem to have been British. Aside from his RAF colleague, the playwright and farceur Ben Travers, who worked in security and had a similarly earthy sense of humour,[50] Dahl made few friends at the embassy, confessing to his mother that his "main pals" were Swiss, Poles and Americans.[51]

It was a comfortable existence – especially when compared to wartime London – and Roald relished many of his diplomatic perks, particularly the tax exemptions and immunities from prosecution for parking offences.[52] Nevertheless, some of the values that prevailed in Washington upset him and exacerbated his sense of dislocation from a familiar world. He despaired of the standards of American radio broadcasting, for example, describing the programmes as "all advertisements", where every thirty seconds some "smooth-voiced bastard" interrupted even the most serious broadcasts to sing the praises of chewing gum, toothpaste or laxatives. He was also critical of a culture where film stars autographed the wings of fighter planes, and where tank manufacturers paid an actor like Clark Gable to "ride one of their trucks out of the factory" simply for the benefit of a "battery of press reporters".[53]

But this was the world with which his job demanded he engage: a world of people, both inside and outside the embassy, who lacked any experience of fighting on the front line and for whom the war itself was often a very distant reality. He found this stressful and sometimes resorted to alcohol in order to stiffen his resolve before stepping out to address his "po-faced, cod-eyed" American audiences. Over the months he spent regularly travelling around the east coast speaking about the RAF, he became an accomplished speaker, although he usually felt his speeches went better if he got "a little pissed"[54] before he started talking. By and large his audiences seem to have liked the former pilot's blunt, straightforward manner, which was mercifully free of English reserve. For his part, Dahl found Americans peculiar – "about as different from us as the Chinese," he declared. "Everything is done in terms of publicity and money."[55]

His first months in Washington put him in a familiar position – that of being an alien. He felt at home neither among the English at the embassy nor with his American audiences. His own company and his imagination offered him much-needed sanctuary. When he returned from the embassy in the evening, he would water the tiny garden, pour himself a whisky, listen to some music and start to write.[56] Almost immediately he turned to gremlins. "The gremlins," he wrote to the editor of *Collier's* magazine, "comprise a very real and considerable part of the conversation of every RAF pilot in the world . . . Every pilot knows what a gremlin is and every one of them talks about gremlins every day of their lives."[57] These "little types with horns and a long tail, who walk about on the wings of your aircraft boring holes in the fuselage and urinating in your fuse-box",[58] would launch Dahl's literary career. Their antics would eventually take him both to Hollywood and to the White House.

CHAPTER NINE

A Sort of Fairy Story

ALL THROUGH THE HOT and humid Washington summer of 1942, Dahl was plagued by headaches caused by the injuries he had suffered in his plane crash. Writing was almost his only consolation, and in this he felt particularly sustained and supported by his imaginary horned friends, the gremlins. He described his new tale to his mother as "a sort of fairy story", and for much of that year, the little creatures with their "wives called Fifinellas, and children which are Widgets or Flipperty-Gibbets, according to their sex",[1] diverted him greatly from both the daily drudgery of his job and his persistent health problems. He wrote the story swiftly, digging deep into his memories of Norse folklore and his love of the countryside, as well as into the fund of RAF gremlin detail he and Douglas Bisgood had compiled on the boat from England. Initially entitled *Gremlin Lore*, his fable chronicled a "tribe of funny little people", who lived happily in a "beautiful green wood far up in the North", walking up and down the trees in their special suction boots, until human beings, "huge ugly monsters", started to chop down their forest and build factories and airstrips on it.[2] Seeking revenge, the gremlins turn on their tormentors, the airmen, and their "big tin birds", causing innumerable inexplicable air accidents, even going so far as to move entire mountains to deceive RAF pilots and make their planes crash. The story combined fantasy, flying and a dash of malice. It was ideal literary territory for Dahl, and the little sprites may even have offered him some kind of psychological absolution for any lingering guilt he felt about wrecking his Gloster Gladiator in the Libyan Desert.

In Dahl's story, a Battle of Britain pilot called Gus – whose exploits bear some resemblance to those of both Dahl himself in Libya and Pat Pattle in Greece* – becomes a victim of gremlin mischief, when a group of these tiny saboteurs bore holes in his Hurricane's wings, making it crash-land and causing him serious injury. Eventually, Gus tames the destructive tendencies of the gremlins through a curious and rather contrived combination of bribery (feeding them used transatlantic postage stamps) and aversion therapy (playing unpleasant tricks on them when they attack aircraft). Brought to heel, the reformed gremlins assist the earthbound pilot to pass his medical examination and so return to his flying. Though subsequently marketed as a children's story, there is little evidence that Dahl felt he was writing a self-consciously juvenile piece. It was simply the story he needed to tell at that time. And he threw himself into it with obsessive energy. It contained many of the elements that would animate future stories: an eye for dark comedy, a misanthropic gaze on human activity, as well as the creation of a race of little creatures who remain invisible to most humans. The relationship between pilot and elf also contained a curious psychological twist: the gremlin with whom Gus communicates bears his own name. He is Gremlin Gus – almost as if the gremlin is an imaginary dark alter ego of the pilot who has first seen him.

When Dahl finished his first draft, he sent it to his bosses for approval on both sides of the Atlantic. It was part of his agreement with the Air Ministry that anything he wrote needed to be vetted by them. In the grand staterooms of the British Embassy and the dingy corridors of wartime Whitehall, earnest British civil servants studied the forty pages of closely typed manuscript and puzzled over how they could use it to Britain's advantage. Many were completely baffled. The convivial Aubrey Morgan, who ran British Information Services in New York, struggled manfully to find meaning in the little creatures, writing a gloriously convoluted internal memo in which he compared them to the "little man who isn't there" or the "noise of butterflies in an adjacent meadow which

---

*Most of the similarities are with Dahl himself. The most striking similarity to Pattle is the fact that Gus flies with a high temperature against doctor's orders, as Pattle did in Athens. Like Pattle, Gus "never had a chance" against the German plane that shot him down. Unlike Pattle, however, he survives.

put a gentleman off his putt". He concluded that he was "somewhat puzzled as to what the purpose of telling such a story can be".[3] But others rapidly realized how gremlins had the potential to raise American public interest in the RAF and the British war effort. In London, the Conservative member of Parliament Ronald Tree, now working for the Ministry of Information, described the piece as "one of the best literary efforts that has appeared on this side [of the Atlantic] since the war began",[4] while the young British movie producer and entrepreneur Sidney Bernstein, who had founded the Granada group of cinemas in 1934, and was now working under Morgan in New York City, swiftly forwarded the story to Walt Disney. Disney cabled back by return expressing his interest in turning it into a movie.[5]

Disney believed the tale had "great possibilities",[6] and wanted to acquire rights in the project. Dahl, however, though greatly flattered by the studio's interest, was cautious and highly protective of his material. He demanded strict controls on how the idea was developed. This was not just because he naturally felt a powerful sense of ownership but also because he believed that in some strange way fate had made him the guardian of this piece of contemporary folklore, and that he owed it both to the Royal Air Force and to his fellow pilots to ensure that their gremlin tormentors were properly looked after. In this context he had already decided that any money he made from the story would be donated to the RAF Benevolent Fund.† His purpose, as he expressed it to his colleague, the Irish writer William Teeling, was "to persuade [Disney] and everyone else in the studio not to misuse the Gremlins at all, to treat them with considerable seriousness, and to confine their exploits entirely to air matters".[7] This watchful, almost obsessive, need to control gremlin destiny made him unpopular with Disney's Washington-based sales representative, Chester Feitel. Feitel had initially taken a liking to Dahl, reporting back to Disney that the author was a "young fellow" who did "not regard himself as a professional writer" and "would probably accept any reason-

---

† A charity established in 1919 to give financial support to airmen and their families who had been injured or killed in the line of duty.

Olaus Dahl c.1890. Roald described his paternal grandfather Olaus as a "prosperous merchant who owned a store in Sarpsborg and traded in just about everything from cheese to chicken-wire". But the records in the parish church in Sarpsborg describe him simply as a "butcher" while other legal documents refer to him as a "pork butcher and sausage maker".

Harald Dahl c.1895. The one-armed craftsman and painter in his early thirties, shortly after he had arrived in Cardiff from Paris to learn his trade as a ship-broker. "Harald was not the easiest of husbands. He could be withdrawn and undemonstrative."

Roald's mother, the "dauntless… fearless" Sofie Magdalene Dahl with her son, "the apple", and dog in the gardens of Ty Mynydd c.1919. Dahl would later describe her as "undoubtedly the primary influence on my own life".

Roald and his three sisters gathering corn in the fields of Ty Mynydd just before it was sold. "Roald later recalled with nostalgia its grand lawns and terraces, its numerous servants, and the surrounding fields filled with shire-horses, hay wagons, pigs, chickens and milking-cows."

Asta, Else, Alfhild and Roald Dahl photographed
while on holiday in Tenby c. 1924.

Roald Dahl with camera at Repton, c.1932. Photography became his passion. He would write later, "I was the only boy who practised it seriously."

Geoffrey Fisher, photographed by Roald Dahl.

Priory House, summer 1931. Roald Dahl and his friend the bespectacled Michael Arnold stand side by side in the middle row, arms crossed. Seated in the front row is his housemaster S.S. Jenkyns. Next to him, with glasses and cravat, the "supercilious and obnoxious" Hugh Middleton. Jack Mendl is second from the left and W.W. Wilson second from the right in the same row. The senior boys "ruled us with fear", Dahl would later write.

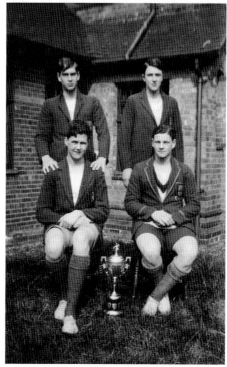

Priory House Senior Fives Team 1931. Roald Dahl is in the back row on the right, standing behind Jack Mendl.

Roald Dahl on a rock in the Great Rattling Brook, Newfoundland, 1934. "If some great giant," Dahl wrote in his diary, "had, in need of a handkerchief, seized up our tent, we would all have drifted away in our sleeping bags."

The explorers who went on the "Long March", Newfoundland, 1934. "Admiral" Murray Levick stands in the middle. To his left, the journalist Dennis Clarke. Roald Dahl is third from the right, Dennis Pearl is on the extreme left.

Tanganyika, 1939. Dahl's car is about to cross the Wami river on the drive to Nairobi, where his flying training would begin.

Louis Dahl playing the mouth organ in Norway and looking as his half-brother described him, "not unlike a native of Honolulu. Brown granite looks white next to his skin." He later used the photograph to illustrate Mr Dippy Dud in the *Shell* magazine.

Roald Dahl and his friend, David Powell, posing in front of a darts board on which has been taped a poster of Hitler's Propaganda Minister, Dr Joseph Goebbels. Dahl was thrown out of the club in Dar es Salaam for similarly throwing darts at a picture of a naked Adolf Hitler.

Leading Aircraftsman Roald Dahl during flying training, Nairobi, 1939.

Roald Dahl during further training as a pilot in Habbaniya, Iraq, 1940. With him is fellow trainee "Filthy" Leuchars.

able deal on our usual basis".[8] He had misjudged his man. Soon he was complaining bitterly about the author's stubborn lack of cooperation. For his part, Dahl took an immediate dislike to Disney's man in Washington, writing to Jim Bodrero, one of the studio's chief illustrators, that he "used to love gremlins very much", until Feitel "damped [his] ardour" for the movie project by accusing him of making all sorts of "complicated demands". Denying that he was being difficult, Dahl continued: "My own Number One Gremlin climbed on my shoulder just as Feitel left the room and whispered, 'That man does not like us much, shall I fix him?' But I told him to lay off."[9] The remark was both humorous and slightly threatening – a combination that he was starting to make his own.

Encouraged by Disney's interest, Dahl was also trying to sell a shortened version of the story to a magazine. He had decided to do so without using an agent, believing he could cut out the middlemen and do their job perfectly well himself. His first choices, *American Magazine, Liberty* and *Collier's Weekly*, all showed interest in the piece, as much for Disney's potential involvement as for the story's own intrinsic merits. In his negotiations, Dahl was disarmingly self-assured. Writing to Thomas Beck, the editor of *Collier's Weekly*, he boasted that Disney had offered him "unusually favourable terms . . . Amongst other things he is going to give me all profits on books, etc. and all profits on merchandise and, in exchange for film rights, all profits on the sale of an article to a magazine."[10] In the end, each magazine prevaricated, perplexed perhaps both by the oddness of the story and by the dogged cockiness of its uniformed young author. There was an impasse. Beck proposed cutting the story in half. Roald refused to countenance this. Vernon MacKenzie, the fiction editor of *American Magazine*, wanted to ask a more experienced writer to work on it with him. MacKenzie admitted to Aubrey Morgan however that he was nervous of proposing this to Dahl because the writer had "so much confidence in his own ability . . . that he might resent the suggestion of collaboration", and then the magazine would lose the story altogether.[11]

Dahl's immediate boss, the air attaché, Commodore William Thornton, was eventually presented with the dilemma. Should he take the project off his obsessive young assistant and hand it to someone else?

Dahl had not invented gremlins. He was simply the first to try and build a coherent story around them. A more experienced writer might do something equally interesting and ruffle fewer feathers. It must have been a tempting option. Providentially for Roald, Thornton cared little for gremlins and did not regard the problem as a priority. Uncertain what to do, he hesitated. And, by this time, Roald had wisely sensed he was in trouble. Aware that Disney's interest was a key card in his hand, he picked up the phone to the only person he trusted to help him, C. S. Forester's agent, Harold Matson.

Matson moved swiftly, cutting out *Collier's* and *American Magazine* completely and concluding a deal instead with the general interest monthly magazine *Cosmopolitan*, with Dahl guaranteed as sole author, albeit writing under the pseudonym "Pegasus".[12] So, when Thornton finally raised the issue with his assistant, Dahl could confidently inform his superior that the publication rights were sorted and that the RAF Benevolent Fund would be benefiting to the tune of over $2,000. Only the agreement with Disney remained to be concluded. However, much to Matson's irritation, Dahl did not ask for his help here, deciding once again to go it alone. This was partly to maximize the revenue for the RAF Benevolent Fund by saving the agent's 10 per cent commission, but also because Dahl sensed that he alone had the means to secure exactly the terms he wanted. He was a canny negotiator, applying himself to the role with energy as well as charm, often acting as if he were not an author but an agent for the gremlins themselves. "My gremlins have been clustering around the contract ever since I received it," he wrote to the senior Disney lawyer, John Rose, "wrinkling their brows, scratching their bald little heads and chanting the words, 'Give, grant, bargain, sell, assign, transfer and set' over and over, and every now and then looking up and saying that, 'It's very complicated.'"[13]

Dahl fought hard to get exactly the rights he wanted, "straining at gnats",[14] as Rose described it, before concluding his deal. In the final stages he was assisted by the eminent attorney Sol Rosenblatt, whom Dahl proudly described as "the best lawyer in the country" and who, he was delighted to find, offered his services for free when he discovered the author's royalties were going to the Royal Air Force. Dahl's attitude to the people around him was always clear-cut. A person was either good or bad, positive or negative. There was no room for shades of grey. Rosenblatt was a good guy. He had waived his "enormous fees".[15] Disney's New York copyright lawyer, Frank Waldheim, on the other hand, was the villain-in-chief. Referred to jokily in some correspondence as "Waldstein" – the name of Roald's favourite Beethoven piano sonata – in letters home, he was also portrayed melodramatically as "a dark cunning little Jew".[16] Likewise, the Disney studio was depicted as ruthlessly, relentlessly commercial. In response to his mother's assumption that it too might be giving its profits away to charity, Dahl commented tartly: "Not bloody likely."[17]

In this particular battle, however, the good guy prevailed. The final contract gave the RAF significant control over how the project evolved and appointed Dahl himself as their representative, to "furnish such advice and suggestions as may enable the British Air Ministry to approve the final version of said motion picture".[18] He was triumphant, crowing to his mother in one of his fortnightly letters about this "marvellous clause" which gave him "full power to disapprove of any part of the film at any stage of its production", and bragging that when Disney had spent "I don't know how many million dollars on making [the film] and I still don't like it, I can just say 'Stuff it up.' And he has to."[19] Such boastfulness had not been so apparent a few weeks earlier when Rosenblatt's aggressive stance caused Dahl to worry that the Disney team might drop the project altogether. Writing effusively to thank him for all his help, Dahl also begged his lawyer "not to make them so angry that they'll chuck the whole thing overboard".[20]

Walt Disney, however, had to weigh up his sense of patriotism with the commercial health of his studio, which was then running a deficit of over $1 million.[21] Before the war, the maximum amount of film produced in any one year had been around 37,000 feet; in 1942–43, the studio produced 204,000 feet – almost all of it commissioned in one way or another by the US military. These included the feature film *Victory Through Air Power*, the Donald Duck cartoon *Der Fuehrer's Face*, training films about flush riveting and spark plugs, and shorts encouraging Americans to pay their taxes on time and informing them how to avoid malaria and venereal disease. These were all made without a profit margin, to help the war effort, so developing more commercial subjects was essential for Walt and his brother Roy, who looked after the business side of the studio.[22] Gremlins here seemed promising material, but the brothers were nonetheless concerned about the intellectual ownership of the creatures, which their researches discovered dated back to the First World War. A memo from Chester Feitel to Roy and Walt Disney after his first meeting with Roald had confirmed that they were not original to Dahl. "The Gremlin characters are not creatures of his imagination," Feitel reported. "They are 'well known' by the entire RAF and as far as I can determine, no individual can claim credit."[23] Walt and Roy liked things more cut and dried. So Walt decided to proceed carefully and use the seven-page *Cosmopolitan* story not only as an opportunity to try out some prototype illustrations but also to see if it flushed out any would-be claimant to rights on the story.

Despite his tenacity in keeping control of the project for himself, Roald was generous about crediting others who had been involved in the story's development, and he was especially open about Douglas Bisgood's role in its evolution.‡ "There is an awfully nice lad called Douglas Bisgood, who may ring you up . . . and ask to come out," he told his mother in October, "I came here on the boat with him . . . He knows all about Gremlins."[24] Indeed, he naively encouraged Bisgood to speak to Disney personally about the film. This proved counterproductive, as Bisgood tried to claim ownership of the project and assert that he was himself the "arch gremlin". Fifinellas and Widgets were "family names, which I claim as being my originals", he told Disney, adding that he was himself planning his own story about them.[25] This, of course, only increased Disney's copyright worries. Concerned, Walt wrote to Dahl wondering "if this fellow will be inclined to cause trouble", and concluding that this sort of complication was precisely why he felt he must "surround" himself "with

---

‡Later he became more forgetful, claiming in "Lucky Break" that he "believed" he was the first to use the word, and in 1989 in a radio interview with Terry Lane that he had "invented the word . . . I don't know anyone else who did".

every precautionary measure".[26] Dahl reassured him that he knew "Bissie" very well, that he was certain Walt did not need to "take anything he says too seriously", and that he was confident his friend would not interfere, "particularly when he finds out how we are treating the matter and what we are doing with the proceeds".[27]

He was right. Though there were a number of other potential gremlin projects in circulation in December 1942, when *Cosmopolitan* published "Introducing the Gremlins", no significant authorial worms emerged from the woodwork – probably because the author of the article was anonymous and it was clear that proceeds were going to the RAF.§ The magazine dealt with the issue cleverly, boldly trumpeting the story as "unquestionably the greatest contribution to living folk-lore in more than a hundred years" and explaining that the author, a "noted gremlinologist", made no claim to be the creator of the little creatures. "'Nobody really knows,' he says, 'how the legend started.'"

Now that the contract was sorted, Dahl turned his critical attention to something that interested him even more: the illustrations. Unsurprisingly, his opinions about the artwork were forthright. Reacting to the drawings that Disney's illustrators had sent to accompany the magazine story, he acknowledged that some were "very close to the mark", but tiny details infuriated him – most strikingly Disney's refusal to incorporate the gremlins' "regulation green bowler hat".[28] He complained to Walt personally about this, and did so even more forcefully behind his back – particularly to the editorial staff of *Cosmopolitan*. Disney "has not got his gremlin at all as it should be", he grumbled. "There should be a great deal more expression on the face, which actually has an almost human appearance. So far as I can see, he has omitted the most important item of all, and that is the bowler hat, which they wear when they are not flying. The Leprechorn [*sic*] or Woffledigit, as I intend to call it, has been represented as an old gnome-like man with six legs, whereas I explain very carefully

§Charles Graves, the author of an account of seven young men who joined the RAF in 1939 called *The Thin Blue Line*, did argue that he had been the first to use the name in print and that, as such, he deserved compensation. But officials from the Air Ministry bullied him into dropping his claim. Bisgood, who died shortly after the war ended, never wrote his book.

in the story that he looks like a wolf." [29] Some of these complaints may now seem comically pedantic, but they reveal how strongly Dahl felt about the world he had created. Time and again, he played his "chief gremlinologist" card – arguing to Disney and his illustrators that only he truly understood the subject matter of the story. "I do wish you could let me see any other tentative drawings which you may make of the little men," he pleaded, "because I really do know what they look like, having seen a great number of them in my time." [30] If Roald was angling for an invitation to Hollywood, then the ploy was successful. Disney suggested he come out for two weeks to the studio in Burbank. And after a short internal discussion, the Air Ministry in London agreed to let him go. On a chilly autumnal day in late November 1942, he boarded an American Airlines plane for Los Angeles.

The two weeks he spent there were exhilarating. He was put up at the luxurious Beverly Hills Hotel, provided with a car for the length of his stay, and introduced to a host of celebrities. On his first night in Tinseltown, Disney threw a party in his honour, where Spencer Tracy, Bill Powell, Dorothy Lamour and Greer Garson all acted out the roles of different gremlins and Charlie Chaplin entertained everyone by pretending to be a Widget. At the same event Roald fell for "a very beautiful dame". She was an actress and socialite called Phyllis Brooks, whose previous lovers had included Cary Grant and Howard Hughes. Roald proudly declared he would "make it his business to organise her" for the rest of his stay. [31] He did. She was probably the first of his Hollywood flings, although their parting was not entirely amicable. Six months later, writing to a colleague who was going out to Los Angeles, Dahl described her as "a well-known character commonly known as Brooksie. She wants to shoot me, so if she sees you, she will probably shoot you as well." [32]

With his youthful good looks and RAF uniform, Roald certainly cut a dashing figure about town. He was a "ladies' man" and "ruggedly handsome", remembered the illustrator Bill Justice. "All the girls went crazy for him. I felt invisible when I accompanied him to parties." [33] When not organizing actresses, giving interviews to the *Los Angeles Times* or singing bawdy songs at the Wrigley Mansion – home of his new friend, the songwriter Hoagy Carmichael – Dahl would be found at the studio, ensconced in Walt's "magnificent" office, complete with sofas, armchairs and grand piano. There, Disney set him and six artists to work on an illustrated book that he intended should precede the proposed movie. Roald was intoxicated by the glamour of the experience, boasting to his mother that it would be the "biggest film he [Disney] has yet made", with the added novelty of using live action performers as well as cartoons.¶ He also took particular pleasure in working with the illustrators – an experience he would not enjoy again until he returned to children's fiction in the 1960s. "I wrote and they drew," he remembered. "As soon as I'd finished a page, it was typed out in the pattern they wanted, sometimes with the type going slantwise across the page and sometimes squiggly. Then they drew pictures all around it, and now and again a full colour picture for the opposite page."[34] Within a week the first draft of the book was finished.

Disney presided over the process with stern benevolence. Dahl came to admire him, although he described him as "quite an erk",** and was shocked to discover that he could barely draw. Yet he was impressed by the way he ran his studio and the fact that all his employees seemed to "worship" him – despite his frequent grammatical errors and his occasional shortness of temper. When one of the artists drew a cover image that he did not like, Roald reported his boss's explosion back to his mother in a comic mixture of American and British vernacular. "Goddamit, Mary, I have to buy the stories, direct the pictures, produce them, but son of a bitch, I'm buggered if I'm going to draw the illustrations as well."[35] Disney, for his part, warmed to the charms of the young airman, nicknaming him "Stalky" because Dahl was so tall, and because he could not pronounce "Roald". But though flattered by the attention he received in Burbank, Dahl was by no means dazzled into submission when it came

---

¶This was apparently suggested by the English-born Eric Knight, who had written *Lassie Come Home*, and who would be killed in a plane crash in January 1943. In a letter to his wife on August 17, 1942, Knight wrote: "This noon I talked with Walt. He is receptive and we kid. He wants me to give him opinions on a swell idea – about Gremlins and Fifinellas and Widgets . . . I suggest he shoots the whole thing as a mixture of real RAF and cartoon – Korkis, "The Trouble with Gremlins".

**In RAF slang, an "erk" was a non-flying member of the air force, usually one of the ground staff.

to the project. He remained feisty and dogmatic, fighting his ground at every turn, and insisting that his text should not be altered even if, as with the green bowler hats, it led to discrepancies between what was written and what was drawn.[36]

He returned to Washington before Christmas with four signed books and a watercolour by Jim Bodrero of two galloping mules with Mexicans on their backs. He told his mother with considerable pride that any one of the artists working on his story could sell a picture for $1,000,[37] but he was not about to try the market with his gift. He also wrote exuberantly to Walt that he had not enjoyed himself so much in a long time and that never had he seen "so many 'good types' as we call them, gathered together under one roof".[38] Energized by his trip, and no doubt also by the sense of fantasy that he had been able to indulge at the studio, Dahl persuaded *Cosmopolitan* to allow the RAF to reprint the story in their Christmas journal. He even ghost-wrote a playful introduction for the magazine, apparently from Disney himself, in which Walt asked his readers if it would be possible to capture a gremlin "and have him crated and shipped to California. I can assure you he'll be treated with the utmost care and consideration at this end".[39]

Disney's own plans were evolving rapidly. After shooting a test reel in November 1942, which was well received by all involved on the project, he abandoned the idea of mixing live action with animation, turning instead to a more conventional, entirely drawn movie. But he remained unsatisfied with the storyline and at one point abandoned Dahl's scenario, experimenting with several alternative ones. One involved the gremlins helping the RAF to defeat the Nazis and featured cameo roles for Hitler and Mussolini. It was dismissed by one of Disney's lawyers as "pure propaganda".[40] Dahl was never sent a copy. Titles considered included *Gay Gremlins, The Helpful Gremlins, The Gremlin Legend, Gremlin Trouble* and *Look! Gremlins.* Eventually, after consulting with more than forty different people, Disney returned to a script outline that was very close to the book Dahl had sketched out on his trip to Los Angeles. By this time, rumours about the project had spread to the publishing houses of London and Dahl had already received a handwritten note from Hamish Hamilton asking if his company could publish the story (with Disney illustrations) in England.[41] In America, "Gremlinmania" had broken out. *Time* and *Newsweek* magazines began debating the origin of the word, going back to the Old English *greme* meaning "to vex", while the malicious imps themselves started appearing all over the place, getting the blame for cock-ups connected with everything from sporting events to coffee rationing. Bob Hope even joked that they had ruined his recent book.

Dahl was on a high, energized by this fantastic aerial world he had created, and delighting in the celebrity status he now felt he had acquired. Writing to Air Marshal Richard Peck, the assistant chief of the Air Staff in London, he chummily dramatized his time in Hollywood, taking personal credit for "wangling the script" into the Disney studio and boasting about the imminent book release, which he claimed was likely to sell half a million copies and thereby greatly benefit the RAF Benevolent Fund. He added, en passant, that it would of course "be essential" for him to go out to Los Angeles again when shooting commenced, to ensure the studio "got certain things correct and accurate".[42] Peck, no doubt irritated by his junior's boastful tone, simply forwarded the letter to his director of public relations, Viscount Stansgate,†† who in turn passed it on to one of his juniors, William Teeling. Teeling, a gifted writer and traveller, who had spent his twenties as a hobo in the United States living with the unemployed and homeless, riding the freight trains in the Dust Bowl and reporting back to *The Times* about his experiences, took an immediate interest in the project and in Dahl himself, whom he clearly viewed as a kindred spirit, telling him that he had "never heard anybody's praises sung so highly as yours" in the corridors of the Air Ministry, and concluding that as far as Dahl was concerned, gremlins were certainly more like "kind gnomes . . . than evil spirits".[43]

Teeling's judgements were not entirely accurate. Some of Dahl's colleagues, like J. B. Hogan, his immediate boss in London, responded well

---

†† Stansgate (1877–1960), formerly William Wedgwood Benn, had just been raised to the peerage, having been a Labour MP for Manchester Gorton since 1937. Benn was a maverick. Although more than sixty years old when war broke out, he reenlisted in the RAF as a pilot officer in 1940, training as an air gunner and flying on several operational missions before being moved to a desk job when his age was discovered. He was eventually promoted to air commodore.

to his enthusiasm and ebullient comic energy, remarking to Roald that "if we all had your sense of balance in these wretched and dark days, life would be far pleasanter".[44] Others, like Isaiah Berlin, felt success had gone to the assistant air attaché's head, and that he had started to become bumptious and overbearing. Berlin described Dahl as "extremely conceited", and recalled him striding around the embassy apparently with visions of himself as "a creative artist of the highest order, and therefore entitled to respect and very special treatment".[45] And higher up the ladder, Dahl's attitudes were making him genuine enemies. In February 1943, Teeling warned him that he had overstepped the mark with Air Marshal Peck and consequently needed to watch his back. He reported that Peck had told another senior air marshal that he did not appreciate receiving personal signals and felt that Dahl "ought to be a little more formal". This overfamiliarity had also "rather alarmed" both air marshals, whose attitude toward their assistant air attaché in Washington had now become "a little chilly".[46] Teeling advised Dahl to tread carefully. But Roald was not about to heed the warning.

Dahl already felt himself undervalued by the RAF top brass. He believed they had shown him scant respect for negotiating such a good contract with Disney, and little appreciation for his decision to hand over his royalties to air force charities. He was grateful for the glamorous times he had had in Hollywood, and for the fact that the RAF had allowed him to be their representative, but he was also very aware that he had written the book in his own time, and was now using up his valuable leave in order to develop the project further. Gradually it became clear to Dahl that many of the apparatchiks in Whitehall simply viewed his gremlins as a source of resentment, irritation, or worse – as an administrative anomaly that needed to be clarified.

In January 1943, the assistant under secretary in the Air Department, Clement Caines, a sixty-one-year-old career public servant, wrote to Air Attaché William Thornton, requesting him to draft a deed of assignment between Dahl and the RAF. This would ensure that Dahl was "acting as a trustee on behalf of the RAF",[47] and that, in the event of his death, the RAF would continue to benefit from the book and the movie. Dahl was stung by the bureaucratic tone of Caines's memo, which threatened to deny him the pleasure of choosing how he would distribute the money amongst needy airmen and their families. Gamely he argued back, and eventually the RAF allowed him to keep 20 per cent of the proceeds for a fund of his own, dedicated to specific individual needs that he had identified. These included buying wireless sets, magazine subscriptions, and sporting equipment for RAF personnel stationed in the United States and helping the mothers of Eagle Squadron pilots who had been killed in action.[48]

The Air Ministry's cool attitude festered in Roald's mind and drove a further wedge between him and his superiors. He wrote to his mother that he thought they had "gone too far", reflecting ruefully that "if you give someone something, they always want more".[49] A month later he complained to William Teeling that he had been "taken aback" by Caines's desire "to tie me down, both when alive and dead, in order to make sure I would not embezzle any of the money which I had promised to give away".[50] It was all the more upsetting because Caines was seeking to distance the RAF from the project, telling the air attaché that he did not want Disney "to describe the film as having been sponsored or approved by the Air Council or the Air Ministry". Caines saved his most cutting blow until last, concluding that the gremlins were, after all, just "a joke",[51] Roald took this as a personal insult. For him, the little creatures were intimately involved with experiences that still bubbled urgently and sometimes uncontrollably in his unconscious. Yet his horned companions were becoming ever more democratized. Gremlin stories were everywhere – and Roald was distraught that the mischievous elves were being turned into "ridiculous figures of fun".[52] He wrote to Disney, desperately asking if there was anything he could do to stop it. "The legend will be ruined," he complained, when everyone sees gremlins "playing with peppermints, bitching up bicycles and trying out toothbrushes."[53] In their defence, he produced an article for *This Week* magazine, begging his readers to "treat them with respect" and declaring that all non-RAF versions were impostors. Only the chosen few were able to see real gremlins. "Allied pilots the world over, navigators, air gunners, radio operators and bombardiers – all are capable of seeing them. BUT NO-ONE ELSE IS. No one in the whole world, but those who fly . . ." [54]

The Gremlins was finally published as a book in April 1943. This time there was no "Pegasus". Now, with the official sanction of Viscount Halifax,[55] the author was clearly credited as Flight Lieutenant Roald Dahl. The book carried the byline "From the Walt Disney Production" and was illustrated by an uncredited Bill Justice, fresh from animating Thumper the Rabbit in Disney's 1942 hit *Bambi*. On the front cover was a fighter plane, with three naughty gremlins boring holes in its fuselage and sawing off its gun turrets. Far from printing half a million copies, Random House printed only 50,000 for the US market. Dahl ordered fifty of these for himself and assiduously posted them off to almost everyone of note he could think of, including Halifax, who sent the author a note of thanks, informing him that he would "make himself familiar" with the gremlins' habits before he passed the book on to his children.[56] He also sent a copy to the first lady, Eleanor Roosevelt, who replied enthusiastically that she found the story "delightful" and hoped the handsome young writer would come and visit her soon.[57] The print run sold out in six months; plans to reprint 25,000 more were only abandoned because of the intensity of the wartime paper shortage.[58]

Despite the book's success, particularly in Australia, where 30,000 copies were sold,[59] and the fact that Disney had even begun merchandising for some of the characters – the Fifinellas and Widgets were particularly popular – the film project was gradually running out of steam.[60] Continued difficulties with the storyline dogged the script. Dahl's own view, that Disney's drawn gremlins lacked sufficient warmth and humanity, may well have been a key, if unspoken factor. The illustrations certainly lack the charm or wit of other contemporary Disney movies, such as *Dumbo* or *Bambi*, or indeed the Kittelsen creatures Dahl remembered from his childhood, and after which he may unconsciously have been hankering. Disney's desire to gamble with the project may well also have been hampered by financial constraints: of his recent films neither *Pinocchio* nor *Fantasia* had yet gone into profit.

Nevertheless, Disney repeatedly asked Dahl back to California to advise on the script, begging him to "come out for a period of at least two months so that, together, we can whip the story into final shape".[61] Without this involvement Disney did not feel that he "could be responsible" to the RAF for the finished treatment. There was no way that Dahl could go to Los Angeles for that length of time. Moreover, one senses that suddenly, after all this enthusiasm, he was becoming bored with the project. It was a typical behaviour pattern. An interest would become obsessive, absorbing, all-consuming. Then, quite suddenly, his own passion for it would wane and he would move on to something else. He eventually went out to Hollywood for ten days in April 1943, reluctantly taking unpaid leave of absence from his job to do so. The studio did not pay him a fee, but it did take care of all his expenses, putting him up at a "palatial suite" at the Beverly Hills Hotel. His Los Angeles schedule was a busy one – he reported to the studio at seven thirty every morning and rarely left until seven at night – but he made sure he found time for relaxation. One evening he had dinner – and perhaps a little more – with Ginger Rogers, at her home "up on top of the hills overlooking the sea". On another he went to Dorothy Lamour's wedding reception, where he reencountered Spencer Tracy, and met Gary Cooper and Marlene Dietrich, with whom he was "most impressed".[62] One day, frustrated at being cooped up in the windowless studio while the sun was shining, he dragged his illustrators off to Hoagy Carmichael's house in the Hollywood Hills and continued their meeting by the swimming pool.

After the illustrators departed, Dahl penned a wistful little piece of verse for Carmichael's two children, Hoagy Bix and Randy Bub. The lines owed a debt to John Gillespie Magee's poem "High Flight", and sing of the lingering regret he felt at no longer being a pilot. However, they also suggest his continued dislocation from the ordinary world around him, as well as his sense of himself as a superman.‡‡

> *When I am old and bent and crinkly-faced*
> *When you are big and strong and muscle-meat,*

---

‡‡John Gillespie Magee (1922–1941) was an Anglo-American pilot and poet who was killed over Lincolnshire when the Spitfire he was flying for the Royal Canadian Air Force was involved in a midair collision. He was nineteen years old. His sonnet "High Flight" has often since been quoted in the face of air disasters. In his speech following the Challenger Space Shuttle disaster, President Reagan reflected that the dead astronauts had "slipped the surly bonds of Earth" to "touch the face of God".

I know you'll learn to fly; you'll like the taste
Of freezing clouds at thirty thousand feet;
You'll like the taste of hail and ice and sleet.

When you come down to earth, you'll have to pay
You'll have the people talk of little things;
You'll have them laugh, and some of them will say:
"It isn't only angels that have wings."

If they do this, you mustn't even yield.
Walk away slowly, never start to run.
Stand in the middle of a poppy field –
Stand on your toes and try to reach the sun.

If someone hits you where it really hurts
Then says "I'll see you in the afternoon" –
Just throw away your most expensive shirts.
Stretch out your hand and gently touch the moon.[63]

All through the summer of 1943, Disney continued to tinker with the movie, despite the diminishing enthusiasm of those around him. Recent polls were not encouraging. They suggested that contemporary moviegoers were increasingly uninterested in war pictures, while an Associated Press article declared that gremlins were now getting "tiresome"; they have "whimsied [the public] to pieces".[64] It was also becoming clear that by the time any film was finished, the war was likely to be over. In July, Disney told Dahl that he thought the film would now be made as a short. He gave as his principal reason the draconian RAF controls on the project: "With the amount of money that is required to spend on a feature of this type, we cannot be subjected to the whims of certain people, including yourself."[65] In August, there was a depressing story conference in which one of Disney's top creatives observed shrewdly that "these little guys" were in many regards simply the pilots' alibi for "their own stupidity, dereliction of duty, and neglect".[66] Disney, however, was reluctant to abandon the project completely and Bill Justice, the illustrator, recalled it "dragging on and on".[67] Finally, in December, Walt wrote off his $50,000 investment and informed Stalky that the movie had been shelved. His official reason was that the distributors felt the public "had become tired of so many war films".[68] Dahl for his part believed that Disney had missed the point. "It could have been successful," he told the Disney studio historian Robin Allan much later, in 1984. "He [Walt] had no feeling for England in any way. Or Europe. It was too English . . . He was not into it. He was a hundred per cent American. A hundred per cent."[69] So the gremlins went underground. But they would continue to scuttle around in Dahl's imagination, and two years later reappeared as the subjects of his first novel. At that point Dahl contacted the studio and asked if he could have the movie rights back. Roy Disney offered them for more than $20,000 – a price the young writer could not possibly afford. And though Disney promised that the studio would not act as "dog in the manger",[70] he argued with some foresight that in the future gremlins might indeed turn out to be "very useful picture material".[71]

Dahl made sure that all his literary royalties went to charity, but out of the sales and syndication of "Shot Down Over Libya" he allowed himself one important luxury – a splendid new set of false teeth, crafted by Lord Halifax's dentist himself, with a plate made out of a "mixture of gold and platinum", and a price tag of $380. This "new set of clackers", as Dahl joyously described them, still left a "tidy hunk" for the RAF,[72] but they were a source of great pleasure to their owner, who believed that in most cases real teeth were more trouble than they were worth. Removing them, in his view, was a radical but undoubtedly prophylactic measure – preferable to years of infections, toothache and expensive dental treatment.

Curiously, this was not an opinion he had formed as a result of his head injuries, but one arrived at while a trainee at Shell. Thus, at the age of twenty-one, just before he went to Tanganyika, he had paid a visit to Leslie Wright, a top Harley Street dentist, to have most of his teeth extracted and artificial replacements fitted. He browbeat his mother into having her teeth removed as well, before turning his evangelical zeal on his siblings. They put up more resistance. But Roald continued to try and persuade them, getting increasingly impatient, foul-mouthed and irrational when Alfhild in particular refused to go. He was delighted when, in the mid-1950s, he persuaded his brother-in-law, Leslie Hansen, to go to an American dentist and have all his teeth extracted. Hansen's subsequent decision not to have any new teeth fitted at all and to live the rest of his life chewing on his gums surprised him. But only momentarily. It soon became yet another eccentricity to savour.

Roald Dahl was revealing himself as a young man who held his opinions with strength, clarity and energy. He was idealistic and high-minded. His views might be wilful and unusual, but they were almost never half-hearted. He liked to be in control and could appear brash and arrogant in the exercise of his authority. The move to Washington had been a huge leap for him and the embassy was not his natural habitat. By no stretch of the imagination was he a born diplomat. He preferred the company of entrepreneurs like Walt Disney or artists like Jim Bodrero to that of men, like Air Marshal Peck, who got annoyed if their internal memos were expressed too informally, and who referred to everyone by their abbreviated job title rather than their real names. His charm and good looks had carried him a long way, and he enjoyed some of the socializing his job entailed. But the hostesses and social market also horrified him to such an extent that he told his mother he usually did not even bother to reply to this sort of invitation when he received it.[73]

He was much happier on his own, in his little house, inventing stories – with a glass of whisky or a bottle of wine at his side. His alternative worlds – his fiction, screenplays and letters home – provided him with an escape valve through which he could deal with all his new experiences and still remain in touch with his own most personal feelings. He found it hard to make close friends, and had little interest in forming deep relationships with women. So he fell back into his familiar role as the outsider, the free spirit, the naughty child. These behaviour patterns could be unpredictable and were sometimes paradoxical. Charming and offensive, boastful and blasé, confident yet diffident, he was impossible to pin down. Even his family in England felt these contradictions. One moment he could be vigorously domineering, berating them about some issue or other, the next he would be affectionately protective – sending home regular packages of cheese, sugar, underwear and lipstick. In Washington he struggled to find anyone who relished those inconsistencies and who he could genuinely call a kindred spirit.

Shortly after Dahl's return from Hollywood, all this began to change. The agent of this transformation was one Gabriel Pascal. Pascal was a native of Transylvania – an urbane rascal, whom Dahl admiringly described as "an amazing scoundrel",[74] "an awful old rogue",[75] and, in a letter to the US vice president, "a great man, a very indiscreet great man".[76] Pascal's early years were shrouded in mystery. He claimed he had been raised by Gypsies, trained as an acrobat, and that he had got his big break in film, while accidentally riding naked on horseback through the set of a silent movie that was being filmed in the Hungarian countryside. He must have looked good, for the director, apparently "enchanted" by what he saw, asked the youth to repeat his appearance several times for the camera.[77] So Pascal got into movies.

Then, while on holiday in the South of France in the twenties, he saw the geriatric playwright George Bernard Shaw wallowing nude in the sea. Pascal swum over to greet the bearded naturist, who was lying on his back, near a big red buoy, "rocking contentedly upon the waves". Pascal's presence initially disturbed him, until the Irishman noticed that he too was swimming *au naturel*. Observing the "wet golden-brown" of Pascal's tanned buttocks, Shaw apparently asked if he was a gypsy. It was a perfect conversation opener. Pascal told Shaw his life story and, after almost an hour in the water, they swam back to the shore, with the older man asking the younger to come and see him if ever he was financially in trouble.[78]

Two years later, a penniless Pascal turned up on the playwright's doorstep. True to his word, Shaw, who had never before sold the film rights of any of his plays, baled Pascal out, selling him the rights to *Pygmalion* for half a crown. The resulting movie, which Pascal produced, starring Leslie Howard, pleased Shaw so much that he declared his producer a "genius".[79] And when Shaw won an Oscar for his screenplay, he offered Pascal the rights to another play: *Major Barbara*. Pascal chose to direct this one himself, shooting on location in London during the height of the Blitz, with the support of another of the Dahl family's favourite rogues, Alfred Chenhalls, who, thanks to his relationship with Leslie Howard, was now involved in wartime propaganda work for the government and a director of Pascal's company.§§

Pascal was now in New York with an ambitious new movie idea: a sweeping allegorical tale about the nature of good and evil that told of "the fight between the children of light and the children of darkness throughout the ages".[80] He was passionate about the project, which was a product of his mystical devotion to the Indian guru Meher Baba, and he had captivated the idealistic liberal vice president Henry Wallace with his plans. A distinguished Iowan agronomist, Wallace also possessed strong mystical tendencies. As a young agricultural journalist with Communist sympathies in Des Moines, he had fallen under the spell of the Russian artist and mystic Nicholas Roerich. Roerich had designed the sets for the infamous premiere of Stravinsky's ballet *The Rite of Spring* in Paris in 1913. But he was also a charismatic radical; a philosopher who wanted to change the world for the better. His fierce intellect and piercing dark eyes, set above a grey-white moustache and beard reminiscent of both an Oriental priest and a Russian revolutionary, gave weight to his belief that all arts, all religions and all cultures would eventually blend into one magnificent peaceful civilization. Roerich's vision influenced many who met him in the early twenties, when he exhibited at the Chicago Art Institute and created stage designs for the Chicago Opera Association. Wallace was one of these acolytes. The two men subsequently exchanged coded letters about sacred chalices and "fragrances from other worlds". Wallace even began giving Roerich money and addressing him as "guru".[81]

By the 1940s, when Roerich was living in India and being hounded by the US Internal Revenue Service for tax evasion, the relationship between them had understandably cooled, but the idealistic vice president remained influenced by his contact with the Russian mystic. As one of his

---

§§In reality, it seems the young David Lean, who had edited *Pygmalion*, did most of the direction on *Major Barbara*, but Pascal paid him $1,000 so that he could have the sole directing credit.

aides, the streetwise Stewart Appleby, would recall: "Very few would have said he was a screwball, but they would have said he was queer."[82] Pascal's intention was that Wallace would provide the vision – and incidentally the money – for his movie.

The two men were a perfect combination. Their ideals and their fascination with Eastern spiritualism made them natural colleagues. But neither was a writer. Pascal needed someone with whom he could exchange ideas, someone also with whom the vice president would feel at ease. He had read *Introducing the Gremlins* and sensed something in Dahl's imagination that might resonate with Wallace. Perhaps it was the love of a fantastical tale? Perhaps it was his connection with Disney? More likely it was his British connections allied to a naive and childish sensibility. Whatever the reason, Pascal decided that he had found the man for the job.

Dahl was swept off his feet by the offer. As he told his mother, with almost breathless excitement:

> *I said – "Well . . ." And the next day I found myself having lunch with the Vice Pres. of the United States and talking to him from one o'clock until 6 p.m. He said he wanted me to give up my job for three months, retire into the mountains somewhere and write the script! I said no, I wouldn't – but if he liked I would try to do it in my spare time. He said O.K. and then rang up Lord Halifax and I had a lot of long talks with him about it. He said "Go ahead." So I suppose I'm going ahead. No one knows, least of all myself, why they should pick on me. Money is apparently no object, because the Vice-Pres. is arranging all that with the U.S. Treasury.*[83]

Soon Dahl was meeting Wallace almost every day to discuss the content and storyline of the movie, and before long the president himself, "old Roosevelt", had been brought into the discussions. All of a sudden, the young air attaché had been catapulted into the highest echelons of Washington life. His Widgets and Fifinellas, so scorned by the top brass of the RAF, had obtained for him the ear of the most influential politicians in the country. For once he did not exaggerate when he told his mother, "we move in high circles – so bloody high that sometimes it is difficult to see the ground".[84]

Soon everyone knew about the project. The *New York Times* announced that the new film would be based on the "philosophy" of the vice president and would "carry an inspirational message to all people from an American angle".[85] The *Washington Times-Herald* interviewed Pascal, who told a reporter that the film would "have its roots in the soil and will treat with the problems facing all humanity in the reconstruction of a postwar world". The paper described Dahl as "a great new writing talent", and revealed that "hundreds of children and youths" would take part in the drama. The cynical correspondent doubted that much would come of it. He thought the project was simply "political propaganda"[86] – designed to help Wallace's bid for the presidency in 1944. But he was intrigued by the involvement of Flight Lieutenant Dahl on the project and by the fact that Pascal had declared that no part of the film would be shot in a studio. It would, he claimed, be filmed entirely in England and the United States. One of the principal locations would be Longlea, the 800-acre Virginia estate of Charles Marsh, a wealthy Democratic newspaper proprietor, who had introduced Pascal to Wallace. At that point, Marsh had not yet met the project's young screenwriter, but their first encounter was imminent. It would be auspicious: the eccentric press baron would become both friend and father figure to the young Dahl and hugely influence the course of his life.

Initially, Roald was almost too overwhelmed with work to realize what was happening. On top of his official duties, the Gremlins movie, and the Wallace project, Pascal had asked him to write a movie adaptation of Paul Gallico's novella *The Snow Goose* (1940). This redemptive, almost sentimental parable, set around an abandoned East Anglian lighthouse during the Dunkirk evacuation, tells of a crippled artist's friendship with a wild and mysterious young girl, and how the two of them nurse an injured snow goose back to health. Its depiction of the relationship, both real and symbolic, between the man and the bird affected Dahl deeply. Many years later he would evoke its mood and subject matter in his own short story "The Swan", and his final book, *The Minpins*. Now, as winter snowflakes fell on the capital, he plunged into writing his screenplay, avoiding all social invitations where possible, and working on it at home in the evenings between eight and midnight while listening to symphonies on his gramophone and drinking French or Californian brandy.[87]

Sitting at his writing table, lost in the world of the imagination, Dahl must have felt destiny was calling him. His short career as a writer had already taken him to Hollywood. Now he was socializing with movie stars and politicians. Exciting projects seemed to be rolling in one after the other. First Disney, now Pascal. Soon it would be the director Howard Hawks asking him to write yet another screenplay.[88] And then there were the short stories, which had begun pouring out of him with prodigious intensity. Dahl sent his second one, "The Sword", about his Tanganyikan houseboy's murder of a wealthy German farmer, to the prestigious *Atlantic Monthly*, which immediately accepted it for publication. His next, also set in Tanganyika, about the snake who suckled milk from a cow, was scribbled down on a five-hour train journey back from New York to Washington. That was slightly harder to sell.[89] However, before long, publishers like Alfred A. Knopf and Simon & Schuster were beating at his door, asking if he had any longer fiction available. But the answer, for the moment, was no. He only had time for his screenplays and short stories.

Apart from those two African tales, most of Dahl's other early stories were concerned with wartime and flying. Some were ingeniously plotted; others were spiritual elegiac meditations on the business of killing or being killed. Many dealt with fear, anxiety and dread, usually from the pilots' point of view, but sometimes also from the viewpoint of a noncombatant. Most were semi-autobiographical and written in the first person. All were constructed in tight, spare, controlled prose. "Only This" is typical – most notably in its simplicity, its imaginative force and the intensity of the feelings evoked. The subject was immensely close to Dahl's heart: a mother whose only son is a bomber pilot. One winter night, alone in her home in the Kent countryside, she hears a vast squadron of planes flying over her house. She climbs out of bed and sits by the window, shrouded in blankets, watching the swarm of dark machines progressing through the night sky. "Now, as she sat there by the open window she did not feel the cold; she felt only loneliness and a great fear . . . She did not see the fields or the hedges or the carpet of frost upon the countryside; she saw only the depths of the sky and the danger that was there." [90] Her mind's eye takes her up to her son's side, where she stays happily for some hours until the raid begins and the plane is hit. As her son struggles to control his machine, she is powerless to help him and ultimately she is left to watch him die. But there is a twist. At the end of the story we realize that it is not the pilot who has died – but his anguished mother. Her imagination has destroyed her.

Dahl never wrote another story in which the mother/child relationship would figure so prominently. The orphaned child, however, who appears in another early story, "Katina" (first published in the *Ladies' Home Journal* in 1944), would become a familiar figure in his future fiction. "Katina" tells of a young Greek girl, orphaned in a German bombing raid, who is adopted by an RAF squadron and witnesses the final days of the Greek campaign, including the fiasco in the olive groves at Argos. Here the landscape of the tale itself becomes human, as the implacable mountains and their ancient deities creep toward the British airmen, as if to crush them with the weight of their history. Pentelikon, one of these "grim and forbidding" peaks, articulates the bleak and misanthropic truth Dahl had perceived there: "Men were foolish and were made only so that they should die." The story closes with a transcendent image of Katina, the angry, innocent child, shaking her fist defiantly at the German bombers who have been ground-strafing the British and Greek aeroplanes.

As I stared, the brightness diffused and became soft and yellow like sunlight, and through it, beyond it, I saw a young child standing in the middle of a field with the sunlight shining in her hair. For a moment she stood looking up into the sky, which was clear and blue and without any clouds; then she turned and looked at me, and as she turned I saw that the front of her white print dress was stained deep red, the colour of blood.[91]

The melodrama, the simple vocabulary, the rhythmic repetition that is almost poetic, the precise yet mystical evocation of place and mood, and the sharp articulation of finely nuanced human feelings were all classic early Dahl ingredients. Most arresting perhaps is that lurking sense of the magical; a characteristic feeling that a very real drama is taking place in a hyperreal, almost ghostly context. Another unpublished early flying story, also set in Greece, explored this fantastical dimension more fully. In "The Ginger Cat", a German bomber unexpectedly lands on the airfield at Elevsis. The commanding officer, Monkey, "a big fine man with a black moustache", rather like "Tap" Jones, Dahl's own CO, cautiously approaches the "huge glass face" of the machine, while around him a hundred or so airmen nervously finger their rifles. Monkey looks up at the cockpit and opens the hatch. As he does so, a ginger cat jumps out, startling him. Casually the animal strolls across the airfield, "taking no notice of him, walking slowly away, soft pawed and very dignified, with its tail in the air and its eyes on the ground".

Monkey and the narrator nervously enter the bomber. It has "a sweet, dusty smell like the smell of a church". There they discover that the wireless operator, pilot and bomb aimer are dead. But the rear gunner is still just alive. They take him out of the Dornier and lay him on the ground. Suddenly he groans. Hearing his cry, the cat stops. It turns and starts walking back toward him, "slowly, delicately, picking its feet up and putting them down". The atmosphere is profoundly sinister. As the animal approaches, the rear gunner starts to writhe and scream. The cat never takes its eyes off him. When it is about two yards away, it stops once more. There the animal stares, "crouched down on the ground, four legs tucked underneath its body, its tail flicking and twitching and its eyes . . . upon the German all the time". Like some kind of supernatural executioner, the cat brings death to the terrified rear gunner. "I saw his face," Dahl writes. "It was turning white, white like the faces of the other three, and his eyes were open, looking up at the sky . . . One moment this man had been a writhing, screaming maniac, and the next he was white and rigid and dead as a stone."[92]

These early war stories contain many of the elements that would make him so famous later on, but the juxtaposition of fantasy and realism is perhaps their most striking quality. It was the hallmark of a style he would pursue for almost twenty years in adult fiction, before returning to writing for children. The immediate reaction of his contemporaries to these tales was almost unanimously positive. The professionals like Harold Matson were struck by their sophistication and confidence of expression. They sensed immediately an individual voice, though Matson wondered if Dahl would last. He thought "A Piece of Cake" "remarkable", but that many of its most striking stylistic aspects might be closely linked to the power of its subject matter. For there were very few writers around in the United States in the early forties with Dahl's experience of aerial combat, a subject for which his spare elegant lyricism was perfectly suited.

Edward Weeks, who edited *Atlantic Monthly* for nearly thirty years between 1938 and 1966, and who published several of Dahl's early stories, praised the care with which he used his words, commenting on the "vividness and beauty"[93] of his storytelling: "Your sense of balance, your economy and your selection are just right. The sentences have a colour and an apparent 'naturalness,' which is a credit to your craftsmanship. Even the old master Maugham would be pleased."[94] Noël Coward too was deeply moved, noting in his diary after reading *Over to You* that the stories "pierced the layers of my consciousness and stirred up the very deep feelings I had during the war and have since, almost deliberately, been in danger of losing".[95]

Dahl was initially reluctant to take money for his writing. And when he did, false teeth apart, any rewards went straight to the RAF Benevolent Fund or his own airmen's charities. Despite Pascal's repeated offers, he refused to take any payment for the filmwork he did for him. His innate decency was undoubtedly the main reason for this, but it is also possible that he feared making money for himself, lest his bosses in Whitehall try to prevent his writing altogether. Yet the absence of commercial gain seems to add to the strange innocent power of these early tales. In November 1943, for example, he sold a story called "Bedtime" to the *Ladies' Home Journal* and donated his $1,000 fee to the widow of an RAF colleague in Washington who had been killed the previous week in a car crash.[96] By then, however, the prospect of having to survive as a professional writer after the war was looming and he was beginning to contemplate changing the status quo. Later that month he posed a situation to his superiors, where one day Flight Lieutenant Dahl might "find himself broke or getting tired of giving all his money away".[97] In that context, he also began looking for alternative representation. Harold Matson had failed to get the proofs of the *Cosmopolitan* article to him in time to make alterations, and Dahl had accused him of failing to "look after his interests" properly.[98] Matson halfheartedly attempted to woo Dahl back, and went on representing him informally for story sales until September 1943, but in Dahl's mind he was already history. A visiting Conservative MP, Victor Cazalet, who was staying with Lord Halifax, took a shine to the embassy's young writer-in-residence, and introduced Dahl to some other potential agents. Eventually, Dahl settled on a woman – "an ancient dame with fuzzy grey hair and a coarse laugh" by the name of Ann Watkins.[99] He would stay with her agency for over thirty years.

Watkins had founded her agency in 1910, and by 1940 she had a small but exclusive list of fiction and nonfiction writers that included Frances Hodgson Burnett, Theodore Dreiser, Carson McCullers, Ezra Pound, Ayn Rand, Dorothy L. Sayers, Gertrude Stein, and two of Dahl's own literary heroes, Ernest Hemingway and Dylan Thomas. Watkins was an eccentric, equally at home in city and country, who dressed flamboyantly in waistcoats and large hats, often with several feathers in them, and came in to work accompanied by two enormous Airedale dogs. She had a sharp, witty sense of humour and a feisty yet maternal attitude toward her clients that could stretch to buying the less successful of them a new pair of shoes, if she felt they needed it. She was, as her former assistant Sheila St Lawrence recalled, "a very emotional person with a lot of empathy . . .

very interested in [Roald] as a young man starting out and knowing he had a road to go down".[100]

When Dahl became a client of the agency, Watkins was already sixty and working only part time, coming into New York for two or three days a week from her country home in Darien, Connecticut. But her influence on Roald was to be significant. She and her successor, Sheila St Lawrence, would become the solid rocks of support, advice and friendship on which his literary career was grounded. Right from the beginning Dahl sensed he had made the right decision, describing his new agent proudly to his mother as "very famous . . . I'm told I'm very lucky to have her".[101] He liked her energy, her sense of fun and the fact that she had called the American Museum of Natural History to check the facts on his African snake story. Subsequently, Watkins and St Lawrence would negotiate film contracts, sell stories to magazines, and act as intermediary, when necessary, between Dahl and his publishers. Watkins and her – almost exclusively female – staff also became Dahl's New York family. He would come to rely on them for everything from literary advice to shopping. At one point he even used them as a temporary storehouse for works of art he was importing. He relished the relaxed professionalism of the Park Avenue office and the lack of snobbery that pervaded the atmosphere there. Most unusually, he often signed letters to the staff there: "Love, Roald."

By the time Dahl became a Watkins client, almost all his filmwork had dried up. Both Pascal projects had been put on ice, partly because two of his producers, Alfred Chenhalls and Leslie Howard, had been shot down and killed by a squadron of eight Luftwaffe fighters over the Bay of Biscay on June 1, 1943. They were passengers in the "Ibis" – one of the tiny number of commercial airliners deliberately downed during the war. Both men may have also been part of the reason the plane was targeted. Initial rumours were that the bon viveur Chenhalls had been mistaken for Winston Churchill, and Churchill himself seems to have believed this was the case. He described the incident characteristically as evidence both of the stupidity of German secret agents and of the "inscrutable work-ings of fate".[102] Recent research, however, has suggested that the target may actually have been Howard himself, a Jew, who had been a ferocious and prominent critic of Nazism and a particularly irritating thorn in the flesh of Hitler's minister of propaganda, Joseph Goebbels.[103] Both he and Chenhalls, it appears, may well have been British agents, returning from a mission to Spain where, under the guise of conducting a Shakespeare Seminar for the British Institute, Howard had actually delivered a secret message from Churchill to the Spanish leader, General Franco, encouraging him to remain neutral.[104]

Back in New York, Pascal took the news of their deaths with apparent equanimity. Now he turned his attention toward a new Shaw project, *Caesar and Cleopatra*, for which he intended to hire the eighty-seven-year-old playwright as screenwriter. Dahl drifted out of his life and it is not clear they ever met again. But the eccentric Transylvanian had already played a significant role in the young writer's story. He had given him a unique introduction to the corridors of US power – and Dahl had seized the opportunity with both hands. By mid-1943, his relationship with Vice President Wallace had moved onto the level of friendship. "One of the most serious minded, fascinating figures in national public life,"[105] as David McCullough would describe Wallace, was now his regular tennis partner. He and the ambidextrous vice president usually played twice a week. "He's very good and luckily I'm a bit better than I used to be," Roald told his mother, "so we both get a lot of exercise and very hot. But it's the only exercise I get."[106] Despite the demise of the film project, Wallace took a paternal interest in the young RAF officer, discussing political ideals with him and recommending vitamin pills for his back and sinus ailments. And charmed by *The Gremlins*, Mrs Roosevelt herself had become a Roald Dahl fan and invited him to dinner at the White House.

All this activity did not go unnoticed by those in Washington whose job it was to further British interests by more unconventional means than those of the press release and the off-the-record briefing. If some senior personnel in the Air Ministry, irritated by Dahl's assertiveness and his brash charm, were plotting to get rid of him, others were quick to realize that a young man in his situation was likely to see and hear things that could be extremely useful to the British war effort. So, inevitably, all through 1943 Dahl moved ever further into the blurry area that separates the worlds of newspapers, propaganda, parties and public meetings from that of intelligence and covert operations. Soon he would be almost entirely lost from view in its murky, swirling fog.

CHAPTER TEN

Secrets and Lies

DAHL HAD BEEN A rebellious teenager, but his defiance was generally a private affair. At Repton, disguised in waders, helmet, wind jacket and goggles, he had roared noisily through town on his illicit motorbike, relishing the annoyance he caused the masters and exulting in the fact that no one in authority recognized him. Even as an old man, he still savoured this gesture which, if discovered, might have led to his being expelled or – at the very least – to one of those "savage beatings that drew blood from your backside". It was a revealing admission, which spoke eloquently of the strength of his interior world. "I never told anyone, not even my best friend," he wrote later. "I had learnt even at that tender age that there are no secrets unless you keep them to yourself, and this was the greatest secret I had ever had to keep in my life so far."[1] Yet, among those who knew him best, Dahl was notorious for being leaky. "He regularly betrayed confidences," his old American friend, Marian Goodman, told me with a chuckle, recalling one incident where Roald destroyed a friendship and wrecked a marriage by an intemperate indiscretion. Mrs Goodman, who first met Dahl in New York in 1954, also recalled with alarm another occasion where he had tried to entertain a group of people at a dinner party with details of a passion of her own that she had foolishly just confessed to him.[2] Eventually she managed to silence him, but only after some effort. His daughter Lucy agreed. "Dad never could keep his mouth shut," she told me. "He gossiped like a girl." She found it almost impossible to imagine that her father had worked in any capacity as a spy during the war.[3] Yet he did. And for the most part he was scrupulously discreet about it.

Dahl's remit to Washington mainly involved dealing with press and public relations, but from the moment he arrived there, he would also have been aware of a complex network of British undercover operations that was being manipulated from New York, by one of the war's most unusual and eccentric figures – the buccaneering Canadian industrialist and businessman William Stephenson. A former boxing champion and pioneering First World War aviator, by the mid-twenties his business acumen and flair for technical innovation had made him a millionaire several times over. Though small of stature, Stephenson's ego and his energy reserves were colossal, and he could compel great loyalty. Noël Coward once told Dahl that Stephenson was the only man for whom he would "go through fire and water".[4] He was also sharp, ruthless and prided himself on getting things done. Churchill admired him for these qualities and – probably on the recommendation of his fellow Canadian Max Aitken – selected Stephenson to run a wartime secret service network based in the United States called British Security Coordination (BSC).* Established initially to promote UK interests in the United States and counter Nazi propaganda, BSC soon become involved in more exotic and clandestine activities, which ranged from training spies in a remote camp on the shores of Lake Ontario to publishing horoscopes from Hitler's former astrologer that predicted the Führer's imminent demise.

BSC represented both branches of British secret service in the United States. The first of them, the Secret Intelligence Service (SIS), also known as MI6, was responsible for foreign intelligence and codebreaking. The more glamorous Special Operations Executive, or SOE, had its headquarters in Baker Street, not far from the house where Sherlock Holmes had solved many a fictional riddle. It was nicknamed "Churchill's Secret

---

*Max Aitken, later Lord Beaverbrook (1879–1964), was minister of supply and aircraft production in the early years of Churchill's War Cabinet. Dahl himself was convinced that Beaverbrook had advised Churchill on Stephenson's appointment. "He [Stephenson] was a close friend, a really genuinely close friend of Beaverbrook," Dahl told Bill Macdonald. "I've been in Beaverbrook's house in Jamaica with him and they were completely like that," he said crossing his fingers. "A couple of old Canadian millionaires who were both pretty ruthless" – Macdonald, *The True Intrepid*, p. 242.

Army" and "The Baker Street Irregulars", and its task was to wage war by all means other than the strictly military – and particularly by espionage and sabotage. Ernest Cuneo, who acted as a liaison between BSC, OSS (the American Secret Service), and the Roosevelt administration, thought Stephenson's outfit was created in this mould, because it was prepared to go "beyond the legal, the ethical, and the proper" to achieve its ends. Cuneo, who was to become a good friend of Dahl's, claimed that, among its many activities, BSC "ran espionage agents, tampered with the mails, tapped telephones, smuggled propaganda into the country, disrupted public gatherings, covertly subsidized newspapers, radios, and organizations, perpetrated forgeries – even palming one off on the President of the United States – violated the aliens registration act, shanghaied sailors numerous times, and possibly murdered one or more persons in this country".[5]

Dahl was fascinated by BSC and initially imagined its enigmatic boss, who worked under the code name "Intrepid", as a "small unknown creature, hiding in a dark room somewhere in New York".[6] Reality was an office on the thirty-fifth floor of the International Building at Rockefeller Center, from where Stephenson coordinated possibly more than a thousand agents, whose activities were directed toward counteracting the significant element in American politics and society that was either overtly isolationist or simply strongly opposed to Great Britain and its imperial interests. Many of these agents were colourful figures infinitely more to the young Roald Dahl's taste than dull embassy bureaucrats. The reckless Ivar Bryce,† who once turned a harmless doodle on his office blotter into a map that Stephenson used to "prove" to Roosevelt that the Germans intended to invade Central America, was one example.[7] Bryce's enthusiasm for espionage was already legendary. He had once tried out a new truth drug on his unsuspecting cousin, Bunny Phillips, and nearly killed him in the process. The pollster and future advertising mogul David Ogilvy

---

†Ivar Bryce (1906–1985) was a wealthy aristocrat of whom Earl Mountbatten was supposed to have remarked: "It's terrible, the advantages he's had to overcome." Dahl found him charming, lazy, but kind – Interview with Roald Dahl, John Pearson Papers, Manuscript Department, Lilly Library, Indiana University, Bloomington, cited in Conant, *The Irregulars*, p. 223.

was another of these intelligence mavericks. "An irreconcilable rebel" and "a misfit",[8] to use his own words, he had run away from his family after flunking out of Oxford University, and worked variously as a cook in a Paris kitchen, a social worker in an Edinburgh slum and a door-to-door salesman hawking Aga stoves, before coming to work for the US pollster George Gallup and eventually for BSC. Finally, there was Bryce's friend, the handsome playboy Ian Fleming, who delighted in the gadgetry of espionage, and would draw on many of his BSC experiences when he devised his James Bond stories. This nonconformist trio were all Stephenson protégés and Dahl would come to be well acquainted with each of them.

Exactly how he stumbled into this world is not entirely clear. His sister Alfhild, whose love of a good story often rivalled her brother's, believed Roald's links with espionage began shortly after he was invalided back to England in 1941. She described how Roald "got in with a lot of funny people" that winter, largely through Alfred Chenhalls and the gun-making Purdey brothers. She recounted a convoluted tale about an Englishman and his half-German, half-Japanese wife whom Roald met on the boat back from Egypt in 1941. In London, Alf and her sister Else fell in with the couple's social circle, but began to suspect that they might be spies for the Vichy French. Alf shared her suspicions with Roald, who promptly had them reported to the authorities. Subsequently, she believed her brother had been "followed and watched" by Secret Servicemen before he was eventually sent for training somewhere on the outskirts of London.[9] Dahl himself, however, never corroborated this story and the official records suggest that he had little contact with the intelligence world until some months after he arrived in Washington. Still, two pieces of circumstantial evidence suggest that his sister's memories may not have been as entirely fanciful as they might at first appear.

In early 1942, Sofie Magdalene and Roald had moved from Ludgershall to nearby Grendon Underwood. It was an important change of location. Station 53a of SOE was based nearby in the grounds of the local big house: Grendon Hall.‡ The station was home to over four hundred sig-

---

‡Grendon Hall and its outbuildings still remain, currently in use as a prison.

nals experts and coders, mostly receiving messages from overseas agents. It was also a training camp for secret agents in France and Norway. Alfhild remembered hearing two trainees speaking Norwegian on the local bus and recalled their shock when she started speaking back to them in their native language. After this incident, she claimed, the entire Dahl family was thoroughly vetted by "Secret Service types".[10] One piece of material evidence also survives that suggests a link between Dahl and Stephenson which predates his arrival in the United States. A memo to Intrepid from a certain "VW" dated February 10, 1942 – some six weeks before Dahl arrived in Washington – has survived among the papers of Stephenson's first biographer, H. Montgomery Hyde. This memo argues the need for the immediate appointment of a "tough and invigorating personality" to the British press team in the US capital: a man who would contrast with the atmosphere of "almost hermit-like seclusion" currently found there.[11] Its author – almost certainly another BSC maverick, the crime writer Valentine Williams, who had arrived in the United States in 1941 to advise Stephenson on "all matters of propaganda" – added that this person should not be one "of the governing class", but "more or less a man of the people".[12]

If this memo was circulated to Harold Balfour, as it might well have been, it is quite plausible that when, a few days later, Balfour found himself at Pratt's sitting next to a tall, straight-talking and abrasively iconoclastic former pilot, he realized that in Roald Dahl he had found exactly the "man of the people" Williams was seeking. If so, right from the outset of his time in Washington, Dahl was loosely one of the BSC team – something that he himself perhaps unintentionally corroborated when he told Canadian television in 1974 that he had been working for Stephenson in Washington for a full year before he first met him.[13]

Whether Dahl arrived in Washington already attached to the intelligence community or simply as a minor embassy official, his task as air attaché would still largely have been the same: to present the RAF to US public opinion in the most favourable possible light. It was not an easy task, for the anti-British lobby was a powerful and diverse grouping. Significant figures included not only pro-Fascists like the former aviator

Charles Lindbergh, and a motley collection of antiwar liberals, but Republican senators such as Gerald Nye, who believed that President Roosevelt himself had connived with the British to allow the US Fleet to be bombed at Pearl Harbor.§ Rex Benson, a senior adviser of Lord Halifax, was shocked to discover that, even in 1942, anti-British sentiment was still the norm at US officer training schools.[14]

Vice President Wallace too shared many of these views, as did Roosevelt himself. But the pro-Communist, Russian-speaking Wallace was much more frank and open about airing anti-imperial opinions than was his more secretive and unpredictable boss. Thus he became an object of profound suspicion for the British – particularly given the frequent scares about the president's own health. Halifax described the prospect that the eccentric Iowan agronomist might overnight become the occupant of the Oval Office as "horrid",[15] while Stephenson was well aware that a lot of BSC's freedom of manoeuvre came from its close relationship with Roosevelt. For him too, a radical in the White House would be a disaster. Both men were consequently delighted to discover that they had a tailor-made mole to hand in the person of their rambunctious new assistant air attaché. Not only did Roald Dahl play tennis and talk politics with the vice president – often until late into the night – he was even distantly related to him through his Norwegian Wallace ancestry. Thus, even if Stephenson had played no part in his initial appointment to Washington, Dahl's unexpected friendship with the vice president made it well nigh impossible for him to avoid being drawn into the secretive Canadian's undercover games.

One of Wallace's closest associates was another buccaneer: Charles Marsh, a self-made newspaper magnate, who had been born in Cincin-

§Curiously, Dahl himself once suggested that he too believed Roosevelt might have known about the planned attack on Pearl Harbor before it occurred. He recalled Stephenson's claim that BSC had bugged the hotel room of Saburo Kurusu, a Japanese diplomat who came to Washington in November 1941, and that the exact date of the Pearl Harbor attack had been mentioned in these taped conversations. Transcripts of the recording were apparently forwarded to Roosevelt, who chose to do nothing about it. When asked whether he believed Stephenson's account, Dahl replied, "I have no way to judge, except Bill didn't usually tell stories like that." He also added that "FDR was a very sensible man and I knew him well. I mean there was no way he'd let the Pacific Fleet be destroyed if he could avoid it. The whole thing doesn't make sense." – Macdonald, *The True Intrepid*, p. 239.

nati, Ohio, in 1887. Beginning as a rookie reporter in Muskogee, Oklahoma, in 1909, Marsh built up a press empire that stretched from Fargo in North Dakota to Massachusetts in the East and Florida in the South. At its zenith, there was hardly a state of the union in which his companies, General Newspapers and Newspapers Inc., did not have an interest, but the focus of his business empire was Texas. A passionate Democrat, whose own desire for the public stage had been thwarted by his brash personality and erratic personal life, Marsh had become content with the role of éminence grise and kingmaker. Yet he was far from self-effacing. He was tall, broad-shouldered and oafishly opinionated: a "smooth talker", as one former business partner described him,[16] who "walked like a bear",[17] and whose restless blue eyes and strong bald dome of a head reminded Lady Bird Johnson of a Roman emperor.[18] He was loud, irreverent, egotistical and coarse: an "idealist",[19] in Dahl's eyes, who played a mean hand of poker, struck a good business deal, entertained lavishly and possessed a well-developed sense of the absurd. He also had a keen eye for talent, a kind heart, and the resources to support his hunches. Marsh was one of the first to back Lyndon Johnson's political career, and even though Johnson would go on to cuckold his mentor, a mutual friend would later write that Charles continued to love Lyndon "like a son".[20] Marsh was similarly drawn to the irreverent young British air attaché and, almost in no time at all, Roald Dahl became another of his surrogate sons.

Initially, Marsh's interest was professional. His strong pro-interventionist views gave him good reason to cultivate Dahl and, as Roald himself later recalled, it was politics that first brought them together:

> *Charles Marsh was a Texan newspaper proprietor. He bought and sold newspapers as though they were cigarette cards. He was a fervent FDR Democrat and although the party valued his ideas and advice, they all kept their distance because somehow or other he frightened them. All, that is, except Henry Wallace, who used to visit Marsh's house in Washington almost every evening when Wallace was Vice-President. Marsh was not all that sympathetic to Wallace's left-wing ideas, but he used him as a channel into the White House.*[21]

Marsh longed to enter the president's inner circle, but Roosevelt regarded him as too much of a wild card and kept him distant. Indeed,
Dahl once bluntly told his friend that "the Great White Indian Chief" –
as he nicknamed Roosevelt – thought of him merely as "a man who owns
a few newspapers".[22] Consequently, Marsh was forced to rely on others –
Dahl among them – to let him know how Roosevelt's mind was working.

Despite the fact that Marsh was almost thirty years older than Dahl,
their rapport was easy and instantaneous. As Marsh's daughter Antoinette
Haskell remembers, Roald very quickly became "family".[23] She sensed
that at first her father had felt sorry for the young airman, who seemed
to have so few British friends, but sympathy soon grew into a profound
appreciation for those qualities that set Dahl apart from his embassy
colleagues: his imagination, his reflectiveness, his creativity and his madcap sense of humour. Antoinette also felt that Roald was looking for a
strong male role model and that her father fit the bill perfectly. It was a
remarkable friendship. Roald quickly became her father's "favourite court
jester"[24] and soon the two of them were "as close as father and son", while
Antoinette herself quickly came to view the lanky Norwegian ex-pilot
almost as a brother.[25] Forty years later, Dahl would touchingly describe
Marsh as his "best friend in the world".[26]

With Marsh, Dahl could joke and indulge his imaginative flights
of fancy. He did not need to mince his words and be diplomatic. They
were "braggarts together", as Antoinette described it, "iconoclasts" and
"fantasists", who played practical jokes that were "elaborate" but also
"sometimes cruel".[27] Under the names of Roald Gordon and Mr C. Bell
Ball, for example, they wrote a series of long-winded letters to a preposterous Californian mystic called Dr Edmund J. Dingle, who dubbed
himself "Preceptor Emeritus of the Institute of Mental Physics". Apparently treating his philosophy with the utmost seriousness, the two men
pushed to the limits of absurdity Dr Dingle's professed belief that his
patented breathing techniques, learned in the high mountains of Tibet,
could prolong human life by up to forty years. But Lord Halifax was
the most frequent target of their jests. For two years Roald sent fictitious
letters to Marsh's home which he addressed to his friend's nonexistent

brother, Stanley. Each was written on embassy notepaper, apparently signed by the ambassador and elaborately sealed with the official red wax. In these, the straitlaced Viscount Halifax, whom Churchill had dubbed "The Holy Fox", voiced his concerns about Marsh's subversive political opinions and confided that he had engaged various agents to gather intelligence on him, including the master of disguise Hermann Horstwessel, the inscrutable Hiruto Hirototo Hiroto, Martin "The Blimp" Levy, and a "negro servant of immense intelligence and knowledge who is known as Mr Clinton, but whose real name is Ambrose Chickenlooper". Special Agent Chickenlooper was charged with investigation of Marsh's relationship with the radical Vice President Schweinhogger. "You will understand how important I consider his information to be," Dahl wrote, parodying Halifax's snobbery, "when I tell you that in spite of the colour of his skin and in spite of the fact that he is neither of the peerage nor descended from a royal house, I still receive him in the privacy of my study." [28]

The tone of this correspondence was enthusiastically disrespectful throughout and filled with scurrilous and lewd gossip about almost everyone in their social circle – whether friend or foe. In some letters, Halifax enthusiastically catalogued his imaginary sexual conquests, and in others Marsh mocked his own secretary and future wife Claudia Haines, describing her as a "martinet" and a cruel, decisive woman.[29] Claudia, of course, was in on the joke too. She typed all Charles's letters. It was innocent, absurd banter: two men letting off steam to each other. But for Roald there was an element of danger in these games. Had he been discovered, he would probably have lost his job. That sense of risk seems to have been part of what made the friendship with Marsh so powerful. "They were lethal together," Antoinette explained. "They were dangerous."[30] One day, Roald took his mentor to visit the British Embassy. "First he tried to shake hands with the messenger at the door, who refused, because he thought he was crazy. Then he poked his head into all the rooms along the corridor and generally had a lot of fun," Roald told a friend. "I wouldn't like to have him around in the Embassy for more than half an hour on end," he concluded. "There would be a riot." [31] With his colourful sense of the absurd and his taste for debunking pomposity,

Marsh was surely a model (if one were needed) for the "geriatric child" Dahl himself would later become.

Marsh also left his mark on Dahl as a philanthropist. In 1947, he would sell many of his newspaper titles and found the Public Welfare Foundation, a nonprofit organization dedicated to improving how people live that remains one of the most active organizations of its kind in America. Marsh espoused the virtue of being an anonymous giver and often boasted that he intended to die broke, having given all of his money away. But while his charitable giving could be comprehensive and global, it often had a very human face. At the Salzburg Festival of 1937, he had befriended a young Austrian pianist and composer called Erich Leinsdorf. The following year Leinsdorf was conducting at the Metropolitan Opera in New York, when Marsh discovered his application to renew his visa had been refused. It seemed Leinsdorf, a Jew, would have to return to a country that had just enthusiastically embraced Nazism. Marsh helped him out, prevailing upon his friend, the Texas congressman Lyndon Johnson to pull strings on Leinsdorf's behalf and enable his visa to be extended. Leinsdorf would go on to become a naturalized American and one of the most significant conductors of his day. It was a typical act of kindness in a man who believed strongly in spreading his money around and using it for the good of others.

Marsh also possessed a sense of the fuzzy dividing line between fantasy and reality that in some respects went beyond Dahl's. Never was this more clearly demonstrated than in the late 1930s, when he embarked on an affair with Alice Glass, a twenty-year-old girl from a small town in Texas, and decided to divorce his first wife, Leona. According to his friend Ralph Ingersoll, he first of all stymied his furious wife's plans to prosecute him under the Mann Act by walking into her lawyer's office and announcing that he would not deny his offences. However, he added, he would also publicly tell the court that the reason he was leaving his wife was because he could not "get a hard on" when in bed with her.[32] During the proceedings, Alice got pregnant. Determined that she should keep the child, Charles devised an ingenious plan to ensure the baby was regarded as legitimate. A few weeks later, as soon as she was of age, Alice was dispatched to England "on holiday", where she wrote to her parents that she had fallen in love with an English soldier by the name of Major Manners and married him at once, because his regiment was soon to be posted to India. Manners even gallantly journeyed all the way from the Himalayas to South Texas to present himself in person to his bride's family and friends.

A few weeks later, her parents received another letter. It contained both good news and bad. The good news was that their daughter was pregnant. The bad news was that her husband was dead. He had, she claimed, been killed by bandits in a border skirmish. Eighteen months later, ostensibly as a widow, and with a small child in tow, she returned to America, where she was swept off her feet by the newly divorced Marsh, who promptly married her and adopted Alice's child, Diana, as his own. The whole episode was in fact an elaborate charade: a fabrication scripted and directed by Marsh in order to make sure that his own child would appear legitimate to the rest of the world. "Major Manners" was a male model. Marsh had spotted him in a clothing advertisement and subsequently hired him to play the role he required.[33]

By the time Dahl met him in 1943, Marsh had been married to Alice for two years and that marriage too was failing. Now in his late fifties, Marsh had begun to sell some of his newspaper titles so that he could spend more time dabbling in philosophy, politics and philanthropy. He held court both in Washington and at Longlea, his rambling brick mock Tudor mansion near Culpeper, in the foothills of the Blue Ridge Mountains in West Virginia, some 60 miles from Washington. Perched on a small hill high above the Hazel River, Longlea had a luxurious freshwater swimming pool, a superb wine cellar and was staffed with a gourmet cook. Dahl described it to his mother as "the most lovely house I've ever seen".[34] Creekmore Fath, a young Texas lawyer and another White House insider who became a protégé of Marsh's, remembered it as "one of the best restaurants in town", a place where everybody came to gossip.[35] However, Marsh's daughter Diana recalled that it was not "a Noël Coward sort of a place". The guests were "mostly Texas friends and cronies, not the smart set".[36] Roald loved it there, "doing tricks and playing crazy practical jokes",[37] although he was equally happy in Marsh's Washington home at the foot of Embassy Row, which Antoinette Haskell recalled as absolutely "jumping with newspapermen and politicians . . . all very glamorous and hush-hush".[38] Stretched out on the sofa there in his RAF uniform, Roald would trade stories with his host and with Henry Wallace, burning the midnight oil and bringing what Ralph Ingersoll described as a "cocky British grace"[39] to their conversation. "You could sit at Charles's house and hear more of what was going on than you'd hear practically any other place in town," reminisced Fath. "I'm afraid we weren't brought up properly as to how to keep secrets."[40] Dahl himself was more realistic about the nature of what was discussed. "Marsh loved it because he got a bit of gossip and he felt closer to FDR," he recollected. "Of course he never got close to FDR. He got very close to Wallace."[41]

It was after one of these conversations with Wallace that Marsh handed Dahl a sheaf of papers to read. Entitled *Our Job in the Pacific*, it was a discussion document on postwar American foreign policy, which Wallace had drafted and which he had left behind for Marsh's comments. To Marsh it all seemed pretty innocuous, but as Dahl scanned the pages of this plan to "emancipate" large parts of the British Empire and thereby ensure an American monopoly of civil aviation, he realized he was looking at information that not only made his own hair "stand on end"[42] but would doubtless do the same to Bill Stephenson's.

Wallace had left the typescript with Marsh. Marsh in his political naivety handed it to me that evening for comments. I saw immediately its importance from the British point of view and excused myself saying that I was going downstairs to read it. I quickly phoned the only contact I knew in BSC and told him to meet me on the road outside Marsh's house fast. I handed the pamphlet through the car window and told him he must be back with it in fifteen minutes. The man buzzed off to the BSC Washington offices and duly returned the pamphlet to me on the dot. I returned it to Marsh without comment.[43]

Dahl, as Wallace himself noted, was "very much excited"[44] by what he had read. He had already been keeping "pretty careful tabs" on Wallace's "communistic leanings", reporting them back to BSC as and when he saw fit.[45] But the pamphlet had little to do with Wallace's socialism. It merely revealed a truth that was obvious to American analysts, but which the British found much harder to swallow: namely, that it was in the US national interest to encourage "an orderly process of transition" among the Asian countries from "colonial subject" states to ones that were free and independent.[46] Dahl, however, saw it in more melodramatic terms. For him it was evidence of treachery: of one ally plotting, as it were, to do down the other after the war was over. And he was not alone in this perception. His timely action in copying the report brought him not only into direct written communication with William Stephenson for the first time, but also to the attention of Churchill himself, who received a copy of the report and was apparently stirred "to cataclysms of wrath" by what he read.[47]¶

When *Our Job in the Pacific* was eventually published in 1944, there was an official complaint from Lord Halifax to Secretary of State Cordell Hull about Wallace's "regrettable" statements. Hull, who had little time for Wallace and his utopian pronouncements, reportedly dismissed the pamphlet as "bunk" or "junk".[48] Dahl, however, told Marsh indignantly that the situation was "very serious" and that he thought it likely Churchill would "ask the President to get a new Vice President". Marsh, not surprisingly, thought his friend was overreacting. "Don't be a child. Grow up," he told Roald. "Don't you know that the most certain way to be sure Wallace will continue to be vice-president is for the word to get around that Churchill is against him?"[49] Wallace's position was nevertheless becoming increasingly precarious. Despite his power base among blue-collar workers and the unions, his political influence was in decline. A year earlier, in July 1943, Roald had told his mother about another

---

¶Though there's no evidence that this was not another of Dahl's exaggerations, it would have been in keeping with Churchill's character. Churchill was certainly aware of Dahl personally. Dahl for his part kept a note, handwritten on House of Commons notepaper, from the former prime minister in 1949. It read: "Your greetings have given me much pleasure. Thank you so much. Winston S. Churchill" – RDMSC 16/1/2.

"rumpus" between Wallace and the president: "Wallace has temporarily lost his prestige, but I think he is on the way up the ladder – not down it, as so many people seem to think."[50] He was wrong. In both disputes between Wallace and other senior figures in the administration – with Cordell Hull in 1942 and Secretary of Commerce Jesse Jones in 1943 – Roosevelt sided against his vice president. Isaiah Berlin read the runes correctly when, in September 1943, he described Wallace as a "distinct political embarrassment to the President".[51]

Wallace himself remained unswervingly loyal to Roosevelt, but he had become an easy target for William Stephenson, who – largely thanks to Dahl's intervention – was now confirmed in his view that the vice president was a "menace",[52] and redoubled his efforts to persuade Roosevelt to drop him from his reelection ticket. His efforts were rewarded when, in the spring of 1944, Roosevelt sent Wallace on a fifty-one-day tour of Russia and China and, in his absence, dumped him from the ticket. In making this decision, the president was probably much more influenced by Wallace's enemies within the Democratic Party than he was by the wiles of Bill Stephenson. The leaking of *Our Job in the Pacific* probably made little or no difference to his decision. Yet, as Wallace's diaries record, Dahl remained close to him throughout these plots, playing tennis with him when his health allowed it, and discussing politics, music and art. It must have been difficult for Dahl, who had admitted neither to Marsh nor Wallace that he had connections with BSC. Though he disagreed with him on many issues, he still admired Wallace's idealism, yet he knew his own actions were helping covertly to undermine him. In a clash of loyalties between his friends and his country, he had sided with the latter. As a reward, Dahl was "seconded into the periphery of BSC",[53] and shortly afterwards promoted to squadron leader.

In the summer of 1943, Dahl was more concerned by what he saw as the failure of British officials to protect the United Kingdom's interests in a postwar aviation settlement than he was by Wallace's political judgements. The politics of aviation itself held little interest for him. That summer he had reluctantly agreed to speak at the Convention of the Aviation Writers Association of America, and while he admitted that some of the delegates were "congenial", he found many others "cantankerous", and told his mother that he wished "they'd go and stuff themselves, each one separately and individually".[54] However, the fact that the British seemed to be acquiescing unnecessarily in the establishment of a US hegemony in civil aviation annoyed him intensely. In a piece called *Post War Air Lines*, which he kept in his papers, he imagined a postwar scenario where a single American carrier became the "largest and most important airline" on the planet. He even invented an acronym for it, "LAMPA", developing a hypothesis where this company eventually gained complete control of the commercial airways of the globe. Thus, he concluded, LAMPA's president and directors would find themselves "controlling . . . the destinies of the world".[55] The paper was alarmist. It was also overtly critical of current British policy. And it irritated his superiors hugely.

The top brass in the Air Ministry had little room for manoeuvre. In an agreement concluded shortly after the United States entered the war, America had guaranteed to supply all UK air transport requirements in return for an undertaking from the British government not to build any new cargo planes until Hitler was defeated.[56] At that point it had seemed like a good idea – Britain was desperate for bombers and fighters. A year later, British air strategists were starting to look on the agreement with more jaundiced eyes. By then it was becoming clear that the United Kingdom was at the forefront of a development that would revolutionize civil aviation: the jet engine. Yet the agreement put a stranglehold on the United Kingdom's ability to exploit this advantage and gave the Americans time to close the technological gap. The British lobbied hard to persuade Roosevelt to loosen its terms, but Assistant Secretary of State Adolf Berle, who coordinated aviation planning, refused to let his transatlantic allies off the hook. As production of American transport aircraft soared, Dahl was aware that the American public were being bombarded with images of a future dominated by easy commercial air travel. Murals and installations such as *Airways to Peace* in New York's Museum of Modern Art demonstrated how, under the hegemony of a benign US carrier, the planet would be transformed into a single global community. It all appeared to confirm his fears that LAMPA was fast becoming a reality.[57]

Dahl was probably unaware how tightly his superiors' hands were tied. If so, their lack of response must have added to his frustrations. Moreover, these anxieties were exacerbated by personal ones of his own when, in 1943, he was unexpectedly thrown out of his home because its owners returned to Washington and summarily terminated his lease. Accommodation was in short supply and he struggled to find anywhere suitable as a replacement. Eventually he heard of an apartment that had just become vacant. A jealous lover had shot his girlfriend there, before turning the gun on himself and committing suicide. Both parties had worked for the combined British and American intelligence network, the Office of Strategic Services. The story fascinated Washington gossips, one of whom observed that, the day after the murder, Dahl was the first person in line to see if the dead girl's apartment might now be available for rent.[58]

"One can't be fussy here," Roald told his mother phlegmatically. "I signed the lease and took the house without ever having seen it."[59] However, within days, his superstitious nature began to play tricks on him. He told the Washington socialite Mary-Louise Patten that he had visited the house at twilight and seen ghosts there, confessing that, as a creative writer and someone who got up at six every morning "to think over the problems of the post-war world", he would find that hard to live with.[60] He gave his mother a lurid description of the apartment: "The last time I went to look at it," he told her, "there was still quite a bit of blood and stuff about, plus bullet holes in the ceiling, and what with one thing and another I thought I'd rather not spend my evenings alone there!"[61] Eventually he sublet the property to the pragmatic Isaiah Berlin, whose only reaction was to ask where he might find "a good cheap plasterer" and "an inexpensive rug of some darkish colour!"[62]

Roald eventually chose alternative accommodation with another colleague at the embassy, but he found it almost impossible to write with anyone else in the house. His problems were mounting. He was suffering severe back pains and struggling with a movie script about the "Dam Busters" mission for the director Howard Hawks.** On the positive

---

** Dahl's version was never made. Another movie, based on Gibson's book, was released in 1955.

side he did get to spend time with the raid's commander, Guy Gibson, and threw a cocktail party for him, to which he invited "all the pretty girls I could think of in town, just so he could take his pick".[63] But this was a rare diversion from the dislocation he felt from his work at the embassy. There he saw himself as an increasingly lone and strident dissenting voice: a muscular patriot, surrounded by opportunists and lazy, self-serving pen-pushers. He was critical of almost everyone around him, complaining to William Teeling, for example, that though the RAF was "on the crest of a wave", the US War Department always seemed to be able to get stories out to the press quicker than the British. Begging for photographs of bomb damage inflicted by the RAF on Germany, he concluded urgently that "to a country which is used to being humbugged by its press, and who knows that it is being humbugged by its press, only seeing is believing".[64]

In that summer of 1943, Dahl received a rare invitation to Hyde Park, the president's country retreat up the Hudson, to spend a weekend with the Roosevelts. Other guests included the Norwegian crown prince Harald and his sisters, and Secretary to the Treasury Henry Morgenthau. Roald made light of the visit, telling his family that he would make sure to tell them whether the president "blows his nose in his fingers . . . eats with his mouth open . . . or laughs at my dirty jokes".[65] However, his closely typed ten-page report on what he found there made fascinating reading for analysts at the embassy, eager to get a private glimpse of how the president's mind was working. His essay teems with details about his experiences there: the small baths in the guest rooms, the sulphurous smell that permeated the water supply, or the eccentric behaviour of the Roosevelts' Aberdeen terrier Fala. An eye for the comic is much in evidence. Examples of Roosevelt "regaling his guests with rather crude stories about dead men"[66] are juxtaposed with a description of the president trying to outrun his bodyguards in his invalid car.

Dahl's charm was powerfully at work in this environment. He knowingly cast himself in the role of entertainer, reflecting later that he had behaved like a "clown".[67] Yet that clowning allowed him a glimpse of the elusive Roosevelt, relaxed and off his guard. This anecdote is typical:

Mrs Roosevelt said, "Well, Franklin used always to walk in his sleep when he was younger. Once, during the time when we used to own an old Ford in the early days of motoring, I wakened up and found him standing at the end of his bed turning an imaginary cranking wheel as hard as he could and saying, 'The damn thing won't start.'" "I said,"
she went on, "Franklin, if you get into the car, I will help you start it. Whereupon he got back into bed and held an imaginary steering wheel, whilst I had to go out in front and pretend to do the cranking. Finally he went back to sleep. In the morning he remembered nothing about it." [68]

Sometimes the conversation became a little more serious, but even then Dahl's observation of peculiar detail is richly manifest. Discussing his pet subject, aviation policy, with Roosevelt and Secretary Morgenthau, Dahl could not help noticing that the latter's trousers "were half unbuttoned".[69] Under the mask of joker, Dahl was also able to ask innocent and uninhibited questions of senior politicians that would have been impossible for the embassy grandees. He spoke directly to the president, for example, about the possibility of his standing for a fourth term of office and Roosevelt told him straight that, if he was to do so, he seriously doubted his chances of winning. FDR must of course have been well aware that his comments would be reported back to British strategists and probably to Churchill himself. So he must have particularly enjoyed telling his house guest how ungrateful he felt Winston had been when he himself defied US public opinion in 1940 and put his neck on the line to conclude the Lend-Lease agreement, without which Britain would probably have been unable to continue fighting the war.†† In this context, FDR was also remarkably unguarded about how he viewed the racial divide that still defined much of America:

The talk drifted around to Winston Churchill again and he said,

††In the deal, various British military bases were leased to the United States in exchange for fifty aging American warships that were essential to the British war effort. According to Dahl, Stephenson himself took a lot of credit for negotiating this deal personally with Roosevelt, maintaining it was "his greatest achievement". Dahl was sceptical, admitting that he "always doubted" whether Stephenson actually met FDR. For the avoidance of doubt he added: "I did" – Macdonald, *The True Intrepid*, p. 248.

*"You know, I was talking to Winston immediately after we had con-
cluded the destroyers-bases deal, when you leased us certain bases in
Newfoundland, Trinidad, British Guiana etc. and Winston said,
'Now how in the heck am I going to explain all this to the British
people? They will say the Americans are taking our territory.' I said,
'Listen Winston, those places are nothing but a headache to you, you
know that. Together they cost the British Treasury five million pounds,
twenty-five million dollars, a year. They are nothing but a headache.
Do you think I want to have your headaches? Because I don't. You can
keep them; furthermore, these places are inhabited by some eight million dark-skinned gentlemen and I don't want them coming to this
country and adding to the problem which we already have with our
thirteen million black men. I tell you Winston, it is just a headache
and you can keep it.'"* [70]

Charles Marsh was mesmerized when Roald sent him a copy of his
report. A few days later – in early August 1943 – Roald wrote again,
advising Charles how he might best get the president's ear. For once the
letter is almost entirely without frivolity and reveals what Roald himself
most valued in his friend's personality. It celebrates Marsh's warmth, generosity, imagination and independence. Encouraging him to forget his
relationship with Wallace and to "work on [his] own", Roald told Marsh
that the president was unused to dealing with "sincere men without personal ambition who ask for nothing in return for what they offer", and
exhorted him to trust in "the force of [his] own personality". Interestingly for one who would later praise the virtues of exaggeration, he tells
Marsh to speak to the president using colours that are not "too bright
and vivid. Paint your picture fast and good," he suggests, "but paint it
gentle, as I know you can . . . Don't go on fiddling with your subject,
just stop talking and see what he has to say." [71] In the end, this counsel
did not do any good. Roosevelt still kept his distance from the eccentric
press baron. But Marsh was full of admiration for the advice he had been
given. "Considering your age," he told Roald, "your wisdom passeth all
understanding." [72]

Shortly after Dahl wrote his piece about Hyde Park, his Whitehall ally, William Teeling, wrote to congratulate him on being promoted to squadron leader. "You should have been one ages ago and from all I hear there is more work done in your office than anywhere else,"[73] he enthused. But Teeling, who was shortly to be elected a Conservative MP for Brighton, was a lone voice in praise of Dahl's activities. Most of the Air Ministry peacocks were convinced that the air attaché needed to be taken down a peg or two. And no one felt this more than Air Marshal William Welsh, who, early in 1943, had been sent from London to Washington as head of the RAF delegation. His animosity to Dahl seems to have been as profound as it was instantaneous. Almost at once, he attempted to bring him to heel, criticizing his "irregular" outside activities and telling Halifax that his young official needed some serious "military discipline". He recommended that Dahl be transferred away from Washington altogether.[74] It is possible Welsh had a personal motive for this hostility. He was nearing the end of his military career and seeking to make contacts with potential future employers in the world of civil aviation in the United States. He cannot have viewed Dahl's continual outspokenness about the postwar situation as particularly helpful to his chances of securing a good appointment.‡‡ On July 14, Roald's "cautious"[75] admirer, J. B. Hogan, thanked him for his useful notes on the weekend at Hyde Park, as it had given him an opportunity "to throw a balanced opinion on your behalf" when faced with criticisms "such as from a quarter you can guess".[76] But Hogan's good opinion was not enough. Welsh eventually prevailed upon the ambassador: at the end of October 1943, Dahl was, in his own words, "kicked out of the Embassy" and recalled to London.[77]

What happened exactly is unclear. Dahl later claimed that the RAF had "sacked" him, but that Bill Stephenson "had me back again in Washington within a week, promoted to Wing Commander".[78] This was an exaggeration. From the papers in his own archive, it seems he left Washington shortly after October 27 and returned on November 21. Ten days

---

‡‡William Welsh (1891–1962) was to resign his commission and join BOAC, the British commercial airline, at the end of 1944. He settled in the United States and married the widow of a US senator. Eventually he became the North American representative for the Society of Motor Manufacturers and Traders.

or so before he departed for London, however, it seems his position was still uncertain. He told his mother that he was looking for a new appointment and hinted that he might already have been approached to work directly with BSC. "I was offered a Staff College Course the other day," he wrote, "but I said I would rather not, because I may be given a more interesting (from my point of view) job, about which I'm afraid I can tell you nothing."[79] When he returned to Washington, little seemed to have changed. It appears he was in a kind of limbo – neither employed formally by the RAF nor by BSC. In December, his ally Hogan wrote to the man he had once affectionately called his "Mr Gremlin",[80] wishing Dahl a Happy New Year, "especially if you leave our sphere of activity for other climes", and adding darkly: "We were right in our surmise that your criticism of the Civil Aviation Appreciation did not altogether find favour in some quarters."[81] Dahl thanked Hogan for his confidential note, adding: "it is a great help to me personally to receive information such as this".[82]

Roald was now well aware that his outspokenness could win him enemies as well as friends. Despite his attempts to do the right thing for his country, his lack of reserve, the passionate zeal with which he held his views, and his inability to keep a low profile and be a team player had proved an Achilles heel. He was, he later admitted, "a tactless sort of fellow and that's the one thing a diplomat mustn't be".[83] It was a problem that seemed to affect him more with the English than with any other nationality. Canadians, in the persons of Stephenson and Max Aitken, now Lord Beaverbrook, for example, responded much more positively to his straight talking and his ability to think for himself. So did Americans like Henry Wallace and Charles Marsh. This lack of connection with the nation whose respect he most craved must have puzzled and perhaps pained him. In a letter written to his agent Ann Watkins's husband, Roger Burlingame, Dahl reflected on this English "indifference to everything" and explored the idea that this was perhaps what made British pilots different from American ones. Their detachment seemed intense because it was brought on by sudden exposure to the reality of violent death. British indifference, he concluded, was quite different. "It is not intense at all because it is always there."[84]

Dahl himself was seldom indifferent. In the early weeks of 1944, even as his destiny hung in the balance, he remained unrepentantly blunt and unguarded in his attitude toward his superiors. He later claimed he was finally "booted out by the big boys" because he had uncovered a "crooked racket" going on with Sir Richard Fairey, the boss of the British private aircraft manufacturer Fairey Aviation, who was being given illicit permission to run a special airplane across the Atlantic for his own personal use.[85] He may well have even hinted that Air Marshal Welsh, who later that year resigned his commission and joined the British commercial airline, BOAC, was turning a blind eye to this corruption.

Dahl was probably working loosely for BSC during the first four months of 1944, but the formal change of his role did not happen until April, when he was replaced as assistant air attaché, and left Washington "on completion of his tour of duty".[86] He flew back for two months to London, at Beaverbrook and Stephenson's request, "to report personally to [them] on the political situation in America".[87] While in London, Dahl also acted as minder for Ernest Hemingway, prior to his departure as a war reporter on the D-Day invasion of Normandy. Dahl had met his hero in New York a few weeks earlier, sparring in a boxing ring with him, before the two men and the boxing coach, George Brown, joined Hemingway's wife Martha Gellhorn at the Gladstone Hotel, where Dahl recalled that they drank champagne and ate caviar from a 2-kilo tin. Subsequently, he had arranged Hemingway's passage over from the United States by contriving to get him hired as a correspondent for the RAF.[88] In London, however, some of Old Hem's lustre began to wear off as Dahl saw that the hard-drinking adventurer, this "strange and secret man" for whom he felt "overwhelming love and respect", was also unexpectedly vain. One day he walked into Hemingway's room at the Dorchester Hotel, to discover him meticulously dripping hair-restorer onto his thinning pate with an eyedropper. Dahl was made to wait while the great author laboriously massaged the tonic into his scalp.

In July, Dahl returned to America, where he was free at last from the petty constraints of the embassy and of RAF officialdom, and he revelled in the company of his buccaneering new colleagues, particularly Max

Beaverbrook, whom he would later describe as "the most dynamic man in the world", with "superhuman" intellectual powers.[89]

Although he was now an official employee of BSC, Dahl's official job title remained "Assistant Air Attaché". A note from Beaverbrook's office, addressed to "Wing Commander R. Dahl, c/o W. L. Stephenson Esq., New York City", thanking him for his advice and help on postwar air policy, which was still "in a state of turmoil", confirmed a rank that was never officially noted in his RAF records.[90]§§

On his return to Washington, Creekmore Fath noted that his friend seemed much more "carefree"[91] than before. And he certainly enjoyed the pleasure of getting back at his detractors.

> *I went to a party, and at the other end of the room was the Air Chief Marshal who'd kicked me out. He strode across and said, "What the hell are you doing here?" I said, "I'm afraid, sir, you'll have to ask Bill Stephenson." And he went even darker purple and walked away. It showed Stephenson's power. The Air Chief Marshal was struck absolutely dumb. Couldn't say a word. Couldn't do a thing about it.*

By that stage, he recalled, "I was working entirely for Bill Stephenson."[92]

Initially, he moved out of the embassy into separate BSC offices in downtown Washington at 1106 Connecticut Avenue NW. A few months later, he relocated to New York – to BSC headquarters in Rockefeller Center – where he probably met Stephenson in person for the first time. The building's fast-moving elevators fascinated him and prefigured the one he would create for Willy Wonka's chocolate factory twenty years later. "They go up and down faster than I have ever dived in an airplane," he told his mother. "Your ears pop and your stomach either comes out of your mouth or drops out of your arse according to whether you are going

---

§§The fact that this new rank, which was awarded at Stephenson's discretion, never appeared on his RAF file later prompted speculation that Dahl had invented it, but in this case his own version was absolutely accurate. "Wing Commander", "Flight Commander", or "Commander" appears on nearly all Dahl's official correspondence between the summer of 1944 and January 1946, when he finally left BSC. It would, in any event, have been quite out of character for him to fabricate something as unimaginative and prosaic as a mere rank.

up or down."[93] In Manhattan, Dahl fully got Stephenson's measure, admiring his quiet, behind-the-scenes exercise of authority, his decisiveness, his ability "to play around with businesses and scientific things",[94] and his striking mental acuity. He was indeed, as Dahl had imagined, "very, very secret" and "extremely private".[95] Yet this studiedly enigmatic exterior also belied something of the self-publicist. In later years Stephenson would boast of BSC as a "labyrinthine apparatus . . . the hub for all branches of British intelligence",[96] and encourage his biographers to paint him as a Machiavellian genius of espionage. The historian Hugh Trevor-Roper was more sceptical. He dismissed Stephenson as a self-serving mythmaker: a puerile grandee, whose assertions were little more than the "dangerous hallucinations" of an isolated old man heading toward second childhood.[97] This judgement was perhaps too harsh. But Dahl, whose respect for Stephenson never faltered and whose delight in hyperbole might have inclined him to echo his former boss's version of events, tended to concur with Trevor-Roper.[98] He certainly did not relish Stephenson's company, describing him later to Stephenson's most recent biographer, Bill Macdonald, as "a totally uncultivated man . . . not a pleasure to talk to . . . If you met him socially, he never had any conversation at all."[99] He gave him the same nickname he had given Isaiah Berlin: "The White Slug".[100]

Stephenson, for his part, understood Dahl's strengths and knew that office politics was not one of them. Instead, his intention was to deploy his new employee's potent ability to dazzle the salons of American high society. Roald, perhaps unaware of his own personal charisma, tended to be self-deprecating about this aspect of his own personality, preferring to think of himself rather as clown than charmer. "I was able to ask pointed questions and get equally pointed replies because, theoretically, I was a nobody," he recalled in connection with President Roosevelt.

> *For instance there might be some argument officially between London and Washington about future operations. I could ask FDR over lunch what he thought, and he could tell me, quite openly, far more than he could say in a formal way. Bleeding this information on the highest level from the Americans was not for nefarious purposes, but for the war ef-*

fort. That's why Bill planted fellows like us . . . I'd walk into FDR's little
side-room on a Sunday morning in Hyde Park and he'd be making mar-
tinis, as he always did. And I would say, "Good morning Mr President"
and we'd pass the time of day. He treated me as a friend of Eleanor. And
he'd say, naively, as if I were nobody much and he was making idle gos-
sip, "I had an interesting communication from Winston today . . ." [101]

Aside from hobnobbing with politicians, Dahl described his main
function with BSC as that of trying to "oil the wheels" [102] that often
ground imperfectly between the British and American war efforts. Much
of this involved dealing with journalists, something at which he was already skilled. His chief contact was the moustachioed political gossip columnist Drew Pearson, whose column, "Washington Merry-Go-Round",
was widely regarded as the most important of its kind in the United
States. Dahl boasted to his mother that it was syndicated to 430 newspapers and that Pearson himself was such an important figure that "no-one
dares open their mouth in his presence".[103] In the official history of BSC,
on which Dahl would later work as one of the anonymous writers, there
is a memorably sharp portrait of the opinionated and often ruthless news-
paperman. There can be little doubt as to who was its author.

Andrew Russell Pearson is a tall, tight-lipped individual, who looks
uncomfortably like a horse, a likeness which is increased by his habit of
snorting as he speaks. He has little sense of humour . . . He had a goat-
ish indifference to the feelings of others, and was quite unperturbed if
one of his disclosures cost a friend or acquaintance his job. [104]

Dahl "fed information" [105] to Pearson, and Pearson returned the compliment, often supplying him with confidential material from Roosevelt's
acerbic and bespectacled secretary for the interior, Harold L. Ickes. "I figure Pearson had something on Ickes," Dahl later recalled, adding that Stephenson "arranged to supply me with carefully chosen information that
I could feed to Pearson in exchange for a lot of high level cabinet stuff",
and that his own reports were forwarded by Stephenson directly to "C"

(Sir Stewart Menzies, chief of the British Secret Intelligence Services).[106] The information Dahl gleaned was varied and exotic, including a report that, as early as 1944, the Americans were planning to land a man on the moon,[107] but much of it was obtained in a self-consciously clandestine manner. Henry Wallace, in particular, had little but contempt for what he perceived as BSC's unnecessary furtiveness and skulduggery. "Why don't they [the British] proceed directly by coming in touch with our American agencies instead of spending all the effort to sell American opinion in an underhanded way?" he had reflected in his daily diary. After all, he added, wasn't this supposed to be a "united" war effort?[108]

The other wheels that Stephenson required lubricating were those that whirred in the salons of the Washington and New York hostesses who helped form public opinion. And if Dahl was something of a neophyte in the area of intelligence and propaganda, in this world of jewels and cocktail parties he was fast becoming a master. The war had created a shortage of eligible young men in both cities and the dashing twenty-seven-year-old RAF officer and author found himself constantly in demand as a guest. He was already a skilled flirt. Beatrice Gould, the co-editor of the *Ladies Home Journal*, who published many of his early stories, was a willing victim of Dahl's "manly beauty" and revelled in her slightly risqué correspondence with him.[109] So too, in their own way, did Ann Watkins and even Eleanor Roosevelt. All were of a type: wealthy, older, sophisticated and married. Roald had a "whole stable" of women to wait on him, recalled Charles Marsh's daughter, Antoinette Haskell, confessing that although her feelings toward Roald were always those of a sister, she had to acknowledge that her father's new protégé was nevertheless "drop dead gorgeous". "He was very arrogant with his women, but he got away with it," she recalled with a chuckle. "The uniform didn't hurt one bit – and he was an ace. I think he slept with everybody on the east and west coasts that had more than fifty thousand dollars a year."[110] His friend Creekmore Fath admiringly described Roald as "one of the biggest cocksmen in Washington".[111]

One of the more exotic salons Dahl frequented was that of Evalyn Walsh McLean, a "fabulous and rather tipsy dame", as he described her to his mother. Widowed and in her early fifties, she had inherited a fortune from her father, who had struck it lucky as a gold prospector in Colorado. She was vulgar, loud and wore large round dark-framed spectacles that made her look somewhat like a startled owl. She was also the proud owner of a gigantic bright blue gem, the Hope Diamond, which had a reputation for bringing misfortune on all who owned it, but inspired little fear in her. Roald described his visits to her house as "like going to the circus and getting a free meal served into the bargain".[112]

> *The woman herself is fantastic and rather stupid . . . She staggers down stairs at about 8.30 covered from head to foot in enormous diamonds and carrying under her arm a horrible little dog, "only six in the country," she says, which bites you whenever it gets a chance . . . I always giggle when I talk to her because standing way above her as I do, I can't help looking down and seeing the closely guarded secret of her finely shaped bosoms. She has enormous pads stuffed into her shirt front, and the effect is very good to anyone who is under 6'5" in height.*[113]

Once a staunch isolationist, McLean had switched sides and was now a devoted supporter of the war effort, but her salon was still full of anti-British types, including her best friend Cissie Patterson, who owned the *Washington Times-Herald*. Dahl's job was to keep his ear to the ground and push the British cause in whatever way seemed most effective. But the comic possibilities of the milieu around him constantly threatened to subvert his intentions. McLean herself flirted constantly with him, calling him, by turns, "dear boy" or "you bastard",[114] and providing a fund of anecdotes with which Roald could entertain his family back in England. A description of supper, with blunt golden cutlery, was typical. On that occasion, bending his knife "almost double" while attempting to cut a piece of steak, Roald shocked his fellow guests – all "dopes" in his eyes – by asking for a steel replacement, then trying surreptitiously to take the gold one home with him as a souvenir.[115]

McLean found Dahl attractive. She also liked his habit of stirring up

political and social controversy at the dinner table. One evening he got
into a heated argument with Frank Waldrup, the managing editor of the
Times-Herald, whom he publicly compared to Joseph Goebbels. Waldrup,
who was already in a bad mood because he had been bitten on the finger
by his hostess's "monkey-dog", took the bait, responding that he thought
the British were instinctively devious and that he did not care for all this
"Winnie and Franklin" stuff.[116] Dahl then upped the ante by likening
Waldrup to Hitler himself. A slanging match ensued that silenced almost
everyone at the table, including Vice President Wallace, who subsequently
chronicled the event in his journal.

It was one of the first examples of something for which Dahl would
become famous: dinner table arguments that escalated into full-blown
rows. In later years these outbursts could be destructive, but on this occasion, at least as far as Mrs McLean was concerned, Roald covered himself
in glory. Her dinner party had become an event. Excited by the controversy, she begged him to come back again the following week. Roald, for
his part, was delighted, departing in high spirits and offering to pluck the
priceless Hope Diamond off her breast and wear it "for good luck" until
he returned. The McLean salon was just the kind of place in which Dahl
thrived: an environment where his iconoclasm and his eagerness to shock
were celebrated. And immersing himself in that world was exactly what
his job with BSC demanded. As Roald once remarked of Evalyn Walsh
McLean: "she runs a good saloon [*sic*] . . . and there are lots of folks to see
and that's my business".[117]

Older women were playing a big part in Roald's life in other ways as
well. When in New York, he usually stayed as a guest at the apartment of
another prominent anglophile, Helen Rogers Reid, the sixty-year-old wife
of Ogden Mills Reid, owner of the *New York Tribune* and the *New York
Herald Tribune*. Dahl described her to his mother as a "charming little
grey haired woman",[118] but as far as Charles Marsh, whom she repeatedly snubbed, was concerned, Mrs Reid was "Horsewhip Helen".[119] She
wielded enormous power in the capital and regularly influenced editorials
in her newspapers. Marsh once described her as "the great female agent
of the British Empire in America".[120] And she was a big fan of Roald

Dahl's. Roald was staying at her apartment when he attended the New York premiere of *Eagle Squadron*, a propaganda movie, co-written by C. S. Forester, about US airmen who had volunteered to fight for the RAF before Pearl Harbor. His date for the evening was the actress Nancy Carroll, a thirty-nine-year-old divorcée, but at the party afterwards it was Congresswoman Clare Booth Luce, the wife of the owner of *Time* and *Life* magazines and a vituperative critic of Henry Wallace's, who caught Dahl's eye.

Mrs Luce, a reluctant anglophile, quickly succumbed to the allure of the glamorous young air attaché, thirteen years younger than she was, and Dahl did not return home that night. "I got home to the house of my host at 9 AM the next morning," he told his mother, "and failed to make my room without being seen to ruffle the bedclothes . . . I had to do a lot of talking to re-establish my reputation."[121] Later, Creekmore Fath claimed that the embassy encouraged the liaison in the hope that Dahl would convert Mrs Luce to a more pro-British position, particularly on Dahl's pet subject, postwar air freedom, which she had opposed in a recent speech in Congress.¶¶ Two months later, Dahl told his mother that he was "working very hard" on her. "I hope to be able to make her change her views a little, and say something better next time she speaks."[122] Eventually, this "assignment" may have proved too much for him. According to Fath (who seems to have lapped up these stories), Dahl told Halifax he was "all fucked out" because Luce "had screwed [him] from one end of the room to the other for three goddam nights". Halifax apparently told him it was his patriotic duty to return to her bed. Isaiah Berlin later dismissed this story as a "wild flight of fancy" that was typical of Dahl. He thought it "inconceivable" that Halifax would ever have talked like that.[123] Berlin was right. But he had missed the point. For Dahl its very improbability made the tale hilariously funny.

A host of wealthy, glamorous older women crossed Dahl's path. Most

---

¶¶Rex Benson summarized the embassy's attitude to Luce when he described her as "a clever hard-boiled ambitious young lady, backed by a wrong-thinking husband for whom success as a big newspaper man and money has been and probably is the main object of living. The less these two try to practise the art of statesmanship the better" – Benson diary, Feb. 8, 1943, cited in Cave Brown, *"C"*, p. 479.

made little impression. Barbara Hutton, whom the press had dubbed the "poor little rich girl", Roald dismissed, rather bitchily, as "quite pleasant, but not so beautiful as her jewellery".[124] Those involved in the arts were usually more to his taste. Aside from Nancy Carroll, Charles Marsh's daughter Antoinette recalled Roald having a brief affair with Leonora Corbett, an actress eight years his senior, and another with the writer Martha Gellhorn, also eight years older, when her marriage to Hemingway began to disintegrate. She found Roald "very, very attractive and slightly mad".[125]

Roald's most significant conquest of 1944 was the oil heiress Millicent Rogers. Rogers was forty-one when she met Dahl. She was quick-witted, well connected, and had something that he found truly irresistible – a great art collection. His description of his first weekend at her mansion in Virginia reads rather like an auctioneer's catalogue:

> I took first weekend for a long time at Easter. Went to the most marvellous and lovely house. Owner is Millicent Rogers, a sort of Standard Oil millionairess, and it was all very fine. It was an old colonial house in South Virginia, and from the back verandahs, long smooth lawns sloped down to the James River, which went on rolling along between gardens of cherry blossom and daffodils. Millicent had ten dachshunds, and a great dane and she had a lot of other things. In the small library (which was huge) there were
>
> a) Degas pastel 5' x 3. Very beautiful.
> b) another Degas pastel, a little smaller.
> c) A Gauguin 5' x 2'
> d) A head of Renoir by Degas
> e) Two Renoirs
> f) Two Corots
> g) One Monet
> h) One Manet

In the next room there were twelve Boucher and some Fragonard.
All very beautiful and carefully bought by M. I had an enormous bed
with gold hanging all around it, and a Norwegian maid to wait on
me. As I say, everything was very fine.[126]

Rogers was in many respects an ideal lover for Dahl. She was not
interested in marriage or fidelity. Indeed, she was probably having an
affair with his friend Ian Fleming at the same time as she was sleeping
with Roald. What she did value was style and good living. Apart from
her estate in Virginia, she had houses in Manhattan, Washington, and a
summer home she had inherited from her father in Southampton, Long
Island. Roald liked her real estate, but found her companions either
disagreeable or dull. "Women with ruby necklaces and sapphire necklaces, and God knows what else sauntered in and out and down below
amidst miles of corridors," he wrote about one weekend in Southampton.
"There were swimming baths, Turkish baths, colonic lavages, heat treatment rooms and everything else which is calculated to make the prematurely aging playboys and playwomen age a little less quickly. I didn't like
it much."[127]

Millicent was infatuated with Roald. She showered the handsome air
attaché with gifts, presenting him with a gold key to her front door as
well as an elaborate Verdura gold cigarette case and lighter. Her Schia-
parelli clothes and her penchant for dressing as Marie Antoinette held
little interest for Roald, who nicknamed her "Curvature", probably because her posture was slightly stooped as a result of childhood rheumatic
fever.[128] Her art collection, on the other hand, continued to be a source of
endless fascination to him. In the summer of 1944, while his own apartment was being repainted and she was in Long Island, she lent Roald
her Washington home. He could not prevent himself cataloguing its
art treasures – mostly more Impressionist, Post-Impressionist and Pre-
Raphaelite paintings, including, in his bedroom, "the finest and largest
Renoir of red roses that you've ever seen, also, a Pissarro, a Sisley and a
Burne-Jones".[129] He enjoyed her Steinway piano, too, and whiled away
the evenings trying to play Bach preludes on it.

None of these encounters seems to have involved him in any serious emotional commitment. They were more lighthearted diversions. But whereas it was said of Ian Fleming that he got off with girls because he could not get on with them, this was not true of Dahl, who truly delighted in female company. Yet, while he enjoyed being with sophisticated and glamorous women, Roald was not disposed to fall in love. In a revealing article for *Ladies' Home Journal* about the nature of desire, which he wrote in 1949, he tried to analyse what made relationships work, speculating that most were built 70 per cent on sexual attraction and only 30 per cent on mutual respect. Consequently, he argued, short-lived affairs, not marriage, formed the best "basis for such activity".[130] To some, this cold-blooded, rather reductive view of human relations was an unattractive aspect of his personality. His friend David Ogilvy, for example, observed that while he may have enjoyed putting notches on his bedpost, his partners were often hurt by his behaviour. "When they fell in love with him, as a lot did, I don't think he was nice to them,"[131] he commented.

One person saw through Dahl's rakish, confident exterior and won his lasting affection. She was the French actress Annabella. Rich, sophisticated and sexually experienced, superficially she might have seemed yet another trophy conquest. But Suzanne Charpentier, as she had been christened, was different. Born in the first decade of the twentieth century, she was the daughter of the man who had brought scouting to France, and she valued courage and loyalty quite as much as glamour. Not that she was any stranger to celebrity. She had been a teenage star, appearing in Abel Gance's famous silent epic *Napoléon* at sixteen, before embarking on movie careers in Paris, London and New York. It was in New York, in 1939, that she married her third husband, the American actor Tyrone Power. Subsequently, she became a US citizen and patriotically toured the country, giving propaganda speeches where boosting the Allied war effort. Her marriage was unconventional. Both parties felt free to indulge in outside relationships. Power was already in love with Judy Garland and, since his death, a number of stories have emerged suggesting that he was also bisexual. Annabella certainly had no reservations about embarking on an affair with Roald.

They first met at one of Evalyn Walsh McLean's parties where Annabella made an immediate impression. "I thought Annabella (the film star) was fine," he told his mother, "and concentrated in that direction. I've seen her many times since. She's an intelligent dame and much fun." [132] Annabella herself later recalled meeting Roald at a first-night party, where he told her a creepy story about a rich man with a penchant for gruesome bets. He liked to wager his expensive Cadillac against the little finger of impoverished and impressionable younger men and women. When he had finished it, Dahl was delighted that, instead of praising his ingenuity or being shocked at its sinister subject matter, she simply asked him: "What happened next?" Their affair began shortly afterwards. It was, she recalled, a "crazy thing", which "came back from time to time when we were thrown into each other's arms". Her conclusion: "It was like we were twin brothers. Romantic? Not really. Physical? Sometimes. But most important, we had a complete understanding and he trusted me." [133] It was an intense and passionate relationship, from which Roald learned a lot about sex, as he admitted to his second wife, Liccy. [134] Their friendship lasted until his death. But would Annabella herself ever have contemplated marrying him? "Certainly not," was the answer she gave Dahl's first biographer, Jeremy Treglown. Her reason: "Because – he was kind of impossible." [135]

Ironically, as 1944 drew to a close and a successful outcome of the war began to seem inevitable, Dahl's sense of ennui and disillusion returned. His letters home lost their vitality. Few things, other than his writing, seemed to offer him amusement and satisfaction. Partly this was to do with his health, which had once again deteriorated. One senses too that his professional double-dealing was beginning to catch up with him emotionally; that the world of secrecy and legitimized betrayal, which had initially intrigued him, had begun to seem repellent. And the deceitful manner in which Roosevelt dropped Wallace as vice president in 1944 must have been painful to observe. Dahl liked Wallace. He did not agree with him on many issues, but he admired his idealism, his love of agriculture, and his honesty. He had drafted speeches for him.[136] He celebrated him as a prophet of a truly democratic America. Yet he had schemed against his friend, this "lovely man", who was "just too innocent and idealistic for the world",[137] and he must have felt some complicity in Wallace's dramatic fall from high political office.[138]

It was not just the vice presidency Wallace lost. Dahl was well aware that the British were also machinating to ensure that if Roosevelt were reelected, Wallace would not get his consolation prize: the State Department job.[139] It was a betrayal of the sort that – until then – was quite alien to Dahl's nature. And it must have disillusioned him. In September, a few days after his twenty-eighth birthday, he visited Wallace and confessed to his friend that he personally had helped undermine him, even admitting that the British had been "scared to death" that he would be offered the job at the State Department. Wallace characteristically took the news on the chin, noting in his diary that he still thought Dahl "an awfully nice boy, of whom I am very fond".[140] It was perhaps a harder blow for Charles Marsh. When Wallace lost the nomination, Marsh's daughter Antoinette Haskell recalled, "it broke Dad's heart".[141]

Whether the mental strain of this deceit and chicanery exacerbated Dahl's back injury is hard to tell, but in August 1944 he told his mother that he was "hobbling . . . like an old man"[142] and that he was visiting a variety of osteopaths and doctors to see what they could do to help. The following week he told her that one particular spine specialist had "muttered something about an operation". However, he continued, "I'm buggered if I am going to allow that. As it is I still limp about the place rather slowly and it hurts quite a lot."[143] For a month or two he tried to fight the pain, joking to one of his doctors that he was "still a little lop-sided",[144] but he remained hopeful that things would get better. Then Washington was hit by the tail end of a hurricane and Roald found himself "shovelling out"[145] a foot of water from his flooded basement. His back pain returned with a vengeance and by October he was in hospital in New York having a lumbar puncture and spinal X-rays. The procedure did not go well. "Unfortunately I had a very severe reaction from it all," he wrote, "with great headaches and pains all over the body, especially in the neck . . . At one point my fingers stood out straight and couldn't move."[146] He felt "too lousy" even to read or write.[147]

In November, events took a turn for the better. Roosevelt won the election, while Wallace appeared to be "in fine form, and going very strong"[148] as secretary of state for commerce. Roald's own health seemed to be improving and on November 18 he was invited to a small private dinner at the White House to celebrate the reelection. There, he noted that Roosevelt too looked "fit and very hearty",[149] despite the fact that he ate almost nothing. However, by December, Roald himself was feeling ill again. He spent a miserable Christmas in Virginia at Longlea with the Marsh family, where Antoinette remembered that he was drinking half a bottle of brandy every morning just to dull the pain. Charles insisted that in the New Year he should go down to Temple, in Texas, where a great friend of his, Dr Arthur Scott, would be able to examine him. Two weeks later, Roald travelled south to the Scott and White Clinic, a huge hospital, set in a landscape filled with "cowpunchers and cattle ranchers and hillbillies and steers and bulls and cows and cowpunchers with piles because they've lived too long on horses and miles and bloody miles of prairie and cowpunchers and cattle ranchers and hillbillies and steers and bulls and cows".[150]

In mid-January 1945, Dahl underwent spinal surgery there to remove a disc. It left him flat on his back for almost four weeks. Marsh paid all his medical bills and insisted he recuperate in Virginia. He spent most of February living at Longlea "in solitary splendour", while working on the proofs of a collection of short stories. But the surgery had been only partially successful. He found he still could not walk without considerable pain, and complained to his mother that getting better was "a bloody slow business".[151]

In March, he returned to Texas for further surgery. A six-inch needle was inserted into his spine prior to his X-ray examination, after which he was confined once more to bed – this time with 11-pound weights attached to his legs. He was "treated like a king"[152] there for eighteen days, reading Dickens, Shakespeare and the Brontës – "a lot of that old stuff, which I'd never read before".[153] But he was still in great pain, although the doctors kept assuring him that the operations had been successful. Finally, puzzled by his apparent failure to respond to treatment, they decided that he had had a particularly violent reaction to an oil they had injected into his spinal cavity in order to make the X-ray images clearer. They decided that they needed to remove the oil. The procedure was a grisly one:

> *It had to be done in the x-ray room under the fluoroscope, so they can watch what they were doing. The first time they tried under local anaesthetic they failed to get the needle in – they had to use a very thick one, because the oil is thick. Three doctors tried for one and a half hours but without success, and I personally did not enjoy it at all. Then, the day before yesterday, they took me up again, and gave me Pentathol, an intravenous anaesthetic, and kept me under two hours while they did the job. Apparently they had quite a time, because I had to be tilted first this way then back so [as] to get the column of oil onto the point of the needle in the spinal column. Anyway they got it all out, and then I had a fairly rough night of it. My breathing when I came back to my room was apparently six to the minute. But I was given lots of glucose intravenously and also penicillin shots all through the night. The next morning – yesterday, I more or less came to and tested my legs and back and found everything cured – so in a day or two I'll be getting up and probably will be back in Washington quite fit and well in about 10 days. It was the first time that they had removed the Lapiadol in this hospital.*** They said that it's very rare for people to get such a reaction from having it in the spine as I had.*[154]

After a week's further recuperation at Longlea, wearing a "sort of bullet proof waistcoat such as Al Capone used to wear. Anyone can shoot at me . . ."[154] Roald returned to Washington, where shortly afterwards he went to have supper at the home of Drew Pearson. One of Pearson's idio-

---

***This was probably Lipiodol, a poppy seed oil used as a radio-opaque contrast agent in radiological investigations.

syncrasies was to keep a few head of cattle for his own personal consumption. Each was named after a prominent contemporary political figure. That evening, much to Roald's delight, Wallace's great rival, Cordell Hull, was served for dinner. But halfway through the meal Roald began to feel unwell and left early. When he got home he was violently ill, with vomiting, diarrhoea and stomach pains. After a few hours contemplating the half-digested remains of the former secretary of state disappearing "down the lavatory", he took himself down to the emergency room in Georgetown University Hospital, where he was diagnosed with acute appendicitis and operated upon immediately. He came out of the anaesthetic to find himself in a ward with two old men who did nothing but "fart all day and have enemas and talk bullshit and then fart some more".[156] He also learned that Franklin Roosevelt had died and that Harry Truman was now President of the United States.

After Roald was discharged from hospital, Marsh again took on the role of his protector, whisking his surrogate son away with him to convalesce for three weeks in California. In La Jolla and Palm Springs, Roald sat by the swimming pool getting a tan, before driving on to Arizona, where the RAF laid on a plane for him to fly back to Los Angeles. On the journey, he celebrated V-E Day with the flight crew, listening to the King's speech on the plane's headphones while high over the Rocky Mountains. In Los Angeles, after two days at the Beverly Hills Hotel discussing gremlin rights with Walt Disney, he went to stay with Hoagy Carmichael, where he spent some more time poolside, before heading back to Palm Springs for a few days with Howard Hawks. He returned to Washington "fine and brown and fit",[157] but also psychologically ready to go back to England.

A chapter of his life was coming to a close. Roosevelt was dead. Wallace was still secretary for commerce, but Dahl had played poker at the University Club several times with the hawkish Harry Truman, and probably suspected that the gentle Wallace would not last long in his administration. Marsh, too, was profoundly suspicious of the new regime. He thought Roosevelt's successor second-rate, accusing him of having grown up in the "political sewers" and castigating his "poor mental equipment, his plotting political life", and his "unattractive personality".[158] He cannot have been surprised when, in 1946, Wallace was fired, as Anthony Cave Brown notes, for "no great crime except his political innocence".[159] Dahl was now desperate to concentrate on writing. In June 1945, he had finally signed an agreement with the publisher Curtice Hitchcock to publish his collection of short stories, *Over to You*. Moreover, he was longing to rejoin his family in England. His half brother Louis had a baby, and now his younger sister Else was also pregnant – "expectorating", as he jokingly called it. Roald felt left out. He might have returned home that summer had Stephenson not thrown him one final surprise and asked him to help write the official history of BSC. For this, Dahl had to go to Canada – to a remote base on the shore of Lake Ontario with the theatrical name of "Camp X".

Now lost in a maze of amorphous industrial estates that have encroached onto what was once fertile farmland, the site of Camp X today is marked only by two nondescript plaques. Commemorating respectively the location of the camp and the career of William Stephenson, they are set into a curving concrete monument, which squats uncomfortably on a small patch of grass in "Intrepid Park" by the shadow of a monolithic warehouse, containing over 3 million cases of wine, and owned by the Liquor Control Board of Ontario. Four flags flutter forlornly there in celebration of the shoreline's more unconventional wartime history. Then, this strange encampment, established in December 1941, teemed with all manner of secret activities, serving both as a sophisticated signals centre and also, more notoriously, as the first training school for spies on North American soil. Techniques of sabotage, of how to kill with a single blow of the knife or blind a man with a box of matches, were all part of the syllabus of Camp X recruits, who also learned how to use codes, write with secret ink, and interrogate prisoners.[160] There, so legend has it, Ian Fleming learned many of the tricks he would later use in his James Bond books.†††

---

†††John Pearson in his *Life of Ian Fleming* argues that Fleming completed the training course at Camp X between 1942 and 1943. David Stafford has cast doubts on this, suggesting that Fleming, like Dahl, was a storyteller with a greater penchant for embroidery and exaggeration than for truthful accuracy.

By the time Dahl arrived, the exploding rats and the cyanide pills had all been put away because, although it still functioned as a signals centre, Camp X no longer dealt in espionage training. Now it was little more than a secure storage location for the BSC records. As the war in Europe had begun to draw to its close, Stephenson had decided that it was too risky for his papers, with their incriminating evidence of illegal British operations in America, to remain on US soil, so in 1944, the entire archive had been packed up from Rockefeller Center and shipped up to Oshawa, by dead of night and under armed convoy, in "some sort of wonderful security truck with an escort",[161] as Dahl later recalled.

Initially, Stephenson had asked an academic historian to write the book, but he found this version too pedantic. He wanted a more glamorous celebration of his achievements left to posterity, so he asked two other of his employees – Dahl and a journalist called Tom Hill – to make the history more racy and readable. It was not an easy task and Dahl's heart was not in it. He spent about three months there avoiding his task, playing the odd round of golf and getting "quite sunburned"[162] walking along the shore of the lake. Wading through a mass of signals and summaries was not Roald's idea of how to celebrate the defeat of Germany. And the run-down Genosha Hotel in Oshawa was a long way from the glamour of Hollywood, New York and Washington. An occasional evening of luxury in Parkwood as a guest of Robert Samuel McLaughlin, the local grandee who was the first president of General Motors of Canada, may have done something to alleviate his ennui and restlessness, but Dahl found Oshawa provincial and the atmosphere of excessive secrecy at Camp X irritated him hugely. Evelyn Davis, one of the office secretaries, recalled that even when her husband Les came over to repair a broken typewriter, the writers all had to cover up all their work and stop talking.[163] Dahl was also fed up with the Ontario liquor laws, which allowed him only one bottle of spirits a month. "It is very disheartening," he complained to his mother, "and bad for one's health."[164]

In August 1945, the atomic bombs fell on Hiroshima and Nagasaki. Soon afterwards, Japan surrendered and the war in the Pacific came to an end. Isolated by Lake Ontario, Dahl continued to work on the BSC history. But despite the good weather and the fact that he was "browner than [he'd] ever been before, really nut brown" – he was desperate to get back to the big city. His book was due out in a few months and he was looking for fresh challenges. His sister Asta wrote to him that she had been posted to Norway with the WAAFs and he considered going out to join her – particularly when he saw a job advertised for an assistant air attaché in Oslo. In the end he decided not to apply because he "couldn't face being in uniform all my life".[165] So he "copped out"[166] of Camp X and returned to New York. Dahl was later dismissive of his three months in Oshawa. "I wrote a little bit of crap," he told Bill Macdonald, "and then thought, 'Christ, I'm not going to do this, it's an historian's job.' And I called Bill [Stephenson] and I said, 'I'm packing this in, I can't write.' And he said, 'Okay, come on back.' And that was it."[167]

Or was it? There remains a slight possibility that other factors influenced Dahl in his decision to abandon his work in Canada. In early 1993, Dahl's daughter Ophelia was contacted by Liz Drake, the wife of a former Canadian soldier. She claimed to have evidence of sinister activities carried out on behalf of BSC in Scotland, which involved the torture of returning Canadian raiders from Occupied France. This torture, she alleged, had been carried out by British marines so that Britain would have "toughened troops ready should Germany occupy the UK". Drake believed that, while writing the history, Dahl had stumbled across the evidence of this "Black War" and had been so "revolted and appalled"[168] by what he read that he asked to be released from his duties. But while she was able to produce evidence that these alleged brutalities had indeed taken place, and circumstantial detail relating them to BSC, Drake was unable to produce anything concrete that directly linked Dahl's withdrawal from writing the Camp X history to this aspect of BSC's work. Nevertheless, it was an intriguing conjecture. BSC's brief was to break rules, to fight a "dirty war", and that is what they did. There was almost certainly a great deal of unpleasant and depressing material in those archives that might well have contributed to Roald's reluctance to complete his task, while the stories he would write after *Over to You* would be darker, more cynical and far less lyrical in tone than their predecessors.

It is also possible Dahl did not really "cop out" at all. In his introduction to the history of BSC, which was unofficially published in 1998, the historian Nigel West concluded that the book was completed "in the late summer of 1945".[169] Dahl was in Canada until September 4. His final letter from Camp X does indeed suggest that he may have been leaving early, but no more than a couple of weeks or so. He had been there already for nearly three months. Reading the book as West presents it, the real puzzle would seem to be what he brought to the project at all; apart from one or two examples – such as the description of Drew Pearson – it is hard to see much evidence of his inimitable literary fingerprint on its arid pages. The book contains no dark secrets about atrocities committed on Canadian volunteers, and fails to shed much light even on the operations that might have inspired James Bond. It is mostly a compendium of minutiae, of interest only to a specialized historian. In short, just the kind of book Roald abhorred.

Dahl always remained uncharacteristically circumspect about his wartime intelligence work and it is possible he took secrets with him to his grave. Alfhild recalled that her brother was always "very discreet" about his time with Stephenson. "He didn't talk to us about it at all,"[170] she told me. This attitude was by and large mirrored in Dahl's reactions to curious outsiders. An early biographer of Stephenson's recalled that "Dahl checked with what he regarded as the proper authorities before talking,"[171] while Bill Macdonald, the most recent biographer of the man called "Intrepid", who visited Roald shortly before his death in 1990, observed his surprise on discovering how many people were now speaking quite openly about BSC. He pointedly assured Macdonald he was not about to reveal any of his own secrets. "'You won't get any from me!' the renowned children's author said emphatically; and then he paused, and sounded more subdued. 'It's a question of honour really.'"[172]

On June 20, 1945, six weeks after V-E Day, Stephenson wrote to Dahl thanking him for what he had done for BSC and summarizing his achievements. "I do not forget", he noted, "that obligation was already owed to you before you joined us in July of 1944, for during the period of your attachment to the British Embassy, there were many occasions when your cooperation – always unstintingly given – was of great use to us. We had, indeed, sufficient cause to know and value your qualities, and that you have done such a good job in the past year is no matter for surprise." He went on to praise Dahl's personal contribution to BSC's activities as one "of particular significance and value", and to assure him that his work would "prove of lasting worth", celebrating Dahl's "considerable initiative", his "capacity for handling extremely delicate situations", his "gift for concise reporting" and his ability "to win the respect and confidence" of his American colleagues.[173]

The letter was one of many similar ones that Stephenson wrote at the time, but there is little doubt that Dahl had made a significant impression on the Canadian spymaster, who continued to stay in touch for many years after the war was over and invite Dahl to his homes in Jamaica and Bermuda. However, by the end of 1945, Dahl was heartily sick of the Great White Slug. Even New York had begun to lose its appeal. He wrote to his mother that he now found the city "slick and chromium-plated and fast and efficient and unpleasant".[174] A week later, despite the fact that he was staying in Millicent Rogers's luxurious apartment, complete with Van Goghs, Gauguins and Cézannes, and despite having been approached to work on a ballet of the Gremlins for the New York City Ballet with the choreographer Leonide Massine, he repeated his sentiments. "I do not like New York very much . . . There are too many bums and everyone, especially the taxi drivers, are so disagreeable."[175]

Dahl finally boarded the *Queen Elizabeth* at the beginning of February 1946 after four formative years in Washington and New York. There he had mixed with statesmen, movie stars, writers and businessmen, and tasted extremes of wealth and luxury. He had become a man of the world, and consorted with a host of glamorous older women. In the world of diplomacy he had tasted success and failure. He had won the respect of North Americans for his straight talking and his initiative and, at the same time, invited the disdain of many from the English governing classes for his brashness and unpredictability. Crucially, he had discovered that he liked the company of buccaneers: men who enjoyed making decisions, who felt no need to shelter behind authority, and who did not care unduly about criticism. One of them, Charles Marsh, was now both his patron and his best friend. And Dahl had changed. He had not lost the enthusiasm, the joie de vivre, the vivid imagination and the powerful desire to entertain that characterized the young man who six years earlier had boarded the SS *Mantola* to Tanganyika, but he no longer craved adventure in the same way. He had experienced enough excitement to last a lifetime, while the realities of war had added a cynical, misanthropic and world-weary aspect to his personality. It was writing now that fascinated him.

In old age, Dahl would often reflect that the war burned out his need for the thrill of danger. In his short story "Someone Like You" (1944), he describes the effect of the war on a young fighter pilot's personality. "From being a young, bouncing boy, he had become someone old and wise and gentle . . . he had become old like a tired man of seventy years. He had become so different and he had changed so much that at first it was embarrassing . . . and it was not easy to know what to say."[176] But while Dahl may have felt the weight of experience on his shoulders, his fascination with politics had not completely vanished. Now, even as his ocean liner steamed across the Atlantic, he saw both his own and his family's futures blighted by a sinister new threat: the mushroom cloud of imminent nuclear holocaust.

In September 1945, shortly before Henry Wallace wrote President Truman an open letter begging the new president to share his atomic secrets with the Russians, Roald had shared his own fears about the future with the former vice president. Wallace noted that though his friend was now "something of a Russophobe", current British policy seemed designed to provoke "the maximum distrust between the United States and Russia and thus prepare the groundwork for World War III".[177] Roald could not but agree with him. The notion that the human race might one day destroy itself haunted him and intensified the struggle between the idealist and the cynic that raged in his mind. In that battle, BSC's arcane world of disinformation and duplicity had already begun to take on a particularly bitter taste. Nothing would ever change that. Despite his tight-lipped loyalty to his country, from now on the world of covert intelligence would always remain a dirty one. Whatever their consequences, honesty and outspokenness would always be a preferable option. A few weeks before Dahl died, concluding an interview about Bill Stephenson, he admitted that from the whole experience of working with him, he had learned nothing at all of any value "except what I disapprove of – the art of secrecy".[178]

CHAPTER ELEVEN

The Scholar-Gypsy

THE ENGLAND TO WHICH Dahl returned in February 1946 was a very different place from that he had left in 1938. Many of its cities were desolate and bomb-damaged and its citizens distressed and disillusioned. A once proud empire seemed to be collapsing into a vacuum of insolvency and bureaucracy, where cunning and chicanery were rapidly becoming the norm. Neither Churchill's "sunlit uplands" nor the "New Jerusalem" ideals of Clement Attlee's new Socialist Britain were much in evidence, while Dahl's own fears about the future began to be realized as soon as the war was over, when the United States abruptly terminated financial support for its transatlantic ally, leaving the British economy well-nigh bankrupt. As a consequence, the new Labour government was forced to export as much of the nation's own produce as it could, while imposing draconian controls on the import of foreign goods. Soon there were food shortages, fuel shortages, and rules for everything. Rationing worsened. Unemployment soared. A crime wave swept the nation. There were queues everywhere.

The writer John Lehmann recalled that it felt as if the British spirit had been crushed by a legion of puritanical officials who believed there was "a virtue in austerity and shabbiness".[1] Staple foods became scarce. Luxuries disappeared altogether. For Elizabeth David, the situation was a "nightmare".[2] Apricots, olives, lemons, almonds, even butter and rice, she recalled, came to be regarded as dirty words, just because they were unobtainable. Power cuts plunged large areas of the country into darkness and cold. Bankers in the City of London were reduced to working by candlelight. Christopher Isherwood, visiting from America, was shocked by what he saw. Gloomy and crumbling, London, he wrote, seemed a "powerfully and continually depressing" place. One of his friends told him that it was now "a dying city". Another simply described postwar Britain as hell.[3]

After almost four years of sophisticated metropolitan existence, Dahl opted to live in the countryside, "amongst the cows and the sheep and the slow spoken types with straw in their hair".[4] His second wife Liccy echoed many in his family when she described him as a "countryman through and through", whose profound love of nature was absolutely central to his character. This went way back into his childhood, perhaps to nostalgic memories of the farm at Radyr. At Repton, his walks and rides through the local countryside had sustained him in dark hours. It was there also that he had found inspiration, excitement, perhaps almost a pattern for his own life, in Matthew Arnold's poem *The Scholar-Gypsy*. Its narrative celebrates an "Oxford scholar poor, Of pregnant parts and quick inventive brain", who, "tired of knocking at preferment's door", forsakes the world of the intellect and goes to live with the Gypsies. He roams the world among "that wild brotherhood", surviving by his wits and remaining always in close touch with the soil.

Roald responded to the poem as viscerally as he did to music. Like a Bach concerto or a Brahms symphony, he told his mother, the work gave him "tickles in the tummy". Its rejection of the "strange disease of modern life" in favour of the simple pastoral ideal – the "unclouded joy" of being a "truant boy" – was an option that had resonated with Roald since, as a child, he had sat up in the trees, writing his diary and collecting birds' eggs. It had inspired him again when he was convalescing from his head injuries in Egypt. Now, with the scars of the war weighing on him, both physically and mentally, its 250 lines exerted a powerful attraction on his psyche. The poem's freewheeling rustic alternative to the dubious glamour of Hollywood, the uncertain allure of London literary circles, and the treacherous corridors of political intrigue gave him, he assured his mother, "exactly the same sensation" as he got when listening to

Beethoven's *Pastoral* Symphony.[5] It would form the psychological canvas against which he would fashion the rest of his life.

He had returned determined to become a full-time writer, while living off a small RAF invalid pension, "about a thousand quid" from his Shell pension fund,[6] and about half of the £5,000 he had inherited from his father's trust fund. From the large garden of his mother's house in Grendon Underwood, he also hoped to grow enough food and vegetables to supplement the family's meagre official rations. His first letter to Ann Watkins brimmed over with excitement at the thought of his new life there. He enthused about his "cottage with straw on its roof and all around fields and cows and sheep having lambs and right now a wind like a vacuum-cleaner".[7] Ecstatic descriptions of rooks "frolicking in the trees",[8] apple blossom "like snow",[9] and drunken village types with names like Old Fizzer were to follow in the next weeks.[10] Soon he purchased a racing greyhound, a "smasher" called Snailbox Lady, who could run 525 yards in just over thirty seconds, and from which he intended to breed a pack of racing dogs. It added to a domestic menagerie, which already included a duckling called Cholly Knickerbocker, a dachshund called Mrs Harris, four more assorted dogs, a parrot, a "repressed"[11] canary called Admiral Canaris after the former chief of German Military Intelligence, and a naughty young magpie, whom Dahl named Walter Winchell after the American gossip columnist, with whom he had had many dealings in the war. He also acquired a "girlfriend who types",[12] but did not bother to mention her name.

This eccentric Arcadia however was by no means immune to the disillusion that was infecting the rest of the country. Dahl was struggling to keep his spirits up and maintain the sense of lightness and whimsy that had been in evidence in some of his early tales, but despair and hopelessness was beginning to animate his fiction. His first collection of short stories, *Over to You,* had been published in the United States in January 1946, just as he was leaving New York. It should have come out a month earlier, but much to Dahl's annoyance, his publishers, Reynal & Hitchcock – or "Ureynall and Stinkpot", as Charles Marsh dubbed them[13] – had delayed publication, which meant that he was forced to leave for

England only a few days after the book appeared.* The reviews had been good, but varied. Nona Balakian in the *New York Times Book Review* celebrated the visionary quality of Dahl's stories and praised his ability to communicate a "sensation . . . that has often nothing to do with us as earthbound creatures". She also commended his ability to inhabit "the narrow margin separating shadow from substance".[14] The *New Yorker* critic, while complaining that the public had now heard from "a great many writing aviators",† warmed to Mr Dahl's "original turn of mind" and, in particular, to two stories from the collection which were "salted with some good low comedy".[15] Another applauded his "savage and piti-ful" humour.[16]

What gave Dahl the most pleasure, however, was a congratulatory let-ter he received from Maxwell Perkins at Scribner's. Perkins was a living legend in the American publishing world – "the king of all the editors", as Dahl would later describe him. A diminutive figure, who "invariably wore his trilby hat on in the office",[17] Perkins was revered by the authors he published, who included Hemingway and F. Scott Fitzgerald. His let-ter concentrated on one of Dahl's most lyrical stories, "Death of an Old, Old Man", which describes an elaborate aerial combat in which a young pilot is killed. Perkins admired its economy, its precision, and declared that "as for the fight, nothing I ever read gave me a better sense of how it is done, and what it is like".[18] He expressed great interest in publishing a novel, should Dahl ever write one.

Before leaving the United States, Dahl had already decided that his next project would indeed be a novel and that it would be based on his beloved gremlins. But this would not be a book for children; it would be something "very different".[19] much darker and more apocalyptic: a

---

*The book marked Dahl's formal break with the RAF Benevolent Fund, which had up until that point received the royalties from all his flying stories. Shortly before V-E Day, he had written to his publisher telling him that he felt he had now "given enough" to the Fund and wanted to start earning money for himself from his literary output – Dahl, Letter to Curtice Hitchcock, 04/20/45 – RDMSC RD 1/1/1/191.

†He was probably thinking chiefly of the French writer Antoine de Saint-Exupéry, who was living in the United States and whose *Pilote de Guerre* (*Flight to Arras*) and *Le Petit Prince* (*The Little Prince*) had been published in 1942 and 1943, respectively. Curiously, a crashed aeroplane in the African desert also plays a key part in the second tale.

critique of the savage nature of humanity and the first novel to address the destructive power of the atom bomb. His own antiwar stance had been slowly evolving throughout 1944–45. Two of his short stories, "Death of an Old, Old Man" and "They Shall Not Grow Old", were considered so negative that they could not be published until the war was formally over, while his final flying story, "Someone Like You", was a biting meditation on the consequences of killing for the psychology of the flyer. "I keep thinking to myself, shall I jink a little," says the prematurely aged protagonist. "Shall I swerve a fraction to one side, then my bombs will fall on someone else. I keep thinking, whom shall I make them fall on; whom shall I kill tonight."[20] The solution for this guilt-stricken pilot is the melancholy oblivion of alcohol. Dahl had tried that himself as a means of dealing with some of his wartime demons. Now he tried something else. He turned his angst, which Ann Watkins was describing as increasingly "melodramatic and bloody",[21] into rage and satire.

The gremlins were transformed. No longer creatures of whimsy, they metamorphosed into something altogether more sinister and evil: twisted, deformed versions of the trolls of Dahl's childhood, living underground, and possessing faces that were "weird and frightening with a deathless, ageless expression in the small black, lidless eyes, with a cunning twist about the small, thick-lipped mouth". The female gremlins, or Fifinellas, liberated from the bland insouciance with which Disney had characterized them, evolved from pert doe-eyed minxes into grotesque fiends, "bald-headed and ugly as hell . . . worse, far worse than the male because the female of any type is always more scheming, cunning, jealous and relentless than the male".[22] As they gleefully willed the human race to destroy itself so that they could take the planet over, Dahl confessed to his agent that the world he had created was "horrifying adult".[23]

World War III was more quick and sudden than either of its predecessors. It lasted only a few months. But the new weapon worked beautifully and the destruction was great . . . The population of the world was cut considerably during that short time. And deep down below the ground the Gremlins heard the distant whoof and roar of huge explosions; they felt the earth tremble . . . A wave of excitement rippled through the whole community. "There they go again!" they shouted exultantly to one another as they listened to the faraway roar of the bombings overhead . . . "But it's better this time. It's quicker this time. Better and quicker, better and quicker, better and quicker." . . . Impatiently they waited to see how great the destruction had been and whether the killing was complete.[24]

While he was writing the book, Dahl's misanthropy seemed to grow exponentially. His view of the atomic bomb as a terrifying agent of destruction was reinforced when, at the end of August 1946, he read John Hersey's article on Hiroshima, which took over almost an entire issue of *The New Yorker.* Hersey's pared-down factual description of the effects of the bomb – which killed 100,000 people – on the lives of just six individuals made a deep impression on Dahl.[25] However, instead of the cool, detached reserve that had characterized his short story writing, he was determined instead to unleash a grand rhetorical tirade against the ordinary man, the "ground person" and "the bullshit in which he wallows",[26] It was dangerous territory. Dahl's ability to see himself as a detached, sometimes godlike figure, wandering the imaginative territory of the skies, and critical of those less free-thinking than he was, had been exacerbated both by his crash and by his combat experiences as a pilot. Both made him feel set apart – liberated from the earthbound existence of most of his fellow mortals. In an unpublished short story from 1945 called "World Leaders", he had God send Zail, a dead airman, back to earth to remind a congress of presidents and prime ministers of their ultimate insignificance. The airman is arrested and brought to the leaders.

It was then that they saw his eyes. When they looked at him it was impossible for them to see anything except his eyes. They were deep blue, the colour of the sky in summer, and behind each one there was a small white flame which burned steadily and with great brightness, for they were the eyes of a thousand men who had been killed in the air. The courage, the truth and the suffering of each of those men and

the strength which this gave to him was reflected in his eyes . . . They
saw in those eyes a strength which was so great that it was beyond their
understanding; then as they looked there was a pale shining around
the place where Zail stood and his face was like the face of an angel.

Zail takes the world leaders on a ride in a supernatural plane, "made entirely of glass".[27] It makes no noise. They fly higher and higher and the world beneath them becomes smaller and smaller until its minuscule scale in the universe is apparent. This perception of himself as "superman" had been one of the motors that drove Dahl's need to write, and his early short stories had often engaged with such detachment, but in a fragmentary, allusive manner. Much was left unsaid as his eye focused on tiny details and minutiae. Now he was moving beyond the cameo and painting his stories on a bigger canvas – a canvas where his sentiments and judgements would be more overt, where his feelings could not so easily be controlled, and where his readers were likely to be less forgiving.

His own politics at the time were complex. Like many from his background, combat had turned him from an instinctive conservative into someone who felt that the suffering of war demanded a more just and transformative peace. It is not clear which way he cast his vote – if he voted at all – in the May 1945 General Election, which swept Winston Churchill's Conservatives from office and brought Clement Attlee's reforming Socialists to power, but it is more than likely Dahl was initially a supporter of the new government. His friend Dennis Pearl remembered how far he had moved from the politics of his schooldays at Repton, where every single boy in the class supported the Conservatives,[28] and where he wrote to his mother that the school had invited a "horrible Labour Man" down for the annual speech day.[29] The time spent with Henry Wallace and Charles Marsh had changed him. He had drunk deep from their cup of idealistic reform, and believed that the time was right for a new world order. Writing his paper *Post War Air Lines* in 1943, Dahl had concluded that "the more that can be done on an international basis after the war, the more likelihood there will be of obtaining a lasting peace".[30]

This internationalism inclined him toward the left, and, as his friend

Lesley Pares, her married name now O'Malley, remembered, his views at that time were "really quite socialist".[31] But in reality Dahl was a radical, advocating world government along with Wallace, Einstein, and his hero, Winston Churchill, whose chilling vision of an iron curtain descending over Europe dividing West from East was now becoming reality.‡ Dahl's attitude to Soviet Russia remained hawkish. It was not the Marxist ideology that appalled him so much as its brutal, violent reality. "I'm not frightened of communism," he declared. "I'm frightened of war. Not frightened of it. Just appalled by it and its coming."[32] As he watched the international situation develop from his home in the Buckinghamshire countryside, the thought of nuclear holocaust preoccupied him to the point of obsession. He discussed the subject at length with Dennis Pearl when he returned home on leave from the army, and he frequently wrote to Charles Marsh about it. However, he was not about to abandon his decision to come home. "I am not yet restless to return to America," he told Claudia Haines. "I think Europe is the place to be right now. The turmoil is bewildering, but there seems to be a centre to the whirlpool and if you watch it you can see where things are going."[33] Writing to Marsh three months later, it was only a question of when, not if, the inevitable hostilities would break out. "Informed London opinion predicts war in the spring of 1949 or spring of 1950 – not this year," he concluded.[34] This deepening fatalism about world affairs was reflected too in a heightened pessimism about human nature itself. "Oh dear the world is really a thick thing," he lamented. "There always has been war before in the world and I suppose there always will be. To try and stop one nation among many from misbehaving periodically is just as difficult as trying to stop crime in a country. You can have policemen and prisons and electrocutions, but still there will always be a crime."[35]

Charles Marsh tried to reassure him. "I am sorry you are so sad," he wrote, urging Roald not to be indignant or pessimistic but to "fight for

---

‡This seriousness of intent did not stop him joking to Marsh that the Russians had "designed an atom bomb to look like a lavatory seat. It has a time fuse attached. It has been installed secretly at UNO headquarters; thus the more constipated the politician the greater the chances he'll be sitting on it when it goes off" – Dahl, Letter to Charles Marsh, 10/28/46 – CMP.

harmony world wide". Marsh deplored the fact that the statesmen of the world wanted to "step up in front of the picture with atomic bombs in both hands", but he argued that the best policy was to face the coming storm with "intelligent gaiety".[36] That, he maintained, was Henry Wallace's approach. Roald had recently told Claudia and Charles that he too was uncertain whether to be "gloomy or gay",[37] but this time his response was scathing in the extreme. He likened Wallace to Neville Chamberlain, "his equally good-natured and well-meaning English colleague, who went to Munich with his umbrella",[38] and told the Marshes that the former vice president had been making such "a fool of himself" that he had not bothered to contact him on Wallace's recent visit to London.[39] If Charles went on kissing the Russians like Wallace, Roald told his friend, sooner or later they would bite off his tongue.[40]

This cynicism could lead him to perceptions that were prophetic. He anticipated, for example, a form of contemporary urban terrorism in his short story "Nineteen Fifty What?" about two shadowy diplomats, who arrive in Washington to inform the president that they have planted atom bombs in fifty-three American cities and will detonate them unless the United States withdraws its troops from Japan.[41] But much of his indignation was based on what he perceived as the injustice of the immediate postwar situation. In a letter to Marsh, admitting that communism might "ultimately be good for the Russian people" – if not for those of America and England – he contrasted the "noble men", Marsh and Wallace, with the "ruthless men", who will always make sure the former "get kicked in the teeth".[42] It was this situation that made the loss of life in the recent war so poignant and that appeared to be leading to the imminent destruction of all he loved. The inevitability of nuclear war, he told Marsh, was "the saddest goddam thought, the saddest, and craziest thought that it is possible to think".[43]

Some Time Never, as his gremlins novel was eventually titled, was Dahl's response to this situation: an attempt not only to write a grand, significant satire about the burning issues of the time, but also a novel that engaged with his own existential struggles. Subtitled "A Fable for Supermen", it begins in familiar territory – in 1940, with a lyrical evocation of the Battle of Britain and the Blitz. It opens, like so many of his early stories, with a controlled description of pilot apprehension, which moves "like the point of a cold needle . . . slowly over the skin of the solar plexus", and evolves into an anxiety that is "deep and dreadful . . . as though everything, all the warmth and the blood and the entrails had been pumped out of your stomach, leaving it empty and ice-cold".[44] This time, however, the apprehension turns out to be more than a prelude to a dogfight or a bombing raid, but a symptom of the terminal distress that flying itself has wrought on one pilot's soul. It is manifested in a battle between caring and indifference, involvement and detachment, connection and isolation: the conflict, as Dahl put it, "between the wish to care and love, and the desire to disbelieve and to forget". The struggle between these two opposing forces – which "fought and clattered in the hollow of your skull", in a battle which "neither won, yet both won all the time" – is the recurrent theme of the novel, and it is clear from early on that nihilism will predominate.[45]

Then it was that you pressed forward against your harness-straps and wanted to jump up in the cockpit and shout at the top of your voice at all those little people on the world below, to tell them all you knew and felt, a hundred true and terrifying things about themselves; to tell them first, to tell them quickly how you loved them all, oh how you loved them all and how you hate them because of that; how you loved them and hated them, each single one of them and especially the tight packed crowds of sallow faces in the Undergrounds and the patient mournful faces of the women in the queues and the vacant empty faces of the soldiers in the streets; to tell them that, and then, to tell them all the other things that seemed so suddenly to come to you; to tell them – and this became the burden of your song – that nothing mattered, nothing, nothing, nothing, not fire nor plague nor murder nor any of the million little things that rule their lives; that henceforth they must not care about the price of gin, the smell of onions, the dying of a wife, a pimple on the cheek, the blast of bombs or sudden death; they must not care . . . simply because such matters did not count . . . nothing

counted . . . that was the simple truth; for the sum total of all things,
of living, loving, hating, dying, adds up, when the sum is carefully
done, to nothing, to precisely nothing.[46]

The tortured protagonist of the first part of the book is Peternip, a pilot with many of Dahl's own characteristics, including a face that is "long and pointed, shaped like an egg, domed on top, pointed at the base", a limping gait that "reminded one somehow of the swing of a mal-adjusted pendulum", and a passion for the music of Bach and Palestrina.[47] His wartime experience directly mirrored Dahl's own, as did the nature of his psychological scars. Both felt prematurely aged. Both felt emotionally blunted. Both felt crippled because they could no longer fly. Roald expressed his own anxieties about this in the letter to Ann Watkins's writer husband, Roger Burlingame, where he suggested that his indifference (which he was trying desperately to overcome) was probably "something to do with flying and the speed at which you fly, and the taking of your danger in small concentrated doses, and the height at which you fly, and the movement, particularly the movement . . ."[48] Now, robbed of this life-giving ecstatic motion, Peternip is sadder and more silent. His reasonable exterior disguises "a black despair, a deep and certain fatalism which made him impatient with the great importance which all men attached to their own individual lives". Loathing politicians and "idealists with their oppressive sincerity", he now "despised all human beings, himself included". And this despair, this loss of rapture and fantasy, will remain uncured. "A solemn person, whose quick and distant eyes told of a mind behind the eyes which travelled often in remote outlandish places far away,"[49] Peternip is killed suddenly, halfway through the book, outside the Queen's Hall after a performance of Brahms's Violin Concerto, when the bomb that launches World War Three hits Central London.

That first atomic war passes swiftly as the novel transforms itself into a futuristic parable about the destruction of humanity. The reader sees the destruction of the human race only from the gremlins' point of view and particularly from that of their "Leader" – a comic distortion of a war-time dictator, whose passion for oratory leads him to study the collected speeches of Winston Churchill and Abraham Lincoln, which he keeps alongside a copy of Samuel Butler's *Erewhon*, whose dysfunctional utopia shares certain similarities with Dahl's Gremlin kingdom – most notably a loathing of machines. Here, satire takes hold. Much of the second half of the book is written in the form of a speech, made by the Leader, on the objectionable moral condition of the human world above him. The principal object of his (and no doubt Dahl's) scorn is not the political system but humanity itself, which has collectively willed this situation into existence. "No single group of individuals was responsible for making lasting peace impossible upon the earth," the Leader declares. "The blame lay only in the nature of the human being himself." [50]

In a tirade of almost Swiftian comic ire, the Leader gleefully enumerates his catalogue of humanity's follies and vices. Mankind is "a mountain of conceit and selfishness . . . a creature who possesses more than any other living creature, wisdom, but more than any other creature he also possesses greed and avarice and a love of power". At the heart of mankind's problems is an obsession with money – the Gremlins describe it as "coin-collecting" – and a fixation on national self-interest, which the Leader likens to a plague. "Nationalifilis", as he comically dubs the epidemic, is "by far the most serious and unpleasant disease from which the human suffers." To prevent it, one would have to make every child in the world blind and deaf, so that "the passages through which the germs enter the body would be blocked". All manner of other human activities are scrutinized and found wanting. Even the physician is stung, leaping from the page as a sanctimonious demon, "pompous and patronising . . . One can almost see the drops of self-adulation dripping from the corners of his mouth. He is the greatest hypocrite of all time." [51]

Through the thick forests of anger and bitterness that often threaten to overwhelm the landscape of *Some Time Never*, a gentler comedy sometimes emerges – particularly when Dahl chooses to settle old scores. "Intelligent men do not take permanent jobs in the armed forces when they choose their careers," he declares, lampooning the six incompetent Air Marshals responsible for defending humanity against the Gremlin menace. And then, deftly, he shows us why.

"The situation," said the Chief of the Air Marshalls again, "is serious. What the hell are we going to do about it?"

"About what?" said the one who was excavating his ear.

"About Gremlins, of course."

"We must fix them," said the one who was scratching his back.

"We must take immediate action," said the one who was cleaning his nails.

"We must issue the necessary orders," said the one who was rustling a bag of coughdrops.

"Absolutely," said the one who was looking out of the window and thinking of his lunch.

"Agreed," said the Chief. He was more intelligent than the others. "But what shall we do first, Sir Hubert," he said, looking sternly at his deputy, "what do you suggest as the first step?"

"Have lunch," said Sir Hubert who was noted everywhere for his snap decisions.

With that the conference broke up.[52]

The novel had begun optimistically, with a quote from the Greek speechwriter Isocrates appealing for a political plan, "which will forever put an end to our hostilities and unite us by the lasting ties of mutual affection and fidelity". It ends in a horrible conflagration of atomic and biological weaponry, as humanity is entirely extinguished.

In his imagination's eye he saw the white-hot flashes in the sky bursting in carefully calculated patterns, covering a continent, scorching the whole face of a continent. He saw the faces of continents scorched black and dry so that nothing lived or grew upon them. He saw the great wind which followed the heat coming down upon the cities, crushing them flat upon the ground, tumbling the towns and piling up the villages into small untidy mounds of stone. He saw salvo upon salvo of huge thin missiles shaped like tall trees shooting up from the surface of the earth in the Eastern Hemisphere, up into the stratosphere and across the world at five thousand miles an hour; he saw them

falling vertically downward to burst one over every city of Europe; he
saw them bursting and he saw appearing clouds of deadly Virus Mist
which floated a while and fell slowly down upon the heads of those
below.[53]

There is one final, almost whimsical, apocalypse. As the Gremlins emerge from their millions of burrows to occupy the surface of the earth, they begin to disappear, to vanish like phantoms at dawn. The planet is left behind, poisoned and devastated. But life itself continues. "Millions and millions of minute living organisms" remain behind to offer some hope for the future. Yet it will be a future without men and women. Dahl's vision of a "mighty monstrous Creature-Earth", for whom mankind is "just a fleeting irritation . . . a great indestructible Creature-Earth, who woke one morning not so very long ago and felt the light touch of a million footsteps on its face and frowned and lay still and said 'ah well, they'll soon be gone,'"[54] anticipates by at least thirty years James Lovelock's "Gaia" theories of the planet as a vibrant, self-regulating organism of its own. It is just one of many original and arresting images that adorn this extraordinary, undervalued and visionary novel. Dahl's daughter Ophelia certainly believed that the book revealed much of her father's deepest, darkest feelings. "He was always very unconflicted about the fact that he felt that human beings were capable of really monstrous things," she told me. "And I think in writing *Some Time Never* he was writing about the capacity that we as humans have to destroy ourselves. I think he was trying to say something about what he'd seen, about the futility of war."[55]

Writing it wore Roald down. His back pain aggravated his melancholy, and after only a month back in England, he told Ann Watkins that he was starting to feel "morose" and that he missed everyone in New York.[56] In June 1946, he, his mother and Asta – who had just returned from her posting to Norway – moved to Grange Farm, a larger house on a hill in nearby Great Missenden. There, Roald converted a cottage in the grounds into a writing studio. Labour restrictions forced him to do most of the decorating himself. Mrs Moore, another pet magpie, lightened the atmosphere somewhat by treading in a bucket of paint and following him around with "white boots", but nevertheless he found the experience "very moribunding".[57] Often the book seemed close to crushing him. In October, he wrote gloomily to Ann Watkins that he was feeling "no love whatsoever" for this "bastard world", and that he knew exactly who were responsible for this. "I loathe, despise and abhor everything to do with the phukking Gremlins," he told her.[58] He had become almost like his alter ego Peternip, whose brain was "clogged and saturated with the impossible and the fantastic".[59] On top of that, he was getting very little professional support either from friends or family. Asta, for example, who had been hired to type the manuscript, told her brother with relish that she thought the story "just didn't work" and that Roald was writing "absolute baloney".[60] As he struggled to complete the novel that Ann Watkins, Maxwell Perkins and others believed was in him, Dahl must have felt he was looking deep into an abyss, wondering whether, like his hero Peternip, "no man can lose confidence and all his faith unless he lose all of himself as well".[61] He was on his own. Those who believed in him most were 3,000 miles away. Two things helped keep him sane. Listening to music. And his dogs.

In December 1946, Dahl completed the "bastard book".[62] Later that day, he took one of his greyhound bitches to be inseminated and fantasized about the life of its canine mate. "What a lovely life it must be to be an expensive and well cared-for stud-dog," he speculated to Ann Watkins, adding jokily that it would of course be nice "to have a say in the choice of bitches".[63] Of his own love life at this time it is hard to form a clear picture except that there was no strong emotional commitment to anyone. Other than the "girlfriend who types", his letters to his transatlantic confidants, Charles Marsh, Claudia Haines and Ann Watkins, reveal nothing.§ Alfhild remembered her brother regularly going up to London to meet "call girls", dating a pretty actress called Ann Darcy, and having "something quite serious" with the widow of a man who had won the VC

---

§Unfortunately Dahl's letters to Ann Watkins for the year 1947 are unaccountably missing from the collection currently housed at Columbia University.

during the war, to whom he gave the bracelet that had been a present to him from Millicent Rogers.[64] But, as so often with affairs of the heart, Dahl played his emotional cards very close to his chest.

His writing does, however, hold out one or two tantalizing clues. In the novel that followed *Some Time Never*, he attempted, unusually for him, to describe several realistic sexual encounters. The principal character in *Fifty Thousand Frogskins*, the swindler Gordon Hawes, is a postwar Don Juan, whose view of women is callous and functional. His attitude contrasts markedly with that of his dimwitted but well-meaning sidekick, Sidney Cubbage. The sex-starved Cubbage, who is desperate for some action with his sweetheart Clarice, thinks women exist on a higher dimension. The sophisticated Hawes disagrees. There's "nothing respectable" about women, he bluntly tells his friend. "Every woman is a whore at heart." Hawes talks about "sexwork" and "womanwork", and keeps body hair from each of his conquests in a bureau, "like an egg-collector's drawers, each in a cellophane envelope". He is drawn to seduction, as he is drawn to making money, regarding "hunting down women" as his entertainment. Remove the exaggeration and the fetishism and this view may reflect something of Dahl's own attitude to sex – at least at this period of his life. Hawes at one point criticizes Cubbage for "glorifying copulation", arguing as Dahl himself might have done that in reality the act is "messy, slightly acrobatic and very undignified. It is indecent," he continues, "even between a bishop and his wife. . . . You try doing it with your wife in a public park. You'll soon find out whether it's indecent or not."[65]

A few days after he had completed the manuscript of *Some Time Never*, Dahl was admitted into the Military Hospital for Head Injuries, near Wheatley, where he spent the Christmas of 1946, because his back pain was so intense that he could no longer walk. His doctors now recommended further surgery on the spine. He was not by nature a complaining patient, but the comparison between the austerity of a British military institution and the luxury of the Scott and White Clinic in Texas was shocking. No longer one of the lucky few, with private room and state-of-the-art service, now he was just one of the many whose new socialist health care, though free, was very far from luxurious. Moreover,

Britain was facing the worst winter in living memory – with extreme cold and fuel shortages so severe that even the hospital could not get enough coal for its boilers.

"Things not so bright here . . . Been pretty ill," Roald told Claudia Haines in a scrawled note that makes plain how painful even the act of writing had become. The hospital was grim – "a remote place, very hot and very cold, very close to mad people, very silent".[66] With Ann Watkins he attempted to make light of the situation. "Of all the godforsaken places in which to be, this is it . . . There's no heating because there's no fuel, and the room is as cold as the tip of an Eskimo's tool. I am flat on the back and floating on a haze of morphine and faraway pain and next week I think an operation on the spine. I do not give a bugger what they do so long as I can sit up in my right senses and get on with some work . . . Pardon this illegible, unintelligible impossible scribble, but I'm sort of writing on the ceiling if you see what I mean."[67] Three days later, "angry" and "half-crazy with pain",[68] he got into a fight with the editor of the magazine that had published his first story.

Before going into the hospital, and while trying to finish *Some Time Never*, Dahl had written an "interlude",[69] a piece of high-class reportage about Gordon Butcher, a humble farmworker, who had accidentally ploughed up a vast hoard of Roman silver in the Suffolk village of Mildenhall, and his deceitful conniving boss, who secreted the silver away, telling Butcher that it was only pewter. It was a tale of avarice and innocence that, Dahl recalled, sent "shivers of electricity all the way down my legs to the soles of my feet"[70] when he came across it in the newspapers. He went up to Suffolk to meet the protagonists, and a few days later the story was complete. Watkins sold it to the *Saturday Evening Post*, who paid $1,000 for it. However, as so often, the magazine found the article overlong and proposed a number of cuts and changes.

Dahl wrote back furiously, arguing that a "clumsy editorial sausage-machine" was destroying many of his "carefully-planned little touches", and reducing his own "individual style" to generic journalese.[71] Ann Watkins, who knew how much Dahl needed the money, tried to smooth over the situation. "Darling," she wrote, "what in the name of heaven, is the use of kicking over the traces and making enemies of editors?"[72] But for once she was unable to change his mind. There was an impasse. Stuart Rose, the *Post*'s editor, refused to publish the piece without cuts and Dahl, notwithstanding his pain and discomfort, stubbornly refused to sanction them. Rose eventually asked Dahl to return the money he had been advanced. Watkins hoped she would be able to sell the piece elsewhere. But no one would take it. Then came another blow. *Over to You*, which had been published in Britain a month earlier, received disappointing reviews – at least by comparison to those it had received in the United States. Increasingly, Roald's future seemed to be hanging on the fate of his ambitious new novel, which he despatched with trepidation to Watkins for her comments when he was discharged from hospital.

A year earlier, Dahl had terminated his relationship with Reynal & Hitchcock, the publishers of *Over to You*. Irritated that publication had been postponed and that the book had consequently missed the lucrative Christmas market, he told Ann Watkins that he thought Curtice Hitchcock "a goddammed liar", adding – with uncharacteristic diplomacy – that although he was through with the firm, there was "no point in being rude at this stage".[73] Hitchcock's unexpected death five months later, aged only fifty-four, simply reinforced a decision Dahl had already made: Maxwell Perkins, and Scribner's, would publish his novel.¶ He was profoundly flattered by the attention of the fiction editor who had discovered Fitzgerald, Hemingway, and Thomas Wolfe, and the dynamic Perkins's confidence in his ability was a vital support to his own self-belief.

Shortly after Roald left the hospital, in January 1947, Perkins sent the convalescing author a long letter, sympathizing over his spine operation, gossiping about their mutual friend "Old Hem", and asking eagerly about the novel, which he had heard was almost complete.[74] Dahl, still in great physical pain and smarting from the rejections of *The Mildenhall Treasure*, was slowly revising his manuscript in the light of Watkins's comments and did not want to submit the book to Scribner's until he felt it

---

¶Dahl later conflated these events, telling Alfred Knopf that he only left Reynal & Hitchcock because "Hitchcock died and the firm disbanded" – Dahl, Letter to Alfred Knopf, 5/13/81 – HRCH KNOPF 553.1.

was ready. These changes took him another five months. The first person to read it at Scribner's was Perkins's close associate and contemporary, the poet John Hall Wheelock, whose protective, almost paternal attitude to Roald mirrored that of Perkins. Wheelock was immediately enthusiastic about the novel, agreeing with Ann Watkins that it was "an important piece of work",[75] and describing it as a contemporary satire in the mould of Jonathan Swift. He wrote to Dahl effusively, describing the "deep impression" the book had made on him, and concluding that it was "a difficult piece of work beautifully carried out".[76] Wheelock added that a copy had been sent to Perkins's home in New Canaan, Connecticut, and that the great man was now in the middle of reading it. Dahl waited anxiously for his verdict.

It never came. Two days after he had received the manuscript, Perkins contracted viral pneumonia and died. He was sixty-two years old. The manuscript of *Some Time Never* – possibly the last thing he ever read – was left on his desk with his notes by its side. Dahl was devastated when he heard the news. A week later, Wheelock wrote to him, thanking him for his letter of condolence and informing him that Max had been intending to tell Dahl of his "admiration for the Gremlin book". Wheelock added that he too had "the greatest confidence" in Dahl's talent and assured him that Scribner's were "very lucky to be your publishers".[77] Celebrating the novel's "outrageous fantasy and wit", he proposed one or two small changes, mostly where he felt the reader's credulity had been strained too far. In doing so, he compared the complex balance of fantastical satire and earthy reality to blowing up a balloon to the point where it is just about to burst but has not yet done so. Still, Wheelock admitted that publishing the novel would be a gamble because it didn't fit into any of Scribner's "usual categories" and might be difficult to sell. "I don't see how it can fail to get splendid press and real recognition from people who know the best when they see it," he continued, but "its conclusions, which have terrifying conviction, will not make it perhaps popular reading."[78]

Dahl had wanted the book illustrated by Mervyn Peake, but was persuaded that it should be published without illustrations. Wheelock believed in the novel, and in the "freshness and vigor"[79] of Dahl's writing, but his conscientious, thoughtful support was no match for Perkins's freewheeling energy and optimism. Moreover, Wheelock himself was overwhelmed, not only by grief at the loss of his closest friend, whom he had known since they were students together at Harvard forty years earlier, but by the volume of work that fell to him following Perkins's death. He simply did not have time to give the manuscript the thorough editing it needed. Dahl may have sensed this, for the self-confidence he showed in dealing with *The Mildenhall Treasure* is entirely absent from his correspondence about *Some Time Never*. One senses uncertainty and nervousness at every turn. Indeed, many of his letters about the novel both to Wheelock and to Ann Watkins seem to invite comment and criticism that was not forthcoming from either of them. His anxieties were doubtless further heightened when, despite the relative commercial success of *Over to You*, which had just earned back its British advance, and had also narrowly missed winning the prestigious John Llewellyn Rhys Prize,** Hamish Hamilton wrote to him to say that they found the novel "a disappointment"[80] and informed him that they did not want to publish it in the United Kingdom.

This reaction was probably not entirely unexpected. Dahl was acutely aware that he lacked a powerful advocate in London. No publisher there responded to him with anything like the warmth and support he received from Hitchcock, Perkins or Wheelock. Nor could he find a representative who really believed in him and wanted to launch his UK career. He had regarded his first UK agent, David Higham, as a "dirty old bastard",[81] and fired him within weeks of his return from the United States. Peter Watt, whom he hired as a replacement on Ann Watkins's recommendation, was now proving to be equally disappointing. Watt was usually "too busy" to see him and Dahl was constantly made aware how low he stood in the agency's pecking order. Eventually, his feelings boiled over into anger. "Do you know," he told Watkins, "I sent Peter Watt the manu-

---

** Dahl lost the prize, which was awarded to a new work by a British writer under thirty-five, on a technicality. After the judges had initially chosen *Over to You* as the winner, the book was declared ineligible for the competition because the collection had already been published in the United States.

script [of *Some Time Never*] and he didn't read it. He wrote back and said 'My reader reports . . .' So I answered in a fury and said, 'For God's sake, man, don't you read the stuff you get?' And he replied, 'No, I haven't time.' A bloody fine agent, Peter Watt." Watt and "his entourage of decrepit and important old men", Dahl concluded, were about as much use to him "as a group of matrons at a tea-party".[82]

It was a massive contrast to the way he was treated by Watkins and her team, who were prepared to do almost anything for him. For years they acted as an unofficial purchasing house for him, sending him everything he asked for – whether model aircraft for his young nephew Nicholas, chocolates for his family, outsize shoes for his six-foot-tall sister Asta, or regular supplies of his favourite Dixon Ticonderoga HB pencils and lined yellow legal pads. This last tradition began in 1946, when Dahl complained about having to write with postwar utility pencils: using them was "like writing with a piece of charcoal on a lump of gravel".[83] The pencils and yellow pads rapidly become talismanic for him. The costs of their purchase and shipping were simply deducted from his next royalty statements.

It took Dahl more than a decade to find anyone in London who believed in him professionally as much as many people did in the United States. Despite the fact that he was an injured pilot, whose only civilian work experience was as a junior manager with Shell, he had immediately felt part of a literary milieu in New York and Washington. He hobnobbed with Hemingway and Lillian Hellman. He got to know C. S. Forester, Ben Travers and Noël Coward, and was welcomed in their Washington and Manhattan circles. The Americans took the handsome, uniformed, opinionated outsider to their hearts. In conformist Britain, and out of uniform, things were different. There, Dahl seemed peripheral rather than exotic, a "misfit", as his niece Anna Corrie described him.[84] He had not been to university. Yet he was neither working class nor an eccentric aristocrat. He was classless. He was political without a party affiliation. He loved good wine and glamorous company, yet he lived in a country cottage with his mother surrounded by a menagerie of animals. On top of that, he lacked a certain literary sophistication. And he knew it. Despite his apparent confidence, to his agents Ann Watkins and her successor Sheila St Lawrence he would admit privately that, for many years, he saw himself as an apprentice to his craft. He felt comfortable revealing his vulnerability to them. And, in return, both women nurtured his talent with warmth and affection. Dahl repaid this handsomely. While he would change publishers regularly in future years, he remained loyal to the Watkins Agency – even after Watkins and St Lawrence had retired and he felt the firm was being badly run. He never forgot his debt to the ancient dame with fuzzy grey hair, who supported him when times were tough and whom he celebrated as "the only one who has never been too busy to see me".[85]

This susceptibility to criticism was probably the reason why, for a man whose opinions were usually forthright and fearless, Dahl rarely reviewed the work of others or contributed to literary debate. In Washington, he had dipped his toe in the water when the *Saturday Review* asked him to review *Desert Episode*, a novel by George Greenfield about the war in North Africa. Dahl did not like it. He told the editor that he had chosen to say "practically nothing" about the book in his review because he thought it was so bad. Instead, he offered a revealing aside on what he himself thought made a writer: "When I opened [the book]," he wrote, "I tried to forget what it had said on the cover about the author having won most of the school colours for games and how later he had won a Double First in English Literature. Especially I tried to forget about the Double First in English Literature because I can imagine how difficult it would be to write a novel after that."[86]†† Matthew Arnold's rustic ideal had encouraged his belief that university education blunted the sensibilities, and that his own autodidactic "gipsy" learning was far preferable to anything a university might offer. Making a fire-balloon, putting a penny on a railway line and letting the train flatten it, or chasing a fire engine to see what disaster lay in store at the end of the journey kept him alive and alert. He felt his responses were fresher, his ear quicker and his eye

---

†† *Desert Episode* would go on to be a great success, selling 35,000 copies in hardback and 450,000 copies in paperback. Greenfield himself would become a well-known literary agent.

sharper as a result of his life outside the groves of academe. These were values he transferred to his own children – and at least two of them came somewhat to regret this. It was only shortly before her father died in 1990, for example, that Ophelia, aged twenty-six, began her degree. Her elder sister Tessa, whose own writing career stalled around the time of her father's death, now wishes that her father had encouraged her to be more academic.[87]

What Dahl never fully acknowledged was that this "gypsy" learning made him feel vulnerable as well as strong. And the tension between those two extremes probably goes some way toward explaining his combative and often self-destructive need to be a literary outsider. Talking to him over lunch or dinner, he was usually more likely to discuss music, politics, wine, medicine, horticulture or painting than a novel he had just read. Music in particular was always a vital part of his existence. In 1947, a press release described his main hobby as "listening for hours to his favourite symphonies, played on an elaborate built-in recording machine".[88] Just after the war he may even have toyed with writing about music professionally. Peternip, his alter ego in *Some Time Never*, becomes a music critic after he is demobbed, while Roald's own wartime copy of Cecil Grey's *History of Music* is filled with the kind of scribbled marginalia that Peternip himself might have penned – thoughts about art, the soul, intellect and the future of Western music, jumbled in amongst a number of more schoolmasterly comments such as "Tosh", "No" and "Wrong . . . Purely Provocative". It was a love that would last for the rest of his life. A guest arriving for lunch or dinner in the 1980s would usually find Gipsy House echoing to Beethoven, Brahms, Tchaikovsky, Bach or Mozart. Roald happily enthused to me about his preferences for one composer over another, and Sir David Weatherall, the haematologist who looked after him in his final illness, was immensely impressed by his detailed knowledge of Mozart operas.[89] But with books it was different.

His interest in other people's writing could often seem halfhearted. I once asked him about other writers he admired and he responded in guarded generalities, praising the elegance and narrative flair of his heroes: Charles Dickens, Ernest Hemingway and Graham Greene. He told me that he found John Le Carré's style convoluted and explained how much he valued clarity and simplicity of expression.‡‡ But he was reluctant to go into details. I was disappointed at his evasiveness, but struck also by how detached he seemed from most contemporary fiction. He thought much of it too self-absorbed, declaring that he would far rather read a new thriller by Elmore Leonard than something nominated for the Booker Prize. In old age, Roald sometimes made exceptions. Long before it was famous, he celebrated Thomas Harris's thriller *The Silence of the Lambs*, for example. Its morbid originality and craftsmanship fascinated him. He even broke his golden rule and offered a pre-publication quote for it – as a favour to Tessa's old friend Amanda Conquy, who worked for Harris's publishers and had sent him the book in the hope that he might endorse it. Notoriously, too, he would get into a tussle with Salman Rushdie over his novel *The Satanic Verses*. But these were the exceptions. On literary matters, he usually kept his head well below the parapet.

When *Some Time Never* was eventually published in the United States in April 1948, it met with faint praise. Roald immediately distanced himself from the novel, telling Ann Watkins that he now thought it was "a bad book". "No-one I've given it to so far likes it," he complained, speculating that it might actually do his writing career more harm than good if it were to be published in Britain.[90] In May, he wrote again telling her that every review of the book "stinks to high heaven" and he was now "depressed about this writing business".[91] He was exaggerating. For while the *New York Times* was critical of its repetitiousness and verbosity, and critics like Bergen Evans – who would later achieve fame as the question supervisor on *The $64,000 Question* on TV – found the "cumbrousness of his supernatural machinery" hard going, there was praise for the moral intent of the book, and also for its lyricism and humour. Evans in particular singled out for special praise the "unquaint realism" of many of its descriptive passages.[92]

---

‡‡In a private letter to his old school friend Douglas Highton, Roald described Le Carré as "grossly overrated. Obscurity is never a virtue. He is either too idle or too incompetent to make the story flow. Clarity is *the* virtue . . . He gets himself into a tangle and then skips over the problem." – Dahl, Letter to Douglas Highton, undated, c. 1984.

But nothing could disguise the fact that *Some Time Never* was less of a glorious rocket than a damp squib. It did not sell, nor did it cause a great controversy. Dahl's dream of being catapulted into the realm of Hemingway and Fitzgerald failed to materialize. It was a bitter disappointment. He had put himself on the line. He had tried to write a fantastical novel of ideas. He had dug deep into his psychology and neuroses, flexing his satirical muscles to the full and penning the first published novel about the atomic bomb. But no one seemed very interested. He agreed to let Collins publish the book in the United Kingdom the following year. His editor there, Peter Wyld, left some "acrid comments" accidentally in the margin of the manuscript, which upset him, but also suggested some judicious cuts. "I feel the book was written in a mood of exuberance," he told Dahl, and consequently suggested that it be "edited in a mood of economy".[93]

Wyld's comment was on the mark, yet there is little evidence that he tried actively to help his young author turn the manuscript around. And when the book appeared in Britain, it was barely noticed. The reviewer in *The Times Literary Supplement* on March 12, 1949, summed up the response of his colleagues when he admitted that although "Mr Dahl can write quite vividly", he found "the whimsical Gremlins mythology . . . an irritating imposition". In Roald's mind, this review sealed the book's fate. He was determined to continue writing, but *Some Time Never* was now something he would try to forget. When the wounds from the book's poor reception healed, the scar tissue they left behind soon became dense and impenetrable. In 1960, after the successes of his third short story collection, *Kiss Kiss*, he would be approached to reprint *Some Time Never* in paperback. His response to Sheila St Lawrence was withering: "Why in God's world anybody should want to paperback that ghastly book I don't know."[94] Later still he told Ophelia that he never wanted to read it again because he thought it would make him feel "vulnerable".[95] And when Liccy once asked if she could read it, he told her that he would rather she did not. In 1971, a fan from Michigan, Mrs J. Goldstein, wrote to him, asking where she could get hold of a copy. "It's not worth reading," he told her bluntly.[96]

The critical rejection of *Some Time Never* marked a turning point. From that moment on, the sensitive author/narrator, so strong a presence in all Dahl's early fiction, began to disappear, increasingly hidden behind a mask of artifice and plot, while his exuberant sense of satirical fantasy also melted into the background. For more than a decade his stories would be characterized by a wit that was hard, brutal and often cruel. At times it would even seem that the sensitive youthful voice which had moved so many of his early readers might be lost for good.

Some Time Never also severed the direct link between writing and flying in Dahl's fiction. Early in 1945, when he sent the manuscript of *Someone Like You* to Ann Watkins, he had apologized for the fact that it was "still more or less on the same old theme . . . If you have a little patience," he continued, "I shall soon get that out of my system."[97] It had taken him three years, but now he had finally done so. Yet finding a new voice was not so easy. Needing money, he experimented in journalism, writing repeatedly to Watkins asking her help in getting him work as a foreign correspondent or as a "staff reporter anywhere in the world".[98] In October 1949, he proposed that he should go out and cover the Greek Civil War, doing "human interest stories on the fighting, the ruined villages, the ruined lives, the girl soldiers, and all such things as that".[99] But because she believed in him as a fiction writer, Watkins did not play ball. Aside from *The Mildenhall Treasure*, his only other attempts at journalism were a piece about Kuda Bux,[100] a Hindu mystic who appeared to be able to see without using his eyes, and one about the two British diplomats, Guy Burgess and Donald Maclean, who mysteriously disappeared in May 1951. It was later revealed that both had been spying for the Russians and had secretly defected to the Soviet Union. This piece is intriguing because it is one of the few places where Dahl attempted seriously to explore the English social milieu in which he himself was now functioning. Curiously, although he was critical of the two spies for their "weakness", he was not unsympathetic to their predicament.

Roald had worked with Maclean at the British Embassy in Washington, and had recognized, where others had not, that he was unstable – a habitual drunkard, who was, as Dahl put it, unable "to resolve the problem of homosexuality versus normalcy". His sex life, however, was not the most abnormal thing about Maclean. Roald sensed, probably from personal experience, that espionage had corrupted him; that he "would probably have given anything to stop his spying, but there is never any stopping in that business once you start". Most revealing of all was his portrayal of Maclean's colleagues in the Foreign Office. When Maclean drunkenly declared that he was a Soviet spy while drinking with them at the Gargoyle Club in Soho, Dahl celebrated the fact that none of them denounced him, because they assumed he was joking. It was, he wrote, "a refreshing change from the howls of the witch-hunters, and the Gestapo of Senator McCarthy and all other forms of Fascism – from which the good Lord deliver us please". On the other hand, he was also critical of the lack of imagination he saw in these weak, overeducated men – "half-successful painters with long side-burns, intellectual writers, bad musicians, queer foreign office types . . . who speak with contempt about everything that is normal, and try to feel strong in each other's company. But they are not strong at all." [101]

Dahl probably sensed that he would always remain an outsider to these university-educated intellectuals. He despised them for their weakness, for their lack of imagination and for the fact that they could not see further than the environment in which they always functioned.

The Foreign Office type, like his colleague in the State Department across the water, is a peculiar bird. He is a hard worker, and he is grossly underpaid for what he does. He is a man of extreme caution, watching his own position and never taking a step which might spoil his chances of promotion. He is obsequious to his superiors and contemptuous of outsiders. He is very good at Latin. But apart from that, and most importantly of all, he seems to be completely out of touch with reality. He undoubtedly still hopes, deep in his heart, that the two culprits have not gone over to Russia at all, but have either joined the Foreign Legion, or slipped into a monastery in France. [102]

Aside from his journalism, Dahl also began a number of creepy short stories, exploring human vices and follies. The most contrived was "Foreign Intelligence", in which a mysterious émigré medic tells the narrator that he has isolated "the centre of intelligence" within the human mind and succeeded in transplanting it into the brain of a rat. A hostile government, he tells the bemused narrator, is now breeding these rats "in regiments" so that they can invade England and kill many thousands of humans in their beds with a single bite to the jugular vein. This implausible story is rendered sinister by the fact that Dahl gives the strange scientist alarmingly rodentine qualities. His head is "large, long . . . with a whole lot of coarse, black hair", and he has a "small, sunken mouth", which continually opens and shuts "like a pair of scissors". At the end, the narrator listens to the "quick click-click" of his footsteps as he disappears into the night.[103]

This hint of the gruesome was to become characteristic of a new phase in Dahl's writing. It was manifested in the tale he had told Annabella in New York about the rich old man who enjoyed betting with impoverished young strangers – staking his expensive car against the little fingers of their left hand. Originally called "The Menace", it was retitled "The Slasher" and then "Collector's Item" before finally appearing as "The Man from the South". But the best of these new tales is "The Dogchild", a bleak wartime parable about human cruelty in which a vindictive German family during the war raises an abandoned Russian orphan as if he were a dog. The tale explores in microcosm the same misanthropic territory of *Some Time Never*. But this time there is no fantasy. The situation here is all too real and there are no sweeping authorial judgements. In their place is the cool eye for detail that had characterized Dahl's flying stories and an understated but unerring sense of surefootedness about the evil he portrays. It is for the reader to witness that in this most savage of worlds, only the child and the dog with which he is kennelled behave with any kind of warmth or dignity. The tale is dark, bitter, brilliant – and still unpublished.

All of these stories were an attempt to find a new voice. The best of them provided a searing glimpse into the dark heart of human behaviour. With others the contrivances of plot were more in the foreground. All of them were characterized by a sharp perception of human flaws and were self-consciously designed to shock. Peter Watt, who now read Roald's manuscripts himself – an honour the author sarcastically commented was only granted to "Kipling, Hugh Walpole, Galsworthy and a woman called Hermione Hornswoggler" [104] – found himself profoundly disturbed by them. He told Dahl they were "the most horrific" tales he had ever read, and that for this reason, "our unenlightened editors" would never publish them.[105] Even Ann Watkins was nonplussed, telling Roald bluntly that, though "beautifully written", the stories were "not exactly what the doctor ordered". She thought their only market would be "a horror magazine", and simply refused to submit them for publication to mainstream magazines because she was quite certain they would be rejected. She encouraged him to try and lighten up, lest he scare the readers of *Good Housekeeping* to death. "That's all I can say to you," she concluded, "except to cheer up and not continue to feel the world is so terrible. Life is worth living, and there are a few good people in this world. By gosh there are." [106] Dahl replied forcefully that if the readers of *Good Housekeeping* continued to devour the "escapist nonsense" that was currently being "dished out to them", they would soon be "scared to death much more violently and more literally".[107]

Sadly, the delights of country living were beginning to wear thin. Despite being surrounded by his family, in the "Valley of the Dahls," as Tessa would later describe it, Roald was dogged by something akin to depression. His contact with children leavened the gloom a little. Forays into the woods and fields with his model aeroplane and his nieces and nephew could not disguise the fact that his relationship with his mother, now in her early sixties, had deteriorated badly. While Roald was "great companions" [108] with his sister Asta, his niece, Lou, remembered hearing from her mother that her uncle had been "unkind" to Sofie Magdalene while he was at Grange Farm and had treated her a bit like a landlady.[109] Lou's twin sister Anna concurred, but suggested that her grandmother, Mormor – "Mother's Mother" in Norwegian – was struggling with her own demons as well.[110] Their father, John Logsdail, had finally succeeded in breaking Harald's trust, thereby releasing some income for her, but she was now suffering from chronic arthritis and often seemed lost in her own world. Increasingly she withdrew from her children, becoming "uncommunicative", "undemonstrative" and "unaffectionate" toward them in a way that she was not with her animals.[111]

It was a difficult time, when neither mother nor son seems to have understood the other. Both were drinking heavily. Roald may have felt that she was incapable of understanding what he had been through in the war, of comprehending why he had changed. Perhaps Sofie Magdalene felt too that now her beloved "apple" was in his early thirties, he should be married, with a proper job. It is hard to make a judgement as so few clues to her inner world have survived and Roald kept none of the letters she wrote him. Yet circumstantial evidence suggests a need to escape her son occasionally, because throughout the entire period that he was living with her between 1946 and 1951 she rented a cottage in Cornwall: Greystones at Praa Sands, near Land's End. It was a place to which she could disappear whenever she needed to be alone with her dogs. That streak of melancholy, of a need for isolation, ran deeply through the Dahl genes. It affected Mormor. It affected her daughter Else. And it affected Roald, whose youngest daughter Lucy told me that she thought "depression" was not quite the right term for it. It was more, she felt, a characteristic Nordic need for "dark solitude, wanting to be dark and alone, which is considered these days as depressed. But then," she continued, "I think, what are the symptoms of depression? Sleep, not wanting to socialize, drinking a lot. He'd fit into all of those categories."[112]

The tense claustrophobia of this life with his mother was made most manifest in the last of Dahl's "personal" stories, "People Nowadays", which he later retitled "The Soldier". It is a melancholy coda to the flying tales, in which the protagonist, a war veteran, is trapped in a cold and joyless marriage, with a wife who has no understanding of what he has suffered. The setting is a location remarkably like Grange Farm, where "through the open window the unhappy couple could hear the water in the millstream going over the dam far down the valley". There, the soldier, haunted by recurrent nightmares and hallucinations, starts to lose his mind. He tries to banish them by recalling the happy memories of his childhood, "seaside holidays in the summer, wet sand and red buckets and shrimping nets and the clear small pools and sea anemones and snails and mussels and sometimes one grey translucent shrimp hovering deep down in the beautiful green water". But his contemptuous wife, with her "hard blue white eyes secret and cunning", cannot understand his behaviour. She offers him no sympathy and only contrives to drive him closer toward madness. Their relationship is described as "strange and difficult". It used not to be like that, Dahl tells us, but now she is "as strange and difficult as they come". The soldier loves her despite the fact that she is an "awful, cruel bitch", and despite the fact that sometimes he gets so angry that he feels violent toward her. In the end, it is his wife who attacks him, smacking her husband across the face "with a quick right hand", and leaving him crying on the bed.[113]

It is fiction, of course. But it is more than possible that Dahl was working out a certain aspect of his troubled relationship with his mother in these nine spare pages. The tone of melancholy tenderness, of a love that has soured because the soldier cannot share the intensity of his wartime experiences, was quite out of keeping with the other more fantastical stories he was writing, and for once Ann Watkins missed its point. "It's a very strange story indeed," she wrote to him, somewhat patronizingly, when he sent it to her. "When you find out what it means, will you please let me know, dear?"[114]

Dahl himself escaped for a month to Jamaica in early 1948, flying via Senegal and Brazil, and staying for two weeks with Hemingway at Sir William Stephenson's house in Hillowton outside Montego Bay – a "dream place" where he went swimming every day on Max Beaverbrook's private beach. He then travelled east along the north coast of the island to spend a few days with Charles Marsh near Ocho Rios. But he ended up staying as the house guest of Pamela Berry, the Marchioness of Huntly, and making his Jamaican "headquarters" with her.[115] The two of them had struck up a friendship on the flight over from Senegal. She was travelling with her two young children – but without her husband, Douglas Gordon, the 12th Marquis of Huntly. Lemina, her seven-year old daughter, recalled that the plane was "so noisy one couldn't have a normal conversation", and that "the man sitting across the aisle" had passed her mother a note asking if she played gin rummy.[116] She did. Roald and Pam played for six and a half hours. Afterwards he boasted that he had taken more than five pounds off her.[117]

Returning to England, the drudge of daily existence quickly wore him down again. He was also desperately short of money. Writing from 10 a.m. to 1 p.m. and 8 p.m. to midnight, always "with the blinds drawn and an electric light on",[118] he turned out material faster than he ever would again. But it was no use. He even tried to write a love story, a piece of "frightful bullshit" which, he told Watkins, could be "turned inside out, washed in soapsuds, put through the mangle, rinsed, ironed and dyed the colour of raspberry jam – if that will help to sell it".[119] Even that failed to find a buyer.[120] In June, he wrote to Watkins telling her that he was going broke, "literally and literarily", and that he was thinking of giving up and marrying a rich woman instead.[121] He even considered taking a job "with some bastard firm of stockbrokers in an effort to make a lot of money in two years – so that I can then write forever at my leisure". Yet he was still defiant. "I'm not disillusioned," he concluded. "I shall continue to write and I truly believe that one day I shall produce a really first-class novel. The stories I'm doing now may not sell, but they are wonderful practice and I learn a little more with each one I do."[122]

Then, quite unexpectedly, the tide turned. *Collier's* magazine bought the tale about the man who collected little fingers. Dahl immediately spent a large part of his fee on a trip to Paris. A month later, there was even better news. The magazine gave him a bonus of $1,000 for the story because it had been judged the best of the year. The news was a massive confidence boost. Dahl described it as "like a shot of Spanish fly to a tired and worn-out sexual athlete".[123] A few months later, he was offered $2,500 to write a piece about love. He could not believe it. "To dangle so much goddam money before the eyes of a writer . . . for a few pages of pure crystalline bullshit," he declared, was a "base crime". Nevertheless, he admitted, "all whores have their price". And in this case $2,500 did the trick. "It made me vomit to do it," he told Watkins when he sent her his piece, "and you know as I do, once a whore, always a whore . . . but send it to them quick and tell them they can cut this one just as much as they like. *And get that dough.*"[124]

The cash from those two stories made Dahl solvent once again. It allowed him to continue writing and sustain his principal daytime pursuit: greyhound racing. This passion was to be one of the main drains on the inheritance his father had left him. At one time Roald had as many as sixteen dogs under the supervision of his trainer, Tommy – an Irishman, with "no teeth and two left eyes and a profound knowledge of all the lousy dirty bastardly tricks in the greyhound racing trade".[125] Dahl rented a cottage in nearby Kirtlington for Tommy and the dogs, and paid him a salary as a trainer, but neither his initial purchase, Snailbox Lady, nor her offspring – which came from the bizarre experiment of mating her with her brother – produced the litters of future champions for which he hoped. Most ended up being given to his mother as pets. However, at Tommy's suggestion, he travelled to Ireland and acquired a dog called Baytown Lark, which he raced at a dog track near Oxford with great success. Though the dogs consumed only a small amount of his time – when he went up once a week to pay Tommy his wages – they and the cunning, wily folk who hung around them intrigued Dahl hugely and fed his literary imagination. Alfhild recalled with delight the substantial winnings that Baytown Lark provided the whole family after his first race, and vividly recollected how much her brother loved[126] the dog-racing fraternity. Alexandra, Asta's daughter, also recollected that Roald struck up a great friendship with a local butcher's assistant, Claud Taylor, a man with "very dark hair, almost patent leather",[127] who grazed his bullocks in the orchard at Grange Farm. He would initiate Dahl into many secret and illicit rural practices, and inspire his next novel.

CHAPTER TWELVE

The Poacher

IN 1975, ROALD DAHL returned to Repton to give a talk. He was nearly sixty years old. In amongst some trenchant criticisms of his old school, he talked at some length about the qualities he felt were necessary in a writer. Fiction writing, he told his audience, was "something you slide into very cautiously and usually through a side door. Only a madman would choose it as the primary way to earn a living until he proved to himself he could bring it off."[1] It was a curious assertion. For Dahl spoke as if he had personally responded to the advice Charles Marsh gave him shortly after he arrived in the United Kingdom and taken "an honest publishing job"[2] before writing full time. In reality, he had done the exact opposite, eschewing any kind of desk job and supplementing the small amount of money he earned from writing with the modest (soon to be exhausted) private income from the trust his father had left for him. He might moan and groan to Ann Watkins about the vicissitudes of writing, but his commitment to his craft would never seriously falter. He had been seized by the desire to tell stories and had responded completely to the compulsion. He had become one of his own madmen. Never was this more clearly apparent than when – after the setback of *Some Time Never* – Dahl decided almost immediately to embark upon another major work of fiction.

He knew from the outset that the book would be quite different from its predecessor – a "good straight novel".[3] Gone was the futuristic setting. Gone was any reference to flying. Gone were the ominous rumblings of nuclear holocaust and human self-destruction. Gone even was the flamboyant satire. Only an acute eye for human cunning and a general air of gloom connected this warts-and-all chronicle of postwar British rural life to its predecessor. Into its fabric he determined to weave all he had learned about greyhounds, poaching, gambling and deception and create a tart comedy of British country manners. The book first began to take shape in May 1948, when he became aware of its themes "maturing slowly in the half-empty barrel of my head".[4] It was a lengthy fermentation. Almost two years later, he had completed only two chapters alongside a mere handful of new short stories.[5] Part of this was due to being afflicted with what he called "imaginative constipation" – a time when "nothing, no work, no stories, nothing would come".[6] Part of it was due to self-confessed laziness. But part of it was also due to the fact that he was still suffering chronic back pain, and had been put in an uncomfortable brace to strengthen his spine. Yet, he was still positive. "If things go right," he told Ann Watkins, "there's just a chance [the novel] will be a good one. No more satiric or metaphysical bullshit like Gremlins. Just ordinary stuff."[7]

This "ordinary" novel would become perhaps the strangest thing he ever wrote – a twisted comic portrait of the four years he spent in Great Missenden and Old Amersham between 1946 and 1950. It is a period that remains shrouded in some obscurity – largely because little documentary evidence of it survives. Roald lived with his mother, so the only letters to her from this period were written on the odd occasions that he travelled abroad. Fortunately, his correspondence with Ann Watkins, and Charles Marsh and Claudia Haines, in New York provides some sort of a window into his thought processes. Yet, as so often with Dahl, these letters often present a front to the world – and usually it is that of entertainer. He is seldom revealing about his interior world, and although the letters are full of gossip, jokes, and information about his writing, there is little about the deep fears and frustrations he was almost certainly feeling, and which, in 1950, would lead to the great crisis of his professional career.

Ann Watkins suspected that the energy of his Washington years had

abated somewhat and that he was now often idle; indeed, when Charles
Marsh tempted him with a free holiday in 1949, he declined, admitting that he was "lazy enough already".[8] "I'm in a bit of a mess," he had
mournfully confided to Marsh the previous year, "because I'm going
through a non money-making period, which doesn't encourage – and
I flourish on encouragement."[9] In place of flying tiny aircraft in exotic
locations, in place of life-and-death struggles in the skies, in place of
life as a celebrity in Washington, Los Angeles and New York, he had
greyhounds, antiques, and gardening. He no longer even had his studio.
At the end of 1948, Roald and his increasingly arthritic mother had
left Grange Farm and moved four miles southeast, to a "smallish white
early Georgian"[10] town house on the High Street of Old Amersham,
which was less isolated and where she could be nearer the local shops.
Asta briefly shared the new house with them as well, but moved out
when she got married to the local vet, Alex Anderson. So mother and
son were there alone. Amersham was not yet the dormitory suburb it
would become later in the fifties when the railway to London was electrified. Then, it was still a thriving ancient market town, with a host of
butchers, grocers and greengrocers dotted along the picturesque main
street.

Wistaria Cottage, where the Dahls lived, had a modest frontage, but
inside the house was large and rambling. Surrounded by two alleyways
on either side, it was configured so that there was an independent top-
floor flat with a separate entrance from one of the alleys. This was where
Roald lived. The position on the High Street suited Sofie Magdalene fine.
Dressed in black and speaking in her thick Norwegian accent, Mrs Dahl
soon became something a local character – telling stories, gossiping and
making psychic predictions about the future of people she had barely
met. Her many eccentricities included subscriptions to the weekly "scandal sheet" the *News of the World*, and to the monthly naturist magazine
Health and Efficiency, which might have been unremarkable in Scandinavia, but in fifties Britain was regarded as semipornographic. Her grandson
Nicky Logsdail vividly recalled its photographs, with nipples and pubic
areas modestly blanked out, and the frisson this caused amongst his own

friends when the magazine was delivered.[11] With some of her new money she also bought a very early black and white television set. Mounted in a grand wood veneer cabinet, her grandchildren clamoured to come over and watch it.

The house also had a substantial garden, where Roald and his mother spent many hours planting fruit trees and building an elaborate rockery. A rickety wooden bridge with a flimsy handrail ran from the bottom of the garden across a tiny stream, the Misbourne, which separated the gardens from a large area of common ground, in the middle of which stood a huge elm tree. Sometimes Roald flew model aircraft in the field with his young nephew Nicholas, who recalled his uncle's shock at discovering that local children had vandalized the ancient tree, lighting a fire in the middle of its huge hollow trunk. Despite his anger at the violation, Roald could not resist taking him into the elm's burned-out interior to see what it smelled like and whether it had any unusual acoustics. At other times, Roald took the boy out in his customized shiny Vauxhall Cresta to seek for adventure. Nicholas remembered with delight how the local blacksmith turned the car into a "three and a half seater" by welding the front seat further back on the chassis, so that Roald could sit more comfortably. He also recalled that his grandmother would sometimes nag his uncle about why he had not married and advise him about the qualities he should look for in a bride. Roald ignored her. In hindsight, Logsdail had the feeling that his uncle's womanizing was both serious and secretive.[12] His sisters seemed never to know what their brother was up to, and were reduced to gossip and speculation. Their suspicions, for example, that Roald was sleeping with the Logsdails' Norwegian nanny were confirmed when one day Roald took her up to London "to see the sights". All she could talk about on her return was the size of the baths at the Savoy Hotel.[13]

A frequent visitor to Wistaria Cottage was Claud Taylor, who lived in a "dark and dingy"[14] flat next to the almshouses that ran off the eastern of the two alleyways on either side of the Dahls' property. Claud was "a storyteller and a bit of a rogue",[15] who sometimes did odd jobs around the house for Sofie Magdalene. He was married, with three small children of his own, and though Dahl would later claim that Claud "had difficulty mustering a sentence of much more than four words", the two men soon became firm friends. What brought them together was a shared love of the natural world, a mutual fascination with gambling, and the desire, as Dahl put it, "to acquire something by stealth without paying for it".[16] Claud soon became Roald's most regular companion. Despite manifest differences of background and wealth, the two men and their families were always on first-name terms and spent a lot of time in each other's company. Claud's daughters, Sue and Jenny, still retain a clear image of their father and Roald "sitting on either side of the hearth in Wistaria Cottage, with two greyhounds stretched out on the floor between them, endlessly plotting how to make their fortunes".[17]

Claud was practical. He helped Roald design and built a portable writing desk – a board covered in green baize from a billiard table, which he could place across the arms of a large armchair. This enabled him to write without pain and quickly became one of his totem writing accessories, along with the lined yellow legal pads and his sharpened Dixon Ticonderoga pencils – always an even number, because odd numbers were unlucky. He would use the desk for the rest of his life. Claud possessed the gypsy spirit Roald so admired and was an expert on all things to do with animals and the countryside. Though eminently respectable – his eldest daughter did not hear her father swear until she was in her twenties – Claud shared Roald's delight in those grey areas of rural legality and taught him much about horse racing, greyhound racing, canasta, and (best of all) poaching.[18] Whether it was leading a cow across woods and fields at dead of night to be secretly inseminated by a prize bull, or bagging pheasants from the woods of Claud's boss, George Brazil, this "sporting type of stealing", and the "delicious element of risk"[19] it generated, thrilled Roald.

Brazil was the local rich man, a "nouveau riche" landowner, who drove around town in a large Rolls-Royce that he replaced every couple of years.[20] He would be the victim of a brilliant poaching stratagem that hinged on the idea of feeding pheasants large raisins that had been laced with sleeping pills. Claud's daughters could both still remember their excitement as the two men set out at dusk for this adventure, with their bags packed with fruit they had slit open, filled with powdered sedatives, and then stitched back up again. Curiously, neither could recall whether the ruse was actually successful, but Jenny did remember that the family had eaten an awful lot of pheasants that winter. Dahl himself was so proud of this ingenious scheme that he recounted it in several different pieces of fiction, most memorably perhaps in 1975 in *Danny the Champion of the World*. In 1949, when he first lit upon the scheme, he was so excited that he wrote immediately to Ann Watkins to explain it to her: "They gobble the raisins then feel sleepy, then go up to roost and then the little buggers sleep so hard that they fall off their bough and we catch them on the way down." "I look at it this way," he concluded. "If anyone poached me, that's how I'd like it to be done." [21]

Dahl included this caper in his new novel, *Fifty Thousand Frogskins* – "frogskins", like "greenbacks", was slang for dollar bills – whose main characters were a pair of comic rural swindlers obsessed with making their fortune through a brilliant and ingenious scam. One of them, the cunning, moustachioed car dealer Gordon Hawes, was modelled on a local character called Ginger Henderson, who owned the filling station at the bottom of Deep Mill Lane, close by Grange Farm, and sometimes joined Dahl and Taylor on trips to the local greyhound races. "Ginger was his great friend," recalled Nicholas Logsdail, "ginger hair, ginger moustache and a total black market dealer . . . a complete spiv . . . Roald would often extol the virtues of his dishonesty." [22] These crooked qualities also informed the character of Dahl's most famous used car salesman, Mr Wormwood, from his 1988 story, *Matilda*. But Wormwood's literary prototype was undoubtedly Gordon Hawes. With his stethoscope round his neck to give an air of expert professionalism, he listens to the engines of the cars he is about to buy, "like a Harley Street surgeon", gently breaking the news to an ignorant driver that the vehicle they are trying to sell him is defective and practically worthless. A con artist, with a "snaky, gleaming look in his eye", Hawes despised English snobbery, but knew how to use it cynically to his own advantage. Although he had never been anywhere near Eton College, for example, he would wear the old school tie, because he was aware that with certain customers it created "an astonishing friendliness". He was astute, selfish and obsessed by money. His dreams of glory consisted only of tricks and hustles that would deliver a thick "wad of crispies"[23] into his own back pocket.

Hawes meets his partner-in-crime, Sidney Cubbage, during the war. Both have served their country from the safety of the Catering Corps. Despite his "impression of slight imbecility" and his "pale expressionless ox-eyes", Cubbage is also sly. But his vices are redeemed by his being "loyal, energetic, wary, comic . . . the perfect stooge in all difficult transactions". Cubbage was modelled on Claud – who had also worked in the Catering Corps in Calgary, Canada – to such an extent that when Dahl later salvaged four stories from the book, the name Sidney was changed to Claud. Cubbage was much the more sympathetic of the two men, despising cruelty to animals, mourning the loss of traditional country values and complaining about the lack of trust in the society around him. Dahl wrote about him with warmth and humanity. "People's changin'," he comments wearily at the outset of the book, and as he does so, "a kind of sadness began to spread all over his face like a cloud".[24] Ann Watkins thought Cubbage by far the most successful character in the novel and described him enthusiastically as "a lovable, understandable, guy".[25] With the antihero Hawes, however, Dahl was less successful, partially because he was less detached about him. For Hawes reflected aspects of his creator's own personality. He was a survivor: an outsider, who lived off his wits, the opponent of "a vindictive and inefficient government".[26] He defied a world of unnecessary officials and regulations. His ingenuity was his trademark. And he loved gambling.

Roald himself had first felt that thrill when he worked for Shell and went to the dog races at Catford. It was in Washington, however, that his fascination with beating the odds matured. There, a clerk in the embassy initiated him into a poker circle. A man called Brett, "a tiny sly fellow", had shown him his personal safe stashed full of hundred-dollar bills. Recounting this story at Repton in 1975, Dahl maintained that at first he thought Brett must have found a way of robbing the embassy and asked whether he could join in. The clerk explained that the money was his winnings from playing bridge and poker at Washington's exclusive University Club whose members were mostly judges and senators, and included the future president, Harry Truman, then Senator for Missouri. Dahl was eager to join – even if his inexperience meant that initially he usually ended up a loser. "So two evenings a week I played in this high powered game in which there were usually at least $500 in the pot," he told his audience. "In the end, I lost all my story money there, mostly to Brett."[27] The losses however did nothing to diminish his enthusiasm.

Although the world of Buckinghamshire "flapping-tracks" was a far cry from Washington's elitist poker circles, it offered a similar gambler's buzz. These ramshackle, unlicensed events took place in unmarked fields, their time and location communicated by word of mouth alone. There, a pack of six greyhounds chased a stuffed white rabbit, pulled on a cord by the "winder", a man at the far end of the field, "frantically turning the pedals of an upturned bicycle with his hands". Dishonesty was rife. A muzzle strapped on one dog so tight that it could not properly breathe, a slender thread of black cotton tying the toes of another together so it was prevented from running at top speed, a sliver of ginger inserted up the anus of a third, so that it bolted down the track to get away from the stinging sensation. Only a year before he died, Roald confessed that his memories of these "sweet days" he spent at the flaps with his greyhounds filled him with "acute nostalgia".[28]

Dahl was not alone in his love of the "flaps". So popular did they become that the government was forced to crack down on the midweek meetings because they were leading to high levels of addictive gambling and absenteeism from work.[29] For Dahl, the events were particularly attractive because they were both a product of the "Scholar-Gypsy" lifestyle he so admired and an expression of defiance against excessive government controls. It was also a place where everyone was an outsider. Toward the end of the novel, Cubbage has an encounter with a ratcatcher called Bunce who – like the bizarre doctor in "Foreign Intelligence" – looks like a rodent. He can kill rats by biting their heads off. He is the same character, "lean and brown with a sharp face and two long sulphur-coloured teeth that protruded from the upper jaw, overlapping the lower lip, pressing it inward",[30] who will later appear in "Claud's Dog".

The ratcatcher is grotesque, but for Claud – as for Dahl – not half as repulsive as the bureaucrats and state officials, with their joyless university intellects, who seem bent on denying ordinary people their simple pleasures. "His [Cubbage's] relationship with the ratman – much as he despised him, much as he hated his cruelty – was a close one," Dahl wrote. "They were both men of the soil of the same county, and the eternal battle against the educated classes, and against officialdom and petty tyranny drew them together." *Fifty Thousand Frogskins* is populated by these small-time crooks – spivs selling black market goods; bookmakers, "scowling, furtive men in thick belted overcoats and trilby hats, watchful, predatory characters with small eyes and closed faces"; "sly, knowing" Jews; and Gypsies, "aloof, unwashed and secretive". In this world of petty sharks and grifters, among "the sewage and the scrapings from the bottom of the cesspools of the big and little towns", Hawes and Cubbage plot the scam that will win them a fortune. For they have managed to acquire two identical greyhounds: one a born loser, and another, "the ringer", who is a natural racer. They plan to pass the latter off as the former and make a fortune from the odds they will receive. Despite the attempts of their adversaries – mostly unscrupulous farmers, government officials, and bookmakers – to foil their plans, Hawes and Cubbage are eventually triumphant. They come home with plenty of "crispies" – all won from that "messy little clump of crooked humanity" that Dahl was so drawn to, "seething, shouting, slobbering and slipping about in the mud".[31] Their success was in sharp contrast to Roald's own. He would later tell Charles Marsh that he had blown all his share of his father's trust fund – possibly as much as £5,000 – on "dog racing and the characters he chose to pal around with of that world."[32]*

While he was working on the novel, Dahl kept in "training", as he called

---

*The fact that Roald squandered his inheritance on greyhounds was also confirmed to me by his wife, Patricia Neal.

it, writing ingenious short stories. "The Sound Machine" was typical. It was in some respects similar to a story he had written as a ten-year-old in the nursery at Cumberland Lodge, which he later described as his "first serious attempt at a short story".[33] In "The Kumbak II", a child discovers that his uncle Aristotle has invented a machine for listening to conversations from the past and uses it to prove that a certain Benjamin Bluebottle is guilty of the murder of Miss Jemima Redbottom. Forty years later, in "The Sound Machine", a similar man invents a device that can detect the noises plants make and therefore hear them cry out in pain. It was another tale about the possibilities of human cruelty, born from the kind of one-line observation or idea that Roald collected in his "Ideas Books" – compilations of characters, situations and ideas that he thought might one day inspire or generate a story. He had been compiling these fictional "germs" since 1945 and would go on doing so for the rest of his life. This one was jotted down simply as "STORY – sound apparatus that could hear trees scream". Sometimes these ideas were sketched out in a short paragraph or two, often unpunctuated. More often than not they were simply notions, hypotheses or information that seemed pregnant with storytelling potential. It might be a fact about dog licensing in Denmark, the description of a urological ward, a thought about the "centre of intelligence" within the human brain. There are details of ingenious scams, ways of murdering people without being detected – such as tickling someone who has a weak heart or giving a diabetic an overdose of insulin.[34]

Some are grotesque – a man who eats his aunt's ashes by mistake – while others are more fanciful and anticipate future children's books. A man who captured "thoughts, jokes and pieces of knowledge" and kept them in a jar rubs shoulders with another who drops his glass eye into a tankard and a radiologist who fires X-rays through the wall of his house to cause his next-door neighbour to become sterile. One reads simply: "Man who grew cherry the size of a grapefruit." Sometimes a newspaper cutting is pasted onto the page, the photograph of a murderer perhaps, with a comment about his eyes, or a collection of unexpected similes and whimsical connections.

People
A pale grey face like a bowl of porridge
Legs like the legs of a chair
Face like crumpled brown paper
A nose like a bathroom tap
A small crooked mouth, shaped like a keyhole

Bach's French Suite No. 4 in E flat is "Oh dear, what can the matter be" [35]

Many were blueprints for later short stories. "German who made Russian child walk like a dog," for example, or "Man with a picture tattooed on his back." † Others were notes on subjects that compelled him – "the curse of nationalism", for example, or this list of human cruelties toward animals:

French woman scraping scales off a live fish, small boys burning ants with a magnifying glass, small boys stoning a toad, the good chef who cuts a lobster in half when it is alive, the geese for foie gras. Feet nailed to plank – in front of fire. Also the ramming of food. In the French markets – skinning frogs alive. They jump about. Recipe. In Shanghai, the little monkey brought in, trussed up, little fire under him to keep his blood running. Good. Cleave head and take out brain to be eaten immediately as a delicacy. USA. The dipping of live turkeys in boiling water in large NY turkey farms. France. Cordon bleu teach you to make the flesh of a boiled trout "bleu", put hand in mouth, pull out guts of live fish before boiling. Woman plucking a live chicken. [36]

In 1949, "The Sound Machine" was accepted by *The New Yorker*, which paid him $1,000 for it. Roald was delighted. He had long wanted the magazine to publish one of his pieces and finally, after many rejections, it had happened. But joy soon turned to anguish when the editor, Harold

---

†These later became "The Dogchild" (unpublished) and "A Picture for Drioli", later retitled "Skin".

Ross, pointed out some inconsistencies and suggested both cuts and re-writes. His letter threw Dahl into a "howling fury". He wrote back accusing Ross of "mincing" his carefully wrought sentences and of presenting his author with an impossible dilemma – whether to abandon writing altogether or become "a sort of literary whore who will sleep with any editor however ugly his face".[37] When Ann Watkins read his letter, which he sent off without her knowledge, she was astonished. "What a boy!" she wrote to him admiringly, "what a boy!"[38] His response had been swift, instinctive and risky. He told Watkins that he was banking on the fact that the staff on the magazine were "an exceedingly reasonable bunch", and that they would not think he was a "conceited little bastard who wants his own way – but merely someone who is trying to find his feet and refuses to have the carpet pulled from under them".[39] The gamble paid off. Ross backed down. Watkins was amazed. He "all but ate crow," she told Roald.[40]

Roald added the tale to a number of other short stories and pieces of journalism he had written since his return to England, and offered the collection for publication. Collins was the first to pass on it. His editor there, Peter Wyld, compared it unfavourably with *Some Time Never*, acidly describing one of the stories as "failed Dorothy Parker" and another as "failed Runyon".[41] Only one tale, he felt, was up to the standard of "Over to You", and that was "The Sword", which Dahl had written seven years earlier. John Wheelock also wrote to him from Scribner's. His words were gentler, his tone more flattering, but his message was the same. A string of other rejection letters followed, mostly without comment, although Harry Maule at Random House celebrated the author's "fiendish imagination" and commented that his stories were "pretty telling exercises in the macabre".[42] Nevertheless, no one felt the collection was either of sufficient literary merit or popular appeal to be worth publishing. It was a blow. More than a year would pass before Dahl sold another story, and so he protected himself, as he admitted, by reverting to childhood – "playing with model airplanes and greyhounds".[43] His young nephews and nieces were the grateful recipients of his energies, joining their "perfect uncle" on walks in the wood or impromptu chases in his car across the countryside in the wake of the plane. All felt their time with him was blessed. This was the carefree escapism Roald would recall nostalgically forty years later, when the stresses and anxieties, the rejections and failures, had all been forgotten.[44]

Of course, he enjoyed this "messing around", but it frustrated him too, because he liked the good things in life. He liked mixing with the wealthy and famous. He liked being the provider of unusual and exotic treats for his family. When he returned from America, his mother had described him arriving "like a Father Christmas with masses of presents for us all".[45] Alfhild too remembered, even in England, that her brother "loved having a good time. And he'd always take his sisters . . . It was important for him to have enough money so the family had a good time, and by that he meant everybody."[46] His current financial situation was making that role impossible. So, by the summer of 1949, Dahl began to consider a career change, albeit one that would still allow him to continue storytelling. "I'm not writing much," he told Watkins in August, admitting that he had been upset by the fight with *The New Yorker* and also by "being told by Collins that the short stories in my last book were no good at all." So he was embarking on another plan. "I am now busy organising a bookmaker's business in London. For the next year or two I shall spend my days taking bets on horses, a thing I've always been fascinated by. You see, I'm broke, and if I can build up an independent business in this way, I'll be able to write just what I want and at the same time tell all the editors and publishers to go and stuff themselves if I want to – not that I haven't been doing that already. But of course I shall keep writing. I shall be a bookie in the daytime . . . leaping across the room to look at the ticker-tape, rushing back, seizing the phone to lay off an enormous bet and having, in short, a lot of fun and excitement."[47]

The plan to be a bookie vanished as quickly as it appeared, but Roald's work as a part-time dealer in antiques and painting was much longer lasting. He was not entirely impoverished. He still had some of his inheritance invested in the stock market and art was in his blood. It had fascinated him since childhood, while his wartime relationship with Millicent

Rogers had begun to open his eyes to the way the art market worked. Soon he was buying works of art for Charles Marsh and his excitement at a picture that took his fancy could be overwhelming. It might be something by the French Expressionist Georges Rouault, whose "brilliant colour and savage satire" electrified him. Dahl bought four of his paintings in 1946. Cézanne had a similar effect. Recognizing a kindred spirit perhaps, he admired the combination of craftsmanship and expressive ambition, describing Cézanne to Charles Marsh as "the greatest of them all . . . a delicate and subtle giant . . . who reached out further towards unobtainable perfection than any other man in any form of art has ever done."[48] Dahl had not acquired these opinions entirely by himself. He had his own formidable tutor: Matthew Smith – one of the most important British painters of the twentieth century.

The two men met for the first time in the autumn of 1941, after Roald had been invalided home from Palestine. The Blitz had abated. Roald had gone up to London and begun to wander in the art galleries around Bond Street. Initially, he simply peered through the windows. Then, "spellbound" by one of Smith's pictures, probably a lush and voluptuous portrait of a woman, he plucked up the courage to enter Tooth's Gallery. He asked the gallery owner where he could see more of Mr Smith's work and was told that the artist had "disappeared". Dahl eventually tracked him down, through a series of forwarding addresses, to a shabby hotel on Piccadilly, near Hyde Park Corner, where he knocked on his door unannounced. From within, one of Bach's Brandenburg Concertos was playing on a tiny gramophone. After several minutes, the door opened and Smith peered out. He looked, as Dahl recalled, "like a small frightened animal coming out of its hole". It was a remarkable first meeting.

"*Mr Smith?*"
"*Yes*"
"*Mr Matthew Smith?*"
"*Yes*"
"*I . . . well . . . I really only came here to tell you how much I*

like your pictures," I said, because that was all I had to say. I did not realize then that he had not long before lost both his sons in the RAF, and that the shock of suddenly seeing a young man standing outside his door in full RAF uniform with wings on his chest must have been tremendous. It bowled him over. "Come in," he said, "Do come in." He was in stocking feet and there were holes in both socks. He began talking very fast. The hands fluttered, the words tumbled out in such a nervous torrent. "I'm sorry it's such a mess. Everything is in a mess. Oh, what an awful mess. Where you going to sit? I can't do things properly. I can't do anything probably these days. I don't know what's the matter with me. How nice to see you. How good of you to come . . ."[49]

Though Smith was more than forty years older, an instant rapport formed between them, and by the time Dahl was posted to Washington, the two men were firm friends. "There was nothing homosexual about it," he told Alice Kadel, the daughter of Smith's mistress and heir, Mary Keene, when she came to interview him shortly after the painter's death in 1959. Kadel thought his statement was strange because that thought had never even crossed her mind. But she recalled that Dahl was not in a good mood that day and that at times he was "aggressive", "unpleasant" and "cold". She warmed to him, though, observing many similarities between Roald and her mother's lover. "Both could seem very worried," she observed, "which gave them enormous charm . . . they gave that impression of wanting to be looked after, and you longed to mother them . . . They touched you somewhere."[50]

When Dahl returned to London two years later for a couple of months in the summer of 1944, Smith invited him to sit for his portrait. Accustomed to painting what Cecil Beaton described as "meaty great nudes and sensuous still lives",[51] the painting was one of the few male portraits Smith ever attempted.‡ It is a vividly colourful piece, with Dahl's blue RAF uniform almost overwhelmed by the surrounding scarlets and oranges. It

---

‡Dahl incorrectly boasted to his mother that it was the "only one he's ever done". He was wrong. Smith also painted memorable portraits of his friend Augustus John and the novelist Henry Green – Dahl, Letter to his mother, 04/18/45 – RDMSC RD 14/5/4/20.

captures well the "languid" quality that had struck Antoinette Haskell in Washington, as well as his sense of detached otherworldliness – qualities not apparent in contemporary photographs. At twenty-five, Roald had been able to access the £5,000 in his trust fund – equivalent to perhaps £175,000 in contemporary purchasing power and more than 38 times his annual salary – and with part of it he purchased two other Matthew Smiths, some watercolours by Smith's great friend Jacob Epstein and a small portfolio of Impressionists and Post-Impressionists. He took them all back to Washington with him, where he told his mother they were "greatly admired".[52] He gave one Epstein to Millicent Rogers and sold another at a good profit. But while he enjoyed dealing, he bought the paintings mostly for the pleasure of looking at them. "Each time I sold a short story," he later wrote, "I would buy a picture. Then, because it took me so long to write another story, I would invariably have to sell the picture I had bought six months before. In those days, fine pictures were inexpensive. Many paintings that today could be acquired only by millionaires decorated my walls for brief periods in the late forties – Matisses, enormous Fauve Rouaults, Soutines, Cézanne watercolours, Bonnards, Boudins, a Renoir, a Sisley, a Degas seascape and God knows what else."[53]

Just as he was fascinated by the deceit involved in greyhound racing, Roald was similarly intrigued by the tricks and ruses of the art world. He learned about restoration, for example, by trying it himself. "The first picture I cleaned was in 1946," he recalled. "It was a Morland belonging to my brother-in-law [John Logsdail] and when I had finished with it, there was nothing left, so I had to paint it back on. I told him that the removal of the dark varnish had, alas, revealed a painting of poor quality and he was quite happy." A blackened decorated mirror, purchased in Uxbridge in "one of the seediest and most dilapidated places you have ever seen", produced greater success, revealing a "brilliantly painted frame full of grotesque heads and shells and fishes . . . almost certainly a Mathias Lock".[54] Fakery too fascinated him. His sister Alfhild recalled him attempting to paint "his own Matisses in five minutes using garden paints",[55] while his nephew, Nicholas – now one of London's most respected dealers in contemporary art – still has one of his uncle's "Monets" hanging in his bedroom.

All this knowledge helped Roald enormously when he started acting as an unofficial art and antiques buyer for Charles Marsh – a lucrative and enjoyable sideline, which helped keep him solvent during the immediate postwar period. The suspicion and cynicism that he had learned at the flapping-tracks came in useful, too. "The antique dealer is never a craftsman," he would write years later. "He is incapable of screwing an ordinary brass handle into a drawer. The only thing he can screw is the customer." [56]

Matthew Smith fed Dahl's passion for painting, and in 1946, the two of them went on the first of several trips to Paris together. The decaying capital made a big impression on Roald, who was excited by its ravaged bohemianism, but also appalled by the poverty and destitution he witnessed there. Smith too loved the city and showed Roald his favourite haunts. Alice Kadel disagreed with those who, like Lesley O'Malley, felt that the relationship between the two men was "like father and son". [57] Knowing Matthew, she felt that, on the contrary, it was probably "quite laddish". [58] In France, Matthew certainly introduced Roald to prostitutes as well as painters and, despite the postwar deprivations, possibly gave his young friend a taste of the world Roald's father Harald had enjoyed fifty years earlier. Dahl was impressed by Smith's relentless sexual energy and told Claudia Marsh how much he enjoyed watching the old man on the prowl. A decade later Roald lamented that his newly knighted friend, at almost eighty, now "fornicates no more than five times a week", [59] while to Charles Marsh he described how, after dinner in London, Smith and he had walked "the full length of Bayswater Road conversing with the whores".

Matthew chased a black one six blocks, and when he caught up with her she said, "You want to come home with me?" Matthew said, "Have a cigarette." "Let's not fick about," the woman said. "Do you or do you not want to come home with me? It'll cost you two pounds." Whereupon the celebrated painter peered closer at her in the dark-

ness, lit a match, held it up to her face and exclaimed, "My God, no."
We talked to eleven more, and when I left him he was travelling fast
towards an enormous woman with yellow hair – both hands in his
pockets.[60]

Back in England, Roald tried to become Matthew's fixer and to "organize" him as he organized his family. For a time, the artist was indeed almost absorbed into the Dahl clan as Roald encouraged him to rent a studio near Wistaria Cottage and took many of his canvases into his own care while it was being renovated. Dahl told Charles Marsh he had fifty-four of them, "stacked in the spare bedroom. I spend hours in there looking at them".[61] But while Smith welcomed "people who would fix things",[62] he was at heart a very private man, who resented being managed, and that loss of control inclined him almost to paranoia. During the move, he became convinced that Roald had stolen one of his canvases – possibly to sell to Charles Marsh – and accused him of being a thief. The accusation shocked Roald to the core, even after he had assured his friend that the missing painting was only being framed. "I hope to hell I shall never be found either mean or cunning or greedy about money or possessions," he told Matthew indignantly. "So far as I'm concerned people can always have what I've got and, if you want to know, that's why I am broke at the moment."[63]

The accusations had been "so horrible",[64] Roald claimed, that they gave him diarrhoea for three days and forced him to go to the doctor. Smith eventually apologized for the "misunderstanding", and the argument was settled. Nevertheless, he remained indignant at his friend's sanctimonious tone, which he described as "damned bad psychology". To some extent this was the pot calling the kettle black. For Smith also claimed that the incident had made him feel unwell – and not just for three days. He told Roald that, as a result of the incident, he had been ill for more than six weeks.[65] Unsurprisingly, he soon relocated to a studio back in London.

Two of Dahl's most famous short stories from this period of his life deal directly with painting and undoubtedly have their origins in his friendship with Matthew Smith. "Nunc Dimittis" is a fanciful tale of a famous portrait painter, who paints his subjects in the nude before adding their clothes, layer by layer. The narrator, a spoiled and wealthy dandy, takes revenge on an obese woman who has slighted him by commissioning a portrait of her from this painter. Once he has received it, like a restorer, he painstakingly removes the top layers of oil, "cautiously testing and teasing the paint, adding a drop or two more of alcohol to my mixture", until the sitter is revealed in her formidable corsets and brassiere, of which the straps were "as skilfully and scientifically rigged as the supporting cables of a suspension bridge".[66] He then humiliates her by displaying the portrait in public. But it is she who ultimately takes the more extreme revenge.

The other, "Skin", is set in Paris in 1946. It tells of an impoverished tattoo artist who, many years before, had persuaded the Russian painter Chaim Soutine to tattoo a portrait of his wife on his back. Now old and ill, the tattooist in Dahl's story falls into the hands of a mysterious, softspoken art dealer, who is eager to obtain this extraordinary living work of art. A sinister hand, "encased in a canary-coloured glove", falls on the tattooist's shoulder as he is promised a life of leisure in exchange for the skin upon his back after he has died. The reader is left in little doubt that the tattooist will meet an unexpectedly early demise. The paintings of Soutine, who had died in France in 1943, mesmerized Roald. Soutine was the archetypal tormented artist. He never washed. His studio reeked unbearably of the rotting carcasses he loved to paint. A colony of bedbugs was once discovered living in his ear. He and Matthew Smith had briefly worked in the same building in Montparnasse and Smith doubtless provided Dahl with many of the narrative details that embellish "Skin" – the "studio with the single chair in it . . . the filthy red couch . . . the drunken parties, the cheap white wine, the furious quarrels, and always, always, the bitter sullen face of the boy brooding over his work".[67] But Dahl's appreciation of Soutine's work went beyond a delight in his extreme bohemian lifestyle in La Ruche and the Cité Falguière. The pinched sensuality of his choirboys and pastry chefs, his bloody studies of animal carcasses and his fascination with the flesh beneath the skin resonated with the misanthropy that currently suffused his own writing. Roald had responded strongly to the hedonistic intensity of Smith's work, but Soutine's viscous, bright oils were more darkly carnal. A decade later he would come to admire and collect the work of an artist whose work took Soutine's decadent vision a league further into darkness: Francis Bacon.

Both of these painting stories were rejected by the magazines to which they were submitted and seemed to confirm Dahl's belief that, while he could still hold his head up in New York, somehow he would never be part of the London club. His most influential ally in London at that time was probably Noël Coward, whom he had met socially in New York and Washington while working for William Stephenson and BSC. Coward was a big fan of Dahl's flying stories and found him good company and "highly intelligent".[68] Dahl, for his part, was critical of Coward for exaggerating his involvement in spying – maintaining that he was "thrilled" by any "piddly little thing"[69] Stephenson asked of him – but he cultivated the friendship because Coward was good company and because he was almost his lone British establishment fan. In the summer of 1946, for example, while Hamish Hamilton were preparing to publish *Over to You*, Coward had given him a huge ego boost in front of his publisher. Hamilton had taken Roald for lunch at the Ivy, when Coward rushed across to them and "gushed" for five minutes about how much he liked the book. "He knew each story almost by heart," Roald told Ann Watkins, "and Ham was greatly impressed."[70]

Intriguingly, Coward too would eventually conclude that Roald was something of a misfit – one whose literary persona no longer seemed to mesh with his outward personality. A few years later, when his next collection of stories, *Someone Like You*, was published, Coward wrote in his diaries that though he found the tales "brilliant" and his friend's imagination "fabulous", he noticed in all of them "an underlying streak of cruelty and macabre unpleasantness, and a curiously adolescent emphasis on sex", which he found odd, because he knew Roald was at heart "a sensitive and gentle creature". Perhaps, Coward wondered, "he has lived in America too long and caught some of the prevalent sex hysteria".[71]

Aside from his family and Claud Taylor, almost all of Roald's closest confidants were indeed Americans, and chief among them was Charles Marsh. For despite being 3,000 miles apart, the two men were in constant, almost interminable, correspondence. Shortly before Roald left the United States, Marsh had sent him a letter confirming the depth of their friendship. "I am so very fond of you that I refuse to be merely your papa," he declared. "Your presence struck me intensely as you first walked into the R Street house living room. In the wear and tear there has been some abrasion as you have seen my clay feet and I have seen yours. But my measure . . . is that your spirit is with me now and tomorrow and yesterday."[72] Charles's own situation had changed, too. Shortly after the end of the war, he had divorced his frosty wife Alice – Antoinette Haskell described her as "about as maternal as an ice-cube"[73] – when he discovered that she was having a number of affairs, including one with his own protégé, Lyndon Johnson. Alice acquired the estate at Longlea in the settlement and Charles purchased a new one in nearby Rappahannock County. Increasingly he came to rely on his secretary Claudia Haines, who became his constant companion and, in 1953, the third and last Mrs Marsh.

Charles's relationship with Roald had always been a mixture of the joker and the mentor. "Work hard. Talk little. Be truly a miser of time,"[74] he had advised within a week of Roald's return to England in 1946, and he remained convinced that his friend was a man of great talent, who needed to follow his own distinctively iconoclastic path to secure his ends. To this end, Charles looked after Roald and opened his home to him. He loaned him money. He encouraged his ambition to be a writer and dissuaded him from going into politics. In return, Roald allowed Charles the unique liberty of addressing him openly, honestly and intimately. Charles's advice could be portentous, even pompous, but it was always given with thought and affection. In 1943, he had urged his friend to seek for "the serene", and to follow his destiny. Counselling him not to "weigh your acts either for self . . . or the demands of others", he exhorted Roald to see his own way through his problems, assuring him that "these weights will lessen if the inside of your spirit, which has nothing to do with the particular, slowly becomes serene". Even then, Marsh had understood the curious tension between toughness and tenderness that animated Dahl's soul, and which very few appreciated. "To this date you have approached life with great sensitiveness," he continued. "Not to hurt people is the first impulse of a generous and sensitive soul. But in the conscious being of not hurting – of not being cruel – comes the complexity of life." He sensed that a crisis lay ahead and urged Roald to "make use" of him, "any time – any place – where you wish me alone in friendship".[75] It was an offer the young writer would not forget.

Throughout the late 1940s, Roald wrote to Charles and Claudia almost once a week. Their letters usually discussed political issues, like nuclear war and the food shortages, but the jokey raillery of close friendship was never far away. Dahl would tell Marsh about the antics of his flatulent goat, named after Marsh's great friend the liberal Democratic senator Claude Pepper, and Marsh would tell him that he had taken up hen-racing. Writing under the pseudonym "Charlie Suet", from the Bureau of British Bullshit, Roald reported on the results of his investigations into "the causes of bow-leggedness in women and other jockeys" as part of the researchers of his "Joy through Length" commission.[76] Charles lampooned the biographical blurb on the back of *Over to You*, inventing scurrilous quotations, which he put into his friend's mouth. Nothing was taboo. On one occasion, Roald recounted the exploits of the Queen's exceedingly hairy "number one lady-in-waiting", the Honourable Eurydice Hislop Pomfret Pomfret, a woman "of extreme age with bandy legs and a great pot-shaped belly", describing luridly how the two of them had made love in Buckingham Palace while testing Her Majesty's beds to make sure they were "ok for springiness and pneumatics".[77] On another, he claimed he had identified Marsh as a "vicious and notorious" rapist called Henry the Rubber. Marsh was then inundated with official letters from Investigator Fingerfucker in New York, and Detectives Slobgollion and Worms of Scotland Yard.[78] On yet another, he drafted a letter to Sidney Rothman, the treasurer of the Stepney Jewish Girls Club, to whom Marsh was sending food parcels, warning Mr Rothman to beware of his ostensible benefactor. Marsh, he advised, had "once bitten off the index finger of a Jewish waiter in a New York restaurant because the man served him salami when he asked for salad" and turned the East Side Club for

Unmarried Yiddish Mothers into a hostel for Arab sailors.[79] They joked about the Scandinavian secret agents Sonya and Yetsofa, and made exotic plans to travel to South America, Greece and Spain. However, in amongst the banter and gossip, which to an outside reader can verge on the tedious and incomprehensible, leap flashes of the profound warmth – the "bond", as Marsh called it – that tied Charles, Claudia and Roald together. "We love you . . . we have been thinking much of you . . . we think more of you away than when you are here . . ."[80] Evidence of it peppers almost every letter.

Claudia adored Roald and sent regular parcels of food and clothing to the Dahl family, along with kitchen gadgets like electric mixers and pressure cookers, throughout these postwar years of austerity. During the winters that immediately followed the war Charles also responded to Roald's impassioned pleas to do something about the "miserable and starving condition of Europe"[81] by shipping food supplies, including vitamins and apples from his new estate at Jesamine Hill, to impoverished and undernourished Londoners in Rotherhithe and in Clement Attlee's Limehouse constituency. Roald resented the complicated paperwork that was required to do this, and railed against the "incompetent, selfish, vindictive, humourless, complacent and ugly" cabinet ministers responsible. "I wish them dead," he told Marsh.[82] However, he agreed to write to the "fat but energetic wife of our prime minister" in the hope that "Mrs Atlee will arrange all the necessary permits etc for getting the apples into the country, for after all they are for the stomach of her husband's constituents." The destitution he had seen in Paris with Matthew Smith had moved him to genuine anger and he was shocked by the indifference of most Americans to European suffering. Their "overall attitude to continental starving (which believe me is frightful and frightening)," he told Charles, "is one that we cannot understand."[83] He imagined the luxurious dinner menus of New York's top hotels being scattered from a plane over the capitals of war-ravaged Europe. What would the Americans' "empty-bellied" allies think, he wondered bitterly, in the face of this excess? And, if they knew, "would the Americans be shamed into doing something?"[84]

Both Marsh and Dahl were instinctive present givers. And Marsh's pleas to his friend not to be cynical, not "to grow sour", but rather to look at "the now",[85] resonated with Roald partly because Charles was such an active proponent of what he preached. In 1947, Marsh founded his Public Welfare Foundation (PWF). Its first grant, the following year, was to buy twenty-eight sewing machines for an organization of Jamaican women, near the hotel Marsh had acquired in Ocho Rios, so that poor children could be clothed and sent to school. Roald styled himself Charles's "English agent and provocateur".[86] His brief was to look out for individual cases of need and hardship. Noël Coward was PWF's agent in Jamaica, while its agents in India included a young Indira Gandhi and a nun in Calcutta called Mother Teresa. Charles also roped in many of Dahl's family and friends as "sub-agents" too, typically giving them $100 to spend on others more needy than they were. Leslie Hansen and Claud Taylor were two of these other recruits. Charles commissioned new work from Matthew Smith's friend the impoverished sculptor Jacob Epstein. He set up a $25,000 trust for Roald and his cousin, Finn, the son of Roald's uncle Truls, who had inherited the family butcher's shop in Oslo and was imprisoned in Sweden during the war for helping Norwegian airmen escape to Britain.[87] Finn later devised a Norwegian forestry scheme to supply timber for the US market, which would form the capital behind a Norwegian branch of the foundation.[88] Jokingly, Roald asked for 10,000 gramophone records as his commission for brokering the deal.[89] By the end of 1949, Marsh was filling out visa forms in an attempt to bring Roald to work for the foundation in New York. Charles and Claudia travelled to Europe several times while Roald was living with his mother and visited them twice in Amersham; but despite their generosity, the other members of the family did not take to the ostentatious Mr Marsh. Perhaps they were too proud to feel comfortable accepting his gifts. Perhaps they regarded him as a dangerous outsider who might steal their brother away. Forty years later, Alfhild described him simply as patronizing and "pushy". Asta said she did not care for the man. Else simply shook her head and said she did not want to talk about him. Her daughter Anna remembered hearing her mother complain that Marsh acted "like Jesus Christ",[90] while Lesley O'Malley dismissed him simply as a "terrible bully".[91] It was a strange attitude to adopt toward the man who had looked after Roald in America and from whom they had received an endless stream of gifts and presents during the hard years of shortages and rationing. But there was a good reason for their animosity. When he came to England in 1950, Marsh had almost driven Alfhild's husband insane.

Leslie Hansen, Roald's brother-in-law, was highly intelligent and unconventional. He drew cartoons and caricatures, but he was also mentally unstable. Roald had known him well before the war because he lived in Bexley. He was, as Roald would later describe him, "even more eccentric" than Alf, "not very prepossessing", and determined never to get a job. The couple spent most of their married life in the thatched cottage in Ludgershall that Alf had bought for her mother in the early days of the war, living "in great frugality on a tiny amount of capital" with their daughter Astri.[92] Despite, or perhaps because of, his idiosyncrasies, Leslie had been completely absorbed into the Dahl family and they all felt protective of him. But he was quite unable to deal either with Charles Marsh's quasi-religious philosophy or his overt generosity. As Roald put it, Charles "toppled an already wobbly brain clean over the precipice".[93] Hansen started to believe that Marsh was Jesus Christ returned to earth, and that he was his disciple. Roald was forced into the role of carer.

Every day he collapsed and jabbered and searched the bible and saw portents and coincidences and said he was dying . . . Well it would have been OK for Charles to be JC and for Leslie to be St Paul if the idea of it hadn't driven him stark staring mad . . . It was as much as one could do to handle him and stop ourselves from being forced to send him to a lunatic asylum . . . I spent hours and hours with him forcing him to realise that Marsh was not Jesus Christ, that he was an ordinary man, rather a good ordinary man nevertheless, who fornicated and joked and made merry just like everyone else . . . I then encouraged him to draw cartoons of Charles (a thing that would previously have been sacrilegious) and he became more cheerful . . . Truly, Claudia, it was a near thing and all pretty awful. The most awful

*thing of all being to hear the small child Astrid saying repeatedly, don't
cry daddy, we won't leave you. Most pathetic thing I've ever heard in
my life. No-one of course cares very much about Leslie. But the terrors
it reflected upon Alf and Astrid are very great.*[94]

After "some terrifying periods",[95] Leslie was eventually restored to
something like his old self, but more than a month after he wrote that
letter, Roald told Claudia that his brother-in-law was still "very bad" and
that in some respects he felt he was the cause of the situation. "I blame
myself more than anyone," he confessed, "because it was I who encouraged Charles to go on seeing him."[96] He begged Charles not to return to
Amersham and henceforth to drop his "mystic bullshit".[97] His brother-
in-law's breakdown added to the pressure of finishing his book, and contributed to the chronic stomach pains from which he now began to suffer.

He confessed his anxieties to Claudia: "Someone who has written as
little as I have finds that in writing one book, you have learned twice as
much by the time you come to the end of it as you knew at the beginning . . . One knows more now. It can all be improved."[98] A certain testi-
ness began to creep into his manner. Amongst his papers for 1950 is a
handwritten list entitled "Things I Hate":

*All piddling spindly tables, specially the kind that slide into each other
   – six of them.*
Women who say "What are you thinking?"
Bookshelves with an unread look.
Men who wear rings that are not absolutely plain.
The larger the ring the worse it is. A diamond worst of all.
*Men who wear bow ties, pointed shoes, shoes in two different leathers,
   tie clips, sock suspenders.*
*Men who have four or five strands of hair and they let it grow long
   and paste it to their domes.*
Men or women who hold a cigarette between thumb and first finger.[99]

A malevolent, acerbic quality certainly pervades some of the grotesques that populate *Fifty Thousand Frogskins*. Dahl's portrait of the two Jewish crooks who sell Cubbage and Hawes the "ringer" is particularly extreme. Not only are they are the cruellest characters in the book; his descriptions of them – "small black eyes," large noses, and "lips, wet and shiny like two small, uncooked chipolata sausages" – disturbed even the unflappable Ann Watkins when she read the manuscript.[100] She told him she found the characters crude and that he should soften his anti-Jewish and anti-religious tone.[101] But that was easier said than done. In his 1951 story, "My Lady Love, My Dove", a wife confesses to her husband that she is "a nasty person". So is he, she tells her spouse reassuringly, persuading him that they should both feel at ease with their nastiness. It was a distinctive aspect of Dahl's own literary genius that he too now felt at ease with his dark side. "With me the ideas that come seem to represent a rather nasty side of my nature," he once declared. "Nasty things happen to all sorts of people. I can't help it. That's the way they come. And yet in real life I'm a perfectly ordinary sort of fellow and I don't usually do nasty things to other people. I don't hunt foxes or shoot animals. I won't even have mousetraps in the house."[102]

Dahl was not just kind to animals. During the war, RAF charities had been the beneficiary of his generosity. In 1946, a family friend who was temporarily unable to send money to a destitute woman he had been supporting in Canada told him about his plight. Dahl wrote to Ann Watkins at once and asked her to send the woman $65 from his own account in New York.[103] He was also a loyal supporter of Marsh's London food aid plans, despite the fact that he believed the poor "do not give a fuck for vitamins and do not understand them".[104] Here was a flash of the cynicism that so often coloured his responses and that, he jokingly confessed to his adolescent audience at Repton, had even been in evidence there back in the 1930s. More than forty years earlier, his "lovely and gentle" contemporary, Denton Welch, had apparently told him this story: Mr Snape, Welch's housemaster and Dahl's own English teacher, had been helping put up a stage for his house play. A boy asked where he could get a vice large enough to hold two big planks together. Without hesitation, Snape muttered to him that he should go to The Priory and look for Roald Dahl. "He's got every vice in the world," he told him.[105]

As *Fifty Thousand Frogskins* neared its conclusion, Dahl's sense of alienation from the British literary establishment was further exacerbated by his dealings with the BBC. Thanks to the patronage of Alfhild's friend, the broadcaster Archie Gordon, Roald had given a "most un-BBC"[106] talk about dog racing in 1948. Following this, the BBC broadcast three of his new stories – early drafts of "The Soldier", "Skin", and "Man from the South". Now, after the failure of *Some Time Never*, his new submissions were increasingly being met with rejection and Roald began to rail against the "discriminating literary gentlemen" of the BBC's Third Programme. Returning from a trip to Central Europe with Charles Marsh, where he had visited Hitler's Eagle's Nest and "gazed out upon the surrounding snowy peaks", he quipped to Gordon that he had "dreamed dreams of glory and conquest – ridiculous, unattainable dreams, such as selling a story to the British Broadcasting Corporation, and sticking a needle through the eye of a camel".[107] He repeated these complaints to Martha Gellhorn, when she came to visit him in Amersham. She for her part was amazed at the "suffocating atmosphere of adoration" with which Roald was surrounded at Wistaria Cottage, recalling that his sisters directed "hatred" toward her, fearful lest she steal their brother away and take him back to America. Gellhorn, who knew how well Dahl had fit in to New York literary circles, was shocked at his isolation from London. She found the whole experience with his family "*very* boring and *very* heavy".[108]

On the other side of the Atlantic things were going a little better. Ann Watkins, "the only sane baby in the business",[109] as Dahl lovingly described her, had sold one of his recent short stories, "Poison" – the tale about the Indian doctor and the snake – to *Collier's*. Within three months CBS bought the rights for both radio and television adaptation, while "The Sound Machine" was listed as one of the best short stories of the year. But the new collection had been refused by everyone. Even Watkins was becoming irritated by her client's "slow and uneven"[110] rate of writing. Grasping the nettle, she told Roald that she would not be able to sell the book unless he dropped the three nonfiction pieces it contained and replaced them with better quality fiction.[111] She told him bluntly that *Collier's* had wanted to commit to his next story, but were put off doing so because he produced new work too infrequently. "Which may, I hope," she added, in a tone that she alone could get away with, "be a lesson to you, my child, on greater productivity."[112] Two months later, Watkins's assistant confirmed the "depressing" news. "We've given that collection of stories a long run," she told Roald, and "with the field covered, we must now admit that it would be best to await the publication of your novel and then bring forth this collection again."[113]

By Christmas 1950, the first draft of the new novel was complete. On Boxing Day, Roald wrote to Ann Watkins that he was doing some revisions, but that he was pleased with the book, which was filled with "stuff I know and have seen which is solid stuff that is true and dirty and sorrowful and amusing". But, he warned her, it would be "very different from everything before".[114] A month later, it was "quite finished . . . No-one has seen a word of it apart from the girl in the village who typed it, who was in turn disgusted, horrified, amused, then disgusted again."[115] He was obviously nervous, warning Watkins that though he liked the book, it was "not very classical", and confessing that he trembled to send it to her. So he didn't. He sent it instead straight to Peter Wyld at Collins, thinking perhaps that Wyld would understand its English subject matter better than she would. It was a mistake. A week later he got a "brief, curt, terrifying letter", from Wyld and his colleague Milton Waldman informing him that the company would not be exercising its option to publish. Dahl then sent the manuscript to Watkins for her opinion, pointing out that Wyld, a devout Christian, and Waldman, a Jew, had probably just been offended by some of the things he had written. "Would you be a sweetie and send me a cable as soon as you read it," he begged, "saying whether it's good or bad or ordinary to put me out of my misery."[116] Watkins took him at his word, sending him a telegram that was terse and unequivocal: FROGSKINS UNPUBLISHABLE PRESENT FORM. CONSTRUCTION UNSOUND. TOO MANY LOOSE ENDS. AIRMAILER UPCOMING.[117]

Maternal and yet thoroughly professional, Watkins followed up her cable the next day with a detailed letter, explaining to Roald that she

found the book "not dirty, but dull . . . For you not nearly good enough."
With judicious cuts and edits, she thought he could probably salvage it.[118]
Dahl, however, did not read her letter. He did not even open it. He was
too scared. He took a plane to Lebanon and from Beirut scribbled her a
postcard, uncharacteristically in turquoise ink:

> *Dear Ann,*
>
> *I got your cable and then I fled. I have not read your letter. I have
> not dared to read it. Perhaps it's chasing me. But I don't think it will
> ever catch me because I am moving fast.*
>
> *Roald.*[119]

It was the great professional crisis of Dahl's career. His saviour, at this
moment of watershed, was his companion in Beirut, his confessor and father figure, Charles Marsh. Charles swept his friend out of England onto
an extended trip, offering him a salaried job working for the Public Welfare Foundation in New York and securing him an indefinite US working
visa. He even put him up in the guest wing of his own apartment.

It was a mark of the love that he felt for Roald and to which their
voluminous correspondence is testimony. Both Charles and Claudia
understood more clearly than anyone else that their friend was in need,
and their remedial actions were swift and transformative. They offered
him a safe, supportive and secure environment in which he could rebuild
himself, and their speedy, decisive action almost certainly saved him from
a more serious breakdown. It was little surprise that Roald dedicated his
next collection of short stories to Charles.§ Indeed, so positive was their
response that Dahl was able to disguise the disaster from family, friends,
perhaps even from himself. He almost managed to disguise it from
posterity. In his own files, he destroyed the letters from Ann Watkins

---

§In her autobiography, Patricia Neal claimed that Dahl initially intended to dedicate the book to her, but
that she had made him change his mind.

and Peter Wyld that dealt with the rejection of *Frogskins*. A copy of the manuscript survived, but nothing else. It was a moment of failure and humiliation over which he rapidly drew a shroud. Were it not for Watkins's own archive, evidence of the rejection might have been lost for good. It was a moment too of watershed. Dahl bid farewell not only to his book but also to greyhounds, life with his mother, and his conviction that he wanted to be a novelist. A chapter in his life had closed. The rural idyll, the "Scholar-Gypsy's" existence, was over.

THIRTEEN

The Master of the Macabre

NEW YORK OFFERED DAHL a refuge from his troubles. It gave him a measure of financial security and he enjoyed being back among friends who believed in him. He was returning to the city that had brought him success and celebrity. Yet he also felt isolated from his family and the English countryside he loved. He missed his greyhounds, his poaching, his garden, his mother, his sisters, and their children. He longed to be flying model aeroplanes with his nephew Nicholas or tickling trout with Claud Taylor. Most of all he missed his independence and the sense of being paterfamilias. He was now thirty-six years old and it disturbed him that he was once again relying on the largesse of Charles Marsh. The rejection of *Fifty Thousand Frogskins* too had taken its toll on his spirits and it would be many months before he would fully recover. Ann Watkins's assistant, Sheila St Lawrence, recalled that her first impressions of Roald at that time were not of a brash, argumentative entertainer but of a quiet, bespectacled man, who struck her as "rather shy and retiring".[1] Charles Marsh and Claudia Haines thought that what their friend needed more than anything was a wife.

Soon Dahl was dating a Hungarian-American divorcée called Suzanne Horvath, who was clever, sophisticated and had a small child from her previous marriage. Horvath was able to beat him at chess – a quality he later confessed he found both attractive and irritating.[2] In the autumn of 1951, he bought her a $200 Patek Philippe watch, which he acquired with the profits he expected to make from two paintings he had purchased in Zurich with Charles Marsh – a Redon oil of a naked boy and a Rouault cartoon of President Woodrow Wilson.[3] Soon afterwards he proposed to her. Still secretive when it came to emotional relationships, he was strikingly unforthcoming about her in his letters and this lack of communication irked his mother, who believed Suzanne was the main reason her son was staying in Manhattan. To Claudia Haines that December she wrote plaintively, "I have not heard from Roald for a very long time. We are all wondering if he has married Suzanne yet."[4] Two days later Roald answered her. "Suzanne is fine. We are not hurrying over getting married. There's no point in that. I see her every day and my guess would be that it will happen about next spring or summer. Financially also it is better to wait."[5] Two months passed and Sofie Magdalene heard nothing more about Suzanne. Then, in February 1952, she received a letter from Roald, informing her that he was planning to wait "a long time yet" before making any final commitment.[6]

If he did share any of his thoughts on his private life, it was with Charles and Claudia, but even with them he was frequently tight-lipped. Sofie Magdalene, sensing that her son was getting cold feet, wrote to Claudia to try and find out exactly what was going on: "I understand that Roald's marriage plans have been shelved for the time being. I am pleased that they will not get married unless they are sure of making each other happy. Roald is not rich enough for keeping a divorced wife. I was not surprised as I had not expected it to come off. I don't know why."[7] At some point in 1952, the relationship formally ended. Exactly why remains a mystery. But it seems Suzanne took the decision to end it. Shortly after Sofie Magdalene heard the news, she wrote again to Claudia in search of more information. "He never says how he is feeling," she complained. "We never found out why Suzanne gave him up – except that it was she that finished it . . . Perhaps it was the best," she concluded ruefully.[8] In reply, Claudia – always a wise and balanced critic – cast an interesting light on "the end of Suzanne", hazarding her opinion that she would not have made Roald a suitable wife. "I think he would always have had to take care of her," she observed, "that she would have taken more from him emotionally and every other way than she had to give."[9]

Liccy, however, who understood Roald's need to "look after" people, reflected later that, for this very reason, she might actually have made a very good match for him.[10]

But just as the relationship with Suzanne Horvath was fizzling out,* Dahl crossed paths unexpectedly with another person who was seeking refuge in Manhattan. In September 1952, Patricia Neal, a twenty-six-year-old actress from Tennessee, returned there after the breakup of her three-year love affair with the Hollywood movie star Gary Cooper. The dark-haired Southern beauty, with her distinctive deep chocolate voice, had just completed a series of live shows for American troops stationed in Korea, which culminated in her almost being raped by a sex-starved soldier in Seoul. She was exhausted. A promising movie career had dissolved in a series of "'disappointments' and 'heartaches'",[11] and now she was returning to the city where she had made her name, winning a Tony Award for best actress at only twenty. That accolade had secured her a movie contract with Warner Bros. in Los Angeles, but none of the thirteen films she subsequently made there had shown her talent in a positive light. In her two movies with Ronald Reagan she was described as "gauche", "embarrassing", "painful", and "ill-at-ease", with reviewers complaining about her inexperience and lack of subtlety. One described her as "a tigress in a cat show".[12] Despite appearances in three movies that would go on to become cult classics – *The Fountainhead, The Breaking Point* and the science fiction classic *The Day the Earth Stood Still* – Neal's confidence was destroyed. The contract with Warners was not renewed.

This professional disappointment was compounded by the failure of her relationship with Cooper. Not only did the understated movie star, almost twice Neal's age, eventually abandon her to return to his wife, he insisted that Pat abort their child. As a consequence, she suffered a serious mental breakdown and unfairly won herself a reputation among the gossip columnists as a home-wrecker.[13] In New York, Neal hoped to regain her self-respect and to remake her career. Not long after her return, she

---

*Suzanne seems to have disappeared from Roald's life soon after he broke up with her. The last reference I could find for her was an address in Reno, Nevada, scribbled in pencil in his address book.

went to audition for her old friend Lillian Hellman, in whose play, *Another Part of the Forest*, she had won her Tony six years earlier. The feisty and stern Hellman, then in her late forties, regarded the young actress as a particular protégée of hers, and when Pat appeared at the auditions for a revival of *The Children's Hour*, Hellman's voice had boomed reassuringly from the back of the auditorium: "Hello, Patsy Neal! Glad you're back in New York where you belong!"[14] Neal, who was underweight and thought she looked "ghastly",[15] did a wonderful audition. Hellman immediately offered her the choice of either leading role in her play about two women teachers who are suspected of being lesbians, and invited her over for dinner, where the guests included Leonard Bernstein and Hellman's old friend and sparring partner, Roald Dahl.†

Dahl confessed years later that at this point both he and Pat were equally "eager to get married", and this may have explained why Hellman seated them next to each other. Both were attractive and eligible. Both were drawn to glamour and celebrity. Both were also straight-talking. Yet both were bruised as well. Pat, like Roald, was also often melancholy. Cooper had broken her heart and she still missed her father, who had died unexpectedly when she was eighteen. "She was not gay," Roald remembered. "She was reserved, holding herself in; obviously pretty shaken all round . . . I think she planned to work hard as an antidote against her personal misfortunes . . . It wasn't a happy girl I was seeing."[16] Nevertheless, both were survivors. They tried to maintain an appearance of ease and keep their problems to themselves.

The relationship did not get off to a good start. Pat had noticed the "lean handsome" man who towered over the other guests as soon as she entered the room and was instantly attracted to him. But Roald was in no mood for flirtation that night. He ignored the young actress seated next to him and instead monopolized Bernstein, whom he regarded as the

---

†Dahl had maintained his friendship with Hellman throughout his postwar years in England. She came to visit him in Amersham and they also met in London when her lover, Dashiell Hammett, was in prison for his political views. "She is now a very unhappy, ill-at-ease woman," Roald wrote to Claudia Marsh, "and I must say I felt sorry for her because she is really so nice. She talked of 'Dash' much of the time and doesn't like the idea of him being in jail. Am afraid that his being there will turn Lillian automatically more and more against her own country" – Roald Dahl, Letter to Claudia Marsh, 10/09/51 – CMP.

"young musical genius"[17] of America, and who was sitting opposite him at the table. "Never once during the entire evening did he look my way," Pat later recalled, remembering that Roald's behaviour had "infuriated" her and that by the time she left Hellman's apartment she had "quite made up her mind that [she] loathed Roald Dahl".[18] Dahl agreed that he had behaved badly. His excuse was characteristic – that once he had got into an argument with Bernstein, "there was no backing off from it".[19] In any event, composers interested him more than actresses. Before he left Hellman's apartment, however, he got Pat's telephone number and called her the following morning to ask her out on a date. She initially refused her "horrible dinner companion".[20] But when he rang again two days later, she weakened and accepted his invitation.

Roald took her to a restaurant owned by John Huston's father-in-law and did his best to impress her. "He was acquainted with just about everybody," Pat wrote later. "And he was interested in everything. He spoke of paintings and antique furniture and the joys of the English countryside. He was as charming that evening as he had been rude the first time we met. I was fascinated. I remember his taking a sip of wine and looking at me for a long moment through the candlelight. 'I would rather be dead than fat,' he said."[21] She had agreed. The evening ended with another audition. Roald took her to meet Charles Marsh, who was staying in the penthouse of a nearby hotel because his own apartment was being refurbished. Neal evidently passed this test, too – and with flying colours. As Roald and Pat were about to leave, Marsh took him aside and whispered in his ear: "Drop the other baggage, I like this one!"[22]

Dahl took his friend's advice to heart. But with his family, he was almost as uncommunicative about Pat as he had been about Suzanne. Her name first appears in his letters home in the context of the opening night of *The Children's Hour*. Roald took his neighbour, Anthony Eden's ex-wife, Beatrice Beckett, to the show – in which he and Charles had each invested $1,000. Lady Eden still fitted into the mould of his favourite female: sophisticated, well connected, temporarily unattached or perhaps with a *mari complaisant*, and normally more than ten years older than he was – the kind of woman who enjoyed his playing what Charles

Marsh's friend, Ralph Ingersoll, described as his "gay blade" role.[23] Roald described Lady Eden to Claudia as "nice but a very long nose – like a banana."[24]

Afterwards, he told his mother that he had waited up with Hellman and other members of the cast into the early morning to read the reviews in the early editions of the papers and that the critics had been almost universally favourable.[25] But he gave no inkling that anything romantic was in the offing. A few weeks later, he sent his mother a cutting from the gossip column of a New York newspaper, which reported that "Patricia Neal is now adored by Roald Dahl". He attached no comment of his own, but when he sent the same clipping to Claudia, he added that the piece was all a "considerable exaggeration".[26]

Tongues were set wagging back in Buckinghamshire, but they all knew better than to ask Roald for details. Instead, Else wrote to Charles and Claudia, who were on holiday in Jamaica, asking whether they knew what was going on. The cutting had "made us all inquisitive", she admitted. "Is it the real thing this time?"[27] Claudia took her time, but eventually she responded positively. An effusive letter from Sofie Magdalene arrived by return: "I am so very pleased to hear from you that you like Pat and think that Roald has at last found the right one. I hope she will like the Dahl family, which is a bit out of the ordinary, as they are all very fond of each other and stick together more than most sisters and brothers do. They *never* quarrel! I am sure Roald wants a family," she added, "as he is unusually fond of and good with children, but that is their business and not mine."[28]

Roald's courtship of Pat was not exactly romantic. "Deliberate," was how Neal would later describe him. "He knew exactly what he wanted and he quietly went about getting it."[29] They were certainly sexually compatible. Pat found Roald attractive, and when she saw photographs of his nephews and nieces, became convinced that the two of them would "make beautiful children".[30] She also responded positively to his individualism, his wit, and the "deft authority" with which he looked down at the world. "When he said 'Well done!'" she recalled, "it was as if God Himself were bestowing the credit."[31] And she was impressed by how well he got on with her friends. He could talk medicine with Edmund Goodman, theatre with her friend Edla Cusick, and stocks and shares with Edla's husband, Peter. He energized her. The gossip columnist Louella Parsons observed that Patricia Neal was a "happy girl" again and that her new escort had once more made her sparkle.[32] Neal herself wrote to her actress friends Jean Valentino and Chloe Carter that she was daily becoming fonder of Roald Dahl. "So who knows? Might work," she concluded, adding hesitantly that "he is cautious too. And I think – stable. You would like him – I think. Very British."[33] It was a pragmatic relationship. But both instinctively drew back from the idea of commitment. Pat's reluctance here was made more intense by the fact that she suspected she was still in love with Gary Cooper. Indeed, her attachment to Roald might well have come to nothing had not Charles Marsh intervened.

"He loved me," said Pat of Dahl's mentor, "and he desperately wanted us to get married."[34] To this end, she recalled how Marsh had forced the issue soon after she met him, by asking her how much money she had in the bank. Though she prevaricated and tried to avoid answering, he eventually made her admit that she had $20,000 saved from her work in the movies. Pat was proud of the figure, but shocked at Marsh's unexpected reply: "Ah yes, that *is* poor," he had murmured.[35] She was surprised that he thought the wealth of his protégé's potential spouse so important, but Charles knew Roald well. This Scholar-Gypsy was also a sybarite. The world of heated indoor swimming pools and vast indoor croquet lawns, of butlers, fine wines, chauffeurs, and private flying boats was by no means everything to Dahl, but its luxury attracted him. As he once admitted to Sheila St Lawrence: "The rich are always interesting."[36]

Pat was flattered that, despite her relative lack of funds, Charles still believed she would make Roald the right wife. However, when Roald unexpectedly asked her to marry him one evening in her dressing room, she was astonished. And, much to his chagrin, she refused. "He looked horrified that I had turned him down," she remembered. But she was still not really sure that she loved him, or indeed that she really wanted to get married at all. At the same time, she knew that her responses were confused. "I did want marriage. And a family. Roald would have beautiful children. What was I holding out for? A great love? That would never come again. When was I going to face reality?"[37] She said no, but a few weeks later she changed her mind.

Perhaps it was this uncertainty that made Roald so uncommunicative. On May 16, 1953, he wrote to his mother about his plans to come back to England in the summer. His dates had changed slightly, he told her, because he had decided to bring Pat with him as well. At that point, he told his mother almost nothing about her – just a little about her family background and a bit more about how much money she was earning. Proudly he boasted that she was being paid $1,000 a week for *The Children's Hour* in New York and that she had just agreed to go on tour in September for a run of five months at $1,250 a week. He told her he thought these figures were "pretty good". And they were – particularly by comparison with what he was earning. "We are considering getting married," he continued, "but there doesn't seem to be any point in hurrying it. She's twenty-six and not been married before, so is almost as cautious as I am. Therefore what we propose to do is to buy a car here in New York, a good second-hand 1951 Jaguar four-seater convertible (open) – about £850 – and ship it direct to Rome. We would then fly to Rome . . . pick up the car and drive slowly up Italy through France, and so to England arriving maybe somewhere around early August."[38]

Dahl told his mother that on the trip they would be sharing all the expenses, including those associated with the car. Then, ever the tease, he added casually, almost as a postscript, that he would try and send his mother a photograph of his new girlfriend – that was if he could find one. A few days later, he sent several. He was much more enthusiastic to Matthew Smith, writing to say that he had just hung one of his paintings in "my girl Pat's flat" and suggesting that Matthew join them on their upcoming trip through France. "You will be crazy about this Pat," he told him.[39]

That trip turned out to be a honeymoon. Pat and Roald were married on July 2, only six weeks after he had written that letter to his mother, in a small church in downtown New York near Wall Street. Despite several warnings against the match from friends like Dashiell Hammett, who

Roald Dahl washing at the airstrip at Elevsis. It was dotted with tents, temporary latrines, washbasins, and grey corrugated-iron hangars along one side.

Pilot Officer Roald Dahl, photographed in Palestine, 1941.

Roald Dahl and Walt Disney with cuddly toys inspired by Dahl's gremlins. For Dahl, the gremlins were often almost real. Negotiating over movie rights, he wrote to one of Disney's animators: "My own Number One Gremlin climbed on my shoulder… and whispered, 'That man does not like us much, shall I fix him?' But I told him to lay off."

The actress Annabella Power, the only one of Dahl's wartime lovers with whom he felt a real emotional connection, photographed in 1939. She recalled that the two of them often behaved "like naughty schoolboys together".

Wing Commander Roald Dahl and his literary hero, Ernest Hemingway, in London, 1944. Dahl thought him "a strange and secret man" for whom he felt "overwhelming love and respect".

Vice President Henry Wallace in 1940. Wallace was perhaps the most left-wing American politician ever to hold high office. A distinguished agronomist, he was also a mystical idealist. Dahl played tennis with him regularly, and connived in making sure that he lost the vice presidential nomination in 1944.

The movie producer Gabriel Pascal with one of his cows in 1945. Dahl admiringly described Pascal, a native of Transylvania, as "an amazing scoundrel", "an awful old rogue", and, in a letter to the US vice president, as "a great man, a very indiscreet great man".

The Roosevelts at Hyde Park, 1943. Photo taken by Roald Dahl. Dahl charmed the President and First Lady, acting like a clown when he stayed with them. "I was able to ask pointed questions and get equally pointed replies because, theoretically, I was a nobody," he recalled.

Dahl's friend and mentor
Charles Marsh around the time
Dahl first met him in 1942.

Portrait of Roald
Dahl, taken for the
publication of *Over
to You*, in 1945.

Portrait of Roald Dahl c.1948

Portrait of Roald Dahl c.1951

Roald Dahl and Patricia Neal on
honeymoon in Rome, 1953.
The trip was not a success.

Patricia Neal and Olivia in
the aviary at Gipsy House.
The aviary was at one time
home to over four hundred
homing budgerigars.

Roald Dahl and Olivia, 1958.

Pat Neal, Tessa, Sue Denson and Olivia in the nursery at Gipsy House, 1961.

Pat, Olivia, Roald and Tessa on holiday in Norway, 1958.

Dahl and Olivia outside the gypsy caravan he had bought from his sister Alfhild. It stands still in the garden of Gipsy House.

thought Dahl "a very silly, dull fellow",[40] and Leonard Bernstein, who thought she was "making the biggest mistake of her life",[41] Pat went ahead – partly one senses because she did not feel strong enough to pull away, and also because she needed to make a commitment to the future rather than continue to dwell on her fractured love affair with Gary Cooper.

Roald too was far from enthusiastic about the wedding. His letters home during the weeks that led up to it were far more preoccupied with his work than with any excitement about the imminent marriage. Charles Marsh once again provided the crucial impetus, presenting Roald with a "huge yellow sapphire ring"[42] to give his bride and offering to host the reception afterwards in his apartment.‡ Claudia Haines, who was herself scheduled to marry Charles in Paris two weeks later, wrote to Sofie Magdalene some ten days before the wedding, expressing her personal pleasure at the engagement. She told Mrs Dahl that Roald and Pat were "as happy as two people can be", while conceding, rather disingenuously, that she and Charles had been very careful to be "enthusiastic without trying to become matchmakers".[43]

Yet even before the knot was tied, the arguments were beginning. Dahl's high-handed behaviour toward Neal's friends provoked a row one evening where she told Roald that he was "rude, arrogant and nasty"[44] and that she wanted to call off the wedding. Roald did not apologize. It was Pat who relented and backed down. She did manage to persuade him to have a church wedding, but he made her agree that it would be small and simple. Under no circumstances was it to be a "showbusiness" event, he told her. He wrote to Pat's mother, Eura, politely explaining that they wanted "to be a bit secret about it",[45] and informing her that no members of either family would be attending. Charles would be best man and there would be just a tiny handful of friends at the ceremony. He took the same line with his own family, telling them that he wanted to get the thing over with the minimum of fuss, and reassuring them that they would all

---

‡Dahl took the ring as a gift, but Neal later claimed Marsh had expected him eventually to pay back its cost. In her memoirs Neal also claimed that the stone was not a sapphire but a marquise diamond.

meet his new bride less than a month later. However, the reporter of *The Buckinghamshire Advertiser* back in England did not miss the opportunity to paint a melancholy picture of the sixty-eight-year-old Sofie Magdalene, sitting alone in her cottage, while 3,000 miles away her playboy son was wedding a Hollywood glamour girl.[46]

The ceremony itself took place in the middle of a heat wave, with the temperature over 100°F. So intense was the heat that, as he was preparing to go to the church, Roald ripped out the silk lining of the new suit he had been persuaded to buy. It was a practical measure, typical of his pragmatic approach to life, but the whiff of brutality shocked Pat, who also later confessed that when they were in bed that night and Roald switched off the light and told her he loved her, she began to cry. Her tears were not tears of relief or delight, but tears of pain. She still longed to be married to Gary Cooper.

Neal would later claim with some bitterness that when she married Dahl, she was the breadwinner. "It was my money when we were married," she declared vehemently when I spoke to her in New York in the spring of 2007. "Roald didn't have any money at all."[47] This was not entirely fair. The writer she had married was by no means the impoverished failure that Charles Marsh had picked up from the floor two years earlier. As Marsh had predicted, returning to the United States had kick-started Roald's writing career. He had abandoned *Fifty Thousand Frogskins*, but Sheila St Lawrence had persuaded him to salvage some of the episodes and turn them into the four "Claud's Dog" short stories, which eventually appeared in his next collection, *Someone Like You*. In response to the energy he felt around him, his productivity also increased markedly. Then *The New Yorker* bought another of his tales: "Taste", about an acquisitive father who stakes his eighteen-year-old daughter's hand in marriage in a bet against a lecherous middle-aged wine connoisseur. Her fate hinges on whether the wine buff can identify the exact vineyard and vintage of an obscure Bordeaux wine by taste alone. After he has won the bet, the expert is revealed as a cheat.

It was more than two years since *The New Yorker* had published "The Sound Machine" and the news of this new sale filled Roald with "almost

unbearable pleasure".[48] Shortly afterwards the magazine bought another new tale, "My Lady Love, My Dove", about the "nasty" suburban couple who bug their guests' bedroom and listen to their conversations. It also published "Skin", the final version of his story "A Picture for Drioli" about the man with the Soutine masterpiece tattooed on his back. Each was typical of the short stories that would make Dahl's name during the 1950s – nuanced, suspenseful, devious, fantastical and often grisly. Sometimes Gus Lobrano, *The New Yorker*'s new fiction editor, turned them down because he found them simply "a little too unpleasant for our general readers".[49]

"Taste", however, had found a powerful admirer in Alfred Knopf. Knopf was another maverick with a big ego. A future colleague, Bob Gottlieb, later described him to me as "a monster . . . a true horror", who indulged in "little boy tantrums" and was a notorious office bully.[50] But Knopf thought Dahl wrote "like an angel"[51] and found the story "stunning". "Please look him up and see what he is and what he has done," he noted to his editor-in-chief, Harold Strauss. "I don't know how we missed this one."[52] One night Alfred read the tale out loud to his shrewd and opinionated wife Blanche. She too thought the story was a winner.

Spurred on by his wife, Knopf contacted Watkins personally to ask if his company could publish a new collection of Dahl's short stories. It was the beginning of a strong mutual admiration between the two men. Roald was flattered by the publisher's praise, and when the deal was eventually signed, Knopf wrote to Ann Watkins to tell her that he was "tickled pink"[53] to have Mr Dahl on his list. Later that year *The New Yorker* offered Dahl a "first reading deal" on any new story he might write in the coming year. His career as a short story writer was back on track. Dahl was therefore not being disingenuous when he claimed to Pat's mother that although it was going to be "a bit strange" to have a wife who earned more money than he did, he was confident he would "always be able to support her".[54]

His letters home in this period are among the most prosaic he ever wrote, possibly because so much of his creative energy was being channelled into his writing. One senses too that, after six years of relative failure in England, he had a point to prove to his family about his commercial successes in America. Money indeed became something of an obsession. No longer were his letters filled with amusing incidents and anecdotes; instead, they were packed with details of his short story sales and of their burgeoning radio, television and film adaptations. There is a distinctly childish pride, as well as a need to prove that he was not just Charles Marsh's poodle, in Roald's boast to his mother that, after only a few months in the United States, he had accumulated the equivalent of £2,000 in the bank – "all made since I arrived, by writing".[55] Marsh offered him advice too about stocks and shares, and his letters home are filled with investment tips and suggestions for his mother and sisters.

Roald would always be grateful for the safety net Charles had provided him, but as soon as he felt financially able, he moved out of Marsh's apartment, renting two small but comfy[56] rooms on the fifth floor above Ralph Ingersoll's apartment on East 62nd Street. Ingersoll was another of Charles's protégés, who would make his fortune working for his mentor, and he and Dahl were in a similar position. Claudia recognized that Roald would "enjoy having a place of his own, where he can work without the many interruptions he is bound to have in a place such as this."[57] Charles owned both apartments and initially charged him only 60 per cent of its market rental value, before Roald insisted on paying the full amount. As he had told his friend two years earlier, "I rather like trying to pay my own way."[58]

There, he reestablished the pattern he had evolved in England, working in the mornings, breaking for lunch – usually with Charles and Claudia – entertaining himself, perhaps at the races, in the afternoon, before returning to write again for a couple of hours before dinner. Content again with being a short story writer, his novelistic ambitions were now entirely behind him. When John Selby of Rinehart Publishers wrote to him in May 1952, praising his story "Skin" and asking politely whether Dahl might have "a novel in [his] system",[59] Roald scrawled on the top of the letter in bold capitals: "NO." Having his own front door meant also that he could listen to music again. So he bought himself a new gramophone, "because I can't do without one". The new machine played

LPs so now Roald had "a whole symphony on one disc."[60] Claudia, who knew that Roald's mother found his absence painful and was aware how little he told her of his personal life, sometimes wrote to give her news about her son's life; gossip, which she reckoned Roald "would probably not think of telling" her.[61] In one of these letters, Claudia told Sofie Magdalene that she thought her son's new autonomy was crucial to his improving mental and physical health. "I think he is enjoying having his own apartment where he can work uninterrupted and be independent. It is not far away and we see him almost every day. Physically I'm sure he is well. He seems to have plenty of energy. Also his work is splendid. That is a great satisfaction naturally to him and I'm sure has some bearings on his physical well-being."[62]

Sofie Magdalene had problems of her own. For nearly a year now she had been trying to sell Wistaria Cottage, and move into the annex of her daughter Else's house in Great Missenden, but she had so far failed to find a buyer – despite the fact that she kept dropping the asking price. Roald encouraged her not to worry about the money, and to move in with the Logsdails anyway, where he felt she would be safer, happier and better cared for. But Sofie Magdalene was stubborn and continued on in Amersham, despite the fact that intruders ventured into her back garden at night and frightened her. Her failing eyesight was also making her liable to trip and fall and, in hindsight, many of her family are now convinced she had become an alcoholic. But she was not lonely. She had her dogs; Claud Taylor and his family were just over the garden wall; and her daughters all lived within half an hour's drive of her house. The in- domitable young woman who had abandoned her own family in Norway to come to Wales, who had survived the early death of her husband and eldest child to raise a family on her own in a foreign land, had evolved into "Mormor" – the ancient, eccentric matriarch.

When she finally moved out of Wistaria Cottage and into the Logs- dails' annex, she arrived, perched on a large armchair in the back of the removal van, surrounded by her dogs.[63] In the thirteen years that remained to her, she came to occupy this new personality completely: still stubborn, still unconventional, still full of stories – mostly about

Norway and the past – but now metamorphosed into a strange, hunched, troll-like hermit, usually dressed in black, with her long grey hair, which had been cut only twice in her life, wound up into a rather scruffy bun. She walked at first with two canes, like a curious black beetle; but after an unsuccessful hip replacement she was confined to a wheelchair with a housekeeper, Mrs Newland, to look after her. Her granddaughter Lou remembered that "everybody was frightened of her".[64] Yet despite her disabilities, Sofie Magdalene's mind was always active. She held court in the glassed-in conservatory at the back of the annex, tending to her plants and reading books and newspapers with a large magnifying glass. Increasingly she became mystical, making predictions about family and friends – many of which came true. Though trapped in her chair, she still radiated a restless, powerful energy. Her grandson Theo later recalled that her large bony hands were "always twitching and her long, spindly fingers, tapping".[65]

Her son's honeymoon was not a success. Alfred Knopf had loaned Roald at least $3,000 to pay for it, but the car that Roald had had shipped over from America at great expense turned out to be unreliable and frequently broke down, while his attempt to show his new wife the great cultural sights of Italy and France went largely unappreciated. He later told his second wife, Liccy, that Pat had spent most of the time in the car asleep, totally uninterested in the paintings, architecture and ancient monuments he had lined up for her to see.[66] She was more intrigued by the tropical fish that swam behind the glass at one end of the tub in the bathroom of the luxurious hotel in which they stayed in Positano. Pat later acknowledged that she had indeed been "very bad" on that honeymoon and that she had spent much of the time inwardly regretting her decision to marry.[67] When she arrived in England, however, things started to look up. The Dahls as a family took her to their hearts immediately. To Else's five-year-old daughter, Anna, Pat seemed like a fairy, "scented and beautiful".[68] Her twin sister Lou agreed. Pat hugged the children, and lavished physical affection on them in a way that was unfamiliar to the more restrained Dahls. They were all "charmed" by her.[69] After she and Roald had returned to New York, Sofie Magdalene wrote to Claudia declaring: "We all love her, and think that she couldn't possibly be nicer and hope that she and Roald will be happy together. We all missed them when they went. Nicky missed Roald so much that he sat in Roald's car all the next morning and the twins were very lost when they did not have Pat here any more. She completely spoiled them."[70]

The reality was not quite so straightforward. Both the twins remembered that Mormor was initially far from impressed when her new daughter-in-law drifted down from her bedroom into the kitchen of Wistaria Cottage each day, almost at lunchtime, wearing a pink chiffon negligée and matching feathered dressing gown. She expected a wife to be able to cook and make a home for her husband and was scornful when she discovered that Pat could scarcely boil an egg. After a few days of quiet resentment, she lost her temper, provoking Roald to exclaim that if his mother was not kinder to his new wife, she would never see her son again.[71] Pat recalled with some distaste the coldness with which Roald had spoken to Mormor and the fact that he had made her cry. Shortly afterwards, the newlyweds moved into the annex at the Logsdails, which Sofie Magdalene herself was about to occupy. Pat and Mormor soon patched up their differences, and when Sofie Magdalene wrote to Claudia Marsh a few weeks after they left, it was Pat's welfare and not her son's that concerned Sofie Magdalene. "I do hope Roald will be nice to her. He is not easy to live with, as he is not always feeling very fit. She said she was glad she had met us as it helped her understand him . . . I do hope they have a child soon," she concluded, "as they are both longing for one." It is a sign of the intimacy she now felt with Claudia that she signed her letter "Mama".[72]

Pat, for her part, had tasted something of what made the Dahl family "out of the ordinary". She had warmed to their closeness and been stung by their tempers. She had seen how they "bitched and complained about each another", but perceived as well how deeply bonded they were. She had also become accustomed to what Nicholas Logsdail would describe as the "strange kind of sexual innuendo, almost lavatorial humour" that characterized their conversation.[73] She had even experienced one of Leslie Hansen's "performances", put on for her benefit the day she arrived. Shortly after dinner, he got down from the table and took a box of matches out of his pocket. He dimmed the lights and the room fell silent. Then he lay down on the floor and struck a match. Carefully raising both legs in the air, he put the flame near his bottom and farted loudly. The match burned with a spectacular and explosive blaze that provoked applause and merriment from everyone in the room. Pat was both "impressed and dismayed". But Leslie was not the only one who surprised her. She had been amazed to discover that Roald preferred to make love in the dark and that he disliked her walking around naked. She could not understand why. She also found that his confidence and that his way of demanding admiration from those around him could sometimes disturb, even frighten her.[74]

These qualities were much in evidence when the Dahls travelled back to New York, via Georgia, where they spent three days with Pat's family. Roald found the Neals boring and parochial. "They're all very pleasant," he reported to his mother, "but pretty dull . . . I wasn't sorry to leave."[75] For Pat, too, it was a miserable visit. After only a few hours, she recalled, Roald retired to his room to read, appearing afterwards only for meals. He annoyed Eura by making plain his distaste for her Southern cooking and by encouraging her only son, Pete, to quit school, abandon his plans to go to college, and go run a filling station instead. For Roald, of course, the latter was a splendidly romantic Arnoldian notion. But the Neals were appalled. "Mother and Nini [Pat's sister] thought he was the rudest thing alive,"[76] Pat remembered. Roald was indifferent to their criticism. He had other things on his mind. He was planning their move to a larger but less expensive apartment on West 77th Street, near Central Park and the Museum of Natural History. He was also deeply concerned about the health of the sixty-six-year-old Charles Marsh who, on the day of his wedding to Claudia, had been taken ill and diagnosed with a cerebral haemorrhage.

Roald was shocked when he saw Charles in New York. "All one side of his face has dropped," he told his mother, adding that Marsh's doctors had informed him that "if he has any excitement . . . that will be the end".[77] Marsh in fact made an unexpectedly swift recovery, and was left just with a slight "crookedness of the mouth and eye".[78] He had not had a stroke at all but an attack of Bell's palsy, a virus that attacks the facial nerve. Nevertheless, his energy and strength were noticeably diminished. Pat meanwhile was occupied with rehearsals for the tour of *The Children's Hour*, which "bored her to death",[79] as she told her mother-in-law, because she was the only significant member of the original cast staying on for the revival. Despite disappointing audiences that led to an early close in Chicago, it was a critical success for Pat. Roald visited her several times during the run, staying for a few days on each occasion. On his first visit, Pat admitted that she had missed him enormously and that it had been a "terrible shock" suddenly to find herself in a series of lonely hotel rooms.[80] She told him she had stayed up all night once in Wilmington crying. But when Roald arrived in Chicago at the end of the tour, he was ecstatic. Alfred Knopf had just published his new collection of stories, *Someone Like You*, and it seemed the book was fast becoming a runaway success.

Knopf had told Roald in March of 1953 that the new short story collection was "about the best thing he'd ever handled",[81] and that he would give it special treatment. He was as good as his word. He pushed the book hard, with big adverts in *The New Yorker* and the *New York Times*. Even so, everyone was astonished by its sales. The first print run of 5,000 sold out within a week, and Knopf had to rush out a second printing. The reviews were almost universally positive. *Time* magazine was the least enthusiastic, calling Dahl an "adroit craftsman", whose tales were "long on plot" and "short on character".[82] *The New York Herald Tribune* was probably the most perceptive when it described him as a conjurer, with "a macabre imagination" and a distinctively offbeat sense of humour – albeit with "a good deal of compassion". The reviewer concluded shrewdly that Dahl had a remarkable ability "to manufacture his own brand of credibility".[83] It was a quality he was to manifest in almost everything he wrote and one that would often mystify critics and publishers alike. But the reading public responded warmly to it, and this word of mouth popularity encouraged further offers of television and movie adaptations. Before long, the book was into its fourth printing and had sold 20,000 copies. The Book-of-the-Month Club picked it up, guaranteeing further sales of 25,000. Not long afterwards, Roald received his first Edgar Award from the Mystery Writers of America. Dahl described the statuette of Edgar Allan Poe as a "ghastly thing . . . I gave it to our char-lady who thought it would be useful as a doorjam in her kitchen." [84]

But if his writing career was blooming, Roald's short but already storm-tossed marriage seemed to be heading straight for the rocks. He had not found living with Pat easy. He felt uncomfortable with a bride who shared few of his interests and he despised her need for constant applause. He found her family, particularly her mother, shallow and dull. It was not a good omen. "Look at the brood mare," he would tell his children years later when they were uncertain whether to pursue a relationship. "The mother will tell you everything." By 1955, Roald was nearly forty. He was accustomed to making his own decisions and, though he had lived as an adult under the same roof as his mother and Asta, he had always had a space there that was entirely his, where he could be secluded from others. He was quite unused to sharing all his living space and simply could not write if there was anyone else around him.

Pat understood this. She told her mother-in-law that she was trying to stay out of the apartment as much as possible in order to give him the "privacy and freedom" he wanted to write, but she admitted it was hard "to get the proper balance". [85] For his part, Roald was increasingly frustrated, not only by his lack of solitude but also by the fact that Pat was not yet pregnant. He found it hard to live with someone who was more famous than he was, and became irritated by the fact that when his name was mentioned in the press, it was often misspelled. Being described as Ronald, Raoul, or even Roger Dahl was bad enough. Worse still was when he was simply referred to as "the husband of Patricia Neal". On top of this, his eyes started to wander toward other women – most notably the heiress Gloria Vanderbilt – while his return to Great Missenden had reminded him how much he missed the English countryside. So, shortly after Pat returned from Chicago, just after Christmas, he turned to her one evening in bed and told her, "nonchalantly", as she remembered it, that the marriage was over and that he wanted a divorce. " 'Don't worry about it now," he said; "just go to sleep.' " [86]

Pat was devastated. But it was hard for her to talk through the situation, because Roald's nervy brother-in-law, Leslie, was staying with them at the time as a house guest, prior to going for treatment to the Scott and White Clinic in Temple, Texas. Leslie's mental state had only marginally improved since Roald left England, and it had taken a colossal effort to persuade him to cross the Atlantic. But Roald was convinced, as usual, that the best American doctors, under his supervision, would be able to solve, or at least mitigate, many of his brother-in-law's problems. Characteristically, he paid for the air trip over – first-class – putting Leslie up in their apartment and paying all his medical costs, which included dental bills in New York as well as countless tests and investigations in Texas. Nothing gave Roald greater delight than giving presents to those who enjoyed receiving them, and he wrote excitedly to his family that Leslie was "having the time of his life" with them.[87]

Ingratitude, on the other hand, was a monstrous sin, as Ashley Miles, the husband of his half sister Ellen, would discover a few weeks later. Miles had first visited the United States in 1952, when Roald put him up in his apartment, loaned him money, and introduced him to many of his friends, including Lillian Hellman. Two years later, he returned and opted to stay with Hellman rather than with Roald, who felt his brother-in-law had snubbed him. Roald raged against being ignored, complaining to his mother that Ashley was a "small-minded twerp",[88] who had spent only fifteen minutes at their apartment and asked nothing about Pat's career or his book. He even hinted that Miles and Hellman were now lovers.

Leslie was quite different. He was deeply appreciative of Roald's generosity and brought out the caring, problem-solving side of his brother-in-law's nature as well as his need to control. Roald had promised Alfhild he would accompany Leslie to Temple and stay there as long as he was needed. Pat, however, refused to go with them. This annoyed Roald and it seems her wilfulness was the immediate provocation for him to deliver his bedtime bombshell. The next day, Pat called the Marshes, briefly explained the situation, and Charles immediately invited her to come and stay with him and Claudia in Jamaica while Roald was in Texas with his troubled brother-in-law. Pat accepted the invitation with alacrity. In Temple, little progress was made in discovering a metabolic cause for Leslie's mental instability and Roald was soon impatient at the lack of positive progress; but – much to his delight – Leslie did have all his teeth removed. They were, he told his mother, "floating in pus" and had "to come out at once".[89] Eventually, Roald bunked off back to New York. "I simply can't wait around here forever," he told his mother, assuring her that his brother-in-law would now "be quite alright alone". When the doctors finally deemed that Leslie was well enough to travel on his own back up to New York, he and Roald made plans to travel to join Pat in Jamaica.

When Pat arrived in Jamaica, she was unsure how much Charles and Claudia knew of her marital problems. She found them remarkably well informed. From Texas, Roald had written them a long letter explaining what he thought had gone wrong and why he doubted the marriage was ever going to work. In a thoughtful and dispassionate analysis of his and Pat's incompatibilities, Roald revealed how strong his powers of self-analysis could be:

> Down here there has been a good deal of time to think, and that's about all I've been doing these last six days. And whichever way I look at it and however hard I try to change my own mind, I still always come to the same conclusion – that I do not believe it is possible for us to live together in complete serenity. She is still far and away the nicest girl I know and is full of the two great qualities – courage and honesty. But that doesn't necessarily mean that we shall feel comfortable and as it were complete in each other's company. It happens to be a fact that when we are alone together in the evenings I find myself feeling extremely uncomfortable because I keep wondering what she is going to do to amuse herself. I read. She doesn't. We talk a little – about theatrical people and the stage, but not much more than that. I know that she longs for the company of her own group of theatrical friends, who I cannot (although I have tried very hard) stand. The two days she was in New York after I had left, she was with them all the time. And I do not blame her at all for this. The blame is equally mine. But I am afraid it only emphasises the point that we both like different people, and also different things.

Of course, there's also the question of one's mother. For years I've seen her (and indeed Claudia, or any other good wife) running a house, keeping it clean, and to a certain extent, serving the man. I don't know how self-sufficient the man is (and I am), yet when he has a woman in the house it is in his nature to expect a certain amount of service. Pat is not able to bring herself to do this. For the last five weeks I have been working. She has not. But I make the coffee in the morning. She stays in bed. I work till lunchtime. Then I get my own lunch out of a can of soup, while she is often still in her bed telephoning.

It seems horrid to be enumerating these little things, but they are the things that start the resentments building up inside one. She is naturally absorbed in herself because she is a fine and successful actress, but I do not believe it is possible to be a successful wife and to be absorbed in yourself at the same time unless you are very clever indeed.

To have a career and to be a wife at the same time is goddam hard work and I've noticed that the few who do it successfully (and it can be done), seem to double their efforts to be a wife in order to compensate for the other. A woman cannot get by saying to herself "I am a successful career person and therefore I do not have to be much of a normal wife. My husband will not expect me to be a normal wife because I have this great career to look after." She can't say that, because unfortunately, and although he makes allowances, he still expects her to be comparatively normal – certainly when she's not working.

Now, Charles, I do not think it would be right for you to try to change Pat by talking to her. I wouldn't want her to know, anyway, that I had told you these things. I am saying them to you simply to ask your advice, and whether you think it would now be a mistake for me to try to go back to her. I believe it would. I think we could run it on for several months, even a year; but it would not be perfectly comfortable, and would fail ultimately. For example, I think it wrong, at this stage to try to have a child (you know how much I want one) and to risk the poor little nipper being born to parents who are liable to

separate, or who may even be separated before he is born. It is wrong.
But Pat, and she may be right, will not live with me under those
conditions, even temporarily. At least that's what she said. Also, when
she refused to come with us to Temple, that seemed to do something to
me. I was all set to go to work and repair the whole business with her,
or anyway to try, and I was so upset and ashamed and guilty that I
would have done anything. It was, as I say the exact moment psycho-
logically when we should have come together again. But she didn't
wish it, and now the mood has passed.

Please don't let her know that I've written you about these things.
But should I, now, in your opinion, come to Jamaica after Temple is
over? I wish to give her the least possible hurt. And to do this, I'll go
anywhere. But it would be unkind and foolish to deceive, or to pro-
long something that must, so far as I can see, gradually fail in the end.
It's probably all my fault.

Love
Roald [90]

Charles's reply, although couched in his customary bizarre ethical generalities, was also perceptive and to the point. He blamed the problem on
what he called "presumptive incompatibility".

Your last line, it's probably all my fault, is inaccurate. What you want
is complete sincerity and you both have it. What she wants is complete
serenity and neither of you have had it during the past weeks at least.
So what is, and where does serenity start and how is it kept going?
Why naturally by service to others. But if each of the two people in
the marriage stake don't put in a hell of a lot of service to one another
they will go bankrupt with great rapidity as they think of their own
affairs.

What you want in a wife is what I have right now. You want a
woman to think of you 80% of the time and to work like hell on the
80% without asking you for direction. You and I as males are willing

to admit it to each other but we will never tell any woman what we want. We want this service deluxe done so graciously that we think a conversation about it vulgar if not stupid.[91]

Charles encouraged Roald to join him in Jamaica, and Roald, thrilled with his friend's "wonderful" advice, told him he would be there in four or five days, when Leslie's treatment was completed. "Please persuade Pat to hang on there," he begged.[92] Meanwhile, Charles listened to Pat's side of the story and returned to those subjects – money and status – that he had already discussed with her and that he felt to be at the heart of their marriage difficulties. "Work hard," he told her, "do all the cooking . . . You must not lie in bed." He also recommended that the two of them pool all their money in a joint bank account. "You can't have the balls in the family," he told her. "Have one bank account and let him write the cheques." If she followed these simple rules, Charles assured her, the marriage would work out fine.[93]

Pat took his advice to heart. When Roald arrived, she told him her new plan at once and almost immediately sensed a thaw in his attitude to her. That evening the Marshes and the Dahls were invited to Firefly, Noël Coward's house, for dinner. Roald and Pat woke next day to discover that Charles, already ill with diabetes,[94] had contracted cerebral malaria from a mosquito bite. Despite round-the-clock care, the fever worsened, and he suffered a series of small strokes, which left his speech and mobility severely compromised. He would never be the same again. The resilient, reliable Marsh, whom Pat had come to think of as "Roald's daddy, practically",[95] had been broken beyond repair.

Roald and Pat returned to New York, leaving Charles in Jamaica. He was, as yet, far too ill to return to the United States. His friend's sudden and unexpected shift from strength to vulnerability caused Roald to reflect on his own life and provoked one of his most profound and revealing letters. In an attempt to console his bedridden mentor, he not only articulated the unremitting daily nature of his own physical pain, but also explained how he had mentally come to terms with that suffering and how it had driven his desire to be a writer.

I just want to tell you this: I am an expert on being very ill and hav-
ing to lie in bed. You are not. Even after you get up and get well after
this one, you still will be only an amateur at the game compared with
us pros. Like any other business, or any unusual occupation, it's a hell
of a tough one to learn. But you know I'm convinced that it has its
compensations – for someone like me it does anyway.

I doubt I would have written a line, or would have had the abil-
ity to write a line, unless some minor tragedy had sort of twisted my
mind out of the normal rut. You of course were already a philosopher
before you became ill. But I predict that you will emerge a double
philosopher, and a super philosopher after all this is over. I emerged a
tiny-philosopher, a fractional philosopher from nothing, so it stands
to reason that you will advance from straight philosopher to super
philosopher.

I mean this. I <u>know</u> that serious illness is a good thing for the
mind. It is always worth it, afterwards. There's something of the yogi
about it, with all its self-disciplines and horrors. And it's one of the
few experiences that you'd never had up to now. So take my view and
be kind of thankful that it came. And if afterwards, it leaves you with
an ache, or a pain, or a slight disability, as it does me, it doesn't mat-
ter a damn; at least not to anyone but yourself. And as you've taught
me so well, that is the only unimportant person – oneself.[96]

Charles's predicament also reinforced Pat's resolution to change her
ways, and encouraged Roald to inject a necessary shot of positive energy
into the troubled marriage. While Pat was on tour and away in Jamaica,
Roald had continued his dalliance with Gloria Vanderbilt. Initially she,
like so many, had found him lofty, opinionated and condescending. But
his charms were powerful. Soon she was flattered by the attention he
showed her and excited when he presented her with one of his handwritten manuscripts, held together by a thread, onto which was attached a
tiny gold greyhound, "an antique key to wind a fob watch".[97] For Roald,
a "stiff prick had no conscience" – so it was perhaps no surprise that even
as he wrote to Charles about the crisis in his marriage, he was also trying

to seduce Vanderbilt. Indeed, according to her memoirs, he almost consummated the relationship just before he went to Jamaica. Roald now put this *affaire* behind him. Equipped with a joint bank account and a more pliant, domesticated wife, he also took steps to deal with two other things that he felt had been disturbing the marriage. First, he sent Pat to a specialist to investigate why, after nine months of marriage, there was still no "bun in the oven".[98] The new gynaecologist diagnosed blocked Fallopian tubes as the cause of her infertility and blew air through them to clean them out. Second, he wrote to his family in Buckinghamshire, and asked them to look for a house near the Logsdails in Great Missenden, which he and Pat could rent – or preferably purchase.

Despite his successes in New York, it was always Roald's intention to return to England. City life held increasingly little excitement for him and he viewed Manhattan, as he pointedly told his friend Marian Goodman, simply as somewhere "to make money".[99] In early 1952 he said much the same to his mother, when he acknowledged that his only reason for being there was "to amass some capital".[100] In that context, the city had delivered for him. But now that he was solvent and successful, he was finding life there increasingly stressful. In an autobiographical fragment in one of his "Ideas Books", he explained his feelings in typically comic terms:

> Now if you are self-employed, as I am, and if you are exceptionally indolent, as I am, then you will discover no finer cure for your indolence than to go and stay for a while in New York City. It costs so much money simply to exist in the place that you find yourself living in a state of perpetual panic. You begin to work feverishly, trying to earn enough money to pay the bills. You dare not stop. You dare not take a day off, not even Sunday. Yesterday, I was reading the paper for a few moments after breakfast, and all of a sudden I leaped out of my chair and cried, "My God, what am I doing! I shall be ruined."[101]

The lure of the English countryside was once again becoming overwhelming. So "slowly and insidiously",[102] Roald began trying to persuade Pat that they should spend half the year there. Eventually she agreed that they should spend the winters (eight months) in Manhattan and the summers in England. In mid-March 1954, Sofie Magdalene sent her son details of a tiny cottage that had come on the market on the outskirts of Great Missenden. It was less than an hour's train journey from London, and a stone's throw from the Logsdails' house, with six acres of land, including an orchard filled with apple and pear trees and two functioning water wells. It was owned by the Stewart-Liberty family, who owned Liberty's in Regent Street, and had been inhabited mostly by tenant farmers and latterly by a solicitor and his young family who had fallen on hard times.[103] Situated on an ancient drove road, which ran from an old medieval abbey up the hill to a mighty beechwood, the property was to be sold at auction on April 8. Both Roald and Pat went "crazy" about the idea of Whitefield Cottage and decided immediately that they wanted to buy it. Sofie Magdalene offered to put up half the money – although she had to persuade her trustees that it was a sound investment.§ Else and John went with her to bid for it. They were successful. Roald and Pat were now the owners of a house they had never actually seen. It had cost just over £4,000.

Almost six weeks later, they arrived in England to supervise building work on the primitive cottage and "remodel, redecorate and completely furnish" it.[104] Electricity needed to be installed, walls knocked down and doorways raised, so Roald and Pat lived with Mormor in the Logsdails' annex until the work was completed. There they took many a glorious walk in the Buckinghamshire countryside, and it was on one of these – after a bout of open-air sex in one of the nearby fields, where Pat had laid down on an ant's nest and got her bottom badly bitten – that Pat was convinced she finally got her "bun in the oven". Above her, she remembered, nature seemed to suggest omens of fertility. "The bright blue sky was skirted with low-hanging clouds." It reminded her, strangely, of "ladies removing their panties".[105] A few days later, on July 27, 1954, the Dahls moved into Little Whitefield, as they had named it, to avoid con-

---

§Ashley Miles, one of the trustees, seems to have objected to her doing so, but was overruled by the others.

fusion with the Logsdails' house, which was also called Whitefields. Roald was in Arcadia once again.

> *There are pheasants to be poached up in the woods across the valley.*
> *There are exciting furniture auctions to go to in vast decaying country*
> *houses all around us. There are wine auctions up in London. There*
> *are horse races to bet on, and small secret greyhound races out in the*
> *fields. There are roses to be budded onto the wild briars in the hedges*
> *around the orchard, and outhouses to be painted, and cherries to be*
> *picked, and the donkey's hooves to be pared, and an old carved frame*
> *to be re-gilded, and a tree-house to be built, and there are mushrooms*
> *to be gathered in the dew-drenched grass of someone else's pasture in the*
> *very early mornings. There are in fact so many things to be done all the*
> *time that it becomes impossible on any single day between April and*
> *September to find a moment for doing what a publisher would call*
> *serious work.*[106]

Roald's relations with his British publishers continued to be problematic. His new collection, *Someone Like You*, had been published in England by George Orwell's publisher, Secker & Warburg, just before his return. The reviews were generally excellent, and shortly after its initial print run, the book went into a second printing. But Dahl, who described Fredric Warburg as "a desiccated, rather constipated old fart, who reads about eight books a year",[107] was dissatisfied. Once again, he found himself comparing London unfavourably with New York. "My book does nothing here," he told Sheila St Lawrence angrily. "No contact from Warburg. No advertising. No books in shops."[108] He was equally uncomplimentary about his UK agent, Peter Watt, who might be "charming," but had "about as much drive as a pair of stilts".[109] The press were generous with their accolades for the book. Improbable, witty, malicious, sophisticated, fresh, horrifying, extravagant, cruel and prescient were some of the many adjectives bandied about, but the most popular of all was "macabre". *Punch* described the best of the stories as "attractively horrible", noting that "the chuckle is not completely separated from the scream", while the *Manchester Evening News* noted that Dahl's view of humanity was neither kindly nor genial, but that he had "a genuine ability for grotesque comic invention". The *Times Literary Supplement* was more reserved, concluding that "the general effect of his work is unpleasant". The critic for *Time and Tide* was perhaps the most perceptive of all when he observed that Mr Dahl "behaves in his work like the mad inventor of a book for boys".[110]

Roald had already shown his remarkable ability to connect with children in many contexts. Within his own family, it was perhaps most striking in the relationship he had developed with his nephew, Nicholas Logsdail, who described him as "the best uncle a boy could wish for".[111] Nicky was the recipient of a stream of presents from his uncle in New York – mechanical guns, model aeroplanes, train sets – mostly the kind of things that fascinated Roald himself. He wrote to him at school every two or three weeks. He also encouraged the young boy's talents as an artist, paying him ten shillings for his painting of the burning elm tree, which he then framed and hung on the wall of his study. He took his nephew poaching and travelled to antique sales with him. He helped him build a huge tree house in the garden, and backed him when he decided he wanted to live in it. He left him on his own in Matthew Smith's studio for a weekend, so he could paint with the great man. And he was quite uninterested in his school exam results.

This led to a situation where Nicholas felt he had a closer relationship with his uncle than he did with his father, for whom – in the words of one of the Dahl nannies – "those girls [Anna and Louise] and their mother were the apple of his eye".[112] "Roald took over my brother, he influenced him utterly," remembered Nicholas's sister, Anna, recalling that this sometimes irritated her father, who would describe his interfering brother-in-law as lazy and unsuccessful.[113] Behind his back, he would often refer to him as "the oaf". Roald encouraged Nicky's sexual adventures. He gave him a gramophone and introduced him to classical music, rhapsodizing about an artist's existence in much the same way he would later celebrate the life of a writer. "It's not work for him," Nicky recalled his uncle saying. "He [Matthew Smith] gets up when he wants to, he goes to bed when he wants to, he doesn't have any obligations to anybody." [114] It was the gypsy ideal all over again: the apparent absence of dreary, day-to-day responsibilities that was almost an extension of the delights of childhood.

The ease with which Dahl could enter a child's mind had been apparent too in his recent story, "The Wish", in which a young boy, left on his own in a room with a multicoloured carpet, persuades himself that he must cross it only by treading on its yellow portions. If he steps on the wrong colours, he will either disappear into a black void or be killed by venomous snakes. The boy's wild imagination takes such hold of him that the reader is left uncertain of his fate when, inevitably, his foot does slip into the danger zone. It is a startling effective piece of prose, and it led Sheila St Lawrence to suggest that Roald should consider writing a book for children. It was a typically sensible suggestion from the woman who was taking over as his literary rock. Ten years younger than he was, Sheila was strong, clever and unintimidated by her client's sometimes eccentric manner. She came from a medical family. Her father was a doctor and her mother had been a Red Cross nurse in the Great War. She had studied mathematics at Columbia University in New York before joining Ann Watkins in 1947 as the office assistant. She had first written to Roald in 1950. "Dear S. S. Lawrence," he had replied. "If you don't mind me saying so that's the damnedest name I ever heard. It's either a ravishing film star or a negro missionary. Henceforth I shall imagine you in the former . . ." [115] She took his frivolity in her stride, responded in kind, and their correspondence was soon characterized by a gossipy, bantering repartee. When Roald returned to New York in 1951, he invited Sheila out one evening to watch an indoor tennis match. The date, she recalled with a grin, went no further than that. As the aging Ann Watkins ventured into the office less frequently, St Lawrence gradually took over dealing with Dahl's literary affairs. Her self-reliant, practical and inventive mind was perfectly suited to Roald's, as was her directness of expression. In the future, he would come to rely as heavily on her judgement as he had relied upon Watkins's. However, it was to be a number of years before he responded to her prescient suggestion about writing for children.

The summer of 1954 saw him working on two new projects – a movie script of Herman Melville's *Moby-Dick* and a theatre project based on three of the most macabre short stories in *Someone Like You*. The film-work was short, intense and unsatisfying. A first draft had already been written by Ray Bradbury, but the director John Huston was unhappy with it and asked Roald to inject something of "the feeling and philosophy of Melville"[116] into the dialogue. Remembering his unsatisfactory movie experiences with Gabriel Pascal, Roald was unsure whether to take up the offer, but eventually decided to do so because the money earned would help pay for the rebuilding and furnishing of Little Whitefield. Yet he did not take to Huston at all. Impressed neither by the director's showy eelskin jacket nor his way of dealing with people, Dahl summed him up as "a queer guy", and one whom he found difficult to read. "I cannot tell whether H is really pleased with what I've done or not," he told Sheila St Lawrence. "I believe what he's actually doing is taking my ideas and my sentences and fiddling around with them himself. He tells you nothing of the final version and won't show it. Really a strange sort of egomaniac, and I feel he could gobble you up if you don't take care."[117] He was not far off the mark. The project ended with Huston refusing to pay Dahl for all his work, and crediting himself as Bradbury's co-writer. The experience reinforced all Roald's suspicious attitudes toward "movie types".

Fortunately, his irritation with the *Moby-Dick* project was swept away by the enticing prospect of becoming a father. Pat noticed with some relief that Roald began calling her "old girl" and "old sausage" as soon as she started to get larger. At the outset of their relationship, she had loathed these endearments, finding them neither affectionate nor sexy, but recently their withholding had come to cause her pain. It consoled her to hear them again. Roald began to anticipate the birth of his child almost as soon as it was conceived, and – with Pat barely six weeks pregnant – he lightheartedly imagined himself into the role of father. "Parenthood is a great strain," he declared. "I can see it all. Nursery books for Knopf. Once upon a time there was a dear little bunny . . ."[118] It was a year since Sheila had suggested he might consider writing for children. Again he skirted by the waters of his destiny, but did not stop to drink.

For the next two years his professional life would be consumed by his one and only stage play, *The Honeys*. Based on three of the short stories in *Someone Like You*, it seemed initially like a good idea. Many of these tales had already adapted well to television and there seemed no reason why they should not work well in the theatre, too. But the reality of the show's production would be fraught with pitfalls and problems. In August 1954, he wrote to Sheila summarizing the plot. It was a typical mixture of the macabre, the moral and the comic.

> *The general idea is to follow a woman (in three acts) through three marriages with three different men . . . In each case the husband is murdered because he deserves it . . . The woman is not really the murdering sort, but is driven to it by intolerable provocation. Actually she's rather a sweet little thing – small, kind, gentle, passionately in search of a cosy little home, a good husband, and domesticity. A woman in search of a decent mate. The fact that she kills them off instead of divorcing them should not obscure the principle moral of the play, which is that a bad husband deserves all he gets. Many women in this world would gladly murder their husbands if they thought they could get away with it (and vice versa), but they are afraid. Crime (in the form of murder) pays all the way through. And good luck to it. Because at the same time, crime (in the form of naughtiness and infidelity) does not pay. Which is interesting, because who is to say which of the two crimes is the worse. The police, society, the church hold one view. Our little woman holds another.*[119]

The excitement of conquering a new genre – and particularly one that was his wife's metier – was probably Roald's primary motivation for spending so much time on the project. His little sketch, *Double Exposure*, written in Bexley before the war, had, until then, been his only other foray into theatrical writing. Perhaps he also hoped writing the play would bring him closer to Pat. He had certainly enjoyed watching the

rehearsals of *The Children's Hour* and liked the collegial nature of the process. "Never seen professional rehearsal before," he told his mother then.
"Liked it. Going again." [120]

Unfortunately, when he returned to New York in the autumn of 1954,
The Honeys turned out to be a horrible experience for everyone involved.
Roald quarrelled with Cheryl Crawford and Carmel Myers, the American
producers. He was unhappy with the casting, particularly Jessica Tandy in
the lead role, and he fought constantly with the director, Frank Corsaro.
And when his "farce comedy" opened on Broadway in the spring of 1955,
it was panned. *The New Yorker*, for example, described it as "tedious" and
"unpleasant". It closed early. Crawford herself seems curiously not to have
grasped what the play was about, describing it in her memoirs as "a story
of insidious evil" [121] rather than a dark comedy, but she did tell Roald that
it was "the most miserable experience" she had ever had in the theatre.[122]
He felt much the same way, having "a perfectly dreadful time" [123] with the
project and becoming "profoundly disillusioned" by it.[124] He told Sheila
St Lawrence that he was considering having a machine gun mounted
on the roof of his house in Great Missenden to defend himself in case
Carmel Myers came to visit.[125] Yet the project refused to die. Despite the
failure in New York, a British producer, Emile Littler, picked the play up
and persuaded Roald to rewrite some of it for a UK production.

So, more than a year after its New York debacle, under the new title
Your Loving Wife, Roald had to go through the humiliation of failure all
over again. The year 1956 was an inauspicious time to be premiering a
tightly constructed, essentially artificial piece of drama. London had just
witnessed the premiere of John Osborne's *Look Back in Anger*, which had
been hailed as the beginning of the "new wave" of British theatre. Gritty
realism was all the rage, and even in the provinces, Dahl's clever escapist satire failed to synchronize with the popular critical pulse. Roald was
quick to pin the blame for its lack of success on others. "The first night
was very bad indeed," he told Sheila St Lawrence after the opening in
Oxford. "I don't think there was anything much wrong with the play, but
the acting was simply atrocious. No style, no speed, no fun. In addition,
our male actor is, I'm afraid, no good at all . . . The whole thing is a bit

of a bloody bore, isn't it?" [126] The budding poet and playwright Adrian Mitchell, criticizing the play's construction, described it in the *Oxford Mail* as "a piece of jerry building", though in Bournemouth audiences seemed to enjoy its sauciness, sophistication and madcap humour. Sheila St Lawrence, however, was horrified at the trajectory the project was taking and the amount of her author's time it was consuming. Eventually she wrote to Roald suggesting that he abandon it. "You've been working constantly for almost two years on this vehicle to the detriment of everything and anything else. It seems perhaps the time has come to divorce yourself from it and start afresh with the stories that we as well as your reading public are clamouring for." [127]

Dahl himself was initially unsure what to do. He was tired of the play, but desperate not to squander the time he had already invested in it. Emile Littler eventually settled the issue when he cancelled the London run and asked for yet more rewrites.

Conference with that prick Littler yesterday. He wants to close the play at the end of the run. Rewrite and recast . . . I said I didn't feel like doing any more at the moment. I'd given him six months work for free after he'd bought the property. He said he wanted someone else to do it. "Who?" He didn't know. "Who would pay this man?" "You would," he said to me. I said, "Will I? Hell." He said, "I won't." I said, "I can't." There it ended. The next move is up to him. I'm leaving him to stew. Will he lose the play by not bringing it to London? I know he doesn't want to lose it. He's going to lose me soon. I'm off to NY as soon as our nurse's entry permit comes through. [128]

Dahl did indeed leave as soon as he could and, in his absence, the play was finally put to rest. Apart from one or two amateur revivals, it has never been professionally produced again.

He returned to New York in October 1956, with his eighteen-month-old daughter Olivia, but without Pat, who had gone to star in a movie produced and directed by Elia Kazan. Olivia Twenty was born in New York on April 20, 1955, and named after her mother's favourite Shakespearean heroine, the date of her birth, and the fact that Roald had $20 in his pocket when he came to visit Pat in hospital. He had been in Boston on tour with *The Honeys* and, much to Pat's disappointment, not present at the birth. She described her new baby to Claudia as "rare and beautiful. I love her and am terrified of her". She longed for Roald to be able to hold her and for him to finish with his other baby, his play. "I want to be married to a short-story writer who has recovered from the theatre," she told Claudia regretfully.[129] The next month they travelled to England to spend the summer there. In Great Missenden, Pat found the demands of motherhood hugely stressful. Though her niece Anna Corrie acknowledged that Pat was "the most wonderful aunt", she also described her as "the most lousy mother".[130] Pat struggled to deal with Olivia, who she believed was almost "at war" with her, "lying in wait" for her mother and screaming loudly whenever she came close.[131] In desperation she handed the child over to her sister-in-law, Else Logsdail, who returned her a few weeks later, quite transformed.[132]

In contrast, Pat could see that Roald was "a very maternal daddy",[133] who happily took on the burden of child care while she was away filming and seemed relatively content that his paternal duties were leaving him little time to write. "There's no doubt that babies are charming," Roald admitted to Sheila, "but they do bugger up the quiet and routine necessary for work."[134] As he told Claudia Marsh, "between you and me I can do without the little buggers until they are six months old. Until then they are nothing but a great whirling blur of wet nappies and vomit and milk and belching and farting."[135] He took measures to deal with the problem, employing a nurse to help, and constructing an isolated work hut in his orchard, where he could write undisturbed. Even so, it was difficult – particularly when Else and her children were away. The following summer, he compared notes with Sheila St Lawrence, who had also recently had her first baby.

I don't go for this rushing about at all. And with my sisters away on holiday, the nurse's day off here gives me a very arduous day. I have the nipper solid from 8 am to bedtime, all meals for her and me,

pramming, bathing, everything. And now, by God, the nurse has to
have a WEEKEND to go and see her mother. That may finish me.
Certainly it won't finish anything else – like a story, for instance . . .
I am going out into the orchard to eat apples.[136]

Baby problems aside, Roald was blissfully happy in Little Whitefield.
He loved his new work hut, describing it to Charles and Claudia as "marvellous . . . only Claud's heifers licking the windowpanes from time to time
and eating the curtains if I leave the windows open".[137] If Pat was home,
in the evening there might be dinners with American actors and writers
who were passing through the United Kingdom. Or, if Pat was away, he
might go out to play poker locally or amuse himself on a midnight adventure with Claud Taylor. Now that he had his own small herd, Claud was
eager to mate his cows illicitly with a huge Black Angus bull in a nearby
field. Achieving this involved stealthy and sometimes hilarious nocturnal
escapades, some of which Roald would later recreate in his novel *My Uncle
Oswald*. It made wonderful entertainment for Charles and Claudia.

Then the fun really started. The bull started jumping them one after
the other in quick rotation and the cows got so excited they started
jumping the bull as well. Claud had a torch and he would shine it
in a bright yellow beam on the bull's prick just as it was entering the
cow, then afterwards he would shine it on again, crying out, "Look at
her! Look at her tail all curling up! She's had it alright! Boy, he really
creamed her up that time! Look at it dribbling out." Then we success-
fully returned the bull to his herd and made the long journey back over
the fields. "Just look at them," Claud kept saying proudly as we walked
along. "They're so bloody tired they can 'ardly stand!"[138]

Roald had been disappointed when Pat, now pregnant again, accepted a part in the Elia Kazan film *A Face in the Crowd* and had to leave
their rural idyll for twenty weeks' filming in the United States. But he
was philosophical. "I tell you," he complained to Claudia, "a career and
motherhood, (or wifehood) do not go together. To hell with the money

she will earn. Who wants that? On the other hand, it would have been madness for me to stop her from doing the film, because to make a Kazan movie is the big ambition, and she would never have forgiven me. I wish I could feed her some magic pills that would rid her of this fierce driving ambition that all actresses seem to have." [139] He longed to settle down in Buckinghamshire and abandon the New York element of their existence.

For a period of five years – 1955–60 – Roald and Pat commuted between Great Missenden and New York, with occasional sojourns in Los Angeles if Pat was working there. In Manhattan, they moved into a bigger apartment on the Upper East Side, between Madison Avenue and the Metropolitan Museum of Art on Fifth. Pat fitted her stage, television and movie work around two more pregnancies, which resulted in the births of a second daughter, Chantal Sophia, in Oxford in April 1957, and a son, Theo, in July 1960. A few days after Chantal had been christened, Roald realized her name rhymed with Dahl and renamed her Tessa. Pat described her to Claudia Marsh as "really cunning . . . with a longer thinner jaw than our moonfaced Olivia . . . She has all her buttons and is a bright little bird." [140] To escape the inevitable hurly-burly generated by young children and the live-in nanny, Roald rented a room in an apartment directly above theirs, which belonged to the playwright Clifford Odets. It looked out onto Campbell's Funeral Chapel and Roald later enthralled his offspring with stories of how he used to watch dead bodies being unloaded there at night. Once he told them he could occasionally still see the corpses twitching. [141] But he found the city itself ever more objectionable: "The merchants are impolite, the bus drivers are truculent, the cab drivers are crazy, and the cops are not to be trifled with," [142] he wrote. He worried about raising a family there, and about the speed with which taxis careened across the streets.

Yet the option to leave New York remained a financial impossibility. Pat was now the significant earner in the family and much of her work was coming from American film and television. Her return to the big screen as the female lead in *A Face in the Crowd* was a huge critical success. The film explored both the US public's susceptibility to being manipulated by television and the emptiness of celebrity. Her character, a radio presenter who picks up a young no-hoper and turns him into a television star, returned her to the movie mainstream. While Pat's career was going from strength to strength, however, Roald's productivity declined markedly as he got bogged down in *The Honeys* and found himself increasingly involved in looking after the children. Repeated rejections from *The New Yorker* were also depressing him. They seemed now to follow a consistent pattern: initial interest, leading to cuts and rewrites, then an "unpleasant exchange"[143] with the new fiction editor, Roger Angell, which culminated in a refusal. Sheila St Lawrence had some success selling them to *Playboy*, but this strained relations with Alfred Knopf, who disapproved of the magazine and told Roald he thought he "ought not to appear in such company under any circumstances".[144] Dahl replied bluntly that he was not rich enough to turn *Playboy* down simply because he disliked the magazine.[145] Alfred Hitchcock's popular television adaptations of earlier stories made up the bulk of his earnings, as Sheila St Lawrence struck a series of lucrative deals with Hitchcock's company for them. "Up to that time Hitch had never paid anyone half the price we got out of him," Ann Watkins's son Mike later told Murray Pollinger in London, "and up to that time he had never agreed to the price we were able to pry out for theatrical exhibits and remakes."[146]

The short stories were taking him ever longer to complete – his next collection, *Kiss Kiss*, took him six years to compile – and they were also becoming ever stranger and more grisly. Alfred Knopf found most of them excessively grim. One in particular – "William and Mary" – about a man whose brain and single eye are kept alive after his death by a surgeon, who leaves them floating in a bowl while a life support machine keeps the brain supplied with oxygenated blood, had made him almost "physically ill" when he read it. He preferred the more sophisticated tales, like his favourite, "Taste", and wrote a long letter explaining why he did not think the new stories were up to the standard of those in *Someone Like You*. "Your numerous admirers will, for the most part, experience a feeling of let down," he warned.[147] Roald himself was increasingly grumpy and beginning to contemplate the end of his career as a short story writer. "Work is going very slowly," he told Sheila St Lawrence. "It always does, I'm afraid, when I don't sell anything."[148] Five months later, he wrote again, telling her that he was "not so much depressed now as puzzled" by the situation, and concluding: "I shall not write any more stories."[149] Sheila responded by once again prodding him to consider writing a children's book: "The more I think about it the more appealing it becomes. It seems to me here is the chance for you to get away from the short story formula, which is imprisoning you at the moment and reindulge yourself in the realm of fantasy writing at which you are so very good. I think you could come up with a book with tremendous appeal to both adults and children."[150] It was a shrewd suggestion and at last, third time around, Dahl took the bait.

For much of his adult life he had enjoyed telling stories to children. During the war, in Grendon Underwood, he had enthralled the young Jeremy Lang with his gremlin tales; on his honeymoon he had visited friends in the South of France and entranced their two young boys with his storytelling. Pat recalled that they followed him as if he were the Pied Piper,[151] mesmerizing the children with his rich voice, his glittering eyes, his sense of fun and his wild, subversive imagination. Now Roald was spending a lot of time with his own children – particularly when Pat was away on movie shoots. "He worked his head off," recalled Marian Goodman. "He raised those kids. He was the mother and the father . . . Pat was wonderful with them when she saw them . . . But when it came to the routine and the drudgery, I think he did more than she did."[152] And it was not all drudgery. A story was never far away. Roald read them traditional fairy tales from Norway or from the Brothers Grimm, Beatrix Potter stories, and absurdist fables such as Hilaire Belloc's *Cautionary Verses*. He also began concocting narratives of his own.

Slowly, blindly, he was edging toward his destiny as a children's writer. Three of his recent adult stories had children as central characters. Two of them, "Royal Jelly" and "Genesis and Catastrophe", were creepy narratives constructed out of the kind of one-liners that filled his Ideas Books. The third, "Pig", was more complex and had reflected all of Dahl's darkest fears about city life. By mid-1959, with his new short story collection completed, he began seriously to consider some plots for a children's story and jotted down a few thoughts. A "Turtle Boy", "the cold-cure inventor (tiny insects in soil?)", "the magic tape-recorder", "the child who could move objects", "tiny humans in hollow tree", and "the child who dreamed of the future, which always came true", were some of the ideas that initially intrigued him.[153] But none seemed quite right. He continued to hesitate despite the fact that increasingly there was no obvious other option. He confessed to Knopf that six years was "too long a time between books even for a slow worker like me. I am longing to do a short novel," he added, "but I don't have a single idea in my head."[154]

Gradually, one or two of his potential children's stories began to acquire a little more flesh in his imagination. The idea of a novel that featured insects, in particular, intrigued him. He had noticed that his own children were always fascinated by animals, but felt that Beatrix Potter and others had slightly cramped his ability to do something original with dogs, cats, rabbits, mice and ducks. "I searched around," he recalled, "but there seemed to be jolly little that had not been written about, except maybe little things like earthworms and centipedes and spiders."[155] It was these tiny, insignificant arthropods he fastened upon. He had also started to speculate what it was that stopped the fruit in his garden from growing endlessly. Slowly, the two ideas began to gel, as he realized that in order to relate his animals to a child protagonist, the child would either have to become very small or the creatures themselves very large. In this case, after considering enormous apples, outsize pears and a gigantic cherry as a possible focus for their adventures, he opted instead for a peach because he thought its flesh and flavours were more exciting and more sensual.[156]

In August 1959, the whole family along with Susan Denson, the nanny, went on holiday to Hankø in Norway, and there the story that would become *James and the Giant Peach* began to germinate. Denson was nineteen years old. She came from a farming family in the Midlands and had possessed very little experience when Pat had hired her the previous summer. But the two women bonded immediately and within hours of her arrival, she was taken away with the family to the Isle of Wight. Now, after a year in New York and Little Whitefield, she seemed like part of the furniture. In Hankø, Roald started to "walk around [his new story] and look at it and sniff it", evaluating it carefully, "because once you start you're embarked on a year's work".[157] And the more he smelled it, the more he liked it. Not long after his return to England, a first draft was underway. Then Alfred Knopf suddenly dropped *Kiss Kiss* from his 1959 autumn publication list. Knopf had made his disappointment with the manuscript of the book only too apparent and Roald felt this postponement advertised his publisher's lack of confidence. He felt betrayed, and as a result his enthusiasm for the new story evaporated. "I think he has behaved very badly," he told Sheila St Lawrence, "especially after being so chummy all these years. And as far as getting a children's book out of me now, he can stuff that one up his arse."[158]

Dahl put the children's story aside and instead spent the rest of that summer buying antiques and researching a US television proposal he had been asked to develop. The aim was to create a drama series out of classic ghost stories and Roald's initial task was to choose the tales. This involved a great amount of enjoyable reading and started promisingly enough when a pilot episode was commissioned after Roald had presented his producer, Alfred Knopf's half brother Edwin, with what he considered to be the twenty-four finest stories. The tale selected for this trailblazer was "The Hanging of Arthur Wadham", by E. F. Benson. Dahl wrote the adaptation himself, and the show was duly shot and edited. By all accounts it was an excellent piece of work. However, its plot hinged on whether a priest should break the sanctity of the confessional or let an innocent man hang, and no one had considered the power of the Catholic lobby on this issue. Concerns about negative Catholic audience reactions conspired to ensure that no network would take it and eventually the series itself was abandoned. For Roald, it was yet another screenwriting disappointment. But it forced him to return to *James and the Giant Peach*.

The story was to some extent a reworking of themes he had explored in his recent adult stories, only in a lighter, more fantastical vein. A newly orphaned boy is sent to live with a relative in the countryside – only in this case the kindly Aunt Glosspan of his parable "Pig" is replaced by two vicious monsters, Aunts Sponge and Spiker. From their first appearance, it was clear that these were villains of a different order from most found in existing children's literature. They were cruel, selfish, greedy, lazy and violent – comic grotesques, whose vices were described with a relish for crude and disgusting detail that was already distinctively Dahl's own.

> *Aunt Sponge was enormously fat and very short. She had small piggy eyes, a sunken mouth, and one of those white flabby faces that looked exactly as though it had been boiled. She was like a great white, soggy overboiled cabbage. Aunt Spiker, on the other hand, was lean and tall and bony, and she wore steel-rimmed spectacles that fixed on to the end of her nose with a clip. She had a screeching voice and long, wet, narrow lips, and whenever she got angry or excited, little flecks of spit would come shooting out of her mouth as she talked.*[159]

The two aunts starve James, beat him mercilessly and work him until he drops. But whereas in his adult tales these "ghastly hags" would almost certainly have prevailed over the young innocent, Roald now felt free to abandon his misanthropy and give his sense of justice and fair play full rein instead. The giant peach, swollen magically, and with James and his outsize animal friends on board, breaks loose from the tree, rolls down the hill, and symbolically crushes the two women, leaving them "ironed out upon the grass as flat and thin and lifeless as a couple of paper dolls cut out from a picture book".[160] One senses the lifting of a weight, an abandonment of the dark energy of the short stories, as the lyrical aspect of his writing sensibility was released from the wraps in which he had stifled it after the failure of *Some Time Never*. No longer is the child a victim. Now he is a resourceful and shrewd problem solver, who takes control of his own destiny and those of his new friends in a series of wonderfully fanciful adventures. At one point, the peach tumbles off a cliff and into the sea, where James saves it from a shark attack by attaching it to a flock of seagulls using threads that have been spun by a giant silkworm. It rises out of the ocean and into the safety of the sky. Returning to the theme of flying liberated Dahl's sense of the rhapsodic as the peach's aerial journey across the ocean is illuminated by euphoric evocations of clouds, nature and stillness. Even New York is redeemed when, after crossing the Atlantic Ocean, the peach eventually lands upon the needle of the Empire State Building. A glorious celebration ensues.

By the time he returned to England in the spring of 1960, *James and the Giant Peach* was already in its second revision. Roald showed it first to Pat and then to Sheila St Lawrence, who both responded with enormous enthusiasm. But Sheila was facing problems of her own. She was a young mother, with three small children. Her husband was often away on business. The previous autumn, her father had fallen ill and now needed her attention. The result was that she had become semidetached from the Watkins Agency, working part time at home. In doing so, she abandoned many of her clients. But not Roald. As her new boss, Ann Watkins's son, Armitage ("Mike") Watkins, put it in a letter to the London agent Laurence Pollinger: "Dahl has been and is her friend and her most special client . . . She knows the minutiae of the Dahl complex – and it is a complex indeed – better than anyone else."[161] *James and the Giant Peach*, on whose evolution she had exerted such an influence, was her main focus of interest. She had prompted and pestered him to write it. Now she was a sympathetic and imaginative editorial critic, to whose suggestions Roald was responding with gusto. In the peach's encounter with the sinister hairy cloudmen, for example (the cloudmen were a reworking of his gremlin "spandules" from 1942), Sheila suggested a number of additional details, including the idea that the shaggy monsters should bombard the peach with gigantic hailstones. In the margin of her letter, Dahl excitedly scribbled "Yes! Yes!" to this and other ideas, which he then incorporated into his next draft.

Sheila understood how much Roald needed this kind of constructive critical response. It was quite different from the syntactical nitpicking that had so irritated him with *The New Yorker*. She knew that he valued his own writing style and was confident of its quality, appreciating how important the "rhythms and patterns" of his prose were to him, and she was aware that they often took many weeks of careful honing before he was satisfied. "He was pleased with himself in a nice way, not a haughty way," she told me. "But he was a clever bloke . . . and one had to be cautious in making comments."[162] Fortunately, she also believed strongly in his talent and simply could not contain her own passion for the new book, which bubbled over with a zesty energy that matched Roald's own. As she liaised deftly between Roald and Virginie Fowler, his old-fashioned and somewhat prickly editor in Alfred Knopf's children's division, she continually reassured him that she knew she was reading a winner. Convinced the book was even better than the two most recent juvenile publishing successes, E. B. White's *Charlotte's Web* and *Stuart Little*, Sheila told Roald she was certain that *James and the Giant Peach* would be "a runaway best seller". "Really, honestly, truly," she wrote when she got the second draft, "it is unbelievably better than ever, and better than ever I thought it could be. I think you've done the undoable, crossed the border between adult and juvenile." [163]

CHAPTER FOURTEEN

A Tornado of Troubles

THE YEAR 1960 BEGAN calmly enough, but it would prove to be tumultuous in many ways. *Kiss Kiss* was published in the United States in March and, despite all Alfred Knopf's reservations, it stormed into the *New York Times* bestseller lists. As Roald and Pat, who was more than five months pregnant, boarded the boat back from New York to England in early April, Roald was pleasantly surprised to find that many of his fellow passengers, including C. S. Forester – the man who had first encouraged him to begin writing almost twenty years earlier – were reading it. Nor had this escaped the notice of two other passengers in the publishing business who were also making the crossing on the *Queen Mary* – the London literary agent Laurence Pollinger and the publisher Charles Pick. The fifty-eight-year-old Pollinger had recently parted from David Higham to set up his own company and was now aggressively looking for new clients. His friend Charles Pick was five years younger, a senior editor at Michael Joseph, and a charismatic bon viveur, whom Pollinger's son, Murray, would describe as "shrewd, cruel, a salesman, utterly through and through". Both were self-made men, who had risen up through the ranks of the publishing business. They were ambitious entrepreneurs – close colleagues, who "fed off each other" professionally.[1] And they had Roald Dahl in their sights.

Behind the scenes there was also the shadowy figure of Armitage Watkins, who had taken over the business from his mother when she formally retired in 1957. The day before Dahl left Manhattan in 1960,

Watkins had taken Pick out to lunch to let him know that Dahl had yet to conclude a UK publishing deal for *Kiss Kiss*. He told Pick that Roald had parted company with his UK agent Peter Watt six years earlier after the publication of *Someone Like You*, and that he had subsequently joined up with Raymond Chandler's agent, Helga Greene. He also hinted that his client's low public profile in the United Kingdom annoyed him and that Dahl was quietly on the lookout for a new British agent.

Armed with this information, Pick and Pollinger seized the opportunity to persuade Roald that they were the team to revitalize his British career. Having "run the gauntlet of the snooty purser", Pick found the Dahls in their cabin. Pat was hunting for a valuable diamond she had mislaid, he later recalled, while Roald was telling her not to bother looking for it.[2] Pick's flattery worked a treat. "I have never been so assiduously and pleasantly wooed and wined and dined as I (and Pat) were on board ship by Messrs Charles Pick and Laurence Pollinger,"[3] Roald wrote excitedly to Sheila on his arrival in England, informing her that from now on he intended Pollinger to represent him in Britain and Michael Joseph to publish both *Kiss Kiss* and the incomplete *James and the Giant Peach*. He also confessed that, although he had already agreed to the terms of the new arrangement, he had not yet informed Helga Greene, admitting that he did feel "a bit embarrassed", as he knew she was already in negotiations with Heinemann and Cape about publishing *Kiss Kiss*. He asked Sheila to do the dirty work and extricate him from his commitment to Greene. "Please guide me in this," he concluded. "I don't want to cross any wires."[4]

Dahl had put St Lawrence in a difficult position. She understood completely why Pick and Pollinger's enthusiasm had been such a tonic to him. She knew how much he wanted to be accepted as a writer in the United Kingdom, and that he longed to spend more time in England with his young family, but that he did not want to do so as long as his own career there was effectively stalled. In that context, his behaviour was understandable. Yet it was also ruthless. Roald had asked her to "ease Helga out very quickly and gently",[5] but this was easier said than done. Greene was almost certain to object. She had been working hard on placing *Kiss Kiss* with a British publisher and would surely feel she was due some compensation. In the event, St Lawrence's letter to Greene was a model of honest diplomacy. "Roald has been restive about his representation in Great Britain for some time," she began.

> *He is, as you must know, very anxious to establish himself to the same extent at home as he has in the States, and he was beginning to feel the need for more aggressive exploitation of his work in England. Before his departure last month, we had discussed his remaining with you. We were both well aware that you had to date very little to work with as far as material was concerned, that you had expended a great deal of time and effort untangling knots made by others; and had done much to prepare the way for launching* Kiss Kiss . . . *Apparently something has gone wrong. This morning I received a frantic cable and letter from Roald asking to be released from his agency commitments immediately.*[6]

Greene responded with quiet dignity, saying that she was neither "upset nor even surprised" to get St Lawrence's letter. "It has seemed to me always," she concluded, "that you were the only person really able to handle him, and therefore his work."[7] The matter was sorted with remarkably little fuss. Roald, delighted that he had got exactly what he wanted, basked in the sunlit honeymoon of his relationship with Pick and Pollinger, enthusing to Sheila about the "real action" they were bringing to his career in Britain.[8] In May 1960, Penguin bought the paperback rights to *Kiss Kiss* and the *Sunday Times* in London published a complete story from the collection. Roald meanwhile relaxed with his family, tinkering with *James and the Giant Peach*, considering potential illustrators, gardening and buying antiques. It was a golden period, as Sue Denson remembered, with Pat doting on Olivia and Tessa, and Roald content and at ease. They seemed, she recalled, a "wonderful team".[9] His nieces, particularly the twins Anna and Lou Logsdail, were on hand most days to help with looking after the children, while Mormor, now in her mid-seventies, was always only five minutes away in the Logsdails' annex. She had installed an elevator so that she could move around the house more easily and Roald visited her almost every day. Sue Denson recalled her sitting "dour and uncommunicative" in her conservatory, listening rather than talking, surrounded by dogs and looking "a bit like a troll". In Little Whitefield, too, animals roamed everywhere, bringing back for Roald fond childhood memories of Radyr, Cumberland Lodge and Bexley. "Pat seems very well. Olivia is learning to read," he told Sheila the following month. "We have two ducks wandering about the lawn, and a nine weeks puppy pissing on the carpets in the house." [10]

By the end of the decade, Roald would demand privacy in his hut and make it clear that he was only to be disturbed there if something important had happened. But in the early days, it seems he was more relaxed – particularly when Pat was away. He struck up a friendship with Alan Higgin, a local teenager, who kept two ancient cars in the orchard. Not only did he let Alan race around the field in his cars, he picked apples with him, often cooked him meals, and sometimes let him sit in the hut and chat with him. Higgin remembered Roald as "just a big kid really".[11] Nearby, a traditional gypsy caravan loitered amongst the trees in gaily painted splendour. Alfhild and Leslie had originally bought it, with some of Charles Marsh's PWF money, for Bert Edmonds, a gypsy neighbour of theirs, who had fallen on hard times and had nowhere to live.[12] When Edmonds died, they sold it to Roald. Now it served not only as a playhouse for the children, who ran naked around it on the long summer days, but also a private tribute to that gypsy ideal which continued to inspire him. A family of gypsies regularly camped each year at the top of the lane. Alan Higgin recalled them as "kind, nature-loving people who had chosen that existence. . . . You weren't afraid of them." [13] Roald loved that. Shortly afterwards, he renamed Little Whitefield "Gipsy House".[14]

Raising children had brought Roald closer to Pat, while Gipsy House was turning into the haven of which he had always dreamed. Not only was he back in the countryside within the bosom of his family, but now he finally seemed to have found an energized and positive agent and publisher working for him an hour away in London, who would complement Sheila St Lawrence, his professional rock in New York. But storm clouds were starting to gather. Laurence Pollinger, for one, was not content with the status quo. He harboured ambitions to poach some of St Lawrence's responsibilities. Perhaps he even sensed that if Roald were to settle permanently in England, he might one day replace her as his principal agent. Roald's own judgement about all this was blurred by the fact that his ego, starved of praise from the London establishment for so many years, was now swollen with regular doses of adulation from Charles Pick and Pollinger himself. The latter was daily at the end of the telephone, plotting, planning, pestering, urging him to move forward. Sheila, by contrast, was 3,000 miles away and distracted by her own domestic problems. In their ten years working together there had never been an angry word between them. Now Dahl was beginning to rock the boat. A destructive row was about to ensue.

It all began with the question of who should handle Dahl's translation rights. Pollinger persuaded Roald that because of his own proximity to European territories, he was in a much better position to handle them. Roald wrote to Sheila explaining his simple geographical logic. But if he thought that, like Helga Greene, she would simply give up her rights without a fight, he was wrong. Irish blood ran in Sheila's veins and she was a combative and feisty negotiator. She believed she could handle these rights just as well as Laurence Pollinger and she resented the potential loss of income and influence involved. She was also stung by the implication that Roald believed Pollinger could do this part of her job better than she could. So she objected. She told him that she wanted to continue to act as his agent for foreign translations and asked him politely to stay out of the discussion, arguing that the author should not be involved in these issues, and that the matter should be decided directly between herself and Pollinger, the UK subagent.

Roald was uncertain how to respond. At first he pretended he did not care how the issue was resolved. "None of it is anything to do with me," he told her, "so must keep out of it. It's up to you to handle as you wish."[15] Two days later, he repeated that line. "You square it with him [Pollinger]. There's no question of taking anything away from you."[16] He was being disingenuous. If he had meant what he said, the matter would have ended there. But he was in a quandary. He believed Pollinger was the right man to maximize his foreign sales. On the other hand, he did not want to hurt Sheila.

In the middle of all this uncertainty, Sheila's father died and she had to go away for a few days to organize the funeral. While she was out of town, Roald decided he must get off the fence and tell her directly what he felt about the situation. So, when Sheila returned to New York, tired and emotional, having just cancelled a long-planned holiday to Greece with her husband and children, she found awaiting her a letter from Roald, which tried to browbeat her into giving up the rights. Its content – a mixture of bullying, pleading, hectoring and childish flippancy – was unlikely ever to achieve the effect he desired. "I know quite well that Laurence P. is a pushing little businessman who wants to get in on everything, but in this case *he* is not pushing so much as *I* am . . . PLEASE let Laurence have a go at this in Europe, sharing his commission with you in the usual way. It doesn't really amount to all that much anyway, so I am not really taking hamburgers out of your children's mouths. Will you be nice and write him a letter at once telling him I've asked you to ask him to go ahead?"[17]

Sheila was devastated. She knew her client's reputation for self-righteous grumpiness and had seen it in action on many occasions. Roger Angell at *The New Yorker* was not the only person who dreaded the "unpleasant altercations" that often ensued in dealings with Roald Dahl. However, she had never experienced this self-righteousness used against her. Now, just when she was most vulnerable, he had turned on her – presumably in the hope that she would crumple. She didn't. She felt a profound sense of injustice, almost of betrayal. In her mind, having assured her that he would not interfere, that he would not take anything from her, Roald had now made it quite plain he wanted her to give up her translation rights to a man who had known him for barely three months. She wrote back, initially criticizing Laurence Pollinger for not behaving like a gentleman. But it was not long before the fact that she was wounded was all too clear. Her first instinct had been to resign completely, she told Roald, "to bow out immediately as your agent in order to avoid any further unpleasantness". But her sense of fair play would simply not allow her to do it.

Roald, I don't know what to do or where to begin. I, unlike Laurence, haven't got you here to persuade or influence or bamboozle.

You have put me in one hell of a position . . . I don't know whether you have lost confidence in my ability or whether the songs of praise from a new voice have gone to your head . . . I should bow to his [Pollinger's] wishes in order to maintain harmony . . . but I refuse to be trampled underfoot after all these years without putting up a fight. Either you have faith in your wildlife or you don't.

I have much to lose by taking this stand and nothing to gain. You as a client, you as a friend, and you and your family's warm and close association over the past thirteen years. These things are important to me. They mean a great deal to me and I value them highly. I don't want to lose them. But I value ethics and fair play too and I do not believe I deserve this display of fair weather sailing.

I will not reread this letter. I cannot . . . It is the principle that has caused me such splitting headaches and sleepless nights.

> *My love to you,*
> *Sheila*[18]

Shocked by what he described as the "tornado of troubles" he had stirred up in her breast,[19] Roald should probably have called Sheila and tried to reason it out. He thought she had overreacted. She probably had. And perhaps some reassurance and sympathy was all the recently bereaved Sheila needed. Yet, although he discussed it with Pat, his eventual response was wheedling, argumentative, and ultimately unfeeling:

Dear Sheila,

. . . Now if you were the one who is pregnant, I could understand the whole thing, but as it is, I thought I was almost doing you a favour, taking this troublesome and unremunerative business to someone else. But see what happened. Pat says you are a woman and what the hell did I expect. Resign as my agent? You must be mad. Pollinger

doesn't mean anything to me. He is brisk and smooth. I have noticed
that he sometimes has a little dandruff in the hairs on the side of his
head and how could one turn everything over to someone like that?

But I still want to talk about it a bit more (if you will keep abso-
lutely calm) and as it's now seven pm and as we have a poor derelict
woman and two children in the house (she was evicted in the rain
this morning by her landlord and her husband has run away). I must
now go down and lend a hand in the house.

Love,
Roald [20]

Roald and Pat had indeed taken in a destitute local family of strangers
and allowed them, with characteristic generosity, to stay as house guests
until, in Alan Higgin's words, they "got themselves a bit sorted out".[21]
Nevertheless, despite this unexpected domestic disruption, next day
Roald wrote again to Sheila. His letter began in a conciliatory manner.
Once again he told her how important she was to him, how much both
he and Pat valued her. But after a few lines the strident, self-righteous
tone returned. It is a uniquely emotional professional letter, revealing just
how much Sheila meant to him, how loyal he felt to her, and how much
he valued her friendship and judgement.

Dear Sheila,

I am enormously worried that my small request about these transla-
tion rights should have upset you so much. Did you, one wonders, as
you hinted in your letter, read into it a general loss of faith in you and
the beginning of a slow, sly slide towards Pollinger. One simply has to
assume that you did. And that is so ridiculous that I don't even want
to talk about it – except to say no-one could have had a better, a more
successful, more clever and also a more marvellous agent and friend
than me. I should be lost with anyone else as far as important business
goes.

I'm concerned because I have from the start made it absolutely clear how much I rely upon you professionally and personally. Godammit – you are even talked about in my will . . . to the effect that your personal advice should be taken in all matters relating to my literary properties and that you should continue to handle them etc. etc . . . You should not require a declaration of faith from me any more than I should or would want one from you. Balls to that. And don't get so bloody emotional. I am not a SHIT. You are not a SHIT. Charles Pick is not a SHIT. It is just possible that Pollinger is a little bit of a shit . . .

I would never have put it up to you if it had meant the loss of any considerable commission to you – although I know this is not what you are concerned about. You are obstinate, that is why you are such a good trader. I am also obstinate, but not quite so obstinate as you. I am ready to give in. But I don't want to. And I think I should tell you I don't want to. I believe we should give it a try . . .

But for God's sake don't fly off the handle. It upsets me as much as it upsets you, and it upsets Pat as much as it upsets me, and if you do it again you might be responsible for her having the baby in the kitchen, and although that would probably make a nice story of sorts, it wouldn't be worth it.

We love you,
Roald [22]

Sheila eventually backed down, proposing a compromise by which she retained the translation rights on *Kiss Kiss* and Dahl's back titles but handed the rights over to Pollinger for *James and the Giant Peach*. But she was still upset. She pointed out to Roald that losing *James* particularly pained her because she felt "like a foster mother" to the story. "Do you recall my letters in 1950–51–52 hounding you to do just such a book?" she asked pointedly, concluding: "I am sorry about my Irish temper. Is this the first you've seen of it?" [23]

Her attitude took the heat out of the situation and provoked Roald to a form of jocular apology:

Dear Sheila,

It is time that we both stopped sulking and feeling injured – and got down to work. I myself haven't done a stroke, not one line, since this "great translation rights affair" came up, and I have been terribly unhappy (though not guilty) about the whole thing. You too have been unhappy. And also angry. But now it is over and it is time to forget it. I think I was right. You think I was wrong. And whenever a situation like that comes up, the best thing to do is to let it ride for a while and allow time to demonstrate who was wrong – if anyone cares.

PLEASE FORGET IT. But what about James? Should I try to do another children's book? Or a play? Or a short novel?

Love,
Roald [24]

The explosion was over, but the poisonous fallout remained. Sheila, whose husband Miran's work was taking him increasingly often to Ireland, began to wonder if she should abandon her career as a literary agent and leave America to join him there. Within a year, she had taken the decision to do so. She would go on to make a permanent new home for herself there. Her choice cost Dahl his most constant, shrewd and loyal adviser – and one he found impossible to replace. Had her resolution to leave New York been affected by her argument with Roald? I asked her this question in 2008, when she was eighty-four and I had tracked her down to a tiny cottage nestling by the edge of Strangford Loch. Absolutely not, she assured me. It was entirely a family matter. And did their quarrel sour the relationship? Time had evidently been a great healer for, despite her quick wits and ready recall of detail, she had no recollection at all of the intensity of the "tornado" that had whirled so fiercely almost half a century before. "Wow. Boy, oh boy. I didn't know I could do it," she exclaimed, her eyes glittering, as I read her the letter she had written nearly fifty years earlier. "Gosh, gracious, snakes alive! I was spitting at him in the same way he was spitting at me. I *must* have been upset," adding, as if in reassurance to her guest, "I'm not usually like that!"

Surprisingly, her boss, Mike Watkins, played no public part in the contretemps. He offered Sheila no support and clandestinely seems indeed to have taken Pollinger's side in the affair. It was almost as if he wanted her to leave. In a private letter to Pollinger, Watkins offered him the rights he wanted and blamed Sheila for the whole dispute, describing it disdainfully as "somewhat of a tempest, which has been transferred from a small pot labelled Vanity, to a larger one marked Pride, to its present container, marked larger, PRINCIPLE".[25] His attitude was puzzling. Sheila St Lawrence still worked for his agency. The rights for which she was fighting were shared between the two of them. He could have been backing her against his London rivals. So, why was he quietly encouraging Pollinger? Perhaps he was threatened by the very closeness of Sheila's relationship with his client. Perhaps he sensed that if her semidetached status from his company ever evolved into full independence, Dahl might well decide to leave him and go with her, so he engineered the wedge that drove Roald and her apart.

There's no doubt Watkins set up Pick and Pollinger, ceding valuable rights of his own to them and making no attempt whatsoever to intercede between Dahl and St Lawrence when the storm blew up. When Sheila decided to go to Ireland, he made little attempt to persuade her to stay on and even discouraged Roald from communicating with her. Watkins probably underestimated his author's own sense of commitment to the agency where he had made his name – although Dahl was increasingly contemptuous of Watkins himself. "I know he is a twerp," he wrote to his publishers at Knopf in 1969, apologizing for his agent's behaviour over *Fantastic Mr Fox*. "He drinks too many martinis at midday and these are beginning to pickle the brain, not that there was a lot of it there to begin with. But his mother was a good agent and a fine friend and I cannot bring myself to leave the firm after twenty-six years. I put up with his nonsense. You should not have to. I shall try and bypass him in future as much as possible."[26] Twelve years later, his verdict was even more damning. "After thirty-nine years experience with this gentleman," he told Anne McCormick, "I can assure you that he understands nothing."[27]

As the row with Sheila began to blow over, Roald found solace going to house sales, like that of Laurence Olivier and Vivien Leigh, ostensibly in search of furniture but more often, Sue Denson felt, out of sheer curiosity. He also began restoring a huge antique mirror he had recently bought – "a real beauty", he told Sheila, "a seven foot high carved Chippendale one with delicate leaves and branches and birds on it and I am presently and patiently scraping 1/8 of an inch of plaster off it to reveal the gold leaf underneath. Five hundred hours work. But worth it. In fact that's all the work I am doing at the moment." [28] He was also investigating the idea of setting up a company in Portugal to own his new copyrights and minimize his UK income tax obligations. It might sound "perfectly ridiculous", he admitted, but he had been encouraged to do so by a "terrific expert." Most significant of all, he had become the father of a strapping young son. Theo Matthew Roald was born on July 30, 1960, and the arrival of an exotic new male in this family of women was the cause of both excitement and fascination. "He has a pair of testicles the size of walnuts and a sharp wicked penis," [29] Roald informed Sheila a fortnight after his birth. Another progress report was despatched three days afterwards: "He's a fine nipper, and his circumcised tool (now healed) glows with promise, like the small unopened bud of some exotic flower." [30]

Six weeks later, the Dahl family's summer idyll was over. On October 1, they boarded a "ghastly Boeing jet" to spend another winter in New York. Roald's love affair with Manhattan was becoming ever more jaundiced. He now viewed it as a violent place, filled with threats and danger. The cab drivers gave him "the willies"; they were "the enemies of the people". One day from his window he watched a tall boy with a "tense white face" running through traffic. Roald identified with the youth. It seemed he was a kind of prophet, warning him that catastrophe was around the corner.[31] Like the child in his short story "The Wish", terrified of stepping on the cracks in pavements or treading on the wrong colour in the carpet, Roald had a premonition of disaster. He had seen the omens, and, as he confessed to himself, "we crack-dodgers *always* take notice of omens".[32]

His short story "Pig" – the masterpiece of *Kiss Kiss* and perhaps the most misanthropic tale he ever penned – had explored his disillusion with the city. Doffing a bloodstained cap to Voltaire's *Candide*, Dahl tells the tale of Lexington, a naive orphan who is raised by his kindly vegetarian relative, Aunt Glosspan, in the Virginia countryside. When she too dies,

Lexington is forced to return to the grim dystopia of Manhattan – a city populated by moronic Irish policemen, who have killed the boy's innocent parents, and corrupt Jewish lawyers, who will swindle the young child out of his rightful inheritance. Finally, around the tale's bitter last corner, lurks the slaughterhouse. There the unsuspecting young lad must come face to face with the true brutality of humanity. Dangling by his ankle from a chain, the confused Lexington meets his end at the hands of a "benevolent . . . wistful . . . cheerful" pig-sticker in rubber boots, who takes him "gently by the ear", before deftly slitting open his jugular vein, thereby conveying him from this, "the best possible of all worlds", into the next.[33] Lexington was the same "white-faced boy" he had recently seen from his window. He had tried to dodge life's dangerous cracks and failed. Soon, this instinct that New York was no place to raise a young family would seem cruelly prophetic. On December 5, 1960, just a few months after "Pig" was published, the pram carrying Roald's sleeping four-month-old baby, Theo, was hit by a cab on the corner of a New York street and crushed against the side of a bus.

Susan Denson had just collected Tessa from nursery school and was bringing her home for lunch. She was pushing Theo in his pram and trying to manage Stormy, one of Ivar Bryce's dogs, at the same time. It was her third winter in New York with the Dahls, and she fitted so well into their family that they had made her one of Theo's godparents. The weather was bitterly cold. They were walking down Madison Avenue and when they reached 85th Street, waited at the crossing for the light to change. When it did, Sue pushed Theo's pram off the sidewalk and out into the road. At that point a cab careened around the corner and crashed into it. The driver panicked. Instead of braking, he stepped on the accelerator, ripping the pram out of the nanny's hands and propelling it 40 feet through the air, before it smashed into the side of a parked bus. Theo's head took the full force of the impact and his skull shattered.*

Both Roald and Pat were within earshot of the accident, but neither

---

*I have reconstructed this version of the crash from various notes and accounts given by Patricia Neal and Roald Dahl within two years of the accident. These include a lengthy interview Neal gave to Lloyd Shearer in the *Long Island Sunday Press*.

saw it. Roald was in Clifford Odets's apartment, writing. Pat, who had only recently finished shooting *Breakfast at Tiffany's*, was in a local shop. She heard the police sirens, but did not initially realize her own son had been injured. An ambulance rushed the tiny child to the nearby Lenox Hill Hospital, along with Susan, Tessa, and the dog. There, Marian Goodman's physician husband Ed recalled, Theo was diagnosed with a "terrific neurological deficit".[34] Almost everyone thought he was going to die.

When Roald and Pat arrived in the emergency room, they faced a dreadful situation. Not only was their tiny child horribly injured, but the doctors were disagreeing publicly about what should be done. It was a challenge to which Roald responded with a sang-froid and clearheadedness that again recalled his ancestor Pastor Hesselberg's actions in the church fire at Grue. Several days later, he wrote the whole experience down on paper in one of his Ideas Books. He did this neither for the lawyers nor for an insurance claim, but for himself. It was a private affair, the reflex action of a writer, an observer, who needed to record every detail of the trauma. This was the flip side of the hyperbolic fantasist. Now the analytical eye of the reporter was at work. I have extracted it at some length because – even in this note form – its cumulative power is remarkable. He called it simply "A Note on Theo's Accident".

I was working on the 7th floor, my phone turned off. I did not get the incoming call from Susan. But I heard a police siren. Then Pat was in the apartment calling to me. We went out, got a cab drove to Lenox Hill Hospital Emergency. Cab driver didn't know entrance, dropped us a block away. Theo was in examination room with two doctors. Susan, Tessa, Stormy were in small waiting room with policeman who drove squad car and policeman in charge of school crossing. Things looked grim. They were giving plasma to Theo. Pat called Dr Zipser. He arrived quickly. They admitted Theo upstairs to paediatric section, in charge of the senior paediatrician, Dr O'Regan. They called in Dr Echelin, senior orthopaedic surgeon, who interrupted an operation to come down and look at Theo. He was in a state of deep shock, colourless, high pulse, temp 102 degrees. They didn't dare move him for x-ray. I suggested portable x-ray. They did this. Also arranged round-the-clock special nurses. But this was general paediatric ward, and none of the nurses nor the floor-doctors were trained in neuro-surgery.

It is now about 3 PM. We called Ed Goodman and Bill Watson for advice . . . They both examined baby, Ed going in with Dr Echelin. Multiple skull fractures were revealed by x-ray. But there were no signs of other bodily injury. Around 8 PM Theo began coming out of shock. Colour in cheeks. Temp down a little. Bill Watson called and suggested we call in Dr Milton Singer as consultant. I checked with O'Regan, who grudgingly acquiesced. Called Milton at home 9/10 PM. He came at once. There now ensued a one-hour argument around bedside between Drs O'Regan, Echelin, Singer (and Watson). Singer said it was essential to do a subdural tap immediately to relieve the pressure on the brain. Drs Echelin and O'Regan said no. It was too early to tamper. Singer refused to budge. In the end, they did the tap, drew off 10 and 8 cc of fluid and blood. O'Regan came bustling out, said to me: "I did not approve of this, and I do not know what the consequences will be." Echelin said the same. I said, "Why did you allow it, then?" They said because Singer was so insistent.

I stayed all night in hospital watching the baby. At 1 AM his temperature went down to 101. At 2 AM it went to 99 and stayed there. He was still having blood and intravenous feeding. His blood count was low, indicating a big loss of blood somewhere. He was also in an oxygen tent. I had a row with nurses about fixing a catheter tube. First she strapped it to his kicking leg! Then she strapped it upwards to the side of his cot. I said "Lay it on the mattress!" Eventually she did.

Next morning, O'Regan came in and called me aside. Saying he couldn't have outside men like Dr Goodman and Watson interfering and examining baby. He was very unpleasant about it. I said I would tell them. I did.

Theo improved slightly through day. They x-rayed him. Found no fracture of cervical spine. I requested O'Regan to make no decisions without Singer's agreement. Echelin said, "I'm not going to ask

Dr Singer's permission for what I do!" I said, "You must all work together." This was Tuesday. I stayed most of the day. So did Pat. The doctors came and went . . . I stayed Tuesday night, watching the inefficient antics of the nurses, trying to advise them as best I could.

Wednesday morning, Singer came in. Theo had had two seizures in the afternoon. Singer prescribed 1/2 cc of Dilantin as sedative. Checked with Echelin. I watched the nurse giving it by dropper. She had 1/2 a small cardboard cup full of the stuff. I protested. Made her check and re-check the order book. She said it was correct. (She should not have given it, only hospital nurse may dispense medicines) Ten minutes later (Anne Bancroft and Harvey† are there) O'Regan enters. The nurse checks dosage. O'Regan says she's given 1/2 oz instead of 1/2 cc. He immediately aspirates it out with a tube. (This is a fifteen times overdose). He then rushes out and proceeds to blame Dr Singer to me. I call in Pat to hear it. We protest. "It would not have happened had I written the order," he says. "Why not?" we say. This was a nurse's error. His general attitude is too much to stand. I call Singer. He arranges for an immediate removal of baby to neurological wing of Presbyterian Hospital. Bill Watson rushes round to help. O'Regan finally (1 hour) turns up, has to give release, which I sign. Bill has blanket to carry baby. O'Regan says "Hey, wait! Who are you?" He then delays still further by doing a complete medical examination of Theo in front of two other doctors. Echelin comes in. He behaves well. I explain to him the reasons for move. Bill Watson carries Theo out in his arms. Harvey is waiting in Bill's car. Bill and Theo, Pat and I get in. Harvey drives to Presbyterian. There Drs Singer and Ransahoff are waiting and efficiency reigns. This is Wednesday evening 9 PM.[35]

---

†Harvey Orkin was Pat's agent – a man she would describe as a "totally appealing, warm and joyful human being." Roald did not initially take to him, describing him in a letter to Charles Marsh as "a loud-mouthed Jewish gent of the worst type." However, when Orkin turned up during the hospital crisis and drove the Dahls from Lenox Hill to Presbyterian Hospital, Roald's perception of him changed radically. "He was the sort of friend who would drive through a storm to help," Pat recalled her husband declaring afterwards. "There was no long line of cars at the curbstone, just Harvey's." (Dahl's own description of events that evening suggests that Orkin drove Dr Watson's car.) – Neal, *As I Am*, pp. 121–122, 218; Roald Dahl, Undated letter to Charles Marsh, c. 1954 – CMP.

It was the beginning of several weeks of horrible uncertainty for the family. New York had been hit by a particularly icy winter and the snow made getting anywhere difficult. Roald slipped and broke his ankle. Pat caught flu and was confined to bed. Sue Denson sat for hours in her "horrible bedroom that faced the brick wall of the next block", wondering if she should return home.[36] But at least under the supervision of Drs. Singer and Goodman at Presbyterian, Theo's medical care was consistent. Housed in an oxygen tent for two weeks, he underwent several operations to drain fluid from his head. The surgery was successful and the doctors became increasingly confident that he would pull through, but no one was sure how badly his brain had been damaged. As there were no serious internal injuries and his head wounds seemed to be healing, Theo came back home to convalesce just before Christmas. Then, a week later, something about his condition began to disturb his parents. He went quiet; he no longer smiled; his reactions seemed dull. Pat and Roald spent New Year's Eve with their neighbour the psychiatrist Sonia Austrian and her husband, Jeffrey. It was they who realized what had happened.[37] Cerebrospinal fluid had built up in Theo's cranial cavity and was pressing on his brain, causing him to go blind.

Roald rushed the baby back to hospital. Ed Goodman recalled that when he examined him, his head felt "like a bag of marbles".[38] The pressure of the buildup of fluid around the brain, he told Dahl, carried with it a severe risk not only of permanent blindness but also of retardation and even death. The doctors immediately extracted the liquid, and fitted a tube to drain any further fluid directly into his heart, where it could easily be reabsorbed. Initially, they were doubtful that the child's sight would return, but it did, and eventually Theo was declared fit enough to go back home on January 14, 1961. No sooner had he got home, than his sight began to deteriorate again. The shunt – the internal drainage tube into his heart – had blocked. Once more the surgeons operated and cleared the blockage. Once more Theo's sight returned, though "much impaired".[39]

It was a pattern that would repeat itself. Each time, Roald and Pat hoped that Theo's body would start absorbing the cerebrospinal fluid naturally and that the implanted tube would become redundant. Each time, their hopes were to be dashed. Theo would come home, appear to be doing fine, then he would lose his sight because the tube had blocked. He would be rushed back into hospital for surgery, often convulsing, leaving his parents to face once more his "huge, desolate, bewildered eyes" [40] when he awoke in the emergency room. Six times in the next nine months, the same thing happened. Every time, there was a chance that Theo's sight would not return, that his brain damage would be worse. After the second emergency, the tube was inserted into the pleura – the membrane around his lung – which involved particularly invasive surgery. It was, as Roald told his mother, with uncharacteristic frankness, "very distressing, the whole thing". [41]

Dahl, of course, was not one to sit back and let things take their course. As soon as he realized that the defective valve was the problem, he abandoned his writing and began to work out how he might improve the situation. He swiftly became something of an expert. On February 18 he wrote his mother: "I don't think much of the tubes that they use here for this work, particularly the valve at the lower end, which is meant to open up between 40 mm and 80 mm water column pressure. This valve is literally nothing but a slit in the plastic tube . . . Do they have anything better in England, something less likely to block and clog?" [42] Sofie Magdalene, now confined to an electric wheelchair but still the materfamilias, asked her stepdaughter Ellen's husband, Ashley Miles, now director of the Lister Institute, for advice. Miles put them in touch with a Scottish neurosurgeon called Wylie McKissock, who had performed similar operations in Britain, but using a different valve. When the family returned to England in May and Theo suffered another relapse in Great Missenden, McKissock fitted this alternative valve, but it too failed to function effectively. Then he tried removing the shunt entirely, in the hope that the hydrocephalus would no longer occur. But this also proved ineffective and the old shunt was installed once more.

But Roald remained determined to find a technical solution to the shunt's deficiencies and quietly worked out what he thought was needed. With typical resourcefulness, he contacted a man with whom he had first corresponded in 1950, when he wanted to buy a miniature steam engine as a present for his nephew Nicholas.[43] Stanley Wade was no ordinary toymaker. He was a craftsman, a self-effacing perfectionist. Ophelia remembered him as "a short, quiet man with twitchy lips that he continually pursed and relaxed".[44] Roald himself described Wade as "a brilliant metal turner, who could turn a minute steel component to an accuracy of ten thousandths of a millimetre".[45] His specialty was making model aeroplane engines and, in particular, the tiny hydraulic pumps that supplied his little aircraft with fuel. These never blocked. When Roald explained his son's problem and asked Wade if he could build something to the specifications Theo required, Wade told him he thought he could.

By this time, too, Dahl had found a kindred spirit in one of McKissock's protégés, a pioneering paediatric neurosurgeon called Kenneth Till, who was consultant at London's premier hospital for sick children in Great Ormond Street and would become Theo's consultant. Till listened with patience to Roald's proposal to design a new valve, and then invited Dahl and Stanley Wade to come and watch him operate, so they could see exactly what was required. Till was impressed by Dahl's knowledge, his grasp of the issues, his tenacity and his psychological detachment. "He had this coolness," he recalled, "I think this perhaps is the word – the coolness to want to know the pros and cons, the whys and wherefores. He didn't have to hold himself in."[46]

Roald struggled to keep writing that summer. He and Pat had arranged a rudimentary communication system between the house and the hut, with a switch in the main house and a flashing light bulb in the hut. One flash was a minor disturbance; two flashes an emergency. The light often flashed twice. In October 1961, Theo nearly died again. He was rushed to hospital in London, suffering from a collapsed lung, and immediately had a double operation to remove the tube and drain the lung. Nine "terrible" days followed with Roald and Pat enduring a "nightmare of suspense in hospital wards and dark, sleazy hotel-rooms near the hospital". Theo was constantly in pain, crying, vomiting and thrashing in his cot, as the doctors hoped against hope that perhaps this time he would recover without the need of the drainage shunt and an eighth craniotomy.

But it was not to be. His head began to swell once more and so a new tube was fitted – still with an old-style valve because the Dahl-Wade-Till version was not yet ready. His recovery was by no means certain. Yet the "small pale baby with an indomitable spirit and a tremendous constitution, swathed in bandages, and surrounded by tubes and drips",[47] pulled through once again. By January 1962 he was back home, but his state of health kept Roald and Pat "on the jump constantly",[48]

Within a year, the Dahl-Wade-Till (DWT) valve was ready. "No more than two centimetres long with six tiny moving steel parts inside it",[49] Till fitted it for the first time on a one-year-old child in May 1962. And it worked perfectly. As he reported in *The Lancet*, the invention was characterized by "low resistance, ease of sterilisation, no reflux, robust construction, and negligible risk of blockage".[50] It was a massive improvement on what had existed previously, and had been realized almost entirely by Dahl's practical initiative and his refusal to accept the status quo. The DWT valve proved a huge advance in treating similar conditions, and because Dahl, Wade and Till had agreed not to make any money from their invention, it cost less than a third of its more inferior predecessors. Before it was eventually superseded, the valve was used successfully on almost three thousand children around the world. Some people may even still have one in their heads today.

It was partly this fascination with invention that drew Roald to the medical world. In *Going Solo*, he would write that all his life he had taken "an intense and inquisitive interest in every form of medicine",[51] and he often described himself as "a frustrated doctor".[52] He had an immensely detached view of his own body and was very amenable to using it for medical experiments. In 1952, for example, he offered himself "as a guinea pig" to Presbyterian Hospital for an electogastrogram. "They are trying out a new machine for plotting electrically what goes on in the stomach," he told his mother. "They stuffed the tube up my nose and right down into the stomach and left it there for two hours. It was rather unpleasant, mainly because of my broken nose, but on the whole not bad and very interesting. The machine said there was nothing wrong with my own stomach, but I'm going again because they find out a lot each time about what's going wrong with the machine."[53] Ed Goodman, the doctor who had performed this procedure, admired his friend's "insatiable curiosity" and agreed that in a different life, he would have made a marvellous doctor.[54] When his sense of fancy overreached itself, Roald even seemed to believe he was one. His second wife, Liccy, told me that once on a long-distance flight, when there was a medical emergency and the steward asked whether there was a doctor on board, she had to restrain him physically from getting up to answer the call.

Being a medical expert was another of what Roald called his "dreams of glory": childlike insomniac fantasies about the brilliant amateur who rises to the needs of the occasion and outdoes the great professional. Usually these reveries were sporting in nature, but they could also be more diverse. The idea of the amateur doctor, rising from his seat to diagnose the sick passenger's illness and effect a brilliant cure, would greatly have appealed to him. He had huge respect for doctors, and particularly for those who pioneered new treatments. But he was also not above teasing them. In *George's Marvellous Medicine* (1981), a young boy devises a complex potion to cure his cantankerous old grandmother of all her illnesses. The "medicine" is concocted from a crazy mixture of household items, including gloss paint, shaving cream, engine oil, anti-freeze, shoe polish and dog flea powder. Dahl dedicated it to "doctors everywhere".[55]

Alongside this scientific streak went another, more illogical, which had its roots in the psychic leanings of his mother. The pragmatic rationalist also had a powerful sense of fatalism and destiny. He told his Manhattan neighbour, Sonia Austrian, that he was convinced the city of New York was in some way to blame for Theo's accident.[56] Pat, by contrast, was desperate to ascribe human blame for the accident and sometimes felt a "sickening clutch of hate" toward her nanny. She was haunted by not knowing what exactly had happened on that corner, and she remained uncertain that Susan was not in some way responsible for Theo's accident. Roald, on the other hand, seems not to have worried about this. He told Pat it would be both cruel and pointless to fire Susan.[57] He took no legal action. Instead, he told his daughter Tessa that he believed a painting of a peacock he had recently purchased was probably responsible. He thought the bird was unlucky. It represented a city whose attractions had now finally withered and from which he longed to escape. He wanted to move permanently back to England.

When the Dahls returned to Great Missenden in May 1961, Whitefield Cottage had changed once more. A local builder, Wally Saunders, had constructed a new annex on the east side of the house. Intended as a guest wing, almost immediately Roald began to use it as a room where he could work on antique restoration. Sue Denson recalled how much energy he put into restoring the frame of the huge Chippendale mirror and Alan Higgin remembered Roald teaching him how to regild it. He had already remodelled the garden, planting it with vegetables and more than two hundred native roses. Through its paths roamed a large menagerie of animals, including tortoises, bantam hens, and a "fucking awful insolent gigantic black rabbit",[58] which lived wild in the orchard. Roald tried halfheartedly and unsuccessfully to run it over with Olivia's tricycle, because it kept eating his vegetables. Most striking perhaps was the elaborate birdhouse, which his brother-in-law Leslie had designed. It was filled with parakeets and four hundred homing budgerigars that flew around the countryside during the day and returned home to roost at night. The birds were a constant source of amusement and fascination to him. "Pat is sitting this moment – and has been for the last hour – on a stool in the aviary," Roald joked to Sheila St Lawrence in 1959, "watching the parakeets fighting and fucking. Twenty-five nest boxes. Forty birds and the mating season is in full swing. They copulate incessantly. Every nine or ten minutes. I can't watch them any more. It gives me a terrible inferiority complex."[59]

Roald now found that he wrote best when he was undisturbed in his hut. It was built out of a single layer of bricks, insulated with polystyrene and divided into two rooms, neither more than six feet wide. In the front room he stored his files, letters and manuscripts in two ancient wooden cabinets, on top of which were perched two tiny model aeroplanes with oak propellers and long slender wings covered in varnished silk. In the opposite corner lay a rubber exercise mat, and several sets of barbells.[60] The backroom was his writing space. There, for four hours a day, he could separate himself from the main house and cut himself off from the world of nannies, nurses, schools and shopping. Seated in a soft leather chair – which he replaced with a chair of his mother's after her death – with his legs up and covered in a warm blanket, he created a world where his imagination could run free. It was not dissimilar to the cockpit of a plane. With the curtains drawn, and only the occasional sound of Claud's cattle chomping the grasses outside to disturb him, his green baize writing board and lined yellow US legal pads in front of him, his sharpened Dixon Ticonderoga in hand, and a tableful of little treasures at his side, he could escape into an alternative existence and become a "truant boy" once more.

He missed his professional relationship with Sheila St Lawrence, but had too much on his mind to try to resurrect it. Sheila had by now moved to Ireland and given up her career as an agent. Despite the fact that she and Roald had been close for thirteen years, that they had families of similar ages, that Sheila had stayed with him through the night at Lenox Hill Hospital on the evening of Theo's accident, and despite her considerable editorial impact on his next book, *Charlie and the Chocolate Factory*, they corresponded less and less frequently, and not at all after 1962. Perhaps if Roald's own life had not been so full of other more pressing disasters, the rift might have been healed. Instead, it almost set a pattern for the future. A close relationship suddenly sundered by a fierce and self-righteous row would become an all-too-familiar trajectory in his life. Sometimes the victim would be professional. Publishers like Bob Bernstein, Bob Gottlieb and Stephen Roxburgh would all be embraced warmly, showered with compliments, then rejected in a flurry of angry and resentful correspondence. With friends and family, the disagreement would usually happen over dinner – typically after several whiskies and glasses of wine, when Roald would become garrulous and hurtful. His friendship with his Repton school friend, Michael Arnold, ended this way, and his relationship with his nephew Nicholas was soured by a meal where Roald "insulted" and "humiliated" Nicholas's young wife. Logsdail believed that, in this instance, alcohol was largely the cause.[61] Dahl's daughter Tessa agreed.

"Daddy was a mean drunk,"[62] she told me, recalling many other fierce domestic rows.

With Sheila St Lawrence, the disagreement was somewhat different – firstly because he made some attempt to patch it up and also because Roald was almost certainly hurt himself by its disintegration. After she moved to Ireland, he would occasionally ask Mike Watkins why she did not write to him. There was never a clear answer. For twenty years, Sheila recalled, there was "no communication, nothing, absolutely nothing" between them. Then, just a few years before his death, he invited her to Dublin for a book signing. To her great regret, she was in the United States when he was in Ireland, and consequently could not make it. They never reconnected.

Ironically, too, despite the energies of the Pick-Pollinger nexus, establishing himself in the United Kingdom proved to be a much slower process than anyone had anticipated. *Kiss Kiss* was eventually published in the autumn of 1960, but although it received generally good reviews, its success was muted by comparison to its popularity in America. John Betjeman wrote to Dahl congratulating him on the collection.[63] From then on, he would always be a fan – affectionately addressing Dahl in superlatives such as "the world's best short story writer"[64] and "best of story writers".[65] Other critics were more measured. H. E. Bates, writing in *The Sunday Times* on October 9, 1960, summed up the general perception when he described Dahl briefly as "a humorist, whose prime speciality is the macabre. Many of his subjects are quite revolting, some are merely diabolically ingenious, others just plain nasty; but nearly all are very funny." Disappointed by the UK sales, Michael Joseph's fervour for *James and the Giant Peach* began to cool, whereas Alfred Knopf in New York remained "crazy" about it, enthusing that it was the kind of children's book he had always wanted to publish,[66] and telling Dahl himself that it was a "little classic".[67] Roald was now finding that Charles Pick did not return his calls. Soon the firm would renege on its agreement to publish the book and Pick himself would leave to join Heinemann. When Roald found out, he was furious. "It smacks a bit of 'Fuck you, Jack, I'm all right,'" he complained to Mike Watkins. "What about the writers they wooed so assiduously with a 'Come to me, I'll look after you . . .'?"[68] Watkins could offer no reply.

Throughout 1961, Roald focused on preparing a new musical version of some of his adult stories,‡ and the illustrations and design for *James and the Giant Peach*. After some indecision, he had eventually agreed that an American, Nancy Ekholm Burkert, should get the job, rather than the distinguished Danish fantasy painter Lars Bo. He had characteristically clear views about the look of the drawings and, perhaps surprisingly, his tastes were neither macabre nor fantastical. His model for James, for example, was Winnie-the-Pooh. Shepard's Christopher Robin "is and always will be the perfect small boy", he told his editor at Knopf. "We should get closer to that . . . A face with *character* is not so important as a face with *charm*. One must fall in love with him."[69] In November 1961, he flew back to New York for the publication of *James and the Giant Peach*, returning home three weeks later with some glowing reviews. The *New York Herald Tribune* (Nov. 12, 1961) described the book as "a richly imaginative fantasy, extremely well-told and convincingly illustrated, concluding simply: 'We love it.'" The *New York Times* was equally positive, terming it a "lively fantasy . . . a magic brew concocted from absurdly nauseating ingredients . . . with never a dull moment." The reviewer was confident that the book would be "received with rapturous attention".[70] In fact, sales were slow and decidedly unspectacular – at least to Dahl's eyes – but the children's department at Knopf assured him that even their most successful books always started slowly.

Roald returned to an English winter so bitter that he had to cut a path almost 100 feet long through the orchard to reach his writing hut.[71] There he began revising the manuscript of a new children's book, *Charlie's Chocolate Boy*. But he found himself starved of advice. Mike Watkins had responded with some insensitivity to the first draft, telling him curtly that the story was excellent, "but not quite up to the level of *James*",[72] and offering no advice, no suggestions, and little enthusiastic encourage-

---

‡This proposed project, devised by the successful English writing team of Ned Sherrin and Caryl Brahms, was in development for many months before Dahl abandoned it, feeling that neither Sherrin nor Brahms had brought sufficient energy and new ideas to the adaptation.

ment. Nor was Laurence Pollinger an editor. He was a dealmaker and a negotiator – as Sheila St Lawrence put it, he was "all business".[73] Dahl did not even bother to send him a draft. In desperation, he begged Mike Watkins to find out where Sheila was living in Ireland and send the draft of the new children's book to her.

To make matters worse, Pat, whose opinion he also sought out and trusted, was away, shooting a new movie in Texas. Earlier in the year, she had received a script entitled *Hud Bannon*, from the director Martin Ritt, who asked if she would consider playing the role of Alma Brown. It was not a huge part, only twenty-five minutes of screen time, but Pat liked the character – "a tall woman, shapely, comfortable and pretty . . . with an indulgent knowledge of the world".[74] The fact that her co-star would be Paul Newman and that Ritt would allow her the opportunity to go home to see her children for a few days when the shooting locations changed from Hollywood to Texas, also led her to accept the offer with alacrity. All through the shoot she sensed a special chemistry between her and Newman, who would later describe working with her as "a delight".[75]§ She flew home at the end of July, and a few days later the family departed for their annual summer holiday in Norway.

The family itself was damaged, but strong. Looking after Theo, whose walking skills were improving fast and whose mind seemed surprisingly undamaged by his trauma, had brought Pat and Roald closer together, and she told a journalist that she no longer constantly challenged him or wished to "have nice fights and make it up in bed". Instead, she acknowledged that constant disagreements simply wore away at the trust her husband needed, observing that after an argument, Roald "simply didn't like me – for days and days".[76] Theo had become a "centring force",[77] assisting the family to settle down more permanently in England. For herself, Pat still missed New York and life on East 81st Street – "that dirty old building with its nutty inhabitants".[78] But despite Tessa deliberately

---

§After her stroke, Patricia came to believe that *Hud* had been shot the following year, after Olivia's death. She told this to the *Life* magazine journalist Barry Farrell and later repeated it in her autobiography *As I Am*, where she recounted a fictitious story about being in a swimming pool with Paul Newman and telling him of Olivia's death. His response, she claimed, was insensitive.

wetting the bed a few times,[79] and initially refusing to go to school, she and Olivia soon adjusted to life in Great Missenden. Roald bought Olivia a glass cabinet for her most precious possessions and she spent hours playing with her miniatures on a little rug that lay in front of it. Sometimes he indulged his own childish side with them, chasing fire engines through the countryside in search of adventure, launching tiny fire-balloons into the summer skies, inventing stories about the witches' tree at the top of the garden, and making Olivia and Tessa's names appear magically on the lawn one morning by sprinkling weedkiller on the grass at midnight. He told his children it was the work of the fairies.

Gradually, even Pat was beginning to come to terms with English rural life. She began describing Little Whitefield as her "permanent home", boasting that the following year, 1963, she had no plans to go to the United States at all. "You see the serenity of this sleepy, leafy place is irresistible to me," she told a reporter from *Housewife* magazine, "and work is not."[80] Her relationship with Roald seemed to have settled into one of a profound companionship that had been tempered and strengthened by cruel adversity. Pat defined herself to the same journalist as a good wife – one who was her husband's "best and truest friend". Surrounded by three children and Roald, on whose face wrinkles were starting to appear, and whose hair was now thinning rapidly, she would later describe the two years after Theo's accident as one of the most beautiful periods of her life. Sue Denson agreed. To her, the Dahls seemed as strong and resilient a family unit as you could imagine.

Each of the children had a different character. Seven-year-old Olivia, the eldest, was fascinated by many of her father's hobbies. She loved painting and making things. To Tessa, she was glorious: "beautiful and willowy, translucent and glowing".[81] Roald delighted in her curiosity, her kindness, and her love of plants and animals. She would spend hours on her own in the bird house, just watching what was going on. Although he had described her as "an irregular little bastard"[82] when she was a baby, and had smacked her when she misbehaved, now that she was a little girl, he found being with her an "enchantment".[83] Sheila St Lawrence was similarly captivated. "We have all fallen in love with Olivia," she wrote to Roald shortly after his daughter's birth. "She is magnificent. I am a bit jealous of her wonderful prettiness and delicacy." [84] She illuminated summers at Gipsy House. "Breakfast on the lawn, Olivia running around naked," Roald wrote Sheila in 1956, "all the huge fruit trees in the orchard now a sea of pink and white blossom and the first delicious young tender spinach picked from the garden." [85] Olivia learned to identify all the roses, reciting their Latin names for her father and listing the qualities that made each of them distinctive. [86] Roald revelled in the time he spent alone with her.

Michael Arnold's son Nicholas recalled too that she seemed to have "something of the angel about her", [87] while her aunt Alfhild fondly remembered her teaching Theo to walk by placing books carefully on the ground and gently persuading him to put his feet one after the other on each book. [88] Tessa, on the contrary was "a little tiger" [89] – a "cat", [90] who was feisty and determined. She was a humorist, too, with a quick sense of wit and an enormous grin. [91] Pat thought she had been moulded in the womb, not by glorious walks in the summer meadows but by "the catwalks and hot studio sets of *A Face in the Crowd*". [92] And Theo? He was a mystery. No one was quite certain how the injuries he had sustained as a baby would affect him when he grew up. Roald was simply pleased that he was alive.

Throughout 1962, life seemed to be settling into the kind of familiar pattern Roald had long desired. Pat was away for eleven weeks shooting *Hud*, but he was blissfully content to stay at home, writing, gardening, and taking the children to and from school when required. He continued revising *Charlie's Chocolate Boy* and even started a new children's book. Then, one day in November 1962, Olivia returned home from school with a note from the headmistress at Godstowe, notifying all parents that there was an outbreak of measles. Pat and Roald were concerned largely for Theo, because he was still so vulnerable to infection. There was no generic measles vaccination available then – the first was licensed in the United States in 1963. However, Dahl knew that gamma globulin could be used to boost children's immunity against the disease and that, although uncommon in England, in America it was a fairly routine prophylactic. Pat once again called her brother-in-law Ashley Miles to see if he could help. Miles agreed to send some. But he only provided enough for Theo. "Let the girls get measles," he told her, "it will be good for them."[93] Three days later, Olivia was covered in spots.

Roald and Pat separated her from her siblings and let the disease take its course. After a couple of days of mild fever, all seemed to be progressing normally. When she awoke on the third day, her temperature had come down and she was sufficiently alert for Roald to teach her how to play chess. She beat him immediately. After eating a good lunch, she went to sleep again at 5 p.m. and did not wake until late the following morning. Only now she did not want to play games, complaining instead that she had a headache. Roald did his best to distract her. He tried to persuade her to make a monkey out of coloured pipe cleaners. But she was not interested. He noticed also that her fingers, usually so dextrous, were fumbling and imprecise. All she seemed to want to do was sleep. Roald and Pat called their GP, Mervyn Brigstocke, who came over in the afternoon. He examined Olivia carefully and, although he agreed that she was strangely lethargic, he found nothing wrong. He left half an hour later. Roald returned to his hut. It was about four o'clock.

Soon afterwards, Roald's sister Else dropped round to see how her goddaughter was faring. She looked in on Olivia, who seemed sound asleep. Sue Denson, the nanny, went down to make Tessa and Theo their tea. At 5 p.m., just as dusk had fallen, Pat went back into Olivia's bedroom and discovered her daughter having convulsions. She stared at her mother with "dead-looking eyes",[94] then suddenly became quite still, "her mouth gaping limply, oozing spit".[95] Pat ran to the switch that connected the hut to the main house and hit it desperately. Four quick flashes brought Roald running. Immediately, he called Dr Brigstocke. While they waited for him to arrive, Pat and Roald cooled Olivia's forehead with cold flannels. But she did not respond. Soon she was unconscious. As soon as Brigstocke saw her, he summoned an ambulance. Olivia's breathing was now shallow and irregular and she needed oxygen. Roald wrapped his limp daughter in an eiderdown and carried her out to the ambulance, which rushed her away to nearby Stoke Mandeville Hospital. There they hoped she could be resuscitated. Pat stayed behind with the other children. Brigstocke went with Olivia in the ambulance. Roald followed behind in his car.[96]

CHAPTER FIFTEEN

Breaking Point

Awful drive. Lorries kept holding us up on narrow roads. Got to hospital. Ambulance went to wrong entrance. Backed out. Arrived. Young doctor in charge. Mervyn and he gave her 3 mg sodium amatol.* I sat in hall. Smoked. Felt frozen. A small single bar electric fire on wall. An old man in next room. Woman doctor went to phone. She was trying urgently to locate another doctor. He arrived. I went in. Olivia lying quietly. Still unconscious. She has an even chance, doctor said. They had tapped her spine. Not meningitis. It's encephalitis. Mervyn left in my car. I stayed. Pat arrived with Else and John. John went out to get some whiskey. Pat went in to see Olivia. Kissed her. Spoke to her. Still unconscious. I went in. I said, "Olivia . . . Olivia." She raised her head slightly off pillow. Sister said don't. I went out. We drank whiskey. I told doctor to consult experts. Call anyone. He called a man in Oxford. I listened. Instructions were given. Not much could be done. I first said I would stay on. Then I said I'd go back with Pat and Else and John. Went. Arrived home. Called Philip [Rainsford] Evans.† He called hospital. Called me back. "Shall I come?" "Yes please." I said I'd tell hospital he was coming. I called. Doc thought I was Evans. He said

---

*Sodium amatol was a barbiturate used to treat catatonic mutism. It is possible the doctors thought Olivia might have had some psychiatrically based catatonia and were trying to quickly determine if this was indeed the case. Because its effects are short-lasting, the medics may also simply have been using it to make sure Olivia remained inert while they performed the lumbar puncture.

†A distinguished paediatrician who had been involved in Theo's treatment.

I'm afraid she's worse. I got in the car. Got to hospital. Walked in. Two
doctors advanced on me from waiting room. How is she? I'm afraid it's
too late. I went into her room. Sheet was over her. Doctor said to nurse
go out. Leave him alone. I kissed her. She was warm. I went out. "She
is warm." I said to doctors in hall, "why is she so warm?" "Of course,"
he said. I left.[1]

No one knows exactly when Dahl wrote this distressingly cool and clinical account of how his daughter died. The meticulous description of her final day, of which this is the conclusion, was written in note form, in a green school exercise book, on whose cover, in capitals, was written one word: OLIVIA. He kept it at the back of a particularly obscure drawer in his hut and told no one about it. His family only discovered it after his own death, twenty-eight years later. Its focus on detail suggests that, like the notes he made after Theo's accident, these series of snapshots were written soon after the event, when the disaster was all still bitterly fresh in his mind. Perhaps it was just the reflex response of the habitual writer. Possibly it was a kind of improvised therapy, an attempt to deal with the fact that his daughter's death had robbed him of the sense of forward momentum he had always previously been able to generate in a time of crisis. It may simply have been an agonizing aide-mémoire that helped ensure that the emotional wound of losing his daughter would never entirely heal. The ugly details of her sudden death, which the soothing analgesic of memory might with time have blurred and fuzzed, would now lurk there forever in a secret corner of his most private space. One glance alone would be sufficient to re-evoke the immediate intensity of those emotions of loss.

For Olivia's death was quite different to Theo's accident. Theo had required his father's active care and attention. Roald was able to channel all his reserves of positive energy into the practical issues of designing the valve that might give his son a normal life again. With Olivia there was nothing he could do to affect the outcome. She was gone and he could not bring her back. Her death left him "limp with despair". And fast behind the sense of loss was a feeling of guilt that somehow he had let his "favourite child" down. "I wish we'd had a chance to fight for her,"[2] he told Mike Watkins a few days after her death. The uncertain sense that somehow he had failed as the family protector, and had not done enough to shield his daughter from the cruelty of the world, would haunt him for years.

Pat was waiting for him when he returned home. She already knew the worst. The doctors at the hospital had called her to break the news. Roald hugged her desperately, his "heavy sobs" spilling onto her shoulder. Then she sensed that he needed to be alone. She knew already he was "destroyed".[3] The paediatrician Dr Evans, who had arrived at the hospital after Olivia died, came early the next morning to Gipsy House and told them that she had been the victim of measles encephalitis, a rare inflammation of the brain which can arise from measles, and which affects one in a thousand cases. He confirmed that large doses of gamma globulin could well have prevented her from getting the disease. Thus, Pat remembered, began the "landslide of anger and frustration"[4] that almost buried the family.

The children were resilient. Theo was too young to understand what was happening, while five-year-old Tessa simply responded to the news by asking her mother if all of Olivia's miniatures were now hers. This upset Pat, but it was exactly what Tessa's aunt Alfhild had done when her elder sister died four decades earlier. Only later would the effects of her elder sister's death on her own psychology become clear to Tessa – to such an extent that even now she finds her mind has "blanked" many memories of Olivia.[5] Pat found surprising consolation from Mormor. Her Norwegian mysticism and "crystal vision" offered a sense that death was not the absolute end. Moreover, Pat knew that her seventy-seven-year-old mother-in-law had suffered in 1920 exactly as she was suffering now. The parallels between the deaths of Astri and Olivia were indeed uncanny. Each had been the eldest child, each the apple of their father's eye, each seven years old when a medical emergency abruptly ended their young lives.

The funeral took place in the nearby village of Little Missenden inside a tiny church, almost a thousand years old, some of whose stones dated back to ancient Saxon England. It was a simple service, "peaceful and short",[6] as Alfhild described it, with family and a handful of friends in attendance. Snow fell as they buried Olivia, inspiring Else to compose a poem comparing that pristine winter canopy to a white blanket that enfolded her grave with love. But it offered Roald little consolation. Sonia Austrian came to visit the family after Christmas and found him absorbed in creating a living monument to his daughter. He had bought two plots in the graveyard and on her grave he and Pat had inscribed a quotation from W. B. Yeats – "She stands before me as a living child." Around it, Roald planted an intricate alpine garden, with rocks chosen from different quarries, and more than two hundred different plants – including tiny Japanese evergreens, a cineraria from Afghanistan and countless varieties of snowdrop. With the help of Valerie Finnis, an expert in alpine plants, who worked at the nearby Waterperry Horticultural School for Women, he was fashioning an exquisite miniature world – understated, but powerful in its sombre organic melancholy – and one that would always require his constant care and attention. As she watched her father's "enormous hands holding a small fork, delicately weeding, forbidding the plants to die", it seemed to Tessa as if her father was being "consumed" by the garden, as if he was "frightened to let go of the last living part of her".[7]

But the garden was not enough to keep Roald's demons at bay. Whereas Pat was able to cry and talk to others about her lost child, Roald kept himself to himself and seemed incapable of acknowledging his wife's suffering. He rapidly put all Olivia's toys and books into a polished oak chest, which he kept in his bedroom. He made Tessa feel that she could never make up for Olivia's loss. He was silent. Pat found him increasingly distant. "He did not talk about his feelings . . . did not want to talk about Olivia . . . he wouldn't let anything come out, nothing."[8] His daily consumption of alcohol increased and he upped the regular dose of barbiturates for his back pain. Sonia Austrian recalled that during her stay there, she "just could not reach him . . . There was no way to talk to him, to do anything, he was totally withdrawn." His normally garrulous, argumentative personality disappeared completely. He spent hours in his hut, at the cemetery, or alone with his mother. The loss destroyed his lust for life. It also damaged his relationship with Tessa and Theo, who understandably felt they had lost their father. "It took him a long while to get out of that," Austrian remembered. "I think he always missed [Olivia], I don't think he ever really got over her death." [9]

Roald struggled to find any kind of consolation. One moment he was the brutal atheist, tearing into Pat's fragile belief in an afterlife and angrily dismissing it as no more than "trashy sentiment", the next found him more uncertain. Less than a month after Olivia died, he wrote to his ex-headmaster, Geoffrey Fisher, the supposed tormentor of his friend Michael Arnold, to ask if he could offer them any spiritual guidance. Pat, whose "mystical self" already believed that she would see her daughter again in heaven, [10] was probably the principal architect of the visit; but Roald went along with her, asking his old French teacher, Henry Davidson ("Peehard"), now secretary of the Old Reptonian Society, to contact Fisher on their behalf. [11] It was a surprising turnaround for such a sceptic, but as Pat recalled, Roald was prepared to give a man who until the previous year had been Archbishop of Canterbury the chance to convince him. On December 18, 1962, he and Pat drove down to Trent Rectory, deep in the Dorset countryside, where Fisher had retired. There the former leader of the Church of England discussed the "hard path" [12] he believed the Dahls would need to tread if they were to overcome their loss. Afterwards, they wrote to Fisher thanking him for his help and enclosing copies of *Kiss Kiss* and *Someone Like You* as a gift.

Superficially, the contact appeared to have been very cordial. But Dahl was always touchy about religion and would later claim that the conversation with Fisher finally convinced him Christianity was a sham. Characteristically, the deciding issue appears to have been what "the Boss" said about the Dahls' family dog, Rowley. Nine years later, Dahl explained his reasoning to his two youngest children, Ophelia and Lucy, by then six and five respectively, on Christmas Day, 1970. They had been to the church at Little Missenden and were carrying some bunches of richly variegated holly to decorate Olivia's grave. Ophelia asked her father why God had allowed her elder sister to die. Roald admitted that he did not know and then told her about his meeting with Fisher and how certain "the Boss" had been that although Olivia was now in Paradise, her beloved Rowley would never join her there. "His whole face closed up," he recalled. "I wanted to ask him how he could be so absolutely sure that other creatures did not get the same special treatment as us, but the look of disapproval that had settled around his mouth stopped me. I sat there wondering if this great and famous churchman really knew what he was talking about and whether he knew anything at all about God or heaven, and if he didn't, then who in the world did? And from that moment on, my darlings, I'm afraid I began to wonder whether there really was a God or not." [13]

Dahl's Christian faith had always been tenuous, but his mystical streak could be surprisingly powerful. More than anything, he feared that some sort of bitter destiny hung over his family. Two years before, in Manhattan, he had blamed a peacock and a white-faced boy for Theo's accident. They had seemed like omens of disaster. He had moved to Buckinghamshire, where he thought himself safe from these sinister forces. Now once again he felt threatened. The similarity between his father's fate and his own weighed heavy on his mind. At one point he seriously considered having a male witch come and exorcise malignant spirits from the house. "I was in a kind of daze," he told the *Life* journalist Barry Farrell later. "Morbid thoughts kept after me. It occurred to me that there must be some kind of tie-up and that kind of thought can run you down, you know, worrying about fate and the meaning of things." [14] Alfhild was also disturbed by her brother's gloomy condition. One day she went to see him and found him contemplating a painting of his lost daughter. He stared at it quietly for a long time, before turning to her and whispering four words: "the face of doom". [15] The picture remained in his hut until the day he died.

Depression – the secret enemy that had stalked Dahl much of his life, and that he had usually fought off with his unique brand of positive energy – now had him in its grip. He tended to view it as "a great self-indulgence", [16] arguing that the only way to cope with grief was "to bury [it] and not wear it on your sleeve and then roll those sleeves up and get down to putting things right". [17] But this time there was nothing he could do. He began to suffer from heart problems. He took to his bed. A sense of the pointlessness of life overwhelmed him. As a sixteen-year-old schoolboy he had struggled to keep that negativity at bay. Responding to the news that a family friend had recently given birth, he had told his mother: "I suppose you have got to give the baby a present; well, give it a millstone with instructions as to how it should be hung around the neck while in the bath."[18] In that teenage nihilism there lurked at least the shadow of a smile. But there was little laughter at Gipsy House in the first months of 1963. It was the coldest winter for years, with temperatures so low that the ink in his hut froze in the bottle. Sporadic bursts of activity punctuated the melancholy gloom. Roald bullied his doctor into getting gamma globulin for Olivia and Tessa's great school friends, Sarah and Amanda Conquy, who also had measles. He tried to puzzle out why Olivia's measles had evolved into deadly encephalitis, hoping he could discover what had made her vulnerable and thereby prevent other children from suffering her fate. But it was beyond him. He retreated into himself, refusing to talk about his pain even to Pat, who was frustrated by what she later described as his "Nordic strain of deep restraint".[19] She wrote to her friends Jean Valentino and Chloe Carter that she felt Roald "truly wanted to die".[20] Sarah and Amanda's mother, Frankie Conquy, recalled that he could not even bring himself to mention Olivia's name, though he framed her paintings and poems and hung them all about the house. Years later, in her autobiographical novel *Working for Love*, Tessa recreated the situation: "My father could not function and my mother, realizing the need for solidarity, rallied herself. For about a year she held our family together."[21] Pat, who longed to talk about her daughter, stoically endured her husband's silence. She told the columnist Louella Parsons that she felt as if the family were living through the Book of Job.[22]

Tessa found her father's behaviour confusing and inexplicable. However hard she tried to help him, however much she tried to console him, he rejected her. *Working for Love* may ultimately be fiction, but it is so closely based on reality that Tessa thought it accurately reflected much of what she was feeling at the time. In the book, she described her father as "beyond help. He could not speak for grief. I remember seeing his beautiful blue eyes fill with tears. I saw him weep in his bedroom, and then when he noticed me, he asked me to leave." In another scene, the narrator Molly (Tessa) describes her father driving to school and asking her to sing a song that her dead sister used to sing. The father ends up shouting: "Why can't you be more like her? Why can't you sing like her? The woods, the walks, the spark, you haven't got it, have you? Why can't you be her?"[23] Pat despaired of his behaviour, wondering if things would ever improve. "It gets worse rather than better," she told friends. "I want him to get a job that will force him to see people and work with others."[24]

Then, as winter turned into spring, hope appeared in the form of an organization called *International Help for Children* (IHC), which assisted illegitimate boys and girls in southern Italy who had been abandoned by their families. Marjorie Clipstone, a neighbour, had brought the pioneering work of Father Mario Borrelli to Roald and Pat's attention. Borrelli, who helped found the charity, had spent many months living as a vagrant among the vagabond children of Naples and had subsequently founded a hostel for these *scugnizzi*, or street urchins. His autobiography had just been published[25] and a documentary about him recently screened on British television. The children's helplessness stirred Dahl. It not only stimulated his natural instinct for generosity and his identification with the underdog, it also motivated him to do something positive. Following the advice to put the self aside that Charles Marsh had given him years earlier, he and Pat put all of Olivia's trust fund into IHC and Roald himself became an active chairman of the Great Missenden branch, which eventually boasted over three hundred members. For the first time in his life he became a committed public campaigner, writing outspoken reports that bristled with eloquent indignation at the human cruelty and injustice he perceived around him.

Alberobello is a small town high up in the mountains above the heel of Italy . . . The inhabitants of Alberobello are poor and backward. They are also shockingly bigoted. In those parts, for example, a child with a deformity is regarded as a disgrace to the family and is liable to be kept locked in the cellar for life. Any woman who becomes pregnant out of wedlock is immediately treated as an outcast, and neither church nor family will give her assistance. And recently, in Alberobello, in this town with a lovely name, there was a case of a twelve and a half year-old girl who had been brutally raped. Her family kicked her out on the spot. She ran for help to the convent, hysterical. The nuns shut the door in her face. Nobody would touch her. She was lost. So you can see that there is a problem here.[26]

While Roald immersed himself in charitable work, Pat found some solace in acting. She and the entire family went to Los Angeles for two weeks, while she filmed an episode of a popular medical television series called *Ben Casey*. When they returned to England, Theo's seizures returned. It seemed his shunt was malfunctioning again. Later in the summer, he lost consciousness and had to be rushed to hospital. Roald assumed that now – at last – his son would get the replacement valve which he had helped design. Kenneth Till, however, proposed removing the device altogether. He had attempted unsuccessfully to do this eighteen months earlier. Now he wanted to try again. It was a gamble. If Theo, who was barely three, could last thirty days without the drain, Till believed he would be in the clear. Roald and Pat agreed to let him go ahead. So, on September 8, for the ninth time in Theo's short life, the surgeons operated to remove the shunt. This time, there would be good news. Theo survived the thirty days without a relapse. His hydrocephalus did not return. He would never need the new valve his father had helped pioneer. For once in the Dahl family's recent history a medical crisis had produced a happy outcome. And there was yet another piece of good news too. "Hot news from the Frog Laboratories in Oxford,"[27] Dahl scribbled to Mike Watkins in October. Pat was pregnant again.

Eventually Dahl's spirits improved sufficiently for him to return to the alternative reality he had started to create almost three years earlier. Just before Olivia's death, he had retitled his latest story *Charlie and the Chocolate Factory* and greatly fleshed out its central character, Willy Wonka – the superhuman genius with an ability to create the most outlandish and exciting sweets the world had ever seen. This extravagant magician – whose name Dahl had refashioned from a boomerang called the Skilly

Wonka his half brother Louis once made for him – possessed a personality that was much like his creator's. He was capricious, entertaining and brilliant. He was an adult, but one with the sensibilities of a child. He was devoid of sentimentality. He was funny. He was private. He was elusive. And he had a dark side. Bad children would get mashed, stretched, transformed into a giant blueberries or boiled into fudge if they stepped out of line in his inventing rooms. On the surface he could seem aloof, but underneath he had a kind heart. It was perhaps the most memorable character Dahl would ever create – a man who lived by his own rules, within his own realm, apparently safe from the world outside his factory walls. When Roald finally closed the door to the hut, pulled the curtains tight, sat down in his chair, wrapped a sleeping bag around his legs and switched on his anglepoise lamp, he too found himself in a world which he controlled completely and where no unpleasant surprises could disturb him. It also was reassuring that this imaginary universe was focused on one of his most favourite things: chocolate.

Ever since he was a child, Roald had been fascinated by sweets – and particularly by chocolate. Beyond boyhood ecstasies among the liquorice bootlaces and multicoloured gobstoppers that lined the walls of Mrs Pratchett's sweetshop in Llandaff, he had honed a palate for chocolate tasting at Repton, where his housemaster had arranged with the marketing department of *Cadbury's* at Bourneville that each year every boy in The Priory would receive a cardboard box containing twelve bars of new Cadbury's chocolate. The box came with a checklist on which its recipient was invited to write comments and award marks. To make it suitably scientific, they always included one "control" bar – a coffee cream. Roald had relished his role as a schoolboy connoisseur – he claimed in *Boy* that he had once commented that one chocolate creation was "too subtle for the common palate",[28] and he fantasized about the extraordinary place where these new recipes were devised. This passion continued into adulthood. One of the talismanic objects he kept beside him in his writing hut was a big silver ball made out of wrappers taken from the chocolate bars he had eaten for lunch each day when he was working at his office in Shell in London in the 1930s. Somewhere between a golf ball and a tennis ball in size, it was so unexpectedly heavy that, when he brought it out and showed it to visitors, few could guess what it was. Most reckoned it was some sort of cannonball.

Roald's own taste in chocolate was itself eclectic. Sometimes it was highbrow. During the war, he arranged for regular boxes of milk and bittersweet chocolate to be sent across the Atlantic to his mother and each of his siblings from a high-end New York chocolatier called Rosemarie de Paris. This little bit of luxury helped relieve the miseries of rationing. But his real enthusiasm was for commercial mass-market chocolates. Most meals at Gipsy House, however grand, concluded with a selection of these familiar brands, produced from a small red plastic box. In an essay in *The Roald Dahl Cookbook*, written in the last year of his life and first published posthumously as *Memories with Food at Gipsy House*, he waxed lyrically about the seven miraculous years between 1930 and 1937 when the greatest of these chocolates – *Mars, KitKat, Aero, Maltesers, Rolo, Smarties* and many others – were all invented. He thought that British children should be taught these dates at school, instead of the reigns of the Kings and Queens of England, and – with a smile – he compared them to other golden ages which, in the arts, had produced Beethoven and Mozart in music, the French Impressionists in art, and Dickens, Balzac and Tolstoy in literature.

The exuberant pleasure in the magic of invention is one of the great qualities of *Charlie and the Chocolate Factory*. In that respect, the book mirrors Dahl's own real-life crisis in the aftermath of Theo's accident; but in other ways its rip-roaring energy and swagger seem to stand at a distance from the pain of Olivia's death and the many continuing anxieties surrounding Theo, to whom the tale is dedicated. Those two disasters partially explain why the story went through six different rewrites, but they do not entirely explain its long gestation, which was also due to an obsessive need to clarify the storyline. Much of the narrative remained constant throughout. The essential nature of the two main characters, for example: the capricious Willy Wonka and the impoverished, spirited and kindly child, Charlie Bucket, never changed. In all versions of the story, Charlie wins one of the "golden tickets" that have been hidden under the wrappers of his most popular chocolate bar, thereby entitling him to a trip around Wonka's extraordinary factory. His fellow winners – there were originally ten – likewise were always grotesque parodies of childish vices such as greed, selfishness, conceitedness, television addiction, or being spoiled. But there the similarities end.

At the beginning, there were no Oompa-Loompa factory workers and no Grandpa Joe to look after Charlie. Nor were any of the child grotesques present in their final form. Characters who were eventually eliminated from the adventure or substantially altered included Elvira Entwistle (the prototype of Veruca Salt), Miranda Grope (who fell into the chocolate river), Tommy Troutbeck (who disobeyed Wonka and ended up in the Pounding and Cutting Room), Bertie Upside (who overheats after eating too many warming candies), Marvin Prune, Violet Strabismus and Herpes Trout. The plot, too, was quite different. It was a detective story in which Charlie strayed from Wonka's gaze long enough to be accidentally coated in quick-drying chocolate. Mistaken for one of Wonka's giant "chocolate boys", he is delivered as an Easter present to Wonka's son, Freddie. Trapped inside his chocolate shell, and left overnight in Wonka's home, Charlie witnesses a burglary. The following morning, when he has been liberated from his cocoa prison, he helps identify the thieves and is rewarded by Wonka with a huge sweetshop of his own, which "occupies a whole block in the centre of the city and is nine stories high".[29] Most strikingly perhaps, in the early drafts, Dahl described Charlie as a "small NEGRO boy", who boldly confronts Wonka with the issue that innumerable parents and educators would ponder in future years. What actually happened to the children who were juiced, stretched, minced, flushed down a rubbish chute or cooked in a fudge-boiler? Shocked that Charlie should think anyone might actually have been hurt in his domain, Wonka's reply is true to form in its innocent naivety: "I run a chocolate factory, you know," he tells the boy indignantly, "not a butcher's shop."[30]

The second draft (the first that Dahl showed to anyone) was completed in 1961, and though Sheila St Lawrence had now officially stopped working as an agent, Roald was eager to have her critical input on the story and wrote to Mike Watkins asking him to forward it to her.[31] That same day he wrote to Sheila personally, telling her that he "valued *enormously*" her comments and would "feel lost" without them.[32] It took her a month to reply, and when she did so, her response was tentative. "I've read *Charlie's Chocolate Boy;* reread it for the children, and then gone over it again myself," she began, admitting that "I have hesitated to write to you for I felt it was not my place . . . I didn't want to be a back-seat driver." Soon however she was enthusing about how much she had enjoyed the book. "I can't tell you how excited I was by the idea of the story. It's marvellous. As soon as I got the gist of where you were going, my mind ran away with all the kinds of candy that could be brought into the story, the smells and feels and colours, and all the wonders that go into cooking and making candies." However, she added, the story was bogged down by details of the plot. "Somewhere, somehow, someplace along the line this initial magical excitement gets lost . . ."[33] She went on to suggest a mass of changes – including having the greedy Augus-tus Pottle (later Gloop) get stuck in a glass pipe after he has fallen in the chocolate river, and having the gloating Hilaire Belloc–like songs about how the bad children get their just deserts delivered by the white-coated factory workers, rather than by a "chorus of tiny whispering voices".[34] In conclusion, she told him. "I'd like to see more humour, more light Dahlesque touches", adding circumspectly that "I hope some of my remarks will produce counter remarks in you that will stir you to flights of fancy to make the book take off and fly as it undoubtedly will."[35]

"Your letter was just what I have been waiting for," Roald replied, continuing that he agreed with "virtually everything you say. Yes – just about everything." Predictably he could not stop himself from telling Sheila that he too had previously considered a number of her suggestions and then rejected them – wrongly, so he now realized. Nevertheless, he acknowledged that he was "most grateful" for her help.[36] A year later, however, the book was still unfinished. Dahl told Mike Watkins that despite Sheila's enthusiasm – she had recently told him she thought the book was "simply excellent" ‡ – he appeared weary of writing for children. He even wrote to Alfred Knopf telling him that he would much prefer to be writing for adults.[37] The US sales of *James and the Giant Peach* (only 2,600 copies in its first year) had horrified him. "Who the hell am I writing these lousy books for?" he asked Watkins angrily.[38] By the summer of 1962, the new story had been through four drafts. The fifth version, renamed *Charlie and the Chocolate Factory*, was the draft that was eventually sent to Virginie Fowler at Knopf. "If she doesn't like it then I guess we will throw it away," Roald commented grumpily to Watkins, adding as a coda: "I do want some money out of it."[39]

Ironically, for several years even the self-confident Dahl failed to see the power – both financially and artistically – of what he had created. Indeed, shortly after the book was finally published in the United States in 1964, he wrote an article for the *New York Times* in which he attacked the vogue for short, expensive picture books, which he felt were dominating the market to the detriment of properly worked-through stories. Admitting that he was uncertain of the value of what he himself had written in this genre – "for all I know they may be worthless" – he concluded that writing them was "a big drain on his batteries" and "an uneconomic diversion".[40]

Virginie Fowler, an experienced but traditional children's fiction editor, certainly had no idea whatsoever that a classic tale had landed in her lap. She liked the book, but had reservations about the literary conventions that it broke and felt that parts of it were vulgar and in singularly bad taste. "This world of children's books has its own set of rules," she wrote to Dahl; "ignoring these rules does cause unnecessary difficulties for a book."[41] Her new boss, the aggressively commercial Bob Bernstein, viewed it differently. He had recently been put in charge of juvenile publications for the new Random House–Knopf–Pantheon group, and sensed at once he was dealing with something out of the ordinary. Not

---

‡This was probably the final exchange between Dahl and St Lawrence until he invited her to meet him in Ireland twenty-five years later. The last mention of her in his letters is in February 1963, where Roald wrote to Mike Watkins, expressing surprise that Sheila had not written to him about Olivia's death. "Incidentally not a word from Sheila – ever," he observed with evident regret. "I wrote to her about Olivia. Perhaps she just *cannot* write" – Dahl, Letter to Armitage Watkins, 02/13/63 – WLC Box 25.

only did he see the remarkable merchandising potential inherent in the tale, he also loved its concept and execution. "It is a wonderful, wonderful children's book,"[42] he enthused to Dahl, recounting how his three sons had received it with rapture. So did Alfred Knopf, who found the book "miraculous", and immediately predicted it would become a classic,[43] largely because it appealed to adults as well as children. His wife Blanche agreed. "Children should adore it," she told Roald, "and – judging by myself – old ladies too."[44]

The venerable Knopfs and Bob Bernstein's children were among the first to appreciate that beyond the coarse humour and madcap violent morality lay a fantasy underpinned by powerful emotional ingredients. A child, starved of opportunities and avenues of self-expression, finds an unexpected soulmate, who believes in him and empowers him to succeed. It was a potent recipe. Willy Wonka may be a confectionery wizard, but he is also the "special friend" that most children long for – the one who recognizes their worth and talent and with whom they can share their vulnerabilities. Many years later Dahl himself would jokingly admit that his child hero had always been a "rather boring little bugger" and that it was really Wonka "who makes the stories".[45] Yet it is perhaps Charlie's very blandness that so readily allows a child reader to implant him- or herself in the story and create their own special relationship with Wonka.

This theme of the unexpectedly transformative friendship would reoccur in many of Dahl's most successful books. It was one with which Dahl himself resonated closely – although he would probably have hated admitting it, because he was so uncomfortable with articulating his own vulnerabilities. In the case of *Charlie and the Chocolate Factory*, that resonance was particularly immediate. Many critics have pointed out the similarities between the top-hatted chocolate magnate and his creator. Both men shared an apparently boundless self-confidence and "No arguments, please" public manner. Both could be grandiose, mercurial, capricious. Both cultivated a sense of mystery around themselves. Both were misunderstood. In all these respects Wonka mirrored his creator. However, Dahl was also Charlie. The little boy's sense of wonder, his vulnerability, his rich inner life of the imagination, his recognition by a powerful maverick, all had parallels in Roald's own personal story. He was not just a show-man. He was also the teenage loner, happiest in his Repton darkroom; the shattered airman, comforted through the desert night by a fellow pilot, or – perhaps most pointedly – the broken writer redeemed by an ir-repressible, eccentric and verbose buccaneer. In that context, Wonka was surely also a veiled tribute to Charles Marsh, who now lay bedridden and near the end of his own life. Both had unquenchable optimism. Wonka's energy-giving pleas to Charlie – "You mustn't despair! Nothing is impos-sible!" [46] – echoed the confidence Marsh had shown in Dahl himself only ten years earlier, when Roald, like his child hero, had faced his own crisis of self-doubt and felt himself rejected and undervalued. For ten years before that, Marsh had encouraged him to write, sorted out his medical problems and baled him out financially. He had even acted as unofficial broker and therapist in his marriage. At all times he had encouraged his young protégé's sense of self-belief and destiny. Dahl had relied on this friend and father figure. But he could do so no longer.

As he completed the book, all of Roald's gurus were either dead or dying. Matthew Smith had passed away in 1959. Henry Wallace lay in Connecticut, debilitated by Lou Gehrig's disease; he would die in 1965. The most important of them all, Charles Marsh, was now under twenty-four-hour nursing care in Washington. He would die, largely forgotten by the world, shortly after the publication of *Charlie and the Chocolate Fac-tory*, on December 30, 1964. Roald barely saw him in his sad final years. It was probably simply too painful for him to witness the decline. [47]

Twenty years earlier, Flight Lieutenant Roald Dahl had been Charlie to Marsh's Wonka. For hours, he had lain on the latter's sofa in wartime Washington and listened to him pontificating about people, politics, and philanthropy. He had learned from him. Now, many of his mentor's ideas and attitudes had become his own. *Charlie and the Chocolate Factory* inhabits the hinterland between the world of the child and that of the adult – territory that Dahl himself was ideally equipped to explore. At the end of the final version of the book, Wonka (now unmarried and child-less) gives his factory to Charlie because he acknowledges he is vulnerable and needs an heir. He could pass his kingdom on to a clever grown-up,

Wonka tells the lad. But he doesn't want to. "A grown-up person won't listen to me; he won't learn. He will try to do things his own way and not mine. So I have to have a child."

Dahl himself, the "geriatric child", who often communicated better with children than with adults, will always be remembered as a Mr Wonka figure – garrulous, exotic, rambunctious. But a part of him, a vulnerable, hidden part, remained the child: the child who absorbed as much as he radiated and who, as a young man, had formed much of his own personality in the company of his swashbuckling, iconoclastic Texan mentor. As a father he passed some of these attitudes on to his own children, but as a writer he passed them on to the world.

Roald's own moral views had powerfully flavoured *Charlie and the Chocolate Factory*. They would be apparent too in a new children's book on which he had just started working when Olivia died – a parable directed against "all the brave deer hunters and duck hunters in the country".[48] Constructed from an assigned 250 words, it was part of a project in which a group of famous adult writers – including John Updike and Arthur Miller, the "so-called giants of the literary world",[49] as Dahl described them – were each paid $2,000 to create a children's story using this limited vocabulary. With the exception of a magical story by Robert Graves called *The Big Green Book*, Roald thought that most of their efforts were "tripe".[50] The other stories were "guaranteed to anaesthetise in two minutes flat any unfortunate child who got hold of them."[51] However, he could not afford to turn down the "monstrous bribe"[52] the publishers had offered him.

His own story, completed in that bitter winter of 1962–63, turns the tables on a group of duck hunters by transforming them into birds, and having the ducks hunt them. It is a clever, witty fable that wears its heart on its sleeve. The story is told by an eight-year-old girl narrator, whose sense of injustice and response to the cruelty she sees about her inspires her to develop magical powers. "I can't stand hunting," she bluntly tells the reader, "I just can't stand it. It doesn't seem right to me that men and boys should kill animals just for the fun they get out of it."[53] His publishers, Crowell Collier, fearful of offending the powerful US gun lobby, sat on the manuscript until their option to publish had expired. Eventually, the rights reverted back to the author.

Dahl then offered the book, which for most of its gestation was known as *The Almost Ducks*, to Virginie Fowler. She turned it down. Three years after its completion, the story was published by Harper & Row as *The Magic Finger*. Fowler's decision soon got her into trouble with her boss, Knopf, who could not believe she had acted so unilaterally. "You took me rather by surprise last week," he complained in a memo,

> *when you told me that Mike Watkins had sold a story by Dahl to Harper for $5,000 . . . You also made it clear that you thought so badly of this particular story that you felt it a great pity that it was going to be published at all, and didn't seem greatly concerned about the fact that an author closely identified with us, and heretofore very important to the house, was going to appear at least once in another imprint . . . I do not think a decision to refuse to publish a story by Roald Dahl should be made without discussions with, and approval by, the very top people in Knopf and Random House . . . I am afraid that we are all more concerned about and embarrassed by what has happened than you can realize.*[54]

From now on, Roald would not have to deal with her again.

The summer of 1963 found Roald and Pat "up to [their] necks in charity work". Pat's new film, now simply titled *Hud*, had opened to "smashing reviews",[55] and the UK charity premiere in Aylesbury had raised almost £1,000 for children's causes of Dahl's choice. The bulk of the proceeds were used to enable twenty of Father Borelli's Neapolitan "urchins", aged between five and eleven, and ten illegitimate girls from Bari to travel to England and stay with families for up to three months. Dahl went to meet the children at Victoria Station. He described their arrival as "an enthralling sight".

> *Their suits were ill fitting, but clean, while their shoes, which in several cases were decorated with fantastic brogue patterns across the*

tops and sides, were often far too large for the feet. Some of them were
carrying very small battered suitcases whose handles had been repaired
with string or wire. One had his possessions in a canvas water-bag.
Another was lugging around an enormous portmanteau made of card-
board. And one very small child, who had no bag at all, was clutching
with both hands a red plastic petrol container – a treasure which he
had undoubtedly swiped at great personal risk from a Naples garage in
the days before he was introduced to Father Borelli.[56]

In late summer, Susan Denson got married and decided she would
leave Gipsy House. The parting was not easy. She had been employed as
the Dahl's live-in nanny for more than four years and been through two
terrible traumas with them. She had become family. In the Gipsy House
nursery, shortly after Olivia's death, Roald and Pat had tried to make her
promise that she would never leave them and offered her the guest house
as a permanent home. Before she could answer, old Mrs Ingram, the
housekeeper, who had overheard their request, piped up and said that Mr
Dahl was being unfair. He was asking too much of a girl so young. Sue
was immensely grateful for the housekeeper's intervention and felt that
when she did tender her resignation a few months later, both Roald and
Pat's attitude toward her cooled swiftly. She also felt she compounded
the frostiness by not asking Tessa to be a bridesmaid at her wedding. She
had intended that both Olivia and Tessa would be her bridesmaids. "I felt
as if they were my children," she told me tearfully. "After Olivia died, I
thought it would simply be too painful for Pat and Roald – and for me
– to see just one daughter going up the aisle . . . I was probably wrong."
Her husband agreed that in retrospect the decision was almost certainly
a mistake,[57] and one that helped ensure that, after Susan left the Dahls'
service, she soon grew apart from them.

Pat was away filming in the summer, so in August 1963 Roald went up
to Scotland to interview some twenty potential candidates for Susan's job.
Some of his old comic energy was clearly returning, for he wrote to Mike
Watkins of the choices he had had to make. "It was an odd experience.
One of them had never boiled an egg. One was still asleep in bed at eleven
am when I called. One answered our advertisement because she thought,

'I'd like to see something of London.' A girl living in a place called Clack-mannan said she'd webbed feet and was a good swimmer. But I found three nice ones and they're all flying down at our expense to be grilled some more. It's a busy life."[58] They eventually chose Sheena Burt, whom Pat described as "a lovely twenty-one-year-old Scottish lass".[59]

When Pat returned home from shooting her latest movie – a thriller called *Psyche 59* – she began to sense a new buzz of anticipation around *Hud*. The New York Film Critics voted her Best Actress of 1963, as did the National Board of Review. A few weeks later she was nominated for an Oscar, but because the ceremonies in Los Angeles were taking place in April 1964, when she would be eight months pregnant, she decided not to attend. She also thought she was a rank outsider for the award. Then, at 5 a.m. on April 13, the phone rang to inform her that she had won. Roald's former lover, Annabella Power, had collected the statuette for her. It was a moment of triumph both for Pat and for the family. Her talent had finally been acknowledged and her own professional future now seemed to be secure. "Not only did my whole industry think I was good enough," she wrote, "but now, finally, a fabulous new career was just around the corner. And we'd make a fortune."[60]

Ophelia Magdalene Dahl was born in May – her name, perhaps consciously, evoking Olivia's – and a few weeks later the entire family decamped to spend the summer in Honolulu, where Pat was co-starring with John Wayne in a movie called *In Harm's Way* – a wartime drama, directed by Otto Preminger. Roald was not happy there. He disliked the "gold taps" style in which they were living. It brought out the Spartan in him. "I don't really like this place," he told Mike Watkins, "and I don't like living like the Aga Khan with a suite of eight adjoining rooms, four bathrooms, three kitchens – all paid for thank heavens, by old Preminger. I don't like luxury living in any form," he concluded somewhat disin-genuously. "It rots the soul." Inspired perhaps by his memories of the intrepid "Iron Discipline" in Tanganyika, he took consolation searching the island for phalaenopsis orchids, then his current hobby, to take back for an orchid house he was planning to create at Gipsy House. He was also befriended by a young and unknown movie director called Robert Altman, who tried to "pressure" him into writing a movie script.[61]

Roald was flattered by the attention and he liked the idea Altman proposed, but he was reluctant to get involved. His wartime experiences had left him suspicious of the genre, and watching Hitchcock shooting one of his short stories at the Royal Albert Hall in 1955 he had found tedious in the extreme. Now he contemplated film and television work only when he needed money. After Theo's accident, for example, he had "made a bloody fool" [62] of himself, introducing an edgy "grand guignol" half-hour US television series called *Way Out*. He had done it to pay hospital bills. From time to time, when he was broke, "a bit of awful movie work in Hollywood" [63] would always tempt him. Normally, he managed to resist the temptation.

Curiously, he had just earned the biggest movie fee of his life, from MGM, and he had done it without writing a sentence of dialogue. Earlier in 1964, Pat had showed him a script of a movie called *36 Hours*, which she felt was very similar to Roald's own short story from 1944, *Beware of the Dog*. The film was indeed a direct parallel to his tale of an RAF pilot who awakes from unconsciousness after baling out of his plane to discover that the hospital he is in is not in England, as he has been told, but in Occupied France, and that the doctors who speak perfect English and are looking after him so assiduously are actually Germans, bent on extracting information from him. MGM's version, scripted by the director George Seaton, involved an American diplomat (James Garner) with knowledge of the D-Day invasion plans, who is kidnapped, drugged and taken to a sanatorium, where German doctors, pretending to be Americans, stage a similar charade. They tell him that he has awakened from a coma long after the war has been concluded. For his own good, they try to make the patient remember his last thoughts before the trauma and thereby reveal details of the invasion plans, which they pretend are of no more than academic medical interest to them. Seaton had made no acknowledgement of Dahl's original story, and Roald immediately sensed an opportunity to extract a substantial sum of money from the studio. He instructed his reluctant agent to do battle with MGM.

The fight was a short one. Watkins initially advised his client to settle for $12,500, [64] but Dahl was confident of the strength of his position and wanted at least $25,000. "We could hold up the whole picture if we wanted to," he argued, "or let them make it and then sue."[65] But the studio refused to increase their offer. So Dahl calmly increased his demand, explaining his resolve to the nervous Watkins in terms of his responsibilities to his family. "As you know I am not personally greedy for money. This property is not mine now. It is in trust for Theo, who may well need funds throughout his life, especially if he becomes an epileptic. The chances of this are even."[66]

MGM still prevaricated, but Dahl – convinced of the justice of his case – held firm. "This is a big matter for me," he told Watkins. "That is why I am making such a song and dance about it. It is not often in a lifetime that a storywriter has a full movie based on his story. He must, therefore, get (for his children) all he possibly can out of it. Every extra thousand counts . . . I think you could tell them that I am in a fighting mood about all this (which I am) and that I intend to get at them or the writer in some way or another if they don't come through."[67] In the end, his tenacity paid off. MGM not only gave Dahl a credit as the originator of the story but a payment of $30,000 made directly into his children's trust account. Dahl's earlier experiences had already left him battle-hardened and cynical about studio executives. "If one does not fight for one's rights with these people," he told Mike Watkins's assistant, Peggy Caulfield, "they will always screw you in the end."[68]

Roald returned to London prior to the publication of *Charlie and the Chocolate Factory*. He had initially wanted the young Maurice Sendak, who had illustrated the Robert Graves children's story *The Big Green Book*, to do the drawings.[69] In the end he was persuaded to choose the slightly more experienced Joseph Schindelman. When the book was published in September 1964, it was an immediate success, provoking none of the controversy it would later cause when made into a movie. The *New York Times Book Review* declared on October 25, 1964, that Roald Dahl, "a writer of spine-chilling stories for adults, proved in *James and the Giant Peach* that he knew how to appeal to children. Now he has done it again, gloriously." The reviewer praised his fertile invention, his rich humour, and his acute observational skill, declaring that Wonka was a "Dicken-

sian" character and that the tale itself made a "lovely book". It was selected as one of the *New York Times*'s books of the year. All over America,
adults and children responded to the story with warmth and enthusiasm.
"It will be read not once, but over and over again", declared the *Tulsa
World*. The *Star News* in Pasadena noted that, while the book was written
for children, it also had "adult appeal". The reviewer for the *Boston Globe*
begged to differ. He thought the descriptions (the Oompa-Loompa Song
about the contents of Wonka's rubbish chute perhaps) might give adult
readers indigestion, but agreed that "the young, with their stainless steel
digestive systems, will take to it with relish". Only one group of people
were unconvinced: the librarians. *The Library Journal* commented primly
that while Mr Dahl's "facility with the pen is unquestioned, his taste and
choice of language leave something to be desired".[70]

After Christmas, the entire Dahl family along with Sheena, the new
nanny, and Angela Kirwan, the sporty twenty-two-year-old daughter of
one of their neighbours, headed to Los Angeles, the city Roald once described as "Gomorrah and destruction and the Lion's den", where "none
of us is Daniel".[71] There Pat was scheduled to star in what would be
John Ford's last movie, *Seven Women*. Her role was that of a missionary
in China, who gives herself up to marauding barbarians in order to save
the lives of the other sisters in the mission. As Martin Ritt, the director
of *Hud*, was away with his wife in Europe directing John Le Carré's *The
Spy Who Came In from the Cold*, the Dahls rented their home on Romany
Drive, Pacific Palisades. It was a big, spacious Hollywood house, filled
with pink marble, and it had a kidney-shaped heated swimming pool and
a sauna. For several weeks, the house – on a street whose name had reminiscences of Dahl's beloved gypsy ideals – seemed auspicious enough. Pat
was now a star. Since the Oscar, her fees had increased hugely and she was
enjoying some of the additional "perks" of increased celebrity. A British
magazine had offered to redecorate Gipsy House for free when they were
away, while she was able to boast to a journalist that she was now being
paid "so much money . . . it's almost ridiculous".[72] She went on to assure the reporter that none of this new success was going to change their
lifestyle and that most of this new money was going straight into a trust

fund for the children. As shooting commenced, what neither of the Dahls had told anyone – not even John Ford – was that Pat was three months pregnant.

On February 17, 1965, the fourth day of filming, she spent much of the time riding a donkey. Ford required Pat to repeat the same sequence of events many times. When he was finished, she was exhausted. Pat's friend, the actress Millie Dunnock, who was also in the movie, dropped her home at around five thirty. Ophelia was asleep, but Tessa and Theo "besieged" her with questions about the day's filming and particularly the donkey.[73] Roald brought her a martini at about six. Then Sheena took the children off to have their baths. Pat followed them. She wanted to bathe Tessa herself. Downstairs, Roald was making her another martini. As she sat on the lavatory seat, a searing pain shot through her head. "Mummy, what's wrong?" Tessa cried, as Sheena helped her mother stagger out of the bathroom and into the bedroom. Roald, who was coming up the stairs with Pat's drink, found her sitting on the bed. "I've got the most awful pain right here," she told him, pressing her hand to her left temple. She told Roald she was seeing double and experiencing what her medical notes later described as "bizarre fantasies" and "peculiar thoughts."[74] Suddenly her head jerked back and she lost consciousness. Roald suspected at once that she was having a stroke. He rushed into his study and called one of LA's top neurosurgeons, Charles Carton, whose home number he had pinned to the wall because the two men had met only recently to discuss bringing the Dahl-Wade-Till valve to the United States.

When he took Dahl's call, Dr Carton initially assumed there was something wrong with Theo, but as soon as Pat's symptoms were described to him, he dispatched an ambulance. Roald returned to the bedroom to find his wife just conscious. She was covered in vomit and could not recognize her own children. Tessa, still naked, was staring at her with a look of "utter desolation".[75] Five minutes later, sirens wailed. "What's that sound?" Theo asked. Sheena told him it was a cat. Tessa however, perhaps remembering the night Olivia died, knew exactly what it was. "It's an ambulance coming for Mummy," she said.

The paramedics put Pat on oxygen and stretchered her out of the house. Roald climbed into the ambulance beside her, asking the driver not to switch on the siren until they were away from the house. It was now 6.20 p.m. On arrival at the UCLA Medical Center's emergency room, Pat was able to talk again, and initially Carton thought she might have just had a seizure. Then she passed out once more. A spinal tap confirmed Roald's initial diagnosis: the fluid was "scarlet with blood".[76] With a lead apron over her abdomen to protect the unborn baby in her womb, the doctors took her in for two and a half hours of detailed X-ray examinations. They discovered that she had already suffered two severe haemorrhages. While Carton was studying the results and working out what to do, she had a third – the most massive of them all. Urgently, he asked Roald's permission to operate, warning him that he doubted his wife would survive the surgery. When Roald asked him what would happen if he said no, Carton told him that his wife "would succumb for certain".[77]

The operation began at midnight and lasted until after 7 a.m. the following morning. The doctors shaved her head, sawing loose a 4- by 6-inch trap door in her skull so they could remove the clots that had formed and inspect the damage the spurting blood had inflicted on the surrounding brain tissue. The surgery revealed that the rupture had been caused by an aneurysm, a genetic weakness in the wall of the artery. Perhaps pregnancy and the stress of a tough day's shooting caused it to burst at that particular moment, but it was a disaster that had simply been awaiting its moment to strike. Carton delicately removed the damaging clots – one of which was located in the part of the brain that controls speech and movement on the right side of the body. Then he put metal clips on the base of the aneurysm and sprayed on a plastic coating to reinforce the artery wall.

Roald stayed in the hospital throughout. Early in the morning, he called Mildred Dunnock, who was staying ten minutes away at the Chateau Marmont Hotel on Sunset Boulevard, and asked if she would go over to Pacific Palisades and tell the children what was happening. Roald himself rang Pat's mother. If her daughter made it through the next ten days, he told her, she might just recover some sort of normal functions. He was being optimistic. As Carton emerged from the operating theatre, he had taken Roald aside and advised him that, even if his wife did pull through, her disabilities were likely to be so severe that he might come to regret her survival.

Pat remained in a coma for almost three weeks, lying on an ice mattress to minimize swelling, and besieged by tubes. Antibiotics to prevent infection and anticonvulsants to prevent further damage to the brain dripped constantly into her system. She was fed both intravenously and through another line into her stomach. The doctors had performed a tracheotomy to assist her breathing, so there was yet another tube coming out of her neck.[78] She made no voluntary movements. Ed Goodman, who flew in from Manhattan to see her, recalled her condition as "pitiful".[79] Roald, he remembered, sat by her side for hour after hour, repeating endlessly, "Pat, this is Roald." Sometimes he would shout in her ear, "Tessa says hello. Theo says hello. Don Mini [Theo's nickname for Ophelia] says hello." Sometimes he lifted an eyelid to see if he could get a response. Millie Dunnock remembered that on one occasion Roald slapped her across the face to see if that would provoke a reaction,[80] but Roald told Dirk Bogarde that this recollection was untrue.§ For days there was no improvement in Pat's condition. On February 20, the *Los Angeles Herald Examiner* reported that there was "little hope". Two days later, *Variety* announced that Pat had passed away, running the headline: "Film Actress Patricia Neal Dies at 39." But on March 10, almost three weeks after the haemorrhage that nearly killed her, Pat began to regain consciousness. Roald was by her side when she falteringly opened a single eye. She could not move. She could not speak. She had no idea where she was or why she was there. The world she saw around her was confusingly blurred and hazy. Anger and fear coursed through her system as she tried to work out what was happening. Alone in her room when everyone had gone, all she could hear was a strange sound swirling round and round in her head: "wubble-wubble-wubble-wubble".[81]

---

§In a much later letter to Bogarde, who played Dahl in *The Patricia Neal Story* (1981), Dahl told him that he "never slapped Pat on the face when she was unconscious (or otherwise). That is a false note. Please don't do it" – Dahl, letter to Dirk Bogarde, 01/09/81 – Dirk Bogarde Collection, Howard Gotlieb Archival Research Center, Boston University.

Roald himself could have been forgiven for wondering whether some malignant neurological spell hung over his family. In 1940, his own head injuries had arguably altered his personality and led to a life of almost continual pain. Shortly after his marriage, a brain inflammation had incapacitated his best friend Charles Marsh. Then his son's skull had been shattered on a New York street corner. Two years after that another brain inflammation had taken his beloved daughter from him. Now his wife lay in her hospital bed, speechless and immobile, her head swathed in bandages after radical cranial surgery. What future lay ahead of her? As he gazed at the "enormous pink cabbage"[82] in front of him, it would not have been surprising if, for a moment, he had reflected on the fictional brain of William Pearl, which he had imagined in his short story *William and Mary*. That "sensitive, lucid, uberous organ", with its "ridges and creases running over his [*sic*] surface",[83] isolated from its body, incapable of expression and communication, with its single eye floating in a basin of Ringer's solution, was shockingly, almost mockingly prophetic of his wife's current situation.

Yet Dahl later claimed that he had not felt fatalistic. He had not thought "in terms of a curse or anything melodramatic", but reflected rather on the strange coincidence of it all. "I don't think I'm capable of taking it beyond that," he told the journalist Barry Farrell. "Superstition is something that one grows out of. You try avoiding all the cracks in the pavement or you touch all the posts in the fence. But then you find out later that it doesn't help. You find out that it's not going to make a bit of difference if you step on the cracks or not. I think I just realise subconsciously that if you start thinking about bad luck, you're going to weaken. The great thing is to keep going, whatever happens."[84]

CHAPTER SIXTEEN

Indomitable

IN THE DAYS IMMEDIATELY following Pat's stroke, Roald spent most of his time at the hospital, by her bedside, arriving there each morning at 6 a.m., and returning home only for meals and to sleep. His responsibilities were immense. On top of all the medical issues, an army of journalists and photographers lurked around the hospital waiting for news, quotes, stories, any scrap of information they could gather about the fate of the Oscar-winning actress who lay, as it seemed, in death's embrace. More than a hundred letters arrived each day from friends and well-wishers. Roald might have been overwhelmed, but it was the kind of crisis he was able to endure because it offered the opportunity to take complete control of the situation and also because he saw the chance of a positive outcome. The image of himself as the lone fighter, struggling against adversity to keep his family alive, was now profoundly ingrained in his psychology. Each crisis seemed only to intensify its presence.

Once again, the odds seemed stacked against him. After three weeks in a coma his wife lay, as she later put it, like "an immense vegetable",[1] on a life-support machine. The damage to her brain was as yet unquantifiable. Her appearance was so upsetting that her sister was warned by her husband not to go to the hospital.[2] At first Theo and Tessa were kept entirely away. A few days after she began to emerge from the coma, however, Roald decided that the children should see their mother. The experience was traumatic. Theo, aged four, was upset. And seven-year-old Tessa was terrified: a mixture of "horror, fear, nausea" welled up inside her as she contemplated "this hideous creature who cackled and moaned . . . this thing that was meant to be my mother. This woman propped up in bed with tubes coming out of every hole . . . She had no hair, she had a black eye patch, she had lipstick smeared over a lopsided mouth."[3]

For days, Pat made little sense. She found it difficult to recognize people, her ability to speak was severely compromised and her right side was paralysed. But despite the pessimism he must have picked up from almost everyone around him, Roald seized on the advice of Charles Carton that immediate and intense stimulation offered perhaps the best hope for his wife's recovery. He set her to work immediately, hiring speech therapists and physiotherapists to help her relearn the simplest things. Sympathy was not high on his list of priorities. He limited the number of visitors she could receive, removed most of the flowers from her room, and destroyed the bulk of her get-well cards, dismissing them all as dangerous indulgences that might drag his wife into the mire of self-pity and distract from her recovery. Within days his draconian plan seemed to be working. Pat's mobility began to improve and doctors were startled at the speed with which she tried to put sentences together. A few days after she had regained consciousness, Roald gave his mother a report on her condition. Its clipped, no-nonsense optimism was typical of the brutally positive attitude he was adopting:

Dear Mama,

Pat is really doing very well. At present she is helped out of bed into a wheelchair for all meals, and also whenever she wants to go to the pot. She understands possibly 50% of everything that is said to her, it may be more. Speech is poor, but she is just beginning to have therapy on that, and it is coming back slowly. She watches one's lips and then copies very well. You tell her to say "Tessa." She tries, fails, then tries again and succeeds. If she has a request to make she usually gets as far as "I want to . . ." or "Can I have . . ." But this will probably come back almost totally in time. She still has no use in her right arm. Her right leg is beginning to move. In herself, she is very

fit and cheerful. She smiles a great deal. She has met and completely
recognised Tessa & Theo . . . I think that in about four days we will
get her home here to the house, with a full time living-in nurse. That
will make things much easier for everyone, and much pleasanter for
her . . . They are going to put a steel brace on her right leg to help her
to walk . . . The children are all fine, and everyone is very braced by
Pat's condition.

Love to all
Roald[4]

Miraculously, barely a week after she began to regain consciousness, and a month after she had suffered the stroke, Pat was discharged from the hospital to convalesce in Pacific Palisades. She left wearing an eye-patch as well as a leg brace. A scarf hid the scars on her shaven head. Assisting her into the car, Roald told the press proudly that his wife was now "fully conscious and her thought processes are perfect . . . She is a tremendous fighter".[5] But when she got home, this bravado was more difficult to maintain. Bouquets of flowers and bowls of fruit from well-wishers arrived at the house daily. Frank Sinatra sent over his chauffeur to deliver a portable gramophone and a stack of records. Pat showed little interest. Roald forced her into daily physiotherapy and speech therapy, and hired Annie, a "fine enormous negress"[6] as a live-in nurse to look after her. But as Pat struggled to put her thoughts into words, to teach herself the names of primary colours, to work out how to use her right arm and feed herself, she became overwhelmed by the awareness of exactly what she had lost. The fact that she was pregnant also made relearning how to walk particularly exhausting. One of the other nurses, Jean Alexander, remembered that to get her to exercise was "like pulling teeth".[7] Roald later described his wife's condition in terms that starkly contrasted with the facade he had put on for the reporters outside the hospital. In reality, Pat had "no initiative". "If left alone, she would sit and stare into space and in half an hour a great black cloud of depression would envelop her mind. Unless I was prepared to have a bad-tempered desperately unhappy nitwit in the house, some very drastic action would have to be taken."[8]

Encouraged by Charles Carton, Dahl therefore embarked on an innovative regime of almost constant mental and physical stimulation. His methods were Spartan – almost reminiscent of the kind of discipline he himself had experienced at school. There was to be no self-pity, no indulgence toward the illness, just a determination to beat all the disabilities. His approach, Pat recalled, "was to get me to do it myself". Hard work would be the key. Though the speech therapist had said that an hour or so a day was all she could initially manage, and that doing more might even be harmful, Roald forced her to do four or five times more than that. He felt that "idleness was far more dangerous than fatigue", Pat later wrote. "And anything was better than vegetating."[9] Frustrated, tired and uncertain of the outcome of her treatment, Pat was frequently deliberately uncooperative, although she could still perform when the occasion demanded. Within a week of being discharged from the hospital, the director Mel Brooks and his wife Anne Bancroft, who had taken over Pat's role in *Seven Women*, invited the Dahls over to their house for dinner. Brooks expected Pat to arrive in a wheelchair, but was astounded to find her walking around the house unaided.[10] Pat herself remembered the occasion as "a fine evening", although she "couldn't follow a word of the conversation".[11]

Carton's wife Claire agreed that Roald's attitude was "extraordinarily instrumental"[12] in the speed of her recovery. To others, Roald's strict approach seemed unnecessarily controlling and strangely lacking in human warmth. Pat's mother Eura, for example, recovering from viral sinusitis in Florida, was desperate to see her daughter, but her doctors had forbidden her to travel. Roald barely communicated with her. Mrs Neal wrote to Dahl's sister Else, complaining that she felt she had been consciously kept away from her crippled daughter. With characteristic tact, Else tried to explain what she felt her brother needed to achieve his ends. Her letter is a fascinating articulation of that detached, buttoned-up quality in Roald that was at its most striking when he was most vulnerable, and that would often baffle outsiders when they encountered it. In this time of crisis, when the family's survival was at stake, Else said, it was not sympathetic relatives but skilled outsiders that her brother needed. He could not allow himself to be exposed to extreme feelings, which might deflect him from his task and interfere with what he believed was necessary for Pat's recovery. "Any strong emotional element" was likely to be "damaging", she concluded. Encouraging Mrs Neal to be patient, Else assured her that since the illness, Roald and Pat's understanding of each other had been "to the exclusion of everyone else," consoling her with the thought that "they have been through so much together that it has strengthened their love and trust of each other".[13] This may have been true. But the absence of tangible affection in that understanding was distressing to almost all who witnessed it.

Roald behaved like a general running a military campaign, demanding absolute adherence to his rules from everyone in the household. Pat's friend Gloria Stern, who came to visit one afternoon, found him reminiscent both of a stage manager and a traffic cop. She admired his "fierce, unrelenting approach", but was disturbed because it also reminded her of "the way one trains a dog".[14] Marjorie Clipstone, their friend from Great Missenden, who was travelling in America, also came to visit. She planned to spend two days in Pacific Palisades. She stayed a month. In a letter to Alfhild, she too painted a disturbed picture of life in Romany Drive, with the seven-year-old Tessa particularly unhappy. Clipstone noticed that Roald spent a lot of time "boosting" his daughter, and she reflected that he "must need a lot of boosting too, even if his stoical independence won't let him ask for it or even accept it easily". Roald's stoicism did relax sufficiently for him to admit to her that he was in "terrible trouble"[15] with his mother-in-law, who had finally come to stay and whose approach to Pat's condition was clashing completely with his. One evening, Eura cooked her daughter a special steak for dinner. Roald was appalled. He took it off the plate, cut it into pieces and passed it around the table, so that everyone could have some of it. "She should share with everybody," Pat remembered him saying. "She should not be treated special."[16] Eura was made to feel so unwelcome that she decided to return home early.

Mrs Neal might have consoled herself that she was by no means the only one whose offers of help were spurned. The recently widowed Claudia Marsh also suggested she fly out and assist Roald. She too was refused, although Claudia understood why. She sensed, like Else, that all Roald wanted was for "everyone to leave him alone" so he could "concentrate on what was completely absorbing him".[17] He was almost entirely focused on Pat's treatment. Helping him were a household of six staff: Sheena Burt; Angela Kirwan; the speech therapist; the physiotherapist; Annie the nurse; and a cleaning woman. Sheena Burt wrote to Sofie Magdalene describing Dahl admiringly as "the only man among all these women . . . such a strong man that one feels one can carry on with his inspiration and guidance".[18] But Sheena was blissfully unaware of the financial implications of Roald's attitude. Though the Ritts had continued to let them use their house rent-free and though Pat's medical insurance paid half of the surgeon's fees and 80 per cent of the hospital bills, running the household in Los Angeles was costing Roald more than $800 a week (perhaps as much as $4,500 by today's values). The family was living off its savings, and the prognosis for Pat's recovery was still highly uncertain. For the "Estimated period of disability," Carton had written on his discharge notes: "Cannot be determined at this time."[19] So, as soon as Pat was declared fit to travel, Roald returned to England. At Gipsy House, he would be able to construct a support system that would be significantly cheaper than the one in California. "I shall be glad to be back," he told his mother.[20]

The family arrived back in Great Missenden on May 17, after breaking the journey for two days in Washington to stay with Claudia Marsh. Cary Grant had driven them to the airport in Los Angeles and Dahl had announced to the waiting reporters that his wife would walk onto the plane unaided. She did. She also handled a fifteen-minute press conference with some aplomb, although her speech problems were manifest for all to see. To the London press, she even cautiously hazarded the view that one day she might return to the stage. In his own version of what happened, Roald merged the two events for maximum effect, claiming that Pat was "unable to answer any of their questions except in monosyllables" while emphasizing his own role in her recovery. "When I told them that one day she would act again, the room went silent," he wrote later. "The reporters stared. I might just as well have announced that the woman was going to sprout wings and fly to the moon." In the same context he also declared that his wife's treatment was being conducted without any direct medical supervision. "I called in no doctors," he announced. "It was a matter that had to be sorted out by the family alone."[21] His was a dauntless, intrepid response to a crisis. Yet part of this survival mechanism involved turning events into a coherent narrative with no grey areas: a story with a challenge, a hero and a positive outcome that would defy the prognoses of other pundits. It was almost one of his "dreams of glory".

A nasty surprise awaited the Dahls when they got home to Gipsy House. The interior was almost unrecognizable. The decorators had stripped out the wooden doors and antique floor tiles, installed bookshelves with fake books in the drawing room, and replaced much of their antique furniture with more fashionable bamboo alternatives. The final flourish was to paint the drawing room dark brown and lay a matching carpet that Roald described as "the colour of elephant turds".[22] A few weeks earlier, the ever watchful Sofie Magdalene had warned her son that all was not well, and criticized Linda Blandford, the journalist in charge of the project. Despite her disabilities, she even offered to sort out the situation. Roald's reply had been characteristically positive: "I don't worry about the chocolate walls and ceiling. Pat did agree to all those colours before she left. And I don't really agree with you about Linda Blandford. I think she has been splendid. You see, she is a professional, doing a job for her magazine, and part of the deal was that she and her decorator, after ascertaining Pat's wishes, should be allowed to go ahead from there on their own . . . She has been marvellous about getting us all sorts of appliances as cheaply as possible through the magazine . . . If we don't like the result, then that is really our fault, not hers. We certainly will not denounce it as soon as we see it. We'll give it a good try. All radical changes are hard to adjust to."[23] As soon as he returned, however, he realized that his mother was right. Immediately, he set to work, ripping out bookcases, repainting the walls, replacing the new doors and removing the new flooring.

While all this was going on, he was devising a strategy for Pat's rehabilitation based, as he saw it, on "common sense" and the avoidance of "inertia, boredom, frustration and depression" in the patient.[24] It involved an increase in the levels of stimulation she had been receiving in Los Angeles. He sent her for physiotherapy at a nearby RAF Military Hospital, where Pat felt as though she were in a boot camp.[25] Then each day, between nine and twelve in the morning and two and five in the afternoon, he arranged for friends and neighbours to visit her. These amateur therapists – Dahl described them as "intelligent, ordinary people, a lot of them retired or housewives whose husbands were working"[26] – read children's books to her and played elementary word games. Some encouraged her to draw pictures, or laid out objects on a tray and got her to try to memorize them. Others stretched her mind with simple crosswords, jigsaw puzzles or arithmetic. Many were initially shocked at her physical appearance. "It was very upsetting," Pam Lowndes told me, recalling Pat's eyepatch and leg brace. "I mean, from a vibrant, lovely-looking woman, she now looked terrible." Pam also remembered Roald's stern command not to "stand any nonsense" from his wife, encouraging her to push Pat as far as she could. But when Roald was not around, Pam recalled, the therapists were not quite so firm with their patient.[27] Dahl probably sensed this, writing later in an introduction to a set of notes for treating recovering stroke victims that "recreation and fun" should also be "an important part of the programme".[28]

In September, Jean Alexander and Gloria Carugati, two of the nurses who had worked with Pat in Los Angeles, came to the United Kingdom to work at the Atkinson Morley Neurological Hospital in Wimbledon, on the outskirts of London. Anne Bancroft paid for their flights over, and on their days off they too joined the roster of helpers at Gipsy House. The atmosphere there was often strained. Humiliated by being pushed into situations that she felt were beyond her, Pat complained vociferously. She would frequently tell her niece Anna Corrie to fuck off when she tried to help her and sometimes her responses were entirely unintelligible. A cigarette came out as an "oblogon", a spoonful of sugar as a "soap driver". A martini was a "sooty swatch". "Inject me again," she would say if she had forgotten something.[29] Tessa described the situation in *Working for Love*: "She would shout and scream. Make up words that we didn't understand and then laugh hysterically. Every day swarms of visitors would come and sit with her. On my father's instructions they would make her study, like a kindergarten child, reading, writing and arithmetic. Matthew [Theo] was more advanced at school than she was." [30]

Pat's frustration was compounded by the fact that friends like the actor Kenneth Haigh, Mormor's companion Mrs Newland, the Kirwans, and Frankie Conquy, the mother of Tessa's best friend Amanda, now seemed more like tutors than comrades. Although these sessions often concluded in tears, Roald insisted they continue. He was convinced that any activity, however stressful, was better than nothing. A few of Pat's friends occasionally wondered if Roald's hectoring manner might be wearing her down, but most of her teachers agreed with Pam Lowndes that he had shown "great vision" in his attitude and were astonished by her progress. "He was not horrid," Lowndes recalled, recalling how easily Pat slumped into despondency and self-pity. "He was abrupt. But then, if Roald shouted, she pulled herself up." [31]

Before long, one of these amateur therapists began to bring a more formal structure to Pat's rehabilitation. Valerie Eaton Griffith was in her early forties. A former manager of an Elizabeth Arden salon in London, she had recently been ill herself and given up work to live nearby with her elderly father. She had time on her hands. Arriving at Gipsy House for the first time, all Roald had told her was that his wife had "to be stimulated a lot". [32] Immediately, Eaton Griffith sensed that Pat needed a coherent strategy for her psychological problems to mesh with Roald's stimulation therapy. Gradually she began devising one, boosting her patient's self-esteem and compiling systematic data about what activities seemed to yield the best results. Roald was delighted. Although he had instigated this rigorous regime, he had also taken a very detached attitude toward the therapy itself. He simply let the helpers get on with their sessions, reserving his own energies, as he put it, for "running the house or earning a living and above all, keeping cheerful". [33] Now he handed Pat's rehabilitation over almost entirely to Eaton Griffith, who worked with her two or three times a week for six hours a day. "Slowly and cunningly," as Pat would later describe it, Val nudged her patient forward. [34]

In his introduction to *A Stroke in the Family* – the pioneering self-help book based on her experience with Pat which Val Eaton Griffith would later write – Roald explained that he had not involved himself directly in his wife's rehabilitation because of the damage that this role change might cause to their marriage. Later, he joked that he simply "stood by and whacked her over the head and saw she was ready to start work at nine each morning", praising her tenacity and humour, but speculating also that his own incentive for her recovery was perhaps more powerful even than her own. "I was often criticised at the time for pushing the patient too hard," he told the Speech Rehabilitation Institute in 1971, "but when you're talking about real life as opposed to vegetable life, you're in a crisis and you don't stop to enquire whether the patient is comfortable or not . . . Nothing was smooth or easy. In fact at one time I took her to a psychiatrist to make sure she didn't intend to carry out her threats of suicide." [35]

Yet, despite all his efforts, it was gradually becoming clear to Roald that the aneurysm had metamorphosed his wife into a quite different person to the one who had returned home from shooting on February 17. The match had never been ideal. It had started shakily, and without Charles Marsh's support would probably have broken down within six months, but it had been galvanized by the arrival of their children and further strengthened by the twin disasters of Olivia's death and Theo's accident. These shared catastrophes had brought Roald and Pat closer together. Now Pat had become the third of these calamities. With her eyepatch and her steel calliper, Tessa felt that her mother had been transformed from a glamorous extrovert into a "terrible burden" that the family had to endure with "silent suffering". [36]

Pat was aware of this too and it only added to her unhappiness. Despite the fact that she would later claim she had been a "gorgeous wife . . . making the beds and doing the cooking", [37] she was, by her own confession, "still no homemaker and no mother". [38] Susan Denson however remembered that, when she was working for the Dahls, she had found Pat to be a warm, loving and proactive mother. Now everything had changed again, and Pat found herself with "no authority" because "Papa", as she now began calling Roald, had completely taken over the running of the house. "My children always had plenty of love for me," she would write later, "but they regarded me as a peer with whom they vied for Papa's attentions. Or they totally ignored me."[39] Tessa, though only ten years old, even tried to usurp her mother's place, imitating her father's attitudes and sometimes acting, by her own admission, as if she was in charge.[40] As a result, Pat was often morose and hostile. Her husband's relentless optimism particularly got on her nerves. "He would tell me I was 42 per cent better than yesterday and 51 per cent better than last week. God I was so sick of his percentages, his plans, his programmes, his world. It was Papa's world now. He was a hero and I was hating him."[41]

Nevertheless, there was still time for celebrations. First, Pat's eyepatch came off. Then, on August 4, 1965, she gave birth to their last child, Lucy Neal Dahl, in Oxford. Within hours of the delivery, she was sitting up in bed, being photographed by the press drinking beer and playing dominoes. To celebrate, Roald gave his wife an ancient Greek ring, made in the fourth century BC. A few days later, he told Barry Farrell, who was now living with the family prior to writing the piece about them for *Life* magazine, that he was certain Pat would act again. Shortly afterwards he made a similar announcement to the press, in language that again was faintly reminiscent of that of an animal trainer. "Pat realizes she must rise to the challenge I have set for her and she is doing it,"[42] he declared.

This kind of statement alarmed Pat because privately she was unsure she would ever recover sufficiently to work again as an actress. She was profoundly aware of the extent of her disabilities: she still could not walk properly and found it almost impossible to remember lines. Sometimes, during her remedial sessions, she would try to recite poetry. Usually she would become confused, mangling the sense, speaking gibberish – often without realizing it. But Roald was convinced that only by maintaining the role of energetic leader and pushing her further than she wanted to go would her rehabilitation succeed. "He never let her develop self-pity," a family friend told a Hollywood reporter. "Every little thing she did accomplished something: she began to rally and this led to her pride in self-accomplishment, so Roald was *not* cruel."[43] Yet this attitude sometimes made even Farrell uneasy. He admired Dahl hugely, but he was nevertheless perturbed when he discovered Pat in the garden only hours after returning from the hospital where she had given birth to Lucy. She was trying to walk without a leg brace for the first time, while Roald was shouting at her "like a drill sergeant" and yelling: "Don't limp! Stride out! It's not onetwo, threefour, onetwo, threefour, it's one, two, three, four, one, two, three, four."[44]

On New Year's Day, 1966, Roald once again publicly raised the stakes on his wife's recovery, telling the press that he felt certain she would be "working again within the year".[45] As a result, movie offers slowly began to come in. Mike Nichols offered her the role of Mrs Robinson in *The Graduate*. Pat knew she was not ready for the part, which was eventually taken by her friend Anne Bancroft. Peter Sellers offered her a cameo in his movie, *What's New Pussycat?* She passed on that as well. Finally, Edgar Lansbury (brother of the actress Angela) offered her the lead in a film version of the Tony Award–winning play *The Subject Was Roses* by Frank Gilroy. Pat liked the part of Nettie – a tough working-class New York mother, whose son (played by Martin Sheen) returns home from fighting in the Second World War to discover that his parents' marriage is failing. The role was gritty, raw, and it suited her mood. It had two other attractions: it was not to be shot until 1968, and the filming would be largely in her beloved New York. Val Eaton Griffith convinced her to accept it. Yet Pat remained anxious that she was not ready.

Val, however, had already persuaded her to deliver a speech in New York in March 1967. Roald had written the text of her address, and Val coached Pat on it daily for a month, before accompanying her on the flight to New York for the celebrity dinner. "An Evening with Patricia Neal" was a fund-raiser for brain-injured children held at the Waldorf-Astoria. Its starry guest list included Leonard Bernstein, Joan Crawford, Yul Brynner, Rock Hudson, Paul Newman, Alistair Cooke, Mel Brooks and Anne Bancroft, and it was Pat's first public appearance since the stroke. Her speech – including a line borrowed from Sonia Austrian to the effect that "Tennessee hillbillies don't conk that easily" – won her a standing ovation, and the event raised $90,000. The adulation stimulated Pat's desire to recover and she began to believe she truly might pull off the movie comeback. That night she too hailed her husband as a "great man" and saluted him for what he had done to force her back into the lime-light. Later, she would articulate her gratitude more eloquently: "I knew at that moment that Roald the slave driver, Roald the bastard, with his relentless courage, Roald the Rotten, as I had called him more than once, had thrown me back into the deep water. Where I belonged."[46]

Pat's newfound confidence began to evaporate when she started to realize how much greater was the challenge of *The Subject Was Roses*. She prevaricated, looking for a way out of her commitment. "It is not my desire to work at all," she told Cindy Adams. "My husband coerced me. He felt that my rehabilitation would only be completed once I was back at work . . . I'm no longer used to the hustle and bustle and rushing and fittings and make-up tests and press interviews."[47] Most challenging of all was a five-page monologue that the director wanted to film from various angles, each time in a single take. The thought of it terrified her. Nevertheless, with Val Eaton Griffith's focused support, she got through most of the filming. Then came the evening when the soliloquy would be shot. The set was closed and teleprompts and cue cards hidden in case she needed them. Roald flew over to New York to support her. She got through the session with some difficulty, but Roald's effusive praise, so rarely given, filled her with delight.

When the film was released in 1968, Pat's performance brought forth a throng of accolades. The critic of *New York* magazine was left "groping for superlatives," while *Time* magazine praised Miss Neal's "vast resources of energy and intelligence" and her "melancholy dignity". "She no longer indicates suffering," the reviewer concluded, "she defines it."[48] The movie won her another Oscar nomination. It seemed to the world that, against all the odds, a star had miraculously been reborn.

The story of how Patricia Neal's clearheaded and determined husband had defied medical convention and masterminded her "return from the dead" quickly became the stuff of popular legend. Roald's "cruel to be kind" approach toward her rehabilitation did indeed revolutionize treat-ment for future stroke victims, mainly through the media publicity that Pat's story attracted. However, there was also an element of self-conscious mythmaking in both their versions of the narrative, which downplayed the enduring physical and mental problems that remained when Pat was away from the limelight. And it drew a veil over something that was obvious to their neighbour Alan Higgin: Pat had changed. Sue Denson, who had tea with her former employer shortly after she had finished *The Subject Was* Roses, agreed. Pat seemed like a different person, she told me. She found her "vindictive" – particularly when it came to Mrs Ingram, the housekeeper, whom Denson believed to have been the mainstay in running Gipsy House and who had recently handed in her notice.[49] Lou Pearl too felt that her aunt was no longer so demonstrative and affectionate, but more obsessive, much less open.

Roald simply refused to see this. His version of events seemed not to acknowledge that there might be a limit to Pat's powers of recovery. It was as if he had planned the story of her return to health in his head and was determined to force reality into the mould of his imagination. No other viewpoint could be tolerated – even from members of his family. Eura Neal thought an article he had written for the *Ladies' Home Journal* about her daughter self-absorbed and inaccurate and wrote to her son-in-law to tell him so.[50] Roald was dumbfounded by her accusations and by the emotional pressure he felt she was trying to exert on his family. "Please, what is it that bothers you? How have I offended you?" he asked. "In a case like this, Pat's family has only one duty – to support the husband who is trying desperately to cure her. Any letters that contain criticisms or demands or requests to her serve no purpose. So for heaven's sake stop them. I will not concede that I have wronged you in any way."[51]

The mythology had been further reinforced during the summer of 1965 while Barry Farrell was living with the family for his *Life* magazine article. For several months, the thirty-year-old Farrell became part of the family. He even went on holiday with them. Starved of male companionship in his almost entirely female world, Roald took the young journalist into his confidence. They took long walks together and often talked until late in the night. Farrell was captivated by Dahl and revelled in his "large small talk". Describing him admiringly as "the best storyteller I know", he confessed that "listening to him often worked a kind of spell on me".

Farrell too had been sceptical about the idea that Pat could return to what she was before her stroke. But he had been turned around. "In the months I had spent visiting Gipsy House," he wrote, "I was always made uneasy by Roald's talk of a 'hundred per cent recovery.' Now Pat's cheerful radiance seemed to bear him out miraculously, and his optimism was infectious: everyone agreed that the change in Pat after only six months made any recovery possible in the end."[52] Four years later, Farrell would expand his article into a more measured book called *Pat and Roald*. It would serve for many years as Dahl's only published biography and set in stone for a generation the legend of his role in his wife's recovery.

Roald's relationship with Farrell was a paradigm of many others he would have with younger professional males in the last twenty-five years of his life. Initially, Farrell was seduced by his charm and charisma – when one was with Roald on his own, he had an uncanny ability to make you feel special – but the contradictions in his personality would inevitably put the friendship under strain. In Farrell's case, he underestimated both how much Roald needed control over his own story and the extent to which he valued his family's privacy. It was a reasonable misjudgement. Roald was probably not dissembling when he appeared to welcome Farrell's presence in Gipsy House. His home was often full of visitors. But, on another level, intruders irritated him. His friend Marian Goodman observed this inconsistent attitude a number of times, recalling that although Roald criticized Pat for sending her publicity photographs and news cuttings to Tessa while she was at school, he himself would often ring gossip columnists and "feed them" stories about his own children. "It's the old story – methinks the lady doth protest too much," reflected Mrs Goodman. "He disliked publicity and would pick it up on somebody else, but then he succumbed himself . . . He loved being interviewed."[53] It took Farrell a long time to understand that his subject's sword was double-edged, and that while he was celebrating their late night têtes-a-têtes, his friend was complaining behind his back about his "endless talk and probings". Dahl told Mike Watkins he only put up with it because of the $100,000 worth of publicity he reckoned the article and book would bring him.[54]

When Roald and Pat eventually read Farrell's manuscript, in 1968, they were shocked by some of his observations – in particular his assertion that Pat's personality had changed after her stroke and that she seemed to be becoming an alcoholic. His observation that she was garrulous, unpredictable and intolerant – even to Val Eaton Griffith – also stung them. Pat later admitted that she had indeed been "rude" and "obnoxious"[55] to Val and that she probably did have an alcohol problem. At the time, however, the wounds were much rawer and even the unshockable Dahls were startled by the picture Farrell had painted of their family.

Roald did not speak to Farrell personally about his concerns. He called Farrell's publishers instead, accusing the author of cruelty and slander, and threatening to block publication unless changes were made.[56] Farrell was forced, as he put it, to censor his manuscript, removing various details, including the circumstances surrounding the departure of the nanny, Sheena Burt, who, he asserted, had slapped Pat's face in frustration at her treatment of the infant Ophelia. Pat herself wrote to Farrell complaining about "the rotten things" he had said about her and claiming that his book portrayed Roald as "the hero" and herself simply as "the bitchy woman". In particular, she resented his insinuation that she was a dipsomaniac. "*I am not a drunk! I am not a drunk! I am not a drunk!*" she railed, adding, only partly in jest, "At least I don't think so!"[57] Yet her nephew and nieces, the Logsdails, agreed with the journalist that a haze of intoxication now hung over Gipsy House and that tempers were often frayed. It was a far cry from the tight family unit Susan Denson recalled in her four years with the Dahls between 1958 and 1962.

A devastated Farrell made the required changes, complaining to Roald and Pat that cutting the manuscript had made him feel "like a whore". "It was not a cruel book," Farrell wrote, arguing that "a great deal was left out . . . to protect your feelings and your privacy. Nonetheless, you attacked it using means that suggested contempt for the work as well as for the friendship of its author . . . I feel stung and betrayed by you and I regret every day that I ever gave an hour to writing the vain, false book that is now to be issued under my name."[58] Roald thought his letter "nasty and childish", and suggested Farrell come over and see them to sort it out. Farrell was too hurt to accept his offer.[59] Ironically, many of the book's falsities were of its author's own making. As a writer, Farrell – who died at the age of forty-nine in 1984 – was not constrained by much fact-checking and his weak research helped establish many fictions about Roald's life as truths in the public's mind. Dahl, the fighter pilot, shot down by enemy fire over Libya; Dahl, the sole inventor of the gremlins; Dahl, the laid-back and successful writer, whose tales were published in *The New Yorker* just as soon as he submitted them. All of these and more were enshrined in *Pat and Roald*. For over twenty years these stories were repeatedly rehashed by a stream of journalists and often by Dahl himself. It was not until 1994 that Jeremy Treglown set many inaccuracies straight and began systematically to unravel the complex web of fictions that Roald had woven around himself.

Farrell's book became the basis of a television film about Pat's stroke called *The Patricia Neal Story*, made in 1981, with Glenda Jackson playing Pat, and the Dahls' near neighbour Dirk Bogarde as Roald. The movie reinforced the image of a resilient Dahl family, led by its charismatic and determined paterfamilias, pulling together to deal with a crisis that would have broken many others. What Roald had achieved in pushing a recovering stroke patient to the limit was indeed remarkable. And Patricia Neal's celebrity status ensured a high profile for this new kind of stroke therapy, while Val Eaton Griffith's book about managing strokes in the family would help many others to deal with similar crises. It also spawned a network of "stroke clubs" across the world. Both book and film, however, encouraged the world to believe that Pat's recovery was complete and that the Dahl family unit was uniquely strong and robust. It wasn't. Serious stresses tugged at its heart, but they were concealed by the compelling narrative Dahl had created around them. He may even have been aware of what he was doing. "I do not display emotions," he told Bogarde, when offering him some tips on how to play him on screen. "They may churn madly inside, but I always keep them there. Unsentimental. I am cool and competent in a crisis. Act swiftly, never get visibly excited." Most tellingly, perhaps, he compared his tenacity in dealing with Pat's stroke to that of completing a book. "All good writers," he explained, "have a very great tenacity and endurance. They do not give up . . . The act of rehabilitating Pat was like writing a long and difficult novel."[60]

Barry Farrell had not known Pat before her stroke, but he observed how it had affected her personality. He described traits that Roald's family told him she had not exhibited before: how she had become fixated by trivia, how she picked up litter obsessively and complained loudly about lights being left on in the house when people went out.[61] "When Pat had her stroke, Pat became more Pat," claims Marian Goodman. "She was the same woman . . . but the self-interest, the self-centredness were more exaggerated. She was just more demanding." Even today, Mrs Goodman still finds these qualities frustrating in her good friend. "Sometimes I'd like to shake her until her teeth rattle," she told me, "but my compassion for her is endless because I realize just what she's been through."[62] Roald too was impressed by Pat's determination. He had seen her progress from an "idiot",[63] whose only vocal means of communication was grunting, to an Oscar nominee in less than three years. Yet, by 1967, admiration was about all that remained of his feelings toward the woman he had once proudly dubbed "my girl Pat". The "wild, gorgeous" woman that the actress Maria Tucci remembered had first been "tamed" by her husband and then brought low by her illness. Speaking to Pat after her stroke, Tucci recalled, was like speaking to "an adorable but rather odd ten-year-old".[64] Roald's physical desire for his wife was dwindling, and for Pat having sex was now "agony".[65] Val Eaton Griffith noted that she had become loud, intolerant and "actressy", making peace in the household almost impossible. "It was extremely hard for all of them," she said, "and *very* hard on Roald."[66]

So, the more complex truths of Pat's recovery remained hidden from the public eye. Occasionally the cat escaped from the bag. Once, Roald told an interviewer that he had compelled his wife into making *The Subject Was Roses*. "Pat's not ambitious," he added. "I really did have to bully her into making another film. She didn't want to do it."[67] Pat herself could be even franker about her defective memory and her limp, admitting to the *National Enquirer* on May 9, 1971, that despite the success of *The Subject Was Roses*, she was well aware that producers were still "fighting shy" of her. Future triumphs however lay in store. In 1972, she won a Golden Globe for her performance in Fielder Cook's *The Home-coming*, although she was disappointed not to get the role in its television spin-off, *The Waltons*. Then, at seventy-three, she stole the show as the pipe-smoking Cookie in Bob Altman's *Cookie's Fortune* (1999). But throughout the 1970s and 1980s, her television and movie appearances became rarer and increasingly she spent her time giving well-paid talks about her life, often on her own or accompanied by Val Eaton Griffith. Her relationship with Roald too had altered dramatically. He was "Papa" Dahl – and she was a dependant. Tessa hated the change. "Like two baby birds in a nest squawking for food, we sat open-beaked, craving his attention," she wrote in *Working for Love*.[68] Eventually it got too much for her. She asked to be sent to boarding school just so that she could get away from a home where, she bluntly told her mother, there were simply "too many babies".[69] It was clear to Roald too that – at least for the short term – he would have to become the major breadwinner. To achieve that end, he decided he had to turn his own talents to a world he instinctively disliked and distrusted: the movies.

In the summer before Pat's stroke, when the family were in Hawaii, Roald had toyed somewhat halfheartedly with writing a fantastical comedy script for a young director, Robert Altman. He liked Altman, he liked his story about First World War fighter pilots and their raid on the Zeppelin base at Friedrichshafen and he particularly liked the title Altman had given the project – *Oh Death, Where Is Thy Sting-a-ling-a-ling?* – which he had plucked from the refrain of an old RAF song, "The Bells of Hell." Roald had worked on the script in Hawaii, but he had other things – like orchids – on his mind, and for several months there seemed little urgency to the project. In any event, he was doing it "for fun".[70] He brushed up his first draft over the autumn in Great Missenden. He was not paid a fee. He had agreed to share the rights with Altman. Payment would come when Altman sold the project to a studio that would accept him as a director.

This was not an easy task. Although he had a stack of television credits, Altman had not yet directed his first feature. The project was still uncertain when the Dahls returned to Los Angeles in January 1965. Just a few days before Pat's stroke, Roald wrote to Mike Watkins, telling him about Cary Grant's enthusiasm to take the lead role. "The snag with Grant," he added, was that he had yet to be convinced that Altman was a "capable director".[71] Grant never was. Nevertheless, the relationship between Dahl and Altman remained trusting, casual, friendly. Too friendly for Watkins, who worried that the agreement between them was "awfully vague". When a hard copy of the contract finally arrived, he told Roald that he only approved it because he knew of his special relationship with Altman.[72] With Pat earning good money, however, Roald was happy to wait until Altman found the right studio. The stroke changed that dynamic overnight. In Roald's eyes, Altman was suddenly transformed from an inexperienced and engaging young director into a stubborn opponent, whose selfishness was preventing him from realizing the cash he now desperately needed for his family.

By April 1965, there was a complete impasse. In Los Angeles, with his wife just out of hospital, Dahl was desperate to sell the project to United Artists, who had offered $150,000 for the script, but only on the condition that Altman gave up directing it. Altman, however, had refused. As a result, the two men had fallen out. "I called Bob, who was a small television director," Roald later recalled, "and I said: 'Look, I need the money!' And he screamed: 'You can tear the bloody thing up, if I don't direct it.'"[73] The conflict was only resolved when Dahl hired a legendary Hollywood agent and dealmaker, Irving "Swifty" Lazar, to help him. "I don't see Altman at all now," he told Watkins later in the month. "The feelings run high between us. The whole thing is a mess and a great pity. He is not behaving well at all. If only we could sell it now, I could get some expense money immediately from a studio for the rewrite, which would make it less of a drain to remain here with this vast household."[74] When the Dahl family returned to England the following month, the issue was still unresolved. Six weeks later, Lazar persuaded Altman to back down. They split the proceeds down the middle. Altman got $75,000 and – after paying Lazar's 10 per cent – Roald collected a fee of $67,500, which he put straight into a trust fund for Theo and Tessa. It made him feel, he told Alfred Knopf, "a bit safer".[75] Altman, however, was devastated by what he saw as his friend's disloyalty. Years later he told Roald's youngest daughter, Lucy, that though he had long since forgiven him, he still felt her father had "betrayed him like no one's ever betrayed me in my life".[76]

Roald got paid another $25,000 for rewriting the script with the new director, David Miller. Miller was an American, in his mid-fifties, who had been directing movies since the 1930s. He had worked with John Wayne and the Marx Brothers, but he had none of Altman's idiosyncratic charm. Roald was distinctly underwhelmed, describing him as "competent . . . but extraordinarily ignorant". He told Peggy Caulfield at the Ann Watkins Agency that Miller would not make "anything brilliant, ever", but concluded that – in view of the $6 million to be invested in the picture – he was doubtless safe.[77] He wasn't. The two men never saw eye-to-eye and, with his money banked, Roald swiftly lost interest in the project. His correspondence suggests that ultimately he was less concerned about the script than whether he would get sufficient expense money to pay for his entire family to come on holiday to Switzerland, where the picture was being shot.

The film was a disaster. After over a month on location, the studio abandoned it, and declared their investment a write-off. "*Sting-a-ling* as you probably know has folded," Roald told Watkins in August 1966. "I'm told they got a writer called Robert Alan Arthur . . . and he fucked the thing up to a point where neither he nor the director knew what they were doing. They shot three minutes of film in five weeks on location."[78] Yet something of the energy of the original project lingered on – at least in Robert Altman's memory. Not long before he died in 2006, the director, then in his eighties, was asked by a journalist how he regarded his own imminent mortality. "I'm aware of it, I do wake up and face it most mornings," he told the interviewer. Then he paused, smiled and simply uttered: "Oh Death, where is thy sting-a-ling-a-ling?"[79]

Dahl's script for the film was not entirely wasted. It had impressed Harry Saltzman and Albert "Cubby" Broccoli, two producers who also had a deal with United Artists. They owned the James Bond movie franchise, and were looking for a screenwriter for their latest *007* project, *You Only Live Twice*. Roald quickly found his name at the top of their screenwriting options. He was in many respects an obvious choice. He had known Ian Fleming well. Both men had worked in espionage for William Stephenson during the war, and both had similar reputations as hard-drinking, gambling, womanizing sophisticates. They also shared the same attitude toward money. "Despicable stuff," Fleming had once remarked to Dahl, adding: "but it buys Renoirs." [80] Roald himself was in need of money now, not so much for Renoirs as for school bills and medical fees. So he was delighted by the approach. He admired Fleming. He thought him one of the few writers worth meeting, describing him as "a sparky, witty, caustic companion, full of jokes and also full of odd obscure bits of knowledge". [81] He told Fleming's biographer that "a great red glow" illuminated the room when Fleming entered it. [82] But he was less enamoured of his friend's writing skills, describing *You Only Live Twice* variously as "tired", "bad", and "Ian's worst book". [83] For his first meeting with the two overweight moguls, Broccoli and Saltzman, Dahl was ushered into "an enormous room". He discovered that they shared his low opinion of Fleming's novel; they told him he could do anything he wanted with the story so long as he didn't change the Japanese location, "mess about" with the character of Bond, or tamper with the franchise's famous "girl formula". [84]

The movie plot was indeed almost completely different from Fleming's book. But it was not all Roald's work. He was given a number of useful suggestions by an established Los Angeles television writer named Harold Jack Bloom, who proposed many of the narrative ideas that were in the final film, including Blofeld's scheme to threaten the Russian and American Space Programs and the idea of faking Bond's death at the opening of the movie. [85] Nevertheless, a lot of the details – giant magnets, a battle between miniature helicopters, and a spacecraft that "swallows" another – were quintessential Dahl. Like the cunning magpie, one of his favourite birds, Dahl picked what he wanted from Bloom's outline and then made it his own. The first draft took him just eight weeks to write, including one week spent on holiday with his family by the sea in Tenby.

After he had delivered it, he wrote to Mike Watkins telling him that "the bosses" were thrilled with the draft, adding with characteristic boastful self-deprecation that he thought the script was "the biggest load of bullshit I've ever put my hand to".[86]

Bloom, whose screen credit read "additional material by", felt he had got the raw end of the deal. In an interview with Jeremy Treglown, he claimed he had created "everything you saw on the screen", and that he and Dahl should by rights have shared the screenwriting credit[87] – a familiar cry in an industry notorious for its ruthless treatment of writers. In the past, Roald himself had felt that sense of injustice, but this time, after a run of bad experiences of his own, he had finally hit the jackpot. He revelled in his regular trips to the Beverly Hills Hotel in Los Angeles, and in the luxury of sending scripts down to London in a chauffeur-driven Rolls-Royce.[88] He also liked working with Lewis Gilbert, describing him in a radio interview as "the only fine, lovely director I've ever worked with" – one who "never changed a word" of the script.[89] Best of all was the money: $165,500.[90]

It transformed the Dahls' finances. Roald boasted to his neighbour Alan Higgin that he would never need to work again because he had "made so much money from that movie".[91] Nevertheless, when Cubby Broccoli offered him the opportunity to adapt Fleming's children's book, *Chitty Chitty Bang Bang*, at a fee of $125,000 with a percentage of profits and an agreement to pay the money into an offshore account, which saved Dahl paying 91 per cent rates of UK income tax,[92] he found he simply could not refuse. But the project did not really excite him. He described the work as "simple, rather childish", and the script as "rubbish". He told Alfred Knopf that he was only doing the work to accumulate sufficient capital to take care of his children should he "croak",[93] as he did not believe in insurance. To Mike Watkins he admitted that he was desperate for Pat to be working again, so that he could abandon movies and get back to writing fiction. "I do not like this film business," he confessed, adding optimistically that Pat was progressing so well that he hoped he would be "a free man" again in just eighteen months' time.[94]

Chitty Chitty Bang Bang was as grim as the Bond film had been gratifying. Roald rapidly fell out with the director, Ken Hughes, who was used to writing his own movies and who contrived to take the script away from him after the first draft,[95] claiming that Broccoli thought Roald's work "a piece of shit". Hughes claimed later that he had written "every fucking word"[96] of the final script on his portable typewriter. He was almost certainly exaggerating. It's hard to believe, for example, that Dahl was not directly involved in devising many of the new characters and storylines – the preposterous Truly Scrumptious, for example, the Kingdom of Vulgaria, or the "toot sweets", which unexpectedly summon all the dogs in the neighbourhood to the candy factory. His fingerprint is most apparent in the film's most memorable character: the sinister "Child Catcher". This spindly, long-nosed monster captures children in a cage baited with candy, sniffing them out in their hiding places with his extremely sensitive nose. He is Willy Wonka's evil doppelgänger, treading that line between the creepy and the comic that Dahl had already made distinctively his own. Aunts Sponge and Spiker had walked it already. Miss Trunchbull and the Grand High Witch would step along it two decades later. But the Child Catcher is perhaps the most terrifying of them all. With good reason, he is often described as one of the scariest characters ever to appear on screen.

Dahl hated the final version of *Chitty Chitty Bang Bang*, and his involvement concluded in an acrimonious dispute between himself and Broccoli over why he was not invited to meet Queen Elizabeth at the charity premiere. It was a classic example of the contradictions in his character. Dahl the iconoclast claimed he did not care about shaking hands with royalty. But being excluded from the top table was infuriating. "I am sure you are aware that I personally don't give a damn whether we met the Royal Family or not," he complained to Swifty Lazar. "What I did care about was Cubby's behaviour and the way I have been treated all through." His exclusion from that limelight reminded him that – despite his growing fame, wealth and status – even self-made men like Broccoli ultimately shied away from him. "I have now produced two worthwhile original scripts for Cubby and as far as I can tell, have done nothing wrong," he told Lazar. "It makes me very cross."[97] It doesn't seem to have occurred to Dahl that his growing reputation for being irascible and unpredictable might have accounted for his exclusion from the royal glad-handing. Yet, despite his protestations that he disliked cinema, his financial successes had rekindled his interest in movies, and he consciously sought out more projects. Illness alone forced him to abandon an adaptation of Aldous Huxley's *Brave New World,* and for a while he seriously contemplated writing a screen adaptation of Ludovic Kennedy's *10 Rillington Place*, about the miscarriage of justice surrounding a real-life serial killer, John Christie.

His reasons for turning down *10 Rillington Place* also offer a revealing insight into Dahl's own aesthetics. In an interview in Los Angeles in 1970, he described the role of writer as that of entertainer, and explained that for him "fantasy" was the best means of performing that function. He wanted to take his audience to somewhere "marvellous, funny, incredible", concluding that he "would never want to write anything that wasn't completely made up or invented".[98] The story of Christie, a mild-mannered Londoner who killed seven women, concealing the bodies behind the wallpaper of his flat, disgusted Dahl because it was much too real and because it lacked wit. "I am sorry but I don't like it," he told William Dozier, the potential producer. "The history of this man Christie is so sordid and so humourless that I cannot see it as entertainment. A macabre story, if it shall be successful, must have a quality about it that makes one smile at the same time that it makes one wriggle. That is the secret . . . Christie's story is a succession of seven carefully premeditated sex murders, all of them too beastly to contemplate. I couldn't do it. I'm sorry. I expect it will be a huge success, but it's not my stuff."[99] The grand guignol fantasy of Ambrose Bierce or Thomas Harris's *The Silence of the Lambs* was much more to his liking. Admitting that the only project that really appealed to him was adapting *Charlie and the Chocolate Factory* into a musical, he declared once again that he was tired of films. All he wanted now was to go back to writing stories and children's books.[100]

He was not quite finished with movies, however. He did adapt *Charlie and the Chocolate Factory*, and the following year, in an attempt to create a project for Pat, he acquired the rights to *Nest in a Falling Tree*, a psychological thriller by a young New Zealander named Joy Cowley. The plot focused on the plight of Maura Prince, an intelligent, sensitive spinster, who falls for a mysterious young handyman without realizing that he is in fact a serial rapist and killer. Maura was a wonderful role for Pat. In his script, he even turned her into a recovering stroke victim. But *The Night Digger*, as the movie was finally titled, never really engaged Roald's full attention perhaps because, like *10 Rillington Place*, the story had little intrinsic humour in it. He tried to inject some, much to Cowley's own delight.[101] But even so, the tale relied on the kind of suspense, built on subtle psychological detail, that was not Dahl's strength. It is testimony to his determination to make things happen for his wife that he pursued the project with such doggedness.

Swifty Lazar was sceptical. He thought the story tame, predictable, "almost Victorian".[102] But Roald was tenacious. Writing in the middle of the night – his five-year-old daughter Lucy used to see his light on in the hut when she got up in the night to go to the bathroom – he told Lazar he thought his finished script might be the best screenplay he had ever done.[103] A number of directors were sent the script, including William Friedkin, Lindsay Anderson, and the young Ken Russell, who liked the story but thought he himself would not be a sufficiently good collaborator.[104] Roald had teamed up with an amiable English producer called Allen Zinn Hodshire, who even approached Robert Altman to direct. "He will see you at once," Roald declared bullishly, "if you tell him that Pat and I want him and Pat especially wants to be directed by him."[105] Unsurprisingly, Altman, still smarting from his fallout with Dahl four years earlier, did not respond and eventually they chose a young Scottish director called Alastair Reid.

Though Roald owned the rights to the story, he needed to strike a deal with an experienced production company in order to access the funds from the studio to make the picture, and he found the process extremely frustrating. He was psychologically ill-equipped for the chicanery and hot air involved in being a movie producer and quickly became impatient with the endless inconclusive meetings. "He floats around like a small jelly," he wrote of one potential producer, "waving his chubby hands and only appearing on the scene when there is nothing to be decided."[106] Finally, he struck a deal with a company called Youngstreet Productions, which had persuaded MGM to put up the money for the project. The new producers turned out to be ruthless. They demanded that Dahl replace the luckless Hodshire with two of their own staff, and Dahl swiftly consented to their demands. His decision to drop Hodshire revealed how tough adversity had made him. It seemed as if he now believed that everyone outside the tight family circle was ultimately disposable if the situation required it. The abrupt parting came as a cruel, unexpected and "staggering" blow to Hodshire,[107] who had given the project a great deal of his own time and energy, and had been working with Roald unpaid, in the expectation that he would receive a producer's fee if and when the film got financed.

Dahl did not like looking backwards, but in this case he soon came to regret what he had done.[108] After the movie was over, he wrote to Hodshire, admitting that he had made a mistake and acknowledging that the deal he had struck left him with little control over the picture's destiny. The letter was a litany of complaints that focused mostly on the director, a "very nasty little man" who had eroded his wife's fragile confidence.[109] Pat too confirmed that she felt undermined by the experience.[110] After the shoot was over, she told a journalist that she was tired of acting. "I don't really care about making films now," she admitted. "I was so ambitious once. But I don't really want to work. I would not care a lot if I don't do another film."[111] Touchingly, she added that she was "just pleased I am married to the man who is my husband".

Dahl, who remained profoundly uninterested in the detail of making films, quickly tired of the project. He seldom turned up on location and never saw any of the rushes. He did not notice that Reid had taken significant liberties with his script until he saw a rough cut of the movie, and then it was too late to do anything. "It was unbelievable," he told Hodshire. "All Pat's big scenes had been cut and the entire film was a mess of pornographic junk with men and women copulating all over the place. We were aghast."[112] When *The Night Digger* opened in America, it received dismal reviews. *The Hollywood Reporter* described it as "lethargic" and *Variety* found it clichéd. The movie was never even released in the United Kingdom. Roald and Pat ironically ended up in the same position as Allen Hodshire because they had agreed to terms that only gave them a share in the profits. There were no up front performance or writing fees so neither of them ever received a penny from it. Yet such was Dahl's desire to create roles for Pat and keep her working that he acquired the rights to two further properties: Donald Harington's thriller *The Lightning Bug* and Rumer Godden's award-winning children's story about an orphan gypsy girl, *The Diddakoi*. He wrote screen versions of both stories, and hawked them around for a while, but neither ever made it into production. He was eventually forced to concede defeat.

After a five-year gap, he returned to writing children's fiction. The Roald Dahl who began a story called *Mr Fox* in the spring of 1968 was a different man to the one who had finished *Charlie and the Chocolate Factory* four years earlier. He was tougher, stronger, even more empowered and determined than before. He had emerged "a little tired" from his "long siege",[113] but also wealthier and more successful. The bank balances in the children's trust funds looked healthy, and paintings by Francis Bacon and the Russian avant-garde Suprematists now hung on his walls alongside the Matthew Smiths. Roald had discovered Bacon in 1958, when the artist shared an exhibition with Matthew Smith, and had seen at once that he was a "giant of his time."[114] Later, he would tell his stepdaughter Neisha Crosland how much he admired the "blend of economy and profound emotion" in his painting.[115] Between 1964 and 1967, Dahl bought four Bacon canvases – none of which cost him more than £6,000.* During the same period, he also purchased a shop on Great Missenden High Street, where one day he hoped to sell antiques.[116] The paintings and the shop were concrete evidence of his success in defeating adversity and gave him considerable satisfaction.

One frosty winter evening in 1965, as Roald went out to check that his aviary was safely locked up, Barry Farrell got an insight into what had kept him going. Roald told him the story of Lady Rachel MacRobert, the American widow of a Scottish baronet, whose three sons had all been pilots.

---

*These were *Landscape at Malabata* (1963), *Three Studies for a Portrait of George Dyer* (1963), *Study for a Portrait of Henrietta Moraes* (1964) and *Head of Lucian Freud* (1967).

In 1938, the eldest was killed in an air crash. In 1941, the second was shot down and killed in Iraq. The third perished a month later when his Wellington bomber ditched over the North Sea. Lady MacRobert was grief-stricken. But she did not dwell on her sorrow. Instead, she calmly took out a pen and made out a check to the Air Ministry for £25,000 to pay for the cost of a new bomber. "I have no more sons to wear the MacRobert badge or carry it in the fight," she told the air minister, "but if I had ten sons, I know they would all have followed that line of duty." The RAF bought the bomber and painted two words on its side: "MacRobert's Reply". This determination to fight on, this refusal to be beaten – Roald told Farrell – had inspired his own tenacity when all seemed set against him. "I can remember being very moved by that," he said. "It was something really dauntless, really indomitable. You simply cannot defeat such people."[117]

By 1970, Dahl's years of extreme adversity were almost over. One sadness remained. His career as an adult fiction writer was in its death throes. Both of his most recent short stories, "The Visitor" and "The Last Act", had been rejected by *The New Yorker*. Roger Angell told Mike Watkins he had turned them down with particular reluctance, because he knew Mr Dahl "always feels a rejection very deeply".[118] As a result, Dahl had decided to return the $100 a year the magazine paid him for the first reading of all his adult short stories. He told Angell sadly that he thought it wrong "to continue to accept this money each year when the stories I am writing are so clearly not to your liking", adding as a wistful coda that he still remembered "with immense pleasure the times when the magazine used to buy my work".[119] *Playboy* finally published "The Visitor", but with unsanctioned cuts, which infuriated Dahl and provoked more outraged letters accusing the literary editor, A. C. Spectorsky, of artistic "murder".[120]

The slow end of Dahl's career as an adult writer was painful, just as the abandonment of his dreams of being a novelist had been twenty years earlier, although he admitted that, as time went by, he found good adult plots harder and harder to come by. And, while the decline of his short story writing might have hurt his pride, it did not dent his wallet. For it was not just the movie scripts that had begun to earn him money. His children's books had taken off as popular bestsellers. By March 1968, *Charlie and the Chocolate Factory* had sold over 600,000 copies in the United States, while *James and the Giant Peach* had topped 250,000. Knopf found they owed their author almost $1 million in royalties.[121]

From today's perspective, it is very hard to believe that it took Dahl almost seven years to find a UK publisher for both these titles. Yet despite their success in the United States, at least eleven major UK publishers rejected them, forcing him once again to take matters into his own hands.[122] "I *refuse* to peddle these two nice children's books all over London at random, to get one rejection after another," he told Mike Watkins in December 1964. "Merely to flog the books round indiscriminately until they have been rejected by all of London is absurd."[123] To Blanche Knopf, he wrote that he was determined no longer to go "cap in hand" to establishment publishers, who would only "reject him right and left". He wanted instead to do his own thing and "break through" their "priggish, obtuse stuffiness".[124] Ignoring the advice of Laurence Pollinger's younger son, Murray, who was now handling his affairs in London and thought his client should continue to try to sell the books to an established name, Roald began to work out his own strategy for publication. A week later he explained it to Mike Watkins.

> *I am digging my toes in hard re James and Charlie over here, refusing to offer them any more to top-rate English publishers. I want to get them printed and colour plated in Czechoslovakia and sold here for a very cheap price through the kind of publisher Murray virtually refuses to deal with – "second-rate fellows." But these "second-rate fellows" are producing over here now the most wonderful books on wildflowers, fungi, butterflies, birds etc. each with 50 lovely plates selling for 15/- and selling well – all printed in Czechoslovakia. I want to do it too. Murray is conventional and hates the idea. "You go for a second-rate house and your books will be regarded as second-rate," he says. To which I reply "Balls. NO mother who buys children's books has the faintest idea who publishes them. The only first-rate things one wants are distribution, marketing and printing."[125]*

Pat's stroke had forced him to put the problem to the back of his mind. Then, out of the blue, he had a stroke of luck. His daughter Tessa gave a copy of *James and the Giant Peach* to a school friend of hers, Camilla Unwin. She just happened to be the daughter of Rayner Unwin, one of the grandees of English publishing, who – as a ten-year-old – had recommended the manuscript of J. R. R. Tolkien's *The Hobbit* for publication to his own father, Sir Stanley Unwin, the major shareholder in the publishing firm George Allen & Unwin. Rayner Unwin, who lived nearby in the village of Little Missenden, noticed that his daughter seemed particularly gripped by the story she was reading and that the book had not been published in the United Kingdom. A few days later, he called Mike Watkins and asked for official reading copies of both *James* and *Charlie*.[126] After he had received them, he wrote to Dahl asking whether he would be interested in doing a deal. In response, he received "one of Roald's most direct and not entirely flattering letters", pointing out bluntly that no UK publisher had yet been prepared to make a "proper commitment" to the books.[127]

However, Roald had also spoken to Murray Pollinger, who confirmed that though Allen & Unwin had a list that was "largely made up of psychology, sociology, anthropology, all the -ologies really", Unwin himself was "the best Indian in the tribe".[128] The two men met and Roald proposed his deal. Unwin was enthusiastic about Dahl's plan to have the books published in cheap editions, proposing to publish *James* and *Charlie* at the same time and have them printed, not in Czechoslovakia but in another "iron curtain" country, East Germany. Together, the two men drew up an unusual agreement, whereby Dahl would receive nothing until the publishers had recouped all their printing costs, but thereafter he would receive 50 per cent of all receipts.[129] It was a gamble. If the books did badly, Roald would receive nothing. But if they did well, he would get far more per copy than the 10 to 20 per cent most authors normally received.

Roald liked gambling. Despite all the rejections, he believed that his books would be successful. And his faith paid off. Both books were published in the United Kingdom in 1967, and within weeks they had both sold out. They were reprinted and the reprints soon sold out, too. The following year, George Allen & Unwin published *The Magic Finger*, and although sales did not match the earlier two titles, it too soon went into profit. And so it was in an atmosphere of ebullient self-confidence that Dahl began work on a "beginner's book" that would become the most autobiographical of all his children's stories: *Fantastic Mr Fox*.

The tale of a wily and incorrigible fox, who ingeniously leads his starving family and friends out of danger when they are pursued by three evil farmers – Boggis, Bunce and Bean – reads in many respects like an allegory of its author's own recent history. Mr Fox is resilient, resourceful and never defeated by his troubles. So impressive is he that all his wife can do is look deep into his eyes and tell him, just as Pat had done: "'My darling . . . You are a fantastic fox.'"[130] In other respects, too, its central character shared many of his creator's qualities – most notably perhaps his poacher's mentality. In the initial draft of the book, Mr Fox's victory over his adversaries is achieved by a piece of simple theft. He digs his way out of trouble by burrowing a secret tunnel into the local supermarket, where his family can help themselves to whatever food they desire.

> *"From now on we've got it made" said Mr Fox. "Every night we can go shopping on Main Street! We can have anything we want! Isn't it fantastic!" And that is just what they did. They are still doing it today. Every night, Mrs Fox makes out a shopping-list. Every night, they all go shopping on Main Street. They get anything they want. And the store-keepers are still wondering where all the stuff goes. The cops are still looking for the robbers.*[131]

When the manuscript arrived at the publishers, Bob Bernstein, now president and CEO of Random House – the company that had acquired the Knopf imprint in 1960 – faced a dilemma. He and his editors felt the book was weak. "The writing is poor, the fantasy is unbelievable and the plot is badly worked out," was one internal reader's verdict. Also, while Dahl was perfectly prepared to celebrate petty larceny if the caper was sufficiently resourceful and cunning, the editorial staff at Random House were much more nervous. They were concerned that the book's apparent glorification of theft would not "go down well with teachers, librarians and parents."[132] And there was another issue. The draft contained a passage in which Mr Fox compared the conflict between the animals and the farmers to human warfare, which he condemned in terms that almost evoked passages of *Some Time Never*. The fact that US military involvement in Vietnam was escalating and that the book was intended for readers as young as four made some of the staff at Knopf very uneasy.

> *"Boggis and Bunce and Bean are out to kill us. You realise that don't you? They have declared war on us. And in a war there is no such thing as stealing. When one country is fighting another country, as they always seem to be doing up there, does the general say to his soldiers, 'You mustn't steal from the enemy?'" "Of course not," said Badger. "They do worse than steal," said Mr Fox. "They bomb and blast and kill and do everything they possibly can to destroy what the enemy has. But you and I are not going to stoop to that level. We are not going to burn Boggis's Chicken House or Bunce's Store House. We could if we wanted to. But we won't. We wouldn't dream of it . . ."*[133]

Bernstein was uncertain how to address this issue with an author who not only had a reputation for being touchy but whose books were now making the company significant sums of money. Moreover Dahl had shown with *The Magic Finger* that he was quite prepared to take his work to another publisher if he felt rejected. Bernstein was uncomfortable with this unfamiliar role as a children's editor and very aware of the fact that Roald could react badly to adverse editorial comment. So he trod with extreme caution. It took him almost a month to respond to the manuscript and gently articulate his editors' concerns. "Am I being too prissy?" he asked about the stealing issue, adding in reassurance that "if we can't convince you to change, in the end we will do it your way".[134] He had left it just a little too long to reply and his letter crossed with a testy telegram from Roald complaining about his "dispiriting and discourteous" delay in acknowledging receipt of the draft.[135] When Roald got Bernstein's letter, his reply was surprisingly measured, but he did not budge on the issue of theft. "Firstly, foxes live by stealing," he argued, adding that if Beatrix Potter had been worried about this issue, half her stories would never have been published. He told Bernstein that the letter had been a "splash of cold water" – and one that had put him "slightly in the doldrums".[136]

For almost four months, nothing happened. There appeared to be a complete impasse. Then the problematic manuscript found itself on the desk of an enterprising young editor at Random House named Fabio Coen. He seized the nettle. To the first problem, he put forward a compromise: the foxes should continue to steal, but instead of raiding a supermarket, Coen proposed they should pilfer the farmyards of their tormentors instead. "If they steal from the farmers," he explained, "it would also hold something of a moral, namely that you cannot prevent others from securing sustenance without yourself paying a penalty."[137] It was a clever solution, and one that involved only a small amount of rewriting. Roald was delighted and his enthusiasm at a good solution to the stalemate bubbled over. "You have come up with suggestions so good that I feel almost as though I am committing plagiarism in accepting them," he told Coen. "So I won't accept them. I'll grab them with both hands . . . No editor with whom I have dealt has ever before produced such a constructive and acceptable idea. I thank you."[138] As if to reward him, when Coen followed up by raising the issue of the "inappropriate" war references, Roald agreed to modify the contentious paragraph. He also agreed to change the title from *The Fantastic Fox* to *Fantastic Mr Fox*.[139] The book was published in the fall of 1970. Once again – despite gloomy predictions from experts in the juvenile division of Knopf – it quickly became a bestseller.

The 1960s were a period of misfortune and triumph for Dahl, a decade in which he emerged out of relative obscurity and into the limelight. He had overcome two dreadful medical emergencies, and though both wife and son were still neurologically damaged, they were both doing far better than most doctors had thought possible. Tessa was still disturbed and unsettled; but his two youngest children, Ophelia and Lucy, seemed mercifully unharmed. The loss of Olivia was a scar that would never heal, and *Fantastic Mr Fox* was dedicated to her memory, but fortitude and hard work were beginning to blunt at least some of this pain. "The Last Act", published in 1966, is one of Dahl's final adult short stories – a shocking tale about a vengeful gynaecologist that Dahl once described as an attempt to describe "murder by fucking".† Yet its sympathetic central character, Anna Cooper, shared one huge similarity with her creator. She has been devastated by the death of a family member – in this case the husband she adored. Her salvation comes from working in an adoption agency, looking after unhappy children, and it is not hard to see Dahl's own sensibility, which had been transformed after Olivia's death by his work with Italian orphans, animating his description of Anna's fading memories of her husband: "The exact sound of his voice was becoming less easy to recall and even the face itself, unless she glanced at a photograph, was no longer sharply etched in the memory. She still thought about him constantly, but she discovered she could do so now without bursting into tears . . ." It seemed, Dahl added, that all Anna had needed was "a good hard job of work to do, and plenty of problems to solve – other people's problems instead of her own".[140]

Through talent, luck and a dogged refusal to be beaten down, he had also become a rich man. Even Pat acknowledged that she had "supported him for many a year", but that Roald had now begun to make "fabulous money".[141] His cellar was well stocked with good Bordeaux and Burgundy, though he was not so precious as to prevent the fourteen-year-old Tessa from decking it out with silver foil for a party she was giving with her friend, Amanda Conquy. He had built a covered swimming pool in the garden, which was freely used by friends and neighbours alike, for whom the Dahls and Gipsy House had now become something of a lovable and eccentric village institution. That sense of Roald as the head of a sprawling family vividly struck the young Amanda Conquy. She remembered what a big presence he was around her, though she found

---

† "Murder by fucking has been something I have wanted to do for years," Dahl wrote, "but I have not had the guts to try it up to now." *The New Yorker* had rejected *The Last Act* because of its unpleasant material. But Dahl told Watkins: "I won't tone it down. That would simply blunt the knife" – Dahl, Letter to Armitage Watkins, 04/09/65 – WLC Box 26.

it "odd" he was at home so much, when everyone else's father was out at work. "He was completely different," she recalled. "No other fathers drove their children to school and were so actively involved in family life . . . No one else had a father who was around at lunchtime during the week. It was very unconventional behaviour in what was a very conventional society."[142]

Fantastic Mr Fox is a celebration both of family life and of the genius of a prodigious paterfamilias. These were two key factors in Dahl's own psychological makeup and he found solace in creating a fable about a family of foxes whose encounters with disaster bring them ever closer together. The Dahl family, however, despite all Roald's efforts, was starting to crumble, and it was crumbling from the top down. Patricia Neal was no Mrs Fox. She was a complex, demanding and extraordinary woman, but one from whom her husband now preferred to keep his distance. That largely unspoken tension was a problem. Sooner or later something was bound to give. Roald had done much with his life. He had fought back from the brink of death. He had shot down and killed men. Flying in his Hurricane over the Mediterranean, he had aspired to touch the face of God. He had mixed with presidents and movie stars. He had slept with some of the most beautiful women in the world. He had made a career out of writing and kept his family together through a series of terrible personal disasters. But he had never yet fallen in love.

CHAPTER SEVENTEEN

The Gentle Warmth of Love

THERE HAD ALWAYS BEEN a degree of sexual tension in Roald's marriage to Pat and this was exacerbated by her stroke. In 1965, when Pat was pregnant with Lucy, Barry Farrell reported a conversation where Roald joked to her that she was getting "a bit long in the tooth" for him. "When you go into hospital to have the baby, I think I'll go into London and find myself a girl," he told her. "Someone not quite so fossilized."[1] Pat bantered back that he too should watch out. He was now so old he might have a heart attack while philandering. However, these jibes had a serious edge. During his marriage, Roald had not always been entirely faithful, but his affairs had generally been transient, leaving scarcely a ripple behind them. They were like his brief wartime fling with the Canadian cosmetics wizard Elizabeth Arden, nearly forty years his senior, whom he sometimes claimed as his "first older woman". He had called at her salon in New York because he had a problem with acne. The cream he wanted was out of stock and, after some discussion, Arden herself appeared. Commanding one of her assistants to make sure new supplies were delivered at once from the factory, she whisked the dashing young air attaché off for lunch and a visit to the races. "It didn't last long," Nicky Logsdail remembered his uncle telling him, "but it cured my spots."[2]

Other old flames were more enduring. Pamela Berry, the Marchioness of Huntly and daughter of the newspaper magnate Lord Kemsley, was one of these. Roald had first encountered her when both were on their way to Jamaica in 1948 and had stayed at her house near Ocho Rios, which was only three miles from Charles Marsh's Jamaica Inn. He liked her independence, her practicality and her sense of adventure – she later became a skilled aeroplane pilot. Her seven-year-old daughter Lemina remembered Roald as "a lovely man", who spent a lot of time with the children. She recalled how he would often take her into the sea, telling her to hang onto his back while he ventured out into deep water – an experience she found both terrifying and exciting, as she couldn't swim.[3] Pam and Roald saw each other a great deal between 1948 and 1952, when she was often absent from her husband, whom Roald described unflatteringly as "a small mousy ex second hand car dealer".[4] He visited her in Scotland, where her husband had a castle, and together with Charles and Claudia, they travelled around Scandinavia. As a teenager, Nicky Logsdail was taken by his uncle to Lord Kemsley's "enormous stately home" in Wales, where he was persuaded to try out his new tent on the front lawn, while his uncle passed the night more comfortably indoors.[5] Roald and Pam saw each other less frequently after Roald's marriage, by which time he had also become good friends with her sister-in-law, Mary Berry, "a very attractive lady", with whom, Sue Denson recalled, he sometimes played poker in London. "She used to come down on the train when Pat was away too," Denson mused. "She had an eye for Roald."[6]

None of these female friendships seems to have destabilized the Dahl family dynamic. But it appears that in 1966, as early as a year after Pat's stroke, Roald may have already been beginning to contemplate the end of the marriage. Tim Fisher recalled that Roald went to seek reassurance once again from his ex-headmaster, in Trent Rectory. By this time Geoffrey Fisher was almost eighty years old, yet Dahl's relationship with him remained full of paradoxes. The "Boss" represented the kind of establishment he affected to despise when he felt strong, but to which he felt drawn in moments of crisis. Fisher was another father figure – a strong older man who had known Roald since he was a rebellious but vulnerable teenager. "I understood Dahl was in a dilemma," Tim Fisher told me; "that he felt he could not leave [his wife] when she needed so much support."[7] Whatever advice the former archbishop gave him, it seems only to have added to Roald's growing sense of uncertainty about his marriage

– a feeling that was essentially foreign to him and that he found difficult to handle. He was used to being the self-righteous, dominant, decision-making paterfamilias, who criticized others but was himself beyond reproach. On this his daughters all agreed. Their father was profoundly uncomfortable with the role or self-image of "the bad guy". Now, however, he faced a dilemma. He had self-consciously created a legend around the rock of his marriage and the primacy of his family. But this story did not allow for the fact that, now the immediate challenge of Pat's recovery had begun to fade, Roald's own dissatisfaction with the relationship was bubbling up once again. And this discontent was further compounded by Pat's altered state. Family meant everything to him, but increasingly Roald found himself isolated and unhappy at the head of the unit he had fought so hard to preserve.

By the autumn of 1967, the complex cocktail of painkillers that comprised his medication was no longer able to deal with his worsening spinal and sciatic pain. His right arm had begun to pulse painfully, making writing difficult, and now his fingers had gone numb. Wally Saunders, his builder, reinforced his bed, so that his back could be better supported at night. But his condition did not improve. Eventually, his doctor persuaded him that he should have a laminectomy to ease the pain. The surgery on the vertebrae of his spine was performed at the Radcliffe Infirmary in Oxford by the same surgeon who had treated him twenty-one years earlier. But it was problematic in the extreme. His wound became infected and would not stop bleeding – despite "massive blood transfusions and antibiotics".[8] Then the lining of his bowel broke down, and a painful fistula developed in the lower colon. After more than two weeks in hospital it became clear that Dahl would probably need a second operation to deal with the problems created by the first one.

His eighty-two-year-old mother usually managed to come to her son's bedside whenever he was in hospital, but she too was now hospitalized after a series of minor strokes. Pat later wrote that she had tried to take his mother's place by Roald's side, but that he only closed his eyes, determined to "suffer in silence".[9] Sofie Magdalene remained in regular touch by telephone. On the morning of November 17, she called to see how

Roald was feeling. It was the fifth anniversary of Olivia's death. Mother and son chatted briefly. It was to prove their last conversation, for Sofie Magdalene died just a few hours later. Roald was distraught. He had no idea she was so near the end.[10] In a poignant parallel with *Only This* – his wartime story about the psychic intimacy between a mother and her son, who is a bomber pilot – everyone's focus had been on the son's welfare, while it was the mother who was quietly dying. Despite her disabilities, she had supported her children to the end, helping Roald through each of his three crises, and living, like the heroine of his story, with "the deep conscious knowing that there was nothing else to live for except this".[11] Her loss seemed to mark the passing of an age.

Roald was too ill to attend the funeral. Her ashes were eventually taken back to Wales, where they were scattered next to her husband Harald's grave in Radyr churchyard – more than forty-seven years after he died. Her loss was a profound one for Roald. She had remained his model for many of the things he valued most: scepticism, resilience, clearheadedness and an insatiable curiosity, combined with a certain nonconformist practicality and joyous sense of fantasy. Right to the end, he sought out her opinion and consulted her for advice. Her toughness and her lack of sentimentality made him feel strong. His sense of the psychic and mystical came from her, as did the instinctive kindness that lurked beneath the rather forbidding exterior. Above all, she had passed on to him her talent for storytelling. There is little doubt that the Norwegian grandmother in Dahl's 1983 novel *The Witches*, "a wonderful storyteller . . . tremendously old and wrinkled, with a massive wide body . . . smothered in grey lace",[12] is his own literary tribute to her.

But at this point the extent of Roald's illness meant that he could not properly mourn her passing. Barry Farrell felt he was just "too deeply engaged in his own survival" to do anything else. A second operation, to deal with the fistula, took place four days later, on November 21. Farrell visited him in hospital shortly afterwards and found him in a forlorn state, "held in traction by a canvas harness attached to a length of clothesline that ran through a pulley above his head to an eleven pound weight that dangled just by the bedstead". He was desolate. "He had lost much of his weight and his face was like a death mask. The harness made red tracings under his cheeks, squeezing the skin into small grey pouches under each eye." After several days in this condition, Roald returned home, "wearied and drastically subdued".[13] Two weeks later, he told Alfred Knopf that he was still "very fragile" and thought he would remain so for several weeks longer.[14] It was a rude and unwelcome reminder of his own physical vulnerability. Perhaps from that moment onwards, he recognized that he could no longer rely on his own strength to hold his damaged family together.

Pat was never going to provide the help and support he needed. Ten-year-old Tessa, who since her mother's illness felt she had shouldered much of the daily responsibility for looking after her siblings, described her mother as "helpless" and "hard to live with . . . She threw tremendous tantrums, and she was very self-involved. She was still a movie star."[15] The household seemed happier and more relaxed when she was away on a television assignment, a speaking engagement or a lecture tour. In 1969, on their annual holiday to Norway, Roald was again hospitalized – this time with severe nosebleeds after a sinus operation. His nostrils were plugged with wads of lint "the size of frankfurters". And he was in agony. "I'm ready to write a new Beginner Book," he told his publisher Bob Bernstein with bitter humour. "It will be called *Hospital Nightmares*. It will start . . . 'Let me tell you some of the really horrible things that can happen to you when you grow up . . .'"[16] Pat came to see him in the hospital ward and brought him some grapes in an attempt to cheer him up. He threw them out the window. She wrote later that she should have realized then that Roald was already growing tired of her.[17]

Three years later, in 1972, Pat was making a commercial for Maxim's Coffee. A thirty-three-year-old stylist called Felicity "Liccy" Crosland had been hired by the production company to be responsible for her wardrobe. Liccy was, and still is, a striking beauty – her father's Indian blood immediately apparent in her raven hair, olive eyes and Mediterranean complexion. She was also an English Roman Catholic aristocrat, whose mother, Elizabeth Throckmorton, had been a descendant of a lady-in-waiting at the court of Elizabeth I who married Sir Walter Raleigh. Her mother defied family convention by marrying a young doctor – later a brilliant thoracic surgeon – whose family hailed from Mangalore in India. His name was Alphonsus Liguori d'Abreu. Liccy herself had married at the age of twenty-one and given birth to three children before she was twenty-five. But her marriage was an unhappy one, and following a separation, in 1973 she divorced, losing custody of her three "girlies" – Neisha, twelve, Charlotte eleven and Lorina ten. She was now supporting herself by working in film commercials.

Liccy's easy charm, her elegance and her pragmatic gaiety were already widely celebrated in the industry, and her director, Adrian Lyne, had asked her to take special care of his "difficult" star and in particular to help sort out her wardrobe. Liccy drove down to Gipsy House uncertain what to expect. She had little idea who Roald Dahl was – although the first line of the script acknowledged the popular reputation he had already acquired. "My husband is a very demanding man," Pat confesses to the camera, as it zooms in on her preparing coffee in the kitchen. It was eleven o'clock in the morning when she arrived and Pat was already drinking a Bloody Mary. She and Liccy discussed her clothes, and an hour or so later Roald returned for lunch. He had been out with Tessa collecting a new car. As soon as he saw Liccy, he experienced a violent and dramatic *coup de foudre*. No words were uttered and barely a look exchanged. It was the same with Liccy, who immediately found his presence "electric". For the battle-hardened fifty-six-year-old author, it was "love at first sight".[18]

Pat had no idea at all what a fire was burning under her nose. She remembered Liccy as a good-looking and hardworking professional who seldom left her side during the shoot. She responded warmly to the younger woman's humour, warmth and her exceptional eye for decor and clothing, and enjoyed her company. Liccy recalled that, the day before the shoot, she went to Pat's hotel to do a final fitting. Afterwards, Roald helped carry her bags to the elevator. Trying to be polite, she pretended that she had read some of his books and told him she particularly enjoyed one called "Someone You Like". He did not correct her mistake, but asked her instead whether she wanted to join them for dinner that evening. Liccy told him she was too busy to accept. A few weeks later, she got another call from Roald inviting her down to Gipsy House for dinner and asking her whether she would mind giving Francis Bacon a lift as well. Liccy accepted the invitation with alacrity, but was devastated when she had to call and cancel because of unexpected filming commitments. After she returned, she invited Roald and Pat to dinner at her Battersea flat, where the other guests were Hugh Hudson, Ridley Scott, and her father.[19] Over supper, Roald asked Pat's permission to have dinner with Liccy at some point in the future, while Pat was away on location.

Pat would later maintain that Liccy "ingratiated herself" into their affections and that, because "she knew how to please",[20] she was able to steal Roald away. "She wanted him and knew how to get him,"[21] she told me. The truth was that Roald made almost all the running. Liccy had felt a spark shoot between them and been excited by the "twinkle in his eye", but she had no idea what a profound effect she had had on him, until she went filming in Paris with Hugh Hudson a few weeks later. Roald had asked her, apparently quite innocently, whether she would mind picking up an umbrella he had left at the home of his old friend, Annabella Power. Annabella had remained a confidante since he met her during the war, and she and Roald always had fun when they got together in New York, Los Angeles, Paris or London. In Manhattan, he had once sneaked her into Gloria Vanderbilt's house while Vanderbilt was away, and the two of them had behaved "like naughty schoolboys".[22] Over the years, she had watched with a wry smile as women ran to him and were mostly rebuffed. She also listened sympathetically when Roald told her about his marriage problems. Liccy, however, had no idea of any of this past history. She simply thought she was running an errand. So she called Annabella one day after the shoot was over, and arranged to collect the umbrella.

She was walking into a setup, which she almost ruined by bringing along Hugh Hudson, because he was a fan of Annabella's and curious to meet her. In the end, however, she went alone. Inside her apartment, Annabella explained that Roald had written to her about his feelings. "He cannot stop thinking about you," she confided. "He's madly in love with you. He thinks you are the most wonderful person in the world."[23] When I interviewed Liccy, who despite just turning seventy still possesses an energy and joie de vivre that would startle a twenty-year-old, she was at pains to let me know that, at this point, nothing had happened between them. "We hadn't even kissed." When she finally asked about the umbrella, Annabella smiled slyly and replied, "What umbrella?" Back in London, Roald took her out to dinner at the Curzon House Club. Afterwards, in the car, they kissed for the first time and Roald told her he wanted to make love to her. It was the start of a ten-year affair that would culminate in divorce for Pat and marriage for Liccy.

To begin with, Roald and Liccy's relationship was completely clandestine, and both intended that it should stay that way. Roald had no idea where this passion would lead him, while Liccy had only recently emerged from her acrimonious divorce, which would be made absolute in November 1974, and was in no mood to be involved in another marriage breakup. The two of them just wanted the simple pleasure of being together. During school terms, their trysts followed a regular pattern. Roald would choose a good bottle of wine from his cellar, then drive to London, stopping off to pick up two fresh Dover sole at the local fishmongers on the way and some *chlodnik* – an ice-cold, creamy beetroot soup with chunks of lobster – from Stefan, the Polish chef at the Curzon House Club. As he waited for Stefan to prepare the soup, he would have a quick flutter on the blackjack tables. Then he would drive over to Liccy's flat for dinner.

It is almost impossible to underestimate what a transformative effect the relationship had on him. At last he had found a companion who shared his love of antiques, paintings, food and good wine. Liccy was young and beautiful, strong and experienced. She was amusing and intelligent. She was an aristocrat, but a subversive one, who enjoyed breaking rules. She needed no looking after. It even seemed as if destiny had cut her out for him when he discovered she had been born in Llandaff – just a few streets away from the Villa Marie, where he himself had first drawn breath. His love for Liccy affected his personality, too. The man his family often found "undemonstrative and cerebral"[24] began to become tactile and loving in ways that startled them. And his letters to Liccy are suffused with this unexpected tenderness and vulnerability.

> *My Darling, for nearly a year and a half, I have been seeing you fairly often. But with each month and each week that goes by, the desire to see you more and more often grows stronger and stronger. So this week is a rough one. Only fifty minutes away from you, but I cannot come. It has become absolutely necessary that I see you and touch you and talk to you every few days, and I suppose that's what real love is all about. Lovemaking is another department, and of course that is also necessary. But the prime necessity, the first longing, the thing that has become vital and essential is "contact", meeting together in a room, sitting down and talking, allowing the warmth to pass from one to another, the marvellous gentle warmth of love.* R[25]

As Liccy's visits to Gipsy House became more and more frequent, the Dahl children and the Crosland girls got to know each other and become friends. Ophelia warmed to what she saw as the Crosland elegance and sophistication, and struck up a good friendship with Charlotte, who felt that the two of them were "really quite similar . . . in a tomboyish way".[26] Liccy's eldest daughter, Neisha, took great solace from the support that Roald was already giving her in her own ambitions to become an artist. They would pore over art books together and he would lend her paintings. She fondly recalled the many journeys to Gipsy House on Sundays, driving up in Liccy's yellow Mini to eat Pat's delicious roast chicken with cream and tarragon sauce that always seemed to be on the lunch menu. Pat, she remembered, was never anything other than warm and hospitable, "very cosy and natural . . . not at all a Hollywood film star in appearance, but quite bohemian". Charlotte and Lorina however were initially quite frightened by Roald. They found it hard to deal with his need to be judgemental and the fact that he could be so combative in conversation. Nevertheless, the two families quickly bonded. Theo even developed a crush on Charlotte. He would sometimes travel down to London, bringing all three girls presents and taking them out to a musical. Eventually, the visits to Gipsy House became so regular that the Crosland girls began to balk at their frequency. "I sometimes felt like the au pair girl," Neisha told me. "Ophelia and Lucy were a lot younger than us in those days and wanted to play kick the can when sometimes we'd rather be meeting our own friends or just hanging out at home."[27]

In *Working for Love*, Tessa gave Liccy the pseudonym "Grace" and recalled that her mother would return from her outings with her new friend, "bags brimming with lampshades, nighties and newfound knowledge".[28] Soon Liccy began to join Roald and Pat for dinner at the Curzon House Club, Dahl's favourite gambling haunt in Mayfair. The club was situated in "one of the most beautiful Georgian houses in London," and the interior gave Dahl a "thrill" every time he walked in there.[29] Pat was no gambler, but Liccy took to the place like a duck to water. "In Felicity, Roald had found someone who adored the tables as much as he," Pat recalled, adding that "she usually wound up a winner".[30] Liccy's positive energy had a galvanizing effect on the Dahl family, and the younger children in particular warmed to her immediately. "We all loved Liccy," Ophelia told me, recalling that she was like a burst of much-needed "jazzy" brightness into the Dahls' broken world. "She was young and seemed to understand teenagers better than either of my parents – one of her friends drove a double-decker bus. At the time I had no inkling that my father was in love . . . only that he seemed lighter when she was around."[31] Tessa, too, was dazzled. It seemed to her as if Liccy had "resurrected" the family.[32]

Pat was still completely unaware of the affair, while the children continued to believe that Liccy was no more than a wonderful family friend, in whose company their father seemed unusually relaxed and happy. As Pat was often away on speaking engagements, Roald had bought a London flat in Battersea – not far from where Liccy lived – with some of the money invested in the children's trust funds. Tessa and Pat increasingly spent time there. When Pat was away and the kids were at boarding school, Roald felt free to call Liccy from Gipsy House whenever he wanted to speak her. But when Pat was in Great Missenden, he would drive out of the village and call her from a local phone box. He was meticulous in his secrecy.

One person, however, tumbled to what was going on. And that was Tessa. A disturbed and rebellious youngster, she had been unhappy at her aunts' boarding school, Roedean, and moved instead to nearby Downe House in Kent, another all-girls boarding school, which she then "walked out of" when she was just sixteen. It was the end of her formal education. Now, just as her father was beginning his relationship with Liccy, she had returned to live at home. There she felt she could help her father, whose approbation she craved, and be a "buffer" between him and Pat.[33] Unfortunately, her actions had the opposite effect. Roald felt cramped by her desire to please, which came across as neediness, and, as Lucy Dahl once commented, "if there was one thing my father hated, it was to be demanded of. He liked to give, but he didn't like to be demanded of."[34] He withdrew from Tessa, while she became increasingly neurotic. To Maria Tucci, the wife of Roald's new editor Bob Gottlieb, who stayed there as a house guest, Tessa was "clearly wild and cracking up . . . She was crazy, selfish and spoiled . . . She was like a disaster in the making."[35] Yet Roald did little to try and take her in hand. He later admitted to Marian Goodman that he was becoming frightened of her.[36]

Tessa now ascribes much of her maladjustment to her early childhood. Even as a toddler, she felt constantly in the shadow of her elder sister who, she sensed, was blessed with a charm and natural radiance she lacked. Though her cousins assured me that all the Dahl children were treated equally, and though Sue Denson even recalled that Tessa had been Roald's favourite, most others agreed that a special glow surrounded Olivia. Her early death seemed to offer Tessa no chance of ever escaping from this shadow. That situation was compounded when Ophelia was born in 1964, for it appeared that, even as a baby, she had inherited her dead sister's mantle. Her name evoked Olivia's. Her personality developed in a similar way. She had similar interests and mannerisms. It seemed to Tessa that her younger sister was Olivia "reincarnated". She certainly felt that her father behaved as if she was. Once again, it seemed, she had another "favourite" to contend with. Moreover, her father, who had an instinctive mistrust of psychiatrists, decided not to take her to an analyst. Instead, so Tessa maintained, he medicated her with barbiturates.

One night, she heard her father arrive back from London. It was quite late. Earlier in the day he had suggested she take a "wonderful new sleeping pill" that he himself had recently been prescribed. She didn't think it strange, as her father had often offered her pills. She had taken it before she went to bed. But it had little effect on her and she was still awake when he returned. She heard him go to the telephone and make a call to Paris. Curious, she went to the top of the stairs to listen. Soon, she realized her father was calling Liccy. "I heard him on the phone and I heard him saying, 'Madame Crosland s'il vous plait' . . . I think he just presumed he'd drugged me sufficiently not to hear . . . But I heard him have this phenomenally amorous conversation, which was nothing like I'd heard him have with anyone else in my life, certainly not Mum." [37]

She returned to bed. Next morning, she called her aunt, Else Logsdail, and went over to see her. She told her everything she had heard. Else tried to calm her down and advised her that, whatever else she did, she should not tell her father. But Tessa was not about to heed this advice, and the next evening she asked her father bluntly if he was going to get a divorce. When he asked her why, she confronted him with her evidence. Caught in the headlights as it were, he exploded, accusing her of prying into his life, of snooping, of being "a nosy little bitch". "I'm fed up with it. I'm fed up with you," he told her. "Get out of my house, I don't have any energy left for little bitches like you." [38] Tessa was stunned. As she was packing her bags to leave, Roald returned and told her that she could stay, but he wanted her to promise that she would talk to Liccy before she told her mother anything. Tessa agreed.

Two days later, she went up to London, where, after some discussion, Liccy presented her with a difficult choice. As neither Roald nor she wanted to hurt Pat, Tessa could either "devastate" her father by forcing him to break off the relationship or share their secret and let things go on. Tessa, hoping she would earn her father's love and become "more of a part of his life", took the latter option and promised not to tell her mother anything. [39]

Pat herself still had no suspicions. She and Roald went to Tobago together on what she described as "a second honeymoon" in January 1974. [40] There, she remembered, he was "outrageously witty" and "charmed everyone. Including me." She came home for some cosmetic surgery on her face, which was still damaged from the stroke. But soon afterwards, Roald seemed to have become "strangely cold" again.[41] That summer, the family suddenly changed their holiday plans. Roald decided not to go to Norway, but to join Liccy, her girls, and a friend of theirs called Phoebe Berens, in Minorca. Neisha recalled that while the Croslands were staying in a picturesque eccentric house at the end of a jetty, the Dahls – who had booked at the last minute – were forced into an unattractive holiday development near a crowded beach. "It was definitely a holiday designed so Mummy and Roald could be together," she chuckled.[42] Cracks in the facade of Roald's marriage were now beginning to appear. Liccy had confided what was going on to her friend Phoebe, and when Pat "bragged" to her about how happy she was with Roald and what a great sex life they were having, Phoebe's look of disbelief began to make Pat unsure of Roald's fidelity. But she upbraided herself for being "a nasty, suspicious tight-ass".[43] In fact, according to Tessa, her father's sex life with her mother was very far from being healthy. "He would confide in me," she recalled, telling her things about his physical relationship with her mother that were "sordid" and "inappropriate".[44]

As the two families came to be more and more in each other's pockets, it was not just Pat who began to be suspicious. Lucy had a hunch her father was "schtupping" Liccy when they got back from that holiday in Minorca and saw that she was in almost every photograph.[45] Then Liccy had her tonsils out and unexpectedly came to stay at Gipsy House to recuperate. Pat later told Lucy that she had caught Roald leaving their bedroom in the middle of the night. "She opened her eyes and he froze and they just looked at each other. Both acknowledged what was happening," Lucy told me. Then Pat "turned over and went back to sleep". Ophelia noticed bottles of wine from Gipsy House cellar in Liccy's flat, while Neisha wondered why there were so many orchids on the table and so many boxes of Roald's favourite Bendicks Mints in the cupboard. Charlotte found aeroplane tickets and an itinerary for Roald and her mother in the bedside drawer. The intrigue was being stretched to the breaking point.

At the root of these machinations was Roald's attempt to balance his

desire to keep his family together with his obsessive, romantic need for
Liccy. Perhaps he hoped that, with time, his desire for her would ebb.
But it was a love that, far from waning, was becoming ever stronger. They
spoke constantly and when she was away he felt the need to write and tell
her how much he loved her.

> *You may think, my darling, that I have a rather dreamy sort of*
> *absent-minded memory, and up to a point you would be right. But it*
> *is only like that with things that I do not really care very much about.*
> *I am able to remember vividly in an absolute detail anything that is*
> *important to me. And so, you see, when you are away, as you are now,*
> *I'm able to console myself just a little bit by living again and again*
> *through the splendid moments of our last meeting and the wonder-*
> *ful one before that and . . . and lots and lots of others. Great times,*
> *marvellous times. Easily the best times of my own particular life and*
> *how can I possibly thank you enough for that. Only, I think, by loving*
> *you a tremendous amount, which is what I do.*[46]

Liccy herself was in a difficult situation. Though she reciprocated his
feelings entirely, she believed that Roald and she would never be able to
live together because he did not want a divorce to rip his family apart.
Tessa agreed that it took her father many years to contemplate separation,
but her reasoning was more cynical. She believed that it was not so much
to do with distressing her mother or his children as it was with disturbing
his writing routine at Gipsy House.

> *He didn't want to lose his house and his hut and he didn't know*
> *what a divorce settlement would do . . . of course he didn't want to*
> *lose his children, but I think he loved the hut most of all. He never*
> *thought he'd write anywhere else . . . There was an equilibrium there.*
> *He had a routine. Every single day of his life was the same. He got up*
> *at the same time, he took the children to school, he made his thermos*
> *of coffee, he answered his letters, he went up to the hut, he worked to*
> *a certain time, he listened to The World and One, he had his Bloody*

Mary, he had his second Bloody Mary, he had his lunch, he had his nap, he watched the horse racing, he put on his bets, he got up, he took his coffee back to the hut. He was up there till about quarter to six. He'd start sniffing the scotch at six, then he'd either drive up to London or he'd have supper at home, then he'd take the dogs out they'd go out and pee and he'd go to bed. Imagine disrupting that. By the time his affair with Liccy was really strong, he'd been doing that for over twenty years.[47]

The complex knot of deceit inevitably began to unravel. Pat maintains that her own suspicions were finally confirmed in the summer of 1975, when she and Roald had supper with Liccy at the Curzon House Club and she felt as if suddenly she had become Liccy's guest. In the cloakroom after dinner was over, she described Liccy turning and giving her a look. "It said very plainly, you have lost him. He is mine. I was sure then and I am sure of it now. No one can ever tell me I misread what was written in her eyes." Next day, in a Knightsbridge restaurant, Pat asked Tessa directly if her father was having an affair with Liccy. Tessa confessed that they were. Pat went berserk, and when she later confronted Roald, she recalled that, rather than feeling embarrassment, he seemed to experience instead "bizarre delight in my distress".[48]

It is likely Pat simply mistook his sheer relief that the lies were over, but her desire to turn Roald into a monster was understandable. She felt deceived and rejected. Her decision to take out her frustrations on her children was less forgivable. She stormed into eleven-year-old Ophelia's bedroom and blurted out the news that her father had betrayed her. Ophelia burst into tears. Roald got into his car and drove to the phone box to call Liccy, who came up to Gipsy House the following day. In a tense and emotional encounter, Liccy and Roald tried to persuade Pat that she was overreacting. Roald told her that he wanted Liccy's companionship but did not want a divorce. Liccy herself simply observed that they had created a situation where no one could be happy.

Pat believed that infidelity, but not divorce, was tolerated within the Dahl family, and felt a pressure from Roald's siblings to let him continue his affair. She also knew the Dahls had always had an uncharacteristically open attitude to sex. Roald had made his own views quite plain in 1949. "The love of two comparative strangers of the opposite sex for each other is neither straightforward, uncomplicated nor especially constant," he had written then, while making a cogent and thoughtful case for cohabitation before marriage, so that young people could "test their love for each other and check their chances of a successful partnership".[49] His own family's experience also resonated with this philosophy. Back in Bexley before the war, Sofie Magdalene – either through ignorance, exhaustion or lack of interest – presided over a household where sex was far from taboo. Alfhild was the most promiscuous, sleeping openly under her mother's roof with several men – including Alfred Chenhalls and Dennis Pearl – before she finally chose to marry Leslie Hansen. Pearl himself also slept with her younger sister, Else, while Chenhalls, a notorious corridor creeper, attempted repeatedly to seduce both Else and Asta.

Almost thirty years later, this history suddenly acquired a new piquancy when the fifty-three-year-old Dennis, now separated from his first wife, fell in love with Else's eighteen-year-old daughter, Lou. Once he could see that their affections were genuine, Roald was one of the first members of the family to give the couple his support, and in 1972 – just as Roald was beginning his affair with Liccy – Dennis and Lou married. Roald, so Lou felt, was pleased that the relationship "entwined" his old friend back into the Dahl family, but for Pat it only seemed to reinforce their unconventional sexual mores. At first she too had chimed in with this unbuttoned attitude. Once, after dinner with a few guests at Gipsy House, Roald had felt tired and gone to bed early. He left a note on the door: "If you want to fuck, wake me up." Pat went upstairs later, read the note and tried unsuccessfully to wake him. The following night, it was she who went to bed early. She too left a note for everyone to see. It read simply: "If you want to fuck, go fuck yourself!"[50]

Since her stroke, however, she had felt increasingly powerless to deal with this strong centripetal family dynamic. So it was Liccy who broke the deadlock, deciding to take matters into her own hands and break off the relationship with Roald. "Because of my respect and affection for

Dahl and one of the antique mirrors he restored.

Roald Dahl. Publicity photograph for *Way Out*, the US television series he presented in 1961.

Roald, Theo and a young friend laying flowers on the intricate alpine garden Dahl had constructed around Olivia's grave. On the headstone was carved the inscription "She stands before me as a living child."

Roald Dahl, Theo and Ophelia playing in the garden of Gipsy House, 1965.

Roald and Pat working on Pat's recovery. Though Dahl was one of the pioneers of intensive stroke recovery, he mostly left it to others to work with his wife, while he got on with earning money and running the home.

Roald Dahl on the set of the movie *Willy Wonka and the Chocolate Factory* with the actors who played the Oompa Loompas, 1970.

Roald Dahl outside Gipsy House with his pet goat Alma.

The Dahl Family outside Gipsy House in the early 1970s. From left to right, Tessa, Roald, Lucy, Theo, Ophelia, Pat.

Felicity (Liccy) Crosland in the mid-1970s. To Tessa, it seemed she had "resurrected" the family.

Liccy in Minorca during her secret affair with Roald.

The Dahls and Croslands outside Brixton Register Office after Roald's wedding to Liccy. From left to right: Sophie (Tessa's daughter), Lucy, Ophelia, Lorina, Charlotte, Neisha, Theo, Tessa, Liccy, Roald.

Roald and Liccy, c. 1988.

Roald Dahl in
his writing hut.

Roald Dahl with
Theo and kite, 1965.

Dahl with Quentin Blake and an early sketch of the BFG.

Dahl the storyteller reading to a group of enthralled children.

you," she wrote to Pat, "I am getting away from you both. In the clear light of day I realised that there is, at the moment, no happiness for any of us . . . I feel very sad at the unhappiness which I have caused you, and hope that in the fullness of time, life will sort itself out."[51] It was a sensible, generous move, but it did not solve anything. Roald was still miserable. He missed Liccy's company and, in his frustration, railed ever more fiercely against Pat. He told Marjorie Clipstone that his wife was "lazy, stupid, a rotten housekeeper, a rotten mother, a rotten everything and he didn't know why he put up with this rotten marriage".[52] Later in 1975, while Pat was in America shooting *Little House on the Prairie*, he wrote to her more calmly in an attempt to explain his position. He told her that he loved her, that he would never think of leaving her, that he had not seen Liccy while she had been away and would not do so until she returned from shooting. However, he wanted her blessing to see Liccy again:

I shall probably look occasionally for her companionship. It is not sex. You think it is. I promise you it isn't. I am very happy right now without sex of any sort. In that respect I somehow feel utterly tired. I feel whacked out. You don't. But you are a bit younger than me. Also I am a huge fellow physically, and I believe that huge fellows, I mean really huge ones of six foot five or six inches, grow physically tired earlier than others. Certainly I feel pretty tired a lot of the times these days . . . So what I would like to do . . . is go on living with you and having you return this love without feeling the least bit jealous of the fact that, now and again, but not very often, I meet Liccy and have lunch with her . . . All of this is obviously a rotten deal for Liccy, and I sort of hope she won't put up with it for long. There is no future in it for her . . . I have told her long ago that there is no chance of me ever leaving you. She knows it. So there is no future for her with me. For her sake though, as well as for mine, the thing should be allowed to tick over until it comes to a natural end. And the best thing you can do to encourage that ending is to be non-jealous and normal. And, at all times, feel absolutely secure in the knowledge that this family will go on as long as I live.[53]

The affair went into abeyance for two years, but the reality of the broken marriage was there for all involved to see. Ophelia remembered that Liccy was "full of sadness and remorse" and that her father was "empty without her".[54] In 1975, the family went on a joyless holiday to Norway. It would be the last time they were there together. Roald's friends were concerned for him. "He was so miserable in that marriage, and so were the children," remembered Marian Goodman. "Pat would come back after an assignment over here and talk about nothing other than herself and the accolades she had received. I think with Felicity it was the first time he was in love".[55] Dennis Pearl knew that at that point, his friend was so in love that "nothing would have persuaded Roald to give up Felicity".[56] Yet the deadlock continued, and his frustrations made him even more cantankerous and argumentative. Tessa, stressed by the tension at home, embarked on a series of affairs herself, mostly with older men, including the fifty-year-old Peter Sellers. Roald bought her a house in Wandsworth, so she could have her own space. By the age of nineteen she was living with another actor, Julian Holloway. And by the age of twenty she was the mother of their baby, Sophie.

Roald was thrilled to have his first grandchild, but Tessa's rackety lifestyle irritated him. In 1980, he wrote to his youngest daughter Lucy, then fifteen, complaining that Tessa had let her small garden go to seed. "Yesterday Wally and I loaded up our Renault with the motor mower (whizzer), spades, forks, rakes, brooms, and drove to five Rose Hill Road. There we worked for four hours tidying up the mess in Tessa's garden. We trimmed the edges of the beds, cut back the shrubs and trees, mowed the grass both back and front and made the place look respectable. Why on earth Tessa and Maureen [Tessa's nanny] can't do it, I don't know? It's really silly to let a garden go to pot, especially a small one. It's so easy to keep nice. There were dog turds everywhere. She *must* shovel those up every day."[57] Tessa's godmother Marian Goodman believed Roald had been too indulgent toward her. She thought he should have stood up to her and made her go back to school after she walked out, rather than letting her drift into modelling and acting. When Marian articulated these criticisms to Roald, she was shocked when he admitted to her that he was "afraid of alienating his kids" and "afraid Tess would hate him for the rest of her life".[58]

Throughout the late 1970s, Roald sought solace in the company of his two younger children, Ophelia and Lucy, who seemed mercifully unscarred by the family disasters. Even today, the two sisters, neither of whom was old enough to remember their mother before she had her stroke, talk about themselves as having quite a different sense of family to Tessa and Theo. Lucy described the situation as if there were "two portions" of the family's life. "There was a tragic era . . . and there was my era, which was calm and lovely."[59] With them, Roald escaped from his own anxieties into a world of youthful innocence and fantasy. He amused himself by playing games with them and telling them stories. The Big Friendly Giant, who lived in the orchard, had legs as long as aeroplane wings and blew happy dreams into their bedroom window through a long pipe, quickly became a favourite. When the two girls were almost asleep one evening, Roald climbed up a ladder and pretended he was the giant, inserting a bamboo cane through the curtains and making a deep guttural *whooshing* sound. Neither Lucy nor Ophelia were fooled by his antics, but both also felt they did not want to disappoint him by telling him so the next morning. They sensed that he too needed "happy dreams" and that these games were possibly more important to their father than they were to them. "He seemed to me, even then," reflected Ophelia, "to have a vulnerable core. So I said nothing."[60] This giant, though later to feature as the main character in *The BFG*, made his first appearance in 1975 in *Danny the Champion of the World*.

Danny, as the original story was called, is perhaps Dahl's most straightforward and lyrical children's book – a touching tale of the relationship between a nine-year-old boy and his single-parent father, which harks back to Roald's beloved gypsy ideals. Danny's father is a benign version of the car dealer Gordon Hawes from *Fifty Thousand Frogskins*. He keeps the same filling station, repairs the same motors, and lives in the same gypsy caravan. Only this time the character is no swindler, but the boy's best friend. Usually Dahl preferred his child protagonists to have more unusual friends – an eccentric giant, a quirky owner of a chocolate factory, a gang of gigantic insects, a schoolteacher, or a pipe-smoking grandmother perhaps – but Danny's father is a thinly disguised portrait of how Roald saw himself. He flies kites, he poaches pheasants with raisins and sleeping pills, he invents fire-balloons that fly high up into the night sky and he smiles with his eyes. He is untrammelled by normal codes and conventions and prepared to break a law if it seems unjust or absurd. Roald had taught ten-year-old Ophelia to drive an ancient Morris Minor around the Gipsy House orchard and scarcely batted an eye when he discovered that, a year later, she was secretly driving it around the lanes of Buckinghamshire to visit her friends. Danny's father too tolerates his son driving his clients' cars while they are being repaired at the garage – although only in an emergency. Like Roald, he was "sparky" rather than "stodgy", nor was he "what you would call an educated man". But, Danny tells his readers, instead he was "a marvellous storyteller".[61]

It is not hard to imagine Roald taking refuge from the strains and stresses of his family life in this idealized world of heroes, villains, and nocturnal adventures in the woods. But hidden within *Danny* – which was optimistically dedicated to "the whole family" – is a kind of apologia to his own younger children, Ophelia and Lucy, about the impending breakup of his marriage. The parallels are all too clear. Danny's mother dies when he is four months old, leaving his father to raise him alone. He washes his son, feeds him and changes his nappies – "not an easy task for a man", he adds, "especially when he has to earn his living at the same time." Danny knows his father adores him and would do anything for him. Yet he also knows that there are things about his father he cannot understand. He has secrets, needs, "powerful yearnings" that cause him to abandon his sleeping son and go off into the woods in the middle of the night – yearnings that a child cannot appreciate. Danny learns during the tale that his father is not perfect. "Grown-ups are complicated creatures, full of quirks and secrets," he concludes. "Some have quirkier quirks and deeper secrets than others, but all of them, including one's own parents, have two or three private habits hidden in their sleeves that would probably make you gasp if you knew about them."[62] Danny's father's secret was the lure of the woods at nighttime and the love of poaching –

something he eventually felt able to share with his son. Roald's yearnings were more complex and troubling, and they would be infinitely more painful to explain.

Sexual anxiety, dysfunction and frustration haunt his last collection of adult short stories, *Switch Bitch*. In an interview with the British writer and journalist Justin Wintle recorded in 1974, the same year the book was published, Roald observed – apparently with some puzzlement – that his writing was now "absorbed with sex". It was a theme, he commented, "which didn't appear at all in the early stories".[63] It was true that it had played no part in the early flying tales, but – as Noël Coward had observed – since the publication of *Someone Like You* in the early 1950s, sex had figured prominently in Dahl's fiction. Mostly this had been in the context of comedy with men portrayed as self-obsessed dupes – hapless victims of cunning, manipulative female predators. Dahl's satirical eye was Swiftian in its observation of the humorous grotesquerie of sex. He wrote to Charles Marsh that in *Kiss Kiss*, he had tried "to show up all women for the brutal lascivious creatures that they really are. The poor man is really nothing but a little body of skin and bones growing inconspicuously out of the base of an enormous prick which he can't even call his own."[64] Only one thing prevented most men from perceiving this, he thought: their own self-importance. In one of his introductions to his 1961 television series *Way Out*, Dahl compared men to frogs, always "blowing out their dewlaps" to attract a mate. "Along comes the female, *hoppity hop-hop* . . . but the male frog is such a *colossal egotist* that he quickly forgets about the female."[65] In another, he introduced his audience to a female spider – "a half-blind savage carnivore who will eat *any* insect she can get hold of *including* the male of the species".[66] The four tales of *Switch Bitch*, however, were of a different order to these comic parables. Though two are ostensibly comedies and feature one of his favourite creations, the buccaneering sexual athlete Uncle Oswald, the others are infused with a bitter tang that mirrored his own personal frustrations and tensions.

With the exception of the sardonic *Two Fables* published for his seventieth birthday, *Switch Bitch* was the last of Dahl's adult story collections. He mourned the end of that part of his career and shared his sense of loss with his great champion, Alfred Knopf. Despite their occasional disagreements, Roald retained a deep personal affection for Knopf, a man whom he believed to be "the best publisher in the world", and whose "personal comradeship" he claimed had meant more to him than that of anyone else in publishing.[67] Knopf certainly returned the compliment. He held his author in great regard. His personal enthusiasm for Roald's short stories had led directly to the publication of *Someone Like You*, and he soon became something of a confessor figure. Roald had confided to him, for example, in 1963, that he felt there was only "a bit of sediment"[68] left at the bottom of his short stories bottle and that he doubted he could prepare another collection in the next two years. Knopf continued to encourage him, praising Roald's "sophistication and intelligence" and urging him not to compromise his "tremendously high standard".[69]

Three years later, despite Pat's stroke, Roald promised his publisher again that he would "come back" with another volume of stories.[70] Knopf, who by then had just abandoned editorial control of his own imprint, responded that he hoped he would live long enough to see it.[71] He did. Yet Roald's belief in himself as a short story writer was failing rapidly, and he no longer had the confidence "to start a story with just the bare bones of a beginning of a plot without knowing the end".[72] Fortunately for him, just as his faith in his talents as an adult writer was waning, his belief in himself as a children's writer began to burgeon.

Shortly after he had finished *Danny the Champion of the World*, Roald wrote Alfred Knopf a letter in which he articulated the joy he got from writing for children. Like a great tree that had taken years to bloom, he was starting to revel in his late-flowering blossom:

> *I'm feeling a bit old myself – now in my sixtieth year. And I can tell you this: that it gets harder and harder to generate the momentum that is necessary for making a new book or a story. I finished the last children's book nine months ago and I've been gardening ever since. But I can also tell you something else: I do not believe that any writer of adult books, however successful or celebrated he may be, has ever gotten one half the pleasure I have got from my children's books. The*

readers are so incredibly responsive and enthusiastic and excited, it's a
real joy to know that this is one's own doing.[73]

That satisfaction was to grow year by year, throughout the remaining
fifteen years of his life. Yet the lingering desire to write adult fiction never
entirely went away. The late 1970s saw him contemplating a comic novel
for adults, based on the Uncle Oswald character, and working on a collection of short stories designed for older children, which would eventually
be published under the title of *The Wonderful Story of Henry Sugar and Six
More*. The last and longest of these concerned a wealthy playboy, Henry
Sugar, who – like the Indian mystic Kuda Bux, whom Dahl had seen and
written about in 1948 – had trained himself to see through playing cards
and consequently make millions at the gaming tables. All of these stories
were suffused with a warmth and emotional empathy that was reminiscent of some of his earliest writing. Henry Sugar, for example, ends
up travelling round the world in a host of disguises with his friend Max
Engelman, "the very best make-up man in the business", making enough
money from defrauding casinos to fund orphanages all over the planet.
Sugar was like Charles Marsh in that he was a man who had shown himself adept at making money, but also felt an "acute revulsion" toward it.[74]
He was also like his creator in that he knew that money could not buy
love.

Roald was still desperately in love with Liccy, but opportunities to
see her during this period of separation were few and far between. All
through 1976, he communicated furtively with her, using the same
public telephone box about ten minutes' drive from Gipsy House. Their
unwanted estrangement only made his feelings for her stronger and more
intense, and when he was deprived of those phone conversations, he became as melancholy as a teenager.

My darling –

The drive to Chesham and back this morning was bleak. There
was no phone call to look forward to. As I passed the little red tele-
phone box on the return journey I very nearly stopped. I wanted to go

*in and dial 01 720 6313 to make the bell jangle all around your flat
and tell your ghost that I was still here and longing for you.*

*That phone box is well-known to me now. When I stand inside
it I can see out over the hedge into a small garden where someone is
growing vegetables with intense pride and care. Two months ago, he
dug it. Then he began to plant it. I have watched his two rows of
potatoes poking up through the soil, and one row of onion seedlings
and one of lettuce and one of shallots and a very fine show of early
radishes. Every time I go in, I can see a change from the day before.
But I've never seen the owner.*

*Are you lying in the sun and browning those long lovely legs of
yours? I am sitting in my orchard hut drinking coffee from my
thermos and telling myself I must start the third short story for
children. This one will be about a boy who discovered he could make
objects across the room move ever so slightly by staring at them. And
last night I dreamed of a marvellous chicken that grew beautiful flowers on itself instead of feathers.*

I rather like that. I rather like you too.

I more than rather like you.

*I love you
R* [75]

The three love letters that Liccy allowed me to see bespeak the tender
intensity of Roald's love for her. This was immediately apparent to almost
all who saw them together. It struck me instantly that first day I met
them in 1985. At that moment I was quite unaware of the complicated
back story, but the power of their relationship was instantly perceptible.
As I got to know them better, I understood that apart from being proud
of both her beauty and her background – he would often embarrass
Liccy by talking about her aristocratic lineage – Roald relished simply
being near her. Though he could still be a dominant and towering force
in Gipsy House – his friend Leonard Figg described him, with a smile,
as "imperious" – Liccy was his match. She radiated physical energy and

strength. She was someone on whom he could rely completely. This was increasingly important to him as he began to come to terms with the fact that he could no longer do everything on his own. As early as 1953, Claudia Marsh had written to Roald's mother from Jamaica to tell her that, because of his injuries, she thought her son needed more rest than other people: "He simply cannot do as much as he wants to and thinks he can."[76] Rest, however, was something that had been in short supply for Roald since then. Yet few were aware of the toll his responsibilities had taken on him, because he hid it so well.

In the early 1970s, his new editor at Knopf, Bob Gottlieb, and his wife, Maria Tucci, came for dinner at Gipsy House and were struck by the easy confidence with which Roald ran everything: supervising the food, leading the conversation, radiating energy all round. At the end of the meal, Tucci recalled him going upstairs for a moment to check that Ophelia and Lucy were both asleep in bed. As he returned, she watched him from the kitchen. He was quite unaware that he was being observed. She was shocked to see the transformation that had taken place. Gone was the mask of the incandescent entertainer; instead, "his whole face had sagged with exhaustion". But the moment Roald saw her, he instantly "pulled himself together" and the two of them had an animated conversation about Russian painters. It was quite clear to Tucci that "everything that looked so perfect was in fact breaking apart", and that Roald himself was in danger of becoming "a truly tragic figure" – a writer who wanted "to control everything in his own life", but was gradually becoming a victim of circumstances and events that were beyond his control.[77]

His ability to disguise his tiredness and ill health was waning. A hip replacement in March 1977 reminded him once again how vulnerable he was and just how little Pat was able or wished to look after him. His old school friend from St Peter's, Douglas Highton, wanted to visit him in hospital in the London Clinic and phoned Gipsy House to ask when would be a good time. Pat, he recalled, was "very offhand, very cold".[78] He was shocked at her lack of warmth, and was touched by the fact that Roald had brought orchids with him into the hospital to keep his spirits up. One particularly grim day Roald called Liccy and told her he simply had to see her. She came over immediately. From then on, they would often meet illicitly if he went away on business trips, Liccy using the name Fiona Curzon when she checked into his hotel. It was the one thing that made him look forward to travel. In almost every other respect, he was now reluctant to leave Great Missenden.

Roald loved Gipsy House and he loved his routine. He loved his hut, he loved listening to music, he loved his games of snooker on Saturday evening, and he loved his orchid house, which also contained a huge cactus that he had inherited from his mother and that periodically required the roof to be raised in order to accommodate it. He was near to his sisters. Olivia's grave was close to hand. His memories of that countryside now went back over thirty years. He had taken full root in the Chiltern soil and become, as Tessa described him, "completely a creature of habit".[79] Though living in London, Tessa was still a frequent visitor. Theo was almost permanently in residence. Like most of his siblings, he had found school disagreeable and ended up with a private tutor, which he infinitely preferred. His injuries limited the speed at which his mind moved, but in almost all other respects he led a relatively normal life. He drove himself to work nearby, and was always at the door to greet guests when they arrived. He, too, liked the regularity of life at Gipsy House. Neisha remembered him as being "adorable, like a puppy", "very programmed" and "very constant in mood – a bit like an old man" whenever they came to visit. He followed her younger sister, Charlotte, around "like a shadow" and was usually in charge of the ice bucket when it came to pre-dinner drinks. He always put on a tie and lots of aftershave before dinner. He was "impeccable". Neisha imagined that he probably changed for dinner even if he and Roald were there on their own. Lucy and Ophelia, however, were quite the opposite and still true to Roald's bohemian ideals. They were "wild", Neisha recalled. "No shoes and socks and a bit snotty and a bit dirty."[80]

In 1978, Pat was featured on the television show *This Is Your Life*, in which well-known personalities unexpectedly reencounter their pasts. Various Hollywood and theatrical stars joined Pat's schoolteachers, her friends and family in paying tribute to her career and to her extraordinary recovery. Roald sat through the whole self-congratulatory jamboree with a studiedly grumpy expression on his face. At the end of it, Pat affectionately reached for his hand. He pointedly withdrew it and put it back in his pocket.[81] She was mortified. But for Roald the celebration simply reminded him what a charade his public existence had become. He missed Liccy terribly and felt daily deprived of his greatest pleasure, her company. He ached for her physically and yearned for her conversation. Above all, he missed the "gentle warmth" of the love that he had discovered so late in life and that had been taken away from him so swiftly. Almost constant pain from his back exacerbated this sense of injustice and brought out the quarrelsome, cantankerous side of his nature. It was a dark period. Even Ophelia began to notice that her father's "lightness" had disappeared.[82] Weekends home from school seemed to drag, she remembered. When Pat's mother wrote to complain that she had been excluded from staying at Gipsy House during the preparations for *This Is Your Life*, Roald dictated a scathing letter telling Eura Neal neither he nor Pat ever wanted to see her again. Pat felt as if "a lifetime of antagonism between them had burst like a ripe boil".[83]

That year Roald went into hospital again for yet another operation on his spine. Far from being fearful of the procedure, he seemed eager for the escape it offered from his domestic environment. "I haven't minded it here at all," he told Ophelia. "I've never had such a peaceful rest since I was a baby in a pram. I've just been lying down and reading and watching a bit of telly – and very few visitors. Lovely. Next week I'm sure I'll be able to go home and that won't be nearly so peaceful."[84] Interviewed on the long-running BBC Radio series *Desert Island Discs* in 1979, he confessed that he longed for isolation. Asked whether he would mind being alone on a desert island, he replied: "I hate to say it, but I would love it."[85]

His secret meetings with Liccy were soon discovered. It was Ophelia who called him on the phone in his hotel room in 1978 when he was supposedly up in Glasgow having a meeting with a potential illustrator and immediately recognized Liccy's voice at the other end of the line.

Ophelia pretended she hadn't done so but she understood immediately what was going on. Her emotions were conflicted. She felt disappointment that the double-dealing was beginning again but also relief that Liccy might be returning to her father's life. Soon she would also come to understand that it was not just the prospect of pleasure that had brought him to Scotland. He was running an errand of mercy.

While en route to Scotland, the vehicle in which Liccy's daughter Charlotte was travelling as a passenger had spun off the road. She was thrown out of the window and subsequently rushed to hospital in a coma, where she was diagnosed with a severely fractured skull. Liccy had called Roald for help almost as soon as she arrived at the hospital and he responded immediately, flying to Scotland to be with her, and offering advice and support with medical treatment. As Charlotte emerged from her coma, she recalled seeing Roald – "this tall, long, lanky man" – leaning over the sink in her room. He too had recently been in surgery. He was asking her boyfriend, who was a medical student, to change the dressing on a wound on his back. "It was all very secret that he was up there," Charlotte added. "But he helped my mother an awful lot." [86] When Charlotte returned to London to convalesce, Ophelia called Neisha and arranged to have lunch with her. "We were huddled up in this Arcade near Sloane Street," Neisha recalled. "I remember how really tight we were . . . and [Ophelia] looked at me and she said: 'Your mum's having an affair with my dad. And this watch, that's not my dad, that's your mum buying it, isn't it?'" For Neisha it was the first time she had been certain of her mother's relationship with Roald, and the deceit of it pained her, yet even then she could see that it was "the biggest love story ever". [87] Charlotte agreed. "I felt hurt," she told me, "but I don't know another couple who were ever so much in love." [88]

Ophelia's vexation too soon subsided. Before long, she was going over to Liccy's flat to pick out the shards of glass that continued to emerge from Charlotte's scalp for many weeks after the accident. "I understood that going to visit Liccy was traitorous," she would write later. "But the truth was I adored her. I was thrilled at the prospect of seeing her again." After a few hours, Liccy would often usher her out, telling her that Charlotte was tired and needed to rest. Sometimes Ophelia would lurk behind and see her father's dark blue BMW pull up outside the flat a few minutes after she had departed. She found it strangely reassuring.

From her flat nearby, Pat became suspicious that the affair had restarted and tried to enlist her younger children as spies. But Ophelia and Lucy were torn between loyalty to their mother and their awareness of just how miserable their father was without Liccy. They remembered how his weariness evaporated when she was around, how she could transform his mood, making him more affectionate, more loving. They could also see that he needed someone to look after him. For his part, Roald could not bear the fact that Liccy was often away filming: he encouraged her to give up this "ruthless, horrible, druggy world" and train as a gilder, so that she could see him more often. She did not take long to heed his advice. Eventually, after taking a crafts course at City and Guilds, she started her own company, Carvers and Gilders, in partnership with three other craftspeople. Explaining the breakup to Sonia Austrian, Roald once admitted, perhaps disingenuously, that all he wanted was someone to make him a cup of tea.[89] Sonia, who was often inclined to take Pat's part against Roald, admitted that she could see why he felt that way, and even Pat would acknowledge that when Roald started to become frail, she was in no position to look after him. It was no surprise that a part of Ophelia longed for Liccy to come and save her "crumbling family".

> *My mother had been abandoned and it felt like we were drowning. It wasn't her fault. She too had loved gardening and antiques but their marriage was sour, old and she had started to resent his talents and his love of solitude. She could do very little on her own and he was still looking after her as he was growing old. He was tired and she was angry with him. She couldn't forgive him for loving Liccy and for lying and now she felt discarded by her husband and her children. It was a terrible conundrum to be in as an adolescent. We tried to make it up to Mom but she saw us all as traitors. How could we love the woman who had betrayed her?*[90]

In 1979, Pat sought sanctuary in the Abbey of Regina Laudis, a Benedictine monastery in Bethlehem, Connecticut, whose abbess, Dolores

Hart, a former movie actress, was reputed to have given Elvis Presley his first screen kiss. It was "an unpretentious place in the New England countryside . . . almost hidden in a valley of pine and maple and surrounded by flowers". Gary Cooper's daughter, Maria, had recommended it. Pat spent three days there quietly trying to come to terms with her failing marriage. The same summer she visited Martha's Vineyard for the first time – with Lucy and Ophelia – staying with Millie Dunnock and her husband. There, she "fell in love" with the island.[91] Theo eventually joined them and they all went to holiday in California, but without Roald, who stayed behind in England.

In 1980, Pat bought a house on the Vineyard at Edgartown, just across from Chappaquiddick. It had once been owned by the whaling captain on whom Herman Melville had reputedly based Captain Ahab. Roald visited it briefly the following summer, commenting wearily to the *Boston Globe* on his way back that "people get tired of being with each other for years – day in, day out. They need some time away from each other."[92] When he got home, he wrote Pat a letter that speaks volumes as to how exhausted he had become.

Darling Pat,

I arrived here this morning feeling as though I had been boiled in a saucepan for days like a dirty handkerchief. I had spent most of the journey over thinking hard about how much I suddenly hate travelling and rushing round at airports and how much I love just sitting in Gipsy House.

I can no longer take the heat. I seem to sweat in it all the time. The actual physical effort of moving my rotten old body around in it is far, far greater than people realize. And it is so painful.

I am not old. Sixty-fiveish is not all that ancient by modern standards and lots of people at that age are bouncing around all over the place. But the combination of two steel hips, no calf muscles (from the spine injury) and six spine operations, has, I honestly believe, added at best, ten years to my age from a physical standpoint. Probably more.

I do try not to display pain openly, but I am never out of it unless I am sitting or lying down, and then only half the time. On this trip I was never out of pain. I take three or four drinks and begin to feel fairly normal under the anaesthetic and then I can do my stuff joking about socially. But that is not the way I want to go on.

I long to sit quietly in Gipsy House which I adore, writing my books and stories which I adore more and playing snooker a couple of times a week which I also adore, and popping up to London twice a week to play blackjack for which I have a passion. Those things are what I like doing in my retarded physical condition. I really do feel that my travelling days are virtually over. I don't mind a couple of hours at a time in my car, puttering around the wine districts of France in cool weather. But that's about the limit.

The Vineyard is not my cup of tea. I would be totally dishonest if I said it was. Neither the heat, nor the crowds, nor my inability to do my work make it congenial. Already (it is now 6 PM and I have been back here ten hours) I am beginning to feel a sense of contentment creeping over me. I am "at home". Tomorrow I can settle down to writing seven days a week. On Wednesday we will play snooker. And the weather is cool, my back is aching less.

I must tell you that during that nightmare rush around Boston Airport when we arrived in a mini plane from the Vineyard with lots of baggage and were trying to get a ticket for Theo (with no porters and no trolleys) I came very close to simply throwing myself out of the large airport window, right through the glass. The urge was enormous, as the back pain was like a red hot knife.

So there we are. The burden of my song is that everybody please excuse me from travelling far distances anymore. I'm not up to it and it's time I said so.

I love everyone in the family, especially you, but just let the old boy vegetate in his own surroundings.

Love
Roald[93]

Though Pat was well aware of the problems and later admitted that the "only time Roald and I were really close was in a time of crisis", she too had not fully faced up to the fact that her marriage might be nearing its end.[94] Increasingly, she was away from home. Roald described her "swashbuckling around America giving lectures (at $4000 each!) to the blue-rinse section of Alaska, Texas, Michigan etc . . . I can think of no worse way to earn a living," he told Dirk Bogarde, "but she's hooked on it."[95] Now, when the two of them were together, the atmosphere was often poisonous. Christmas 1980 was particularly bad. Ophelia found it "unbearably tense",[96] while for Pat it was "depressing" and "grotesque". Roald was colder than ever and her own children seemed particularly distant. The grim holiday celebrations culminated one evening in the revelation that Roald was seeing Liccy again. Pat was "frantic".[97] It was clear to her now that she had to get away. She phoned Sonia Austrian in New York, who invited her to come and stay until she had decided what to do.

That night, Pat remembers, she whispered in Roald's ear as he was sleeping that she wished he were dead. The next day at the airport the whole family came to see her off. As she went through the gate, she looked back over her shoulder and saw Roald roaring with laughter. It was "the most horrendous sight of my life", she wrote. "He looked like Satan. I did not turn back again."[98] Ophelia however felt that her mother's description was probably coloured by her own mood and recalled instead how "distressed" and "unhappy" her father had been.

Eventually, after a year of bitter soul-searching, Pat found some sort of comfort in the monastery in Bethlehem and, encouraged by Tessa and her new husband, James Kelly, she agreed to file for divorce. She felt hatred toward Roald, bitterness toward Liccy, and desperation at the thought that her marriage was about to end. The stroke had "robbed her of her past". Now her anchor in the present was being removed. She was scared she would end up a "fucking bag lady". Acknowledging that there had never been "any real affection . . . no real love" in their relationship, she admitted that what hurt her most was the fact that Roald had been disloyal.[99] In 1982, she told one journalist: "The fact that I am about to have a divorce is really hideous for me . . . I'm not sure what's going to happen."[100]

She bought an apartment in New York on the Upper East Side overlooking the East River. In early July 1983, in a London court, almost thirty years after they were married, Patricia Neal and Roald Dahl were granted a divorce based on uncontested and unspecified complaints about Roald's behaviour. Neither was present. Pat still maintains she was "screwed" [101] financially in the divorce settlement, but that this was her lawyer's fault more than it was Roald's, who later more than made it up to her. That Christmas, she returned to Gipsy House and took what belongings she wanted. About to take a picture that Olivia had painted, she hesitated, remembering how griefstricken Roald had been at her death. She decided to leave it for him. [102]

CHAPTER EIGHTEEN

Explosions Are Exciting

THOUGH HAPPIER WITH LICCY than he had been for many, many years, Roald nevertheless maintained a justified reputation in the final years of his life as an outspoken, immoderate and hot-tempered troublemaker. Before I met him for the first time in 1985, I was warned that he might be cantankerous. "Impossible" was I think the word my boss, Nigel Williams, used. I did indeed sense danger occasionally when things were not going quite right during the shooting of our programme, but throughout both filming and editing, I was struck primarily by his humorous good temper. But there was always a sense that this approval was conditional; that if one put a foot wrong, things might change for the worse. When invited for dinner, every guest had to expect personal questions about sex, religion, money or politics; nothing was taboo. Almost any opinion could be aired at the table. In the end, however, Roald liked to have the last word. As Pat Neal would put it: "Success did not mellow my husband. Quite the contrary, it only enforced his conviction that although life was a two-lane street, he had the right of way." [1]

He was well aware of his own irascibility, complaining – albeit with wit – about the annoying trivia of daily life and occasionally venting his spleen about more serious issues that seemed to him to be unjust, usually without any thought of the consequences of his outbursts. "My faults and foibles are legion," he had written as early as 1972. "I become easily bored in the company of adults. I drink too much whisky and wine in the evenings. I eat far too much chocolate. I smoke too many cigarettes.

I am bad-tempered when my back is hurting. I do not always clean my finger-nails. I no longer tell my children long stories at bedtime. I bet on horses and lose money that way. I dislike Mother's Day and Father's Day and all the other Days and all the cards that people buy and send out. I hate my own birthday. I am going bald."[2] Over the next thirteen years he grumbled to *The Times* that schools no longer gave children homework; he questioned the efficiency of the X-ray machines at airports that did not detect his two steel hips; he argued that television companies rather than the athletes should boycott the 1980 Moscow Olympics, and criticized the verbosity and stylistic longwindedness of "the President and 23 distinguished members of The Writer's Guild".[3] And he sounded off in public about subjects that were rather more controversial – police brutality, the fatwa on Salman Rushdie, and the 1982 Lebanon War. In these contexts, he did not hesitate to air viewpoints that offended and sometimes alienated people. Propriety, diplomacy and sensitivity had no part in this discourse, nor did he appear to consider how damaging or hurtful to others his need to be provocative might appear. Everyone – even in his family – knew that his emotional fuse could be a short one and that, in the wrong mood, he could be pigheaded and wounding. His son Theo put it like this: "Dad had a good temper and he had a bad temper. He would tell you if he didn't like something – just flat out. He had his feelings about everybody, opinions. It was either yes or no. You didn't want to get on the wrong side of him. He liked breaking the rules, but he always liked to be right. He was a very self-opinionated man."[4]

Liccy ascribed this moodiness and irascibility largely to his ill-health and, in particular, to the chronic back pain that dominated much of his daily life. But there was something more fundamental as well. Most people who knew him were struck at some point by what Sheila St Lawrence described as Roald's "overpowering personality", and his "need to dominate".[5] When directed at those not strong enough to take it, however, this belligerent unconventionality could sometimes produce distressing consequences. His niece Lou Logsdail, for example, was once so angered by her uncle's insensitive remarks about her father that she had to leave the dinner table, while Lesley

O'Malley, who thought Roald was "more difficult with men than with women", once fell victim to his love of subversion in a more playful way. Ophelia recalled her father "jazzing up" a dinner party when O'Malley foolishly declared she could always tell the difference between butter and margarine. Challenging her to a blind tasting, Roald disappeared into the kitchen, returning with two pieces of bread – "I've put butter on one and margarine on the other," he told her. "Go on, tell us which is which?" O'Malley tasted both repeatedly and was eventually forced to admit that she was completely flummoxed. Roald then confessed mischievously that he had in fact put butter on both pieces of bread.[6] Pam Lowndes described him to me as a guest who could be "rude . . . aggressive and abusive", but reflected that he more than compensated for these faults with his refreshing lack of convention and engagingly "warped" sense of humour. "He didn't temper anything . . . and he hadn't any patience with people who couldn't stand up to him," she recalled, concluding fondly: "Gosh, he was an amusing man."[7]

Callie Ash, the Dahl's South African cook and housekeeper in the mid 1980s, also tasted these extremes of behaviour. On her first evening at Gipsy House, Roald – who had picked her up a few hours earlier from the station and carried her immensely heavy bags to the car – attacked her for being a privileged and exploitative white settler. Callie felt she was given no opportunity to point out to him that she had a very liberal family background. A few months later when her mother came to visit and brought with her two bottles of fine South African wine as a gift, Roald ostentatiously declared that they were piss, and poured them down the sink without tasting them. Yet, conversely, Callie soon found herself part of the Dahl pack, and felt treated by Roald "almost like a daughter". When she was trying to gain British citizenship two years later, and needed to show the authorities that she had £150,000 of funds available, Roald calmly wrote her out a cheque for that amount and put it into her bank account, leaving it there for several years.

Dahl's neighbour, the diplomat and landowner Leonard Figg, recalled that although Roald could be uncivil in company, many of those to whom he was rude deserved it.[8] Marian Goodman agreed, maintained that generally Roald "bullied bullies", but her husband felt that the "caustic and corrosive" aspects of Roald's character stemmed largely from the fact that he had a "chip on his shoulder".[9] Dr Goodman was surely right that this need to be controversial in public was exacerbated by Roald's sense of irritation that sometimes he was not taken as seriously as he would have wished. Abandoning any desire to impress the establishment, he had settled therefore for the role of irritant, stirring up any consensus that seemed to him too complacent and delighting in being a thorn in the flesh of what he perceived as authority or received wisdom.

Ophelia recalled, with a smile, that "there was always a lack of sophistication to my father's arguments".[10] That was something that Marian Goodman too observed. She noticed his pugilistic desire to "take on" other male opponents. "He liked to shock," she remembered, adding that he particularly enjoyed being combative with someone who was well known. She described a dinner party she had once hosted in New York where Roald was sitting next to the celebrated *Life* photographer Alfred Eisenstaedt. After a few glasses of wine, Roald hazarded the opinion that photography was not a genuine art form. The comment seemed gratuitously provocative. An argument ensued and Eisenstaedt was eventually driven from the table. Years later, Lucy Dahl, by then living on Captiva Island, off the coast of Florida, introduced her father to a neighbour of hers, the painter Robert Rauschenberg – thinking they would get on well. "Dad ended up picking a fight with him about art," she recalled. "The whole evening was a disaster."[11] Mrs Goodman concluded philosophically that "Roald wasn't always fair" and that he was "a very contradictory person". Ophelia concurred, sensing that when her father was with "the person he loved most of all", he was able to feel stronger and less vulnerable. However, she too reflected that, while he might have become cosier at home, he never lost his relish for getting involved in controversy, often without too much heed for any consequences.[12]

Tessa's school friend Amanda Conquy remembered Roald possessing an almost adolescent desire to annoy. There was a lot of "sitting around and talking at Gipsy House", she told me, in an atmosphere that was "terrifically gossipy". Occasionally, the mood would change and Roald would start to pick fights, becoming "awkward" and "cussed," although usually "in a playful way . . . very childlike really".[13] To Conquy, much of it seemed lighthearted. She recalled a summer holiday spent with the family in Norway when she was twelve, where Roald ostentatiously sent the soup back twice in the restaurant of the hotel they were staying in because it was not hot enough. Even as a six-year-old, Ophelia found the incident profoundly embarrassing. "Emboldened by alcohol," she remembers her father advancing toward the offending waiter and pushing his bowl of asparagus soup aggressively into the man's chest, so that the pale green liquid slopped over the rim and onto his starched white shirt. The waiter, "shocked and humiliated" by such belligerence, retreated into the kitchen. Roald, as Conquy recalled the incident, returned to the table with a grin and told the kids that, in the kitchen, the staff would all be spitting into the soup as they reheated it.

Restaurants often seemed to provoke this confrontational aspect of his personality. With Liccy in France, he once sent back some crème fraiche, insisting (despite her repeated assurances to the contrary) that the cream was off. Most spectacularly, he once stood up in the middle of dinner at the Curzon House Club and silenced the entire restaurant, announcing to the diners that the club, which had recently changed hands, had been vulgarized and was going to the dogs. Two bodyguards marched him out of the building.

In this context, Roald's behaviour was perhaps no more than boorishness exacerbated by alcohol, something Lucy acknowledged when she recalled that it was drink that always made him lose his "inner governor". These were the times when Roald was, as his three-year-old son Theo once called him, "just a wasp's nest".[14] Tessa, who was with her father that evening in the Curzon House Club, recalled that he was not so much angry as "rather pleased with himself" when he sat down after his tirade. She thought he had made the scene simply to impress her rich Greek boyfriend. Possibly his behaviour was also a reflection of both the "anarchy" and the "delight in notoriety" his publisher Rayner Unwin recalled. Reflecting on the paradox that Dahl seemed in an instant able to switch from being absolutely charming to absolutely intolerable, Unwin reckoned that when he decided to leave Allen & Unwin over *Danny the Champion of the World*, the root cause was probably the fact that they simply were not "giving him enough attention". Unwin was quite sanguine about the parting, reflecting that he had gone into the relationship with his eyes open, fully aware of Dahl's reputation as a "difficult" author.[15]

Tom Maschler at Jonathan Cape, where Dahl subsequently moved, thought this decision was largely to do with the fact that Cape had a specialist children's department, which Allen & Unwin did not. But the fact that Jonathan Cape had offered Dahl an outstandingly good royalty on hardback copies of his books and that Maschler was a neurotic extrovert, who overtly celebrated his new author's "enormous zeal for life", doubtless also helped sway Roald's decision Cape's way. In this case, the transition was managed with the minimum of bad feeling. Dahl's fallout with Alfred Knopf in the early 1980s was a much more sour and drawn-out affair.

When the sixty-eight-year-old Knopf sold his publishing company to Random House in 1960, he negotiated a deal whereby he stayed on for five years as editor-in-chief, before officially retiring. He left the running of his imprint first in the experienced hands of Bob Bernstein, then forty-three, who became president and CEO of Random House the following year, and was himself succeeded, in 1968, by a brilliant young editor who had arrived from Simon & Schuster called Bob Gottlieb. Gottlieb was earnest, bushy-haired, and he possessed a formidable intellect. Bernstein described him as "one of the great editors of our time . . . with judgement, brains and speed".[16] He would go on to become editor of *The New Yorker*.

Roald was initially bowled over by both men. He liked the way Bernstein handled him, praising him for being "a sly fellow and a great persuader".[17] He also admired his shrewd business acumen, manifested, for example, by his aggressive pursuit of Hershey's over merchandising for *Charlie and the Chocolate Factory*. When Bernstein and his wife Helen came to London, Dahl took them both gambling at the Curzon House Club and taught them how to play blackjack. He gave them a valuable Henry Moore lithograph as a present and arranged for them to go and meet the sculptor at his home in Hertfordshire. Bernstein remembered Roald at that time as "charming and wonderful".[18] Gottlieb went further. He thought his boss "worshipped" Dahl.

Gottlieb was more reserved, but he too was at first enchanted by his new author – despite the stresses of having to deal with Alfred Knopf, who had decided to stay on in the building although he no longer had any editorial responsibilities. To Gottlieb, old Knopf seemed less like a legend and more like a bully. He likened his own professional situation to "having King Lear in the kitchen".[19] There was little love lost between them. Furthermore, Gottlieb – who was not a children's editor – was compelled to take on the editing of Roald's books. This was partly because Dahl was a special favourite of Knopf's, and also because Bob Bernstein was worried that Roald would be offended if he worked with anyone lower down the hierarchy. Gottlieb recalled that no one in the juvenile division at Knopf particularly wanted to work with Dahl, anyway.

To begin with, everything went smoothly. Roald was excited by Gottlieb's intellectual zip, describing him admiringly in correspondence as "that splendid man Gottlieb",[20] and exuberantly celebrating the birth of his editor's child, "the Gottlieblich Gottliebling Gottliebchen".[21] Gottlieb too found it "fun" working with Dahl and was aware that his new author, at least for the moment, adored him.[22] When he and Maria Tucci visited Gipsy House, she found the place captivating – "quite magical".[23]

But Dahl's business relationship with Bob Bernstein was starting to come under strain, as he tried to push up his initial per book royalty share on *Fantastic Mr Fox* from 10 per cent to 15 per cent. He first presented this proposal directly to Fabio Coen, who was in England on a business trip – ambushing Coen after he had enjoyed "a good supper" at Gipsy House and Pat had gone upstairs to bed. "He fell off his chair," Roald told Mike Watkins, "picked himself up again, wiped his forehead, took a deep breath and said this was impossible." Roald then offered him another alternative: he would make the same arrangement that he had made with Rayner Unwin – a 50:50 share of all risk and a 50:50 split of all profits. At this suggestion, Coen, so Roald described it, became like

Violet Beauregard in *Charlie and the Chocolate Factory*. His face "became magenta and he began to splutter".[24] Coen returned to New York to relay the proposal back to his boss. During May 1969, Bernstein and Dahl tussled out the deal by letter in a negotiation that was testy but by no means abusive, as they exchanged detailed figures and forecasts. Much of this negotiation was conducted directly between Dahl and his publishers – and from now onwards, this would often be the pattern. Murray Pollinger told me he found it "a joy" working with Roald, "because he was such a sharp businessman. He knew what he wanted. He was tricky, he was very good at tactics."[25]

At the beginning of June 1969, the negotiation appeared to be drawing to a close. Bernstein made what appeared to be a final offer. "I'm sorry you doubt my figures," he told Roald. "Despite the fact that you doubt them, they are accurate. These are the terms we can offer." He concluded on a lighter note, informing Dahl that he and his wife would probably be coming to Britain in the autumn and would be "delighted to visit you even if you're sulking and writing for Harper's".[26] Bernstein thought this would settle the matter. He felt that Dahl had made significant gains and that his loyalty to Knopf would lead him to accept the offer. However, he underestimated his opponent's love of gambling and was shocked when Dahl stuck to his guns and told Bernstein he was formally going to withdraw *Fantastic Mr Fox* from Knopf at the beginning of July unless his terms were accepted.

Roald of course was also bluffing. Very early on in the negotiations he had told his agent, "I do not under any circumstances wish to leave Random House. They have been extremely good with *Charlie* and *James* and I have a good personal relationship with Bob Bernstein."[27] Two months later, he confirmed that position. "I do *not* want to leave Knopf," he repeated. "I have a sort of feeling that if I do, they might lose enthusiasm for *Charlie* and *James* and let the sales fall off."[28] His brinkmanship, however, was gradually poisoning the relationship between himself and Bernstein, who called Mike Watkins and told him that his client had been "foolish", "unreasonable", and that he had been personally offended by Dahl's lack of faith in his figures.[29]

Roald did not want to push Random House "to the limit", so he asked his agent "to compromise and be friends" instead.[30] But Watkins failed to take control of this delicate situation. All he had to do was advise Bernstein to back off a bit. He didn't. The deal was almost agreed when, on July 2, Bernstein wrote to Roald, in jocular mode, urging him to stick with being an author rather than trying to be a publisher. He had no idea that he was waving a red rag at a bull. Roald flew into a rage. He told Watkins that Bernstein's attitude was all "bollocks". "I am a seller," he continued, "and as a seller, I have the right to ask any damn price I like. He, as the buyer, has the right to say no thanks. What he has not got the right to do is to tell me to keep out of the price-talk business. Publishers would all be happy if writers did that. Frankly I am a bit narked with BB. Those enormous professions of friendship and behind it all the mailed fist and the ruthless business man."[31] A few days later, in a huff, Roald went off on holiday with his family to Norway. The deal remained unconcluded.

It was Bob Gottlieb who settled the impasse when Roald returned to England. In the first flood of admiration for the clever young editor, Roald told Watkins he was convinced that Gottlieb was "a fine friend and staunch ally", who was not interested in finance, but in writers. "Having appointed himself as the official go-between," he continued, "I think he has put a stop once and for all to the semi-acrimonious exchanges that have been taking place between Bernstein and myself."[32] Gottlieb's success was achieved largely as a result of his own personal charisma and also because he was able to convince Roald that his own agent had handled the negotiations badly. Making Mike Watkins the fall guy was an effective ploy. Roald never had much respect for him and increasingly did not even bother to consult him – even on important decisions. On October 20, Roald wrote telling him that it was time to "stop wrangling" over the contract. "I want to sign it," he continued. "I trust Bob Gottlieb. He is not in the business of doing dirt to writers. Just the opposite. For this reason I am prepared to sign whatever contract he puts before me . . . I will take his word for it."[33] For the moment, the relationship with Random House was still functioning, although Gottlieb berated Watkins for making "a complex set-piece for Roald's official gaze what could have been settled between us on the phone in ten seconds".[34] From now on, however, the focus of Roald's literary affairs would move to London.

Throughout this period, Dahl was also starting to emerge out of the shadows into the London limelight that he both craved and detested. But it was a difficult transition. His reputation as a dangerous oddball was enhanced by the growing success of his children's books, but it also ensured that he remained removed from the respectable literary mainstream, for whose respect he still vestigially hankered. Even in 1981, he was still pondering how his first novel *Some Time Never* might have succeeded and how its failure could be ascribed to Max Perkins's premature death. He confessed his feelings to Alfred Knopf in a letter which revealed how – after more than thirty years – the old wound still smarted: "My faith in [Perkins] was absolute. It was going to be a good book, thanks to Max. But one week after I delivered the manuscript, he died . . . Without Max, I felt lost, and somehow drifted into short-story writing."[35]

At some level, short stories and children's writing made Dahl feel like a second-class literary citizen, and increasingly, both in the United States and Britain, he felt like an outsider to the writing community. Yet he openly disparaged English literary intellectuals, preferring the company of actors, artists or artisans – perhaps because these university-educated literati in some way intimidated him. Liccy recalled going with him once to a dinner hosted by the octogenarian aesthete Peter Quennell, where the conversation was so erudite that Roald felt entirely excluded. He departed early, tense and irritated. It had been the same thirty years before when, in 1956, Sheila St Lawrence asked him to deliver a present to a client of hers, the left-wing novelist and radio personality Marghanita Laski. Roald prevaricated for weeks about going, but eventually – months after he was supposed to take the gift over – he and Pat drove down to her "lovely little house" on Hampstead Heath for dinner. "The woman scares the daylights out of me," Dahl later told Sheila. "She also bores one a bit. She's too bloody intellectual for words. Everything is translated into social theories and she uses words I've never heard of and asks questions which take two hundred and fifty words to speak. She's deadly earnest all the time, not gay at all, and I'm afraid has little sense of humour. But quite a character, as you said." [36] It was a rare admission of insecurity.

This vulnerability had consequences. Roald felt that he needed to make his mark, to strike back against the consensus and be radical, shocking, abrasive. However, until the early 1970s, he had had no forum in which to do so. His reputation – at least in the United Kingdom – was as an eccentric rural maverick, who had married a glamorous actress and was now a highly commercial author. His writing itself had courted no controversy until *Charlie and the Chocolate Factory* became a bestseller. That success, at least in England, was achieved largely by word of mouth. For many years, almost all serious children's publishers continued to look down their noses at it and consider it vulgar. Even today, some still do. One publisher confessed that she was proud to have turned the book down – twice. In America, too, its success was achieved despite the hostility of many librarians, who similarly found it brash and tasteless and refused to put it on their shelves. In 1961, the influential *Library Journal* gave even *James and the Giant Peach* a decidedly sniffy critique. Despite acknowledging "some interesting and original elements" in the book, the reviewer, Ethel L. Heins, complained about its violent language and the grotesque characterizations of Aunts Sponge and Spiker. "Not recommended," was her considered conclusion. [37] "May the Lord protect me from Madame Ethel L. Heins," [38] Roald commented ruefully in response, deciding wisely that to be placatory was the most sensible course of action. When asked by the *New York Times* in 1968 to write a piece that was critical of librarians, Dahl circumspectly refused. He told Mike Watkins that he did not wish "to complain in public about the attitude of librarians towards my books. I am well aware of this attitude. I also believe it to be quite misguided. But anything I write in the *Times* will only serve to aggravate it. One cannot make a zebra change its slippers . . ." [39]

That cautious approach was not to last. For, the following year, quite unexpectedly, and largely through no fault of his own, *Charlie and the Chocolate Factory* became something of a cause célèbre. Soon after news leaked out that there were plans to turn the book into a film, the producer David Wolper received a letter from the National Association for

the Advancement of Coloured People (NAACP) objecting to the project
on the grounds that the book was racist. This thinking stemmed from
the fact that Wonka's factory workers, the Oompa-Loompas, had been
portrayed as African Pygmies "from the very deepest and darkest part of
the jungle where no white man had ever been before".[40] For Roald, this
conclusion came as a complete shock. Not only had he never intended
this fanciful detail to cause offence, he had also quite failed to appreciate
fully the ferocity of the social tide that eddied around almost every public
project within the United States at that time. Civil rights were a burning
issue, the Black Panther movement was at its height, and Martin Luther
King, Jr., had recently been assassinated. For the NAACP, the Oompa-
Loompas seemed clearly to reinforce a stereotype of slavery that American
blacks were trying to overcome. Exaggerated rumours quickly spread that
the organization would picket any cinema which screened the movie and
that even the use of the word "chocolate" in the title had implied racist
overtones. The producers were put under pressure to change both the
nature of the Oompa-Loompas and the title of the film.

Lillian Hellman waded in to support Roald, writing to the NAACP
on his behalf, but the reply she received was unequivocal. "The objection
to the title 'Charlie and the Chocolate Factory' is simply that the NAACP
doesn't approve of the book, and therefore doesn't want the film to encourage sales of the book. The solution is to make the Oompa Loompas
white and to make the film under a different title."[41] Roald was only too
willing to change the colour of the Oompa-Loompas and did so with
alacrity, but the people at the NAACP were adamant that the title of the
movie also had to change because they did not want it to promote the
book. Roald told Bob Bernstein he was "shattered" by this unreasonable
attitude, complaining that he could not understand why the NAACP
viewed his story as a "terrible dastardly anti-negro book". Angrily, he
described their attitude as "real Nazi stuff".[42] To Alfred Knopf he wrote
more sadly: "The book is banned by the NAACP. They thought I was
writing a subtle anti-negro manual. But such a thing had never crossed
my mind."[43] Curiously, he seems to have forgotten that he had initially
wanted to make Charlie a black boy, because he failed to mention it in

any of the correspondence that surrounded the furore. Eventually a compromise was reached. Roald agreed to "de-negro"[44] the Oompa-Loompas in both book and movie, transforming them in the latter into dwarves with green hair and orange skin. The movie's title was altered to *Willy Wonka and the Chocolate Factory*.

Roald eventually came to tolerate the film, acknowledging that there were "many good things" in it.[45] But he never liked it. Even after it was acknowledged as a classic, he would dismiss it as "crummy".[46] He found the music trashy, attempting to cut the song "The Candyman" when the movie opened in the United Kingdom, and he loathed the director, Mel Stuart, who he felt had "no talent or flair whatsoever".[47] He also disliked many of the small changes to his script that had been made by David Seltzer, the young screenwriter Stuart had hired to do rewrites, believing these had watered down "a good deal of the bite" in his own original draft.[48] He had serious reservations about Gene Wilder's performance as Wonka, which he thought "pretentious"[49] and insufficiently "gay [in the old-fashioned sense of the word] and bouncy".[50] He regretted that the producers had chosen neither Spike Milligan nor Peter Sellers to play the role. At Roald's request, Milligan had shaved off his beard to audition for the director, while Sellers had called Dahl personally "begging to play the part".[51] Both were rejected in favour of Wilder. Roald was so annoyed that, despite his own $300,000 writing fee, he considered disassociating himself entirely from the movie and "campaigning against it on TV and magazines in the US".[52] That was the high watermark of his rage. Eventually, as its popularity helped boost his book sales, his disapproval mellowed, but he remained "enormously depressed"[53] by the experience. It would prove his final foray into movies as a writer. From then on, as Murray Pollinger recalled, "he had no interest in working for the movies. He hated working for the movies, he hated people in the movies. Always."[54]

The racism rumpus gained him notoriety – something Rayner Unwin thought was good for book sales, because it was clear to him that there was nothing intentionally racist in Dahl's writing and because he knew that books that "irritated librarians" generally entertained children.[55] However, it provoked a period of intense – and with hindsight, almost comic – anxiety at Knopf. There, editors went through all Dahl's new material, scrutinizing it for anything that might unintentionally cause offence. Fabio Coen became concerned about using the word "spades" in *Fantastic Mr Fox*. When he told Roald, the latter responded unexpectedly with a zeal worthy of Dr Bowdler. "I will try to think of another word for *spade*. Shovel will not do because that is used in the story for *mechanical shovels*. *Black with rage* will certainly change."[56] But within two years his attitudes had relaxed somewhat and a more familiar ironic detachment had returned. In an early draft of *Charlie and the Great Glass Elevator*, Dahl had depicted the President of China using a yellow telephone and speaking on it in a silly accent. Coen was concerned about the racist implications of this, too. Although the offending passage was indeed eventually excised, Roald's first reaction now was that his editor had overreacted. "Re the Boxer rebellion in Fabioland," he bantered to Bob Gottlieb, "I am polling Mike [Watkins's] office . . . to see if there is a chink in my armour."[57]

Strangely, perhaps, it was not until the NAACP controversy that librarians began to complain about racism in *Charlie and the Chocolate Factory*. It seems none of them had noticed it until then. The letter that Dahl received from four of them who lived in Madison, Wisconsin, was typical. They informed him "with great dismay" that they had found the book to contain "passages with racist implications". This was especially unfortunate, they added, "as there are too few really fine authors writing for children, and you are certainly one of the best". However, the book had robbed the "little black creatures . . . of all humanity" and this was now forcing them "to question its place" on their shelves.[58] Dahl replied that he was "flabbergasted to learn how much unwitting offence I had given to some people," and assured them that the situation was being put right as soon as possible.[59] It was. Future editions of the book contained no references to African Pygmies, only to dwarves with "golden-brown hair" and "rosy white" skin.[60] Then, confident that his reputation was now restored among the juvenile literature intelligentsia, Roald sent a discarded section of the book about Marvin Prune – one of the characters he had eventually dropped from it – to the distinguished children's literature journal, *The Horn Book Magazine*. He thought that they might want to publish it.

The extract provoked a completely unexpected backlash from the editor, Paul Heins, who commissioned the Canadian children's writer Eleanor Cameron to write an article entitled "McLuhan, Youth and Literature". The piece was an attack on the ideas of her fellow Canadian, the media theorist and critic Marshall McLuhan. McLuhan of course was an apostle of the television age, who had coined such phrases as "the global village" and the "medium is the message". A professional academic, a self-conscious intellectual, a creature of university campuses, drawn to jargon and theory, who argued that television had shown itself to be an extension of the human body's nervous system, he was about as far away from the values of Roald Dahl as it was possible to imagine. Dahl almost certainly had no idea who McLuhan was and would have despised his ideas as much as he detested the effect that television was having on his own children. He had certainly given the "goggle-box" short shrift in *Charlie and the Chocolate Factory* – most notably when the Oompa Loompas beg all parents to throw their "nauseating, foul, unclean, repulsive" television sets away and replace them instead with a "lovely bookshelf". Television "kills imagination dead", Dahl had declared, by hypnotizing kids with a stream of "shocking, ghastly junk".[61]

Not for the first time, he was destined to be misunderstood. Cameron ignored all this common ground between them and chose to see *Charlie and the Chocolate Factory* instead as a herald of a terrible new age of post-television juvenile fiction. Admitting that teachers across the United States found that the book held pupils spellbound whenever it was read out loud in class, she nevertheless derided it as "the very worst" of contemporary children's fiction. "The book is like candy," she argued, "in that it is delectable and soothing . . . but leaves us poorly nourished with our taste dulled for better fare." She contrasted it unsympathetically with one of Dahl's own favourite books, E. B. White's *Charlotte's Web*, and – warming to her task – bizarrely asserted that *Charlie and the Chocolate Factory* had "overtones of sadism". Everything about it was "phony". Comparing it to "one of the more specious television shows", or a biblical epic of Cecil B. DeMille's – "with plenty of blood and orgies and tortures to titillate the masses" – Cameron declared that Willy Wonka was nothing but "the perfect type of TV showman with his gags and screechings. The exclamation mark is the extent of his individuality." She found the book cheap, tasteless, ugly, and sadistic; and, quoting T. S. Eliot, she wondered whether it might actually harm children.[62]

It was a ferocious and unexpected attack. Not surprisingly, Roald felt personally wounded by it. And his response was predictable. Forgetting about zebras and their slippers, he decided to pick up his pencil and reply to Cameron's "vicious" comments with a piece that was equally inflammatory. How could she suggest that he would ever want to write a book that would harm children, he enquired, when he had fought such a long battle to restore his son's health? It was "an insensitive and monstrous implication". He resented the "subtle insinuations" she had made about his character and the "patronizing attitude" she was adopting toward the teachers of America. She was "completely out of touch with reality". He added pointedly that he had been telling bedtime stories to his own children every day for fifteen years and that he thought these 5,000 stories had helped make them "marvellous and gay and happy".[63] It was not perhaps his best defence, but then cool, rational argument was not his way when he was both hurt and angry. He would probably have been much better off telling the magazine's readership how his stories were encouraging children the world over to read books and that many of them loved his stories so much that they felt impelled to write and tell him so. "The current rate of letters from children in the US is between fifty and sixty a week," he had written to Mike Watkins in 1966. "I try to answer them all with a postcard."[64]

Roald was always a diligent and engaging correspondent, and if he was in the right mood and thought a child's letter particularly imaginative, he or she would receive a fuller and more memorable response. When the sports journalist and television anchorman Keith Olbermann was seven years old and "Head of Maps" in his class at school, he wrote to Dahl from Hastings-on-Hudson in New York and told him, at some length, about his own writing ambitions and successes. Roald's reply was thoughtful, generous and full of gentle ironic humour. "My dear Keith," he began.

> *It was wonderful to receive a letter from a fellow author. It meant so much more than the usual ordinary message from a mere reader. As "Head of Maps" you will be able to calculate very easily what a long way your letter had to travel in order to reach me in this little village. Thousands of miles . . . The postman, an elderly fellow who comes on foot, knocked on the door this morning and said "I have a letter from you from K. Olbermann of Hastings, USA." I said, "How do you know?" He said, "It says so on the envelope." He is a very inquisitive postman and he likes to know who is writing to me. "Who is Olbermann?" asked the postman. I opened the letter and read it. "He is a writer," I said. "He has written more books than me . . ."*

Olbermann's parents later told the local newspaper that the letter had given the boy "the kick of his young life". Mrs Olbermann added that it "just about proves that there still are some very nice people left in this old, beat-up world. If all adults acted with such loving attention to children, would it not be wonderful?"[65]

Dahl was quite sincere when he argued that he thought children alone were decent judges of whether a book written for them was any good or not. In 1962, he had written to a child critic of *James and the Giant Peach* to tell him that, "up to now, a whole lot of grown-ups have written reviews, but none of them have really known what they were talking about because a grown-up talking about a children's book is like a man talking about a woman's hat". It was an approach that, in the future, would come to define his attitude towards adult critics who disparaged his work.[66] But, despite letters of support from many teachers and librarians, he remained bitterly upset by Cameron's article and the equally unpleasant follow-up letter from a celebrated children's science fiction writer, Ursula K. Le Guin. Le Guin acknowledged that one of her children had been "truly fascinated" by *Charlie and the Chocolate Factory*, describing how, as soon as her daughter finished the book, she would start rereading it. Her conclusion was not that the book had made a wonderful connection with the child's inner world, but that, under its influence, her "usually amiable" daughter became "quite nasty".[67]

Roald was "stopped cold" by these criticisms. He wrote to Richard Krinsley at Random House that the article had caused him "to lose my appetite for doing another book. I haven't written or wanted to write a line since then. I am playing chess with Theo, Ophelia and Lucy, and I am cultivating my orchids. I don't mind ordinary bad reviews, but I do mind those that imply personal bad taste and the possibility that I'm causing actual harm to young readers. This has temporarily taken away from me the intense pleasure I get from writing for children and with it, the enthusiasm and drive."[68]

His disillusion did not last long. In a few months he completed *Charlie and the Great Glass Elevator*, his sequel to *Charlie and the Chocolate Factory*, and had soon embarked upon *Danny the Champion of the World*. Then, with his hankerings to be an adult writer still not entirely spent, and perhaps encouraged by Gottlieb's reputation as a fiction editor, Roald decided once again to try his hand at a comic novel for grown-ups, *My Uncle Oswald*. This rollicking picaresque comedy, set in 1919, was ostensibly drawn from the diaries of Dahl's fictional uncle, Oswald Henryks Cornelius – an early twentieth-century Casanova, who had first appeared in his 1964 short story, "The Visitor". Using the charms of his glamorous assistant, Yasmin Howcomely, and the world's most powerful aphrodisiac as bait, the sophisticated, worldly and cynical Oswald attempts to make his fortune gathering sperm from the world's greatest geniuses in order to sell it to women who want to have brilliant children. Inspired by a request from *Playboy* magazine for another Oswald tale for their twenty-fifth anniversary edition, Roald told a journalist that this one had simply "refused to stop" and grown into a book.[69] He would later describe it as "the longest and dirtiest story" he had ever written.[70] It was also one that he took a particular pleasure in researching, for he wickedly enlisted the help of a number of local librarians to check biographical information about famous writers, artists, musicians and scientists in the 1920s, relishing the fact that they had no idea of the context in which their researches were going to be used. On the title page of the first draft, he wrote: "I hate the pompous, And I hate all pomp. But I love the romptious, And I love a romp."[71]

Roald's notes for the novel make entertaining reading. "D H Lawrence: Went to Italy in 1919 (Frieda) Impotent! Ravel: Kept Siamese cats. Never married. Diaghilev (homo) so no but tempted."[72] He corresponded earnestly with scientists in Cambridge about the art of preserving semen and with experts at the Milk Marketing Board in the UK about the precise details of insemination techniques. By December 1978, he told Bob Gottlieb that the book was "now two inches thick" and that its subject was "fucking".* Gottlieb replied that he very much wanted to see it, and jokingly noted that "as for fucking, I seem to remember it".[73] From the correspondence between them, it is clear that Gottlieb enjoyed editing *My Uncle Oswald*, persuading Dahl that there were too many painters in the first draft and that he needed more "giants of the day" in the narrative. Later he persuaded him to take out a particularly scurrilous section about the size of Stravinsky's penis. "I think you should eliminate the size of his pizzle," he commented. "Madame S is still alive (and wonderful) and I feel she would be distressed."[74] Roald was delighted with Gottlieb's input. "You did a marvellous job. More or less all your points valid. Some super. Huge thanks."[75]

The book was eventually published with a short introduction from Dahl, declaring his uncle's diaries to be a document of "considerable scientific and historical importance". This comic conceit allowed him the opportunity to elaborate once more upon one of his favourite subjects: the ridiculous nature of male sexual behaviour. Once again the male was presented as a strangely pathetic creature, dominated by the needs of his penis. Among many bizarre comic vignettes, the cerebral Sigmund Freud flaps his arms "like an old crow" and hysterically tries to analyse what is happening to him as "his doodly came alive and stuck out as though he

---

*Curiously, Dahl was adamant that *Uncle Oswald* was not about sex. "It is a monstrous thing for a serious writer to write explicit sex," he declared. "*My Uncle Oswald* is a *parody* of all those awful books . . . Look at John Updike and *Couples*. That's rubbish, just rubbish!" – Roald Dahl interviewed in *Publisher's Weekly*, June 6, 1980.

had a walking-stick in his trousers". Yasmin, who has disguised herself as a boy so she can seduce the homosexual Marcel Proust, discreetly disposes of the banana she has used to fool him, before getting trapped in an embrace that reminds her somewhat of a "mechanical lobster". The self-righteous George Bernard Shaw, on the other hand, once dismissed as "all hen and no cock", turns out to have been a virgin.[76] Oswald's cultivated eye observes the follies of human behaviour with a detachment that is reminiscent of his creator's. But did Dahl in fact see himself as Uncle Oswald? That was just "wishful thinking", he told the Australian journalist Terry Lane a year before he died. "I would like to have been like him and I think that all men would like to be like him."[77]

At the same time as Roald was writing *My Uncle Oswald*, other, more commercial, concerns were weighing on his shoulders. For much of the 1970s, Knopf had paid the American royalties at his request in the form of a salary, around $60,000 to $75,000 per annum.[78] It was an efficient way of dealing with the fact not only that a writer's income could be very inconsistent but that Britain had immensely high rates of personal taxation. Even after Margaret Thatcher came to power in 1979 and began to cut taxes, the rate of tax payable on earned income over £20,000 was still 60 per cent, and on interest and dividends above this 75 per cent, so it was hardly surprising that Roald began to focus on how to get the balance of his royalties – which amounted to more than $1.25 million – out of the United States with the minimum of interference from "the voracious Revenue men".[79]

In 1970, on advice from a tax lawyer recommended to him by Cubby Broccoli, Dahl had sold the copyrights of his short stories to a company in Liechtenstein called *Anric*. All the revenues from the popular Anglia Television series *Tales of the Unexpected* were remitted to this company, which paid Dahl a salary as and when he invoiced them. It was managed by a banker from Lausanne called Gerard Schlaeppi. Now Dahl decided to set up a subsidiary company, a "Societé Anonyme" improvidently called *Icarus*, also registered in Switzerland, into which he asked Knopf to pay all these outstanding book royalties. It was a scheme he would later describe to Tom Maschler as "semi-legitimate".[80]

Bob Bernstein went along with these plans, but then informed Roald that there was a catch. In order for the procedure to get round the US IRS requirements, *Icarus* had to provide the publishing house with a service that appeared to justify these payments. The lawyers at Knopf, sensing an opportunity to tie down their fractious author, proposed a contract where the royalties would be paid over in four instalments – as if they were advances for four new books.

The four-book deal cost him more than $100,000 in legal fees to negotiate and set up.[81] *My Uncle Oswald* would be the first of these four books, to be followed by three shorter children's books. But almost at once the agreement began to go sour. Moreover, he felt – for the first time in his life – controlled by his publishers and consequently under pressure to write fast. *My Uncle Oswald* was virtually complete, but the children's books were not yet begun. By the time he started *The Twits* and *George's Marvellous Medicine*, which would become the second and third of these short books, there were already problems administering the plan. Unusual royalty splits with Dahl and his new illustrator Quentin Blake needed attention, and agents' percentages had to be factored in. Further redrafting was required. Dahl was soon confused by his own creation. "This all gets a bit complicated and is really too much for me," he told Gottlieb in January 1980.[82] A month later, Gottlieb, who had tried to keep himself clear of the business side of the arrangement, responded that he too was perplexed by it. "The only thing I can see clearly is that you are in as much of a muddle as I am about the business side of everything. I hate it."[83]

When it came to literary matters, things were thankfully simpler. Gottlieb liked the earthy humour of *The Twits*, a comedy about a grotesque husband and wife who delight in playing unpleasant tricks on each other. "I like it VERY MUCH," he told Roald. "You're right: what we want (or *should* want) for these little ones is stuff with meat, not the yuchy [*sic*], sweetly pretty material we're exposed to."[84] He suggested removing a particularly graphic passage about nose-blowing and also a few changes to the text that might have made it more comprehensible to an American audience. Roald agreed to drop the nose-blowing, but rejected most of his other suggestions. "Do they Americanise the *Christmas Carol* before publishing it, or the novels of Jane Austen?" he asked. "Let the kids figure it out for themselves. Let them also figure out 'long knickers.'"[85]

With *George's Marvellous Medicine*, too, Gottlieb's "literal mind"[86] was able to offer Roald some useful advice about issues of scale and about the "emotional payoff" at the end. But behind these cordial exchanges, the strain of delivering these new short books in order to collect royalties he had already earned was beginning to tell. The editors in Random House's children's division were also becoming ever more resentful of their author's remoteness and hauteur. Frances Foster, who was editing the book as it were under Gottlieb's cover, told her boss that she thought the ending was flawed, but felt she would have either "to hold her tongue" or "bide her time" before she could say anything to her author. By now, as well, the artifice of the *Icarus* arrangement was beginning to chafe with everyone. Dahl had begun playfully enough, sending his manuscripts "direct" to Random House, "at the request of my employers, *Icarus S.A.*"[87] However, a month later, Gottlieb complained to Dahl about the "hideous contract", which was time-consuming and complex to administer.[88] Now Roald was asking for increased royalties on the two new books, which would require further changes to the agreement.

Knowing that there was dissatisfaction with the ending of his latest manuscript, Random House's legal department suggested that the firm hold up the next payments until Dahl finished rewriting it. "*Icarus* has demanded payment due for delivery of *George's Marvellous Medicine*," their lawyer wrote to Gottlieb, "but under our contract, payment is due on delivery of a manuscript in content and form acceptable to [Random House]. I understand that the manuscript for the above title was delivered in February, or perhaps sooner, but that Roald Dahl has been asked to re-write the last chapter. If that is the case, the payment will not be due until he has rewritten the manuscript to make it satisfactory."[89] The arrangement, which Roald had devised to benefit himself, was now starting to work against him.

Furthermore, Roald could not charm Gottlieb as he had charmed Alfred Knopf, Sheila St Lawrence, Ann Watkins or Tom Maschler. So when, in March 1980, he wrote to Gottlieb, politely asking for a supply of his favourite pencils, the request was not treated as a priority. Roald had written with these pencils ever since the war. For years, Ann Watkins and Sheila St Lawrence had sent them out to England for him. It was probably a sign of his deteriorating relationship with Mike Watkins – no longer his main agent, but now a subagent to Murray Pollinger – that he had started turning to his publishers instead. But Gottlieb was a busy man. He was editing perhaps a dozen other books and he was not used to looking after his authors that way. For three months, Dahl's letter went unanswered. In June, he followed it up again. "Quite a long time ago I wrote, either to you or addressing it to your secretary, asking if someone could buy for me and send over: 1 gross DIXON TICONDEROGA PENCILS, 2 5/10 MEDIUM. Did anyone get the message?" Lest Gottlieb should think him importunate, he added: "I've used no other pencils since I started writing thirty-seven years ago. They little erasers [*sic*] on top. I'd be awfully grateful if someone could do this for me. Airmail. Let me know how much and I'll send a cheque (check)."[90]

A week later, Gottlieb's assistant replied: "I'm afraid we've not had too much luck. No one seems to carry Dixon Ticonderoga any longer. The enclosed is the closest we could come, and the salesman assured us that these were very similar to the Ticonderoga. But, since they're $65.00 for a gross I thought it would be a good idea for you to give them a try before purchasing that many."[91] Unfortunately, no one had appreciated how important these pencils were to Roald. "They don't have erasers on top. They are too hard. And they are the wrong colour,"[92] he wrote back, asking if she would mind phoning the Joseph Dixon Crucible Co. in Jersey City to find out if they were still manufacturing them. Curiously, the pencils were not that hard to come by. They were and still are standard in many US schools, so it is strange that Gottlieb's assistant failed. Yet from the contact details and prices scribbled on the letter, she had clearly tried at least five local stationery stores. Roald, of course, was unaware of this. To him, it seemed that his American publishers were now unwilling even to supply their author with one of the key fetishes he required to perform his craft. The conclusion was obvious: he was no longer appreciated or valued at Random House.

That summer, the royalty storm continued to simmer. Gottlieb, who didn't care how the royalties were paid "as long as they were legal", found Roald's demands increasingly "exaggerated . . . dotty . . . unrealistic and unmeetable", recalling that "waves of hostility" were growing apace between them. Roald himself was ill, tired and under stress. His marriage to Pat was on its last legs. He wrote to old Alfred Knopf to see if he could help. But by now this King Lear had played out his last rages and was powerless to assist him. "At the office I only know what I am told," he wrote to Dahl, "and don't ask too many questions, so I know of your troubles only from you. I hope, for sentimental reasons, that they will not drive you from the firm, which I think still bears a fine reputation."[93] If Mike Watkins had been more sensitive and manipulative, he might yet have headed off the storm. But Roald no longer trusted Watkins's judgement and Watkins now did little more for him than simply collect his percentages. Sooner or later there was bound to be an explosion.

In August 1980, Roald sent Gottlieb the last of his four titles, a book of scurrilous and witty poems for children called *Dirty Beasts*. "*Icarus* has asked me to forward the enclosed to you direct to save time," he wrote, adding that "Tom Maschler and his gang have seen each one as it's come along and we have collaborated closely upon the correct and most economical proper length this book should be. They all seem to be enormously high on it . . . I believe this completes the contract between you and *Icarus* and no doubt you will be dealing with Mr Schlaeppi regarding what you owe him."[94] Gottlieb replied with a lengthy critique of the book, and concluded by reminding him that he was "no longer involved with the contract side". Business stuff was not his domain, he insisted; it put him in a "no win" situation.[95] Three weeks later, Roald had still heard nothing and he was furious. "I would like to hear from you or from someone that the nefarious four book contract between Knopf and the foreign company has now been completed," he fumed. "That would be a small act of grace and thoughtfulness. I have felt that fucking contract clutching at my throat like a bloodsucking vampire ever since it was written."[96] Gottlieb replied that the Juvenile Department would get back to him, and on October 20, Dahl received a letter saying that the manuscript had been accepted and that the final sum of money could be released.

Two months later, Murray Pollinger wrote to Gottlieb to complain that, despite his "repeated enquiries", Mr Schlaeppi had still not received any money. Dahl was now irritated by everything that Random House did. In January 1981, he wrote to Gottlieb complaining about the print size of his name on the front cover of *The Twits*. Gottlieb agreed that his name should indeed be bigger, but otherwise his response was decidedly testy. "I had nothing to do with the making of the book," he reminded him. "When I'm through with my 'editing,' it all gets passed along to our friends on the 6th floor where I believe Frances Foster looks after you. Remember: I have nothing whatsoever to do with Knopf's juvenile division. My single function with them has been as a volunteer editor for you. I'm not the publisher, designer, boss or anything. Which is why the various disagreeablenesses of the past several years have been particularly disagreeable for me: I've had the unpleasant role of messenger boy between or among conflicting parties, without the authority to resolve things as I would here on the 21st floor. I'll pass along your strictures to Frances, and no doubt you'll be hearing from her." [97] To Roald, this must have read like a put-down; he would certainly have been stung by this reminder that, despite his successes, he was still merely part of the "juvenile division", and that the brilliant Gottlieb was only dealing with him on sufferance.

When Frances Foster innocently followed up the next day to defend her jacket design, she did her best to be conciliatory. "I wish we could keep you happy! I can't tell how much it distresses me to have you disappointed . . . For me, it goes with saying that you are THE *author* on the list we most want to please – and it seems we don't do a very good job of it. Maybe we can do something about that? I think we might come closer to keeping you happy with your juvenile books if we were in closer and more direct touch with you – at the same time freeing Bob Gottlieb from his spot in the middle?" [98] For Dahl, this was the last straw. With Tom Maschler in London assiduously "looking after him", supervising "every detail" of his books "including illustrations and lay-out", [99] Random House's attitude by contrast seemed offhand and dismissive.

Dahl wrote to the Legal Department complaining again about the "monstrously unfair contract" that "had been foisted" upon him and objecting to the fact that Bob Gottlieb had declined to intervene personally on his behalf. "He refuses to take sides or to protect me," he complained, and the result was that – now he was a "free man" again – Dahl was considering moving to another publisher. "These words are not spoken lightly," he concluded. "I have served your house well since 1943 and am still a close friend and regular correspondent of Alfred Knopf. How I wish he were still in his office so that he could bang a few heads together. I suggest you let me hear from you pretty quickly otherwise I shall tell Bob [Gottlieb] to call it a day." [100] That same day Dahl also wrote to Gottlieb himself, accusing him of failing to "protect" him from "the slings and arrows" of the Random House legal team, and accusing them of having "pulled the wool" over his eyes over the "thorny matter of the four-book contract". He concluded by reiterating his threat to leave Knopf after the publication of *Dirty Beasts*. "I damn well mean it." [101]

Gottlieb turned the tables on him. Complaining that over the last two years Roald's comments had been "unmatched" in his experience for "overbearingness and lack of civility", he complained that recently Roald had begun "to address others here – who are less well placed to answer you back – with the same degree of abusiveness. For a while I put your behaviour down to the physical pain you were in and so managed to excuse it. Now I've come to believe that you're just enjoying a prolonged tantrum and are bullying us." This was how his letter concluded:

> *Your threat to leave Knopf after this current contract is fulfilled leaves us far from intimidated. Bernstein and I will be sorry to see you depart, for business reasons, but these are not strong enough to make us put up with your manner to us any longer. I've worked hard for you editorially but had already decided to stop doing so; indeed, you've managed to make the entire experience of publishing you unappealing for all of us – counter-productive behaviour, I would have thought.*
>
> *To be perfectly clear, let me reverse your threat: unless you start acting civilly to us, there is no possibility of our agreeing to publish*

you. Nor will I – or any of us – answer any future letter that we con-
sider to be as rude as those we've been receiving.

Regretfully,
Bob[102]

Gottlieb told me he had applied what he called his "fuck-you" principle. "You take any amount of shit [from writers] because it's their book,
they're the ones who are tense and sensitive and then there comes a moment when you can't do it any more and then you're free to say, 'Go Fuck
Yourself,' because with very few exceptions there is no one writer who is
crucial to your enterprise."[103] He maintained that when he sent the letter,
everyone at Random House "stood on their desks and cheered".[104]

At Gipsy House, the letter was read with astonishment. Two days
later, Dahl sadly wrote to the eighty-nine-year-old Alfred Knopf, enclosing photocopies of his correspondence with Gottlieb and explaining why
he was leaving the firm. "I am, as I hope you know, a very easy man to
get on with," he maintained. "And in my thirty-seven years of writing
have never before had a row with a single publisher. I live quietly in the
country and get on with my business. It is only when someone really does
behave badly to me that I become aroused. I certainly would not try to
bully a publisher or throw my weight around. I will spare you the gory
details of this fracas but I just wanted to let you know. Our friendship
will continue always . . ."[105]

In hindsight, Gottlieb thought "something snapped" in Dahl. His
"big problems" were with Bernstein, he recalled. "At one point it became
clear that he thought we were just a bunch of blood-sucking Jews . . .
We were Jews, but very generous . . . Everyone had gone out of his way
to keep Roald happy and give him what he wanted. He was clearly out
of control."[106] Roald disagreed. Ignoring the fact that he had got himself
into this pickle only because he wanted to avoid paying income tax, he
still felt swindled by Random House. His amour propre had been dented.
Badly. Five years later he would still be complaining sharply about how
Random House had "done the dirty" on him.[107] His next US publisher,

Roger Straus, recalled vividly how bitter Dahl was about the affair, while Roald himself would later assert that Random House had treated him not as the author of "six semi-classics" but as "a kind of excrescence who got in the way of the publisher's grand design".[108]

However, Gottlieb and Bernstein's opinion that there was anything overtly anti-Semitic in Roald's attitude toward them is hard to prove. In all the correspondence surrounding the furore that I examined, the fact that both were Jewish was never mentioned. More than twenty-five years on, neither of them could recall a specific incident. They simply recollected a general sense that this was the case. Possibly Roald said something to either of them over the telephone. Yet this is unlikely. All of the negotiations took place at a time when he hardly ever made a transatlantic call. In any event, many of the closest people around him and on his side of the argument – from Alcan Copisarow and Murray Pollinger's wife Gina, to Tom Maschler at Cape and his new American publisher, Roger Straus, were Jewish. So, of course, was Alfred Knopf, whom Roald tried to protect from the worst of the row, "for fear it would shorten his life".[109] Perhaps Gottlieb and Bernstein's memory was coloured by their former client's most notorious foray into contemporary politics, which occurred two years later, when Dahl reviewed a book about the 1982 Israeli invasion of Lebanon.

God Cried was a 140-page, large-format book of reportage about the atrocities committed against the people of Beirut by the invading Israeli Army. It was written by an Australian war reporter, Tony Clifton, and focused on the large number of civilian casualties sustained in the conflict. A series of graphic photographs, mainly showing the innocent victims of the warfare – including a number of severely mutilated and dead children – illustrated the text.[110] Tessa suggested to the editor, Naim Attallah, that her father, who had in the past donated money to Palestinian educational charities through International Help for Children,† might want to review it for another of his publications, *The*

---

†Some of the money from the premiere of *Hud*, for example, was used to educate Palestinian refugees in Ramallah.

Literary Review. She knew also that Roald had recently met and been impressed by the British surgeon Pauline Cutting, who had worked in Beirut's hospitals during the invasion.[111]

Roald refused at first. He hated reviewing. But once he got the book, his sense of injustice was stirred. His response to both the text and the "heartrending" images was overwhelming. He changed his mind. The result was a two-and-a-half-page article entitled "Not a Chivalrous Affair". It began:

> *In June 1941, I happened to be in, of all places, Palestine, flying with the RAF against the Vichy French and the Nazis. Hitler happened to be in Germany and the gas-chambers were being built and the mass slaughter of Jews was beginning. Our hearts bled for the Jewish men, women and children, and we hated the Germans.*
>
> *Exactly forty-one years later, in June 1982, the Israeli forces were streaming northwards out of what used to be Palestine into Lebanon, and the mass slaughter of the inhabitants began. Our hearts bled for the Lebanese and Palestinian men, women and children, and we all started hating the Israelis.*[112]

Referring frequently to his own "glowing memory" of the beauties of the Palestinian landscape and "the kindness of its people", Dahl condemned the Israeli government, using the kind of inflammatory rhetoric he had practised over many a dinner, but seldom in print. Marian Goodman felt he was using his desire to shock in order to defend what he perceived as the victims in this particular conflict. "If anybody was a big loudmouth, he'd hit him right back with the same treatment," she told me. "But if somebody couldn't defend themselves, he never attacked. He was protective."[113] In this instance his rhetoric, though sympathetic to the Palestinians, got the better of him, and some of the article reads as if it was written deliberately to irritate Jewish readers. Most inflammatory was the repeated comparison of Israel to Nazi Germany. Menachem Begin, and his minister of defence, Ariel Sharon, were branded as war criminals, whose actions condemned the whole nation. "Must Israel, like

Germany, be brought to her knees before she learns how to behave in this world?" Dahl concluded.[114] He despatched the review as soon as he had written it, with a note to the editor: "If I have said anything inaccurate or injudicious, do let me know."[115]

When Liccy saw what he had written, she was horrified. Amazed that he had not shown it to her before he sent it off, she sensed immediately that his unrestrained anger was certain to offend Jews in ways he had not begun to imagine. She urged him to change it. But he refused. His response to her was the equivalent of the Duke of Wellington's "publish and be damned". He went away with her on holiday. Upon their return, he found that an enormous row had indeed ignited in his absence. Years of press releases about Dahl's "macabre imagination" and his "nasty mind" had caught up with him: all over the media he was branded as an anti-Semite. He was bombarded with angry letters and phone calls. He even received death threats. He tried to put the record straight in a letter to *The Times*, claiming that to call him anti-Jewish was as foolish as to call him anti-Arab simply because he was critical of Colonel Qaddafi. "I am not anti-Semitic," he declared. "I am anti-Israel."[116] But it was too late. He made matters much worse when, over the phone to Mike Coren of *The New Statesman* a few days later, he confided that he felt there was "a trait in the Jewish character that does provoke a certain animosity, maybe it's a kind of lack of generosity towards non-Jews . . . Even a stinker like Hitler didn't just pick on them for no reason."[117]

The comment was significant in many ways. It showed that, even in public, when his back was against the wall, Dahl was likely to become antagonistic rather than conciliatory. It manifested the bluntness that had been apparent since his plane crash in the desert and made clear how little he now cared about what other people – particularly in the literary establishment – now thought of him. So, in another context – in this case a quarrel with an American film producer – he did not think twice about describing the man, in a private letter to Dirk Bogarde, as "the wrong sort of Jew", and exaggerating his faults accordingly. He simply applied the principle he used in his writing for children. He told Ophelia's friend Todd McCormack, the son of the author and agent Mark McCormack, who came to film an interview with him: "I find that the only way to make my characters really interesting is to exaggerate all their good or bad qualities and so if a person is nasty or bad or cruel, you make them very nasty and very bad and very cruel. And if they're ugly, you make them extremely ugly. That I think is fun and makes an impact."[118] In this spirit, the offending producer's faults were catalogued to Bogarde, almost as if he were a character in one of Dahl's children's books. "His face is matted with dirty, black hair. He is disgustingly overweight and flaccid though only forty-something, garrulous, egocentric, arrogant, complacent, ruthless, dishonourable, lascivious, slippery."[119] Doubtless, Bogarde felt Dahl had made his point.

This kind of invective, quoted out of the frame of reference of its author's frequently explosive tongue, sounds extreme. But for Roald it was simply par for the course. His adult correspondence, over more than fifty years, had been peppered with rude generalizations about all number of people and nationalities that, at one time or other, had irritated him. The English, French, Dutch, Germans, Swedes, Irish, Iraqis and Americans joined the Israelis – or the Jews – in being victims. Nor were friends or family members exempt. Neisha Crosland recalled how Roald had "absolutely crucified" one boyfriend she brought over to dinner at Gipsy House because he had been to university and fancied himself an intellectual.[120] Her sister Charlotte concurred. "He used to squash him like a fly," she told me.[121] Ophelia had realized as a child that, when he got involved in an argument, whether public or private, her father was always inclined to exaggeration and hyperbole to get his way: "I learned early on that he wasn't interested in the matter of the argument. He simply wanted to cause a stir."[122]

At the dinner table those who knew him best understood that the onslaught would soon blow over. In a more public forum, things were not so simple. And when he ventured into that territory, Ophelia, for one, was less tolerant of her father's behaviour. "I wasn't as keen on his rather more controversial public side," she told me. "And I still try and think about why he needed to do that. Some of it was about very strongly held opinions and some of that I respect a lot because he really didn't do things in order to be popular and he didn't say things so that he could gain public approval. In fact, if he felt strongly about something, he would say it often really without thinking about the consequences very much or who he might be hurting by doing such a thing."[123] Murray Pollinger too felt that, in this context, because Roald was "not a broad intellectual", he would often simply say things that were "badly prepared and not well expressed". Nevertheless, Pollinger believed, it was his client's need to outrage convention, to "be a provocateur . . . to say outrageous things just to get a reaction", that was the principal motivation behind his most notorious foray into the media limelight. "In the whole of my thirty years with Roald," he assured me, "I could never perceive a crack or a peek at any anti-Semitism on his part. Not once."[124]‡ For others, of course, that point of view was more difficult to appreciate.

By the end of his life, Roald had grown into an accomplished performer and distinctive public speaker. This evolution was a slow and gradual one. Always comfortable with being shocking over dinner, during the war he was a nervous and reluctant speechmaker, who needed a stiff drink to get him onto the platform. Though he had presented *Way Out* in 1961 with some style and panache, for much of the 1960s and 1970s he eschewed public appearances. "My trouble is that I am not a performer in any way," he told the audience at a children's book festival in 1971. "Short of reading from my books, which I presume have already been read, I am really no good at speaking to anyone, let alone a group of children. I would gladly come and do my 'thing' as you call it if only I had a 'thing' to do, but I don't. I cannot believe that my presence alone drifting among the children would create much pleasure or give much enlightenment."[125] Four months later, in similar vein, he turned down an

---

‡Curiously, in a letter to *The Times* on September 15, 1983, Roald claimed that he had "quite a few pints of Jewish blood in [his] own veins through [his] Norwegian grandmother Hesselberg, and [his] great grand-great-grandfather, who was called Preuss". The Preuss connection to the Dahl ancestry remains obscure. Ellen Wallace (b. 1856) was his "grandmother Hesselberg," and she was primarily of Scottish descent. Her father was George Wallace and her mother Sophie Bergithe Maria Huun (b. 1835). That either the Huuns or the Preusses were Jewish was extremely unlikely, because – apart from a tiny number of Sephardi Portuguese – Jews were banned from entering Norway until 1851. Even in 1892, there were only 214 Jews in the whole of the country – See Ingrid Muller, *The Jewish Community of Oslo*, www.dmt.oslo.no/english/jews-in-norway.

invitation to speak to the Round Table of Uxbridge: "Firstly, I am a rotten speaker, and secondly, I would rather stick to my own trade. If once I started going round making speeches I would become that awful creature which we see quite often around the place – 'the writer-speech maker.'" [126]

But a decade later he was appearing regularly on television chat shows, introducing *Tales of the Unexpected,* and entertaining sales representatives, master carvers, medical foundations and university debating societies with subversive and risqué perorations. At some point in his speech he would usually stretch the limits of what was expected, and inject a frisson of danger – the dodgy practices of antique dealers, the perils of masturbation, the attraction of a pert bottom in tight jeans, the filthy natures of men with beards, or the antics of "randy" television presenter Bruce Forsyth: all were grist to the mill of a man who had now become a skilled and subversive humorist. But the primal desire to annoy was never far away. At Oxford University, prior to arguing that romance was bunk, he managed to irritate Rupert Soames, then the president of the Union, by gratuitously declaring over dinner that his grandmother, Winston Churchill's wife Clementine, was a "boring non-entity". [127] It was typical of his need to cause a stir.

A couple of months after he had written the review of *God Cried*, Roald Dahl was profiled by Peter Lennon for *The Times*. There Dahl acknowledged that, because that piece was "written so fast and so emotionally", he had perhaps somewhat overplayed his hand. Lennon concluded that it seemed Dahl had simply "refused to accept the conventions of international political debate". [128] This was true. He would do the same when, in 1989, he was almost a lone voice in the British media criticizing the novelist Salman Rushdie, when a fatwa (an Islamic death sentence) was issued against him by Ayatollah Khomeini of Iran, after Rushdie had supposedly slurred the Prophet Mohammed in his novel *The Satanic Verses*. It was ironic that Roald, who called Rushdie a "dangerous opportunist" [129] because he had put the lives of his publishers and their employees at risk, also attacked Rushdie for not having exercised self-censorship before he published his book.

In an interview conducted shortly before he died, Dahl refused to comment on this incident, because it stirred up such passions in people. "The only thing I want to say is that every writer should be his own censor – up to a point. I don't hold with all this 'I'm a member of the Society of Authors' stuff. They seem to think that unlike other people they have a God-given right to publish exactly what they want. All of us should exercise a degree of censorship. In my children's books there's a wild degree of censorship. I eschew all sexual matters. And violence as well." [130] Here again, of course, the pot was calling the kettle black. In most contexts almost everyone who knew him agreed that he had precious little capacity for self-censorship. Nor was he interested in consistency. Making a point with force was much more important.

There were other strong inner conflicts that lay behind these outbursts. "Roald had a great sense of justice," his nephew Nicholas told me. "But he just couldn't get his head round it in relation to himself." Logsdail thought in this respect his uncle was like many of the great painters he had represented as a gallery owner. "They're so insightful, they're so clever, but when they reflect upon themselves they don't get it, because they can't apply the same things to themselves that they see in the world. They see themselves apart . . . Roald was so black and white. What he really wanted was the middle ground. Yet he never found it." [131] Logsdail felt strongly too that the family's sense of not belonging to the English middle classes was tied into this conundrum, that his uncle was perhaps so fearless of public opinion because he did not feel he truly fitted in.

But something more fundamental may have lurked behind this need to stir. Murray Pollinger thought that Roald would float an opinion he did not hold – "Isn't Beethoven a crummy musician?" – just to get conversation going. Ophelia however thought that, at some level, this perverse trait was tied into the misanthropy that had developed in her father during the war. "He felt that everybody was capable of great acts of cruelty," she told me, sensing that this was somehow linked to his need to shock. "That was important because he felt life was shocking . . . and I think he felt there was something truthful and real about shocking people." [132] During his interview with Peter Lennon, too, Dahl admitted that, in his view, adults were "not likeable people",[133] adding that he usually felt happier with children. They were more straightforward and easier to handle.

Roald had, in any event, long celebrated the need to become irate. In an article written for the *New York Times* in December 1983, he had praised Alfred Knopf for possessing this quality, describing him as "a terrible wrathful man with a slow fuse burning in one end of his belly and a stick of dynamite in the other. This is nice," he concluded, "because explosions are exciting."[134] D. H. Lawrence was another of his literary heroes, whose polemical writing appealed to him greatly. "Any article that is worth anything at all is almost certain to be contentious," he once wrote in a letter to Mike Watkins. "Lawrence, who was the best of all critics, never wrote an uncontentious piece in his life. Everything he said boiled and bubbled with wrath and contempt."[135] Nevertheless, Liccy was frequently frustrated that Roald seldom, if ever, slept on a decision.[136] He liked to act spontaneously and his responses were, as Neisha recalled, more often "from the heart than from the head".[137] Moreover, because he was unaccustomed to being challenged, he found it almost impossible ever to back down gracefully. His niece Astri recalled that Roald "always made important decisions within the family and no one questioned them".[138] Nicky Logsdail was far from being alone when he told me that he could not ever remember his uncle apologizing about anything.

In 1971, Roald quarrelled with the headmistress of Ophelia and Lucy's junior school, Godstowe. He had contributed some money to rebuild one of the classrooms and wrote to Patricia Fitzmaurice-Kelly, complaining bitterly that now he had seen the work, he felt "cheated" and "conned". His language was intemperate and characteristically inflammatory – the classroom was no more than a "hole" that would "never be tolerated in any village school in England today".[139] Miss Fitzmaurice-Kelly however held her own. Claiming she was "shattered" by his letter, she calmly answered his criticisms, offered to return his money and suggested that, if he felt so strongly, perhaps he should make other arrangements for his children's education.[140] It was a situation reminiscent of the great "tornado of troubles" with Sheila St Lawrence a decade before.

This time, however, Roald reflected upon his own temperament before responding. "I agree that the tone of my letter, and indeed some of the phrases I used, were unforgivable. But my trouble is I get so carried away by it all, I forget completely the impact these things may have upon the reader." Interestingly, he then backed down completely. "I simply must repair this quarrel, and with you of all people, for whom I have a massive admiration. I wouldn't dream of annulling my deed of covenant whatever happened, and I don't want my daughters to go to another school. So if you accept my apologies for having said the things I said and if you come with us to the premiere of *Willy Wonka and the Chocolate Factory*, I will in future try to write only books and stories, not letters."[141]

But neither Olympian detachment nor standing on the sidelines was part of his nature. He was too impulsive, too spontaneous. In 1988, he and Liccy were driving through Hyde Park when they saw several policemen beating up a black man who was resisting arrest. Roald filed a formal complaint against the police for brutality. "He was really appalled by this, almost in a naive kind of way," his daughter Ophelia recalled, "and he was not, by any stretch of the imagination, anti-police. But I think he had a well-honed, if simplistic sense of fairness and he thought he had seen something unjust."[142] The case went to court. There, the police used the fact that Dahl was a fiction writer against him, and although he claimed that, on the contrary, this made him "adept at observing situations and noting details",[143] other witnesses contradicted his account of events. The defence implied that he had exaggerated reality and the case was dropped. Once again, it seemed, his need for hyperbole, which served him so well as a writer of fiction, had become counterproductive in a public context. The fact that, once committed to a position, he was seldom able to find a neutral, let alone reverse, gear could make him seem unreasonable, insensitive and oddly inconsistent. This made him easily misunderstood. Like one of his favourite characters, the Big Friendly Giant, it seemed his words often came out not quite as he intended. When accused of not making sense, the Giant's response was childishly simple and might have been appropriate too for his creator: "What I mean and what I say is something different."[144]

CHAPTER NINETEEN

The Wizard and the Wonderman

THROUGHOUT THE 1970S AND 1980s, Roald's confidence in his ability to penetrate a child's mind became increasingly profound. As he himself aged, and his body became ever more painful and unreliable – by the mid-1980s he was almost two inches shorter than he had been in his twenties – his perceptions about childhood and about how children think became ever more certain. Even as he approached seventy, this naive eye remained startlingly undimmed: "The mind of a child is a dark wood. It is full of secret half-civilized thoughts that are forgotten like dreams a short time afterwards," he wrote. "And it is no easy matter for the adult to recall totally and with absolute clarity some forty or fifty years later just what it was like to be a little boy, or a little girl. I can do it. I am certain I can."[1] The daily pile of fan mail from young readers bore out his conviction and fed a sense of certainty about his destiny and stature as a children's author that was some consolation for any disappointment he felt about his exclusion from the inner citadel of literary London. Critics and librarians might still disparage his work, but a powerful constituency of young fans, devoted to him and his books, offered an alternative, constant source of gratification and fodder for his self-esteem. This perception empowered him. He began to talk about himself as their representative and spokesman. The misanthrope, who his daughter Ophelia recalled had "never really trusted adults", was becoming the "geriatric child" redeemed by the youth of his adoring readers.

In January 1982, Roald wrote a letter to the thirty-two-year-old

Stephen Roxburgh at Farrar, Straus & Giroux, introducing himself to his new editor. "I must warn you," he told Roxburgh, "that you are not, alas, taking on a sprightly young writer of thirty, with years and years of work before him. I am sixty-five and a half. I have two steel hips and a spine that has suffered no less than six laminectomies (from war injury). So how much more there is in me I simply do not know. I doubt there is an adult novel or even a new collection of short stories. But I *would* like to go on writing books for children as long as the old fire keeps smouldering. I love work and am unhappy if I am not at it seven days a week."[2] Although illness would stalk him throughout the 1980s, and death would eventually claim him late in 1990, this last decade of his life would be by far the most productive of his career – despite the fact that he viewed writing still as more craftsmanship than inspiration, sticking to his mantra that what the writer needed was "an infinite capacity for taking pains . . . you really have to get down to it and work and work and work and work . . . Rewrite and rewrite and rewrite."[3]

Much of this new productivity was due to Liccy, who gave up her own job at Carvers and Gilders and set about changing the nature of Gipsy House. Her arrival there was not without stresses. The years of deceit had left a legacy of resentment and anger. Roald's children initially somewhat begrudged her presence in their home, while Liccy's three girls felt somewhat "swallowed up by the Dahl pack".[4] From being one of three, Neisha recalled, she was now "one of many". Liccy, however, was determined to set a new agenda. She and Roald had decided between themselves that they would not attempt to have any children together, so that at least would minimize disruption to the status quo. She also focused on making the house calmer, more comfortable and more stable. It would be prettier. It would be more private.

The swimming pool and greenhouse were pulled down to make way for a separate guest annex and a snooker room – all away from the main house. The old guest room on the ground floor, now a drawing room, became their master bedroom. The garden was redesigned. The open house policy that his nephews and nieces remembered affectionately from earlier days became more restricted. Roald complained bitterly about the building work. "The entire inside is being ripped out and redesigned," he told his old schoolfriend Douglas Highton. "Dust and bricks and dusty labourers are in every room except one, in which we cook and sit and eat."[5] Tessa recalled that she could never remember her father as fractious and bad-tempered as he was when the remodelling was going on. But the end result provided him with a restful, tranquil environment that eased his final years enormously.[6]

Almost everyone was aware how much happier he seemed with Liccy around him. She delighted in looking after him and both glowed in each other's presence. "I know few couples that loved one another the way they did," Tom Maschler told me. "She took care of everything."[7] Roald himself paid tribute to his new wife – they had married quietly in 1983 at Brixton Town Hall – ghosting an article in 1985 about life in Gipsy House for his Australian housekeeper, Sandy Anderson, who had helped nurse him through another operation – this time for suspected bowel cancer. "Felicity is a lovely woman of forty-six," he declared. "She is beautiful, cheerful, clever . . . and everything a wife should be. She cares for her husband totally and without her I doubt very much if he could keep going. He is obviously deeply in love with her and she with him and it is a fine thing to watch them when they are together."[8] Even his own children, who initially felt resentment toward her, had to admit that their father was transformed. Lucy thought that Liccy "stimulated" and "fulfilled him in a way no one had done before",[9] because she was strong, energetic, positive and not in the least bit needy. Ophelia noticed that her father had relaxed physically. "He seemed comfortable kissing people on the cheek, and suddenly he was embracing us more often and with less brusqueness."[10] Charlotte thought Roald, for his part, made her mother "stronger, because she had been struggling a bit before", while observing that her need "to control" was almost as great as Roald's.* Quentin Blake sensed that Liccy brought Roald a kind of new "equilibrium" because she

---

*Paradoxically, Charlotte also admitted that in usurping her own father's role and lavishing his generosity and affection on the Crosland girls, Roald sometimes exerted a control over them that was, in retrospect, "cruel" to her own father – Charlotte Crosland, Conversation with the author, 03/12/10.

was not a "competing ego".[11] Everyone noticed that his writing productivity increased dramatically.

Now, after years of distractions, in love and surrounded by this newfound stability, Roald was able to concentrate more fully on his most particular pleasure, his writing. In a radio interview in 1970, he described the almost sensual delight he got when he went up to his hut, closed the door and sat down in his chair.

> *You become a different person, you are no longer an ordinary fellow who walks around and looks after his children and eats meals and does silly things, you go into a completely different world. I personally draw all the curtains in the room, so that I don't see out the window and put on a little light which shines on my board. Everything else in your life disappears and you look at you bit of paper and get completely lost in what you're doing. You do become another person for a moment. Time disappears completely. You may start at nine in the morning and the next time you look at your watch, when you're getting hungry, it can be lunchtime. And you've absolutely no idea that three or fours hours have gone by. So when you meet a musician or a writer, you shouldn't be surprised that they look exactly like ordinary people, because in that part of their lives they are . . . All the best artists that I've known, like Hemingway and Steinbeck and EB White and Thurber, behave very normally in their private lives . . . They are ordinary people who have a secret compartment somewhere in their brain which they can switch on when they become quite alone and go to work.[12]*

Freed from the "financial evils"[13] of the Random House four-book deal, he felt ready to embark upon a longer children's book, his first for five years. He worked on it for most of 1981, and in October wrote to Dirk Bogarde that he was "feeling a little light . . . because yesterday I finished the longest children's novel I've done so far, the end of about 600 hours work, seven days a week".[14] The story had begun with something he scribbled in an Ideas Book many years before: "The man who captured and kept in bottles – Ideas from the brain – Thoughts – Pieces of knowledge – Jokes – I saw them thrashing around furiously in their jars."[15] He had explored this character briefly in *Danny the Champion of the World*. Now he would devote a whole book to the Big Friendly Giant – *The BFG*.

Dedicated to Olivia on the twentieth anniversary of her death, the book would become Roald's own favourite of all his works. However, as with so many of his longer stories, it had a complex journey to completion. The first draft had a male hero called Jody, while the BFG himself spoke barely a word of "gobblefunk" – the mangled English that would come to define his eccentric and lovable personality. "As I am telling you before, I know exactly what words I am wanting to say," the BFG declared to the eventual heroine, Sophie, who was named after Roald's first grandchild, "but somehow or other they is always getting squiff-squiddled around."[16] Both idiosyncratic language and new protagonist were in place when Roald sent a completed draft to Stephen Roxburgh at Farrar, Straus & Giroux. Tom Maschler at Cape thought it ready for publication in the United Kingdom and Roald was already quietly excited about it. Yet he sensed it might be further improved, although he did not think he had enough energy left for any significant rewrites. "I think it is the longest children's book I have done," he told Roxburgh,

> *and I believe that in time it will become as well established as either "Charlie" or "James", both of which have been going some twenty years with undiminished sales. I am a severe self-critic and have been a long time in the business, so I am not giving this opinion lightly. But listen, do you as an editor have any suggestions to make about this book? I don't mean major changes. I couldn't do that. But I would welcome criticisms of a more minor nature. A wrong word. An unnecessary sentence. A bad paragraph. A poor joke. You see, Tom Maschler is a great picture editor, probably the greatest. But he is not by nature a word man.*[17]

Roxburgh and Dahl were made for each other in many ways. An academic specialist in Victorian children's literature, Roxburgh had become disenchanted with university life and joined Farrar, Straus in 1978 as an assistant in their small but prestigious children's book department. His talents were such that by 1981 he had become editor-in-chief. He was thrusting, hardworking and he bubbled over with energy; but he was nervous of dealing with Dahl. He had also been warned by both Murray Pollinger and Tom Maschler that his new author did not take kindly to editing. Nevertheless, he believed the manuscript he had been sent could be polished. So he took a deep breath and wrote Roald a "meticulous" letter, eleven pages long, with many small observations alongside some much more significant suggestions about how *The BFG* might be improved structurally and how the giant's bizarre language might be further refined. He even told Roald that he thought some passages of the book had gone too far in offending a significant part of his potential market: the librarians. With some trepidation, he despatched his comments.

He need not have worried. Roald wrote back enthusiastically with his own lengthy commentary on these notes. For Roxburgh, this response was "an editor's dream".[18] For Roald, it was even better. He had rediscovered the kind of thoughtful, sensitive critical voice that he had not really experienced since the days of Ann Watkins and Sheila St Lawrence. And he embraced this new force in his life with an enthusiasm that bubbled over into gobblefunk.

> *I am absolutely swishboggled and sloshbungled by the trouble you have taken and by the skill of your editorial work on The BFG. In nearly forty years of dealing with publishers, I have never seen a job like it. Gottlieb's maximum was two pages of comments. Maschler's nil. Rayner Unwin's nil. Michael Joseph nil, etc . . . Ninety-eight percent of your comments were thoroughly sound and a couple of them were vital . . . The whole thing must have driven you round the twist. It nearly drove me the same way going through them. But it was all marvellously worthwhile . . . You are right that frobscottle* [a delicious fizzy liquid, whose bubbles travel downwards] *and whizzpoppers* [extravagant noisy farts brought on by drinking

frobscottle] *should not be an isolated incident never to be mentioned again. So I've gone even further and had the BFG doing a whizzpopper for the Queen. Slightly vulgar, perhaps. But you and I know that the children will love it. And this is a book for children. To hell with the spinster librarians of your country. By now I am impervious to their comments. The louder they shout, the better the book does.*

Only one thing in your letter disturbs me. You say in the final paragraph ". . . the book could be published just as it is and be quite successful . . ." It's the word "quite" that worries me. It has two meanings. One is "moderately", the other is "thoroughly". The former is the more common usage, and if that is what you meant, then you've got me fretting. I honestly think that I have yet to write a children's book that is only moderately successful, and I hope this one isn't it. Anyway, I do thank you enormously for the blood, sweat and tears you have spent on my behalf.[19]

Roxburgh's response in turn was swift and to the point: "I stand corrected. The BFG will be *thoroughly* successful . . . And I stand flabberstacked by your kind words. Praise from you is praise indeed. The scenes you reworded are terrific. The new scene in which the BFG whizzpops for the Queen is simply one of the funniest things I have ever read. The entire office is laughing out loud."[20]

When Roxburgh told Roald that he would be visiting London, he was immediately invited for lunch to Gipsy House. Yet he was unsure the meeting was such a good idea. Would he and his author have anything to talk about? "I came from a teeny little town on the wrong side of the tracks in Massachusetts," he told me later. "And now, here I was in England – with the great Roald Dahl." As he boarded the train for the forty-minute ride from London to Great Missenden, he hoped he would get away from the meeting without doing anything stupid or embarrassing. Roald collected him at the station. Over lunch, any anxieties soon dissolved and it was immediately apparent to both men that they were on the same wavelength.[21] The "shy, intimidated editor", who was still in awe of his author, discovered not only that he and his author had literary tastes in common – both were admirers of Hemingway – but that they were also keen wine buffs and knowledgeable about woodwork and carpentry. Roxburgh at one time had worked finishing cabinets.

He returned to London later that afternoon relieved that the encounter had passed without an explosion, but unaware what a striking impression he had made. The following evening, after a day of meetings, he arrived back at the house of a friend in Chelsea to discover that Roald had driven down to London and personally delivered him the manuscript of his new book: *The Witches*. He had also left a message informing his young editor that he had not shown it to anyone else. When Roxburgh called Tom Maschler to ask what he should do, Maschler had just one piece of advice – to drop whatever he was doing and read the manuscript now. "Dahl's not in a hurry until he's in a hurry," he told him. That night, Roxburgh read the script, and the following morning he returned on the train to Great Missenden to discuss it with Roald.[22]

The BFG was not only the first book on which Roald collaborated with Stephen Roxburgh, it was also the first long book on which he would work with the illustrator who would become synonymous with almost his entire children's oeuvre: Quentin Blake. Blake had first worked on a Dahl book in 1978, when – in response to Roald's complaints that Maschler had failed to find him an illustrator for *The Enormous Crocodile*, his first book for really very young kids – Murray Pollinger's wife, Gina, suggested the forty-six-year-old artist as a potential collaborator.[23] Gina was a celebrated and successful children's literary agent in her own right, and Roald respected her and frequently sought her advice. Maschler, who later took credit for having conceived the pairing, agreed, and the combination was an instant success. Blake's colourful, witty, yet slightly dangerous illustrations were a sparkling counterpoint to Roald's anarchic description of a greedy, cunning reptile hunting children down in the African jungle.

The team then worked together again on two of the Random House four books – *The Twits* and *George's Marvellous Medicine* – where Quentin's witty caricatures brilliantly animated the two hideous practical jokers, as well as George's grumpy grandmother, with her "pale brown teeth" and "small puckered up mouth like a dog's bottom".[24] Curiously, the illustrations for *Dirty Beasts*, which Blake himself would reillustrate in 1984, were originally drawn by Rosemary Fawcett. More curious still was the fact that, until they started working on *The BFG*, writer and illustrator did not meet each other except in Tom Maschler's office at Jonathan Cape.

Blake remembered that initially their relationship was formal. "I was rather nervous and frightened of him," he admitted.[25] And the collaboration on *The BFG* did not get off to a good start. Maschler had asked Quentin only to provide twelve illustrations for the book's twenty-four chapters. Roald insisted on more. "I hope I am not right in thinking that because Quentin is not sharing in the royalties of this book he has done a rather quicky job and got away with as few illustrations as possible,"[26] he complained. When, a few days later, he discovered that Quentin indeed was not to blame, Maschler was the recipient of an incendiary letter:

> There is no way in which I will permit a major children's book of mine to be published with only twelve illustrations. It cannot be difficult for you to imagine my astonishment when I discover (from Roger Straus) that you were unwilling to pay Quentin more than £300 for illustrating The BFG. Of course he gave you only twelve pictures! This is cheeseparing to the ultimate degree. It is also an insult to my book. You have got yourself into this difficulty and I'm afraid you are going to have to get yourself out of it as best you can. I will not agree to your publishing The BFG unless properly and fully illustrated in the same manner as all the others . . . I do not wish to have a long telephonic conversation about this and I don't wish to be browbeaten. I am too upset for that. I want to be left in peace while this is properly resolved, which it must be as soon as possible.[27]

Maschler quickly backed down, and Quentin was offered a better deal, which involved starting all over again from scratch. It was during this process that Roald and Quentin finally met on their own and Quentin began to realize just how precisely Roald imagined his stories, and how close in particular he was to the character of the BFG. Initially, Dahl had described his character wearing a black hat, apron and large black boots. But when Roald saw Quentin's drawing, he knew at once that the giant needed to look softer and more lovable. During the course of his discussions with Quentin on this new look, he posted his illustrator one of his own gigantic Norwegian sandals in a "lumpy brown paper parcel"[28] to help him get the character right.

But the giant was not entirely modelled on his creator. There were a number of other sources, including Dahl's ever present builder, Wally Saunders, whose huge ears influenced the BFG's. "I have been working hard with Quentin Blake to make *The BFG* look curious and comical," Roald told Roxburgh. "I think we have about got it now and this necessitates a change in my brief description of the clothes he was wearing."[29] He was absolutely confident about his judgement, Quentin recalled, citing as an example the sequence toward the end of the story where the aggressive child-eating giants are rounded up and captured. "We must see helicopters," Roald had told him. "Children like helicopters." Quentin responded well to this enthusiasm and, aside from the general teasing and banter that went with the territory, there was never any animosity between them. "My belief is that if you collaborate with the book, with the words, then you collaborate with the author," he told me. Roald "might try and wind me up", he added, but his intention was "always affectionate".[30]

Writing *The BFG* had taken "quite a lot of electricity out of the battery".[31] Dahl admitted, but even while he was impatiently waiting for it to charge up again, he had begun work on *The Witches*. His youngest daughter, Lucy, saw Liccy's hand behind this increased productivity. She felt her father wanted to impress Liccy, that she was about the only person around whom he felt he had to behave. "But I think she pushed him too," she reflected. "I think she knew that there was still a burning fire there . . . I don't think it was a conscious decision to say, 'Get back on the horse and write something brilliant, because you've still got it in you.' I think it all worked organically. He was happy doing it, and she was happy watching it happen."[32] Tom Maschler too was "filled with admiration" to see how Roald, though ill and obviously in pain, continued to grapple with his craft. "He was incredibly ambitious for his own work and he was always trying to surpass himself," he told me.[33]

In 1984, Dahl began writing another book for very young readers, *The Giraffe and the Pelly and Me* – a story about a little boy who starts a window-cleaning company, with the help of his friends: a giraffe, a pelican and a dancing monkey. Its thirty-two colourful pages, superbly illustrated by Quentin Blake, are the literary equivalent of a soufflé – simple, light and easily devoured. But behind this effortless façade lay seven months of hard work, and a file of discards and rewrites that exceeded 300 pages. Dahl later described writing this story as "the hardest thing in the world".[34] Once again Stephen Roxburgh was a crucial part of the mix. His obsessive attention to the detail of editing was such that he likened himself to "the vampire of legend who is caught by the morning sun because he must pick up every grain of sand sprinkled on the threshold that stands between him and his coffin".[35] Roald's own view was less elaborate. "Three cheers for Stephen Roxburgh!" he told Roger Straus.[36]

The physical pain he was suffering made working both harder and easier. Now that Liccy was around and his children were moving into adulthood, he was freed up from struggling with many of his previous responsibilities. A series of accomplished cooks and housekeepers were on hand to make life at Gipsy House even more comfortable. His beloved garden too had largely been handed over to Liccy and to professionals. "Gardening is for the birds if you are sixty or over," he told Dirk Bogarde. "I see all these old farts digging their allotments across the lane, straining their backs and bending their bones . . . I don't garden any more. I supervise."[37] So, when he was not bedridden, as Stephen Roxburgh recalled he often was, his available energy could be focused on writing. For years he had longed for this situation and it had been denied to him. "I am an old man full of metal," he declared, describing his body as a "rickety structure" that preferred "sitting comfortably in an armchair with a writing-board on the lap and the feet resting on a suitcase" to being out of doors.[38] Yet other pleasures were not entirely abandoned. He still went gambling, if less frequently than before, and never recklessly (he usually risked only £200), while he indulged his passion for wine by going "banco"[39] on the excellent 1982 Bordeaux vintage, buying over a thousand cases of the very greatest wines, a few of which still lie, unconsumed, in the Gipsy House cellar.

Looked after by Liccy and surrounded by his family, Dahl now seemed like an ancient lion at the head of his pride. In 1988, Tom Maschler and his managing director, Graham Carleton Greene, invited Roald for a birthday dinner in a private room at London's Garrick Club. They told him he could invite whomever he wanted. Ever the family man, his first choices were Liccy and the available children. As special guests he added the broadcaster Frank Delaney, the actress Joanna Lumley, and Francis Bacon, whom he had not seen for some time. Lumley was surprised that she had been invited because the only time they had previously met – on a live television show – Roald had "snapped" at her and she felt that she irritated him. However, she was flattered at the invitation and particularly eager to meet Bacon, who – much to everyone's surprise – turned up "at eight o'clock on the dot, smartly dressed and not remotely drunk". Lumley remembered what good company Roald was that evening, how he talked about fiction writing being the highest form of any kind of creative art, and how Bacon's "little round black eyes sparkled" when Dahl began to talk to him across the large table halfway through dinner. Delaney then "butted in" on their conversation, annoying Dahl and provoking him to announce that the meal was ended and he was going home. "We all had to suddenly swallow our chocolate mousse," Lumley recalled, "and leave our undrunk wine and fight for our coats . . . It was a ghastly end to a fabulous evening."[40]

Dahl's sense of himself as a naughty schoolboy never left him. Nor did his sense of exuberance or his belief that life needed to be filled with "treats". He relished giving unusual and unexpected presents. Quentin Blake recalled Roald putting two oysters into his hand as he was leaving Gipsy House because a basket of seafood that he had ordered had just arrived. His stepdaughter, Neisha, enthused about his zestful eagerness, that "twinkle in the eye" that she found so attractive. Even his dreams of glory were undiminished. "In my old age, I spend my life having dreams of glory," he told Todd McCormack. "I'm always winning the golf Open Championship or tennis at Wimbledon or something like that. I go through long thinks about this lying in the dark . . . trying to get to sleep . . . imagining every little detail of what happens . . . I lie in bed and dream up that I've beaten them all, and everyone's surprised. It's great fun, it's the same with books. You associate with the heroine or the hero . . . You pretend it's you."[41] And sometimes he could even laugh at himself. In 1984, responding to news that a school in Norfolk had just named one of its houses after him, he wrote to the head teacher: "I'm a bit bowled over and of course enormously honoured . . . Already I can see the children lining the edge of the playing field during house matches and yelling 'Come on, Dahl!', 'Up Dahl!' and many other personal obscenities."[42]

Stephen Roxburgh was a key ingredient in this newfound enthusiasm. Roger Straus described Roald's relationship to his editor as a "mad attachment". Dahl "sort of fell in love with him", he told me, recalling rumours spreading around Farrar, Straus that plans were even afoot for Roxburgh to marry one of Roald's daughters.[43] Roxburgh acknowledged that he had indeed "adored" Roald and felt like "a kind of disciple" when he was with him, while Roald revelled in the attention he was receiving from the kind of literary intellectual who would often not give him the time of day. It seemed the more they worked together, the deeper this professional relationship was becoming. Roxburgh found his author "enormously responsive" to "every level of detail" of his criticisms – "from broader conceptual issues, structural issues, right down to the structure of sentences". The two men also enjoyed each other's company. Roald "loved to be provocative . . . to make you respond", Roxburgh remembered. "He liked nothing better than to get you fired up."[44]

No one was happier with these new developments than Dahl's British literary agent, Murray Pollinger, who from 1979 had taken over his global representation. He had worked for Dahl since the author joined his father, Laurence Pollinger, in 1960, and though the two men were never intimate, over twenty years an immense kinship and loyalty had developed between them. Murray too had initially "hero-worshipped" his client, finding him "dynamic, dashing, just huge". "I loved his hugeness," he told me, affectionately recalling a party in New York in 1961, where towering above everyone else, and quaffing double martinis as if they were water, Roald "had to stand with his legs wide apart in order to look people in the eye and hear what they were saying".[45] Murray, by contrast, was slender, spare, polished and self-consciously elegant. Ophelia recalled that he would only drink tea if it was served in a china cup, while Wendy Kress, Roald's last secretary, remembered him as "ramrod-straight, greased hair, old-fashioned . . . always a gentleman".[46]

Laurence was rather different. Murray described his father as "a Victorian tyrant [who] ran a very harsh home and governed the business the same way",[47] and any initial loyalty Roald might have felt toward him was soon transferred to his son, who dealt with his day-to-day UK affairs. Roald also admired the judgement of Murray's wife, Gina, and was delighted when he and Pat were made godparents to their son, Edmund. Thus the Pollingers too were absorbed into the extended Dahl family. "We saw Murray's nipper last Sunday," Roald wrote to Mike Watkins in 1964. "Fine child. He and Gina are like a couple of parrots who have just seen their first egg hatch out. They sit on the edge of the nest, preening their feathers and making little clucking noises in their throats."[48]

A few months later, Roald attended a family gathering at the Pollingers. "Laurence was there acting ostentatiously the part of the generous grandfather," he told Watkins. "By that I mean he was dispensing pennies – only pennies – one at a time to his three other grandchildren. He said, 'I give them pennies every time I see them.' 'How often do you see them?' I asked. This question made him uncomfortable, and there was a good deal of nose-blowing to make his reply inaudible. So I asked the question again. The answer was, 'Quite often, old man, about two or three times a year.' His maximum financial liability therefore, to each child, was ninepence per annum."[49] When, five years later, Murray fell out with his father and resigned from the agency, leaving "without a penny", Roald was "the most effusive"[50] of a nucleus of about a dozen of his clients, including Laurie Lee and Penelope Lively, who backed him to set up on his own. Murray "has handled my affairs for a long time now with extreme efficiency and he is the only person who knows the intricacies of these many contracts", he told Laurence Pollinger. "Were someone else to step into his shoes now, I should be the loser. I know you would not want that."[51] The same day he wrote to Mike Watkins to tell him that he proposed "to stand by [Murray] 100%".[52] He did.

Murray was forever grateful for this display of loyalty. "Is my face red," he declared. "You make me a bit ashamed of my close relatives . . . that you should have been stirred up to write as you did . . . I am deeply grateful for your loyalty, expressed in such robust and irrefutable letters. This means an enormous amount to me at a time like this, and I am unable to find words meaningful enough to thank you."[53] The two families' lives were further intertwined when Roald dedicated *Charlie and the Great Glass Elevator* to his godson Edmund – apart from Charles Marsh, the only person outside the direct family ever to receive such a dedication. Then, in 1976, by a bizarre twist of fate, the shunt he had helped to design for Theo saved Edmund's life – after his godson was admitted to hospital as the result of a minor car accident and a routine scan revealed severe neurological problems. It was hardly surprising that Murray felt his client was always "a tower of strength to our family when we were really up against it".[54]

Dahl and Pollinger made a good team. Pollinger liked the fact that his client was "such a sharp businessman"[55] and was always in the thick of things when it came to deals and negotiation, but while Gina sometimes got involved in editorial discussions, Murray stayed almost entirely out of them. "He never challenged Roald," Roxburgh recalled. "He never offered an opinion . . . His domain was the business part."[56] However, while Pollinger might celebrate Dahl's negotiating skills, he was to learn that his client could get out of his depth when it came to other financial issues. Early in 1986, Dahl received a letter from the UK Inland Revenue asking for details about his Swiss companies, *Icarus* and *Anric*. His lawyer went to see the tax inspector, Mr C. G. White at the Inland Revenue, and reported that White was going to instigate a "substantial enquiry" into Roald's "overseas employment arrangements". He added threateningly that these investigators were usually "reasonably determined and unreasonably aggressive".[57]

Dahl had regretted *Icarus* almost as soon as he set it up. A year after its creation, he admitted to his lawyer that he was "thoroughly fed up with everything" and that – as he was "a moron when it comes to accounts and figures" – he wanted his UK income paid directly so that he could "pay my tax on it immediately".[58] But his foreign earnings were so inextricably wound up in the Swiss companies and he had spent so much money setting them up that unravelling those did not seem an option. The investigation changed all that. And it did not get off to a good start. Roald, in his own words, "made a cock" of filling in the initial forms, and as a result Mr White became "rather ratty".[59] It was soon evident too that his accountant's initial strategy of giving minimal information was proving counterproductive. So Roald took Liccy's advice and hired a new lawyer and accountant: Bill Geffen and Alan Langridge.

Their plan was to reveal everything to the Revenue, ascribing any anomalies in the two Swiss companies to the fact that Dahl was unworldly in matters of finance. In this they were not being disingenuous. His final tax lawyer, Martin Goodwin, would later describe his client's approach to figures, with a smile, as "somewhat unsophisticated",[60] although Geffen and Langridge may have been stretching the truth a little when they suggested that Roald actually had been intimidated by his Swiss banker, Mr Schlaeppi.[61] By September 1986, Roald was firmly behind the new plan. "We should help White in every way we can," he told Geffen. "I personally believe he is well-disposed towards me now and I will bend over backwards to keep it that way. I do not want to string this affair out."[62] It was not surprising. The previous year Roald had had three major bowel operations and, in his own words, "only just survived". He was still "in and out of hospital constantly and . . . under prolonged and massive doses of two different antibiotics".[63]

He knew he was likely to suffer a hefty penalty. Late in September, he paid £400,000 on account to the Inland Revenue and another £100,000 three months later. However, the deliberations continued. Before Christmas he suggested to Wendy Kress, his secretary, that perhaps they might send Mr White a Christmas present, to encourage him to move a bit more swiftly. Liccy had to explain to him why she did not think this was a good idea. When he eventually received a proposal from the Inland

Revenue for the final settlement of the affair, he confessed to Alan Lang-ridge his complete lack of comprehension of the minutiae of the deal. "I personally understand almost nothing of Mr White's letter, but I feel he is trying to be helpful," he told Langridge. "I have given orders for the dissolution of the Swiss companies *Icarus* and *Anric* . . . I have no further comment because I simply do not understand the rest of it." [64]

In January 1987, the settlement was eventually agreed. In all, he owed £717,000. He paid the debt by closing his Swiss operations altogether and by renegotiating the sale of his US paperback rights from Bantam to Penguin – a stratagem devised by Roger Straus, who had discovered a technicality in Dahl's contract that allowed him to do this if Bantam came under new ownership.† Roald was grateful to his publisher for this and thanked his accountant for his "magic work" in dealing with the investigation. [65] When, in September 1987, he finally received the "epoch-making" note from the Inland Revenue informing him that the whole business was irrevocably settled, he confessed that he was thinking of framing it. [66] Mr White wound up by thanking Dahl for his "patience and co-operation", but characteristically it was Roald himself who had the last word. "Your last paragraph gave me more pleasure than my first bicycle on my ninth birthday," he wrote in reply, adding: "Now that our business is concluded, I am able without prejudice to send you a small token of thanks for the sympathetic way you helped me out of my embar-rassment." [67] Dahl sent him signed copies of some of his children's books.

Throughout the 1980s, his books became ever more successful. *The Witches*, which was published in 1983, a year after *The BFG*, and dedicated to Liccy in the year he married her, was another massive hit with the public. Roald's correspondence with Roxburgh over the book is intriguing for the robust but respectful way in which various discus-sions, both textual and political, were handled. "He was impatient . . . he wanted to move quickly . . . I was going over there three or four times a year," [68] Roxburgh told me, explaining, with a chuckle, that his own lib-eral outlook naturally made him a trifle uneasy about a story that focused

---

†Bantam had recently been sold to the Newhouse magazine group.

on a bunch of two-faced, vicious bald hags with clawlike fingers, who descend on the sleepy English seaside town of Bournemouth in an attempt to ensure that every single child in England is "rrrubbed out, sqvashed, sqvirted, sqvittered and frrrrittered".[69]

Roald was convinced Roxburgh was overreacting. First he pointed out, justifiably, that the boy hero's grandmother, who plays a crucial role in the story, was "the nicest person in the whole thing", so it was unfair to accuse him of being misogynistic. Then, observing that he was "not as frightened of offending women as you are", he pointed out that "this sort of problem arises in all my children's stories and I ignore it". Nevertheless, he thanked Roxburgh for taking so much trouble, and reminded him in exaggerated terms that he had never had an editor like him before. Once again he found sanctuary in his understanding of his audience. "I must keep reminding you that this is a book for children and I don't give a bugger what grown-ups think about it," he concluded.[70]

The book was significant, too, not only for its rollicking narrative and its creepy humour but for a particularly daring plot, in which – halfway through the tale – the Grand High Witch turns the boy narrator into a mouse, and from then on the reader sees the world from a rodent perspective. Moreover, in the final pages, Dahl uses this device to handle issues of love and death with extraordinary sensitivity, adroitness and lack of sentimentality. For him, the mouse's short lifespan was not something to be glossed over. The moment when the narrator realizes that his new mouse-life will be short, and that he and his eighty-six-year-old grandmother will probably die together, is not one of sadness but of childish tenderness and profound unspoken emotion. As the mouse and the grandmother snuggle up together, her lace dress tickling his nose, they discuss the extraordinary rate at which a mouse's heart beats. The grandmother tells him how she can hear it humming when he is lying next to her on the pillow at night in bed.

The two of us remained silent in front of the fire for a long time after that, thinking about all these wonderful things. "My darling," she said at last, "are you sure you don't mind being a mouse for the rest of your

*life?" "I don't mind at all," I said. "It doesn't matter who you are or
what you look like as long as somebody loves you."*[71]

Quentin Blake, who illustrated the book, was greatly impressed by
the deft way Roald addressed this situation; but equally striking was the
way the work once again unself-consciously celebrated the triumph of an
unlikely loving friendship over any conventional family values. This was
one of Dahl's most powerfully "subversive" qualities – and one that was
little appreciated or acknowledged in his lifetime. It was also something
that mattered hugely to him. Liccy recalled that when the director Nicholas Roeg showed him the original version of his movie adaptation, Roald
wept at this final scene of love between the grandmother and the mouse.
That this version, which was so faithful to the ending of the book, was
later abandoned for an alternative where the mouse turns back into a boy,
appalled him. He felt that Warner Bros had completely missed the point.

The Witches, as published, contained flashes of unexpected biographical detail about its author. The unnamed narrator, who loves playing with
mice, whose parents were Norwegian and who travels to his homeland
every summer for wonderful holidays with his large storytelling grandma,
were brief glimpses of what had originally been a much lengthier portrait
of Roald's own childhood that appeared in the opening pages. Roxburgh
was tenacious in his belief that this sequence of three chapters actually belonged elsewhere, and eventually he persuaded Roald to drop them. They
were not put to waste. Roxburgh already had other plans for them. "Perhaps it might not be repulsive for you to consider a book on your early
childhood/boyhood?" he suggested.[72] The seed fell immediately on fertile
ground and soon Roald, who had responded that he regarded "straight"
autobiography as "the height of egotism",[73] was roughing out drafts of
a new manuscript and sending all his childhood letters to his mother –
which she had kept in bundles "neatly tied up in blue ribbons" – over to
Roxburgh in New York for him to study.[74] A year later, *Boy* – arranged
with photographs, extracts from his letters, documents and illustrations –
was ready for publication.

Boy, and its successor *Going Solo*, published two years later, in 1986, were, as Roxburgh anticipated, immensely popular with young readers. By now what Murray Pollinger described as "the Roald Dahl phenomenon" was in full spate.[75] The books were, as Quentin Blake described them, "hybrids of true autobiography, recollections and his own imagination", because Roald "would always take a story in a direction that made it more interesting than in a way that made it more accurate". But in editing the book, Roxburgh revealed some truths to Dahl about himself – the fact that his mother was so important to his development, for instance. This provoked Dahl to suggest to Roxburgh that he might want to write his official biography. Roxburgh was "surprised, honoured, and flattered"[76] to receive the offer, accepting it calmly, but acknowledging that if Roald had "second thoughts, for whatever reason", he would happily withdraw.[77]

The idea was that the book would be completed after Dahl's death, but Roxburgh began work on it immediately – copying much of Dahl's correspondence and briefly interviewing Roald's sisters when he was in Great Missenden. When he returned to New York, he even went to visit Claudia Marsh, then in her late eighties. Twenty-one year-old Ophelia revealed how close Stephen had become to the family when she wrote suggesting that he and his girlfriend ought to come over to Great Missenden to write it. "You could stay here for the rest of your lives," she joked. "You could be Chief Logsman, snooker coach and write the book. Perhaps we could draw his life story out over, say, twelve volumes . . ." She reminded him how he fitted in, "nice and mellow", and that both her father and Liccy liked having him around. When her father referred to their occasional political differences, she jested that this was "probably a phase he was going through".[78] It was the high water mark of their friendship.

By the mid-1980s, all Roald's children were adults. Ophelia was about to travel to Haiti and discover her life's passion in Third World medicine. Tessa was married to an American financier, James Kelly, and was living not far away from Gipsy House. She had given birth to another daughter, Clover, in 1984 and a son, Luke, in 1986. Meanwhile, Lucy had married and was living on Captiva Island off the coast of Florida with her husband Michael. Her father had not approved of the match. Driving with her in the bridal car on their way to the ceremony, Roald, ever the subversive, offered to give her the cost of the reception – tens of thousands of pounds – if she changed her mind and abandoned the wedding. Theo was still living at home. Surprisingly, however, for a man who set such store by his family, all of Roald's children were in some way critical of how their father had raised them. Lucy wonders now whether he should have set more boundaries, agreeing with her stepsister Neisha that the Dahl children were too often allowed to run wild. As teenagers, at one time or another, all of them had experimented with drugs. To feed her habit, Lucy became an accomplished thief, raiding her father's stash of gambling money, his wine cellar and even pawning the gold cigarette case his mother and sisters had given him before the war.[79]

In hindsight, Lucy felt that her father simply did not understand teenagers, and that this was perhaps why, despite the fact that he himself had experienced such a miserable time at Repton, he sent all his children away to boarding school. Although Ophelia enjoyed the experience, Tessa and Lucy did not. Lucy recalled that when she begged her father not to send her away, he simply replied that she needed to be "toughened up". It was the way he had behaved when she competed in show-jumping contests. He would drive over to watch her take part, then leave her to walk home on her own, pretending he had never been there, and not realizing that she had spotted him in the crowd wearing his distinctive yellow hat. She felt he was "uncomfortable with open affection". Just as Roald had done at St Peter's, Lucy feigned illness to try to escape her fate, inventing severe headaches that led to painful medical examinations. When the moment came to go back to school, she even tried sabotaging her father's car so that he could not drive her there. Eventually, she set fire to one of the school buildings and was expelled. She was "never really disciplined" for this offence by her father, she recalled, but when he came to the school to collect her after the incident, she remembered that he found it impossible to talk to her about it. Instead, he sent her back to London to live with Tessa. "He didn't know what to do with me, he had no idea. I don't think he was very interested in adolescents. He didn't like them. I don't think he could identify with them at all."[80]

Dahl's attitude to his teenage children revealed something too about his own attitude to adolescence – an emotional period he seldom explored in conversation and that he eschewed almost entirely in his writing. It seems that for him, as for many children's writers, the advent of sexuality spelled the end of an enchanted world of innocence and fantasy – adulthood intruding rudely into the scented garden of youth. In an unpublished article written for the *Sunday Express Magazine* and titled "Things I Wish I'd Known When I Was Eighteen", he claimed, probably truthfully, that teenage sex was something about which he knew very little.

I am very glad I did not have to go through the horrors of promiscuity that torture today's children. In this benighted age, girls and boys treat the sexual act rather as rabbits do, or cattle . . . Some of you may not believe this, but I promise you that a young man in the 1930s would have to court a girl for six months before he got anywhere near the mattress. He would have to ply her with flowers, give her meals he could ill-afford and behave generally with immense circumspection. If he tried anything too early, he got the boot. And even if he did happen to have a success at the end of this long and arduous hunt, he never shacked up with the girl afterwards. Today a girl will "move in" with a boy or vice versa with no more fuss than if one was moving in an old sofa. They go on holidays together without a blink and often never see each other again afterwards. I am so happy, therefore, that I was not swept into this particular dustbin when I was eighteen.

As far as drugs were concerned, he argued that he would like to see senior boys and girls in all schools throughout the land attending, as part of their education, regular meetings of Narcotics Anonymous. "It's no good giving them a few lectures and showing a few films," he wrote. "Make them sit and listen to the dreadful tales of drugging and thieving that the young addicts at NA meetings have to tell. Once a week for the last year of school should be compulsory."[81]

Lucy was most critical of her father for the way he dealt with Theo. She remembered the period in the late 1970s – after Tessa had left home, and when Ophelia was at boarding school – when she was often alone with Theo and her father. She felt sorry for her brother because Roald seemed to demand so much of him. "I watched everything," Lucy told me. "Dad was always pushing him too far and I think Theo felt that he was always disappointing him." When his son was sixteen, Roald decided his education was over, dismissing his tutor and taking the unilateral decision that he should become a baker. After sending him to a local college to learn his craft he set him up in business with a local firm that had been facing financial difficulties. He invested much-needed capital in the enterprise, selling one of his Francis Bacons – *Landscape at Malabata* – to raise the £50,000 he needed. "Theo was so unhappy," Lucy recalled. "He would have to get up at three in the morning and be at work at four. He'd come home with cuts and burns all the way up his arms. It was never going to work."

After the bakery collapsed, Roald tried to set up an antiques business for his son, committing a further £50,000 to the business, and filling up the empty swimming pool at Gipsy House with so much stock that it looked like an "antiques supermarket".[82] The enterprise was a "big deal" for Roald, who believed that the business would be "Theo's whole future",[83] but it too was destined for failure because Theo, unlike his father, was simply not interested in furniture.

Theo, who – like so many sons of dominant, successful men – craved his father's approval, was frequently worn down by his apparent failure to live up to Roald's high standards. "He worshipped his father, smoked a pipe, and tried so much to be like him," Roald's secretary, Wendy Kress, recalled, adding that Theo loathed any uncertainty, change or upheaval. Once, she remembered, Roald had just come out of hospital, and Liccy was driving him to the Isle of Wight for a few days' recuperation. Roald had just bought a small portrait by his favourite painter, Van Gogh, and wanted to bring it with him to hang in his hotel bedroom. So he wrapped the painting in a tartan blanket and gave it to Theo to put in the car. Ophelia, who was packing the car, thought it was crazy to take the picture, so sent him back inside with it. There his father berated him for not having put the picture in the car. "He was aimless, paralysed," Wendy reflected; "he didn't know what to do, wandering around with a Van Gogh under his arm."[84] Eventually, Theo would find some measure of contentment working at the local supermarket. Some years after his father died he married and settled down in Florida, where he started his own family.

Meanwhile Roald was struggling with his last long children's book: *Matilda*. Almost all the people who read an early draft thought he had gone off the rails. The heroine, Matilda Wormwood, was "born wicked", and the story focused a great deal on gambling and cheating at the race tracks. The story climaxed at a race course, with Matilda using her telekinetic powers to manipulate the result of a horse race and therefore help her favourite teacher solve her financial problems. She died doing so. Gina Pollinger had serious reservations about this initial version. "I was shocked," she recalled, adding that the storyline seemed unnecessarily "savage" and "aggressive".[85] Stephen Roxburgh saw the first draft and thought it was so "hopeless"[86] he did not even immediately acknowledge receipt of the manuscript. This hesitation hurt Roald, who – for the first time – had to chase his editor for a response. He knew himself that there were problems with the draft. "I had awful trouble with it," he admitted later. "I got it wrong . . . the main character, the little girl kept changing."[87] It was a situation that even Roger Straus could see "depressed him . . . and made him scratchy".[88] As a result his warmth toward Stephen Roxburgh began to wane.

Sensing this cooling, Roxburgh tried hard to put things right, to reestablish his old relationship with his author. He flew over to see him three separate times to discuss revisions, but the process only exhausted Dahl and made him wonder whether he could any longer go on writing books of that length. "I started the whole book again," he told Todd McCormack in 1988. "I rewrote every word . . . It was a very interesting experience, which I've never had to do before, but maybe in my old age I'm getting not so good at it and it takes longer . . . I'm fairly happy with [the book] now. I think it's OK. But it certainly wasn't before."[89] The mellow atmosphere of his working relationship with Stephen Roxburgh, however, had disappeared. Roxburgh recalled an argument over dinner about whether Merlot or Cabernet grapes were picked first, where both he and Roald defended their territory without humour. "It was like an old marriage," he said. "We would just sort of snip at each other. And that aggravated me."[90] Roger Straus thought his colleague had become too grand, that he "had decided he knew more about Roald's work than Roald knew himself".[91] Roxburgh disagreed, but sensed that his own obsessiveness might be "wearing [Roald] down". He thought his author simply "wanted to be left alone". A comic dimension crept in, too. On his most recent visits to Gipsy House, Roxburgh had arrived sporting a beard, something he knew Dahl hated. Wendy Kress thought Stephen now looked "scruffy . . . creepy . . . a bit like a hippie". She too speculated that perhaps he had just got a little too big for his boots.[92] As Murray Pollinger recalled: "this clean-shaven, keen editor who Roald put so much faith in . . . had not only gone down the tubes, but had actually grown a bloody beard too".[93]

The editing of *Matilda* proved to be protracted. Roald complained to Liccy not that Roxburgh had too much energy, but that he had too little. Furthermore, as he was also now responsible for contractual negotiations as well as artistic ones, Roxburgh found himself negotiating a contract for the book after the revisions had been completed. Characteristically, Roald refused to accept FSG's initial offer. Roxburgh responded by hinting that perhaps the publishers deserved the proposed royalty split because of the amount of time they had put into editing the book. Appearing to put a price on the cost of editing infuriated Dahl. He readily acknowledged Roxburgh's help, but wrote that he had "never before heard of a publisher who actually made a charge in this way for editorial work". However, it was the fact that Roald sensed Roxburgh did not really value the book that rankled more than anything. In the end this was probably the key influence in his decision to take it to a different publisher. In a long letter he attempted to explain his decision to move to Penguin:

> . . . *I am not even sure that you like the final version of Matilda. The most I could get out of you on the phone when I called to see if you had gotten it after three weeks was (and these two words are seared on my memory) "It works." This contrasted very strongly with Cape's attitude. They were enthusiastic and rolled up their sleeves and went*

right ahead making plans to publish in the spring . . . So all in all, I
would be dishonest if I did not tell you that I feel pretty uncomfort-
able about this whole business . . . My duty is to my own family in the
long term, and I must not allow sentiment to prevent me from getting
the best terms I can for my works. Both Liccy and Ophelia agree re-
luctantly and with great sadness that I am right to go elsewhere now,
especially as your present duties in FSG are going to prevent you in
the future doing the kind of super-editing that you did for me in the
past.[94]

For his part, Roxburgh tried to argue that his author should have left contractual matters to his agent, and that "the rhetoric of negotiations" was
not "the language of friends".[95] He deplored the antagonistic attitude that
seemed to have entered the argument, and apologized if he was in any
way responsible for this. But it was no good. The relationship had come
to an end.

Roald was also ill. His recent bowel operations, though successful, had left him exhausted. Peter Mayer at Penguin promised him
new energy and a better royalty deal. Roger Straus tried to persuade
him to change his mind, but Roald was adamant. A reminder that
Straus had helped his author out of his million pound tax liability
made him hesitate for a moment, before Roald simply replied that it
wasn't "gentlemanly" of Straus to mention that. "But we'll always be
friends."[96] Roxburgh's biography died with Roald's move to Penguin,
but there was no antagonism left behind. Only a vague sense of regret.
For his part, Roald had once again moved on, while Roxburgh, though
disappointed, remains justifiably proud of the six books they published
together and still treasures his close association with Roald. "He'd
involved me in his life," he reflected. "And there was a great personal
affection and admiration. He was a father figure for me – there's no
question about that." He also well understood his author's psychology. "He dealt with superlatives . . . The best, the brightest, the most
famous, the richest . . . if your star fell out of the constellation . . . you
quickly became the lowest, meanest, stupidest, vilest of things. He saw
things in black and white."[97]

The financial advantages of the move to Penguin aside, Dahl quickly found a kindred spirit in Liz Attenborough, the youthful publishing director at Puffin Books. She found him "extraordinarily professional", and – once he had got over her youth – he delighted in the fact that she usually answered the phone herself, and was not always protected by a secretary. Soon they were sharing gossipy stories about their respective families and he was asking her children to comment on a new manuscript. He admired her passionate commitment to children's literature, while delighting in the fact that she regularly made charts and lists for him about which of his many books was selling best.[98]

Financial success meant a lot to Dahl. "He had a great sense of being able to enjoy money, but he was not one of those people who could enjoy it in a vacuum," Ophelia reflected. "He liked handing money around and being generous with it. But he was consistently surprised by the sort of treats and delights that it could buy and the very serious things that money could do." She recalled a short essay she once had to write at school entitled "The Best Things in Life Are Free". She had spoken to her father about it and he told her bluntly that some of the best things in life were not free – like many of "the best medical interventions", for example. "He knew they were trying to get me to say that the woods and the fields are just wonderful, delightful things that we can all enjoy for free but he didn't delight in anything so obvious," she told me.[99]

In a similar vein, Dahl refused to insure his paintings. His reasons were threefold. "Firstly, I hang them on my walls only for their beauty and for the pleasure they give. Once you start insuring them, it means that you are becoming overly conscious of their value, and this will tend to supersede in your mind their aesthetic beauty. Secondly, I do not insure because I know damn well how simple it is for villains to penetrate the files of insurance companies. Thirdly, I don't think it makes any sense for a thief to nick them. He'd have an awful job getting rid of any of my better paintings, and I myself would never, on principle, negotiate to buy them back. So he's stuck with them. If the house burns down, then that's just bad luck. I would miss my pictures terribly, but money would be no compensation for their loss."[100]

In 1975, at the speech to pupils at Repton, he had reiterated Charles Marsh's dictum that money was only good "if you spread it around".[101] And his final years saw acts of considerable generosity both to individuals and to the many charities that he supported. He wrote a short book called *The Vicar of Nibbleswicke* whose rights he auctioned in aid of the Dyslexia Institute. He raised money for Great Ormond Street Children's Hospital, and other medical charities. In 1987, he donated his manuscript of *You Only Live Twice* to the writers' charity PEN. But the bulk of his giving was done quietly and on a personal level. A story recalled by Liz Attenborough was typical. She had been invited to dinner at Gipsy House and brought with her a letter from a woman with two young daughters so disabled they required special motorized wheelchairs, which cost £10,000 each. The woman had written in the hope that Puffin might be able to help her raise the money and Attenborough had brought a book with her for Roald to sign in the hope she might be able to sell it and put the cash toward the purchase of the wheelchairs. When Roald saw the letter, he was so struck by the women's plight that he went upstairs and brought down a complete set of his work. He and Quentin Blake (also a dinner guest that night) signed each book. Then, a week later, Roald called Attenborough. He told her he had just phoned the mother and had a long talk with her about her daughters' problems. The conversation had concluded with Dahl writing her a check for £10,000 to cover the cost of one wheelchair, and advising her where she might get help with purchasing the second. Attenborough was flabbergasted. "I'm sure I was the only one he told . . . It was typical. He was always doing things like that."[102]

Sick or injured children were most usually the recipients of this generosity, but others were beneficiaries too. He increased Pat's divorce settlement, gave financial support to his nephews and nieces, and regularly rewarded those who worked for him with gifts that ranged from Christmas turkeys and geese to foreign holidays.

Some saw this relationship as a bit like that of a "master to his serfs",[103] but most saw it as simple benevolence combined with a total lack of snobbery. Small acts of kindness had always meant a great deal to him. On holiday with his family in Switzerland in the 1980s, he noticed that the operator of the funicular that took guests from the hotel down into the centre of Zurich was getting enormous pleasure from smoking a humble little cigar. He seemed to be able to make one last forever, taking a contented puff or two while the car trundled up or down the mountainside, then leaving the smouldering stub on a ledge while he went out to collect tickets from the passengers about to board the car. One day, in Zurich, Roald bought the most expensive cigar he could find, and when the driver left the car, he quietly replaced the chewed stub with the grand new one. He did not stay to see the look on the man's face when he found it. Knowing that he would be delighted was quite enough. Similarly, when Tom Maschler had a nervous breakdown and was recovering in France, Roald wrote him an extremely long, entertaining letter about what was going on back in London – just to cheer him up. Maschler was astonished. "It had poems, gossip, bits of stories, it was a whole world," he recalled. "A little book, written just for me. It was an extraordinary act of generosity." [104]

He was assiduous, too, in answering letters from the constituents who mattered most to him: his young readers. A sick child in a remote hospital in Nebraska, a small boy in New Zealand whose mother had asked him to encourage her backward child with his reading, an English school in Abu Dhabi that was holding a charity auction and wanted an article of his clothing to sell, a small girl in New South Wales with multiple sclerosis. All received replies. Few were ignored. "He loved being with children," Murray Pollinger recalled. "He would always have a word with each of them, get a reaction from them." [105] He shared their sense of fantasy. He knew that storytelling was a powerful force for good and that there was something deathly about nonfiction. "The nicest small children, without the slightest doubt, are those who have been fed upon fantasy," he had written years before in the *New York Times*, while "the nastiest are the ones who know all the facts".[106] Alfred Knopf had been farsighted when, in the mid-sixties, he described Dahl as "one of the wizards, one of the wondermen of this age".[107] Twenty years later, the middle-aged wizard had become the grand old master of his craft. He knew how to shock, he knew how to scare, he knew how to keep his readers on the edge of their seats with excitement. He knew how to make them smile and how to make them roar with laughter. In learning his trade, he had evolved into something of a zealot: a committed supporter of countless literacy campaigns. His "passionate purpose", as he described it, had become to teach children "to be comfortable with a book and to read a book".[108] He wanted to take them out of their everyday environment, filled with chores and schoolwork, where "nothing was fabulous anymore", and to lift them into some kind of "marvellous or funny or incredible place".[109]

He was now almost content with his status as a subversive. He was proud of being the voice of youth in a world that sometimes seemed to despise children as much as it seemed to despise him. Only a couple of months before he died, he jotted down some notes for a lecture. To children, he reflected, grown-ups were giants, and consequently, "whether it is the mother or the father or the teacher", all were subconsciously "the enemy". "This fact is not generally realised by adults," he continued. "When I write a book which vilifies parents or teachers, e.g. *Matilda*, children absolutely love it . . . This is because the children shout, 'Hooray, here at last is a grown-up who understands what it is like to be one of us.'"[110] He had outlined this philosophy more than ten years earlier in an article that reads almost as a manifesto for his craft:

> *What makes a good children's writer? The writer must have a genuine and powerful wish not only to entertain children, but to teach them the habit of reading . . . [He] must be a jokey sort of fellow . . . He must like simple tricks and jokes and riddles and other childish things. He must be unconventional and inventive. He must have a really first-class plot. He must know what enthrals children and what bores them. They love being spooked. They love suspense. They love action. They love ghosts. They love the finding of treasure. They love chocolates and toys and money. They love magic. They love being made to giggle. They love seeing the villain meet a grisly death. They love a hero and they love the hero to be a winner. But they hate descriptive passages and flowery prose. They hate long descriptions of any sort. Many of them are sensitive to good writing and can spot a clumsy sentence. They like stories that contain a threat. "D'you know what I feel like?" said the*

big crocodile to the smaller one. "I feel like having myself a nice plump juicy child for my lunch." They love that sort of thing. What else do they love? New inventions. Unorthodox methods. Eccentricity. Secret information. The list is long. But above all, when you write a story for them, bear in mind that they do not possess the same power of concentration as an adult, and they become very easily bored or diverted. Your story, therefore, must tantalize and titillate them on every page and all the time that you are writing you must be saying to yourself, "Is this too slow? Is it too dull? Will they stop reading?" To those questions, you must answer yes more often than you answer no. [If not] you must cross it out and start again.[111]

CHAPTER TWENTY

No Point in Struggling

IN JANUARY 1990, ROALD took Liccy, Ophelia, and Liccy's youngest daughter, Lorina, on holiday to Jamaica. They stayed on the north coast of the island, at the Jamaica Inn – the intimate colonial-style lodge that Charles Marsh had founded shortly after the Second World War. For Roald, the hotel and its environs were filled with nostalgic memories: in the 1940s, William Stephenson, Pam Huntly, Lord Beaverbrook, Noël Coward and Ian Fleming had all walked on the beach and quaffed sundowners on the veranda with him. Now all but one of them were ghosts. There too Charles Marsh had helped to patch up Roald's failing marriage with Pat, before suddenly falling victim to the mosquito bite that gave him cerebral malaria.

Roald, however, was not there to indulge in memories. Though seventy-three, and walking a bit like an arthritic giraffe, he was still living very much in the present, and revelling in the company of people he loved – a grizzled lion surrounded by three glamorous lionesses. Ophelia, who had recently moved to Boston, where she was about to start a degree at Wellesley College, recalled the holiday as "a giant punctuation mark" – the last time she could recollect her father "unburdened by the weight of illness". With her sitting next to him on the beach, under one of the large thatch umbrellas, he whiled away his time reading, dreaming up lewd limericks – something he had always enjoyed – and studying the other guests, "like a life guard", before selecting one around whom he would start to weave a fanciful story. He had felt run-down, but the Caribbean sunshine, the company, and the lack of pressure invigorated him.

Twenty-six-year-old Lorina on the other hand was not feeling well at all. She had a persistent headache and felt as if something was continually buzzing in her ear; at one point she asked Ophelia to see if she could peer inside because she thought an insect might be trapped down there. A quiet, self-contained beauty, who had recently become a fashion editor at *Harper's*, Lorina's features and skin colour revealed more of her family's Indian blood than either of her sisters. Roald had nicknamed her "The Burmese Cat" because of her slenderness and inscrutability, and often took delight in trying to provoke responses out of her. He seldom succeeded. When the buzzing and the headaches did not go away, Roald called in a local doctor who diagnosed an ear infection and gave her some antibiotics. Back in London, another physician would misdiagnose her symptoms as labyrinthitis – a viral infection of the inner ear. In reality she was suffering from an undiagnosed and aggressive brain tumour. Oblivious of the impending disaster, Lorina continued to "get on" with her busy and exciting life, unaware just what a tiny amount of it remained to her. Shortly after she returned from Jamaica, she went to South Africa to supervise a shoot there for the magazine.

Back in England, the February weather had been unseasonably warm and mild, with temperatures in the mid-60s F. and narcissi and daffodils blooming in the garden of Gipsy House several weeks earlier than usual. The forecast promised more warmth and mildness. One evening, at about eleven o'clock, the telephone rang. Roald and Liccy were in their bedroom. Ophelia was sitting at the end of the bed, massaging Liccy's feet. She picked up the phone. An unfamiliar voice asked for Mr Dahl. Ophelia passed the phone over to her father. "Everything stopped at that moment," she recalled. "I stood at the end of their bed and watched my father's face as he held the phone. He said nothing. His mouth opened and he raised his scared eyes to me. I knew then that Lorina was dead and that nothing for Liccy would ever be the same again."[1] She had died at the airport of a sudden aneurysm caused by the tumour on her brain.

The disaster plunged Liccy and Roald into despair and turned spring back into deepest winter. Liccy was inconsolable, and Roald's inability to ease his wife's distress upset him deeply. Though powerless to help, he did his best to be positive. When Liccy said that she wanted to be buried next to her daughter, he bought the next six plots in the graveyard. Lucy remembered her father trying to keep the show on the road – even at the funeral. "Everything was very businesslike," she told me. She had flown in from Florida and was surprised when afterwards Roald told her simply "to go back home and get on with my life". She felt it was a sign of his need to cover up his own vulnerability, of his "inability to be able to withstand the pain", and reflected that he was behaving in the same way he had thirty years earlier when Olivia had died. "I think he made an unconscious decision not to open his heart after [Olivia's death]. I think he slammed his heart shut for any form of mourning and loss . . . and he never really opened it up again . . . Olivia was the one thing he never spoke about – ever." [2] Lorina's death seemed also to accelerate his own illness, for he soon began to decline physically in a way that took everyone around him by surprise. "It was tragic, awful," Charlotte told me, remembering how suddenly he began to deteriorate. "He sort of blamed himself. It was the last straw . . . He felt a curse had struck again." [3] Neisha was aware that her mother had to cut short her own grieving in order to look after him.

Before Roald went to Jamaica, he had been suffering from blurred vision. He had been travelling to London twice a month to have half a pint of blood removed, on the premise that this might ease the pressure on the capillaries in his eyes. This experimental technique appeared to be working, though he found it left him unexpectedly weak. Nevertheless, despite this unwanted lassitude, he was still basking in the calm that Charles Marsh had urged him to find within himself and which he seemed to have discovered living with Liccy. Four years earlier, he had attempted to describe this feeling. "A kind of serenity settles upon you like a warm mist," he wrote. "The real struggle is over. Every movement becomes slower. You have all the time in the world. There is no rush. The never-ending fight to achieve something excellent has ended." [4] This statement did not imply that he had given up writing, or that he had sacrificed his standards, only that, after *Matilda*, he no longer felt any great pressure to complete things until he felt they were truly ready. Now he was working on a number of smaller projects: a tale about two middle-aged people and a tortoise, set in a high-rise block of flats; a railway safety guide; a cookbook; a lyrical description of the cycle of the seasons; two adult fables and what would be his valedictory children's story, *The Minpins*. The act of writing still excited him, much as it had when, as a young flight lieutenant in Washington, he burned the midnight oil writing his flying stories. Nearly fifty years later, he was a little bit more sanguine about the process. But only marginally so. "Nothing can prevent the old fires of excitement rekindling once I am well into a story or a book," he noted. "The momentum still gathers and the drive towards the last pages becomes as relentless as ever." [5]

Though his bones ached "like mad", he was never bored, and while the prospect of his own mortality moved ever more clearly into view, death itself held no terrors for him, not only because he had looked it in the eye many times before, but also because of his oddly Peter Pan–like psychology that could view almost everything as an awfully big adventure. "The curious thing is that although I am strictly speaking an old man, I find it impossible to think of myself as being in the least bit ancient," he wrote. "My body may be rusting to pieces, but my mind is something absolutely separate and is as young as ever. I believe that mentally I am a sort of overgrown child, a giggler, a lover of childish jokes and knock-knocks, a chocolate-and-sweet-eater, a person with one half of him that has failed completely to grown up." [6] That "spark of naughtiness" that delighted his nephew Nicholas Logsdail, that "need to snigger" that his niece Alexandra Anderson remembered, that "love of horrid detail" that Quentin Blake recalled, combined with his apparently endless fascination for the new and the unexpected to keep Roald completely engaged with the world. He might lose his temper from time to time, but his outlook on the universe around him remained essentially sunny. It was without fear, bitterness or ennui. And almost all his final books bear gentle witness to this lightness.

Esio Trot is a charming tale about a middle-aged single man, Mr Hoppy, who ingeniously wins the love of his neighbour, Mrs Silver, with a spell that apparently makes her pet tortoise, Alfie, grow bigger. Quentin

Blake described it succinctly as a "love story set in two rooms". A fable without a single wicked or grotesque character, Blake felt the narrative was built largely around Roald's feelings for Liccy,[7] and that there was a great deal of his creator to be detected in Mr Hoppy's penchant for ingenious and imaginative problem solving. It was a surprising perception perhaps. Mr Hoppy was shy, reticent and nervous – not at all like the persona Roald presented to the public. Yet Wendy Kress, while acknowledging that her boss was humorous, pugnacious and often tried to get a rise out of her, also characterized him as essentially "introspective, shy, and totally untactile."[8] The magic spell to make Mrs Silver's tortoise grow bigger – "Esio Trot, Esio Trot, Teg reggib reggib! Emoc no, esio trot, worg pu, ffup pu, toohs pu! Gnirps pu, wolb pu, llews pu! Egrog! Elzzug! Ffuts! Plug! Tup no taf, Esio Trot, Tup no taf! No, teg no, elbbog doof!" – was, of course, not magic at all, but an amusing word game that disguised the fact that Mr Hoppy had bought a collection of tortoises of different sizes from the pet shop and devised a way of replacing one with another every few days without Mrs Silver noticing. The novelist Susan Hill, reviewing the book for *The Times* on May 20, 1990, commented that this was "a Roald Dahl we have never before encountered, newly mellowed, telling a silly, endearing story in a straightforward way – no rudeness, no dark underside, nothing for parents and teachers to complain about".

Esio Trot was a trifle, and an unusual one, in that there was not a child anywhere to be seen in its 60 pages. *The Minpins*, on the other hand, was much more characteristic late Dahl in that its hero is a warmhearted and mischievous child, who longs for adventure and eventually finds it in "The Forest of Sin", discovering a race of tiny people in the woods, learning to fly on the back of a swan, and ultimately destroying a terrifying monster deep within the heart of the forest. In tone and subject matter, the tale in many ways harked back to Roald's own Scandinavian roots, but it also doffed a cap to his old friends, the gremlins. Like their malevolent wartime cousins, the Minpins too wore suction boots to get around above ground, but instead of hitching a ride on Hurricanes and Spitfires, they flew on the backs of birds. This idea of flying on birds had featured in the Norwegian fairy tales of Theodor Kittelsen that Roald

had been read as a child, and had stayed with him ever since. Ophelia remembered her father telling her a tale he had invented when she was very
young about a tiny pink pill that miniaturized the swallower to such an
extent that he or she was able to fly on the back of a budgerigar.[9] According to Tom Maschler, Roald first started talking to him about *The Minpins* in the early 1980s, but had then put it aside. He picked it up again in
1989 when he started to feel his strength ebbing.

In hindsight, the book reads like a poetic farewell. Its scale is grander,
its tone more lyrical and its range more monumental than anything he
had written since *Some Time Never*. For someone who had made his name
by shattering some of the conventions of children's literature, it was also
curiously old-fashioned and metaphysical – particularly when it came to
evoking the ecstasy of flying. Moreover, for the first time since he had
worked with Quentin Blake, Roald suggested that another illustrator,
less quirky and more epic in style, should illustrate the book. The reason
he chose Patrick Benson becomes transparently clear in the final pages,
where Little Billy realizes that soon he will be too big to fly on Swan's
back, and so the great white bird takes the boy on one final flight: a mysterious and transcendental flight that is pregnant with symbolic significance. Adolescence looms for Little Billy. Soon the magic of childhood
will be over for him and he will have to face the drab world of adulthood.
For Roald, a different, more absolute journey lay ahead, but the terms of
reference were curiously the same. Both were leaving familiar territory
and venturing into new landscapes, both too would have to bid farewell
to the ones they loved most. Awesome vistas of sky, water and rocks overwhelm the tiny boy and the bird on their elemental flight, and evoke the
infinite and benign power of nature that had seemed to redeem all the
flaws of humanity at the end of *Some Time Never*.

> *Swan flew through the night for what seemed like hours and hours
> until they came to a gigantic opening in the earth's surface, a sort of
> huge gaping hole in the ground, and Swan glided slowly round and
> round above this massive crater and then right down into it. Deeper
> and deeper they went into the dark hole. Suddenly there was a bright-*

ness like sunlight below them, and Little Billy could see a vast lake
of water, gloriously blue, and on the surface of the lake thousands
of swans were swimming slowly about. The pure white of the swans
against the blue of the water was very beautiful.[10]

Tom Maschler remembered that Roald was profoundly focused on the
book in his last months. "He didn't stop until he knew it was right."[11]

Mortality preoccupied him in more mundane ways, too. And he busied himself with sorting out his financial affairs. In November 1989, he
complained grumpily to Jonathan Cape that his royalty payments were
taking considerably more than six months to be processed, and were
being paid to him without interest added. His own high street bank account was paying him 14 percent per annum interest, he pointed out, so
the publishers were making many thousand of pounds out of these delays.[12] He also upset Murray Pollinger by refusing to make any long-term
future commitment to his agency, unless Murray was prepared either to
bring in "a younger partner of whom I approve, or . . . make an arrangement with another agency that is large enough to provide . . . continuity
for my heirs in the future."[13] He tried to get Pollinger to take on Amanda
Conquy, who was working at Heinemann, and threatened at one point
to sell all his copyrights, because he was worried that Pollinger could
not guarantee that his agency would be run by "competent and caring"
staff for the next thirty or forty years. Murray, unsurprisingly, took this
criticism personally. But he probably had not yet realized that behind the
pugnacious rhetoric lurked a new context: Roald was planning carefully
for the world that would exist after he was gone.

In November 1989, his accountant Alan Langridge had encouraged
him to consult Martin Goodwin, a specialist tax lawyer, because he was
concerned about how best to look after his copyrights after his death.
Over lunch at Gipsy House in January 1990, Dahl probed him with
questions about the best way to look after his literary legacy and Goodwin was aware that Liccy too was "a big part" of that discussion. "She
seemed," he told me, "very much involved with all the books and it was
clear Roald trusted her completely." He also became aware that Roald and

Liccy were planning to write a book together – a compendium of favourite Dahl recipes, combined with a collection of biographical anecdotes about the family. It would be called *Memories with Food at Gipsy House.*

Goodwin suggested that Dahl might be able to minimize future inheritance tax liabilities and ensure Liccy's control over the exploitation of his works by forming a partnership with her to which he could transfer all his existing copyrights. "At high speed" Roald decided to go ahead with the plan, creating Dahl & Dahl, and arranging for Goodwin to make another trip to Gipsy House so that he could help explain the plan to the children. The visit was, as Goodwin remembered, "not a consultation exercise but an information exercise". Roald himself was predictably direct: "I'm leaving everything to Liccy," he told his children. "I trust her absolutely to do right by you and to do right by the copyrights, and you must too." [14] Lucy recalled her own and her siblings' shock when they realized that – apart from certain substantial specific gifts and legacies – it seemed they were being cut out of their father's will. At one point she asked whether there were any limits on Liccy's control and she remembered clearly Goodwin's reply: "Yes, she can take whatever percentage she likes." Roald had simply muttered: "Good." Lucy was "horrified", as Goodwin went back to London and their father sloped off into his bedroom to have a rest.

Lucy told me that the children had all been brought up to believe that they would be left plenty of money when their father died, so they were stunned. "Suddenly our inheritance had gone to zero," she told me somewhat melodramatically, "and we knew he wasn't going to last more than six months." After some discussion, Tessa and Ophelia convinced Lucy to venture back into their father's bedroom to tell him how they felt. "I walked in . . . He was lying on his bed watching television, obviously exhausted . . . And I said to him, 'Dad, we're not sure that we quite like this plan that you've just told us about . . . We're not sure we like the fact that everything's being left to Liccy and nothing's being left to us.' And he said, 'Well, if you don't trust Liccy, you can fuck off!' " Nowadays Lucy tells that story with a throaty chuckle not dissimilar to her father's, acknowledging what a good job her stepmother has made of running the estate over the last twenty years and how fairly the income has been distributed. Nevertheless, at the time she felt that the decision "turned" the Dahl children once more against Liccy. "We didn't like her very much, because she had just taken everything that was supposed to be ours."[15] In fact, Roald had not forgotten his children's interests. Having failed to persuade Amanda Conquy to leave her job at Heinemann and join the Pollinger agency, he then asked her to be one of the executors of his will. Amanda was initially astonished at the request – which she accepted – but rapidly realized he had asked her largely as "an insurance card" to make sure his children felt represented in the decision-making.[17]

As he became weaker, Roald's interest in public honours began to wane. Everyone around him knew that he had craved a knighthood for many years, and that he had tried, unsuccessfully and sometimes clumsily, to lobby for one. His ill-judged public utterances in the early 1980s had probably put paid to any chance of that happening. But even without the *God Cried* affair and the final Salman Rushdie outburst, one senses it was unlikely that cautious government officials would have ever bestowed the honour on such a notorious maverick. In 1985, he was offered the lower rank of an OBE. He turned it down.[17] Politically, he was a fan of Margaret Thatcher's and once bought her flowers, but his conservatism was never doctrinaire and always unorthodox. So it was something of a surprise when in 1988 he was unexpectedly asked to serve on a government Literacy and Education Committee that had been commissioned to report on the state of reading in the nation's schools. Perhaps he saw it as a way to redeem his reputation. If he did, it was an error of judgement, for he did not last long on the committee. His secretary, Wendy, remembered that he was "bored out of his mind" and eventually resigned. He was replaced by a right-wing expert on linguistics.

His own physical decline first became apparent when, in April 1990, while visiting Tessa in hospital after she had had a minor operation, Roald suddenly found that he had not the strength to get out of his chair. Tests revealed that he was suffering from sideroblastic anaemia, a condition that, while chronic, was not life-threatening. With steroids and regular blood transfusions it appeared he could keep the illness at bay for several more years. In the summer, there was a reconciliation with Pat, who returned to Gipsy House to celebrate Theo's thirtieth birthday. For many years she had been embittered by Roald's rejection. In her autobiography, she admitted that, in this period, she often could not get the thought of Liccy out of her mind: "Like a venom, it poisoned the times I should have been concentrating on other things." [18] But Roald had been generous to her since they divorced and there were other consolations. She had felt more involved in her children's lives since her separation and since Lucy and Ophelia had returned to the United States. She also felt she had come closer to God, and that this had given her an unexpected capacity to forgive. Soon, Liccy and she would bury the hatchet and become friends once more.

Within weeks Roald was back at the John Radcliffe Hospital in Oxford, where tests began to suggest that his anaemia was evolving into myelofibrosis – a rare form of leukaemia. He was delighted when other tests revealed that, despite years of high alcohol consumption, his liver was still in pristine condition. Visiting him in the hospital, Ophelia found him more reflective than usual. He talked to her about his experiences in the war and also about the possibility of her writing his biography, but he also discussed a story he had started writing about a girl who wanted to talk to her dog. She began to find her father increasingly childlike, vulnerable and innocent. "He had lost his sureness," she later wrote. "I began to feel a greater need to protect him." [19] Yet, even in extremis, his mischievous nature and love of breaking rules did not desert him – and it was particularly evident when it came to smoking in hospital. One day he singed his eyebrows trying to light his cigarette furtively on a communal gas ring. Another time he got stuck while craning out of the window to puff away on one of his Cartier "gaspers" without being detected. It took a gaggle of nurses to drag him back inside, while an irate patient in the neighbouring room complained that clouds of cigarette fumes were billowing in through his window. On another occasion, because dogs were not allowed in the hospital, he tried to arrange for Chopper, his pet Jack Russell, to be hauled in a basket to his window several storeys up, just so he could see him.

The junior houseman, Tom Solomon – now himself a distinguished neurologist – was repeatedly struck by his patient's irrepressible sense of humour in the face of an illness that he knew was incurable. And Roald's consultant haematologist, Sir David Weatherall, recalled his "enormous charm" and the extraordinary impact he had on the staff who were treating him. Roald gave each of the nurses nicknames – one was "the Russian ballerina" – and when the hospital authorities experimented with nurses wearing ordinary clothes rather than uniform, Roald sent Liccy out to buy new outfits for all of them. "He thought the idea was ridiculous," Liccy recalled. "Not only did it mean that the patient was unsure who was a nurse and who wasn't, but he felt it was a terrible imposition on the nurses themselves." Yet he despatched Liccy to Marks and Spencer to buy a selection of shirts and cardigans and invited all of them into his room to choose what they wanted. "It was like a market stall," Liccy remembered with a fond chuckle.[20]

Through it all, Roald was never gloomy or morose. "I've been a bit off colour these last few months," he wrote to his young fans late that summer, "feeling sleepy when I shouldn't have been and without that lovely old bubbly energy that drives one to write books and drink gin and chase after girls." But, he added, his young readers should not consign him to the grave just yet. "I usually manage to climb out," he told them. "I've done it many times before."[21]

He was in and out of hospital throughout September and October. In mid-November, Ophelia flew in from Boston for a long weekend and was shocked at her father's decline. He could hardly walk to the car. His imminent mortality was transparently clear to her now, although his joie de vivre was sufficiently intact that he still took enormous pleasure one evening in teaching her exactly how to decant a bottle of vintage port. She flew back to Boston two days later, returning to her apartment only to find a message from Lucy asking her to come back immediately because he had taken a turn for the worse and been readmitted to the hospital. She closed the door of her flat and headed straight back to the airport. Tom Solomon recalled Roald's sister Else sitting by his bedside and telling him that he had nothing to fear from death. But when

Ophelia got to the hospital, her father seemed to have rallied. He told her that he had just had the worst day he could remember since he crashed his plane in 1940. "I think I almost bought it," he told her. In a slow, "whispery" voice, he started to ponder which of his children would be able to get themselves out of the burning plane. "I am not frightened of falling off my perch," he told her. "If Olivia can do it, so can I." [22] He was becoming weaker by the hour, incontinent, and now the pain was incessant. "The nights were long and sad," Ophelia recalled. "Talking became an enormous effort." [23]

There was debate within the family as to what to do. Liccy wanted to keep him alive as long as possible. His children felt he was suffering too much. They wanted him to be given morphine, which might hasten the end but relieve his pain. At night, in his hospital room, Tessa heard her father talking in his sleep to his mother and to Olivia, "as if he were visiting them . . . And then he'd wake up and say to me 'Teddy, what are we going to do?'" This went on for several nights, but each morning, just when Tessa was certain it was clear he needed this ultimate pain relief, Liccy's arrival would cause him to "perk up as if there was nothing wrong and he wasn't in pain at all". [24] To Ophelia, it seemed as if her father was fighting now "just for Liccy". [25] His breathing became ever more laboured and he was fitted with an oxygen mask. By the night of November 22, a crisis seemed to be approaching. Though impossibly weak, Roald had finally managed to heal a rift between himself and Tessa. After nights of sleeping in his room at the hospital, Tessa had decided to go and stay with friends in Oxford. As she left the room, she spontaneously went over to kiss her father's "mossy" forehead. She knew he hated physical contact, but as she did so, the man she hailed as "the love of her life", who had always been so reticent in showing her affection, quietly whispered that he loved her "very much indeed". Tessa was so overwhelmed that she pulled off her glasses and smashed them against the wall. [26]

Later that night, Roald became very thirsty. Ophelia tried to get him to drink some water, but found he had not the strength to swallow. He went back to sleep. Carefully she peeled a tangerine and dribbled some of its sweet juice onto his parched lips. He woke again and looked at her. "You know, I'm not frightened," he repeated. "It's just that I will miss you all so much." It was the last sentence he would utter. Not long afterwards, Liccy came in from her camp bed in the next room. Now she too could see that he was so near the end there was only one option left. At about three in the morning, Solomon recalled, the Dahl family, which had previously seemed to him somewhat dysfunctional, suddenly "pulled together." As a nurse prepared to administer some morphine, Roald appeared to be completely unconscious. Ophelia and Liccy put on a tape of Tchaikovsky's Violin Concerto – one of his favourite pieces.

But Roald had one more surprise left for them. As the needle pricked his skin, he opened his eyes and muttered: "Ow, fuck!" They were to be his final words. As he died, Liccy cradled him in one arm, while her other hand covered his eyes, "lightly as though coaxing him to sleep". Tessa stood at the end of the bed, "her arms folded, like a sentry guarding him".[27] Lucy waited outside. She had already exchanged her final words with her father. He had exhorted her to look after her children.[28]

An hour or so after he passed away, the press began to call the hospital. Some wanted to know if the rumour was true that he had died of AIDS. A reputation for notoriety haunted him even at the end. Later, driving back to Gipsy House through the Vale of Aylesbury where Roald had lived so much of his life, Liccy and Ophelia sat in the car in silence. There seemed to be nothing to say. Then, quite suddenly, two white doves swooped down out of the trees and flew along beside them – their wings almost touching the passenger window of the car. The birds travelled with them for almost a mile before disappearing back into the woods. Both Liccy and Ophelia felt as if they had witnessed a gesture from another world.

Lucy thought her father had died at the right time. Death as a concept had never been taboo at Gipsy House, and she recalled a dinner years earlier where her father, Else and Alfhild had discussed sending off for a do-it-yourself euthanasia kit, because none of them wanted an existence that had lost its dignity. "I think he was tired and he was ready," she told me. "If he'd been offered another ten reasonable years he would have taken them, but I think the illness had worn him out. I think he knew that he wasn't going to lick it. At that time Tessa was wealthy, because she'd just divorced James. Ophelia was fine. I was married, with two children . . . Theo was fine. Everyone was fine and I think that's what he needed to know. I felt like he'd cleared his desk. Everything was organized."[29]

Ophelia felt that he had passed away with "plenty of regrets", but that his sense of humour was perhaps the most important thing in his life and he was beginning to lose even that. "I think he wanted to let go, to be free of pain, and he wanted to be allowed to stop struggling," she told me. That attitude was a long way from the fierce will to live that had characterized his ancestor's behaviour in the church fire in Grue 170 years earlier, and that had animated so many episodes of Roald's life – most notably perhaps his decision to pull himself from his burning aeroplane in 1940. Yet it was strangely reminiscent of the death of the fighter pilot in one of his earliest stories, *Death of an Old, Old Man*:

> *He relaxed his body and all the muscles in his body because he had no further wish to struggle. How nice it is not to struggle, he thought. There is no point in struggling. I was a fool to have struggled for so much and so long; I was a fool to have prayed for the sun when there was a black cloud in the sky . . . This is so much better; this is ever so much better because there is a wood somewhere that I wish to walk through and you cannot walk struggling through a wood. There is a girl somewhere that I wish to sleep with, and you cannot sleep struggling with a girl. You cannot do anything struggling; especially you cannot live struggling, and so now I am going to do all the things that I want to do, and there will be no more struggling.*[30]

A couple of days after Roald died, David Weatherall sent Liccy the following tribute: "In thirty years of clinical practice I cannot remember ever being so moved or privileged in caring for a patient. Roald was quite unique. I have never seen anyone have such an effect on the medical and nursing staff – the sense of loss at every level was quite extraordinary. You all must be very proud of him. I was so glad he retained his extraordinary intellect to the end, and that he died with the calm and dignity which was so important to him."[31] Tom Solomon too remembered that he had had "a good death". It seemed entirely appropriate to everyone that he had died on Children's Day. Many were stunned when they heard the news. It was hard to imagine such a big man, such a force of nature, had departed. Astri Newman had thought him almost "immortal", as had Quentin Blake, who reflected that, though increasingly "battered", it seemed Roald would "go on for ever".

Several weeks after her father died, Ophelia went back into the hut. Nothing had been moved. The floor was still covered in dust, cobwebs and cigarette ash. Her father's Dixon Ticonderoga pencils were still "sharpened like thin rockets . . . pointing upwards ready to pick up the story exactly where he had left it off".[32] On his green baize board was a sheaf of the lined yellow paper on which he always wrote. There were rough notes sketched out for the beginning of a story – even a few illustrations. "The cleverest man in the world is called Mr Billy Bubbler," was how it began.

> *He can invent just about anything you want. He has a marvellous workshop full of wheels and wires and buckets of glue and balls of string and huge pots full of thick foaming stuff that gives off smoke in many colours. There are old motorcar tyres, baskets of carrots and electric machines and sewing machines and fizzy-drink machines and bath tubs and cow's teeth and rice puddings and old shoes and everything else Mr Bubbler needs to make his wonderful inventions.*[33]

There were other ideas left incomplete as well. The story of Cathy and her dog Zip who go into the woods and meet a gypsy woman who teaches the young girl how to talk to her pet. A tale about a child who could predict the future in her dreams. The outline of several ghost stories and – perhaps most fascinating of all – a story where the characters in the book become aware that they are only alive when a child reads them, and so in order to prolong their existence, they try to seek that child out in real life before he or she has finished reading the book.[34]

Though his body had run out of steam, it was clear Dahl's inventive brain had been whirring away in his little hut, dreaming up stories until he was admitted to the hospital for the last time. Stephen Roxburgh, for one, was unsurprised to discover that there were incomplete tales left behind. He was convinced Roald "had more big books in him". It was simply the physical energy to go through with them that was lacking. "I think until he stopped going out to that hut, he was writing," Roxburgh reflected.[35] Tom Maschler agreed. "Many writers write their masterpiece when they're twenty-five or thirty and then it's downhill all the way," he noted, maintaining that Dahl could have written another twenty books if he'd lived another twenty years and that some of them might have been "even better than anything he had written previously".[36] To that extent, Roald left with a fund of untold stories that were lost to the world. Yet rarely has a writer lived such an extraordinary and eventful life. Without his writing his life would still have been a remarkable one. He had lived it with energy, passion and commitment, and remained true to one of his favourite fragments of verse, four lines written by the American poet Edna St Vincent Millay:

> *"My candle burns at both ends,*
> *It will not last the night;*
> *But ah, my foes, and oh, my friends –*
> *It gives a lovely light."*[37]

The CEO of Penguin Books, Peter Mayer, quoted those lines at Roald's funeral in the ancient church in Great Missenden, where a huge number of friends turned up to bid him farewell. In his eulogy, Mayer remembered him not only as a great writer and a supreme "family man" but also as "a benefactor and protector". Aside from paying tribute to Dahl's countless acts of philanthropy, Mayer also unexpectedly thanked him for having been so "caring" to him personally during the Salman Rushdie crisis. It was an unexpected revelation from a man whose decision to publish *The Satanic Verses* Dahl had openly criticized. Roald took fierce issue with him, Mayer explained, but at another level, he also wanted to help his friend. "He sought me out and wrote to me and sent me things to ponder," he told the mourners. "He tried to figure out how I could go forward in what had become a publishing drama . . . He disagreed with me . . . and still with brains and hands and heart wanted to protect me."[38] There was the paradox of Roald Dahl. He was like a firework: unpredictable, volatile and exciting. He could delight you, but he was dangerous, too. Get too close and you would likely be burned. However indignant and hotheaded he might appear, his intemperateness could rapidly be defused by humour or kindness. You never quite knew what he would do next.

For his children, of course, Roald would always be a consummate father – flawed perhaps, like all parents, but always loyal and loving. He could never be replaced. His sisters, nephews and nieces, too, lost a powerful force that had bound the wider family together. Roald had been "like a guru", as Nicky Logsdail described him, for over forty years, and with his departure the ties binding them together began to come loose. No one could replace his irrepressible, sometimes "monstrous" energy,[39] and the family gradually dispersed. His closest colleagues felt they had lost a man of genius. Twenty years after his death, both Murray Pollinger and his wife still describe him in these terms, mourning the loss of a fire that had seemed "unquenchable",[40] while for Tom Maschler he was a storyteller who ranked "second to none . . . A one-off with a seam of genius."[41] To other adults who knew him less well he was a showman, a loyal friend, a generous host, a benevolent employer, an affable companion at the snooker table, a name-dropper, a poseur, an unreliable witness, or simply someone of whom one needed to be wary.

Notwithstanding his macabre reputation, almost no one who spent any time with Roald Dahl ever found him sinister. Quentin Blake was typical. "I don't think I ever thought he was dark, actually," he told me; "difficult perhaps . . . but I think you got the sense that in broad principle he wanted his own way, if you see what I mean."[42] Sometimes he could veer off the tracks, but at other times his perceptions were sharp and almost always decisive. His decision to give Liccy control of his estate and not have it run by a committee would certainly prove to be a shrewd one. With Amanda Conquy – who left her job in publishing six months after

Roald died – to help her run it, she has managed his legacy with love, professionalism and ambition. She has presided over the development of a wide range of film, theatre, opera, musical and concert adaptations of his work. She has opened a museum and story centre named after him, and started a medical charity in his memory devoted to helping young people suffering from brain and blood disorders. Carefully, like a proud and skilful gardener, she has watched Dahl's literary reputation grow enormously over the last twenty years. Despite occasional flashes of resentment, her stepchildren are now among the first to acknowledge this.

I always thought there was something of Charles Darwin in Roald. Both men were fascinated by the natural world, both loved observing small behavioural details in humans and animals. Both constructed stories out of what they had seen, and both articulated their hypotheses with imaginative fearlessness. Roald of course was more fantasist than scientist. But that desire to search for ultimate knowledge fascinated him deeply. He longed to reach beyond the mundane and the humdrum into richer and more fertile alternative universes. Doing so in his fiction might open the door to either pleasure or pain, but whatever he was doing in real life, a part of his mind was always somewhere else. Liccy described his restlessness at night, when he seldom slept more than three or four hours. Roald too explained how difficult he sometimes found it to sleep when his mind was somewhere else. "Your mind is whirring and when you lie down in bed and put the light out, your mind is working on [a book] all the time," he told Todd McCormack. "It's a devastating process actually, because you can't get rid of it until you've finished it. You really can't get rid of it."[43] Ophelia was also acutely aware of this detachment. "Even when he sat reading to himself, his middle finger tapped to some secret rhythm," she recalled.[44] He was like Klausner, the amateur inventor, in his early short story "The Sound Machine", for whom the tangible world immediately around him was only the humblest of starting points for what might eventually be perceived – if only one could find a way to do so.

"I believe," he said, speaking more slowly now, "that there is a whole world of sound about us all the time that we cannot hear. It is possible

*that up there in those high-pitched inaudible regions there is exciting
music being made, with subtle harmonies and fierce grinding discords,
a music so powerful that it would drive us mad if only our ears were
tuned to hear the sound of it."*[45]

Stephen Roxburgh was probably right when he said that above all else
Roald Dahl was a "family man". But he also valued himself very highly
as a writer. Graham Greene, whose skill Dahl admired hugely, and whom
he had visited in Antibes with Ophelia in 1988, once said that he viewed
his own books as his children. For Roald, too, this was the case. Each
of them was a distillation of inspiration and craftsmanship, and each
occupied a special place in his heart. They had been seeded not in the
"normal life" but in that other world, the imagination, where "one's mind
changes" and the writer ceases to be a "normal man".[46] He had nourished
them all in the privacy of his writing hut and he took pleasure in the skill
and beauty of their construction. He had defended many of them against
criticism and rejection. He loved them.

To the outside world, Dahl might make light of his talent and argue
that in general writers took themselves too seriously, maintaining that
he was "simply an entertainer" whose job was "to entertain his public."
Privately, however, he saw himself as much more than this. He found the
process of finishing a book immensely painful and would wander around
afterwards "like a mother who has lost her children".[47] Ophelia told me
he could be "unhinged" by the experience.[48] As a storyteller, the fantastic
would always triumph over the literal, lest he succumb to his "constant
unholy terror of boring the reader".[49] Objectivity or truth was never his
aim. "I think the best way of entertaining children is writing fantasy,"
he argued. "I would never want to write anything that wasn't completely
made up or invented."[50] Adults sometimes had problems with this attitude. Children never did. That was why he was so surefooted with them.

By the end of his life, Roald Dahl had connected with a vast number
of children. His daily postbag was filled with hundreds of fan letters and
he could proudly boast that children all over the world would invite him
into their houses for a cup of tea. To deal with the rejection that he still
felt from many adult critics, he had taken to praising child readers over

adult ones. It was a petulant defence perhaps, but understandable in light of the generally dismissive attitude that still prevailed toward him in the publishing world, and that was evident in many of the obituaries that followed his death in 1990. But it was genuine, too.

He would have been amazed and proud at how things have changed in twenty years, at the respectability now afforded to children's literature and the praise heaped upon his work by current exponents of the genre, from J. K. Rowling and Philip Pullman to Anthony Horowitz and Michael Rosen. In a world awash with literary prizes, it is hard to imagine that Dahl won only one major award in his lifetime for his children's fiction. This change of his own status and that of the genre he championed would doubtless have given him enormous pleasure, for he craved fame and recognition, but at his heart he knew it was an empty need. Knowing that, through storytelling, he had touched the interior worlds of millions of children was infinitely more rewarding. He described the sensation it gave him just before he died: "Sometimes it gives me a funny feeling that my writing arm is about six thousand miles long and that the hand that holds the pencil is reaching all the way across the world to faraway houses and classrooms where children live and go to school. That's a thrill all right." [51] I doubt he could wish for a finer epitaph.

Acknowledgements

I AM HUGELY GRATEFUL to so many people who helped me with this book. To begin with I must thank Roald Dahl's Estate and in particular Ophelia Dahl who invited me to write it and who ensured me free access to her father's remarkable archive. Roald's other children – Tessa, Theo, and Lucy – have also given generously of their time and allowed me access to many of their own private papers. Patricia Neal and Liccy Dahl too have been unstinting with their cooperation.

The wider Dahl family have also been enormously accommodating. I was fortunate to interview Roald's three sisters, Alfhild Hansen, Else Logsdail and Asta Anderson, before their deaths. Subsequently many of their children also spared their valuable time to talk to me, seeking out letters and photographs in old drawers, trunks and attics and loaning them to me, often for several weeks at a time. In particular I would like to mention Astri Newman, Anna Corrie, Lou Pearl and her husband Dennis, Nicholas Logsdail and Alexandra Anderson. Louis Dahl's children, Bryony and Ashley Dahl, were also immensely obliging, as was Oscar Dahl's great-grandson, Roald, whom I tracked down in France. After driving him down to Gipsy House one evening for dinner, I was subsequently able to claim that I had introduced Liccy to Roald Dahl.

Witnesses who offered invaluable interviews and information on aspects of Dahl's family background and childhood included: John Cleese, Johan Petter Hesselberg, Reidun Jebsen, Peter Persen, Herbert E. Roese, Eleanor "Tull" Strømsland, Marianne Strømsland, Olivier Beaurin-Gressier, Nicholas Arnold, Nancy Deuchar, Rachel Drayson, Margaret

Edwards, Tim Fisher, Douglas Highton, Sir Charles Pringle and Ben Reuss. On Roald's time as a fighter pilot I am grateful for the help of Barbara Dods, Deb Ford, John Lowe, Lesley O'Malley (formerly Pares) and Robert Stitt; and on his years in Grendon Underwood to Pat Brazier, Pauline Hearne and Jeremy Lang. On his wartime exploits in Washington I am grateful for the assistance of Jennet Conant, Jonathan Cuneo, Antoinette Haskell, Robert Hegeman, Norm Killian and Bill Macdonald. Most of all, I owe special gratitude to Robert Haskell, the current guardian of all the letters Roald wrote to his grandfather, Charles Marsh. Robert was also a most generous host, allowing me to study the huge trove of letters while staying on his farm in Virginia and driving me to see his grandfather's homes, both at Longlea and in Rappahannock County.

Others who helped me with information on Dahl's later life include: Linda Ambrose, Miran Aprahamian, Sonia Austrian, Liz Attenborough, Veronica and Marius Barran, Bob and Helen Bernstein, Quentin Blake, Amanda Conquy, Sarah Conquy, Charlotte Crosland, Neisha Crosland, Sophie Dahl, Michael de las Casas, Sue Elder, Paul Farmer, Christopher Figg, Sir Leonard Figg, Ed and Marian Goodman, Martin Goodwin, Bob Gottlieb, Alan Higgin, Callie Hope-Morley, Alice Kadel (formerly Keene), Luke Kelly, Wendy Kress, Lemina Lawson Johnson, Sheila Lewis Crosby (formerly St Lawrence), Pam Lowndes, Joanna Lumley, Tom Maschler, Rosie Mennem, Jane Pepper, Gina and Murray Pollinger, Stephen Roxburgh, Wally Saunders, Tom Solomon, Roger Straus, Jenny Taylor, Maria Tucci, Rayner Unwin, Sue Vivian (formerly Denson), Sir David and Lady Weatherall and John Wilkinson.

I would like to thank Amanda Conquy for reading the manuscript so diligently and for her thoughtful criticism, and I am greatly indebted to Cherie Burns for generously sharing information gleaned during her researches for her forthcoming biography of Millicent Rogers, to be published by St Martin's Press in 2011.

The book could not have been written without the assistance of a number of key institutions and archives: Heather Mountjoy, the Archivist of the Glamorgan County Records Office; Averil Goldsworthy, the Chairman of the Welsh Norwegian Society; Paul Stevens, the archivist of Repton School; John Golding, the housemaster of The Priory; various archivists at Shell; Justin Warwick and Emily Cox at the British Schools Exploring Society; Miss Hammond-Smith at the RAF Museum; Rob Brown who runs the 112 Squadron website; Anthony Richards at the Imperial War Museum in London, who gave me access to the private papers of GJ Thwaites and WG Rockall of 80 Squadron; Dave Gale, who kindly proofread the chapter relating to the Battle of Athens; Adam Dixon at the Howard Gotlieb Archive at Boston University; Henry Hardy at Wolfson College; Patrice S. Fox at the Harry Ransom Centre for the Humanities at the University of Austin, Texas; Jeremy Johnson at the Guildhall; Trish Hayes at the BBC Written Archives Centre; Jacque Roethler of the Special Collections Library at the University of Iowa in Iowa City; and last, but by no means least, Tara C. Craig at the Rare Book and Manuscript Library of Columbia University.

Barney Samson and Diane Sullivan both helped me initially to gather and organize my material. Diane had worked with me at the BBC in 1985 when I made my first television film about Roald, and gave up hours of her own time freely to transcribe his wartime letters. More recently, Jake Wilson has been the most tireless and perceptive of ferrets, chasing out information from the most inaccessible places, and always keeping me on my toes. I am lucky to have had the benefit of his sharp and subtle sensibility. Liz Whittingham, the first archivist at the Roald Dahl Museum and Story Centre, also helped get me started on the book, but I could not have completed it without the kindness, industry, clear-headedness and generosity of her successor, Jane Branfield. To her, I owe an enormous debt of gratitude.

On the production side of the book my thanks are due to a host of people – principally Caroline Dawnay, but also Olivia Hunt and St John Donald at United Agents in London, Zoë Pagnamenta in New York and Michael Siegel in Los Angeles. Sarah Hochman, my editor at Simon & Schuster in New York, and her assistant Michele Bové dealt patiently with my many questions and quibbles. I am immensely grateful to them as I am to Arabella Pike, Robert Lacey, Richard Johnson and John Bond at HarperPress in London, David Rosenthal also at Simon and Schuster, and

Dinah Forbes at McLelland and Stewart in Toronto. I was lucky enough to benefit from all their advice and experience. Alan Samson too was kind enough to read the book at an early stage and offer me his thoughts.

I am grateful to Deborah Rogers for steering me toward the mercurial Bob Gottlieb and to Drs Shawn and Jo Libaw for their hospitality in New York and Los Angeles, as well as for offering unofficial medical advice when I requested it. It goes without saying that any errors in that department are all my own.

Finally, I would like to doff my cap too to my great friends Peter Ash and Stephen Walker. They were the first people to read the manuscript and their enthusiasm, encouragement and advice helped keep me going when the end seemed to be receding ever further into the distance. My thanks are also due to John Manger for suggesting that I write the book with a single reader in mind and to the sparky Thorvald Blough for being that person – at least in my imagination. I have yet to hear his verdict on the book.

Most of all my thanks are due once more to Liccy and Ophelia Dahl, who trusted a neophyte with writing Roald's biography. From the beginning they urged me, above all else, to "make him come alive". I have tried to do this at all times, but whether I have vindicated their decision only time will tell.

Notes

A Note on quotations from Dahl's manuscripts and letters

Roald Dahl was not the greatest of spellers. I have generally corrected errors in his spelling unless their inaccuracy is either particularly funny or telling.

Abbreviations used in the Notes

CMP – Charles Marsh Papers (in possession of Robert Haskell)
FSG – Farrar, Straus Giroux Archives, New York
GHPP – Gipsy House Private Papers
HGC – Howard Gotlieb Archival Research Center, Boston University
HRCH – Harry Ransom Center for the Humanities, The University of Texas at Austin
LDC – Lucy Dahl Collection
PNC – Patricia Neal Collection
RDMSC – Roald Dahl Museum and Story Centre
WLC – Watkins Loomis Collection at Columbia University

PROLOGUE: *Lunch with Igor Stravinsky*

1. Roald Dahl, interviewed in *A Dose of Dahl's Magic Medicine,* 09/28/96.

CHAPTER ONE: *The Outsider*

1. *Memoirs of Gunder Paulsen (1821–1872),* MS at University of Oslo, translated by Anne Livgaard Lindland.
2. Dr Johan Petter Hesselberg, Letter to the author, 01/07/08.
3. Dr Johan Petter Hesselberg, Letter to the author, 01/07/08.
4. I am most grateful to Dr Johan Petter Hesselberg, who supplied me with many of the Hesselberg family details. He also recalls visiting Roald Dahl one day in the late 1980s, after the publication of *Boy,* and telling him these stories over the dinner table at Gipsy House.
5. Ophelia Dahl, Conversation with the author, Boston, 11/01/07.
6. These were perhaps most notably articulated in Eleanor Cameron's attack on *Charlie and the Chocolate Factory* in her article "McLuhan, Youth and Literature", *The Horn Book Magazine* (October 1972).
7. *Bookmark,* BBC Television, 1985.
8. Roald Dahl, *Boy* (London: Jonathan Cape, 1984), p. 9.
9. Ibid., p. 51.
10. Ibid.
11. Louise (Lou) Pearl, Conversation with the author, 05/09/08.
12. Douglas Highton, Conversation with the author, 11/08/07.
13. Alfhild Hansen, Interviewed in *A Dose of Dahl's Magic Medicine,* 09/28/86.
14. Christiania, Probate Court, Record Protocol no. 15, Series D, 8/7-1922-4/12-1923, p. 113.
15. *Boy,* p. 13.
16. Sarpsborg Church Register, MINI 1, 1859–1869.
17. Felicity Dahl, Conversation with the author, 11/19/06.
18. *Boy,* p. 15.
19. Sarpsborg Church Register, MINI 1, 1859–1869, and Kristiania Census, 1900.
20. Stephen Roxburgh, Conversation with the author, 03/14/09.
21. Alexandra Anderson, Conversation with the author, 11/14/07.
22. *Boy,* p. 15.
23. Ibid.
24. Alfhild Hansen, Conversation with the author, 08/07/92.
25. Henrik Ibsen, *Ghosts* (1881).
26. Kingsley Amis, *Memoirs* (London: Hutchinson, 1991), pp. 305–7.
27. Roald Dahl (Oscar's great-grandson), Conversation with the author, 02/08.
28. *Boy,* p. 15.
29. Ibid.
30. Roald Dahl, *Hairy Faces* (?1986) – RDMSC RD 6/2/1/125.

CHAPTER TWO: *Shutting Out the Sun*

1. B. G. Charles, *Old Norse Relations with Wales* (Cardiff, 1934).
2. Herbert Roese, "Cardiff's Norwegian Links", *Welsh History Review*, vol. 8, no. 2 (December 1996).
3. Hjalmar Karlsen, quoted in *A Little Bit of Norway in Wales, Recollections of Norwegian Seamen's Churches*, Norwegian Church Cultural Centre, Cardiff, 2006.
4. Peter Persen, Conversation with the author, 06/10/07.
5. The album belonged to Harald's daughter Ellen and is now in the possession of his granddaughter Bryony.
6. Bryony Dahl, Conversation with the author, 01/17/08.
7. Marriage Settlement of Marie Baurin-Gressier – RDMSC RD 20/08.
8. Felicity Dahl, Conversation with the author, 08/28/07.
9. Bryony Dahl, Conversation with the author, 01/17/08.
10. The house, in Fairwater Road, Llandaff, is now called Ty Gwyn.
11. Ellen Dahl, remembered by her niece Bryony Dahl.
12. Alfhild Hansen, Conversation with the author, 08/07/92.
13. Louise (Lou) Pearl, Conversation with the author, 09/05/08.
14. Tessa Dahl, Conversation with the author, 10/22/07; Astri Newman, Conversation with the author, 10/15/07; and Else Logsdail, "Casseroled Ptarmigan" in *Memories with Food at Gipsy House* (London: Viking, 1991), p. 61.
15. Margaret Edwards, Conversation with the author, 01/07/98.
16. According to his sister Alfhild Hansen, he weighed 8 pounds, or about 3.6 kilos.
17. J. Harry Williams, Letter to Roald Dahl, 10/02/76 – RDMSC RD 16/1/2.
18. Alfhild Hansen, Conversation with the author, 08/07/92.
19. J. Harry Williams, Letter to Roald Dahl, 10/02/76 – RDMSC RD 16/1/2.
20. Newspaper cutting found in Harald's wallet – RDMSC RD 20/07.
21. Alfhild Hansen, Conversation with the author, 08/07/92.
22. Louise (Lou) Pearl, Conversation with the author, 05/09/08.
23. Alfhild Hansen, Conversation with the author, 08/07/92.
24. *Boy*, p. 21.
25. Ibid.
26. Journal of Harald Dahl (trans. Else Dahl), courtesy of Ophelia Dahl. This journal, once in the possession of Else Dahl, seems to have gone missing since her death. This is the only extract I have been able to trace.
27. Alfhild Hansen, Conversation with the author, 08/07/92.
28. Ibid.

CHAPTER THREE: *Boy*

1. Roald Dahl, *Charlie's Chocolate Boy* – WLC Box 23.
2. Roald Dahl, *The BFG* (London: Jonathan Cape, 1962), p. 38.
3. Roald Dahl, *Matilda* (London: Jonathan Cape, 1988), p. 10.
4. *Treasure Islands*, Interview with Julia Eccleshere, BBC Radio 4, April 15, 1988.

5. *Memories with Food at Gipsy House*, reprinted as *The Roald Dahl Cookbook* (New York: Penguin, 1996).

6. Alfhild Hansen, Interviewed in *A Dose of Dahl's Magic Medicine*, 09/28/86.

7. Asta Anderson, Conversation with the author, 1997.

8. *Boy*, p. 53.

9. Ibid., p. 62.

10. Bryony Dahl, Conversation with the author, 01/17/08.

11. Glamorganshire County Record Office Probate Office, 05/20/20, to Oscar Dahl; Shipowner and Sofie Magdalene Dahl, widows Effects £158, 917 10s.

12. Roald Dahl, *James and the Giant Peach* (New York: Knopf, 1960), pp. 1–2.

13. *Boy*, p. 23.

14. Roald Dahl, *More About Boy* (London: Puffin Books, 2008), p. 19.

15. Ibid., p. 21.

16. *Boy*, p. 35.

17. Mrs Ferris, quoted in Jeremy Treglown, *Roald Dahl* (New York: Harcourt Brace & Co., 1994, cited hereafter as Treglown), p. 19.

18. *Boy*, p. 33.

19. Ibid., p. 46.

20. Ibid., pp. 48, 71–72.

21. John Cleese, Conversation with the author, 1999.

22. Douglas Highton, Conversation with the author, 11/08/07.

23. *Boy*, p. 71.

24. Douglas Highton, Conversation with the author, 11/08/07.

25. Ibid. See also Dahl, Letter to his mother, 01/23/27 – RDMSC 13/1/2/19.

26. Dahl, Letter to his mother, 03/17/26 – RDMSC 13/1/1/42.

27. Dahl, Letter to his mother, 03/10/26 – RDMSC 13/1/1/37.

28. *Boy*, p. 103.

29. Dahl, Letter to his mother, 09/23/25 – RDMSC 13/1/1/1.

30. *Boy*, p. 90.

31. Roald Dahl, St Peter's School Report – RDMSC 13/2/1–51.

32. Dahl, Letter to his mother, 05/29/27 – RDMSC 13/1/2/39.

33. Dahl, St Peter's School Report – RDMSC 13/2/1–51.

34. Dahl, Letter to his mother, 06/02/29 – RDMSC 13/1/4/16.

35. Dahl, St Peter's School Report – RDMSC 13/2/1–51.

36. Douglas Highton, Conversation with the author, 11/08/07.

37. Roald Dahl, Interviewed for *International School Publications*, 03/06/79 – RDMSC RD 12/1/10/1.

38. Douglas Highton, Conversation with the author, 11/8/07.

39. Dahl, Letter to his mother, 10/02/27 – RDMSC 13/1/3/3.

40. Dahl, Letter to his mother, 09/25/27 – RDMSC 13/1/3/2.

41. Dahl, Letter to his mother, 06/05/27 – RDMSC 13/1/2/41.

42. Dahl, Letter to his mother, 12/1/27 – RDMSC 13/1/3/7.

43. Roald Dahl, *The Roald Dahl Diary* (London: Jonathan Cape, 1991).

44. Dahl, Letter to his mother, 11/29/25 – RDMSC 13/1/2/16.

45. Dahl, Letter to his mother, 11/29/25 – RDMSC 13/1/1/16.

46. Dahl, Letter to his mother, 02/14/26 – RDMSC 13/1/1/31.

47. Dahl, Letter to his mother, 06/03/27 – RDMSC 13/1/2/40.

48. Dahl, Letter to his mother, 02/27/27 – RDMSC 13/1/2/28.

49. Dahl, Letter to his mother, 03/13/27 – RDMSC 13/1/2/30.

50. Dahl, Letter to his mother, 02/05/28 – RDMSC 13/1/3/20.

51. Dahl, Letter to his mother, 03/10/29 – RDMSC 13/1/4/08.

52. Dahl, Letter to his mother, 11/21/26 – RDMSC 13/1/1/37.

53. Dahl, Letter to his mother, 11/13/27 – RDMSC 13/1/3/11.

54. Dahl, Letter to his mother, 02/06/27 – RDMSC 13/1/2/23.

55. Roald Dahl, *Children's Books* (1988) – RDMSC RD 6/2/1/30 and 6/2/1/36.

56. Roald Dahl, Examination Paper – RDMSC 13/1/2/32.

57. Dahl, Letter to his mother, 02/06/27 – RDMSC 13/1/2/24.

58. Justin Wintle and Emma Fisher, *The Pied Pipers* (London: Paddington Press, 1974), p. 111.

59. *Desert Island Discs*, BBC Radio, 10/27/79.

60. Wintle and Fisher, *The Pied Pipers*, p. 60.

61. Copy of *Boy* in the possession of Douglas Highton.

62. *Boy*, pp. 97, 65.

63. Ibid., pp. 113, 112, 114.

64. *Boy – First Draft* – RDMSC RD 2/23/1/106.

65. Dahl, Letter to his mother, 02/28/28 – RDMSC 13/1/3/23.

66. Dahl, Letter to his mother, 01/20/27 – RDMSC 13/1/2/18.

67. Dahl, Letter to his mother, 02/13/27 – RDMSC 13/1/2/25.

68. Dahl, Letter to his mother, 07/08/28 – RDMSC 13/1/3/39.

69. Dahl, Letter to his mother, 03/24/29 – RDMSC 13/1/4/10.

70. Dahl, Letter to his mother, 10/29/29 – RDMSC 13/1/3/09.

71. Dahl, Letter to his mother, 11/17/29 – RDMSC 13/1/5/14.

72. Dahl, Letter to his mother, 03/25/28 – RDMSC 13/1/3/28.

73. Dahl, Letter to his mother, 12/09/29 – RDMSC 13/1/5/18.

74. Dahl, Letter to his mother, 10/24/26 – RDMSC 13/1/2/6.

75. Dahl, Letter to his mother, 02/07/26 – RDMSC 13/1/1/29.

76. Dahl, Letter to his mother, 06/17/28 – RDMSC 13/1/3/35.

77. Dahl, Letter to his mother, 02/05/28 – RDMSC 13/1/3/20.

78. Dahl, Letter to his mother, 08/01/29 – RDMSC 13/1/4/17.

79. Dahl, Letter to his mother, 04/03/27 – RDMSC 13/1/2/34.

80. Douglas Highton, Conversation with the author, 11/08/07.

81. Ben Reuss, Conversation with the author, 02/09/98.

82. Asta Anderson, Conversation with the author, 1997.

83. *The Roald Dahl Diary*, December.

84. Else Logsdail, Conversation with the author, 1997.

85. Asta Anderson, "Cauliflowers and Shrimps" in *Memories with Food at Gipsy House*, p. 106.

86. Asbjørnsen's collections had been published in Norway between 1883 and 1887; Moe's collection was published in 1907.

87. In Norwegian, the picture is known as *Syg Kjaerlighed*. It was painted in 1893.

88. Leif Østby, *Theodor Kittelsen* (Oslo: Dreyers Forlag, 1975).

89. Alfhild Hansen, Conversation with the author, 08/07/92.

90. *The Roald Dahl Diary.*

91. *Boy*, p. 79.

92. Roald Dahl, *Danny the Champion of the World* (London: Jonathan Cape, 1975) p. 73.

CHAPTER FOUR : *Foul Things and Horrid People*

1. Ben Reuss, Conversation with the author, 02/09/98.

2. Denton Welch, *Maiden Voyage* (London: Routledge, 1943), p. 24.

3. Thomas Arnold, Letter to the Rev. John Tucker, 03/02/1828.

4. Cited in Alan Hamilton, "Children Say Farewell to Roald Dahl", *The Times,* Nov. 30, 1990.

5. *Boy*, p. 126.

6. *Boy – First Draft* – RDMSC RD 2/23/1.

7. Nancy Deuchar, Conversation with the author, 12/04/07.

8. Tim Fisher, Conversation with the author, 09/17/07.

9. *Boy*, p. 146.

10. Sir Charles Pringle, Conversation with the author, 12/05/07.

11. Rachel Drayson, Letter to the author, 10/20/07.

12. Nancy Deuchar, Conversation with the author, 12/04/07.

13. Dahl, Letter to his mother, 03/19/33 – RDMSC RD 13/1/8/31.

14. Graham Greene, *A Sort of Life* (London: Bodley Head, 1971), p. 72.

15. *Boy – First Draft* – RDMSC RD 2/23/1/147.

16. *Boy*, pp. 143, 140, 128.

17. Roald Dahl, "Galloping Foxley" in *Collected Stories* (New York: Knopf, 2006), p. 420.

18. Tim Fisher, Conversation with the author, 09/17/07.

19. *Boy – First Draft* – RDMSC RD 2/23/1/154.

20. *Boy*, p. 126.

21. *Boy – First Draft* – RDMSC RD 2/23/1/166.

22. Ibid. – RDMSC RD 2/23/1/166–7.

23. Ibid. – RDMSC RD 2/23/1/161.

24. Ibid. – RDMSC RD 2/23/1/158.

25. Ibid. – RDMSC RD 2/23/1/159.

26. Tim Fisher, Conversation with the author, 09/17/07.

27. *Bookmark*, BBC Television, 1985.

28. *Boy – First Draft* – RDMSC RD 2/23/1/160.

29. *Boy – First Draft* – RDMSC RD 2/23/1/156. Middleton was killed in a car crash in Assam in 1937, only four years after he left the school.

30. *Boy*, p. 128.

31. "Galloping Foxley", p. 420.

32. *Boy*, p. 129.

33. *Boy – First Draft* – RDMSC RD 2/23/1/151.

34. *Galloping Foxley*, pp. 417–18.

35. Alfhild Hansen, Conversation with the author, 08/07/92.

36. Repton School Reports – RDMSC RD 13/2/58–90.

37. Dahl, Letter to his mother, 01/18/30 – RDMSC RD 13/1/5/9.

38. Dahl, Letter to his mother, 05/30 – RDMSC RD 13/1/5/38.

39. Dahl, Letter to his mother, 01/31 – RDMSC RD 13/1/6/22.

40. Dahl, Letter to his mother, 03/15/31 – RDMSC RD 13/1/6/27.

41. Dahl, Letter to his mother, 12/30 – RDMSC RD 13/1/6/14.

42. Dahl, Letter to his mother, 12/31 – RDMSC RD 13/1/7/27.

43. Dahl, Letter to his mother, 11/31 – RDMSC RD 13/1/7/18.

44. Dahl, Letter to his mother, 05/30 – RDMSC RD 13/1/5/46.

45. Dahl, Letter to his mother, 04/31 – RDMSC RD 13/1/6/33.

46. Dahl, Letter to his mother, 09/02/30 – RDMSC RD 13/1/5/24.

47. Dahl, Letter to his mother, 06/31 – RDMSC RD 13/1/6/43.

48. Ben Reuss, Conversation with the author, 02/09/98.

49. Nicholas Arnold, Conversation with the author, 01/16/08.

50. Dahl, Letter to his mother, 02/33 – RDMSC RD 13/1/8/26.

51. Dahl, Letter to his mother, 05/01/32 – RDMSC RD 13/1/7/39.

52. Dahl, Letter to his mother, 12/32 – RDMSC RD 13/1/8/15.

53. Ben Reuss, Conversation with the author, 02/09/98.

54. *Boy*, p. 149.

55. Dahl, Letter to his mother, 06/31 – RDMSC RD 13/1/6/48.

56. David Atkins, "Writers Remembered: Roald Dahl", *The Author*, vol. CIII, no. 1 (Spring 1992), p. 24.

57. Roald Dahl, Untitled speech about teaching English in schools, c. 1965 – RDMSC RD 6/2/1/23.

58. Dahl, Letter to his mother, 10/31 – RDMSC RD 13/1/7/7.

59. Roald Dahl, *Nursery Rhymes* – RDMSC RD 13/3/39.

60. Roald Dahl, *Dreams* – RDMSC RD 13/3/3/23.

61. Atkins, "Writers Remembered: Roald Dahl", p. 24.

62. He used it most publicly in a BBC Television interview with Sue Lawley – BBC, *Wogan with Sue Lawley,* 1988.

63. Roald Dahl, *Laughter* – RDMSC RD 13/3/3/1.

64. Dahl, Letter to his mother, 06/03/34 – RDMSC RD 13/1/9/42.

65. Dahl, Letter to his mother, 01/18/30 – RDMSC RD 13/1/6/14.

66. Atkins, "Writers Remembered: Roald Dahl", p. 24.

67. Dahl, Letter to his mother, 01/18/30 – RDMSC RD 13/1/5/9.

68. *Boy – First Draft* – RDMSC RD 2/23/1/149.

69. Dahl, Letter to his mother, 02/04/34 – RDMSC RD 13/1/9/24.

70. *Boy – First Draft* – RDMSC RD 2/23/1/155.

71. Dahl, Letter to his mother, 01/31 – RDMSC RD 13/1/7/10.

72. Welch, *Maiden Voyage*, pp. 30, 66, 48.

73. Ibid., pp. 55–56.

74. Sir Charles Pringle, Conversation with the author, 12/05/07.

75. Anna Corrie, Conversation with the author, 10/08/07.

76. Dahl, Letter to his mother, 07/33 – RDMSC RD 13/1/8/44.

77. Nancy Deuchar, Conversation with the author, 12/04/07.

78. Atkins, "Writers Remembered: Roald Dahl", p. 24.

79. James Methuen-Campbell, *Denton Welch, Writer and Artist* (London: Tartarus Press, 2002), p. 22.

80. Atkins, "Writers Remembered: Roald Dahl", p. 24.

81. Dahl, Letter to his mother, 01/33 – RDMSC RD 13/1/8/20.

82. Dahl, Letter to his mother, 05/33 – RDMSC RD 13/1/8/37.

83. Dahl, Letter to his mother 05/07/33 – RDMSC RD 13/1/8/35.

84. Dahl, Letter to his mother 05/14/33 – RDMSC RD 13/1/8/36.

85. Dahl, Letter to his mother, 05/33 – RDMSC RD 13/1/8/37.

86. S. S. Jenkyns, Letter to Mrs Dahl, 06/14/33 – RDMSC RD 13/1/8/43.

87. Dahl, Letter to his mother, 06/33 – RDMSC RD 13/1/8/42.

88. Ben Reuss, Conversation with the author, 02/09/98.

89. Nicholas Arnold, Conversation with the author, 01/16/08. Nicholas, one of Michael Arnold's three sons, did not care to say what the subject of the argument had been.

90. *Boy*, p. 131.

91. Ben Reuss, Conversation with the author, 02/09/98.

92. *Boy*, p. 132.

93. Ben Reuss, Conversation with the author, 02/09/98.

94. Asta Anderson and Else Logsdail, Conversation with the author, 01/03/98.

95. *Boy*, p. 132.

96. Dahl, Letter to his mother, 05/15/33 – RDMSC RD 13/1/7/42.

97. *Boy*, p. 132.

98. The book is now in the Repton School Archives.

99. Roald Dahl, Speech to Boys at Repton, Nov. 21, 1975 – RDMSC RD 6/1/1/25.

100. Dahl, Letter to his mother, 11/32 – RDMSC RD 13/1/8/15.

101. Dahl, Speech to boys at Repton, Nov. 21, 1975 – RDMSC RD 6/1/1/25.

102. John Bradburn, Letter to *The Daily Telegraph* 05/06/88.

103. *Boy*, p. 148.

104. Dahl, Letter to his mother, 05/07/33 – RDMSC RD 13/1/8/35.

105. Dahl, Letter to his mother, 12/30 – RDMSC RD 13/1/6/17.

106. Else Logsdail, Conversation with the author, 01/03/98.

107. Dahl, Letter to his mother, 02/04/34 – RDMSC RD 13/1/9/24.

108. Ben Reuss, Conversation with the author, 02/09/98.

109. Ophelia Dahl, Conversation with the author, 03/18/08.

110. Letter from B. L. L. Reuss quoted in Treglown, p. 31.

111. Dahl, Repton School Report (Summer 1934) – RDMSC RD 13/2/90.

CHAPTER FIVE: *Distant Faraway Lands*

1. Roald Dahl, *Newfoundland Journal* – *"The Long March"* – RDMSC RD 13/5/1.

2. Dahl, Letter to his mother, 08/13/34 – RDMSC RD 13/1/9/57.

3. Dennis Clarke, *Public School Explorers in Newfoundland* (London: Putnam, 1935).

4. Dahl, *Newfoundland Journal* – *"The Long March"* – RDMSC RD 13/5/1.

5. Dahl, *Newfoundland Journal* – RDMSC RD 13/5/2.

6. Dennis Pearl, Conversation with the author, 01/03/98.

7. Dahl, *Newfoundland Journal* – RDMSC RD 13/5/2.

8. Dahl, *Newfoundland Journal* Notes – RDMSC RD 13/5/1.

9. *Boy*, p. 154.

10. Memoir of Mr MacPherson, Outpost Archive Centre, Shell/BP, The Hague.
11. Ibid.
12. Dahl, Letter to his mother, 07/14/36 – RDMSC RD 14/2/8.
13. Antony Pegg quoted in Treglown, p. 33.
14. Dahl, Letter to his mother, 02/32 – RDMSC RD 13/1/7/32.
15. Alfhild Hansen, Conversation with the author, 08/07/92.
16. Alexandra Anderson, Conversation with the author, 11/14/07.
17. Dahl, Letter to his mother, 12/31 – RDMSC RD 13/1/7/20.
18. Dahl, Letter to his mother, 09/33 – RDMSC RD 13/1/9/4.
19. Dahl, Letter to his mother, 11/32 – RDMSC RD 13/1/8/14.
20. Dahl, Letter to his mother, 06/33 – RDMSC RD 13/1/8/40.
21. Dahl, Letter to his mother, 07/33 – RDMSC RD 13/1/8/52.
22. Dahl, Letter to his mother, 08/35 – RDMSC RD 14/2/1.
23. Dahl, Letter to his mother, 08/13/35 – RDMSC RD 14/2/2.
24. Roald Dahl, *Double Exposure*, unpublished sketch (c. 1938) – RDMSC RD 9/1.
25. Dahl, Letter to his mother, 08/13/35 – RDMSC RD 14/2/2.
26. *Boy*, p. 155.
27. Roald Dahl, Speech for Sunday Express Book Award, 11/29/89 – RDMSC RD 6/1/2/35.
28. Roald Dahl, "A Book That Changed Me", *The Independent*, July 15, 1990 – RDMSC RD 6/2/1/39.
29. Dahl, Letter to his mother, 03/03/29 – RDMSC RD 13/1/4/07.
30. Roald Dahl, Article for the 50th anniversary of Dartford Golf Club – RDMSC RD 6/2/1/43.
31. Treglown, p. 34.
32. In a letter to his mother from Tanganyika dated October 16, 1938, Roald boasts that with a handicap of two he may well be the best player in the territory – RDMSC RD 14/3/07.
33. Dennis Pearl, Conversation with the author, 01/03/98.
34. Ibid.
35. Ophelia Dahl, Conversation with the author, 03/17/08.
36. Treglown, p. 37.
37. Dahl, Letter to his mother, 04/14/36 – RDMSC RD 14/2/7.
38. Dennis Pearl, Conversation with the author, 01/03/98.
39. Atkins, "Writers Remembered: Roald Dahl", p. 24.
40. Alfhild Hansen, Conversation with the author, 08/07/92.
41. Louise (Lou) Pearl, Conversation with the author, 05/09/08.
42. Dahl, Letter to his mother, 05/20/34 – RDMSC RD 13/1/9/40.
43. Louise Pearl, Conversation with the author, 05/09/08.
44. Alfhild Hansen, Conversation with the author, 08/07/92.
45. Dennis Pearl, Conversation with the author, 01/03/98.
46. John Wilkinson, Conversation with the author, 10/18/07.
47. Treglown, p. 36.
48. Louise Pearl, Conversation with the author, 05/09/08.
49. Felicity Dahl and Louise Pearl, Conversations with the author, 03/14/08 and 05/09/08.

50. Roald Dahl, *Going Solo* (London: Jonathan Cape, 1986), p. 13.
51. Dahl, Letter to his mother, 10/38 – RDMSC RD 14/3/6.
52. Dahl, Letter to his mother, 10/38 – RDMSC RD 14/3/1.
53. Dahl, Letter to his mother, 10/16/38 – RDMSC RD 14/3/7.
54. Dahl, Letter to his mother, 10/28/38 – RDMSC RD 14/3/9.
55. *Going Solo*, p. 32.
56. Dahl, Letter to his mother, 12/08/38 – RDMSC RD 14/3/15.
57. Dahl, Letter to his mother, 04/02/39 – RDMSC RD 14/3/31.
58. Dahl, Letter to his mother, 07/11/39 – RDMSC RD 14/3/45.
59. Dahl, Letter to his mother, 02/26/39 – RDMSC RD 14/3/26.
60. Dahl, Letter to his mother, 07/13/39 – RDMSC RD 14/3/49.
61. Dahl, Letter to his mother, 02/39 – RDMSC RD 14/3/21.
62. Dahl, Letter to his mother, 11/25/38 – RDMSC RD 14/3/13.
63. Dahl, Letter to his mother, 03/05/39 – RDMSC RD 14/3/27.
64. Felicity Dahl, Conversation with the author, 03/10/10.
65. Dahl, Letter to his mother, 01/39 – RDMSC RD 14/3/19.
66. Dahl, Letter to his mother, 03/05/39 – RDMSC RD 14/3/27.
67. Dahl, Letter to his mother, 03/19/39 – RDMSC RD 14/3/28.
68. Dahl, Letter to his mother, 05/28/39 – RDMSC RD 14/3/39.
69. Dahl, Letter to his mother, 04/02/39 – RDMSC RD 14/3/31.
70. Dahl, Letter to his mother, 04/09/39 – RDMSC RD 14/3/32.
71. Dahl, Letter to his mother and sisters, 11/25/38 – RDMSC RD 14/3/13.
72. Dahl, Letter to his mother, 11/25/38 – RDMSC RD 14/3/13.
73. *Going Solo*, p. 34.
74. Dahl, Letter to his mother, 01/39 – RDMSC RD 14/3/19.
75. *Going Solo*, p. 34.
76. Dahl, Letter to his mother, 11/38 – RDMSC RD 14/3/14.
77. *Going Solo*, p. 61.
78. *Charlie's Chocolate Boy – First Draft*, 1961 – RDMSC RD 2/7/1.
79. Dahl, Letter to his mother, 05/14/39 – RDMSC RD 14/3/37.
80. Dahl, Letter to his mother, 05/02/39 – RDMSC RD 14/3/22.
81. Dahl, Speech to Boys at Rapton, Nov. 21, 1975 – RDMSC RD 6/1/1/25, and Australian Broadcasting Corporation, Radio interview with Terry Lane, 1989.
82. Roald Dahl, "Poison", in *Collier's* magazine, June 3, 1950 – RDMSC RD 4/18/5.
83. Dahl, Letter to his mother, 10/14/39 – RDMSC RD 14/3/58.
84. Dahl, Letter to his mother, 08/27/39 – RDMSC RD 14/3/52.
85. Dahl, Letter to his mother, 03/26/39 – RDMSC RD 14/3/29.
86. Dahl, Letter to his mother, 08/13/39 – RDMSC RD 14/3/51.
87. Dahl, Letter to his mother, 05/14/39 – RDMSC RD 14/3/37.
88. Dahl, Letter to his mother, 04/16/39 – RDMSC RD 14/3/33.
89. Dahl, Letter to his mother, 12/38 – RDMSC RD 14/3/17.
90. Dahl, Letter to his mother, 03/05/38 – RDMSC RD 14/3/27.
91. Dahl, Letter to his mother, 12/38 – RDMSC RD 14/3/16.
92. Roald Dahl, Letter to Ann Watkins, 12/08/43 – RDMSC RD 1/1/70.
93. Dahl, Letter to his mother, 12/16/38 – RDMSC RD 14/5/2/40.

94. Dahl, Letter to his mother, 06/05/39 – RDMSC RD 14/3/40.
95. Dahl, Letter to his mother, 07/11/39 – RDMSC RD 14/3/45.
96. Dahl, Letter to his mother, 06/05/39 – RDMSC RD 14/3/40.
97. Winston Churchill, Speech to the House of Commons, Oct. 5, 1938.
98. Dahl, Letter to his mother, 04/09/39 – RDMSC RD 14/3/32.
99. Dahl, Letter to his mother, 03/19/39 – RDMSC RD 14/3/28.
100. Dahl, Letter to his mother, 09/30/39 – RDMSC RD 14/3/57.
101. Dahl, Letter to his mother, 05/14/39 – RDMSC RD 14/3/37.
102. Dahl, Letter to his mother, 08/27/39 – RDMSC RD 14/3/54.
103. Report by Sir Mark Young to Malcolm MacDonald on measures taken after the outbreak of war, 09/15/39 – Public Record Office, CO 323/1657/82.
104. Dahl, Letter to his mother, 09/15/39 – RDMSC RD 14/3/55.
105. Roald Dahl, "The Sword", *Atlantic Monthly* (August 1943), p. 79.
106. Roald Dahl, "Lucky Break", in *The Wonderful Story of Henry Sugar and Six More* (London: Jonathan Cape, 1977), p. 220.
107. *Going Solo*, pp. 71, 73.
108. Ibid., pp. 79, 83.
109. Ibid., p. 80.
110. Dahl, Letter to his mother, 09/30/39 – RDMSC RD 14/3/57.
111. Dahl, Letter to his mother, 10/14/39 – RDMSC RD 14/3/58.
112. Dahl, Letter to his mother, 11/14/39 – RDMSC RD 14/3/62.
113. Ibid.
114. Dahl, Letter to his mother, 11/18/39 – RDMSC RD 14/3/63.
115. *Going Solo*, p. 87.
116. Dahl, Letter to his mother, 12/04/39 – RDMSC RD 14/3/65.
117. *Going Solo*, p. 94.
118. Dahl, Letter to his mother, 08/14/40 – RDMSC RD 14/4/3.

CHAPTER SIX: *A Monumental Bash on the Head*

1. Alfhild Hansen, Conversation with the author, 08/07/92.
2. See Derek O'Connor, "Roald Dahl's Wartime Adventures", *Aviation History* (January 2009).
3. *Going Solo*, p. 96.
4. Dahl, Letter to his mother, 02/20/40 – RDMSC RD 14/4/7.
5. Dahl, Letter to his mother, 02/26/40 – RDMSC RD 14/4/8.
6. Dahl, Letter to his mother, 06/24/40 – RDMSC RD 14/4/20.
7. Dahl, Letter to his mother, 02/20/40 – RDMSC RD 14/4/7.
8. *Going Solo*, p. 8, and Dahl, Letter to his mother, 03/14/40 – RDMSC RD 14/4/10.
9. Dahl, Letter to his mother, 05/03/40 – RDMSC RD 14/4/17.
10. Dahl, Letter to his mother, 06/26/40 – RDMSC RD 14/4/24.
11. Dahl, Letter to his mother, 07/24/40 – RDMSC RD 14/4/28.
12. *Going Solo*, p. 98.
13. Dahl, Letter to his mother, 08/28/40 – RDMSC RD 14/4/32.
14. Dahl, Letter to his mother, 05/17/40 – RDMSC RD 14/4/19.

15. *Going Solo*, p. 105.
16. Dahl, Letter to his mother, 11/20/40 – RDMSC RD 14/4/38.
17. *Going Solo*, p. 105.
18. Roald Dahl, "Shot Down Over Libya", *Saturday Evening Post*, Aug. 1, 1942.
19. Dahl, Letter to his mother, 11/20/40 – RDMSC RD 14/4/38.
20. Roald Dahl, *Beware of the Dog*, first published in *Harper's* (October 1944); collected in *Over to You*, 1946; *Collected Stories*, (Everyman), p. 49.
21. *Going Solo*, p. 112.
22. Ibid., p. 113.
23. Dahl, Letter to his mother, 1/20/40 – RDMSC RD 14/4/38.
24. Forced Landings and Flying Accident cards in RAF Museum, London, NW9.
25. *Going Solo*, pp. 105–6.
26. Letter to the author from Mr G. Day, Ministry of Defence (Air Historical Branch), 07/23/07.
27. *Going Solo*, p. 100.
28. O'Connor, "Roald Dahl's Wartime Adventures", p. 46.
29. Ophelia Dahl, "Memories of My Father", unpublished MS.
30. Roald Dahl, Letter to Barbara McDonald, 04/24/53, donated to Roald Dahl Museum and Story Centre by her daughter, Deb Ford.
31. Roald Dahl, "A Piece of Cake" (1942) in *Collected Stories*, pp. 129–30.
32. Dahl, Letter to his mother, 01/29/41 – RDMSC 14/4/44.
33. Dahl, Letter to his mother, 01/02/41 – RDMSC RD 14/4/42.
34. Lesley O'Malley (née Pares), Conversation with the author, 1998.
35. Dahl, Letter to his mother, 02/17/41 – RDMSC RD 14/4/46.
36. Dahl, Letter to his mother, 03/07/41 – RDMSC RD 14/4/48.
37. *Going Solo*, p. 118.
38. Roald Dahl, Interviewed by Peter Lennon in *The Times*, Dec. 12, 1983.
39. See Ophelia Dahl, *Memories of My Father*, unpublished MS.
40. See Ryan Hall, Richard C.W. Hall, and Marcia J. Chapman, "Definition, Diagnosis and Forensic Implications of Postconcussional Syndrome", *Psychosomatics*, 46 (June 2005), pp. 195–202.
41. *James and the Giant Peach*, p. 95.
42. *The Minpins* (London: Jonathan Cape, 1991), p. 41.
43. *The Wonderful Story of Henry Sugar and Six More*, p. 116.
44. Dahl, Letter to his mother, 03/07/41 – RDMSC RD 14/4/48.

CHAPTER SEVEN: *David and Goliath*

1. Roald Dahl, Address Book – RDMSC AC 1/185.
2. "Jonah" Jones, C.O. of 84 Squadron, cited in T. H. Wisdom, *Wings Over Olympus, The Story of the Royal Air Force in Libya and Greece* (1942), p. 169.
3. Roald Dahl, *Katina, Collected Stories*, pp. 26–27.
4. *Going Solo*, (FSG), p. 122.
5. Ibid., p. 123.
6. Roald Dahl, "The Ginger Cat", unpublished short story, 1945 – RDMSC RD 5/14/1–3.

7. *Going Solo*, p. 123.

8. Ibid., pp. 124, 130, 128.

9. Ibid., p. 124.

10. Roald Dahl, "Death of an Old, Old Man", *Collected Stories*, p. 87.

11. *Going Solo*, p. 134.

12. James Oswald Gale, *Unpublished Memoirs*. Flight Lieutenant Gale was Equipment Officer for 33 Squadron. He remained in the RAF after the war, rising to the rank of air commodore.

13. Keith Skilling, quoted in Wikipedia article on flying Hawker Hurricanes, August 2008.

14. *Going Solo*, p. 134.

15. Dahl, Letter to Roger Burlingame, 04/28/45 – RDMSC RD 1/1/1/200.

16. Roald Dahl, Letter to Harold Matson, 05/13/42 – RDMSC RD 1/1/1/3.

17. *Katina*, p. 37.

18. *Going Solo*, p. 152.

19. Interview with Vernon "Woody" Woodward of 33 Squadron, quoted in Hugh Halladay, *Woody: A Fighter Pilot's Album* (Toronto: Canav Books, 1987).

20. Gale, *Unpublished Memoirs*.

21. Christopher Buckley, *Greece and Crete 1941* (London: HMSO, 1952), p. 97.

22. *Going Solo*, p. 169.

23. *Katina*, p. 42.

24. *Going Solo*, p. 172.

25. *Katina*, p. 43.

26. Gale, *Unpublished Memoirs*.

27. Dahl, Letter to his mother, 05/06/41 – RDMSC RD 14/4/52.

28. *Going Solo*, p. 201.

29. Dahl, Letter to his mother, 05/15/41 – RDMSC RD 14/4/54.

30. *Going Solo*, pp. 187–88.

31. Dahl, Letter to his mother, 06/28/41 – RDMSC RD 14/4/57.

32. Dahl, Letter to his mother, 06/20/41 – RDMSC RD 14/4/56.

33. *Going Solo*, pp. 193–94, 198.

34. Ibid., p. 199.

35. Dahl, Letter to his mother, 06/28/41 – RDMSC RD 14/4/57.

36. Alfhild Hansen, Conversation with the author, 08/07/92.

37. Roald Dahl, "My Time of Life", *The Sunday Times*, Oct. 4, 1986.

38. *Going Solo*, p. 208.

39. Alexandra Anderson and Louise Pearl, Conversations with the author, 11/14/07 and 05/09/08.

40. Ophelia Dahl, Conversation with the author, 03/17/08.

41. Roald Dahl, *Searching for Mr Smith*, 1979, Browse & Darby Catalogue, 1983.

42. *Bookmark*, BBC Television, 1985.

CHAPTER EIGHT: *Alive but Earthbound*

1. Roald Dahl, Letter to John Logsdail, 06/08/40 – in possession of Louise Pearl.

2. Elizabeth Bowen, "London 1940", in *Collected Impressions* (London: Longmans Green & Co., 1950).

3. Else Logsdail and Asta Anderson, Conversations with the author, 01/03/98.

4. Alfhild Hansen, Conversation with the author, 08/07/92.

5. Ibid.

6. Ibid.

7. Astri Newman, Conversation with the author, 10/15/07.

8. Pat Brazier, Conversation with the author, 10/04/09.

9. Jeremy Lang, Conversation with the author, 12/01/08.

10. Ibid.

11. Pauline Hearne, Letter to the author, 09/12/09.

12. Roald Dahl, *The Gremlins* (New York: Walt Disney/Random House, 1943).

13. Barry Farrell, *Pat and Roald* (London: Hutchinson, 1970), p. 68, and Wintle and Fisher, *The Pied Pipers*, pp. 102–3.

14. Wintle and Fisher, *The Pied Pipers*, p. 103.

15. William Stevenson, *A Man Called Intrepid* (Guilford, CT: Lyons Press, 1976, p. 169.

16. Ibid.

17. Roald Dahl, Notes to prospective biographer Stephen Roxburgh – HRCH KNOPF.

18. Dahl, Letter to his mother, 04/14/42 – RDMSC RD 14/5/1/1.

19. Dahl, Letter to his mother, 04/21/42 – RDMSC RD 14/5/1/2.

20. Dahl, Letter to his mother, 04/14/42 – RDMSC RD 14/5/1/1.

21. Dahl, Letter to his mother, 04/21/42 – RDMSC RD 14/5/1/2.

22. Quoted in Treglown, p. 56.

23. Michael Ignatieff, *Isaiah Berlin: A Life* (New York: Henry Holt, 1998), p. 111.

24. *Time* magazine, April 7, 1941.

25. Dahl, Letter to his mother, 05/13/42 – RDMSC RD 14/5/1/4.

26. Stevenson, *A Man Called Intrepid*, p. 169.

27. Treglown, p. 56.

28. "Lucky Break", p. 225.

29. Ibid., p. 229.

30. At the time, Dahl calculated $300 was worth about £76 – Dahl, Letter to his mother, 05/13/42 – RDMSC RD 14/5/1/4.

31. Harold Matson, Letter to Katherine Swan, 05/11/42 – RDMSC RD 1/1/1.

32. "Lucky Break", p. 229.

33. The earliest surviving MS dates from 1945, when he rewrote the story for inclusion in his collection of stories *Over to You*.

34. *Going Solo*, p. 101.

35. Dahl, Letter to his mother, 08/07/42 – RDMSC 14/5/1/11.

36. Dahl, Letter to his mother, 05/13/42 – RDMSC RD 14/5/1/4.

37. "Lucky Break", p. 227.

38. Dahl, "Shot Down Over Libya", *Saturday Evening Post*, Aug. 1, 1942.

39. "Lucky Break", p. 233.

40. He did so, for example, in a letter to Thomas Beck, the editor of *Collier's* magazine, in August 1942 – RDMSC RD 1/4/8.

41. For example, Wintle and Fisher in *The Pied Pipers*, p. 102.

42. *Boy*, p. 160.

43. *Going Solo*, p. 101.

44. Dahl, Letters to his mother, 05/13/42 and 06/42 – RDMSC RD 14/5/1/4 and RD 14/5/1/5.

45. Information supplied by Astri Newman.

46. Dahl, Letter to his mother, 10/04/42 – RDMSC RD 14/5/1/17.

47. Dahl, Letter to his mother, 12/15/42 – RDMSC RD 14/5/1/24.

48. Dahl, Letter to his mother, 10/20/42 – RDMSC RD 14/5/1/18.

49. Dahl, Letter to his mother, 12/15/42 – RDMSC RD 14/5/1/24.

50. In a letter to his mother, Roald described Travers as "about the dirtiest little man I have ever met, but extremely nice and terribly funny" – 09/04/42 – RDMSC 14/5/1/14.

51. Dahl, Letter to his mother, 12/15/42 – RDMSC RD 14/5/1/24.

52. Dahl, Letter to his mother, 04/21/42 – RDMSC RD 14/5/1/2.

53. Dahl, Letter to his mother, 08/07/42 – RDMSC RD 14/5/1/10.

54. Dahl, Letter to his mother, 05/13/42 – RDMSC RD 14/5/1/4.

55. Dahl, Letter to his mother, 08/07/42 – RDMSC RD 14/5/1/10.

56. Ibid.

57. Roald Dahl, Letter to James Beck, 08/20/42 – RDMSC RD 1/4/8.

58. Dahl, Letter to his mother, 06/22/42 – RDMSC RD 14/5/1/6.

CHAPTER NINE: *A Sort of Fairy Story*

1. Dahl, Letter to his mother, 06/22/42 – RDMSC RD 14/5/1/6.

2. Roald Dahl, *Gremlin Lore* – RDMSC RD 2/1/1.

3. Aubrey Morgan, Letter to Air Commodore William Thornton, 08/21/42 – RDMSC RD 1/4/1/9.

4. Dahl, Letter to his mother, 06/22/42 – RDMSC RD 14/5/1/6.

5. Walt Disney, Cable to Sidney Bernstein, 07/14/42 – RDMSC RD 1/4/1/5.

6. Ibid.

7. Roald Dahl, Letter to William Teeling, 11/30/42 – RDMSC RD 1/4/1/74.

8. Internal Disney Memo quoted in Jim Korkis, "The Trouble with Gremlins", *Hogan's Alley Magazine*, 15.

9. Roald Dahl, Letter to Jim Bodrero, 08/03/42 – RDMSC RD 1/4/1.

10. Roald Dahl, Letter to Thomas Beck, 08/20/42 – RDMSC RD 1/4/1/8.

11. Vernon MacKenzie, Memorandum to Aubrey Morgan, 08/20/42 – RDMSC RD 1/4/1/10.

12. Harold Matson, Telegram to Roald Dahl, 09/01/42 – RDMSC RD 1/4/1/18.

13. Roald Dahl, Letter to John Rose, 08/25/42 – RDMSC RD 1/4/1/12.

14. John Rose, Letter to Roald Dahl, 08/27/42 – RDMSC RD 1/4/1/17.

15. Dahl, Letter to his mother, 10/04/42 – RDMSC RD 14/5/1/17.

16. Dahl, Letter to his mother, 09/04/42 – RDMSC RD 14/5/1/14.

17. Dahl, Letter to his mother, 10/04/42 – RDMSC RD 14/5/1/17.

18. Quoted in Korkis, "The Trouble with Gremlins".

19. Dahl, Letter to his mother, 11/10/42 – RDMSC RD 14/5/1/20.

20. Roald Dahl, Letter to Sol Rosenblatt, 10/01/42 – RDMSC RD 1/4/1/46.

21. Korkis, "The Trouble with Gremlins".

22. Charles Solomon, *The Disney That Never Was* (New York: Hyperion, 1995), p. 50.

23. Leonard Maltin, *Introduction to The Gremlins* (Milwaukie, OR: Dark Horse Books, 2006).

24. Dahl, Letter to his mother, 10/01/42 – RDMSC RD 14/5/1/16.

25. Douglas Bisgood, Letter to Walt Disney, 09/20/42, quoted in Korkis, "The Trouble with Gremlins".

26. Walt Disney, Letter to Roald Dahl, 10/01/42 – RDMSC RD 1/4/1/48.

27. Roald Dahl, Letter to Walt Disney, 10/07/42 – RDMSC RD 1/4/1/52.

28. Roald Dahl, Letter to Walt Disney, 09/02/42 – RDMSC RD 1/4/1/21.

29. Roald Dahl, Letter to Edmond Witalis, 09/30/42 – RDMSC RD 1/4/1/45.

30. Roald Dahl, Letter to Walt Disney, 09/02/42 – RDMSC RD 1/4/1/21.

31. Dahl, Letter to his mother, 11/27/42 – RDMSC RD 4/5/1/21. Brooks (1915–1995) went on to become the first American female civilian to travel to the Pacific theater of war, eventually marrying the politician Torbert Macdonald, who had once been John F. Kennedy's roommate.

32. Roald Dahl, *Notes on Visiting Los Angeles* 06/24/43 – RDMSC RD 1/4/1/139.

33. Bill Justice, *Justice for Disney* (Dayton, OH: Tomart Publications, 1992), quoted in Korkis, "The Trouble with Gremlins".

34. Dahl, Letter to his mother, 11/27/42 – RDMSC RD 14/5/1/21.

35. Ibid.

36. Roald Dahl, Letter to Walt Disney, 10/07/42 – RDMSC RD 1/4/1/52. This was an impasse that was never resolved. In the published version of the book, the text refers to the gremlins wearing "green derbys", or bowler hats, but all the drawings show them in flying helmets.

37. Dahl, Letter to his mother, 11/27/42 – RDMSC RD 14/5/1/21.

38. Roald Dahl, Letter to Walt Disney, 12/02/42 – RDMSC RD 1/4/1/79.

39. Roald Dahl, Letter to Air Commodore William Thornton, 11/18/42 – RDMSC RD 1/4/1/68.

40. Korkis, "The Trouble with Gremlins".

41. Hamish Hamilton, Letter to Roald Dahl, 08/25/42 – RDMSC RD 1/4/1/15.

42. Roald Dahl, Letter to Air Marshall Peck, 12/08/42 – RDMSC RD 1/4/1/80.

43. William Teeling, Letter to Roald Dahl, 02/11/43 – RDMSC RD 1/4/1/96.

44. J. B. Hogan, Letter to Roald Dahl, 08/23/42 – RDMSC RD 1/4/1/14.

45. Treglown, p. 69.

46. William Teeling, Letter to Roald Dahl, 02/11/43 – RDMSC RD 1/4/1/96.

47. Clement Caines, Letter to Air Commodore William Thornton, 01/25/43 – RDMSC RD 1/4/1/95.

48. Dahl, Letter to his mother, 12/05/42 – RDMSC RD 14/5/1/23, and Letter to William Teeling, 03/16/43 – RDMSC RD 1/4/1/107. Eagle Squadrons were RAF Squadrons made up of volunteer American pilots who joined up to fight Hitler before the United States formally entered the war after Pearl Harbor.

49. Dahl, Letter to his mother, 02/13/43 – RDMSC 14/5/2/4.

50. Roald Dahl, Letter to William Teeling, 03/16/43 – RDMSC RD 1/4/1/107.

51. C. G. Caines, Asst. Under Secretary of State for Air, Letter to Air Commodore William Thornton, 01/25/43 – RDMSC RD 1/4/1/95.

52. Roald Dahl, Letter to Walt Disney, 01/01/43 – RDMSC RD 1/4/1/85.

53. Roald Dahl, Letter to Walt Disney, 05/19/43 – RDMSC RD 1/4/1/129.

54. Roald Dahl, *Stop Picking on Gremlins*, MS, 03/09/43 – RDMSC RD 1/4/1/105.

55. Dahl, Letter to his mother, 02/13/43 – RDMSC RD 14/5/2/4.

56. Viscount Halifax, Letter to Roald Dahl, 04/29/43 – RDMSC RD 1/4/1/124.

57. Eleanor Roosevelt, Letter to Roald Dahl, 05/27/43 – RDMSC RD 1/4/1/136.

58. Lucille Ogle, Letter to Roald Dahl, 12/07/43 – RDMSC RD 1/4/1/145.

59. Roy Disney, Letter to Roald Dahl, u.d. – RDMSC RD 1/4/1/154.

60. The RAF Benevolent Fund earned $368 from gremlin merchandising in 1943 – RDMSC RD 1/4/1/132.

61. Walt Disney, Letter to Roald Dahl, 05/26/43 – RDMSC RD 1/5/1.

62. Dahl, Letter to his mother, 04/17/43 – RDMSC 14/5/2/11.

63. Dahl, Letter to his mother, 04/17/43 – RDMSC 14/5/2/11.

64. Korkis, "The Trouble with Gremlins".

65. Walt Disney, Letter to Roald Dahl, 07/02/43 – RDMSC RD 1/5/1.

66. Walt Disney Archive cited in Korkis, "The Trouble with Gremlins".

67. Justice, *Justice for Disney*, cited in ibid.

68. Walt Disney, Letter to Roald Dahl, 12/18/43 – RDMSC RD 1/4/1/147.

69. Robin Allan, *Walt Disney and Europe* (London: John Libby & Co., 1999), p. 186.

70. Roy Disney, Letter to Roald Dahl, 04/24/45 – RDMSC RD 1/4/1.

71. Roy Disney, Letter to Roald Dahl, 04/17/45 – RDMSC RD 1/4/1.

72. Roald Dahl, Letter to J. B. Hogan, 09/03/42 – RDMSC RD 1/4/1/23.

73. Dahl, Letter to his mother, 12/15/42 – RDMSC RD 14/5/1/24.

74. Dahl, Letter to his mother, 03/23/43 – RDMSC RD 14/5/2/9.

75. Dahl, Letter to his mother, 06/17/43 – RDMSC RD 14/5/2/19.

76. Roald Dahl, Letter to Henry Wallace, 01/13/43 – RDMSC RD 15/5.

77. Valerie Pascal, *The Disciple and His Devil* (New York: Dell Publishing, 1970), p. 72.

78. Ibid., pp. 73–75.

79. Ibid., pp. 83–87.

80. The reference is from a 1947 biography of Wallace by Dwight Macdonald cited in Philip Kopper, *Anonymous Giver: A Life of Charles Marsh* (Washington, D.C.: Public Welfare Foundation, 2000), p. 77.

81. John C. Culver and John Hyde, *American Dreamer, the Life and Times of Henry Wallace* (New York: W. W. Norton, 2000), pp. 134–35.

82. Columbia University Oral History, *Reminiscences of Paul H. Appleby*, p. 12.

83. Dahl, Letter to his mother, 12/28/42 – RDMSC RD 14/5/1/26.

84. Dahl, Letter to his mother, 01/07/43 – RDMSC RD 14/5/2/1.

85. Thomas M. Pryor in the *New York Times*, Jan. 10, 1943.

86. Andrew R. Kelley in the *Washington Times-Herald*, Jan. 11, 1943.

87. Dahl, Letter to his mother, 01/07/43 – RDMSC RD 14/5/2/1.

88. Dahl, Letter to his mother, 04/17/43 – RDMSC RD 14/5/2/11. Hawks would also pester Dahl for a screenplay about Guy Gibson and the "Dam Buster" raid, which happened that summer – Roald Dahl, *Notes on Los Angeles*, 06/24/43 – RDMSC RD 1/4/1/139.

89. Roald Dahl, "An Eye for a Tooth", later retitled "Teat for Tat" and finally "An African Story" when it was included in his first anthology, *Over to You*.

90. Roald Dahl, "Only This", first published in *Ladies' Home Journal*, 1944, from *Collected Stories*, p. 19.

91. "Katina", p. 38.

92. "The Ginger Cat" – RDMSC RD 5/14/1–3.

93. Edward Weeks, Letter to Roald Dahl, 12/20/43 – RDMSC RD 1/1/1/82/1.

94. Edward Weeks, Letter to Roald Dahl dated "Lincoln's birthday," 02/12/43 – RDMSC RD 1/1/1/18.

95. Graham Payn and Sheridan Morley, eds., *The Noël Coward Diaries* (London: Weidenfeld & Nicolson, 1982), Jan. 29, 1946, p. 50.

96. Dahl, Letter to his mother, 11/27/43 – RDMSC RD 14/5/2/38.

97. Roald Dahl, Letter to Mr King, 11/24/43 – RDMSC RD 1/1/1/61.

98. Roald Dahl, Letter to Harold Matson, 10/01/42 – RDMSC RD 1/2/1/45.

99. Dahl, Letter to his mother, 10/12/43 – RDMSC RD 14/5/2/34.

100. Sheila Lewis Crosby (née St Lawrence), Conversation with the author, 07/21/08.

101. Dahl, Letter to his mother, 10/12/43 – RDMSC RD 14/5/2/34.

102. Winston Churchill, *The Second World War*, vol. 4: *The Hinge of Fate* (1950), p. 742.

103. See Ian Colvin, *Flight 777* (London: Evans Bros., 1957), and Ronald Howard, *In Search of My Father* (London: William Kimber & Co., 1981).

104. Cited in José Rey-Ximena, *El Vuelo del Ibis* (Madrid: Ediciones Facta, 2008).

105. David McCullough, *Truman* (New York: Simon & Schuster, 1992), p. 294.

106. Dahl, Letter to his mother, 06/27/43 – RDMSC RD 14/5/2/16.

CHAPTER TEN: *Secrets and Lies*

1. Roald Dahl, *My Year* (London: Jonathan Cape, 1993), pp. 38–39.

2. Marion Goodman, Conversation with the author, 03/11/07.

3. Lucy Dahl, Conversation with the author, 10/09/08.

4. Roald Dahl, Note in his address book – RDMSC AC 1/185.

5. Ernest Cuneo Papers, Box 107, CIA file – FDR Library, Hyde Park, cited in Thomas E. Mahl, *Desperate Deception – British Covert Operations in the US 1939–44* (Washington D.C.: Brassey's, 1998), pp. 15–16. Cuneo was a young Washington lawyer who had worked closely with the Democratic New York mayor, Fiorello La Guardia. He eventually married a Canadian employee of Stephenson's who worked at BSC – Jonathan Cuneo, Conversation with the author, 03/20/07.

6. Roald Dahl, Interview for *A Man Called Intrepid*, CBC Television, 1974.

7. Ivar Bryce, *You Only Live Once, Memories of Ian Fleming* (London: Weidenfeld & Nicolson, 1984), pp. 62–63.

8. Joel Raphaelson, ed., *The Unpublished David Ogilvy* (New York: Crown, 1986), p. 101.

9. Alfhild Hansen, Conversation with the author, 08/07/92.

10. Alfhild Hansen, Conversation with the author, 1997.

11. See Mahl, *Desperate Deception*, p. 202.

12. H. Montgomery Hyde Papers, Churchill College, Cambridge, 3-21, February 1942.

13. Roald Dahl, Interview for CBC documentary *A Man Called Intrepid*, 1974.

14. Reginald "Rex" Benson, *Diaries*, cited in Anthony Cave Brown, *"C": The Secret Life of Sir Stewart Graham Menzies, Spymaster to Winston Churchill* (New York: Macmillan, 1987), p. 480.

15. H. G. Nicholas, ed., *Washington Despatches 1941–45: Weekly Political Reports from the British Embassy* (Chicago: Chicago University Press, 1981), p. 381.

16. Eugene Pulliam quoted in Kopper, *Anonymous Giver: A Life of Charles Marsh*, p. 37.

17. Antoinette Haskell, Conversation with the author, 01/14/98.

18. Cited in Kopper, *Anonymous Giver*, p. 66.

19. This was how Roald Dahl described him to his prospective biographer, Stephen Roxburgh – FSG Archives.

20. George Brown, the construction magnate, cited in Kopper, *Anonymous Giver*, p. 64.

21. Roald Dahl, Letter to Anthony Cave Brown, 10/04/85 – RDMSC RD 16/1/2.

22. Roald Dahl, Letter to Charles Marsh, undated, probably early 1944 – CMP.

23. Antoinette Haskell, Conversation with the author, 01/14/98.

24. Ralph Ingersoll, *But in the Main It's True* (unpublished biography of Charles Marsh), 1975, Howard Gotlieb Archival Research Center, Boston University.

25. Antoinette Haskell, Conversation with the author, 01/14/98.

26. Roald Dahl, Letter to Anthony Cave Brown, 10/04/85 – RDMSC RD 16/1/2.

27. Antoinette Haskell, Conversation with the author, 01/14/98.

28. Lord Halifax (Dahl), Letter to "Stanley Marsh," 12/02/44 – CMP.

29. Charles Marsh, Letter to Roald Dahl, 07/27/45 – CMP.

30. Antoinette Haskell, Conversation with the author, 01/14/98.

31. Roald Dahl, Letter to Helen Ogden Reid, 06/29/43 – RDMSC RD 15/5/96.

32. Ingersoll, *But in the Main It's True*.

33. Ibid.

34. Dahl, Letter to his mother, 03/19/43 – RDMSC RD 14/5/2/8.

35. Cited in Jennet Conant, *The Irregulars: Roald Dahl and the British Spy Ring in Wartime Washington* (New York: Simon & Schuster, 2008), p. 20.

36. Kopper, *Anonymous Giver*, p. 70.

37. Antoinette Haskell, cited in Conant, *The Irregulars*, p. 23.

38. Kopper, *Anonymous Giver*, p. 74.

39. Ralph Ingersoll, *But in the Main It's True*, 1975 (unfinished), chap. 8, p. 2, Howard Gotlieb Archival Research Center, Boston University.

40. Kopper, *Anonymous Giver*, p. 98.

41. Dahl cited in ibid., p. 70.

42. Ibid., p. 80.

43. Roald Dahl, Letter to Anthony Cave Brown, 10/04/85 – RDMSC 1/16/2.

44. Diaries of Henry Agard Wallace, 10/03/44, University of Iowa, Special Collections, Iowa City, Iowa.

45. Roald Dahl, Letter to Anthony Cave Brown, 10/04/85 – RDMSC 16/1/2.

46. Henry A. Wallace, *Our Job in the Pacific* (New York: Institute of Pacific Relations, 1944), p. 24.

47. Roald Dahl, Letter to Anthony Cave Brown, 10/4/85 – RDMSC RD 16/1/2.

48. Hull apparently made the comment to the Dutch ambassador, Alexander Loudon. See Nicholas, ed., *Washington Despatches 1941–45*, p. 376.

49. Diaries of Henry Agard Wallace, 10/03/44, University of Iowa, Box 19, NB 32, p. 2.

50. Dahl, Letter to his mother, 07/17/43 – RDMSC RD 14/5/2/23.

51. Berlin quoted in Nicholas, ed., *Washington Despatches 1941–45*, p. 250.

52. Cave Brown, *"C"*, p. 484.

53. Roald Dahl, Letter to Anthony Cave Brown, 10/04/85 – RDMSC RD 16/1/2. The first reference to his new rank is found in a letter to his mother, 06/17/43 – RDMSC RD 14/5/2/19.

54. Dahl, Letter to his mother, 06/25/43 – RDMSC RD 14/5/2/20.

55. Roald Dahl, *Post War Air Lines* – RDMSC RD 15/5.

56. The Air Ministry believed the Arnold-Powers Agreement of June 1942 established that "as a long term policy [the RAF] were led to rely on America for transports while we concentrated on medium and heavy bombers". See Jeffrey Engel, *Cold War at 30,000 Feet* (Cambridge, MA: Harvard University Press, 2007), p. 30.

57. Even the Air Ministry in London was forced to conclude that it was out of the question for Great Britain to compete with the United States in civil aviation until at least 1950. For more detail on this complex issue, see ibid., pp. 31–45.

58. Mary Louise Patten, Letter to Joe Alsop, 07/30/43, cited in Conant, *The Irregulars*, pp. 171–72.

59. Dahl, Letter to his mother, 07/17/43 – RDMSC RD 14/5/2/23.

60. Mary Louise Patten, Letter to Alsop, 07/30/43, cited in Conant, *The Irregulars*, p. 172.

61. Dahl, Letter to his mother, 07/23/43 – RDMSC RD 14/5/2/24.

62. Mary Louise Patten, Letter to Alsop, 07/30/43, cited in Conant, *The Irregulars*, p. 172.

63. Dahl, Letter to his mother, 10/12/43 – RDMSC RD 14/5/2/34.

64. Roald Dahl, Letter to William Teeling, 05/31/43 – RDMSC RD 15/5/104/1–2.

65. Dahl, Letter to his mother, 06/25/43 – RDMSC RD 14/5/2/20.

66. Roald Dahl, *Visit to Hyde Park* – RDMSC RD 15/5/94/5.

67. Bill Macdonald, *The True Intrepid* (Raincoast Books, 2001), p. 244.

68. Dahl, *Visit to Hyde Park* – RDMSC RD 15/5/94/6.

69. Dahl, *Visit to Hyde Park* – RDMSC RD 15/5/94/3.

70. Dahl, *Visit to Hyde Park* – RDMSC RD 15/5/94/9.

71. Roald Dahl, Letter to Charles Marsh, undated, 08/43 – CMP.

72. Charles Marsh, Letter to Roald Dahl, 08/17/43 – CMP.

73. William Teeling, Letter to Roald Dahl, 08/10/43 – RDMSC RD 15/5/83/1.

74. Charles Marsh Papers at Lyndon B. Johnson Library, University of Texas, Austin, cited in Conant, *The Irregulars*, pp. 179–80.

75. Dahl's own comment, scribbled at the foot of a letter to him from J. B. Hogan, 07/14/43 – RDMSC RD 15/5/91.

76. J. B. Hogan, Letter to Roald Dahl, 07/14/43 – RDMSC RD 15/5/91.

77. Roald Dahl, Transcript of Canadian Broadcasting Corporation documentary on William Stephenson, cited in Conant, *The Irregulars*, p. 180.

78. Roald Dahl, Letter to Anthony Cave Brown, 10/04/85 – RDMSC RD 16/1/2.

79. Dahl, Letter to his mother, 10/19/43 – RDMSC RD 14/5/2/35.

80. J. B. Hogan, Letter to Roald Dahl, 12/07/42 – RDMSC RD 15/5.

81. J. B. Hogan, Letter to Roald Dahl, 12/43 – RDMSC RD 15/5/68.

82. Roald Dahl, Letter to J. B. Hogan, 01/29/44 – RDMSC RD 15/5/59.

83. *Desert Island Discs*, BBC Radio, 10/27/79.

84. Roald Dahl, Letter to Roger Burlingame, 04/28/45 – RDMSC RD 1/1/1/200.

85. Macdonald, *The True Intrepid*, p. 238.

86. W. Roxburgh, Letter to Albert L. Cox, 05/12/44 – RDMSC RD 15/5/40.

87. Roald Dahl, Letter to Anthony Cave Brown, 10/04/85 – RDMSC 16/1/2.

88. Roald Dahl, Draft of a speech, undated – RDMSC RD 6/1/1/5.

89. Roald Dahl, *Notes on Dinner with Max Beaverbrook, William Stephenson, Michael Henderson – Montego Bay*, c. 1947, from *Ideas Book* No. 1 – RDMSC RD 11/1, p. 30.

90. Peter Masefield, Office of Lord Privy Seal, Letter to Roald Dahl, 08/19/44 – RDMSC RD 15/5/45.

91. Conant, *The Irregulars*, p. 177.

92. Stevenson, *A Man Called Intrepid*, pp. 17, 169.

93. Dahl, Letter to his mother, 07/22/44 – RDMSC RD 14/5/3/14.

94. Stevenson, *A Man Called Intrepid*, p. 17.

95. Roald Dahl, Interview with Bill Macdonald, quoted in *The True Intrepid*, p. 239.

96. William Stephenson, *Point of Departure, A Foreword by Intrepid* in Stevenson, *A Man Called Intrepid*, p. xi.

97. Hugh Trevor-Roper, "*Superagent*", Review of Stevenson's *A Man Called Intrepid* in *The New York Review of Books*, May 13, 1976.

98. Dahl told Bill Macdonald that while he thought Stephenson's contributions to the war effort were outstanding, he also felt that "in his later life, the ex-spy chief was trying to get attention" – Macdonald, *The True Intrepid*, p. 238.

99. Ibid., p. 246.

100. Antoinette Haskell, Conversation with the author, 01/14/98.

101. Stevenson, *A Man Called Intrepid*, p. 170.

102. Macdonald, *The True Intrepid*, p. 241.

103. Dahl, Letter to his mother, 12/08/43 – RDMSC RD 14/5/2/39.

104. Nigel West, ed., *British Security Co-ordination* (London: St Ermin's Press, 1998), p. xi.

105. Roald Dahl to Davis Haines, cited in Kopper, *Anonymous Giver*, p. 79.

106. Roald Dahl, Letter to Anthony Cave Brown, 10/04/85 RDMSC RD 16/1/2.

107. Roald Dahl, Letter to Bill Macdonald, 08/03/90, cited in *The True Intrepid*, p. 250.

108. Diaries of Henry Agard Wallace, 06/16/43, University of Iowa, Special Collections, Iowa City, Iowa

109. Beatrice Gould, Letter to Roald Dahl, 01/06/44 – RDMSC RD 1/1/1/87.

110. Antoinette Haskell, Conversation with the author, 01/14/98.

111. Creekmore Fath cited in Treglown, p. 59.

112. Dahl, Letter to his mother, 01/13/44 – RDMSC RD 14/5/3/1.

113. Dahl, Letter to his mother, 11/03/44 – RDMSC RD 14/5/3/6.

114. Ibid.

115. Dahl, Letter to his mother, 03/29/44 – RDMSC RD 14/5/3/8.

116. Diaries of Henry Agard Wallace, 1935–46, University of Iowa, Special Collections, Iowa City, Iowa.

117. Ibid.

118. Dahl, Letter to his mother, 02/21/43 – RDMSC RD 14/5/2/5.

119. Diaries of Henry Agard Wallace, 1935–46, University of Iowa, Special Collections, Iowa City, Iowa.

120. Roald Dahl, Letter to Charles Marsh, undated, probably early 1948 – CMP. Amongst the support Mrs Reid offered Dahl was $36,000 of free advertising space in her newspapers for *The Gremlins* and an introduction to one of his heroes, Paul Robeson, whose records Dahl had collected since childhood.

121. Dahl, Letter to his mother, 07/09/42 – RDMSC RD 14/5/1/8.

122. Dahl, Letter to his mother, 02/21/43 – RDMSC RD 14/5/2/5.

123. Treglown, p. 60.

124. Dahl, Letter to his mother, 03/31/43 – RDMSC RD 14/5/2/10.

125. Cited in Treglown, p. 59.

126. Dahl, Letter to his mother, 04/18/44 – RDMSC RD 14/5/3/10.

127. Dahl, Letter to his mother, 08/25/44 – RDMSC RD 14/5/3/19.

128. Antoinette Haskell, Conversation with the author, 01/14/98; also Letter from Charles Marsh to Roald Dahl, 12/22/46 – RDMSC RD 16/1/1. From evidence gathered by Cherie Burns for her forthcoming biography of Millicent Rogers (St Martin's Press, 2011), it seems that the heiress may have suffered from scoliosis or curvature of the spine.

129. Dahl, Letter to his mother, 08/05/44 – RDMSC RD 14/5/3/16.

130. Roald Dahl, *Love*, in *Ladies Home Journal* (May 1949).

131. Treglown, p. 77.

132. Dahl, Letter to his mother, 03/11/44 – RDMSC RD 14/5/3/6.

133. Treglown, p. 79.

134. Felicity Dahl, Conversation with the author, 10/22/08.

135. Treglown, p. 79.

136. Roald Dahl, *What I would do if I were him and had to give a speech* – RDMSC RD 15/5/92/1–2.

137. Dahl cited in Culver and Hyde, *American Dreamer, the Life and Times of Henry Wallace*, p. 343.

138. As early as February 1944, William Stephenson had reported to London that the president was going to "jettison" Wallace – H. Montgomery Hyde, *The Quiet Canadian* (London: Hamish Hamilton, 1962), p. 192.

139. Cited in Culver and Hyde, *American Dreamer*, p. 373. Wallace eventually got the Commerce Department portfolio previously held by Jesse Jones; he was fired in 1946. In 1948, Wallace unsuccessfully stood for the presidency as an Independent Progressive.

140. Diaries of Henry Agard Wallace, 1935–46, University of Iowa, Special Collections, Iowa City, Iowa.

141. Conant, *The Irregulars*, p. 267.

142. Dahl, Letter to his mother, 08/09/44 – RDMSC RD 14/5/3/17.

143. Dahl, Letter to his mother, 08/18/44 – RDMSC RD 14/5/3/18.

144. Roald Dahl, Letter to George van Riper, 09/04/44 – RDMSC RD 15/5/33.

145. Dahl, Letter to his mother, 09/16/44 – RDMSC RD 14/5/3/21.

146. Dahl, Letter to his mother, 10/24/44 – RDMSC RD 14/5/3/26.

147. Roald Dahl, Letter to Ann Watkins, 10/23/44 – RDMSC RD 1/1/1/144.

148. Dahl, Letter to his mother, 11/10/44 – RDMSC RD 14/5/3/28.

149. Dahl, Letter to his mother, 11/18/44 – RDMSC RD 14/5/3/29.

150. Dahl, Letter to his mother, 01/08/45 – RDMSC RD 14/5/4/1.

151. Dahl, Letter to his mother, 03/45 – RDMSC RD 14/5/4/9.

152. Roald Dahl, Letter to Claudia Haines, undated – CMP.

153. Dahl, Letter to his mother, 03/26/45 – RDMSC RD 14/5/4/13.

154. Ibid.

155. Roald Dahl, Letter to Claudia Haines, undated – CMP.

156. Dahl, Letter to his mother, 04/18/45 – RDMSC RD 14/5/4/20.

157. Dahl, Letter to his mother, 05/21/45 – RDMSC RD 14/5/4/26.

158. Charles Marsh, *How Truman Came Through*, 07/28/44 – Papers of Henry Agard Wallace, University of Iowa, Special Collections, Iowa City, Iowa.

159. Cave Brown, "*C*", p. 486.

160. Hyde, *The Quiet Canadian*, pp. 227–28.

161. David Stafford, *Camp X* (Toronto: Lester and Orpen Dennys, 1986), pp. 253–54.

162. Dahl, Airgraph to his mother, 07/06/45 – RDMSC RD 14/5/4/35.

163. Evelyn Davis, Interview with Norm Killian, 03/07.

164. Dahl, Airgraph to his mother, 08/10/45 – RDMSC RD 14/5/4/40.

165. Dahl, Airgraph to his mother, 08/01/45 – RDMSC RD 14/5/4/37.

166. Roald Dahl, Letter to David Stafford cited in Stafford, *Camp X*, p. 253.

167. Macdonald, *The True Intrepid*, p. 243.

168. Liz Drake, Letter to Ophelia Dahl, 04/02/93.

169. West, ed., *British Security Co-ordination*, p. xi.

170. Alfhild Hansen, Interview with the author, 08/07/92.

171. Bill Stevenson, Letter to David Ogilvy, University of Regina 83-7, Box 9 801.4.

172. Macdonald, *The True Intrepid*, p. 238.

173. William Stephenson, Letter to Roald Dahl, 06/20/45 – RDMSC RD 15/5/2.

174. Dahl, Letter to his mother, 09/08/45 – RDMSC RD 14/5/4/44.

175. Dahl, Letter to his mother, 09/15/45 – RDMSC RD 14/5/4/45.

176. Dahl, "Someone Like You", in *Collected Stories*, p. 76.

177. Diaries of Henry Agard Wallace, 17/10/45 – University of Iowa, Special Collections, Iowa City, Iowa.

178. Macdonald, *The True Intrepid*, p. 246.

CHAPTER ELEVEN: *The Scholar-Gypsy*

1. John Lehmann, *The Ample Proposition* (London: Eyre & Spottiswood, 1966), pp. 30, 70.

2. Artemis Cooper, *Writing at the Kitchen Table* (New York: Ecco Press, 1999), pp. 131–32.

3. Christopher Isherwood, *London Magazine* (August 1956), pp. 45–47. See also David Kynaston, *Austerity Britain* (London: Bloomsbury, 2007).

4. Roald Dahl, Letter to Charles Marsh, 02/20/46 – CMP.

5. Dahl, Letter to his mother, 01/10/41 – RDMSC RD 14/4/43.

6. Wintle and Fisher, *The Pied Pipers*, p. 104.

7. Roald Dahl, Letter to Ann Watkins, 02/20/46 – WLC Box 22.

8. Roald Dahl, Letter to Ann Watkins, 04/02/46 – WLC Box 22.

9. Roald Dahl, Letter to Ann Watkins, 04/10/46 – WLC Box 22.

10. Roald Dahl, Letter to Ann Watkins, 03/30/46 – WLC Box 22.

11. Roald Dahl, Letter to Charles Marsh, 02/20/46 – CMP.

12. Roald Dahl, Letter to Ann Watkins, 04/10/46 – WLC Box 22.

13. Charles Marsh, Letter to Roald Dahl, undated (probably January 1946) – CMP.

14. *New York Times Book Review*, Feb. 10, 1946.

15. *The New Yorker*, Feb. 2, 1946.

16. Orville Prescott, *New York Times Book Review* – undated cutting in Charles Marsh Papers.

17. Roald Dahl, Speech for Sunday Express Book Award, 11/29/89 – RDMSC RD 6/1/2/35.

18. Roald Dahl, Letter to Ann Watkins, 09/14/45 – WLC Box 22.

19. Roald Dahl, Letter to Charles Marsh, 04/02/46 – CMP.

20. "Someone Like You" in *Collected Stories*, pp. 76–77.

21. Ann Watkins, Letter to Roald Dahl, 02/45 – RDMSC RD 1/1/1/174. Dahl replied antagonistically that if his stories seemed to be "melodramatic and bloody" that was because "life itself happens to be that way" – 02/07/45 – RDMSC RD 1/1/1/175.

22. Roald Dahl, *Some Time Never* (New York: Scribner's, 1948), pp. 8, 57–58.

23. Roald Dahl, Letter to Ann Watkins, 02/20/46 – WLC Box 22.

24. *Some Time Never*, p. 145.

25. "My God I wish I had gone to Hiroshima to do what Hersey did," Roald wrote to Ann Watkins, 11/17/46 – WLC Box 22.

26. Roald Dahl, Letter to Ann Watkins, 04/10/46 – WLC Box 22.

27. Roald Dahl, *World Leaders*, unpublished (c. 1945) – RDMSC RD 5/15.

28. Dahl, Letter to his mother, 10/31 – RDMSC RD 13/1/7/9.

29. It was the Lord Chancellor, John Sankey, who the young Dahl erroneously dismissed as "something to do with the exchequer" – Letter to his mother, 05/30 – RDMSC RD 13/1/5/39.

30. *Post War Air Lines* – RDMSC RD 15/5.

31. Lesley O'Malley, Conversation with the author, 1992.

32. Roald Dahl, Letter to Charles Marsh, 11/09/47 – CMP.

33. Roald Dahl, Letter to Claudia Haines, 04/20/46 – CMP.

34. Roald Dahl, Letter to Charles Marsh, 07/19/46 – CMP.

35. Roald Dahl, Letter to Charles Marsh, 09/05/46 – CMP.

36. Charles Marsh, Letter to Roald Dahl, 09/10/46 – RDMSC RD 16/1/1.

37. Roald Dahl, Letter to Claudia Haines, undated – CMP.

38. Roald Dahl, Letter to Charles Marsh and Claudia Haines, 09/26/46 – CMP.

39. Roald Dahl, Letter to Charles Marsh and Claudia Haines, 04/17/47 – CMP.

40. Roald Dahl, Letters to Charles Marsh, 07/22/47 – CMP.

41. Roald Dahl, "Nineteen Fifty What?", unpublished story – RDMSC RD 5/7.

42. Roald Dahl, Letter to Charles Marsh, 11/09/47 – CMP.

43. Roald Dahl, Letter to Charles Marsh, 09/28/46 – CMP.

44. *Some Time Never*, pp. 8, 44–45.

45. Ibid.

46. Ibid., p. 46.

47. Ibid., pp. 29, 129.

48. Roald Dahl, Letter to Roger Burlingame, 04/28/45 – RDMSC RD 1/1/1/200.

49. *Some Time Never*, pp. 129, 29.

50. Ibid., p. 125.

51. Ibid., pp. 112, 160, 167.

52. Ibid., pp. 103–4.

53. Ibid., pp. v, 221.

54. Ibid., 243–44, 204.

55. Ophelia Dahl, Conversation with the author, 03/17/08.

56. Roald Dahl, Letters to Ann Watkins, 03/30/46, 05/16/46 – WLC Box 22.

57. Roald Dahl, Letter to Nancy in Ann Watkins's office, 06/25/46 – WLC Box 22.

58. Roald Dahl, Letter to Ann Watkins, 10/01/46 – WLC Box 22.

59. *Some Time Never*, p. 79.

60. Asta Anderson, Conversation with the author, 01/03/98.

61. *Some Time Never*, p. 79.

62. Roald Dahl, Letter to Charles Marsh, undated – probably 11/47 – CMP.

63. Roald Dahl, Letter to Ann Watkins, 12/03/46 – WLC Box 22.

64. Alfhild Hansen, Conversation with the author, 08/92.

65. Roald Dahl, *Fifty Thousand Frogskins*, pp. 87, 111, 121 – RDMSC RD 3/2/2.

66. Roald Dahl, Letters to Claudia Haines, undated, presumably December 1946 – CMP.

67. Roald Dahl, Letter to Ann Watkins, 12/23/46 – WLC Box 22.

68. Roald Dahl, Letter to Ann Watkins, 12/26/46 – WLC Box 22.

69. Roald Dahl, Letter to Charles Marsh, 09/05/46 – CMP.

70. Roald Dahl, Preface to "The Mildenhall Treasure" in *The Wonderful Story of Henry Sugar and Other Stories*.

71. Roald Dahl, Letter to Ann Watkins, 11/27/46 – RDMSC RD 1/1/2/18/1–2.

72. Ann Watkins, Letter to Roald Dahl, 12/04/46 – RDMSC RD 1/1/2/19.

73. Roald Dahl, Letter to Ann Watkins, 12/45 – WLC Box 22.

74. Maxwell Perkins, Letter to Roald Dahl, 01/20/47 – RDMSC RD1/1/2/27.

75. Ann Watkins, Letter to Roald Dahl, 06/02/47 – RDMSC RD 1/1/2/52.

76. John Hall Wheelock, Letter to Roald Dahl, 06/09/47 – RDMSC RD1/1/2/53.

77. John Hall Wheelock, Letter to Roald Dahl, 06/24/47 – RDMSC RD1/1/2/55.

78. John Hall Wheelock, Letter to Roald Dahl, 07/21/47 – RDMSC RD1/1/2/65.

79. John Hall Wheelock, Letter to Roald Dahl, 11/06/47 – RDMSC RD1/1/2/94.

80. Jamie (Hamish) Hamilton, Letter to Roald Dahl, 08/26/47 – RDMSC RD 1/1/2/73.

81. Roald Dahl, Letter to Ann Watkins, 03/30/46 – WLC Box 22.

82. Roald Dahl, Letter to Ann Watkins, 01/25/48 – WLC Box 22.

83. Roald Dahl, Letter to Ann Watkins, 11/04/46 – WLC Box 22.

84. Anna Corrie, Conversation with the author, 10/08/07.

85. Roald Dahl, Letter to Ann Watkins, 03/30/46 – WLC Box 22.

86. Roald Dahl, Letter to Miss Hazard (*Saturday Review*), 9/11/45 – RDMSC RD 1/1/1/252.

87. Tessa Dahl, Conversation with the author, 01/17/09.

88. *Saturday Evening Post*, Sept. 13, 1947 – WLC Box 22.

89. Sir David Weatherall, Conversation with the author, 10/07/09.

90. Roald Dahl, Letter to Ann Watkins, 04/12/48 – WLC Box 22.

91. Roald Dahl, Letter to Ann Watkins, 05/01/48 – WLC Box 22.

92. *New York Times Book Review*, June 24, 1948; *Saturday Review*, April 3, 1948.

93. Peter Wyld, Letter to Roald Dahl, 05/26/48 – RDMSC RD 1/1/2/123. In the type-
    script that survives in the Roald Dahl Museum and Story Centre, there is no trace of
    these "acrid comments".

94. Roald Dahl, Letter to Sheila St Lawrence, 06/24/60 – WLC Box 24.

95. Ophelia Dahl, Conversation with the author, 03/17/08.

96. Roald Dahl, Letter to Mrs J. Goldstein, 10/11/71 – RDMSC RD 1/1/7/180.

97. Roald Dahl, Letter to Ann Watkins, 01/02/45 – RDMSC RD 1/1/1/159.

98. Roald Dahl, Letter to Ann Watkins, 04/18/48 – WLC Box 22.

99. Roald Dahl, Letter to Ann Watkins, 10/04/49 – WLC Box 22.

100. Roald Dahl, "The Amazing Eyes of Kuda Bux", 07/48, *Argosy* (July 1952) – RDMSC
     RD 4/24/1.

101. Roald Dahl, Unpublished article on Burgess and Maclean, 07/51 – RDMSC RD 5/6.

102. Ibid.

103. Roald Dahl, "Foreign Intelligence", unpublished story, 1947 – RDMSC RD 5/5.

104. Roald Dahl, Letter to Ann Watkins, 05/01/48 – WLC Box 22.

105. Peter Watt, Letter to Roald Dahl, 02/13/48 – RDMSC RD 1/1/2/109.

106. Ann Watkins, Letter to Roald Dahl, 01/30/48 – RDMSC RD 1/1/2/107.

107. Roald Dahl, Letter to Ann Watkins, 01/15/48 – WLC Box 22.

108. Alfhild Hansen, Conversation with the author, 08/92.

109. Louise (Lou) Pearl, Conversation with the author, 05/09/08.

110. Anna Corrie, Conversation with the author, 10/08/07.

111. Louise Pearl, Conversation with the author, 05/09/08.

112. Lucy Dahl, Conversation with the author, 10/09/08.

113. Roald Dahl, "The Soldier", in *Collected Stories*, pp. 200, 192, 199.

114. Ann Watkins, Letter to Roald Dahl, 03/02/48 – RDMSC RD 1/1/2/112.

115. Dahl, Letter to his mother, 02/26/48 – RDMSC RD 14/5/5/2.

116. Lemina Lawson Johnson, Letter to the author, 11/30/09.

117. Dahl, Letter to his mother, 02/10/48 – RDMSC RD 14/5/5/1.

118. Roald Dahl, Letter to Ann Watkins, 07/26/48 – WLC Box 22.

119. Roald Dahl, Letter to Ann Watkins, 05/25/48 – WLC Box 22.

120. The story, called "Meet My Sister", was eventually published as "Girl Without a Name"
     by *Today's Woman* in November 1951 and by *Woman's Journal* in December 1951 –
     RDMSC RD 4/21.

121. Roald Dahl, Letter to Ann Watkins, 06/08/48 – WLC Box 22.

122. Roald Dahl, Letter to Ann Watkins, 01/15/48 – WLC Box 22.

123. Roald Dahl, Letter to Ann Watkins, 07/21/48 – WLC Box 22.

124. Roald Dahl, Letter to Ann Watkins, 11/16/48 – WLC Box 22.

125. Roald Dahl, Letter to Ann Watkins, 07/15/46 – WLC Box 22.

126. Alfhild Hansen, Conversation with the author, 08/07/92.

127. Alexandra Anderson, Conversation with the author, 10/14/07.

CHAPTER TWELVE: *The Poacher*

1. Roald Dahl, Speech to Boys at Repton, Nov. 21, 1975 – RDMSC RD 6/1/1/25.
2. Charles Marsh, Letter to Roald Dahl, 02/18/46 – RDMSC RD 16/1/1.
3. Roald Dahl, Letter to Charles Marsh, 04/06/48 – CMP.
4. Roald Dahl, Letter to Ann Watkins, 05/01/48 – WLC Box 22.
5. Roald Dahl, Letter to Ann Watkins, 04/28/50 – WLC Box 22.
6. Roald Dahl, Letter to Charles Marsh and Claudia Haines, 10/29/49 – CMP.
7. Roald Dahl, Letter to Ann Watkins, 04/28/50 – WLC Box 22.
8. Roald Dahl, Letter to Charles Marsh and Claudia Haines, 01/25/49 – CMP.
9. Roald Dahl, Letter to Charles Marsh, 04/06/48 – CMP.
10. Roald Dahl, Letter to Charles Marsh, 09/20/48 – CMP.
11. Nicholas Logsdail, Conversation with the author, 04/24/08.
12. Ibid.
13. Tessa Dahl, Conversation with the author, 01/17/09.
14. Roald Dahl, "Introduction" to *Ah Sweet Mystery of Life* (London: Michael Joseph, 1989), p. vii.
15. Sue Elder (née Taylor), Conversation with the author, 02/12/09.
16. Dahl, "Introduction" to *Ah Sweet Mystery of Life*, p. viii.
17. Sue Elder and Jenny Taylor, Conversations with the author, 02/12/09 and 10/27/09.
18. Jenny Taylor, Conversation with the author, 10/27/09.
19. Dahl, "Introduction" to *Ah Sweet Mystery of Life*, p. viii.
20. Jenny Taylor, Conversation with the author, 10/27/09. Brazil later became the model for Victor Hazel in *Danny the Champion of the World*.
21. Roald Dahl, Letter to Ann Watkins, 10/08/49 – WLC Box 22.
22. Nicholas Logsdail, Conversation with the author, 04/24/08.
23. Dahl, *Fifty Thousand Frogskins*, pp. 157, 123, 28 – RDMSC RD 3/2/2.
24. Ibid., pp. 35, 31, 5.
25. Ann Watkins, Letter to Roald Dahl, 02/27/51 – WLC Box 22.
26. *Fifty Thousand Frogskins*, p. 62.
27. Dahl, Speech to Boys at Repton, Nov. 21, 1975 – RDMSC RD 6/1/1/25.
28. Dahl, "Introduction" to *Ah Sweet Mystery of Life*, pp. viii, ix.
29. See Kynaston, *Austerity Britain, 1945–51*, p. 201.
30. Roald Dahl, "The Ratcatcher", from "Claud's Dog" in *Collected Stories*, p. 314.
31. *Fifty Thousand Frogskins*, pp. 172, 52–53, 51 – RDMSC RD 3/2/2.
32. Ralph Ingersoll, *But in the Main It's True* (unpublished biography of Charles Marsh), 1975 – Howard Gotlieb Archival Research Center, Boston University.
33. Roald Dahl, *The Kumbak II* – RDMSC RD 5/4.
34. Roald Dahl, *Ideas Book* No. 1 – RDMSC RD 11/1.
35. Ibid.
36. Ibid.
37. Roald Dahl, Letter to Harold Ross, 04/14/49 – RDMSC RD 1/1/2/174.
38. Ann Watkins, Letter to Roald Dahl, 04/19/49 – RDMSC RD 1/1/2/175.
39. Roald Dahl, Letter to Ann Watkins, 04/14/49 – WLC Box 22.
40. Ann Watkins, Letter to Roald Dahl, 04/20/49 – RDMSC RD 1/1/2/176.

41. Peter Wyld, Letter to Roald Dahl, 04/20/49 – RDMSC RD 1/1/2/177/1.

42. Harry Maule, Letter to Ann Watkins, 08/09/49 – WLC Box 22.

43. Roald Dahl, Letter to Ann Watkins, 04/29/49 – WLC Box 22.

44. Dahl, "Introduction" to *Ah Sweet Mystery of Life*, p. vii.

45. Sofie Magdalene Dahl, Letter to Charles Marsh, 11/04/45 – CMP.

46. Alfhild Hansen, Conversation with the author, 08/07/92.

47. Roald Dahl, Letter to Ann Watkins, 08/01/49 – WLC Box 22.

48. Roald Dahl, Letter to Charles Marsh, undated, probably 1946 – CMP.

49. *Searching for Mr Smith* (1979) in Browse & Darby catalogue, 1983.

50. Alice Kadel, Conversation with the author, 08/14/09.

51. Cited in Malcolm Yorke, *Matthew Smith: His Life and Reputation* (London: Faber & Faber, 1997), p. 179.

52. Dahl, Letter to his mother, 09/23/44 – RDMSC RD 14/5/3/22.

53. Roald Dahl, Article for *Architectural Digest* (July 1980) – RDMSC RD 6/2.

54. Roald Dahl, Speech to the Association of Master Carvers, Nov. 2, 1982 – RDMSC RD 6/1/1.

55. Alfhild Hansen, Conversation with the author, 08/07/92.

56. Roald Dahl, Speech to the Association of Master Carvers, Nov. 2, 1982 – RDMSC RD 6/1/1.

57. Lesley O'Malley (née Pares), Conversation with the author, 1998.

58. Alice Kadel, Conversation with the author, 08/14/09.

59. Roald Dahl, Letter to Claudia Marsh, 06/09/57 – CMP.

60. Roald Dahl, Letter to Claudia Haines, 08/26/52 – CMP.

61. Roald Dahl, Letter to Charles Marsh and Claudia Haines, 05/22/50 – CMP

62. Alice Kadel, Conversation with the author, 08/14/09.

63. Roald Dahl, Letter to Matthew Smith, undated (c. June 1950), Guildhall Art Gallery (No. 966).

64. Ibid.

65. Matthew Smith, Letter to Roald Dahl, 06/28/50 – RDMSC RD 16/1/2.

66. Roald Dahl, "Nunc Dimittis" (originally entitled "Twenty Years Younger") in *Collected Stories*, p. 157.

67. Roald Dahl, "Skin" (originally "A Picture for Drioli") in ibid., pp. 177, 165.

68. Payn and Morley, eds., *The Noël Coward Diaries*, May 22, 1951, p. 69.

69. Macdonald, *The True Intrepid*, p. 247.

70. Roald Dahl, Letter to Ann Watkins, 06/04/46 – WLC Box 22.

71. Payn and Morley, eds., *The Noël Coward Diaries*, Sunday, Feb. 14, 1954, p. 231.

72. Charles Marsh, Letter to Roald Dahl, 07/27/45 – CMP.

73. Antoinette Haskell, Conversation with the author, 01/14/98.

74. Charles Marsh, Letter to Roald Dahl, 02/18/46 – RDMSC RD 16/1/1.

75. Charles Marsh, Letter to Roald Dahl, 06/27/43 – RDMSC RD 15/5/95/1.

76. Roald Dahl, Letters to Charles Marsh, undated – CMP.

77. Roald Dahl, Letter to Charles Marsh and Claudia Haines, 02/07/49 – CMP.

78. Roald Dahl, Letters to Charles Marsh, undated and 05/25/49 – CMP.

79. Roald Dahl, Letter to Charles Marsh, 07/30/47 – CMP.

80. Charles Marsh, Letters to Roald Dahl, 06/11/46 and 12/22/46 – RDMSC RD 16/1/1.

81. Roald Dahl, Letter to Charles Marsh and Claudia Haines, 09/26/46 – CMP.
82. Roald Dahl, Letter to Charles Marsh, 07/20/47 – CMP.
83. Roald Dahl, Letter to Charles Marsh, 05/20/46 – CMP.
84. Roald Dahl, Letters to Ann Watkins and Charles Marsh, 05/20/46 – WLC Box 22 and CMP.
85. Charles Marsh, Letter to Roald Dahl, 10/12/47 – RDMSC RD 16/1/1.
86. Roald Dahl, Letter to Charles Marsh, 07/26/46 – CMP.
87. Charles Marsh, Memo to Claudia Marsh, 08/19/50 – CMP.
88. The agreement was signed at the Grand Hotel in Oslo on Aug. 17, 1950, and witnessed by Claudia Haines.
89. Roald Dahl, Letter to Charles Marsh, 07/26/46 – CMP.
90. Anna Corrie, Conversation with the author, 10/08/07.
91. Lesley O'Malley (née Pares), Conversation with the author 1998.
92. *Memories with Food at Gipsy House*, p. 107.
93. Roald Dahl, Letter to Claudia Haines, 10/04/50 – CMP.
94. Ibid. Dahl here incorrectly refers to his niece as Astrid, rather than Astri.
95. Roald Dahl, Letter to Claudia Haines, 10/23/50 – CMP.
96. Roald Dahl, Letter to Claudia Haines, 11/18/50 – CMP.
97. Roald Dahl, Letter to Claudia Haines, 10/04/50 – CMP.
98. Roald Dahl, Letter to Claudia Haines, 11/18/50 – CMP.
99. Roald Dahl, Handwritten note, c. 1950 – RDMSC RD 1/1/2/244
100. *Fifty Thousand Frogskins*, pp. 8–10 – RDMSC RD 3/2/2
101. Ann Watkins, Letter to Roald Dahl, 02/27/51 – WLC Box 23.
102. Roald Dahl, Speech to Boys at Repton, Nov. 21, 1975 – RDMSC RD 6/1/1/25.
103. Roald Dahl, Letter to Ann Watkins, 06/04/46 – WLC Box 22.
104. Roald Dahl, Letter to Charles Marsh, 07/26/46 – CMP.
105. Roald Dahl, Speech to Boys at Repton, Nov. 21, 1975 – RDMSC RD 6/1/1/25.
106. Archie Gordon, Internal Memo to Miss Rowley, BBC Written Archives, Caversham – RCONTI (1948–54).
107. Roald Dahl, Letter to Archie Gordon, 09/05/51, BBC Written Archives, Caversham – RCONTI (1948–54).
108. Martha Gellhorn cited in Treglown, p. 84.
109. Roald Dahl, Letter to Ann Watkins, 08/01/49 – WLC Box 22.
110. Jean Macy (Ann Watkins Agency), Letter to Ned Brown at Columbia Artists, 12/27/49 – WLC Box 22.
111. Ann Watkins, Letter to Roald Dahl, 03/02/50 – WLC Box 22.
112. Ann Watkins, Letter to Roald Dahl, 03/14/50 – WLC Box 22.
113. Jean Parker Waterbury, Letter to Roald Dahl, 05/25/50 – WLC Box 22.
114. Roald Dahl, Letter to Ann Watkins, 12/26/50 – WLC Box 23.
115. Roald Dahl, Letter to Ann Watkins, 02/07/51 – WLC Box 23.
116. Roald Dahl, Letter to Ann Watkins, 02/14/51 – WLC Box 23.
117. Ann Watkins, Telegram to Roald Dahl, 02/26/51 – WLC Box 23.
118. Ann Watkins, Letter to Roald Dahl, 02/27/51 – WLC Box 23.
119. Roald Dahl, Postcard to Ann Watkins, 03/15/51 – WLC Box 23.

CHAPTER THIRTEEN: *The Master of the Macabre*

1. Sheila Lewis Crosby (née St Lawrence), Conversation with the author, 07/21/08.
2. Felicity Dahl, Conversation with the author, 01/29/09.
3. Roald Dahl, Letter to Claudia Haines, 09/10/51 – CMP.
4. Sofie Magdalene Dahl, Letter to Claudia Haines, 16/12/51 – CMP.
5. Dahl, Letter to his mother, 12/18/51 – RDMSC RD 14/5/16/7.
6. Dahl, Letter to his mother, 02/27/52 – RDMSC RD 14/5/7/6.
7. Sofie Magdalene Dahl, Letter to Claudia Haines, 03/27/52 – CMP.
8. Sofie Magdalene Dahl, Letter to Claudia Haines, 01/04/53 – CMP.
9. Claudia Haines, Letter to Sofie Magdalene Dahl, 01/17/53 – RDMSC RD 14/5/8/3.
10. Felicity Dahl, Conversation with the author, 11/03/09.
11. Neal, *As I Am*, p. 152.
12. Critic in *The New Yorker* writing about *The Hasty Heart*.
13. Patricia Neal, Conversation with the author, 03/21/07.
14. Neal, *As I Am*, p. 154.
15. Patricia Neal, Conversation with the author, 03/21/07.
16. Barry Farrell, *Pat and Roald* (London: Hutchinson, 1970), pp. 124–25.
17. Dahl, Letter to his mother, 12/30/52 – RDMSC RD 14/5/7/33.
18. Neal, *As I Am*, p. 155.
19. Farrell, *Pat and Roald*, pp. 124–25.
20. Neal, *As I Am*, p. 155.
21. Ibid.
22. Patricia Neal, Conversation with the author, 03/21/07.
23. Ingersoll, *But in the Main It's True*, Howard Gotlieb Archival Research Center, Boston University.
24. Roald Dahl, Letter to Claudia Haines, undated (?1952) – CMP.
25. Dahl, Letter to his mother, 12/19/52 – RDMSC RD 14/5/7/32.
26. Roald Dahl, Note to Claudia Haines, undated – CMP.
27. Else Logsdail, Letter to Charles Marsh and Claudia Haines, 01/15/53 – CMP.
28. Sofie Magdalene Dahl, Letter to Claudia Haines, 06/23/53 – CMP.
29. Neal, *As I Am*, p. 159.
30. Patricia Neal, Conversation with the author, 03/21/07.
31. Neal, *As I Am*, p. 157.
32. Louella Parsons, untitled article, 06/16/53, cited in Stephen Michael Shearer, *Patricia Neal: An Unquiet Life* (Louisville, KY: University Press of Kentucky, 2006), p. 153.
33. Patricia Neal, Letter to Jean Valentino and Chloe Carter, 03/03/53, cited ibid., p. 154.
34. Patricia Neal, Conversation with the author, 03/21/07.
35. Neal, *As I Am*, p. 158.
36. Roald Dahl, Letter to Sheila St Lawrence, 01/16/54 – WLC Box 23.
37. Neal, *As I Am*, p. 162.
38. Dahl, Letter to his mother, 05/16/53 – RDMSC 14/5/8/18.
39. Roald Dahl, Letter to Matthew Smith, 05/14/53 – Guildhall Art Library (No. 682).
40. Diane Johnson, *Dashiell Hammett: A Life* (New York: Random House, 1983), p. 211. Pat Neal also suggested to me that Hammett had been physically attracted to her and

that this may have influenced his negative reaction to Roald – Patricia Neal, Conversation with the author, 03/21/07.

41. Neal, *As I Am*, p. 166.
42. Dahl, Letter to his mother, 05/23/53 – RDMSC RD 14/5/8/19.
43. Claudia Haines, Letter to Sofie Magdalene Dahl, 06/20/53 – RDMSC RD 14/5/8/21.
44. Neal, *As I Am*, p. 167.
45. Roald Dahl, Letter to Eura Neal, 05/26/53, cited in Shearer, *Patricia Neal*, p. 156.
46. *The Buckinghamshire Advertiser*, July 10, 1953.
47. Patricia Neal, Conversation with the author, 03/21/07.
48. Roald Dahl, Letter to Ann Watkins and Sheila St Lawrence, 09/04/51 – WLC Box 23.
49. Gus Lobrano, Letter to Sheila St Lawrence, 06/20/52 – WLC Box 23. He was referring in this case to "Nunc Dimittis".
50. Bob Gottlieb, Conversation with the author, 06/24/08.
51. Alfred Knopf, "Introduction" to *Recent Publications by Borzoi Books* (Winter 1953).
52. Alfred Knopf, Memo to Harold Strauss, 03/21/52 – HRCH KNOPF 102.8.
53. Alfred Knopf, Letter to Ann Watkins, 06/17/52 – WLC Box 23.
54. Roald Dahl, Letter to Eura Neal, 05/26/53, cited in Shearer, *Patricia Neal*, p. 156.
55. Dahl, Letter to his mother, 02/52 – RDMSC RD 14/5/7/5.
56. Dahl, Letter to his mother, 03/21/52 – RDMSC RD 14/5/7/8.
57. Claudia Haines, Letter to Sofie Magdalene Dahl, 12/03/51 – CMP.
58. Roald Dahl, Letter to Charles Marsh, 01/25/49 – CMP.
59. John Selby, Letter to Roald Dahl, 05/28/52 – RDMSC RD 1/1/2/305.
60. Dahl, Letter to his mother, 05/18/52 – RDMSC RD 14/5/7/15.
61. Claudia Haines, Letter to Mrs Dahl, 10/03/52 – RDMSC RD 14/5/7/21.
62. Claudia Haines, Letter to Mrs Dahl, 04/25/52 – RDMSC RD 14/5/7/12/1.
63. Anna Corrie, Conversation with the author, 10/08/07.
64 Louise (Lou) Pearl, Conversation with the author, 05/09/08.
65. Theo Dahl, Conversation with the author, 09/17/07.
66. Felicity Dahl, Conversation with the author, 11/20/06.
67. Patricia Neal, Conversation with the author, 03/21/07.
68. Anna Corrie, Conversation with the author, 10/08/07.
69. Sofie Magdalene Dahl, Letter to Claudia Marsh, 08/09/53 – CMP.
70. Sofie Magdalene Dahl, Letter to Claudia Marsh, 09/13/53 – CMP.
71. Patricia Neal, Conversation with the author, 03/21/07.
72. Sofie Magdalene Dahl, Letter to Claudia Marsh, 10/01/53 – CMP.
73. Nicholas Logsdail, Conversation with the author, 04/24/08.
74. Neal, *As I Am*, p. 165.
75. Dahl, Letter to his mother, 09/17/53 – RDMSC 14/5/8/24.
76. Neal, *As I Am*, p. 180.
77. Dahl, Letter to his mother, 09/17/53 – RDMSC RD 14/5/8/24.
78. Dahl, Letter to his mother, 10/03/53 – RDMSC RD 14/5/8/26.
79. Patricia Neal, Letter to Sofie Magdalene Dahl, 09/21/53 – RDMSC RD 14/5/8/25.
80. Patricia Neal, Letter to Sofie Magdalene Dahl, 10/17/53 – RDMSC RD 14/5/8/29.
81. Dahl, Letter to his mother, 03/14/53 – RDMSC 14/5/8/11.
82. *Time* magazine (December 1953).

83. John Hutchens, Review of *Someone Like You* in *New York Herald Tribune*, Nov. 21, 1953.

84. Roald Dahl, Letter to Harold Strauss, 04/29/60 – HRCH KNOPF 280.1 (1960).

85. Patricia Neal, Letter to Sofie Magdalene Dahl, 03/29/54 – RDMSC RD 14/5/9/14a.

86. Neal, *As I Am*, p. 180.

87. Dahl, Letter to his mother, 01/11/54 – RDMSC RD 14/5/9/3.

88. Dahl, Letter to his mother, 05/03/54 – RDMSC RD 14/5/9/20.

89. Dahl, Letter to his mother, 01/11/54 – RDMSC RD 14/5/9/3.

90. Roald Dahl, Letter to Charles and Claudia Marsh, January 1954 – CMP.

91. Charles Marsh, Letter to Roald Dahl, 01/19/54 – CMP.

92. Roald Dahl, Letter to Charles Marsh, undated, January 1954 – CMP.

93. Neal, *As I Am*, p. 180.

94. Claudia Marsh, Letter to Sofie Magdalene Dahl, 03/22/65 – RDMSC RD 14/5/11/13.

95. Patricia Neal, Conversation with the author, 03/21/07.

96. Roald Dahl, Letter to Charles Marsh, undated, 1954 – CMP.

97. Gloria Vanderbilt, *It Seemed Important at the Time* (New York: Simon & Schuster, 2004), pp. 138, 142.

98. Patricia Neal, Letter to Sofie Magdalene Dahl, 03/29/54 – RDMSC RD 14/5/9/14a.

99. Marian Goodman, Conversation with the author, 03/11/07.

100. Dahl, Letter to his mother, 01/24/52 – RDMSC RD 14/5/7/3.

101. Roald Dahl, undated MS (probably mid-1950s) in *Ideas Books* No. 4 – RDMSC RD 11/4/14/1.

102. Farrell, *Pat and Roald*, p. 128.

103. Jane Pepper, Conversation with the author, 07/27/09.

104. Roald Dahl, Letter to Charles and Claudia Marsh, undated, 1954 – CMP.

105. Neal, *As I Am*, p. 184.

106. Dahl, undated MS (probably mid-1950s) in *Ideas Books* No. 4 – RDMSC RD 11/4/14/1.

107. Roald Dahl, Letter to Sheila St Lawrence, 09/08/53 – WLC Box 23.

108. Roald Dahl, Letter to Sheila St Lawrence, 06/24/54 – WLC Box 23.

109. Roald Dahl, Letter to Sheila St Lawrence, 09/08/53 – WLC Box 23.

110. David Hughes, Undated review in *Time and Tide* – WLC, Box 23.

111. Nicholas Logsdail, Conversation with the author, 04/24/08.

112. Susan Vivian (née Denson), Conversation with the author, 11/03/09.

113. Anna Corrie, Conversation with the author, 10/08/07.

114. Nicholas Logsdail, Conversation with the author, 04/24/08.

115. Roald Dahl, Letter to Sheila St Lawrence, 09/05/50 – WLC Box 23.

116. Roald Dahl, Letter to Sheila St Lawrence, 06/16/54 – WLC Box 23.

117. Roald Dahl, Letter to Sheila St Lawrence, 07/02/54 – WLC Box 23.

118. Roald Dahl, Letter to Sheila St Lawrence, 09/06/54 – WLC Box 23.

119. Roald Dahl, Letter to Sheila St Lawrence, 08/09/54 – WLC Box 23.

120. Dahl, Letter to his mother, 11/26/52 – RDMSC RD 14/5/7/29.

121. Cheryl Crawford, *One Naked Individual* (New York: Bobbs-Merrill, 1977), p. 254.

122. Cheryl Crawford, Letter to Roald Dahl, 05/20/55 – RDMSC RD 1/1/3/186.

123. Neal, *As I Am*, p. 186.
124. Roald Dahl, Letter to Cheryl Crawford, 05/16/55 – RDMSC RD 1/1/3/185.
125. Roald Dahl, Letter to Sheila St Lawrence, 07/02/54 – WLC Box 23.
126. Roald Dahl, Letter to Sheila St Lawrence, 10/02/56 – WLC Box 23. The male actor Dahl was referring to was probably Meredith Edwards.
127. Sheila St Lawrence, Letter to Roald Dahl, 09/27/56 – RDMSC RD 1/1/3/257.
128. Roald Dahl, Letter to Sheila St Lawrence, 10/08/56 – WLC Box 23.
129. Patricia Neal, Letters to Claudia Marsh, 04/27/55 and 05/06/55 – CMP.
130. Anna Corrie, Conversation with the author, 10/08/07.
131. Patricia Neal, Conversation with the author, 03/21/07.
132. Neal, *As I Am*, p. 190.
133. Ibid.
134. Roald Dahl, Letter to Sheila St Lawrence, 06/13/55 – WLC Box 23.
135. Roald Dahl, Letter to Claudia Marsh, 06/09/57 – CMP.
136. Roald Dahl, Letter to Sheila St Lawrence, 09/03/56 – WLC Box 23.
137. Roald Dahl, Letter to Charles and Claudia Marsh, 07/56 – CMP.
138. Roald Dahl, Letters to Charles and Claudia Marsh, 07/56 and 08/04/57 – CMP.
139. Roald Dahl, Letter to Charles and Claudia Marsh, 07/56 – CMP.
140. Patricia Neal, Letter to Claudia Marsh, 04/27/57 – CMP.
141. Ophelia Dahl, *An Awfully Big Adventure*, BBC, 01/12/98.
142. Roald Dahl, *Ideas Book* No. 4 – RDMSC RD 11/4.
143. Roger Angell, Letter to Sheila St Lawrence, 09/09/58 – WLC Box 24.
144. Alfred Knopf, Letter to Roald Dahl, 08/05/59 – HRCH KNOPF 253.1 (1959).
145. Roald Dahl, Letter to Alfred Knopf, 08/11/59 – HRCH KNOPF 253.1 (1959).
146. Armitage "Mike" Watkins, Letter to Murray Pollinger, 09/29/65 – RDMSC RD 1/2/2.
147. Alfred Knopf, Letter to Roald Dahl, 04/26/57 – HRCH KNOPF 253.1 (1959).
148. Roald Dahl, Letter to Sheila St Lawrence, 04/29/57 – WLC Box 24.
149. Roald Dahl, Letter to Sheila St Lawrence, 09/14/57 – WLC Box 24.
150. Sheila St Lawrence, Letter to Roald Dahl, 06/05/57 – RDMSC RD 1/1/3/282.
151. Neal, *As I Am*, p. 173.
152. Marian Goodman, Conversation with the author, 03/11/07.
153. Dahl, *Ideas Book* No. 3 – RDMSC RD 11/3/14–24.
154. Roald Dahl, Letter to Alfred Knopf, 05/02/60 – HRCH KNOPF 280.1 (1960).
155. Ophelia Dahl, *Memories of My Father*, unpublished MS.
156. Roald Dahl, Interview with Todd McCormack, *The Author's Eye* (1986).
157. Ibid.
158. Roald Dahl, Letter to Sheila St Lawrence, 05/05/59 – WLC Box 24.
159. *James and the Giant Peach*, p. 5.
160. Ibid., p. 40.
161. Armitage Watkins, Letter to Laurence Pollinger quoted in Laurence Pollinger, Letter to Roald Dahl, 08/16/60 – RDMSC RD 1/1/4/195.
162. Sheila Lewis Crosby, Conversation with the author, 07/21/08.
163. Sheila St Lawrence, Letter to Roald Dahl, 04/27/60 – WLC Box 24.

CHAPTER FOURTEEN: *A Tornado of Troubles*

1. Murray Pollinger, Conversation with the author, 10/30/08.
2. Charles Pick, *Finding New Authors*, pp. 59ff – FSG.
3. Roald Dahl, Letter to Sheila St Lawrence, 04/06/60 – WLC Box 24.
4. Ibid.
5. Roald Dahl, Letter to Sheila St Lawrence, 05/04/60 – WLC Box 24.
6. Roald Dahl, Letter to Sheila St Lawrence, 05/06/60 – WLC Box 24.
7. Helga Greene, Letter to Sheila St Lawrence, 05/16/60 – WLC Box 24.
8. Roald Dahl, Letter to Sheila St Lawrence, 05/13/60 – WLC Box 24.
9. Sue Vivian, Conversation with the author, 11/02/09.
10. Roald Dahl, Letter to Sheila St Lawrence, 06/17/60 – WLC Box 24.
11. Alan Higgin, Conversation with the author, 08/04/09.
12. Astri Newman, Conversation with the author, 10/15/07.
13. Alan Higgin, Conversation with the author, 08/04/09.
14. Wally Saunders, Conversation with the author, 08/97.
15. Roald Dahl, Letter to Sheila St Lawrence, 05/20/60 – WLC Box 24.
16. Roald Dahl, Letter to Sheila St Lawrence, 05/22/60 – WLC Box 24.
17. Roald Dahl, Letter to Sheila St Lawrence, 06/24/60 – WLC Box 24.
18. Sheila St Lawrence, Letter to Roald Dahl, 07/02/60 – WLC Box 24.
19. Roald Dahl, Letter to Sheila St Lawrence, 07/11/60 – WLC Box 24.
20. Ibid.
21. Alan Higgin, Conversation with the author, 08/04/09.
22. Roald Dahl, Letter to Sheila St Lawrence, 07/12/60 – WLC Box 24.
23. Sheila St Lawrence, Letter to Roald Dahl, 07/31/60 – WLC Box 24.
24. Roald Dahl, Letter to Sheila St Lawrence, 08/17/60 – WLC Box 24.
25. Armitage Watkins, Letter to Laurence Pollinger quoted in Laurence Pollinger, Letter to Roald Dahl, 08/16/60 – RDMSC 1/1/4/195.
26. Roald Dahl, Letter to Bob Bernstein and Bob Gottlieb, 10/20/69 – RDMSC RD 1/4/2/75.
27. Roald Dahl, Letter to Anne McCormick, 02/10/81 – RDMSC RD 1/1/10/9.
28. Roald Dahl, Letter to Sheila St Lawrence, 09/06/60 – WLC Box 24.
29. Roald Dahl, Letter to Sheila St Lawrence, 08/17/60 – WLC Box 24.
30. Roald Dahl, Letter to Sheila St Lawrence, 08/20/60 – WLC Box 24.
31. Dahl, *Ideas Book* No. 4 – RDMSC RD 11/4/17/1.
32. Dahl, untitled MS (dated December 1960) in *Ideas Book* No. 4 – RDMSC RD 11/4/17/1.
33. Roald Dahl, "Pig", in *Collected Stories*, p. 634.
34. Dr Edmund Goodman, Conversation with the author, 01/12/98.
35. Roald Dahl, *A Note on Theo's Accident* – RDMSC RD 11/2.
36. Susan Vivian, Conversation with the author, 11/02/09.
37. Sonia Austrian, Conversation with the author, 01/15/98.
38. Dr Edmund Goodman, Conversation with the author, 01/12/98.
39. Roald Dahl, Untitled speech, c. 1971 – RDMSC RD 6/1/17.
40. Neal, *As I Am*, p. 220.

41. Dahl, Letter to his mother, 02/26/61 – RDMSC RD 14/5/10/8.
42. Dahl, Letter to his mother, 02/18/61 – RDMSC RD 14/5/10/10.
43. See Roald Dahl, Letter to America's Hobby Center, 04/26/50 – WLC Box 22.
44. Ophelia Dahl, *Memories of My Father*, unpublished MS.
45. Roald Dahl, Address to the Speech Rehabilitation Institute, April 29, 1971 – RDMSC RD 6/1/1/6.
46. Kenneth Till, Interview with Jeremy Treglown cited in Treglown, p. 143.
47. Roald Dahl, Letter to Sheila St Lawrence, 10/20/61 – WLC Box 25.
48. Roald Dahl, Letter to Armitage Watkins, 01/13/62 – WLC Box 25.
49. Dahl, Address to the Speech Rehabilitation Institute, 1985 – RDMSC RD 6/1/1/7.
50. Kenneth Till, "A Valve for the Treatment of Hydrocephalus", *The Lancet*, 1 (1964), p. 202.
51. *Going Solo* (FSG 1986), p. 110.
52. See Dahl, Address to the Speech Rehabilitation Institute, 1985 – RDMSC RD 6/1/1/7.
53. Dahl, Letter to his mother, 11/26/52 – RDMSC RD 14/5/7/29.
54. Dr Edmund Goodman, Conversation with the author, 01/12/98.
55. Roald Dahl, *George's Marvellous Medicine* (London: Jonathan Cape, 1981).
56. Sonia Austrian, Conversation with the author, 01/15/98.
57. Neal, *As I Am*, pp. 217, 219.
58. Roald Dahl, Letter to Sheila St Lawrence, 06/24/57.
59. Roald Dahl, Letter to Sheila St Lawrence, 03/13/59 – WLC Box 24.
60. Farrell, *Pat and Roald*, p. 65.
61. Nicholas Logsdail, Conversation with the author, 04/24/08.
62. Tessa Dahl, Conversation with the author, 01/17/09.
63. John Betjeman, Letter to Roald Dahl, 01/01/61 – RDMSC RD 16/1/2.
64. John Betjeman, Letter to Patricia Neal, 01/23/61 – RDMSC RD 16/1/2.
65. John Betjeman, Letter to Roald Dahl, 02/04/63 – RDMSC RD 16/1/2.
66. Sheila St Lawrence, Letter to Roald Dahl, 09/12/61 – WLC Box 25.
67. Alfred Knopf, Letter to Roald Dahl, 07/05/60 – HRCH KNOPF 280. 1(1960).
68. Roald Dahl, Letter to Armitage Watkins, 01/26/62 – WLC Box 25.
69. Roald Dahl, Letter to Virginie Fowler, 08/20–22/60 – WLC Box 24.
70. Aileen Pippett in *New York Times*, Nov. 12, 1961.
71. Roald Dahl, Letter to Armitage Watkins, 01/13/62 – WLC Box 25.
72. Armitage Watkins, Letter to Roald Dahl, 08/22/61 – WLC Box 25.
73. Sheila Lewis Crosby, Conversation with the author, 07/21/08.
74. Neal, *As I Am*, p. 241.
75. Paul Newman, Interview with Stephen Michael Shearer, 09/30/03, in Shearer, *Patricia Neal*, p. 222.
76. Patricia Neal, Interviewed by Lloyd Shearer for *Long Island Sunday Press* (1963).
77. Neal, *As I Am*, p. 229.
78. Patricia Neal, Letter to Sonia Austrian, 05/17/60, in possession of Ophelia Dahl.
79. Patricia Neal, Letter to Sonia Austrian, 07/26/61, in possession of Ophelia Dahl.
80. Barbara Paul, "An American in Buckinghamshire", *Housewife* (January 1963).
81. Tessa Dahl, *Working for Love* (New York: Delacorte Press, 1989), p. 23.
82. Roald Dahl, Letter to Sheila St Lawrence, 06/30/55 – WLC Box 23.

83. Roald Dahl, *Olivia* – RDMSC RD 7/2.

84. Sheila St Lawrence, Letter to Roald Dahl, 08/08/55 – RDMSC RD 1/1/3/209.

85. Roald Dahl, Letter to Sheila St Lawrence, 05/21/56 – WLC Box 23.

86. Anna Corrie, Conversation with the author, 10/08/07.

87. Nicholas Arnold, Conversation with the author, 01/16/08.

88. Alfhild Hansen, Conversation with the author, 08/07/92.

89. Neal, *As I Am*, p. 198.

90. Nicholas Arnold, Conversation with the author, 01/16/08.

91. Patricia Neal, Letter to Sheila St Lawrence, 08/14/57 – WLC Box 24.

92. Neal, *As I Am*, pp. 198–99.

93. Ibid., p. 230.

94. Patricia Neal, interviewed by Lloyd Shearer for *Long Island Sunday Press* (1963).

95. Neal, *As I Am*, p. 231.

96. Dahl, *Olivia* – RDMSC RD 7/2.

CHAPTER FIFTEEN: *Breaking Point*

1. Dahl, *Olivia* – RDMSC RD 7/2.

2. Roald Dahl, Letter to Armitage Watkins, 11/26/62 – WLC Box 25.

3. Neal, *As I Am*, p. 233.

4. Ibid.

5. Tessa Dahl, Conversation with the author, 10/22/07.

6. Alfhild Hansen, Letter to Eura Neal cited in Shearer, *Patricia Neal*, p. 228.

7. Tessa Dahl, *Working for Love*, pp. 36–37.

8. Patricia Neal, Conversation with the author, 01/15/98.

9. Sonia Austrian, Conversation with the author, 01/15/98.

10. Neal, *As I Am*, pp. 240, 238.

11 In a letter to Dahl dated 12/10/62 Davidson wrote that he hoped the visit in particular will be "all you wife wanted" – RDMSC RD 16/1/2.

12. Lord Fisher of Lambeth, Letter to Roald Dahl, 12/14/62 – RDMSC RD 16/1/2.

13. Roald Dahl, *A Christmas Message for Children – What I Told Lucy and Ophelia About God* – RDMSC RD 7/1/3/1.

14. Farrell, *Pat and Roald*, pp. 78, 135.

15. Alfhild Hansen, Conversation with the author, 08/07/92.

16. Roald Dahl, Interviewed by Stephen Merrick in *Argosy* (August 1986).

17. Roald Dahl, Interviewed in *A Dose of Dahl's Magic Medicine*, 09/28/86.

18. Dahl, Letter to his mother, 05/33 – RDMSC 13/1/8/38.

19. Neal, *As I Am*, p. 238.

20. Patricia Neal, Letter to Jean Valentino and Chloe Carter, 11/29/62, cited in Shearer, *Patricia Neal*, p. 229.

21. Tessa Dahl, *Working for Love*, p. 45.

22. Louella Parsons, untitled article, 02/19/63 – NYPL.

23. Tessa Dahl, *Working for Love*, pp. 35, 38–39.

24. Patricia Neal, Letter to Jean Valentino and Chloe Carter, 09/02/63, cited in Shearer, *Patricia Neal*, p. 234.

25. *A Streetlamp and the Stars: The Autobiography of Father Mario Borrelli* (New York: Coward-McCann, 1963).

26. International Help for Children, Report No. 3, 1964 – WLC Box 26.

27. Roald Dahl, Letter to Armitage Watkins, 10/24/63 – WLC Box 25.

28. *Boy*, p. 134.

29. Roald Dahl, *Charlie's Chocolate Boy, Draft II* – RDMSC RD 2/7/1/2.

30. Ibid.

31. Roald Dahl, Letter to Armitage Watkins, 08/14/61 – WLC Box 25.

32. Roald Dahl, Letter to Sheila St Lawrence, 08/14/61 – WLC Box 25.

33. Sheila St Lawrence, Letter to Roald Dahl, 09/16/61 – WLC Box 25.

34. Dahl, *Charlie's Chocolate Boy, Draft II* – RDMSC RD 2/7/1/2.

35. Sheila St Lawrence, Letter to Roald Dahl, 09/12/61 – WLC Box 25.

36. Roald Dahl, Letter to Sheila St Lawrence, 09/16/61 – WLC Box 25.

37. Roald Dahl, Letter to Alfred Knopf, 04/19/63 – HRCH KNOPF 375.6 (1963).

38. Roald Dahl, Letter to Armitage Watkins, 09/14/62 – WLC Box 25.

39. Roald Dahl, Letter to Armitage Watkins, 09/03/62 – WLC Box 25.

40. Roald Dahl, "Let's Build a Skyscraper But Let's Find a Good Book First", *New York Times Book Review*, Nov. 1, 1964 – WLC Box 26.

41. Virginie Fowler, Letter to Roald Dahl, 05/21/63 – HRCH KNOPF 375.6 (1963).

42. Bob Bernstein, Letter to Roald Dahl, 04/26/63 – HRCH KNOPF 375.6 (1963).

43. Alfred Knopf, Letter to Roald Dahl, 07/06/64 – HRCH KNOPF 403.5 (1964).

44. Blanche Knopf, Letter to Roald Dahl, 07/16/64 – HRCH KNOPF 403.5 (1964).

45. Roald Dahl, Letter to Peggy Caulfield, 02/24/78 – RDMSC RD 1/1/9/106.

46. *Charlie and the Chocolate Factory* (Viking Edition), p. 158.

47. Kopper, *Anonymous Giver*, p. 136.

48. Roald Dahl, Letter to Alfred Knopf, 02/04/63 – HRCH KNOPF 375.6 (1963).

49. Roald Dahl, Introduction to *Roald Dahl's Book of Ghost Stories* (New York: Farrar, Straus & Giroux, 1983), p. 15.

50. Roald Dahl, Letter to Alfred Knopf, 04/19/63 – HRCH KNOPF 375.6 (1963).

51. Introduction to *Roald Dahl's Book of Ghost Stories*, p. 15.

52. Roald Dahl, Letter to Alfred Knopf, 02/04/63 – HRCH KNOPF 375.6 (1963).

53. Roald Dahl, *The Magic Finger* (London: Puffin Books, 1995 ed.), p. 8.

54. Alfred Knopf, Memo to Virginie Fowler, 05/04/65 – HRCH KNOPF 454.8.

55. Patricia Neal, Letter to Armitage Watkins, 06/03/63 25 – WLC Box 26.

56. International Help for Children, Report No. 1, March 1964 – WLC Box 26.

57. Susan and John Vivian, Conversation with the author, 11/03/09.

58. Roald Dahl, Letter to Armitage Watkins, 08/20/63 – WLC Box 25.

59. Neal, *As I Am*, p. 244.

60. Ibid., p. 248.

61. Roald Dahl, Letter to Armitage Watkins, 07/13/64 – WLC Box 26.

62. Dahl, Letter to his mother, 03/18/61 – RDMSC RD 14/5/10/15.

63. Roald Dahl, Letter to Sheila St Lawrence, 09/14/57 – WLC Box 24.

64. Armitage Watkins, Letter to Roald Dahl, 01/24/64 – WLC Box 26.

65. Roald Dahl, Letter to Marion McNamara, 01/20/64 – WLC Box 26.

66. Roald Dahl, Letter to Armitage Watkins, 02/16/64 – WLC Box 26.

67. Roald Dahl, Letter to Armitage Watkins, 03/31/64 – WLC Box 26.

68. Roald Dahl, Letter to Peggy Caulfield, 04/27/64 – WLC Box 26.

69. Roald Dahl, Letter to Armitage Watkins, 03/01/64 – WLC Box 26.

70. Miscellaneous Reviews – undated – WLC Box 27.

71. Roald Dahl, Letter to Dirk Bogarde, 01/09/81 – Dirk Bogarde Collection, Howard Gotlieb Archival Research Center, Boston University.

72. Arno Johanson, "Pat Neal: Her Luck Has Changed At Last", *Parade* magazine, Oct. 14, 1964.

73. Neal, *As I Am*, p. 253.

74. Patricia Neal's medical notes, compiled by Charles Carton, January 1965 – Copy in Possession of Ophelia Dahl.

75. Roald Dahl, "My Wife Patricia Neal", *Ladies' Home Journal* (September 1965).

76. Dahl, Letter to his mother, 02/27/65 – RDMSC RD 14/5/11/6.

77. Roald Dahl, Speech to the Speech Rehabilitation Institute, April 29, 1971, reworked in 1985 – RDMSC RD 6/1/1/7.

78. *Time* magazine, March 26, 1965.

79. Edmund Goodman, Conversation with the author, 01/12/98.

80. Neal, *As I Am*, p. 256.

81. I used a number of sources in assembling my account of the twenty-four hours that followed the stroke. These include Patricia Neal's own medical notes; firsthand descriptions given by Roald and Pat to Barry Farrell in *Pat and Roald*; Dahl's own article "My Wife Patricia Neal" for *Ladies' Home Journal* in September 1965; Patricia Neal's autobiography, *As I Am*; and Tessa Dahl's fictionalized autobiography, *Working for Love*. I have also consulted contemporary letters from Dahl himself, as well as those from Sheena Burt, Angela Kirwan, Margaret Ann Vande Noord and Eura Neal to members of the Dahl family in England during the crisis. Most of these are in the collection at the Roald Dahl Museum in Great Missenden. To flesh these out, I also used interviews with Patricia Neal, Else Logsdail, and Tessa Dahl, and consulted Jeremy Treglown's *Roald Dahl* and Stephen Michael Shearer's *Patricia Neal, an Unquiet Life*. Where there are differences and discrepancies in the versions of events – and there are many – I have generally relied upon the medical records and the earliest accounts of those actually present.

82. Patricia Neal, Speech given at An Evening with Patricia Neal, March 1967 – WLC Box 27.

83. Roald Dahl, *William and Mary*, in *Collected Stories*, pp. 477, 482.

84. Farrell, *Pat and Roald*, p. 137.

CHAPTER SIXTEEN: *Indomitable*

1. Neal, *As I Am*, p. 254.

2. Margaret Ann Vande Noord, Letter to Sofie Magdalene Dahl, 02/24/65 – RDMSC RD 14/5/11/5.

3. Tessa Dahl, *Working for Love*, pp. 61, 76.

4. Dahl, Letter to his mother, 03/16/65 – RDMSC RD 14/5/11/12.

5. Art Berman, "Patricia Neal Partly Paralyzed, Five Months Pregnant, Husband Says," *Los Angeles Times*, March 19, 1965.

6. Dahl, Letter to his mother, 03/27/65 – RDMSC RD 14/5/11/15.

7. Jean Alexander, Interview with Stephen Michael Shearer, 09/16/2003, cited in Shearer, *Patricia Neal*, p. 260.

8. Roald Dahl, Introduction to Val Eaton Griffith, *A Stroke in the Family* (Harmondsworth, UK: Penguin, 1970), p. 50.

9. Neal, *As I Am*, pp. 259, 262.

10. Louella Parsons, "Hollywood Snapshots" (n.d.) PNC, cited in Shearer, *Patricia Neal*, p. 260.

11. Neal, *As I Am*, p. 265.

12. Claire Carton, Conversation with Stephen Michael Shearer, cited in Shearer, *Patricia Neal*, p. 260.

13. Else Logsdail, Letter to Eura Neal, 03/22/65, PNC, cited in ibid., p. 261.

14. Neal, *As I Am*, p. 263.

15. Marjorie Clipstone, Letter to Alfhild Hansen, 04/24/65 – RDMSC RD 14/5/11/20.

16. Neal, *As I Am*, p. 265.

17. Claudia Marsh, Letter to Alfhild Hansen, 03/04/65 – RDMSC RD 14/5/11/8.

18. Sheena Burt, Letter to Sofie Magdalene Dahl, 04/27/65 – RDMSC RD 14/5/11/22.

19. Patricia Neal's medical notes, compiled by Charles Carton, January 1965. Copy in the possession of Ophelia Dahl.

20. Dahl, Letter to his mother, 04/11/65 – RDMSC 14/5/11/18.

21. Dahl, Introduction to Eaton Griffith, *A Stroke in the Family*, p. 9.

22. Patricia Neal, Interview with Stephen Michael Shearer, June 2005, cited in Shearer, *Patricia Neal*, p. 261.

23. Dahl, Letter to his mother, 04/21/65 – RDMSC RD 14/5/11/19.

24. Dahl, Introduction to *Notes for Treating Recovering Stroke Patients* – RDMSC RD 12/5/6/49.

25. Neal, *As I Am*, p. 272.

26. Roald Dahl, ABC Radio interview with Terry Lane, 1989.

27. Pam Lowndes, Conversation with the author, 02/22/10.

28. Roald Dahl, introduction to *Notes for Treating Recovering Stroke Patients* – RDMSC RD 12/5/6/49.

29. Neal, *As I Am*, p. 254.

30. Tessa Dahl, *Working for Love*, p. 87.

31. Pam Lowndes, Conversation with the author, 02/22/10.

32. Valerie Easton Griffith, Interview with Stephen Michael Shearer, cited in Shearer, *Patricia Neal*, p. 272.

33. Dahl, Introduction to *Notes for Treating Recovering Stroke Patients* – RDMSC RD 12/5/6/49.

34. Patricia Neal, Speech given at An Evening with Patricia Neal, March 1967 – WLC Box 27.

35. Roald Dahl, Speech to the Speech Rehabilitation Institute, April 29, 1971 – RDMSC RD 6/1/1/6.

36. Tessa Dahl, *Working for Love*, p. 112.

37. Patricia Neal, Conversation with the author, 03/21/07.

38. Neal, *As I Am*, p. 279.

39. Neal, *As I Am*, pp. 289, 275, 310.

40. Tessa Dahl, Conversation with the author, 10/22/07.

41. Neal, *As I Am*, p. 271.

42. Bob Thomas, "Pat Neal Hopes to Work," *Los Angeles Mirror-Times*, Jan. 31, 1966, cited in Shearer, *Patricia Neal*, p. 273.

43. Gereon Zimmermann, "Does Everyone Love Pat Neal? Oh Yes!" *Look* magazine, Feb. 18, 1969, p. 84.

44. Farrell, *Pat and Roald*, p. 111.

45. Neal, *As I Am*, p. 290.

46. Ibid., 294.

47. Patricia Neal, Interview with Cindy Adams, *Long Island Press*, April 3, 1968 – WLC Box 27.

48. Judith Crist, *New York* magazine, cited in Shearer, *Patricia Neal*, p. 289; *Time* magazine, Oct. 18, 1968.

49. Susan Vivian, Conversation with the author, 11/02/09.

50. Dahl, "My Wife: Patricia Neal," *Ladies' Home Journal* (September 1965) – RDMSC RD 6/3/8.

51. Roald Dahl, Letter to Eura Neal, 11/01/65, cited in Shearer, *Patricia Neal*, p. 268.

52. Farrell, *Pat and Roald*, pp. 126, 139.

53. Marian Goodman, Conversation with the author, 03/11/07.

54. Roald Dahl, Letter to Armitage Watkins, 06/22/65 – WLC Box 26.

55. Neal, *As I Am*, p. 285.

56. Dahl and Farrell shared the rights to the book 50:50. See Armitage Watkins, Letter to Murray Pollinger, 10/13/66 – WLC Box 27.

57. Patricia Neal, Letter to Barry Farrell, 02/10/69 – WLC Box 28.

58. Barry Farrell, Letter to Roald Dahl and Patricia Neal, 05/20/69 – WLC Box 28.

59. Roald Dahl, Letter to Armitage Watkins, 05/27/69 – WLC Box 28.

60. Roald Dahl, Letter to Dirk Bogarde, 01/09/81 – Dirk Bogarde Collection, Howard Gotlieb Archival Research Center, Boston University.

61. Farrell, *Pat and Roald*, p. 211.

62. Marian Goodman, Conversation with the author, 03/11/07.

63. Roald Dahl, Interview by Michael Parkinson, BBC Television, 1982.

64. Maria Tucci, Conversation with the author, 06/24/08.

65. Neal, *As I Am*, p. 267.

66. Val Eaton Griffith cited in Treglown, pp. 208–09.

67. Untitled newspaper article – PNC, cited in Shearer, *Patricia Neal*, p. 284.

68. Tessa Dahl, *Working for Love*, p. 110.

69. Neal, *As I Am*, p. 289.

70. Roald Dahl, ABC Radio interview with Terry Lane, 1989.

71. Roald Dahl, Letter to Armitage Watkins, 01/23/65 – WLC Box 26.

72. Armitage Watkins, Letter to Roald Dahl, 10/28/64 – RDMSC RD 1/1/5/220.

73. Roald Dahl, ABC Radio interview with Terry Lane, 1989.

74. Roald Dahl, Letter to Armitage Watkins, 04/09/65 – WLC Box 26.

75. Roald Dahl, Letter to Alfred Knopf, 07/26/65 – HRCH KNOPF 657.3.

76. Lucy Dahl, Conversation with the author, 10/09/08.

77. Roald Dahl, Letter to Peggy Caulfield, 10/18/65 – WLC Box 26.

78. Roald Dahl, Letter to Armitage Watkins, 08/23/66 – WLC Box 27.

79. Missy Schwartz, Interview with Robert Altman, *Entertainment Weekly*, June 12, 1966.

80. Pearson, *The Life of Ian Fleming*, p. 240.

81. Roald Dahl, Speech given at Chesham High School, Jan. 13, 1978 – RDMSC RD 6/1/15.

82. Pearson, *The Life of Ian Fleming*, p. 231.

83. Roald Dahl, ABC Radio interview with Terry Lane, 1989, and Letter to Armitage Watkins, 03/21/66 – WLC Box 27.

84. Roald Dahl, Draft of article for *Playboy* magazine, June 1967 – RDMSC RD 6/2/1/5.

85. See Harold Bloom, Letter to Henry Saltzman, 03/08/67 – RDMSC RD 1/5/5.

86. Roald Dahl, Letter to Armitage Watkins, 04/13/66 – WLC Box 27.

87. Treglown, p. 178.

88. Farrell, *Pat and Roald*, p. 152.

89. Roald Dahl, ABC Radio interview with Terry Lane, 1989.

90. The basic figure was $125,000 (see his Letter to Armitage Watkins, 03/21/66 – WLC Box 27). However, with rewrites and additional fees the sum came to $165,500. Dahl put his entire fee into a trust fund in Nassau for Theo and paid Armitage Watkins 1 percent from his own account. The total figure was calculated from the fact that Dahl paid Watkins $1,655 – RDMSC RD 1/5/5.

91. Alan Higgin, Conversation with the author, 08/04/09.

92. Albert "Cubby" Broccoli, Letter to Roald Dahl, 07/29/66 – RDMSC RD 1/5/5, and Roald Dahl, Letter to Armitage Watkins, 07/07/66 – WLC Box 27.

93. Roald Dahl, Letter to Alfred Knopf, 16/12/66 – HRCH KNOPF 524.12.

94. Roald Dahl, Letter to Armitage Watkins, 07/07/66 – WLC Box 27.

95. Roald Dahl, Letter to B. Indick, 07/13/77 – RDMSC RD 1/1/9/67.

96. Ken Hughes quoted in Treglown, pp. 183–84.

97. Roald Dahl, Letter to Irving Lazar, 12/20/68 – RDMSC 1/5/5.

98. Roald Dahl, *Bedtime Stories*, 1970 – RDMSC RD 12/1/2.

99. Roald Dahl, Letter to William Dozier, 04/02/68 – RDMSC 1/5/5.

100. Roald Dahl, Letter to William Dozier, 03/28/68 – RDMSC 1/5/5.

101. Joy Cowley, Letter to Roald Dahl and Patricia Neal, 08/29/70 – RDMSC RD 1/5/9.

102. Irving Lazar, Telegram to Roald Dahl, 03/19/69 – RDMSC RD 1/5/9.

103. Roald Dahl, Letter to Irving Lazar, 07/20/69 – RDMSC RD 1/5/9.

104. Ken Russell, Letter to Roald Dahl, undated – RDMSC RD 1/5/9.

105. Roald Dahl, Letter to Allen Hodshire, 08/20/69 – RDMSC RD 1/5/9.

106. Roald Dahl, Letter to Joe Schoenfeld (at William Morris), 12/19/69 – RDMSC RD 1/5/5.

107. Allen Hodshire, Letter to YoungStreet Productions, 09/14/70 – RDMSC RD 1/5/9.

108. Roald Dahl, Letter to Irving Lazar, 10/12/70 – RDMSC RD 1/5/9.

109. Roald Dahl, Letter to Allen Hodshire, 05/27/71 – RDMSC RD 1/5/9.

110. Shearer, *Patricia Neal*, p. 293.

111. Rex Reed, "Pat Neal's Portrait of Courage," *New York Sunday Times*, Nov. 8, 1970.

112. Roald Dahl, Letter to Allen Hodshire, 05/27/71 – RDMSC RD 1/5/9.

113. Roald Dahl, Interviewed by Stephen Merrick in *Argosy* (August 1966).

114. Roald Dahl, Letter to Claude Gallimard, 10/29/71 – RDMSC RD 1/2/3/146.
115. Neisha Crosland, Conversation with the author, 03/20/09.
116. Patricia Neal, Letter to Sofie Magdalene Dahl, 02/09/65 – RDMSC RD 14/5/11/2.
117. Farrell, *Pat and Roald*, p. 138.
118. Roger Angell, Letter to Armitage Watkins, 04/19/65 – WLC Box 26.
119. Roald Dahl, Letter to Armitage Watkins, 04/27/65 – WLC Box 26.
120. Roald Dahl, Letter to A. C. Spectorsky, 04/17/65 – WLC Box 26.
121. On March 31, 1968, Knopf's six-month royalty statement showed that Dahl had earned $681,658 for *Charlie*, $252,714 for *James*, $17,290 for *Kiss Kiss*, and $15,074 for *Someone Like You* – HRCH KNOPF 1334.5.
122. Michael Joseph, Hamish Hamilton, Hart-Davis, Chatto & Windus, Golden Pleasure Books, Hutchinson, The Bodley Head, Faber & Faber, Weidenfeld & Nicolson, Collins and Cassell had all rejected them – Armitage Watkins, Letter to Roald Dahl, 04/22/65 – WLC Box 26.
123. Roald Dahl, Letter to Armitage Watkins, 12/02/64 – WLC Box 26.
124. Roald Dahl, Letter to Blanche Knopf, 11/27/64 – HRCH KNOPF 1334.5.
125. Roald Dahl, Letter to Armitage Watkins, 12/5/64 – WLC Box 26.
126. Armitage Watkins, Letter to Roald Dahl, 07/22/65 – WLC Box 26.
127. Rayner Unwin, Conversation with the author, 01/04/98.
128. Murray Pollinger, Conversation with the author, 10/30/08.
129. Murray Pollinger, Letter to Armitage Watkins, 11/25/65 – WLC Box 26, and Rayner Unwin, Conversation with the author, 01/04/98.
130. Roald Dahl, *Mr Fox, Third Draft*, 1968 – RDMSC RD 2/9/3.
131. Roald Dahl, *Mr Fox, First Draft*, 1968 – RDMSC RD 2/9/1.
132. Walter Retan (Random House), Letter to Bob Bernstein, 07/16/68 – HRCH KNOPF 1334.5.
133. Roald Dahl, *Boggis, Bunce and Bean* (early draft of *Fantastic Mr Fox*) – RDMSC RD 2/9/6/46.
134. Bob Bernstein, Letter to Roald Dahl, 07/17/68 – RDMSC RD 1/1/6/205/2.
135. Roald Dahl, Telegram to Bob Bernstein, 07/18/68 – HRCH KNOPF 1334.5.
136. Roald Dahl, Letter to Bob Bernstein, 07/21/68 – RDMSC RD 1/1/6/206.
137. Fabio Coen, Letter to Roald Dahl, 11/20/68 – RDMSC 1/4/2/1/1–2.
138. Roald Dahl, Letter to Fabio Coen, 11/25/68 – RDMSC RD 1/4/2/2.
139. Fabio Coen, Letter to Roald Dahl, 05/13/70 – RDMSC RD 1/2/3/15.
140. Roald Dahl, *The Last Act* in *Collected Stories*, p. 697.
141. Patricia Neal, *An Awfully Big Adventure*, Music Link International, 1998.
142. Amanda Conquy, Conversation with the author, 02/22/10.

CHAPTER SEVENTEEN: *The Gentle Warmth of Love*

1. Farrell, *Pat and Roald*, p. 102.
2. Nicholas Logsdail, Conversation with the author, 04/24/08.
3. Lemina Lawson Johnson, Letter to the author, 11/30/09.
4. Roald Dahl, Letter to Charles Marsh and Claudia Haines, 05/22/50 – CMP.
5. Nicholas Logsdail, Conversation with the author, 04/24/08.

6. Susan Vivian, Conversation with the author, 02/11/09.
7. Tim Fisher, Conversation with the author, 09/17/07.
8. Roald Dahl, Letter to Alfred Knopf, 12/14/67 – HRCH KNOPF 482.1.
9. Patricia Neal, Conversation with Stephen Michael Shearer, June 2005; also Neal, *As I Am*, p. 299.
10. Alexandra Anderson, Conversation with the author, 11/14/07.
11. Dahl, "Only This" in *Collected Stories*, p. 19.
12. Roald Dahl, *The Witches* (London: Jonathan Cape, 1983), pp. 14–15.
13. Farrell, *Pat and Roald*, pp. 204–6, 215.
14. Roald Dahl, Letter to Alfred Knopf, 12/14/67 – HRCH KNOPF 482.1.
15. Tessa Dahl, Conversation with the author, 10/22/07.
16. Roald Dahl, Letter to Bob Bernstein, 08/11/68 – HRCH KNOPF 1334.5.
17. Neal, *As I Am*, p. 309.
18. Felicity Dahl, Conversation with the author, 11/20/06.
19. Felicity Dahl, Conversation with the author, 02/05/10.
20. Neal, *As I Am*, pp. 320, 318.
21. Patricia Neal, Conversation with the author, 03/21/07.
22. Annabella Power, cited in Treglown, p. 208.
23. Liccy Dahl, Conversation with the author, 02/05/10.
24. Ophelia Dahl, Conversation with the author, 03/17/08.
25. Roald Dahl, Letter to Felicity Crosland, undated, Felicity Dahl Collection.
26. Charlotte Crosland, Conversation with the author, 03/12/10.
27. Neisha Crosland, Conversation with the author, 03/20/09.
28. Tessa Dahl, *Working for Love*, p. 127.
29. *The Gipsy House Cookbook*, p. 21.
30. Neal, *As I Am*, p. 320.
31. Ophelia Dahl, *Memories of My Father*, unpublished MS.
32. Tessa Dahl, *Working for Love*, p. 130.
33. Tessa Dahl, Conversation with the author, 10/22/07.
34. Treglown, p. 199.
35. Maria Tucci, Conversation with the author, 06/24/08.
36. Marian Goodman, Conversation with the author, 03/11/07.
37. Tessa Dahl, Conversation with the author, 10/22/07.
38. Tessa Dahl, *Working for Love*, p. 152.
39. Tessa Dahl, Conversation with the author, 10/22/07.
40. Patricia Neal, Conversation with the author, 03/21/07.
41. Neal, *As I Am*, pp. 325–26.
42. Neisha Crosland, Conversation with the author, 03/20/09.
43. Neal, *As I Am*, p. 327.
44. Tessa Dahl, Conversation with the author, 10/22/07.
45. Lucy Dahl, Conversation with the author, 10/09/08.
46. Roald Dahl, Letter to Felicity Crosland, 09/19/74 – Felicity Dahl Collection.
47. Tessa Dahl, Conversation with the author, 10/22/07.
48. Neal, *As I Am*, pp. 331–32.
49. Roald Dahl, "Love", *Ladies' Home Journal* (May 1949).

50. Louise (Lou) Pearl, Conversation with the author, 05/09/08.
51. Felicity Crosland, Letter to Patricia Neal (1975), cited in Neal, *As I Am*, p. 337.
52. Neal, *As I Am*, p. 336.
53. Ibid., p. 339.
54. Ophelia Dahl, *Memories of My Father*, unpublished MS.
55. Marian Goodman, Conversation with the author, 03/11/07.
56. Dennis Pearl cited in Treglown, p. 214.
57. Roald Dahl, Letter to Lucy Dahl, 10/16/80 – Collection of Lucy Dahl.
58. Marian Goodman, Conversation with the author, 03/11/07.
59. Lucy Dahl cited in Treglown, p. 198.
60. Ophelia Dahl, *Memories of My Father*, unpublished MS.
61. *Danny the Champion of the World*, p. 17.
62. Ibid., pp. 10, 38, 33.
63. Wintle and Fisher, *The Pied Pipers*, p. 110.
64. Roald Dahl, Letter to Charles and Claudia Marsh, 08/31/55 – CMP.
65. Roald Dahl, Introduction to *The Croaker* – RDMSC RD 8a/2.
66. Roald Dahl, Introduction to *I Heard You Calling Me* – RDMSC RD 8a/2.
67. Roald Dahl, Letter to Alfred Knopf, 09/19/74 – HRCH KNOPF 653.2.
68. Roald Dahl, Letter to Alfred Knopf, 11/18/63 – HRCH KNOPF 375.6.
69. Alfred Knopf, Letter to Roald Dahl, 11/26/63 – HRCH KNOPF 375.6.
70. Roald Dahl, Letter to Alfred Knopf, 12/16/66 – HRCH KNOPF 524.12.
71. Alfred Knopf, Letter to Roald Dahl, 12/21/66 – HRCH KNOPF 524.12.
72. Wintle and Fisher, *The Pied Pipers*, p. 110.
73. Roald Dahl, Letter to Alfred Knopf, 1/11/75 – HRCH KNOPF 653.2.
74. *The Wonderful Story of Henry Sugar and Six More*, pp. 192, 179.
75. Roald Dahl, Letter to Felicity Crosland, 05/14/76 – Felicity Dahl Private Collection.
76. Claudia Haines, Letter to Sofie Magdalene Hesselberg, 01/17/53 – RDMSC RD 14/5/8/3.
77. Maria Tucci, Conversation with the author, 06/24/08.
78. Douglas Highton, Conversation with the author, 11/08/07.
79. Tessa Dahl, Conversation with the author, 10/22/07.
80. Neisha Crosland, Conversation with the author, 03/20/09.
81. Shearer, *Patricia Neal*, p. 320.
82. Ophelia Dahl, Conversation with the author, 03/17/08.
83. Neal, *As I Am*, p. 346.
84. Roald Dahl, Letter to Ophelia Dahl, undated – Ophelia Dahl Private Collection.
85. *Desert Island Discs*, BBC Radio, 10/27/79.
86. Charlotte Crosland, Conversation with the author, 03/12/10.
87. Neisha Crosland, Conversation with the author, 03/20/09.
88. Charlotte Crosland, Conversation with the author, 03/12/10.
89. Sonia Austrian, Conversation with the author, 01/15/98.
90. Ophelia Dahl, *Memories of My Father*, unpublished MS.
91. Neal, *As I Am*, pp. 348, 350.
92. Roald Dahl, Interview with Susan Slavetin, *Boston Globe*, 1980.
93. Roald Dahl, Letter to Patricia Neal, undated – PNC.

94. Neal, *As I Am*, p. 352.
95. Roald Dahl, Letter to Dirk Bogarde, 10/07/81 – Howard Gotlieb Collection, University of Boston.
96. Ophelia Dahl, *Memories of My Father*, unpublished MS.
97. Neal, *As I Am*, p. 358.
98. Ibid.
99. Patricia Neal, Conversation with the author, 03/21/07.
100. Joe Leyden, *Houston Post*, March 1982 – PNC, cited in Shearer, *Patricia Neal*, p. 332.
101. Patricia Neal, Conversation with the author, 03/21/07.
102. Neal, *As I Am*, p. 366.

CHAPTER EIGHTEEN: *Explosions Are Exciting*

1. Neal, *As I Am*, p. 308.
2. Roald Dahl, Autobiographical Statement (1972) – RDMSC RD 6/2/1/9.
3. Roald Dahl, Letters to *The Times*, 08/20/77, 09/20/80, 06/20/80 (RD 1/2/6/151), and 08/02/85.
4. Theo Dahl, Conversation with the author, 09/17/07.
5. Sheila Lewis Crosby, Conversation with the author, 07/21/08.
6. Lesley O'Malley (née Pares), Conversation with the author, 1992.
7. Pam Lowndes, Conversation with the author, 02/22/10.
8. Sir Leonard Figg, Conversation with the author, 02/22/10.
9. Marian Goodman, Conversation with the author, 03/11/07.
10. Ophelia Dahl, Conversation with the author, 1998.
11. Lucy Dahl, Conversation with the author, 10/09/08.
12. Ophelia Dahl, Conversation with the author, 1998.
13. Amanda Conquy, Conversation with the author, 01/05/98.
14. Patricia Neal, Letter to Sonia Austrian, 01/24/64 – Ophelia Dahl Collection.
15. Rayner Unwin, Conversation with the author, 01/04/98.
16. Robert Bernstein, Conversation with the author, 06/25/08.
17. Roald Dahl, Letter to Bob Bernstein, 05/08/68 – HRCH KNOPF 1334.5.
18. Robert Bernstein, Conversation with the author, 06/25/08.
19. Robert Gottlieb, Conversation with the author, 06/24/08.
20. Roald Dahl, Letter to Yvonne MacManus of Leisure Books, 05/14/71 – RDMSC RD 1/1/7/138.
21. Roald Dahl, Letter to Bob Gottlieb, 03/16/71 – RDMSC RD 1/1/7/106.
22. Robert Gottlieb, Conversation with the author, 06/24/08.
23. Maria Tucci, Conversation with the author, 06/24/08.
24. Roald Dahl, Letter to Armitage Watkins, 04/14/69 – WLC Box 28.
25. Murray Pollinger, Conversation with the author, 10/30/08.
26. Bob Bernstein, Letter to Roald Dahl, 06/03/69 – WLC Box 28.
27. Roald Dahl, Letter to Armitage Watkins, 03/08/69 – WLC Box 28.
28. Roald Dahl, Letter to Armitage Watkins, 06/07/69 – WLC Box 28.
29. Armitage Watkins, note of phone conversation with Bob Bernstein, 06/10/69 – WLC Box 28.

30. Roald Dahl, Letter to Armitage Watkins, 06/18/69 – WLC Box 28.

31. Roald Dahl, Letter to Bob Bernstein, 07/07/69 – WLC Box 28.

32. Roald Dahl, Letter to Armitage Watkins, 09/03/69 – WLC Box 28.

33. Roald Dahl, Letter to Armitage Watkins, 10/20/69 – WLC Box 28.

34. Bob Gottlieb, Letter to Armitage Watkins, 10/22/69 – WLC Box 28.

35. Roald Dahl, Letter to Alfred Knopf, 05/13/81 – HRCH KNOPF 553.1 (1981).

36. Roald Dahl, Letter to Sheila St Lawrence, 07/05/56 – WLC Box 23.

37. Ethel L. Heins, review of *James and the Giant Peach* in *Library Journal*, Nov. 15, 1961.

38. Roald Dahl, Letter to Sue Mason, 02/05/62 – HRCH KNOPF 1334.7.

39. Roald Dahl, Letter to Armitage Watkins, 01/12/68 – WLC Box 27.

40. *Charlie and the Chocolate Factory*, p. 73.

41. John Morsell, Letter to Lillian Hellman, 12/03/69 – RDMSC RD 1/5/8/27/1.

42. Roald Dahl, Letter to Bob Bernstein, 10/01/69 – RDMSC RD 1/5/8/16/1.

43. Roald Dahl, Letter to Alfred Knopf, 07/25/70 – HRCH KNOPF 530.2.

44. Roald Dahl, Note to Armitage Watkins, undated – WLC Box 28, also Letter to Rayner Unwin, 04/05/72 – RDMSC RD 1/4/3/32.

45. Roald Dahl, Letter to Stan Margulies, 05/04/71 – RDMSC RD 1/5/8.

46. *Desert Island Discs*, BBC Radio, 10/27/79.

47. Roald Dahl, Letter to Irving Lazar, 12/01/70 – RDMSC RD 1/5/8/101. A rich variety of adjectives critical of Mr Stuart can be found in this letter and in another letter to Lazar, written in September 1970 – RDMSC RD 1/5/8/58.

48. Roald Dahl, Draft letter to David Wolper – RDMSC RD 1/5/8/54.

49. Roald Dahl, Letter to James Stuart (Quaker Oats), 06/28/71 – RDMSC RD 1/5/8.

50. Roald Dahl, Letter to Stan Margulies, 05/04/71 – RDMSC RD 1/5/8.

51. Roald Dahl, Letter to Irving Lazar, 01/70 – RDMSC RD 1/5/8.

52. Roald Dahl, Draft telegram to David Wolper – RDMSC RD 1/5/8/58.

53. Roald Dahl, Letter to James Stuart, 06/28/71 – RDMSC RD 1/5/8.

54. Murray Pollinger, Conversation with the author, 10/30/08.

55. Rayner Unwin, Conversation with the author, 01/04/98.

56. Roald Dahl, Letter to Fabio Coen, 12/3/69 – RDMSC RD 1/4/2/92.

57. Roald Dahl, Letter to Bob Gottlieb, 03/23/72 – RDMSC RD 1/4/3.

58. Librarians of Madison Public Library, Letter to Roald Dahl, 04/20/72. RDMSC RD 1/3/9/167/1–2.

59. Roald Dahl, Letter to Librarians of Madison Public Library, 04/25/72 – RDMSC RD 1/3/6/9/167/3.

60. *Charlie and the Chocolate Factory*, p. 85.

61. Ibid., p. 146.

62. Cameron, "McLuhan, Youth and Literature," *The Horn Book Magazine*. "The author of a work of imagination is trying to affect us wholly, as human beings, whether he knows it or not; and we are affected by it, as human beings, whether we intend to be or not" – T. S. Eliot, *Essays Ancient and Modern* (New York: Harcourt, 1936), p. 102.

63. Roald Dahl, "*Charlie and the Chocolate Factory*: A Reply," *The Horn Book Magazine* (February 1973).

64. Roald Dahl, Letter to Armitage Watkins, 05/22/66 – WLC Box 27.

65. Roald Dahl, Letter to Keith Olbermann cited in the *Greenburgh* [N.Y] *Independent*, April 7, 1966 – WLC Box 27.

66. Roald Dahl, Letter to Michael Untermeyer, 01/13/62 – WLC Box 25.

67. Ursula K. Le Guin, Letter to the Editor of *The Horn Book Magazine* (April 1973).

68. Roald Dahl, Letter to Richard Krinsley, 12/20/72.

69. Roald Dahl, Letter to Richard Story at *Travel and Leisure*, 01/23/79.

70. Roald Dahl, Interview with Parkinson, BBC Television, December 1978.

71. Roald Dahl, *My Uncle Oswald*, first draft – RDMSC RD 2/1/15/4.

72. Roald Dahl, Notes for *My Uncle Oswald* – RDMSC RD 2/15/2/9–14.

73. Bob Gottlieb, Letter to Roald Dahl, 12/78 – RDMSC RD 1/1/9/130.

74. Bob Gottlieb, Letter to Roald Dahl, 05/04/79 – RDMSC RD 1/5/16.

75. Roald Dahl, Letter to Bob Gottlieb, 05/18/79 – HRCH KNOPF 8237.

76. Roald Dahl, *My Uncle Oswald* (London: Michael Joseph, 1979), pp. 164, 184, 189.

77. Roald Dahl, ABC Radio interview with Terry Lane, 1989 – RDMSC RD 12/1/35.

78. Roald Dahl, Letter to Armitage Watkins, undated (1972 file) – WLC Box 28.

79. Roald Dahl, Letter to Marion McNamara (Ann Watkins Inc.), 01/07/69 – WLC Box 28.

80. Roald Dahl, Letter to Tom Maschler, 05/11/87 – FSG.

81. Roald Dahl, Letters to Roger Straus, 01/07/82, and Tom Maschler, 05/11/87 – FSG.

82. Roald Dahl, Letter to Bob Gottlieb, 01/29/80 – HRCH KNOPF 823.8.

83. Bob Gottlieb, Letter to Roald Dahl, 02/12/80 – HRCH KNOPF 823.8.

84. Bob Gottlieb, Letter to Roald Dahl, 10/08/79 – HRCH KNOPF 823.7.

85. Roald Dahl, Letter to Bob Gottlieb, 12/04/79 – HRCH KNOPF 823.8.

86. Bob Gottlieb, Letter to Roald Dahl, 04/05/80 – HRCH KNOPF 823.8.

87. Roald Dahl, Letter to Bob Gottlieb, 01/24/80 – HRCH KNOPF 823.8.

88. Bob Gottlieb, Letter to Roald Dahl, 02/28/80 – HRCH KNOPF 823.8.

89. Gerald Hollingsworth, Memo to Bob Gottlieb, 03/18/80 – HRCH KNOPF 823.8.

90. Roald Dahl, Letter to Bob Gottlieb, 06/08/80 – HRCH KNOPF 823.8.

91. Karen Latuchie, Letter to Roald Dahl, 06/14/80 – HRCH KNOPF 823.8.

92. Roald Dahl, Letter to Karen Latuchie, 07/01/80 – HRCH KNOPF 823.8.

93. Alfred Knopf, Letter to Roald Dahl, 06/10/80 – HRCH KNOPF 550.7.

94. Roald Dahl, Letter to Bob Gottlieb, 08/06/80 – HRCH KNOPF 823.8.

95. Bob Gottlieb, Letter to Roald Dahl, 09/09/80 – HRCH KNOPF 823.8.

96. Roald Dahl, Letter to Bob Gottlieb, 09/22/80 – RDMSC RD 1/4/11.

97. Bob Gottlieb, Letter to Roald Dahl, 02/03/81 – HRCH KNOPF 823.8.

98. Frances Foster, Letter to Roald Dahl, 02/04/81 – HRCH KNOPF 823.8.

99. Roald Dahl, Letter to Bob Gottlieb, 02/10/81 – HRCH KNOPF 823.8.

100. Roald Dahl, Letter to Anne McCormick (Legal Department), 02/10/81 – RDMSC RD 1/1/10/9.

101. Roald Dahl, Letter to Bob Gottlieb, 02/10/81 – HRCH KNOPF 823.8.

102. Bob Gottlieb, Letter to Roald Dahl, 03/05/81 – HRCH KNOPF.

103. Bob Gottlieb, Conversation with the author, 06/24/08.

104. Bob Gottlieb cited in Treglown, p. 233.

105. Roald Dahl, Letter to Alfred Knopf, 03/12/81 – HRCH KNOPF 553.1.

106. Bob Gottlieb, Conversation with the author, 06/24/08.

107. Roald Dahl, Letter to Janet Schulman, 10/15/86 – RDMSC RD 1/1/10/88.

108. Roald Dahl, Letter to Gerald Harrison (Random House), 05/21/87 – FSG.

109. Roald Dahl, Letter to Roger Straus, 01/07/82 – FSG.

110. Tony Clifton and Catherine Leroy, *God Cried* (London: Quartet Books, 1983).

111. Felicity Dahl, Conversation with the author, 11/20/06.

112. Roald Dahl, "Not a Chivalrous Affair," *The Literary Review* (August 1983).

113. Marian Goodman, Conversation with the author, 03/11/07.

114. Dahl, "Not a Chivalrous Affair".

115. Roald Dahl, Letter to Gillian Greenwood, 06/27/83 – RDMSC RD 1/2/7.

116. Roald Dahl, Letter to *The Times*, Sept. 15, 1983.

117. Dahl quoted in Mike Coren, "Tale of the Unexpected", *The New Statesman*, Aug. 26, 1983.

118. Todd MacCormack, *The Author's Eye*.

119. Roald Dahl, Letter to Dirk Bogarde, 01/09/81 – Howard Gottlieb Collection, University of Boston.

120. Neisha Crosland, Conversation with the author, 03/20/09.

121. Charlotte Crosland, Conversation with the author, 03/12/10.

122. Ophelia Dahl, *Memories of My Father*, unpublished MS.

123. Ophelia Dahl, 03/17/08.

124. Murray Pollinger, Conversation with the author, 01/22/98.

125. Roald Dahl, Letter to Whitworth Festival, 01/14/72 – RDMSC RD 1/2/3/173.

126. Roald Dahl, Letter to Mr R. A. Bowles, Programme Secretary, The Round Table of Uxbridge, 05/19/72 – RDMSC RD 1/2/3/197.

127. Jeremy Stubbs, Conversation with the author, 10/08/07.

128. Peter Lennon, Interview with Roald Dahl, in *The Times*, Dec. 22, 1983.

129. Roald Dahl, Letter to *The Times*, Feb. 27, 1989 – RDMSC RD 1/6/17.

130. Roald Dahl, ABC Radio interview with Terry Lane, 1989 – RDMSC RD 12/1/35.

131. Nicholas Logsdail, Conversation with the author, 04/24/08.

132. Ophelia Dahl, Conversation with the author, 03/17/08.

133. Roald Dahl, Interview with Peter Lennon in *The Times*, Dec. 22, 1983.

134. Roald Dahl, "Let's Build a Skyscraper", *New York Times Book Review*, Christmas 1964.

135. Roald Dahl, Letter to Armitage Watkins, 10/01/64 – WLC Box 26.

136. Felicity Dahl, Conversation with the author, 11/19/06.

137. Neisha Crosland, Conversation with the author, 03/20/08.

138. Astri Newman, Conversation with the author, 10/15/07.

139. Roald Dahl, Letter to Patricia Fitzmaurice-Kelly, 11/09/71 – Ophelia Dahl Collection.

140. Patricia Fitzmaurice-Kelly, Letter to Roald Dahl, 11/16/71 – Ophelia Dahl Collection.

141. Roald Dahl, Letter to Patricia Fitzmaurice-Kelly, 11/17/71 – Ophelia Dahl Collection.

142. Ophelia Dahl, Conversation with the author, 03/17/08.

143. Roald Dahl, Letter to Police Complaints Commission, 07/89 – RDMSC RD 1/6/9.

144. *The BFG*, p. 52.

CHAPTER NINETEEN: *The Wizard and the Wonderman*

1. Roald Dahl, "Books Remembered and Books of Today", later published in *WETA* magazine (March 1990) as "Roald Dahl Speaks Out" – RDMSC RD 6/2/136.

2. Roald Dahl, Letter to Stephen Roxburgh, 01/07/82 – RDMSC RD 1/4/14/8/1–2.

3. Roald Dahl interviewed for *Bedtime Stories*, Los Angeles, 1970.

4. Neisha Crosland, Conversation with the author, 03/20/09.

5. Roald Dahl, Letter to Douglas Highton, undated (c. 1984) – Property of Douglas Highton.

6. Tessa Dahl, Conversation with the author, 10/22/07.

7. Tom Maschler, Conversation with the author, 02/09/98.

8. Roald Dahl, *Ten Days with Roald Dahl*, 06/17/85 – RDMSC RD 6/7.

9. Lucy Dahl, Conversation with the author, 10/11/08.

10. Ophelia Dahl, *Memories of My Father*, unpublished MS.

11. Quentin Blake, Conversation with the author, 01/19/09.

12. Roald Dahl, interviewed for *Bedtime Stories*, Los Angeles, 1970.

13. Roald Dahl, Letter to Stephen Roxburgh, 12/29/81 – RDMSC RD 1/414/6.

14. Roald Dahl, Letter to Dirk Bogarde, 10/07/81 – Howard Gottlieb Collection, University of Boston.

15. Roald Dahl, *Ideas Book* – RDMSC RD 11/2.

16. *The BFG*, p. 56.

17. Roald Dahl, Letter to Stephen Roxburgh, 12/29/81 – RDMSC RD 1/4/14/6.

18. Stephen Roxburgh, Conversation with the author, 01/13/98.

19. Roald Dahl, Letter to Stephen Roxburgh, 03/01/82 – RDMSC RD 1/4/14/21.

20. Stephen Roxburgh, Letter to Roald Dahl, 03/05/82 – RDMSC RD 1/4/14/27.

21. Stephen Roxburgh, Conversation with the author, 03/13/09.

22. Ibid.

23. Gina Pollinger, Conversation with the author, 04/10/09.

24. Roald Dahl, *George's Marvellous Medicine* (1981), p. 8.

25. Quentin Blake, Conversation with the author, 01/06/98.

26. Roald Dahl, Letter to Tom Maschler, 02/17/82 – RDMSC RD 1/4/14/16.

27. Roald Dahl, Letter to Tom Maschler, 02/21/82 – RDMSC RD 1/4/14/17.

28. Quentin Blake, Conversation with the author, 01/06/98.

29. Roald Dahl, Letter to Stephen Roxburgh, 04/07/82 – RDMSC RD 1/4/14/34.

30. Quentin Blake, Conversations with the author, 01/06/98 and 01/19/09.

31. Roald Dahl, Letter to Stephen Roxburgh, 01/07/82 – RDMSC RD 1/4/14/8/1–2.

32. Lucy Dahl, Conversation with the author, 10/09/08.

33. Tom Maschler, Conversation with the author, 02/09/98.

34. Roald Dahl, Article on *The Giraffe and the Pelly and Me*, written for the Jonathan Cape in-house newsletter 06/25/85 and subsequently published in *The Roald Dahl Treasury* – RDMSC RD 6/2/1/21.

35. Stephen Roxburgh, Letter to Roald Dahl, 09/26/84 – FSG.

36. Roald Dahl, Letter to Roger Straus, 08/17/84 – FSG.

37. Roald Dahl, Letter to Dirk Bogarde, 10/22/81 – HGC.

38. Roald Dahl, Untitled autobiography for Knopf pamphlet – RDMSC RD 6/2/1/18.

39. *Memories with Food at Gipsy House*, p. 227.

40. Joanna Lumley, Conversation with the author, 01/18/09.

41. Roald Dahl, Interview with Todd McCormack, *The Author's Eye*.

42. Roald Dahl, Letter to Mr Kentzer, Headmaster of Redgate Middle School, 09/17/84 – RDMSC RD 1/2/8/52.

43. Roger Straus, Conversation with the author, 01/15/98.

44. Stephen Roxburgh, Conversations with the author, 03/13/09 and 01/13/98.

45. Murray Pollinger, Conversation with the author, 10/30/08.

46. Wendy Kress, Conversation with the author, 08/05/09.

47. Murray Pollinger, Conversation with the author, 10/30/08.

48. Roald Dahl, Letter to Armitage Watkins, 05/15/64 – WLC Box 26.

49. Roald Dahl, Letter to Armitage Watkins, 10/31/64 – WLC Box 26.

50. Murray Pollinger, Conversation with the author, 10/30/08.

51. Roald Dahl, Letter to Lawrence Pollinger, 02/14/69 – RDMSC RD 1/2/2/241.

52. Roald Dahl, Letter to Armitage Watkins, 02/14/69 – WLC Box 28.

53. Murray Pollinger, Letter to Roald Dahl, 03/04/69 – RDMSC RD 1/2/2/253.

54. Murray Pollinger, Conversation with the author, 04/10/09.

55. Murray Pollinger, Conversation with the author, 10/30/08.

56. Stephen Roxburgh, Conversation with the author, 03/13/09.

57. John Libson, Letter to Roald Dahl, 05/02/86 – GHPP.

58. Roald Dahl, Letter to John Radstone, 04/29/80 – GHPP.

59. Roald Dahl, Letter to Murray Pollinger, 05/23/86 – GHPP.

60. Martin Goodwin, Conversation with the author, 02/23/10.

61. Bill Geffen, Draft Report to the Inland Revenue, July 1986 – GHPP.

62. Roald Dahl, Letter to Bill Geffen, 09/26/86 – GHPP.

63. Roald Dahl, Letter to C. G. White of The Inland Revenue, 07/28/86 – GHPP.

64. Roald Dahl, Letter to Alan Langridge, 01/13/87 – GHPP.

65. Roald Dahl, Letter to Alan Langridge, 02/23/87 – GHPP.

66. Roald Dahl, Letter to Alan Langridge, 09/16/87 – GHPP.

67. Roald Dahl, Letter to C. G. White of the Inland Revenue, 09/16/87 – GHPP.

68. Stephen Roxburgh, Conversation with the author, 03/13/09.

69. *The Witches*, p. 73.

70. Roald Dahl, Letter to Stephen Roxburgh, 04/22/83 – FSG.

71. *The Witches*, p. 197.

72. Stephen Roxburgh, Letter to Roald Dahl, 04/28/83 – RDMSC RD 1/4/15.

73. Roald Dahl, Letter to Stephen Roxburgh, 05/16/83 – FSG.

74. Stephen Roxburgh, Conversation with the author, 03/13/09.

75. Murray Pollinger, Conversation with the author, 04/10/09.

76. Stephen Roxburgh, Conversations with the author, 01/13/98 and 03/13/09.

77. Stephen Roxburgh, Letter to Roald Dahl, 05/03/85 – FSG.

78. Ophelia Dahl, Letter to Stephen Roxburgh, 09/25/85.

79. Lucy Dahl, Conversation with the author, 10/09/08.

80. Ibid.

81. Roald Dahl, "Things I Wish I'd Known When I Was Eighteen," Unpublished article for the *Sunday Express Magazine* – RDMSC RD 1/2/7.

82. Roald Dahl, Letter to Lucy Dahl, 02/09/82 – LDC.

83. Roald Dahl, Letter to Lucy Dahl, 02/11/82 – LDC.

84. Wendy Kress, Conversation with the author, 08/05/09.

85. Gina Pollinger, Conversation with the author, 04/10/09.
86. Stephen Roxburgh, Conversation with the author, 03/13/09.
87. Interview with Todd McCormack, *The Author's Eye*.
88. Roger Straus, Conversation with the author, 01/15/98.
89. Interview with Todd McCormack, *The Author's Eye*.
90. Stephen Roxburgh, Conversation with the author, 03/13/09.
91. Roger Straus, Conversation with the author, 01/15/98.
92. Wendy Kress, Conversation with the author, 08/05/09.
93. Murray Pollinger, Conversation with the author, 04/10/09.
94. Roald Dahl, Letter to Stephen Roxburgh, 01/15/88 – RDMSC RD 1/4/20.
95. Stephen Roxburgh, Letter to Roald Dahl, 01/26/88 – RDMSC RD 1/4/20.
96. Roger Straus, Conversation with the author, 01/15/98.
97. Stephen Roxburgh, Conversations with the author, 03/13/09 and 01/13/98.
98. Liz Attenborough, Conversation with the author, 02/08/10.
99. Ophelia Dahl, Conversation with the author, 03/17/08.
100. Roald Dahl, "Gipsy House," *Architectural Digest* (June 1980) – RDMSC RD 6/2/1/16.
101. Roald Dahl, Speech to Boys at Repton, Nov. 21, 1975 – RDMSC RD 6//1/25.
102. Liz Attenborough, Conversation with the author, 02/08/10.
103. Anna Corrie, Conversation with the author, 10/08/07.
104. Tom Maschler, Conversation with the author, 02/09/98.
105. Murray Pollinger, Conversation with the author, 04/14/09.
106. Roald Dahl, "Let's Build a Skyscraper," *New York Times Book Review*, Nov. 1, 1944.
107. Alfred Knopf, Letter to Roald Dahl, 12/21/66 – HRCH KNOPF 524.12.
108. Roald Dahl, ABC Radio interview with Terry Lane, 1989.
109. Roald Dahl, Interview with Helen Edwards, for *Bedtime Stories*, California, July 1970.
110. Roald Dahl, *Notes for Dr Streule's lecture to Bristol*, September 1990 – RDMSC RD 6/2/1/41.
111. Roald Dahl, *A Note on Writing Books for Children* (sent to *The Writer*, Boston, Oct. 4, 1975) – RDMSC RD 6/2/1/12.

CHAPTER TWENTY: *No Point in Struggling*

1. Ophelia Dahl, *Memories of My Father*, unpublished MS.
2. Lucy Dahl, Conversation with the author, 10/09/08.
3. Charlotte Crosland, Conversation with the author, 03/12/10.
4. Roald Dahl, "My Time of Life," *The Sunday Times*, October 1986 – RDMSC RD 6/2/1/27.
5. Roald Dahl, "On Grandmothers," *Puffin Post*, July 20, 1982 – RDMSC RD 6/2/1/20.
6. "My Time of Life."
7. Quentin Blake, Conversation with the author, 01/19/09.
8. Wendy Kress, Conversation with the author, 08/05/09.
9. Ophelia Dahl, Conversation with the author, 03/17/08.
10. Roald Dahl, *The Minpins* (London: Jonathan Cape, 1991), p. 43.
11. Tom Maschler, Conversation with the author, 02/09/98.
12. Roald Dahl, Letter to Anthony Cheetham, 11/17/89 – RDMSC RD 1/2/9.

13. Roald Dahl, Letter to Murray Pollinger, 11/16/89 – RDMSC RD 1/2/9/3.

14. Martin Goodwin, Conversation with the author, 02/23/10.

15. Lucy Dahl, Conversation with the author, 10/09/08.

16. Amanda Conquy, Conversation with the author, 02/22/10.

17. Roald Dahl, Letter to N. L. Wicks, 11/18/85 – RDMSC RD 16/1/2.

18. Neal, *As I Am*, p. 363.

19. Ophelia Dahl, *Memories of My Father*, unpublished MS.

20. Felicity Dahl, Conversation with the author, 02/06/10.

21. Roald Dahl, Newsletter No. 2 for Puffin Books, ?Summer 1990. [No. 1 is dated April 1990; No. 3 was published after his death] – RDMSC AC 56.

22. Ophelia Dahl, Conversation with the author, 03/17/08.

23. Ophelia Dahl, *Memories of My Father*, unpublished MS.

24. Tessa Dahl, Conversation with the author, 10/22/07.

25. Ophelia Dahl, Conversation with the author, 03/17/08.

26. Tessa Dahl, Conversation with the author, 10/22/07.

27. Ophelia Dahl, *Memories of My Father*, unpublished MS.

28. Lucy Dahl, E-mail to the author, 10/13/08.

29. Lucy Dahl, Conversation with the author, 10/09/08.

30. "Death of an Old, Old Man" in *Collected Stories*, p. 94.

31. David Weatherall, Letter to Felicity Dahl, undated – Felicity Dahl Collection.

32. Ophelia Dahl, *Memories of My Father*, unpublished MS.

33. Roald Dahl, *Mr Bubbler Notes* – RDMSC RD 11/3/23.

34. Roald Dahl, Notes and Sketches – RDMSC RD 11/3/3, RD 11/3/19, and RD 11/3/24/3.

35. Stephen Roxburgh, Conversation with the author, 03/13/09.

36. Tom Maschler, Conversation with the author, 02/09/98.

37. Edna St Vincent Millay, *A Few Figs from Thistles* (1920).

38. Peter Mayer, Tribute given at Roald Dahl's funeral, Nov. 29, 1990.

39. Nicholas Logsdail, Conversation with the author, 04/24/08.

40. Murray and Gina Pollinger, Conversation with the author, 04/10/09.

41. Tom Maschler, Conversation with the author, 02/09/98.

42. Quentin Blake, Conversation with the author, 01/19/09.

43. Interview with Todd McCormack, *The Author's Eye*.

44. Ophelia Dahl, *Memories of My Father*, unpublished MS.

45. Roald Dahl, "The Sound Machine" in *Collected Stories*, p. 204.

46. Roald Dahl, Speech to the Oxford Union, May 29, 1981 – RDMSC RD 6/1/6.

47. Roald Dahl, Conversation with the author, 1985.

48. Ophelia Dahl, Conversation with the author, 03/17/08.

49. Roald Dahl, Untitled article (1965) – RDMSC RD 6/2/1/23.

50. Roald Dahl, Interviewed by Helen Edwards for *Bedtime Stories*, California, July 1970.

51. Roald Dahl, *Ten Days with Roald Dahl*, 06/17/85 – RDMSC RD 6/7.

Bibliography

SHORT STORIES – FIRST PUBLICATION

"The Sword" – *Atlantic*, August 1943

"Katina" – *Ladies' Home Journal*, March 1944

"Only This" – *Ladies' Home Journal*, September 1944

"Beware of the Dog" – *Harper's*, October 1944

"Missing: Believed Killed" – *Tomorrow* magazine, November 1944

"They Shall Not Grow Old" – *Ladies' Home Journal*, March 1945

"Madame Rosette" – *Harper's*, August 1945

"Death of an Old, Old Man" – *Ladies' Home Journal*, September 1945

"Someone Like You" – *Town and Country*, November 1945

"Collector's Item" (later renamed "Man from the South") – *Collier's*, September 1948

"The Sound Machine" – *The New Yorker*, September 1949

"Poison"—*Collier's*, June 1950

"Girl Without a Name" – *Today's Woman*, November 1951

"Taste" – *The New Yorker*, December 1951

"Dip in the Pool" – *The New Yorker*, January 1952

"A Picture for Drioli" (later renamed *Skin*) – *The New Yorker*, May 1952

"My Lady Love, My Dove" – *The New Yorker*, June 1952

"Mr Feasey" – *The New Yorker*, August 1953

"Lamb to the Slaughter" – *Harper's*, September 1953

"The Devious Bachelor" (later renamed "Nunc Dimittis") – *Collier's*, September 1953

"Edward the Conqueror" – *The New Yorker*, October 1953

"Galloping Foxley" – *Town and Country*, November 1953

"The Way Up to Heaven" – *The New Yorker*, February 1954

"Parson's Pleasure" – *Esquire*, April 1958

"The Champion of the World" – *The New Yorker*, January 1959

"The Landlady" – *The New Yorker*, November 1959

"Mrs Bixby and the Colonel's Coat" – *Nugget*, December 1959

"A Fine Son" (later renamed "Genesis and Catastrophe") – *Playboy*, December 1959

"In the Ruins", first published in the programme of the World Book Fair, June 1964

"The Visitor" – *Playboy*, May 1965

"The Last Act" – *Playboy*, January 1966

"The Great Switcheroo" – *Playboy*, April 1974

"The Butler Did It" (later renamed "The Butler") – *Travel and Leisure*, May 1974

"Bitch" – *Playboy*, July 1974

"Ah, Sweet Mystery of Life" – *The New Yorker*, September 1974

"The Hitchhiker" – *Atlantic Monthly*, August 1977

"The Umbrella Man" in *Tales of the Unexpected* (New York: Vintage ed., Random House, 1979)

"Mr Botibol" in *More Tales of the Unexpected* (London: Michael Joseph, 1980)

"Vengeance Is Mine, Inc." in *More Tales of the Unexpected*

"The Bookseller" – *Playboy*, January 1987

"The Surgeon" – *Playboy*, January 1988

SHORT STORY COLLECTIONS

Over to You (New York: Reynal & Hitchcock, 1946)
    ("Death of an Old, Old Man", "An African Story", "A Piece of Cake", "Madame Rosette", "Katina", "Yesterday Was Beautiful", "They Shall Not Grow Old", "Beware of the Dog", "Only This" and "Someone Like You")

Someone Like You (New York: Alfred A. Knopf, 1953)

> ("Taste", "Lamb to the Slaughter", "Man from the South", "The Soldier", "My Lady Love, My Dove", "Dip in the Pool", "Galloping Foxley", "Skin", "Poison", "The Wish", "Neck", "The Sound Machine", "Nunc Dimittis", "The Great Automatic Grammatizator", "Claud's Dog: The Ratcatcher", "Rummins", "Mr Hoddy" and "Mr Feasey")

Kiss Kiss (New York: Alfred A. Knopf, 1960)

> ("The Landlady", "William and Mary", "The Way Up to Heaven", "Parson's Pleasure", "Mrs Bixby and the Colonel's Coat", "Royal Jelly", "Georgy Porgy", "Genesis and Catastrophe", "Edward the Conqueror", "Pig" and "The Champion of the World")

Switch Bitch (New York: Alfred A. Knopf, 1974)

> ("The Last Act", "Bitch", "The Great Switcheroo" and "The Visitor")

The Wonderful Story of Henry Sugar and Six More (New York: Alfred A. Knopf, 1977)

> ("The Boy Who Talked with Animals", "The Hitchhiker", "The Mildenhall Treasure", "The Swan", "The Wonderful Story of Henry Sugar", "Lucky Break: How I Became a Writer" and "A Piece of Cake")

Two Fables (London: Viking, 1986)

> ("The Princess and the Poacher", "Princess Mammalia")

BOOKS – FIRST PUBLICATION

The Gremlins. Walt Disney/Random House, 1943
Some Time Never: A Fable for Supermen. Scribner's, 1948*
James and the Giant Peach. Alfred A. Knopf, 1961
Charlie and the Chocolate Factory. Alfred A. Knopf, 1964
The Magic Finger. Harper & Row, 1966
Fantastic Mr Fox. Alfred A. Knopf, 1970
Charlie and the Great Glass Elevator. Alfred A. Knopf, 1972
Danny the Champion of the World. Alfred A. Knopf, 1975
The Enormous Crocodile. Alfred A. Knopf, 1978

---

*The English version of this book was published as *Sometime Never*. For consistency, I have used the American version *Some Time Never* throughout.

My Uncle Oswald. Michael Joseph, 1979

The Twits. Jonathan Cape, 1980

George's Marvellous Medicine. Jonathan Cape, 1981

Roald Dahl's Revolting Rhyme. Jonathan Cape, 1982

The BFG. Jonathan Cape, 1982

Dirty Beasts. Jonathan Cape, 1983

The Witches. Jonathan Cape, 1983

Roald Dahl's Book of Ghost Stories. Farrar, Straus & Giroux, 1983.

Boy: Tales of Childhood. Jonathan Cape, 1984

The Giraffe and the Pelly and Me. Jonathan Cape, 1985

Going Solo. Jonathan Cape, 1986

Matilda. Jonathan Cape, 1988

Rhyme Stew. Jonathan Cape, 1989

Esio Trot. Jonathan Cape, 1990

The Vicar of Nibbleswicke. Random Century Group, 1991

The Minpins. Jonathan Cape, 1991

Roald Dahl's Guide to Railway Safety. British Railways Board, 1991

Memories with Food at Gipsy House (with Felicity Dahl). Viking, 1991;
    later reprinted as *The Roald Dahl Cookbook*

The Roald Dahl Diary (later renamed *My Year*). Jonathan Cape, 1991

The Roald Dahl Treasury. Jonathan Cape, 1997

More About Boy. Puffin Books, 2008

UNPUBLISHED WORK (SELECTED)

"The Kumbak II", short story, 1926

"The Ginger Cat", short story, c. 1945

"World Leaders", short story, c. 1945

"Foreign Intelligence", short story, 1947

"The Dogchild", short story, 1948

"Nineteen Fifty What?", short story, 1950

"Maclean and Burgess: The Great Vanishing Trick", article, 1951

PLAYS

The Honeys. Performed at the Longacre Theater, New York, 1955

SCREENPLAYS AND TELEPLAYS FOR COMPLETED FEATURE FILMS AND TELEVISION DRAMA

Lamb to the Slaughter, for *Alfred Hitchcock Presents*, April 13, 1958
William and Mary, for *Way Out*, March 1, 1961
You Only Live Twice, 1967
Chity Chitty Bang Bang (with Ken Hughes), 1968
Willy Wonka and the Chocolate Factory, 1971
The Night Digger, 1971

SELECTED JOURNALISM

"Shot Down Over Libya," *Saturday Evening Post* (August 1942).
"Let's Build a Skyscraper," *New York Times Book Review*, Nov. 1, 1944.
"He Plowed Up $1,000,000" (later renamed *The Mildenhall Treasure*), *Saturday Evening Post* (September 1947).
"Love," *Ladies' Home Journal* (May 1949).
"The Amazing Eyes of Kuda Bux," *Argosy* magazine (July 1952).
"My Wife: Patricia Neal," *Ladies' Home Journal* (September 1965).
"What I Told Ophelia and Lucy About God," *Redbook* (November 1970).
"Charlie and the Chocolate Factory: A Reply," *The Horn Book Magazine* (February 1973).
"A Note on Writing Books for Children," *The Writer* (Boston) (October 1975).
"Gipsy House," *Architectural Digest* (June 1980).
"On Grandmothers," *Puffin Post* (July 1982).
Searching for Mr Smith, Browse & Darby Catalogue, 1983.
"Not a Chivalrous Affair," *The Literary Review* (August 1983).
"My Time of Life," *The Sunday Times*, Oct., 1986.
"Roald Dahl Speaks Out," *WETA* magazine (March 1990).

SECONDARY SOURCES – PUBLISHED WORKS

Allan, Robin. *Walt Disney and Europe*. London: John Libby & Co., 1999.

Amis, Kingsley. *Memoirs*. London: Hutchinson, 1991.

Asbjørnsen, Peter Christian, and Jørgen Moe. *Norske Folkeeventyr*, 1841–44, trans. by George Webbe Dasent as *Popular Tales from the Norse*. Edinburgh: Edmonston & Douglas, 1859.

Atkins, David. "Writers Remembered: Roald Dahl," *The Author* (Spring 1992).

Berman, Art. "Patricia Neal Partly Paralyzed, Five Months Pregnant, Husband Says," *Los Angeles Times*, March 19, 1965.

Borrelli, Mario. *A Streetlamp and the Stars. The Autobiography of Father Mario Borrelli of Naples*. New York: Coward-McCann, 1963.

Bowen, Elizabeth. *London 1940* in *Collected Impressions*. London: Longmans Green & Co., 1950.

Bryce, Ivar. *You Only Live Once. Memories of Ian Fleming*. London: Weidenfeld & Nicolson, 1984.

Buckley, Christopher. *Greece and Crete 1941*. London: HMSO, 1952.

Cameron, Eleanor. "McLuhan, Youth and Literature," *The Horn Book Magazine* (October 1972).

Cave Brown, Anthony. *"C": The Secret Life of Sir Stewart Graham Menzies, Spymaster to Winston Churchill*. New York, Macmillan, 1987.

Charles, B. G. *Old Norse Relations with Wales*. Cardiff, 1934.

Churchill, Winston S. *The Hinge of Fate*. Boston: Houghton Mifflin, 1950.

Clarke, Dennis. *Public School Explorers in Newfoundland*. London: Putnam, 1935.

Clifton, Tony, and Catherine Leroy. *God Cried*. London: Quartet Books, 1983.

Coldstream, John. *Dirk Bogarde, The Authorised Biography*. London: Weidenfeld & Nicolson, 2004.

Colvin, Ian. *Flight 777: The Mystery of Leslie Howard*. London: Evans Bros., 1957.

Conant, Jennet. *The Irregulars: Roald Dahl and the British Spy Ring in Wartime Washington*. New York: Simon & Schuster, 2008.

Cooper, Artemis. *Writing at the Kitchen Table*. New York: Penguin, 2000.

Cox, Brian. *Cox on Cox: An English Curriculum for the 1990s*. London: Hodder & Stoughton, 1991.

Crawford, Cheryl. *One Naked Individual*. Indianapolis: Bobbs-Merrill Company, 1977.

Culver, John C., and John Hyde. *American Dreamer, the Life and Times of Henry Wallace*, London: W. W. Norton, 2000.

Dahl, Tessa. *Working for Love, A Novel*. New York: Delacorte Press, 1989.

Day, Barry, ed. *The Letters of Noël Coward*. New York: Alfred A. Knopf, 2007.

Engel, Jeffrey. *Cold War at 30,000 Feet*. Cambridge, MA: Harvard University Press, 2007.

Farrell, Barry. *Pat and Roald*. London: Hutchinson, 1970.

Forester, John. *Novelist & Storyteller: The Life of C. S. Forester*. Lemon Grove, CA:, 2000.

Graves, Charles. *The Thin Blue Line*. London: Hutchinson, 1941.

Greene, Graham. *A Sort of Life*. London: The Bodley Head, 1971.

Greenfield, George. *Desert Episode*. London: Macmillan, 1945.

Hall, Ryan C. W., Richard C. W. Hall, and Marcia J. Chapman, "Definition, Diagnosis and Forensic Implications of Postconcussional Syndrome," *Psychosomatics*, Journal of the Academy of Psychosomatic Medicine, 46 (June 2005).

Halladay, Hugh. *Woody: A Fighter Pilot's Album*. Toronto: Canav Books, 1987.

Hodgson, Lynn-Philip. *Inside Camp X*. New York: Mosaic Press, 2000.

Howard, Ronald. *In Search of My Father: A Portrait of Leslie Howard*. London: William Kimber & Co., 1981.

Hyde, H. Mongomery. *The Quiet Canadian*. London: Hamish Hamilton, 1962.

Ibsen, Henrik. *Ghosts* (1881), trans. R. Farquharson Sharp. New York: J. M. Dent & Sons, 1911.

Ignatieff, Michael. *Isaiah Berlin: A Life*. New York: Henry Holt, 1998.

Johanson, Arno. "Pat Neal: Her Luck Has Changed At Last," *Parade* magazine, Oct. 14, 1964.

Johnson, Diane. *Dashiell Hammett: A Life.* New York: Fawcett Columbine, 1983.

Justice, Bill. *Justice for Disney.* Dayton, OH: Tomart Publications, 1992.

Keene, Alice. *The Two Mr Smiths: The Life and Work of Sir Matthew Smith.* London: Lund Humphries, 1995.

Knopf, Alfred. *Introduction to Recent Publications.* Borzoi Books, Catalogue, 1953.

Kopper, Philip. *Anonymous Giver: A Life of Charles Marsh.* Washington, DC: Public Welfare Foundation, 2000.

Korkis, Jim. "The Trouble with Gremlins", *Hogan's Alley Magazine,* 15 (2007).

Kynaston, David. *Austerity Britain 1945–51.* London: Bloomsbury, 2007.

Lehmann, John. *The Ample Proposition.* London: Eyre & Spottiswoode, 1966.

Macdonald, Bill. *The True Intrepid.* Raincoast Books, 2001.

Mahl, Thomas E. *Desperate Deception – British Covert Operations in the US 1939–44.* Washington, DC: Brassey's, 1999.

Maltin, Leonard. Introduction to *The Gremlins.* Milwaukie, OR: Dark Horse Books, 2006.

Maschler, Tom. *Publisher.* London: Picador, 2005.

McCullough, David. *Truman.* New York: Simon & Schuster, 1992.

Methuen-Campbell, James. *Denton Welch, Writer and Artist.* London: Tartarus Press, 2002.

Moorehead, Caroline. *Martha Gellhorn, a Life.* New York: Vintage, 2004.

Muller, Ingrid. *The Jewish Community of Oslo.* Web site of Det Mosaiske Trossamfund, www.dmt.oslo.no.

Neal, Patricia. *As I Am.* New York: Simon & Schuster, 1988.

Nicholas, H. G., ed. *Washington Despatches 1941–45: Weekly Political Reports from the British Embassy.* Chicago: Chicago University Press, 1981.

O'Connor, Derek. "Roald Dahl's Wartime Adventures," *Aviation History* (January 2009).

Ogilvy, David. *Confessions of an Advertising Man.* New York: Atheneum, 1976.

Østby, Leif. *Theodor Kittelsen.* Oslo: Dreyers Forlag, 1975.

Pascal, Valerie. *The Disciple and His Devil.* New York: Dell Publishing, 1970.

Paul, Barbra. "An American in Buckinghamshire," *Housewife* magazine (January 1963).

Payn, Graham, and Sheridan Morley, eds. *The Noël Coward Diaries.* London: Weidenfeld & Nicolson, 1982.

Pearson, John. *The Life of Ian Fleming.* London: Jonathan Cape, 1966.

Raphaelson, Joel, ed. *The Unpublished David Ogilvy.* New York: Crown, 1986.

Reed, Rex. "Pat Neal's Portrait of Courage," *New York Sunday Times,* Nov. 8, 1970.

Rey-Ximena, José. *El Vuelo del Ibis.* Madrid: Ediciones Facta, 2008.

Roese, Herbert E. "Cardiff's Norwegian Links," *Welsh History Review,* vol. 8, no. 2 (December 1996).

Schapmeier, Edward L., and Frederick Schapmeier. *Prophet in Politics: Henry A. Wallace and the War Years, 1940–65.* Ames, IA: Iowa State University Press, 1970.

Shale, Richard. *Donald Duck Joins Up: The Walt Disney Studio During World War II.* Ann Arbor, MI: UMI Research Press, 1982.

Shearer, Stephen Michael. *Patricia Neal: An Unquiet Life.* Louisville: University Press of Kentucky, 2006.

Shores, Christopher, Brian Cull, and Nicola Malizia. *Air War for Yugoslavia, Greece and Crete 1940–1941.* London: Grub Street, 1987.

Solomon, Charles. *The Disney That Never Was.* New York: Hyperion, 1995.

Stafford, David. *Camp X.* Toronto: Lester and Orpen Dennys, 1986.

Stephenson, William. "Point of Departure, A Foreword by Intrepid," in Stevenson, *A Man Called Intrepid.*

Stevenson, William. *A Man Called Intrepid.* Guilford, CT: Lyons Press, 1976.

Thomas, Andrew. *Hurricane Aces, 1941–45.* Long Island City, NY: Osprey Publishing, 2003.

Till, Kenneth. "A Valve for the Treatment of Hydrocephalus," *The Lancet,* 1964.

Treglown, Jeremy. *Roald Dahl: A Biography.* New York: Harcourt, Brace & Co., 1994.

Trevor-Roper, Hugh. "Superagent," Review of *A Man Called Intrepid* in the *New York Review of Books*, May 13, 1976.

Vanderbilt, Gloria. *It Seemed Important at the Time.* New York: Simon & Schuster, 2004.

Wallace, Henry A. *Our Job in the Pacific.* New York: Institute of Pacific Relations, 1944.

– – – , and John Morton Blum. *The Price of Vision: The Diary of Henry A. Wallace, 1942–46.* Boston: Houghton Mifflin, 1973.

Welch, Denton. *Maiden Voyage.* London: Routledge, 1943.

West, Nigel, ed. *British Security Co-ordination.* London: St Ermin's Press, 1998.

Williams, David. *A Little Bit of Norway in Wales. Recollections of Norwegian Seamen's Churches.* Norwegian Church Cultural Centre, Cardiff, 2006.

Wintle, Justin, and Emma Fisher. *The Pied Pipers.* London: Paddington Press, 1974.

Wisdom, T. H. *Wings Over Olympus: The Story of the Royal Air Force in Libya and Greece.* London: George Allen & Unwin, 1942.

Yorke, Malcolm. *Matthew Smith, His Life and Reputation.* London: Faber & Faber, 1997.

Zimmermann, Gereon. "Does Everyone Love Pat Neal? Oh Yes!" *Look* magazine, Feb. 18, 1969.

UNPUBLISHED SOURCES

Appleby, Paul H. *Reminiscences.* Department of Oral History, Columbia University.

Dahl, Ophelia. *Memories of My Father.*

Dahl, Roald. *Transcript of Interview.* John Pearson Papers, Manuscript Department, Lilly Library, Indiana University, Bloomington.

Gale, James Oswald. *Memoirs.*

Gordon, Archie. Papers, BBC Written Archives, Caversham, Surrey.

Hyde, H. Montgomery. Papers, Churchill College, Cambridge.

Ingersoll, Ralph. *But in the Main It's True* (unpublished biography of Charles Marsh, 1975). Howard Gotlieb Archival Research Center, Boston University.

Marsh, Charles. *How Truman Came Through* (1944). Papers of Henry Agard Wallace, Special Collections, University of Iowa.

Paulsen, Gunder. *Memoirs, 1821–1872*, trans. Anne Livgaard Lindland. University of Oslo.

Wallace, Henry Agard. *Diaries 1935–46.* Special Collections, University of Iowa.

SELECTED INTERVIEWS ON RADIO AND TELEVISION

Interview with Helen Edwards for *Bedtime Stories*, California, July 1970.

Roald Dahl, Interviewed for *A Man Called Intrepid*, CBC Television, 1974.

Parkinson, BBC Television, December 1978.

Bookmark, BBC Television, 1985.

A Dose of Dahl's Magic Medicine, an appreciation of the writer Roald Dahl (audiotape) 9/28/1986 – RDMSC RD 12/1/27.

Todd McCormack, *The Author's Eye*, 1986.

Television interview with Sue Lawley – *Wogan with Sue Lawley*, 1988.

Radio interview with Terry Lane, April 1989, © Australian Broadcasting Corporation, 1990.

An Awfully Big Adventure, BBC Television Jan. 1, 1998.

Index